Benchmark Papers in Electrical Engineering and Computer Science

Series Editor: John B. Thomas
Princeton University

Published Volumes and Volumes in Preparation

SYSTEM SENSITIVITY ANALYSIS / Jose B. Cruz, Jr.
RANDOM PROCESSES: Multiplicity Theory and Canonical Decompositions / Anthony Ephremides and John B. Thomas
ALGEBRAIC CODING THEORY: History and Development / Ian F. Blake
PATTERN RECOGNITION: Introduction and Foundations / Jack Sklansky
METHODS OF ENVIRONMENTAL MODELING / R. H. Pantell and D. Daetz
CLASSIC PAPERS IN CONTROL / George J. Thaler
COMPUTER-AIDED DESIGN / S. W. Director
CIRCUIT THEORY / M. E. Van Valkenburg
DIGITAL FILTERS: Design, Theory, and Application / Bede Liu
NONLINEAR SYSTEMS STABILITY / J. K. Aggarwal
NONLINEAR SYSTEMS: Processing of Random Signals / A. H. Haddad
FUNDAMENTALS OF DATA COMPRESSION / Lewis E. Franks
NATURAL LANGUAGE QUESTION-ANSWERING SYSTEMS / Robert Chien
DATA COMPRESSION / Lee Davisson
MODELING AND PHYSICAL FOUNDATIONS OF RANDOM PROCESSES / Robert Lugannani
NONPARAMETRIC PATTERN CLASSIFICATION / T. J. Wagner
SEMICONDUCTOR DEVICE ANALYSIS / James F. Gibbons
INTERSYMBOL INTERFERENCE / Kung Yao
BANDLIMITED SIGNAL EXPANSION / Kung Yao
FORMAL LANGUAGES / Jack E. Carlyle and Sheila A. Greibach
N-PORT NETWORK THEORY / Nhan Levan
RANDOM PROCESSES—LINEAR ESTIMATION, VOLUMES I AND II / Thomas Kailath
SEMICONDUCTOR SURFACE PHENOMENA / Peter Mark

Benchmark Papers
in Electrical Engineering
and Computer Science

A *BENCHMARK*™ Books Series

PATTERN RECOGNITION:

Introduction and Foundations

Edited by
JACK SKLANSKY
University of California at Irvine

Dowden, Hutchinson & Ross, Inc.
Stroudsburg, Pennsylvania

Benchmark Papers in Electrical
Engineering and Computer Science, Volume 4
ISBN: 0–87933–045–7

Library of Congress Cataloging in Publication Data

Sklansky, Jack, comp.
Pattern recognition.

(Benchmark papers in electrical engineering and computer science, v. 4)
Bibliography: p.
1. Artificial intelligence. 2. Pattern perception. 3. Perceptrons. I. Title.
Q335.S55 001.53'4'08 73-12568
ISBN 0-87933-045-7

Manufactured in the United States of America.

Exclusive distributor outside the United States and Canada: John Wiley & Sons, Inc.

Acknowledgments and Permissions

PERMISSIONS

The following papers have been reprinted with the permission of the author and the copyright owners.

American Psychological Association—*Psychological Review*
"The Perceptron: A Probabilistic Model for Information Storage and Organization in the Brain"

Association for Computing Machinery
Communications of the ACM
"Syntax-Directed Interpretation of Classes of Pictures"

Journal of the Association for Computing Machinery
"Sequential Operations in Digital Picture Processing"

Basil Blackwell, Publisher—*Mind*
"Computing Machines and Machine Intelligence"

Edinburgh University Press—*Machine Intelligence IV*
"Linear Skeletons from Square Cupboards"

Institute of Electrical and Electronics Engineers, Inc.
Artificial Intelligence
"Threshold Logic in Artificial Intelligence"

IEEE Transactions on Communication Technology
"The Divergence and Bhattacharyya Distance Measures in Signal Selection"

IEEE Transactions on Electronic Computers
"An Algorithm for Linear Inequalities and Its Application"
"Computer Interpretation of English Text and Picture Patterns"
"Minimum-Perimeter Polygons of Digitized Silhouettes"
"The Illinois Pattern Recognition Computer ILLIAC III"
"A Parallel Computer Organization and Mechanization"

IEEE Transactions on Information Theory
"On the Effectiveness of Receptors in Recognition Systems"
"A Modified Sequential Recognition Machine Using Time-Varying Stopping Boundaries"
"Threshold Training of Two-Mode Signal Detection"
"Signal Detection by Complex Spatial Filtering"

IRE Transactions on Electronic Computers
"An Optimum Character Recognition System Using Decision Functions"
"On the Encoding of Arbitrary Geometric Configurations"

IRE Transactions on Information Theory
"Learning to Recognize Patterns in a Random Environment"
"Pattern Recognition by an Adaptive Process of Sample Set Construction"
"Three Models for the Description of Language"
"The Logic Theory Machine: A Complex Information Processing System"

Proceedings of the IRE
"Pattern Detection and Recognition"

H. D. Landahl—*Bulletin of Mathematics and Biophysics*
"A Logical Calculus of the Ideas Immanent in Nervous Activity"

Spartan Books—*Self-Organizing Systems 1962*
"A Test for Linear Separability as Applied to Self-Organizing Machines"

Series Editor's Preface

The "Benchmark Papers in Electrical Engineering and Computer Science" series is aimed at sifting, organizing, and making readily accessible to the reader the vast literature that has accumulated on both subjects. Although the series is not intended as a complete substitute for a study of this literature, it will serve at least three major critical purposes. First, it provides a practical point of entry into a given area of research. Each volume offers an expert's selection of the critical papers on a given topic as well as his views on its structure, development, and present status. Second, the series provides a convenient and time-saving means for study in areas related to but not contiguous with one's principal interests. Last, but by no means least, the series allows the collection, in a particularly compact and convenient form, of the major works on which present research activities and interests are based.

Each volume in the series has been collected, organized, and edited by an authority in the area to which it pertains. In order to present a unified view of the area, the volume editor has prepared an introduction to the subject, has included his comments on each article, and has provided a subject index to facilitate access to the papers.

This volume, *Pattern Recognition: Introduction and Foundations,* has been edited by Professor Jack Sklansky of the University of California at Irvine. It contains twenty-six papers basic to an understanding of the foundations of pattern recognition and its relationship to engineering and computer science. In addition, Turing's classic "Computing Machines and Machine Intelligence" has been included as an appendix. The volume can serve as a guide for a first course in pattern recognition or as an entree to research in this area. It should prove useful, also, to the more casual reader who may be interested in the historical foundations of this relatively new and exciting field.

We believe that this series will provide a manageable working library of the most important technical articles in electrical engineering and computer science. We hope that it will be equally valuable to students, teachers, and researchers.

John B. Thomas

Preface

The subject of pattern recognition in modern science and technology is something like a eutectic point—a point in intellectual space where many disciplines come together, and moreover, a point from which, I believe, many new disciplines will develop. Thus, in teaching graduate courses in pattern recognition, I found that much of my material came from widely scattered sources, some of which cannot be obtained at many university libraries. I was, therefore, quite pleased to accept Professor Thomas's invitation to bring under one cover a set of basic papers on pattern recognition.

I have exploited this opportunity to include papers that have not only pedogogical value as introductions to various segments of pattern recognition technology, but also historical value as foundation stones in the building of this technology. Thus, several of the papers in this volume are so significant, so frequently cited, that they qualify as classics.

This book is intended not only as a source of basic material for graduate and senior level courses at colleges and universities, but also as a reference for computer scientists, engineers, psychologists, and other professional workers, as well as a source of historical information on the development of ideas on machine intelligence.

I am grateful to Demetrice Burgess at the University of California, Irvine, for taking on much of the heavy burden of correspondence and other secretarial work associated with this book.

Jack Sklansky

Contents

III. FEATURE SELECTION AND REDUCTION

IV. AUTOMATA, LINGUISTICS, AND HEURISTICS

V. IMAGE PROCESSING

VI. PICTURE MACHINES

APPENDIX. MACHINE INTELLIGENCE

Contents by Author

Introduction

The phenomenal growth of digital computer technology since the late 1940s has stimulated both a technological and an intellectual revolution. Part of this revolution is concerned with the use of computers as an artificial intelligence, i.e., as the brain of a machine for analyzing, detecting, recognizing, and describing patterns in apparently erratic data. As a result, *pattern recognition* has come to mean the study of artificial, as well as natural mechanisms that analyze, detect, recognize, and describe patterns in sensory and/or numerical data. Pattern recognition, in fact, has grown into an interdisciplinary field that includes areas of engineering, computer science, biology, psychology, and medicine.

This book is a collection of basic papers in that segment of pattern recognition covering engineering and computer science. Thus we are concerned here with *recognition machines* and *recognition technology*.

The simplest form of recognition machine is a sorter of data into classes. A block diagram of such a machine is shown in Fig. 1. Other aspects of recognition technology include searching for patterns, detecting them, determining their locations in the field of perception, and describing or summarizing them.

Although the field of pattern recognition is relatively new, the number of applications that have been implemented and studied is quite large. These include radar detection, patent searches, character recognition, speech recognition, diagnosis of radiographs, document retrieval, analysis of blood cells, fingerprint identification, theory of human learning, and analysis of bubble chamber photographs.

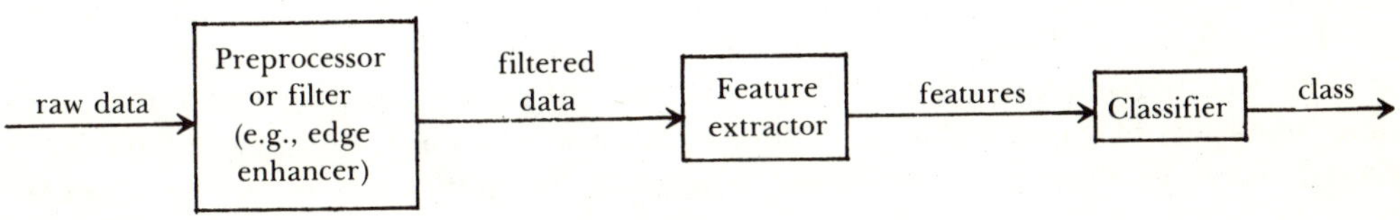

Figure 1

Although discussions of recognition processes appear in very early works of philosophy and psychology (e.g., Plato's "Forms" [McK] and Wertheimer's "Gestalts" [Kof]), the study of recognition machines probably began with the works of McCulloch and Pitts [McCu] and Norbert Wiener [Wie] in 1943 and 1948, respectively. McCulloch and Pitts looked upon machines, particularly information-processing machines, as a means for modeling the brain; consequently their recognition machines were built of large numbers of artificial neurons (threshold gates). Wiener, on the other hand, took an engineering viewpoint and looked upon recognition technology as a means for building sensory prosthetic devices (i.e., devices for replacing the lost senses of vision and hearing in the blind and deaf).

In 1950, A. M. Turing published a delightfully written prophetic article, *Computing Machinery and Intelligence* [Tur], reproduced in the Appendix. This article was a precursor of the entire field of study known today as *artificial intelligence.* Artificial intelligence is concerned with the software and theoretical aspects of the construction of intelligent machines. Since recognition is a major part of intelligence, and since pattern recognition is concerned with hardware as well as software, the fields of pattern recognition and artificial intelligence overlap, but neither contains all of the other.

In 1956, there appeared a landmark in the development of linguistics, intelligent machines, and automata theory: Noam Chomsky's "phrase-structure" model of the syntax of languages [Chom]. Later Chomsky's ideas on generative grammars were tied to Turing's concepts of computability and tape-reading automata, as well as Narasimhan's and others' concepts of the syntactic approach to the design of automatic pattern recognizers.

Also in 1956, Allen Newell and Herbert Simon [New] introduced the use of a *list language* (i.e., a language especially designed for operations on lists) and the concept of heuristic techniques of searching through trees (lists of lists of lists, etc.) for machine intelligence. The impact of these techniques on pattern recognition technology began to be felt with the automatic recognition of mathematical proofs and is currently being applied to the discovery of organic chemical compounds (State University of New York, Stony Brook, New York), path planning in robots (Stanford Research Institute, Menlo Park, California), and speech recognition (Carnegie–Mellon University, Pittsburgh, Pennsylvania).

The next significant impact on the field of pattern recognition came as a contribution to computer engineering: S. H. Unger's "spatial computer" [Ung]. Unger demonstrated how a parallel organization of a large number of identical information processing devices can recognize simple visual figures such as alphabetic characters, much as the retina and the optic nerve perform elementary preprocessing of the field of view of the eye. Unger's paper was the predecessor of many other parallel processing machines, one of the most ambitious of which was B. McCormick's ILLIAC III [McCo].

In 1958, the McCulloch–Pitts viewpoint was given a great boost by Rosenblatt's work on the "perceptron" [Ros-1]. This work was the prototype of dozens of machines (and hundreds of papers) that were similar in basic concept to the perceptron, even though some of these machines were developed independently of the perceptron.

Among the most well known of the perceptron-like machines were Gamba's "PAPA" [Pal], Widrow's "Adeline" [Wid], and Steinbuch's "Learning Matrix" [Ste].

Chow [Chow-1] and Sebestyen [Seb-1, Seb-2] were among the first to show how statistical decision theory may be applied to the design of pattern classifiers.

The application of switching theory and "majority-decision" or "threshold logic" to the classification of binary-valued feature vectors* was pioneered in 1956, 1959, and the early 1960s by Von Neumann [Von]; Muroga, Toda, and Kondo [Mur-1]; McNaughton [McN]; Paull and McCluskey [Pau]; C. K. Chow [Chow-2]; R. O. Winder [Win-1, Win-2]; and Cohn and Lindaman [Coh]. About the same time, an alternative approach to this problem, based on linear programming and game theory, was developed by Minnick [Min]; and Muroga, Toda, and Takasu [Mur-2].

The 1960s was a decade of rapid growth for pattern recognition technology. During this decade hundreds of papers appeared on the subjects of pattern classification, training procedures, picture processing algorithms, cellular recognition machines, and the application of recognition technology to practical problems. Among these applications were optical character recognition, scene analysis, fingerprint identification, analysis of bubble chamber tracks, analysis of blood cells, vector cardiograms, and the mapping of chromosomes and lunar landscapes.

This field is still in a phase of rapid growth. The future of the field will, I believe, move in the following directions: (1) pattern recognition by man–machine interaction; (2) the application of pattern recognition technology to tree searching, problem reduction, and other techniques of artificial intelligence; (3) further developments in the invention and use of picture languages, and the matching of these languages to specific problems; (4) improvements in the theory of machine learning and the design of training procedures; and (5) extensive use of pattern recognition techniques in practical problems, e.g., computer-aided medical diagnosis, sensory prosthetic devices, monitoring of industrial and agricultural processes (in both production and management), remote sensing of the earth's resources, public transportation systems, exploration of planets by robots, computer-aided architectural design, and computer-aided instruction of visual and auditory concepts (such as perspective drawing, recognition of speech buried in noise, electromagnetic theory, kinematics, orthopedics, and radiology).

The papers in this book were selected for their value as introductions to segments of pattern recognition technology as well as for their impact on the development of this technology. Many of them have achieved a degree of importance that qualifies them as classics.

The papers are grouped partly according to the traditional major building blocks of a pattern recognizer: (1) a preprocessor or image processor (for acquiring the raw data and enhancing the detectability of the embedded signals); (2) a feature extractor (for extracting the raw features, selecting the best of raw features, and/or reducing the dimensionality of the feature space); and (3) a classifier (for assigning the observed data to a particular class). This grouping forms Parts I, II, and III

---

*A feature vector is a vector each of whose elements is a "feature," "property," or "measurement" of a pattern.

of the book. The fourth part is concerned with a class of models (deterministic and probabilistic automata) and languages (phrase-structured languages and list languages) for representing schemes of automatic recognition. The topic of Part V, computer-aided image processing, is already recognizable as a major subfield of computer science and engineering. The last part of the book discusses the architecture of special-purpose computers for analyzing pictures. The Appendix contains Turing's classic paper on machine intelligence.

Deterministic Classifiers

I

Editor's Comments on Papers 1 Through 5

The simplest nontrivial approach to the subject of pattern recognition is that of deterministic classification. In this approach one assumes that each member of any of the considered classes of patterns is a d-dimensional vector in feature space. Each component of this vector is a property or feature of the observed pattern. Thus each pattern occupies a point in feature space. Usually, one assumes that the entire class of patterns occupies a connected, compact region in feature space (the compactness hypothesis). In the study of deterministic classifiers one also usually assumes that regions of feature space occupied by distinct classes are nonoverlapping, i.e., that patterns from different classes necessarily have different feature vectors. For this type of model, the following techniques have been developed: (1) threshold logic, (2) gradient descent, and (3) game theory and linear programming.

A very early discussion of the concept of threshold gates or artificial neurons as a means of recognizing elementary logical events was presented in a classic paper by McCulloch and Pitts [McCu], reprinted in this part. This paper was a significant contributing factor to later research on reliability enhancement by majority logic [Von], threshold learning [Skl-3, Skl-4, Ros-1, Ros-3], and linear separability [Sin].

McCulloch's concept of neuron logic was later formalized as "threshold logic." The use of threshold logic for pattern classification is described in this part by R. O. Winder [Win-2]. Refinements and other formalizations of this concept appeared as the "gradient descent" procedure and game theory. The gradient descent procedure is described here by Ho and Kashyap [Ho], using the theory of automatic control systems developed during the 1960s. Game theory technique, which is closely related to linear programming, is presented in Singleton's paper [Sin].

An approach to the use of classification theory as a neurophysiological model of human vision was presented by F. Rosenblatt in his now famous "perceptron." Even though he described his model from a statistical viewpoint, the underlying learning process is, in an important respect, deterministic. Among his basic assumptions were that the regions occupied by each class in feature space (the class regions) do not overlap—i.e., that there is no ambiguity in the identity of any feature vector—and furthermore that these regions can be separated by hyperplanes. These assumptions lead to theorems that state the conditions under which the training process converges to a solution deterministically (as opposed to convergence in probability, in distribution, etc.).

For historical as well as tutorial reasons, it is of interest to read Rosenblatt's first-known publication on his model [Ros-1]. This paper is the last selection in this part.

Reprinted from *Bull. Math. Biophys.*, 1943, **5**, pp. 115–133

1

A LOGICAL CALCULUS OF THE IDEAS IMMANENT IN NERVOUS ACTIVITY

WARREN S. MCCULLOCH AND WALTER PITTS

FROM THE UNIVERSITY OF ILLINOIS, COLLEGE OF MEDICINE,
DEPARTMENT OF PSYCHIATRY AT THE ILLINOIS NEUROPSYCHIATRIC INSTITUTE,
AND THE UNIVERSITY OF CHICAGO

Because of the "all-or-none" character of nervous activity, neural events and the relations among them can be treated by means of propositional logic. It is found that the behavior of every net can be described in these terms, with the addition of more complicated logical means for nets containing circles; and that for any logical expression satisfying certain conditions, one can find a net behaving in the fashion it describes. It is shown that many particular choices among possible neurophysiological assumptions are equivalent, in the sense that for every net behaving under one assumption, there exists another net which behaves under the other and gives the same results, although perhaps not in the same time. Various applications of the calculus are discussed.

I. Introduction

Theoretical neurophysiology rests on certain cardinal assumptions. The nervous system is a net of neurons, each having a soma and an axon. Their adjunctions, or synapses, are always between the axon of one neuron and the soma of another. At any instant a neuron has some threshold, which excitation must exceed to initiate an impulse. This, except for the fact and the time of its occurrence, is determined by the neuron, not by the excitation. From the point of excitation the impulse is propagated to all parts of the neuron. The velocity along the axon varies directly with its diameter, from less than one meter per second in thin axons, which are usually short, to more than 150 meters per second in thick axons, which are usually long. The time for axonal conduction is consequently of little importance in determining the time of arrival of impulses at points unequally remote from the same source. Excitation across synapses occurs predominantly from axonal terminations to somata. It is still a moot point whether this depends upon irreciprocity of individual synapses or merely upon prevalent anatomical configurations. To suppose the latter requires no hypothesis *ad hoc* and explains known exceptions, but any assumption as to cause is compatible with the calculus to come. No case is known in which excitation through a single synapse has elicited a nervous impulse in any neuron, whereas any neuron may be excited by impulses arriving at a sufficient number of neighboring synapses within the period of latent addition, which lasts less than one quarter of a millisecond. Observed temporal summation of impulses at greater intervals is impossible for single neurons and empirically depends upon structural properties of the net. Between the arrival of impulses upon a neuron and its own propagated impulse there is a synaptic delay of more than half a millisecond. During the first part of the nervous impulse the neuron is absolutely refractory to any stimulation. Thereafter its excitability returns rapidly, in some cases reaching a value above normal from which it sinks again to a subnormal value, whence it returns slowly to normal. Frequent activity augments this subnormality. Such specificity as is possessed by nervous impulses depends solely upon their time and place and not on any other specificity of nervous energies. Of late only inhibition has been seriously adduced to contravene this thesis. Inhibition is the termination or prevention of the activity of one group of neurons by concurrent or antecedent activity of a second group. Until recently this could be explained on the supposition that previous activity of neurons of the second group might so raise the thresholds of internuncial neurons that they could no longer be excited by neurons of the first group, whereas the impulses of the first group must sum with the impulses of these internuncials to excite the now inhibited neurons. Today, some inhibitions have been shown to consume less than one millisecond. This excludes internuncials and requires synapses through which impulses inhibit that neuron which is being stimulated by impulses through other synapses. As yet experiment has not shown whether the refractoriness is relative or absolute. We will assume the latter and demonstrate that the difference is immaterial to our argument. Either variety of refractoriness can be accounted for in either of two ways. The "inhibitory synapse" may be of such a kind as to produce a substance which raises the threshold of the neuron, or it may be so placed that the local disturbance produced by its excitation opposes the alteration induced by the otherwise excitatory synapses. Inasmuch as position is already known to have such effects in the case of electrical stimulation, the first hypothesis is to be excluded unless and until it be substantiated, for the second involves no new hypothesis. We have, then, two explanations of inhibition based on the same general premises, differing only in the assumed nervous nets and, consequently, in the time required for inhibition. Hereafter we shall refer to such nervous nets as *equivalent in the extended sense*. Since we are concerned with properties of nets which are invariant under equivalence, we may make the physical assumptions which are most convenient for the calculus.

Many years ago one of us, by considerations impertinent to this argument, was led to conceive of the response of any neuron as factually equivalent to a proposition which proposed its adequate stimulus. He therefore attempted to record the behavior of complicated nets in the notation of the symbolic logic of propositions. The "all-or-none" law of nervous activity is sufficient to insure that the activity of any neuron may be represented as a proposition. Physiological relations existing among nervous activities correspond, of course, to relations among the propositions; and the utility of the representation depends upon the identity of these relations with those of the logic of propositions. To each reaction of any neuron there is a corresponding assertion of a simple proposition. This, in turn, implies either some other simple proposition or the disjunction or the conjunction, with or without negation, of similar propositions, according to the configuration of the synapses upon and the threshold of the neuron in question. Two difficulties appeared. The first concerns facilitation and extinction, in which antecedent activity temporarily alters responsiveness to subsequent stimulation of one and the same part of the net. The second concerns learning, in which activities concurrent at some previous time have altered the net permanently, so that a stimulus which would previously have been inadequate is now adequate. But for nets undergoing both alterations, we can substitute equivalent fictitious nets composed of neurons whose connections and thresholds are unaltered. But one point must be made clear: neither of us conceives the formal equivalence to be a factual explanation. *Per contra!*—we regard facilitation and extinction as dependent upon continuous changes in threshold related to electrical and chemical variables, such as after-potentials and ionic concentrations; and learning as an enduring change which can survive sleep, anaesthesia, convlusions and coma. The importance of the formal equivalence lies in this: that the alterations actually underlying facilitation, extinction and learning in no way affect the conclusions which follow from the formal treatment of the activity of nervous nets, and the relations of the corresponding propositions remain those of the logic of propositions.

The nervous system contains many circular paths, whose activity so regenerates the excitation of any participant neuron that reference to time past becomes indefinite, although it still implies that afferent activity has realized one of a certain class of configurations over time. Precise specification of these implications by means of recursive functions, and determination of those that can be embodied in the activity of nervous nets, completes the theory.

II. The Theory: Nets Without Circles

We shall make the following physical assumptions for our calculus.

1. The activity of the neuron is an "all-or-none" process.
2. A certain fixed number of synapses must be excited within the period of latent addition in order to excite a neuron at any time, and this number is independent of previous activity and position on the neuron.
3. The only significant delay within the nervous system is synaptic delay.
4. The activity of any inhibitory synapse absolutely prevents excitation of the neuron at that time.
5. The structure of the net does not change with time.

To present the theory, the most appropriate symbolism is that of Language II of R. Carnap (1938), augmented with various notations drawn from B. Russell and A. N. Whitehead (1927), including the *Principia* conventions for dots. Typographical necessity, however, will compel us to use the upright '*E*' for the existential operator instead of the inverted, and an arrow ('→') for implication instead of the horseshoe. We shall also use the Carnap syntactical notations, but print them in boldface rather than German type; and we shall introduce a functor S, whose value for a property P is the property which holds of a number when P holds of its predecessor; it is defined by '$S(P)(t) \;.\!\equiv\!.\; P(Kx) \;.\; t = x'$)'; the brackets around its argument will often be omitted, in which case this is understood to be the nearest predicate-expression [***Pr***] on the right. Moreover, we shall write S^2***Pr*** for $S(S($***Pr***$))$, etc.

The neurons of a given net $\mathcal{N}$ may be assigned designations 'c_1', 'c_2', $\cdots$, 'c_n'. This done, we shall denote the property of a number, that a neuron c_i fires at a time which is that number of synaptic delays from the origin of time, by 'N' with the numeral i as subscript, so that $N_i(t)$ asserts that c_i fires at the time t. N_i is called the *action* of c_i. We shall sometimes regard the subscripted numeral of 'N' as if it belonged to the object-language, and were in a place for a functoral argument, so that it might be replaced by a number-variable [***z***] and quantified; this enables us to abbreviate long but finite disjunctions and conjunctions by the use of an operator. We shall employ this locution quite generally for sequences of ***Pr***; it may be secured formally by an obvious disjunctive definition. The predicates 'N_1', 'N_2', $\cdots$, comprise the syntactical class '***N***'.

Let us define the *peripheral afferents* of $\mathcal{N}$ as the neurons of $\mathcal{N}$ with no axons synapsing upon them. Let $N_1, \cdots, N_p$ denote the actions of such neurons and $N_{p+1}, N_{p+2}, \cdots, N_n$ those of the rest. Then a *solution of* $\mathcal{N}$ will be a class of sentences of the form S_i: $N_{p+1}(z_1) .\equiv. Pr_i(N_1, N_2, \cdots, N_p, z_1)$, where Pr_i contains no free variable save z_1 and no descriptive symbols save the N in the argument [Arg], and possibly some constant sentences [sa]; and such that each S_i is true of $\mathcal{N}$. Conversely, given a $Pr_1({}^1p^1{}_1, {}^1p^1{}_2, \cdots, {}^1p^1{}_p, z_1, s)$, containing no free variable save those in its Arg, we shall say that it is *realizable in the narrow sense* if there exists a net $\mathcal{N}$ and a series of N_i in it such that $N_1(z_1) .\equiv. Pr_1(N_1, N_2, \cdots, z_1, sa_1)$ is true of it, where sa_1 has the form $N(0)$. We shall call it *realizable in the extended sense*, or simply *realizable*, if for some n $S^n(Pr_1)(p_1, \cdots, p_p, z_1, s)$ is realizable in the above sense. c_{pi} is here the realizing neuron. We shall say of two laws of nervous excitation which are such that every S which is realizable in either sense upon one supposition is also realizable, perhaps by a different net, upon the other, that they are equivalent assumptions, in that sense.

The following theorems about realizability all refer to the extended sense. In some cases, sharper theorems about narrow realizability can be obtained; but in addition to greater complication in statement this were of little practical value, since our present neurophysiological knowledge determines the law of excitation only to extended equivalence, and the more precise theorems differ according to which possible assumption we make. Our less precise theorems, however, are invariant under equivalence, and are still sufficient for all purposes in which the exact time for impulses to pass through the whole net is not crucial.

Our central problems may now be stated exactly: first, to find an effective method of obtaining a set of computable S constituting a solution of any given net; and second, to characterize the class of realizable S in an effective fashion. Materially stated, the problems are to calculate the behavior of any net, and to find a net which will behave in a specified way, when such a net exists.

A net will be called *cyclic* if it contains a circle: i.e., if there exists a chain $c_i, c_{i+1}, \cdots$ of neurons on it, each member of the chain synapsing upon the next, with the same beginning and end. If a set of its neurons $c_1, c_2, \cdots, c_p$ is such that its removal from $\mathcal{N}$ leaves it without circles, and no smaller class of neurons has this property, the set is called a *cyclic* set, and its cardinality is the *order* of $\mathcal{N}$. In an important sense, as we shall see, the order of a net is an index of the complexity of its behavior. In particular, nets of zero order have especially simple properties; we shall discuss them first.

Let us define a *temporal propositional expression* (a *TPE*), designating a *temporal propositional function* (*TPF*), by the following recursion:

1. A ${}^1p^1[z_1]$ is a *TPE*, where p_1 is a predicate-variable.

2. If S_1 and S_2 are *TPE* containing the same free individual variable, so are SS_1, $S_1 \mathrm{v} S_2$, $S_1 . S_2$ and $S_i . \sim S_2$.

3. Nothing else is a *TPE*.

THEOREM I.

Every net of order 0 *can be solved in terms of temporal propositional expressions.*

Let c_i be any neuron of $\mathcal{N}$ with a threshold $\theta_i > 0$, and let c_{i1}, c_{i2}, $\cdots$, c_{ip} have respectively n_{i1}, n_{i2}, $\cdots$, n_{ip} excitatory synapses upon it. Let c_{j1}, c_{j2}, $\cdots$, c_{jq} have inhibitory synapses upon it. Let κ_i be the set of the subclasses of $\{n_{i1}, n_{i2}, \cdots, n_{ip}\}$ such that the sum of their members exceeds θ_i. We shall then be able to write, in accordance with the assumptions mentioned above,

$$N_i(z_1) \,.\equiv .\, S\left\{\prod_{m=1}^{q} \sim N_{jm}(z_1) \,.\, \sum_{a\epsilon\kappa_i} \prod_{s\epsilon a} N_{is}(z_1)\right\} \tag{1}$$

where the 'Σ' and 'Π' are syntactical symbols for disjunctions and conjunctions which are finite in each case. Since an expression of this form can be written for each c_i which is not a peripheral afferent, we can, by substituting the corresponding expression in (1) for each N_{jm} or N_{is} whose neuron is not a peripheral afferent, and repeating the process on the result, ultimately come to an expression for N_i in terms solely of peripherally afferent N, since $\mathcal{N}$ is without circles. Moreover, this expression will be a *TPE*, since obviously (1) is; and it follows immediately from the definition that the result of substituting a *TPE* for a constituent $p(z)$ in a *TPE* is also one.

THEOREM II.

Every TPE *is realizable by a net of order zero.*

The functor S obviously commutes with disjunction, conjunction, and negation. It is obvious that the result of substituting any S_i, realizable in the narrow sense (i.n.s.), for the $p(z)$ in a realizable expression S_1 is itself realizable i.n.s.; one constructs the realizing net by replacing the peripheral afferents in the net for S_1 by the realizing neurons in the nets for the S_i. The one neuron net realizes $p_1(z_1)$ i.n.s., and Figure 1-a shows a net that realizes $Sp_1(z_1)$ and hence SS_2, i.n.s., if S_2 can be realized i.n.s. Now if S_2 and S_3 are realizable then S^mS_2 and S^nS_3 are realizable i.n.s., for suitable m and n. Hence so are $S^{m+n}S_2$ and $S^{m+n}S_3$. Now the nets of Figures 1b, c and d respectively realize $S(p_1(z_1) \vee p_2(z_1))$, $S(p_1(z_1) . p_2(z_1))$, and $S(p_1(z_1) . \sim p_2(z_1))$ i.n.s. Hence $S^{m+n+1}(S_1 \vee S_2)$, $S^{m+n+1}(S_1 . S_2)$, and $S^{m+n+1}(S_1 . \sim S_2)$ are realizable i.n.s. Therefore $S_1 \vee S_2$ $S_1 . S_2$ $S_1 . \sim S_2$ are realizable if S_1 and S_2 are. By complete induction, all *TPE* are realizable. In this way all nets may be regarded as built out of the fundamental elements of Figures 1a, b, c, d, precisely as the temporal propositional expressions are generated out of the operations of precession, disjunction, conjunction, and conjoined negation. In particular, corresponding to any description of state, or distribution of the values *true* and *false* for the actions of all the neurons of a net save that which makes them all false, a single neuron is constructible whose firing is a necessary and sufficient condition for the validity of that description. Moreover, there is always an indefinite number of topologically different nets realizing any *TPE*.

THEOREM III.

Let there be given a complex sentence S_1 *built up in any manner out of elementary sentences of the form* $\mathbf{p}(\mathbf{z}_1 - \mathbf{zz})$ *where* **zz** *is any numeral, by any of the propositional connections: negation, disjunction, conjunction, implication, and equivalence. Then* S_1 *is a* TPE *and only if it is false when its constituent* $\mathbf{p}(\mathbf{z}_1 - \mathbf{zz})$ *are all assumed false—i.e., replaced by false sentences — or that the last line in its truth-table contains an* '**F**',*—or there is no term in its Hilbert disjunctive normal form composed exclusively of negated terms.*

These latter three conditions are of course equivalent (Hilbert and Ackermann, 1938). We see by induction that the first of them is necessary, since $p(z_1 - zz)$ becomes false when it is replaced by a false sentence, and $S_1 \vee S_2$, $S_1 . S_2$ and $S_1 . \sim S_2$ are all false if both their constituents are. We see that the last condition is sufficient by remarking that a disjunction is a *TPE* when its constituents are, and that any term

$$S_1 . S_2 \;.\;.\;.\;.\; S_m . \sim S_{m+1} . \sim \;.\;.\;.\;.\; \sim S_n$$

can be written as

$$(S_1 . S_2 \;.\;.\;.\;.\; S_m) . \sim (S_{m+1} \vee S_{m+2} \vee \;.\;.\;.\;.\; \vee S_n),$$

which is clearly a *TPE*.

The method of the last theorems does in fact provide a very convenient and workable procedure for constructing nervous nets to order, for those cases where there is no reference to events indefinitely far in the past in the specification of the conditions. By way of example, we may consider the case of heat produced by a transient cooling.

If a cold object is held to the skin for a moment and removed, a sensation of heat will be felt; if it is applied for a longer time, the sensation will be only of cold, with no preliminary warmth, however transient. It is known that one cutaneous receptor is affected by heat, and another by cold. If we let N_1 and N_2 be the actions of the respective receptors and N_3 and N_4 of neurons whose activity implies a sensation of heat and cold, our requirements may be written as

$$N_3(t) :\equiv: N_1(t-1) \,.\, \mathrm{v} \,.\, N_2(t-3) \,.\, \sim N_2(t-2)$$
$$N_4(t) \,.\equiv.\, N_2(t-2) \,.\, N_2(t-1)$$

where we suppose for simplicity that the required persistence in the sensation of cold is say two synaptic delays, compared with one for that of heat. These conditions clearly fall under Theorem III. A net may consequently be constructed to realize them, by the method of Theorem II. We begin by writing them in a fashion which exhibits them as built out of their constituents by the operations realized in Figures 1a, b, c, d: i.e., in the form

$$N_3(t) \,.\equiv.\, S\{N_1(t) \,\mathrm{v}\, S[(SN_2(t)) \,.\, \sim N_2(t)]\}$$
$$N_4(t) \,.\equiv.\, S\{[SN_2(t)] \,.\, N_2(t)\}\,.$$

First we construct a net for the function enclosed in the greatest number of brackets and proceed outward; in this case we run a net of the form shown in Figure 1a from c_2 to some neuron c_a, say, so that

$$N_a(t) \,.\equiv.\, SN_2(t).$$

Next introduce two nets of the forms 1c and 1d, both running from c_a and c_2, and ending respectively at c_4 and say c_b. Then

$$N_4(t) \,.\equiv.\, S[N_a(t) \,.\, N_2(t)] \,.\equiv.\, S[(SN_2(t)) \,.\, N_2(t)].$$
$$N_b(t) \,.\equiv.\, S[N_a(t) \,.\, \sim N_2(t)] \,.\equiv.\, S[(SN_2(t)) \,.\, \sim N_2(t)].$$

Finally, run a net of the form 1b from c_1 and c_b to c_3, and derive

$$N_3(t) \,.\equiv.\, S[N_1(t) \,\mathrm{v}\, N_b(t)]$$
$$.\equiv.\, S\{N_1(t) \,\mathrm{v}\, S[(SN_2(t)] \,.\, \sim N_2(t)\}\,.$$

These expressions for $N_3(t)$ and $N_4(t)$ are the ones desired; and the realizing net *in toto* is shown in Figure 1e.

This illusion makes very clear the dependence of the correspondence between perception and the "external world" upon the specific structural properties of the intervening nervous net. The same illusion, of course, could also have been produced under various other assumptions about the behavior of the cutaneous receptors, with correspondingly different nets.

We shall now consider some theorems of equivalence: i.e., theorems which demonstrate the essential identity, save for time, of various alternative laws of nervous excitation. Let us first discuss the case of *relative inhibition.* By this we mean the supposition that the firing of an inhibitory synapse does not absolutely prevent the firing of the neuron, but merely raises its threshold, so that a greater number of excitatory synapses must fire concurrently to fire it than would otherwise be needed. We may suppose, losing no generality, that the increase in threshold is unity for the firing of each such synapse; we then have the theorem:

THEOREM IV.

Relative and absolute inhibition are equivalent in the extended sense.

We may write out a law of nervous excitation after the fashion of (1), but employing the assumption of relative inhibition instead; inspection then shows that this expression is a *TPE*. An example of the replacement of relative inhibition by absolute is given by Figure 1f. The reverse replacement is even easier; we give the inhibitory axons afferent to c_i any sufficiently large number of inhibitory synapses apiece.

Second, we consider the case of extinction. We may write this in the form of a variation in the threshold θ_i; after the neuron c_i has fired; to the nearest integer—and only to this approximation is the variation in threshold significant in natural forms of excitation—this may be written as a sequence $\theta_i + b_j$ for j synaptic delays after firing, where $b_j = 0$ for j large enough, say $j = M$ or greater. We may then state

THEOREM V.

Extinction is equivalent to absolute inhibition.

For, assuming relative inhibition to hold for the moment, we need merely run M circuits $\mathcal{T}_1, \mathcal{T}_2, \cdots \mathcal{T}_M$ containing respectively 1, $2, \cdots, M$ neurons, such that the firing of each link in any is sufficient to fire the next, from the neuron c_i back to it, where the end of the circuit $\mathcal{T}_j$ has just b_j inhibitory synapses upon c_i. It is evident that this will produce the desired results. The reverse substitution may be accomplished by the diagram of Figure 1g. From the transitivity of replacement, we infer the theorem. To this group of theorems also belongs the well-known

THEOREM VI.

Facilitation and temporal summation may be replaced by spatial summation.

This is obvious: one need merely introduce a suitable sequence of delaying chains, of increasing numbers of synapses, between the exciting cell and the neuron whereon temporal summation is desired to hold. The assumption of spatial summation will then give the required results. See e.g. Figure 1h. This procedure had application in showing that the observed temporal summation in gross nets does not imply such a mechanism in the interaction of individual neurons.

The phenomena of learning, which are of a character persisting over most physiological changes in nervous activity, seem to require the possibility of permanent alterations in the structure of nets. The simplest such alteration is the formation of new synapses or equivalent local depressions of threshold. We suppose that some axonal terminations cannot at first excite the succeeding neuron; but if at any time the neuron fires, and the axonal terminations are simultaneously excited, they become synapses of the ordinary kind, henceforth capable of exciting the neuron. The loss of an inhibitory synapse gives an entirely equivalent result. We shall then have

THEOREM VII.

Alterable synapses can be replaced by circles.

This is accomplished by the method of Figure 1i. It is also to be remarked that a neuron which becomes and remains spontaneously active can likewise be replaced by a circle, which is set into activity by a peripheral afferent when the activity commences, and inhibited by one when it ceases.

III. The Theory: Nets with Circles.

The treatment of nets which do not satisfy our previous assumption of freedom from circles is very much more difficult than that case. This is largely a consequence of the possibility that activity may be set up in a circuit and continue reverberating around it for an indefinite period of time, so that the realizable ***Pr*** may involve reference to past events of an indefinite degree of remoteness. Consider such a net $\mathfrak{N}$, say of order p, and let $c_1, c_2, \cdots, c_p$ be a cyclic set of neurons of $\mathfrak{N}$. It is first of all clear from the definition that every $\boldsymbol{N}_s$

of $\mathfrak{N}$ can be expressed as a *TPE*, of $N_1, N_2, \cdots, N_p$ and the absolute afferents; the solution of $\mathfrak{N}$ involves then only the determination of expressions for the cyclic set. This done, we shall derive a set of expressions [*A*]:

$$N_i(z_1) . \equiv . Pr_i[S^{n_{i1}} N_1(z_1), S^{n_{i2}} N_2(z_1), \cdots, S^{n_{ip}} N_p(z_1)], \quad (2)$$

where Pr_i also involves peripheral afferents. Now if n is the least common multiple of the n_{ij}, we shall, by substituting their equivalents according to (2) in (3) for the N_j, and repeating this process often enough on the result, obtain S of the form

$$N_i(z_1) . \equiv . Pr_1[S^n N_1(z_1), S^n N_2(z_1), \cdots, S^n N_p(z_1)] . \quad (3)$$

These expressions may be written in the Hilbert disjunctive normal form as

$$N_i(z_1) . \equiv . \sum_{\substack{a \varepsilon \kappa \\ \beta_a \varepsilon \kappa}} S_a \prod_{j \varepsilon \kappa} S^n N_j(z_1) \prod_{j \varepsilon \beta_a} \sim S^n N_j(z_1), \text{ for suitable } \kappa, \quad (4)$$

where S_a is a *TPE* of the absolute afferents of $\mathfrak{N}$. There exist some 2^p different sentences formed out of the p N_i by conjoining to the conjunction of some set of them the conjunction of the negations of the rest. Denumerating these by $X_1(z_1), X_2(z_1), \cdots, X_{2^p}(z_1)$, we may, by use of the expressions (4), arrive at an equipollent set of equations of the form

$$X_i(z_1) . \equiv . \sum_{j=1}^{2^p} Pr_{ij}(z_1) . S^n X_j(z_1) . \quad (5)$$

Now we import the subscripted numerals i,j into the object-language: i.e., define Pr_1 and Pr_2 such that $Pr_1(zz_1, z_1) . \equiv . X_i(z_1)$ and $Pr_2(zz_1, zz_2, z_1) . \equiv . Pr_{ij}(z_1)$ are provable whenever zz_1 and zz_2 denote i and j respectively.

Then we may rewrite (5) as

$$\begin{aligned}&(z_1) zz_p : Pr_1(z_1, z_3) \\ &\quad . \equiv . (Ez_2) zz_p . Pr_2(z_1, z_2, z_3 - zz_n) . Pr_1(z_2, z_3 - zz_n)\end{aligned} \quad (6)$$

where zz_n denotes n and zz_p denotes 2^p. By repeated substitution we arrive at an expression

$$\begin{aligned}&(z_1) zz_p : Pr_1(z_1, zz_n\, zz_2) . \equiv . (Ez_2) zz_p\, (Ez_3)\, zz_p \ldots (Ez_n) zz_p . \\ &Pr_2(z_1, z_2, zz_n(zz_2 - 1)) . Pr_2(z_2, z_3, zz_n(zz_2 - 1)) \ldots\ldots\end{aligned} \quad (7)$$

$Pr_2(z_{n-1}, z_n, 0) . Pr_1(z_n, 0)$, for any numeral zz_2 which denotes s. This is easily shown by induction to be equipollent to

$$\begin{aligned}&(z_1)zz_p : . Pr_1(z_1, zz_n zz_2) :\equiv: (Ef)(z_2)zz_2 - 1 f(z_2 zz_n) \\ &\leqq zz_p . f(zz_n zz_2) = z_1 . Pr_2(f(zz_n (z_2+1)), \\ &f(zz_n z_2)) . Pr_1(f(0), 0)\end{aligned} \tag{8}$$

and since this is the case for all zz_2, it is also true that

$$\begin{aligned}&(z_4)(z_1)zz_p : Pr_1(z_1, z_4) \;.\equiv. (Ef)(z_2)(z_4 - 1) . f(z_2) \\ &\leqq zz_p . f(z_4) = z_1 f(z_4) = z_1 . Pr_2[f(z_2+1), f(z_2), z_2]. \\ &Pr_1[f(\mathrm{res}(z_4, zz_n)), \mathrm{res}(z_4, zz_n)],\end{aligned} \tag{9}$$

where zz_n denotes n, $\mathrm{res}(r,s)$ is the residue of r mod s and zz_p denotes 2^p. This may be written in a less exact way as

$$\begin{aligned}N_i(t) .\equiv. (E\phi)(x)t - 1 . \phi(x) \leqq 2^p . \phi(t) = i . \\ P[\phi(x+1), \phi(x) . N_{\phi(0)}(0)],\end{aligned}$$

where x and t are also assumed divisible by n, and Pr_2 denotes P. From the preceding remarks we shall have

THEOREM VIII.

The expression (9) *for neurons of the cyclic set of a net* $\mathfrak{N}$ *together with certain* TPE *expressing the actions of other neurons in terms of them, constitute a solution of* $\mathfrak{N}$.

Consider now the question of the realizability of a set of S_i. A first necessary condition, demonstrable by an easy induction, is that

$$(z_2)z_1 . p_1(z_2) \equiv p_2(z_2) . \rightarrow . S_i \equiv S_i \begin{Bmatrix} p_1 \\ p_2 \end{Bmatrix} \tag{10}$$

should be true, with similar statements for the other free p in S_i: i.e., no nervous net can take account of future peripheral afferents. Any S_i satisfying this requirement can be replaced by an equipollent S of the form

$$\begin{aligned}(Ef)(z_2)z_1(z_3)zz_p : f \varepsilon Pr_{mi} \\ : f(z_1, z_2, z_3) = 1 . \equiv . p_{z_3}(z_2)\end{aligned} \tag{11}$$

where zz_p denotes p, by defining

$$\begin{aligned}Pr_{mi} = \hat{f}[(z_1)(z_2)z_1(z_3)zz_p \;: . f(z_1, z_2, z_3) = 0 . \mathrm{v} . f(z_1, z_2, z_3) \\ = 1 : f(z_1, z_2, z_3) = 1 . \equiv . p_{z_3}(z_2) : \rightarrow : S_i].\end{aligned}$$

Consider now these series of classes α_i, for which

$$\begin{aligned}N_i(t) :\equiv: (E\phi)(x)t(m)q : \phi\varepsilon\alpha_i : N_m(x) .\equiv. \phi(t, x, m) = 1 . \\ [i = q+1, \cdots, M]\end{aligned} \tag{12}$$

holds for some net. These will be called *prehensible* classes. Let us define the *Boolean ring* generated by a class of classes κ as the aggregate of the classes which can be formed from members of κ by repeated application of the logical operations; i.e., we put

$$\mathcal{R}(\kappa) \overset{.}{=} p`\hat{\lambda}[(\alpha,\beta):\alpha\,\varepsilon\,\kappa \rightarrow \alpha\,\varepsilon\,\lambda : \alpha,\beta\,\varepsilon\,\lambda\,.\rightarrow.-\alpha,\alpha\,.\,\beta,\alpha\vee\beta\,\varepsilon\,\lambda]\,.$$

We shall also define

$$\overline{\mathcal{R}}(\kappa)\,.=.\,\mathcal{R}(\kappa) - \iota`p` - ``\kappa\,,$$

$$\mathcal{R}_e(\kappa) = p`\hat{\lambda}[(\alpha,\beta):\alpha\,\varepsilon\,\kappa\rightarrow\alpha\,\varepsilon\,\lambda\,.\rightarrow.-\alpha,\alpha\,.\,\beta,\alpha\vee\beta,S``\alpha\,\varepsilon\,\lambda]$$

$$\overline{\mathcal{R}}_e(\kappa) = \mathcal{R}_e(\kappa) - \iota`p` - ``\kappa\,,$$

and

$$\sigma(\psi,t) = \hat{\phi}[(m)\,.\,\phi(t+1,t,m) = \psi(m)]\,.$$

The class $\mathcal{R}_e(\kappa)$ is formed from κ in analogy with $\mathcal{R}(\kappa)$, but by repeated application not only of the logical operations but also of that which replaces a class of properties $P\,\varepsilon\,\alpha$ by $S(P)\,\varepsilon\,S``\alpha$. We shall then have the

LEMMA

$\boldsymbol{Pr}_1(\boldsymbol{p}_1,\boldsymbol{p}_2,\cdots,\boldsymbol{p}_m,\boldsymbol{z}_1)$ is a *TPE* if and only if

$$(\boldsymbol{z}_1)(\boldsymbol{p}_1,\cdots,\boldsymbol{p}_m)(E\boldsymbol{p}_{m+1}) : \boldsymbol{p}_{m+1}\,\varepsilon\,\overline{\mathcal{R}}_e(\{\boldsymbol{p}_1,\boldsymbol{p}_2,\cdots,\boldsymbol{p}_m\})\;\boldsymbol{p}_{m+1}(\boldsymbol{z}_1) \equiv \boldsymbol{Pr}_1(\boldsymbol{p}_1,\boldsymbol{p}_2,\cdots,\boldsymbol{p}_m,\boldsymbol{z}_1) \qquad (13)$$

is true; and it is a *TPE* not involving 'S' if and only if this holds when '$\overline{\mathcal{R}}_e$' is replaced by '$\overline{\mathcal{R}}$', and we then obtain

THEOREM IX.

A series of classes $\alpha_1,\alpha_2,\cdots\alpha_s$ *is a series of prehensible classes if and only if*

$$\begin{aligned}&(Em)(En)(p)n(i)(\psi) :.\,(x)m\,\psi(x)=0\vee\psi(x)=1 : \rightarrow : (E\beta)\\ &(Ey)m\,.\,\psi(y)=0\,.\,\beta\,\varepsilon\,\mathcal{R}[\hat{\gamma}((Ei)\,.\,\gamma=\alpha_i))\,.\vee.\,(x)m\,.\\ &\psi(x)=0\,.\,\beta\,\varepsilon\,\overline{\mathcal{R}}[\hat{\gamma}((Ei)\,.\,\gamma=\alpha_i)] : (t)(\phi) : \phi\,\varepsilon\,\alpha_i\,.\\ &\quad\sigma(\phi,nt+p)\,.\rightarrow.\,(Ef)\,.\,f\,\varepsilon\,\beta\,.\,(w)m(x)t-1\,.\\ &\quad\quad\phi(n(t+1)+p,nx+p,w)=f(nt+p,nx+p,w).\end{aligned} \qquad (14)$$

The proof here follows directly from the lemma. The condition is necessary, since every net for which an expression of the form (4) can be written obviously verifies it, the ψ's being the characteristic functions of the S_a and the β for each ψ being the class whose designation has the form $\prod_{i\varepsilon a} Pr_i \prod_{j\varepsilon\beta_a} Pr_j$, where Pr_k denotes α_k for all k. Conversely, we may write an expression of the form (4) for a net $\mathcal{N}$ fulfilling prehensible classes satisfying (14) by putting for the Pr_a Pr denoting the ψ's, and a Pr, written in the analogue for classes of the disjunctive normal form, and denoting the α corresponding to that ψ, conjoined to it. Since every S of the form (4) is clearly realizable, we have the theorem.

It is of some interest to consider the extent to which we can by knowledge of the present determine the whole past of various special nets: i.e., when we may construct a net the firing of the cyclic set of whose neurons requires the peripheral afferents to have had a set of past values specified by given functions ϕ_i. In this case the classes α_i of the last theorem reduced to unit classes; and the condition may be transformed into

$$\begin{aligned}&(E\,m\,,n)\,(p)\,n(i\,,\psi)\,(Ej)\;:.\;(x)m : \psi(x)=0\;.\mathrm{v}.\;\psi(x)=1 :\\ &\quad\phi_i\;\varepsilon\;\sigma(\psi\,,n\,t+p)\;:\rightarrow:\;(w)\,m(x)t-1\;.\;\phi_i(n(t+1)\\ &\quad+p\,,n\,x+p\,,w)=\phi_j(n\,t+p\,,n\,x+p\,,w)\;:.\\ &\quad(u\,,v)\,(w)m\,.\,\phi_i(n(u+1)+p\,,n\,u+p\,,w)\\ &\quad=\phi_i(n(v+1)+p\,,n\,v+p\,,w).\end{aligned}$$

On account of limitations of space, we have presented the above argument very sketchily; we propose to expand it and certain of its implications in a further publication.

The condition of the last theorem is fairly simple in principle, though not in detail; its application to practical cases would, however, require the exploration of some 2^{2^n} classes of functions, namely the members of $\mathcal{R}(\{\alpha_1\,,\cdots,\alpha_s\})$. Since each of these is a possible β of Theorem IX, this result cannot be sharpened. But we may obtain a sufficient condition for the realizability of an S which is very easily applicable and probably covers most practical purposes. This is given by

THEOREM *X*.

Let us define a set K of S by the following recursion:

1. Any *TPE* and any *TPE* whose arguments have been replaced by members of K belong to K;

2. If $Pr_1(z_1)$ is a member of K, then $(z_2)z_1\,.\,Pr_1(z_2)$, $(Ez_2)z_1\,.$

$Pr_1(z_2)$, and $C_{mn}(z_1)$. **s** belong to it, where C_{mn} denotes the property of being congruent to m modulo n, $m < n$.

3. *The set* **K** *has no further members*

Then every member of K is realizable.

For, if $Pr_1(z_1)$ is realizable, nervous nets for which

$$N_i(z_1) . \equiv . Pr_1(z_1) . SN_i(z_1)$$
$$N_i(z_1) . \equiv . Pr_1(z_1) \vee SN_i(z_1)$$

are the expressions of equation (4), realize $(z_2)z_1 . Pr_1(z_2)$ and $(E\ z_2)z_1 . Pr_1(z_2)$ respectively; and a simple circuit, $c_1, c_2, \cdots, c_n$, of n links, each sufficient to excite the next, gives an expression

$$N_m(z_1) . \equiv . N_1(0) . C_{mn}$$

for the last form. By induction we derive the theorem.

One more thing is to be remarked in conclusion. It is easily shown: first, that every net, if furnished with a tape, scanners connected to afferents, and suitable efferents to perform the necessary motor-operations, can compute only such numbers as can a Turing machine; second, that each of the latter numbers can be computed by such a net; and that nets with circles can be computed by such a net; and that nets with circles can compute, without scanners and a tape, some of the numbers the machine can, but no others, and not all of them. This is of interest as affording a psychological justification of the Turing definition of computability and its equivalents, Church's λ — definability and Kleene's primitive recursiveness: If any number can be computed by an organism, it is computable by these definitions, and conversely.

IV. Consequences

Causality, which requires description of states and a law of necessary connection relating them, has appeared in several forms in several sciences, but never, except in statistics, has it been as irreciprocal as in this theory. Specification for any one time of afferent stimulation and of the activity of all constituent neurons, each an "all-or-none" affair, determines the state. Specification of the nervous net provides the law of necessary connection whereby one can compute from the description of any state that of the succeeding state, but the inclusion of disjunctive relations prevents complete determination of the one before. Moreover, the regenerative activity of constituent circles renders reference indefinite as to time past. Thus our knowledge of the world, including ourselves, is incomplete

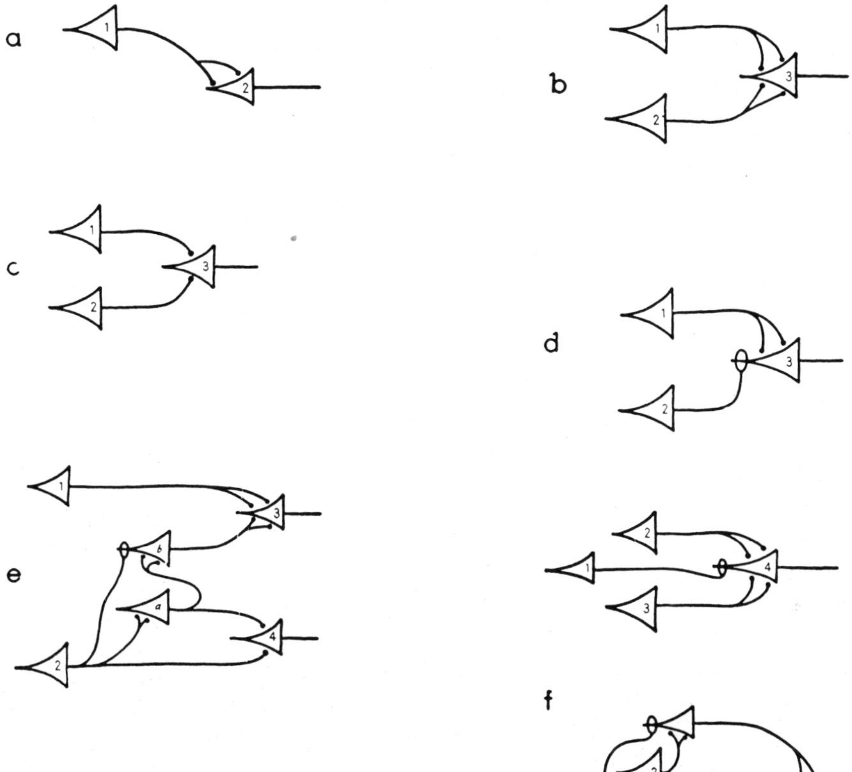

FIGURE 1

as to space and indefinite as to time. This ignorance, implicit in all our brains, is the counterpart of the abstraction which renders our knowledge useful. The role of brains in determining the epistemic relations of our theories to our observations and of these to the facts is all too clear, for it is apparent that every idea and every sensation is realized by activity within that net, and by no such activity are the actual afferents fully determined.

There is no theory we may hold and no observation we can make that will retain so much as its old defective reference to the facts if the net be altered. Tinitus, paraesthesias, hallucinations, delusions, confusions and disorientations intervene. Thus empiry confirms that if our nets are undefined, our facts are undefined, and to the "real" we can attribute not so much as one quality or "form." With determination of the net, the unknowable object of knowledge, the "thing in itself," ceases to be unknowable.

To psychology, however defined, specification of the net would contribute all that could be achieved in that field—even if the analysis were pushed to ultimate psychic units or "psychons," for a psychon can be no less than the activity of a single neuron. Since that activity is inherently propositional, all psychic events have an intentional, or "semiotic," character. The "all-or-none" law of these activities, and the conformity of their relations to those of the logic of propositions, insure that the relations of psychons are those of the two-valued logic of propositions. Thus in psychology, introspective, behavioristic or physiological, the fundamental relations are those of two-valued logic.

EXPRESSION FOR THE FIGURES

In the figure the neuron c_i is always marked with the numeral i upon the body of the cell, and the corresponding action is denoted by 'N' with i as subscript, as in the text.

Figure 1a $N_2(t) \,.\!\equiv.\, N_1(t-1)$

Figure 1b $N_3(t) \,.\!\equiv.\, N_1(t-1) \vee N_2(t-1)$

Figure 1c $N_3(t) \,.\!\equiv.\, N_1(t-1) . N_2(t-1)$

Figure 1d $N_3(t) \,.\!\equiv.\, N_1(t-1) . \sim N_2(t-1)$

Figure 1e $N_3(t) \,:\!\equiv:\, N_1(t-1) . \vee . N_2(t-3) . \sim N_2(t-2)$

$N_4(t) \,.\!\equiv.\, N_2(t-2) . N_2(t-1)$

Figure 1f $N_4(t) \,:\!\equiv:\, \sim N_1(t-1) . N_2(t-1) \vee N_3(t-1) . \vee . N_1(t-1) . N_2(t-1) . N_3(t-1)$

$N_4(t) \,:\!\equiv:\, \sim N_1(t-2) . N_2(t-2) \vee N_3(t-2) . \vee . N_1(t-2) . N_2(t-2) . N_3(t-2)$

Figure 1g $N_3(t) \,.\!\equiv.\, N_2(t-2) . \sim N_1(t-3)$

Figure 1h $N_2(t) \,.\!\equiv.\, N_1(t-1) . N_1(t-2)$

Figure 1i $N_3(t) \,:\!\equiv:\, N_2(t-1) . \vee . N_1(t-1) . (Ex)t-1 . N_1(x) . N_2(x)$

Hence arise constructional solutions of holistic problems involving the differentiated continuum of sense awareness and the normative, perfective and resolvent properties of perception and execution. From the irreciprocity of causality it follows that even if the net be known, though we may predict future from present activities, we can deduce neither afferent from central, nor central from efferent, nor past from present activities—conclusions which are reinforced by the contradictory testimony of eye-witnesses, by the difficulty of diagnosing differentially the organically diseased, the hysteric and the malingerer, and by comparing one's own memories or recollections with his contemporaneous records. Moreover, systems which so respond to the difference between afferents to a regenerative net and certain activity within that net, as to reduce the difference, exhibit purposive behavior; and organisms are known to possess many such systems, subserving homeostasis, appetition and attention. Thus both the formal and the final aspects of that activitv which we are wont to call *mental* are rigorously deduceable from present neurophysiology. The psychiatrist may take comfort from the obvious conclusion concerning causality—that, for prognosis, history is never necessary. He can take little from the equally valid conclusion that his observables are explicable only in terms of nervous activities which, until recently, have been beyond his ken. The crux of this ignorance is that inference from any sample of overt behavior to nervous nets is not unique, whereas, of imaginable nets, only one in fact exists, and may, at any moment, exhibit some unpredictable activity. Certainly for the psychiatrist it is more to the point that in such systems "Mind" no longer "goes more ghostly than a ghost." Instead, diseased mentality can be understood without loss of scope or rigor, in the scientific terms of neurophysiology. For neurology, the theory sharpens the distinction between nets necessary or merely sufficient for given activities, and so clarifies the relations of disturbed structure to disturbed function. In its own domain the difference between equivalent nets and nets equivalent in the narrow sense indicates the appropriate use and importance of temporal studies of nervous activity: and to mathematical biophysics the theory contributes a tool for rigorous symbolic treatment of known nets and an easy method of constructing hypothetical nets of required properties.

LITERATURE

Carnap, R. 1938. *The Logical Syntax of Language.* New York: Harcourt, Brace and Company.

Hilbert, D., und Ackermann, W. 1927. *Grundüge der Theoretischen Logik.* Berlin: J. Springer.

Russell, B., and Whitehead, A. N. 1925. *Principa Mathematica.* Cambridge: Cambridge University Press.

Reprinted from *Artificial Intelligence,* IEEE Publ. S–142, 1963, pp. 107–128

2

THRESHOLD LOGIC IN ARTIFICIAL INTELLIGENCE

BY

R. O. WINDER

Artificial Intelligence, Threshold Logic, Computers, McCulloch-Pitts Neuron, Probabilistic Approach, Synthesis, Switching Theory, Gates, Bayes Nets, Networks

THRESHOLD LOGIC IN ARTIFICIAL INTELLIGENCE*

R. O. Winder RCA Laboratories

Summary: Threshold logic is the mathematical study of a class of logical functions which have been widely used in the field of artificial intelligence. These functions have been called threshold functions, linear-input functions, majority functions, etc., and are identical with the functions realized by the McCulloch-Pitts neuron. The first section of the paper compares a standard probabilistic approach for the synthesis of such a device with a (more successful) new switching theoretic method. A survey of threshold logic constitutes the remainder of the paper.

INTRODUCTION

Threshold logic, a new and active area of switching theory, has been primarily motivated by an interest in certain computer devices called "threshold gates". The logical functions performed by such gates -- called threshold functions, linear-input functions, majority functions, etc., - have been given a great deal of mathematical attention. A switching function f of n arguments is a threshold function when there exist weights $a_1, a_2, \ldots a_n$ and a threshold T (all real numbers) so that

$$f(x_1, \ldots, x_n) = \begin{cases} 1 & \text{if} \sum_{i=1}^{n} a_i x_i \geq T, \\ 0 & \text{if} \sum_{i=1}^{n} a_i x_i < T. \end{cases}$$

Recently, the interesting possibilities of a second major field of application have become apparent: To define complicated decision functions of many variables, students of artificial intelligence almost invariably have used the simple and natural idea of "linear separation" -- their basic functions have turned out to be threshold functions. It seems that both biological and engineering reasons lie behind this: First, the psycho-physiological theories of learning and perception (e.g. Hebb) have employed theories of neural nets (McCulloch and Pitts); these neural models are in fact typical threshold gates. Second, investigators of self-adjusting switching devices have found neuron-like elements to be easily controllable.

* The research reported in this paper was sponsored by the Electronics Research Directorate, Air Force Cambridge Research Laboratories, Office of Aerospace Research, under Contract AF19(604)-8423.

I feel that threshold logic has much to offer students of artificial intelligence. Furthermore, an increased interaction will surely produce interesting new developments in threshold logic, For instance, in the next section we will consider an important common area between the fields: The synthesis of a single threshold gate for purposes of pattern recognition. The frequently used probabilistic approach to the problem will be outlined, its main shortcomings discussed, and an alternative given, which arises from the switching theoretic point of view. It will be shown that the probabilistic results are always worse than the crudest form of the switching theoretic results.

The remainder of the paper is a general survey of the relevant sections of threshold logic. A guide to the literature is provided, specifically slanted towards the student of artificial intelligence. This is an attempt to stimulate the interest of such people in threshold logic, to make the literature easily accessible, and to encourage their continued attention.

TWO METHODS OF THRESHOLD GATE SYNTHESIS

The optical recognition of characters is a commercially important problem; much of what is said below is significant in this area. Pattern recognition, a generalization of character recognition, plays many roles in artificial intelligence. As Minsky* sees it, for instance, one wants a computer to categorize the various problems presented to it into patterns, in order to choose suitable methods of solution. To do this, the computer determines, for each incoming problem, whether or not it satisfies each of a list of *properties*. (Exactly the analogous thing is usually done in optical character recognition.) If we call this list of properties an *input vector*, then the final step in the process is: Given an input vector, to determine into which category the given problem is to be put; each category has a set of associated methods to be used in solving the problem. Without loss of generality, we will restrict outselves to the question of determining whether or not the given input vector belongs to a *single* given pattern.

This reduces the problem to switching theory: To accomplish the last step in pattern recognition, a certain switching function of the input vector must be computed. (If the input vector belongs to the pattern, the value of the function for that vector is 1, otherwise 0.) Theoretically, switching theory could be used to realize such a function. However, because often the number of inputs is far too large to be handled by conventional switching theory, and because the function cannot be completely specified in practice, the following procedure is often followed to design a decision network. (We follow Minsky's excellent discussion of the matter.*)

* Marvin Minsky, "Steps Towards Artificial Intelligence", *PROC IRE*, Vol. 49, pp. 8-30, January 1961.

Bayes Nets

We make several assumptions. First, we "assume that the situation is basically probabilistic" (Minsky). Next, we assume that we know, or can estimate, certain conditional probabilities: The probability of the ith property holding, given that the input vector belongs to the pattern. Finally, we assume that these probabilities are, in a sense described below, independent. Now we can design a system which is able to compute the probability that a given input vector should be assigned functional value 1 or 0 (in or out of the pattern). When several possible patterns are being considered, the system might classify by choosing the pattern with the highest probability. More generally, we specify levels of confidence, so that the machine may fail to classify certain unusual problems; in our case of a single pattern, a confidence level $\Lambda > 1/2$ would be used.

More explicitly, suppose the inputs are associated with variables

$$\vec{x} = (x_1, x_2, \ldots\ldots, x_n)$$

and a particular instance of the inputs is represented by

$$\vec{\xi} = (\xi_1, \xi_2, \ldots\ldots, \xi_n).$$

We are assuming that we know the probabilities

$$p_i = Pr(x_i = 1 \mid f(\vec{x}) = 1)$$

$$r_i = Pr(x_i = 1 \mid f(\vec{x}) = 0)$$

and

$$p_0 = Pr(f(\vec{x}) = 1).$$

From these we obtain the related probabilities:

$$1 - p_i = Pr(x_i = 0 \mid f(\vec{x}) = 1)$$

$$1 - r_i = Pr(x_i = 0 \mid f(\vec{x}) = 0).$$

The independence assumption is that

$$Pr(\vec{x} = \vec{\xi} \mid f(\vec{x}) = 1) = \prod_{i=1}^{n} Pr(x_i = \xi_i \mid f(\vec{x}) = 1)$$

and similarly with $f(\vec{x}) = 0$.

Now we use the Bayes law, writing

$$Pr(f(\vec{x}) = 1 \text{ and } \vec{x} = \vec{\xi}) = Pr(f(\vec{x}) = 1 \mid \vec{x} = \vec{\xi}) \cdot Pr(\vec{x} = \vec{\xi})$$

$$= Pr(\vec{x} = \vec{\xi} \mid f(\vec{x}) = 1) \cdot Pr(f(\vec{x}) = 1).$$

Thus

$$\Pr(f(\vec{\xi}) = 1) = \Pr(f(\vec{x}) = 1 \mid \vec{x} = \vec{\xi})$$
$$= \Pr(\vec{x} = \vec{\xi} \mid f(\vec{x}) = 1) \cdot \frac{\Pr(f(\vec{x}) = 1)}{\Pr(\vec{x} = \vec{\xi})} .$$

Three alternatives face us: 1.) We can write $\Pr(\vec{x} = \vec{\xi})$ in terms of the probabilities given us,* yielding somewhat more complicated rules than we obtain below, or 2.) We can follow Minsky's discussion, taking at this point a maximum over the quantities

$$\Pr(\vec{x} = \vec{\xi} \mid f(\vec{x}) = 1) = \prod_i \Pr(x_i = \xi_i \mid f(\vec{x}) = 1)$$

for the various patterns (f's), or 3.) We can assume at this point that the $\vec{\xi}$ are equiprobable, so that $\Pr(\vec{x} = \vec{\xi})$ is independent of $\vec{\xi}$. For purposes of simplicity of illustration, we make this last assumption; it will make other future computations simpler also.

If $\Pr(f(\vec{\xi}) = 1)$ is calculated to be greater than some confidence level, then, we will ask the machine to guess that $f(\vec{\xi}) = 1$ (i.e. to classify an incoming problem into the corresponding category). Otherwise, $f(\vec{\xi}) = 0$. We convert this calculation into the characteristic threshold function form as follows:

$$\Pr(f(\vec{\xi}) = 1) \geq \Lambda \qquad \text{if and only if}$$

$$\Pr(\vec{x} = \vec{\xi} \mid f(\vec{x}) = 1) \geq \Lambda \cdot \frac{\Pr(\vec{x} = \vec{\xi})}{\Pr(f(\vec{x}) = 1)} \qquad \text{if and only if}$$

$$\prod_i \Pr(x_i = \xi_i \mid f(\vec{x}) = 1) \geq \Lambda \cdot \frac{\Pr(\vec{x} = \vec{\xi})}{\Pr(f(\vec{x}) = 1)} \qquad \text{if and only if}$$

$$\prod_i \frac{\Pr(x_i = \xi_i \mid f(\vec{x}) = 1)}{\Pr(x_i = 0 \mid f(\vec{x}) = 1)} \geq \theta \qquad \text{(for appropriate } \theta\text{) if and only if}$$

$$\sum_i \log \frac{\Pr(x_i = \xi_i \mid f(\vec{x}) = 1)}{\Pr(x_i = 0 \mid f(\vec{x}) = 1)} \geq \log \theta \qquad \text{if and only if}$$

$$\sum_i a_i \, \xi_i \geq T,$$

where

$$a_i = \log \frac{\Pr(x_i = 1 \mid f(\vec{x}) = 1)}{\Pr(x_i = 0 \mid f(\vec{x}) = 1)} ,$$

and $T = \log \theta$. T can be calculated from the various probabilities that we know, as are the a_i, but the general philosophy here is to generate the a_i as specified, and to pick the T so as to optimize performance.

* cf. M. E. Maron, "Design Principles for an Intelligent Machine", IRE TIC, Vol IT-8, pp. 179-185, September 1962.

Now: I would like to discuss the following question -- If we intend to use a threshold function for the recognition procedure, does the above point of view provide the best, or even good, sets of weights a_i?

Saul Amarel (RCA Laboratories) has suggested to me that the independence assumption is a very severe one, and that only a small proportion of threshold functions might actually be realized by the above procedure. This observation has motivated the investigations reported below -- indeed, using the same data, a <u>simpler</u> rule will be shown to work better, and allow of a startling improvement; nonprobabilistic switching theory viewpoint is applied to obtain these results.

We facilitate a comparison by considering the following situation: All 2^n of the $\vec{\xi}$ are given equal probability of occurring, and each $f(\vec{\xi})$ is specified. We assume f is a threshold function. Probabilities are simply obtained by counting frequencies: Let f_{x_i} be the restriction of f obtained by setting $x_i = 1$, $f_{\bar{x}_i}$ obtained by setting $x_i = 0$, and let m(f) be the number of different $\vec{\xi}$ such that $f(\vec{\xi}) = 1$. Schematically, suppose the 2^n possible $\vec{\xi}$ are mapped as in the diagram ($f(\vec{\xi}) = 1$ in the shaded area, 0 otherwise):

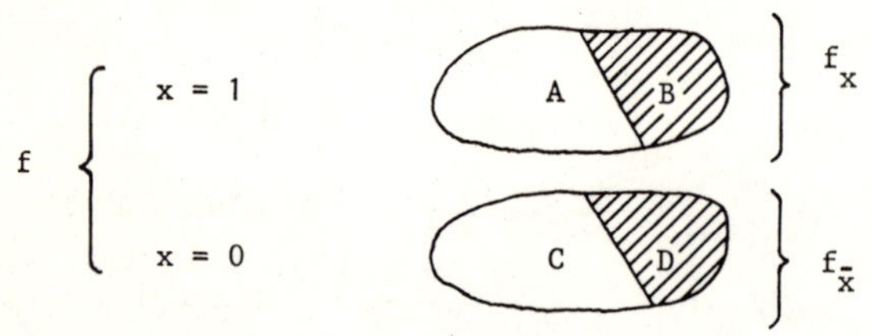

If A, B, C, and D are the number of input vectors $\vec{\xi}$ in the four regions, respectively, then $A = m(\bar{f}_x)$, $B = m(f_x)$, $C = m(\bar{f}_{\bar{x}})$, and $D = m(f_{\bar{x}})$. Note that $m(f) = B + D = m(f_x) + m(f_{\bar{x}})$, $m(\bar{f}_x) + m(f_x) = 2^{n-1}$, etc. Since the $\vec{\xi}$ are equiprobable, we have

$$p_i = \frac{m(f_{x_i})}{m(f)}$$

$$r_i = \frac{m(\bar{f}_{x_i})}{m(\bar{f})}$$

$$p_o = \frac{m(f)}{2^n}$$

<u>Theorem</u>: The independence assumptions hold only for constant functions and functions which are the identity (or complement) in some argument.

<u>Proof</u>: If f is constant (0 or 1), the independence is trivial, so suppose f is not a constant function. By simple properties of threshold functions, we now know that we can, without loss of generality, assume that $f(0) = 0$ and $f(\vec{1}) = 1$, where

$$\vec{0} = (0, 0, \ldots, 0)$$
$$\vec{1} = (1, 1, \ldots, 1).$$

Thus

$$Pr(\vec{x} = \vec{1} \mid f(\vec{x}) = 0) = 0,$$

so that if the independence assumptions hold,

$$0 = \prod_i r_i = \prod_i \frac{m(\bar{f}_{x_i})}{m(\bar{f})} .$$

But one of the factors must be zero, so for that i,

$$\begin{aligned} m(f) &= 2^n - m(\bar{f}) = 2^n - [m(\bar{f}_{x_i}) + m(\bar{f}_{\bar{x}_i})] \\ &= 2^n - m(\bar{f}_{\bar{x}_i}) \geq 2^n - 2^{n-1} = 2^{n-1} \end{aligned} \qquad 1.)$$

On the other hand

$$Pr(\vec{x} = \vec{0} \mid f(\vec{x}) = 1) = 0,$$

so by the independence assumption

$$0 = \prod_i (1 - p_i) = \prod_i \left(1 - \frac{m(f_{x_i})}{m(f)}\right) .$$

Again some factor, say the jth, must be zero:

$$m(f) = m(f_{x_j}). \qquad 2.)$$

But now, from 1.) and 2.),

$$2^{n-1} \leq m(f) = m(f_{x_j}) \leq 2^{n-1} ,$$

so all the terms are equal. Thus for some j, f_{x_j} must be the constant 1. Also, since $m(f_{\bar{x}_j}) = m(f) - m(f_{x_j}) = 0$, $f_{\bar{x}_j}$ must be the constant 0. Thus $f(\vec{x}) = x_j$.

END OF PROOF.

Thus we have shown that for any interesting threshold function, with equi-probable input combinations, the independence assumptions in fact don't hold. The theorem can probably be extended to more general input distributions, - possibly to arbitrary distributions. This substantiates Saul Amarel's conjecture, and suggests that the Bayesian approach can be improved upon. In the next section we consider a different viewpoint.

Geometric Synthesis

A standard switching-theoretic geometric interpretation of threshold functions is as follows: The inputs take on values ± 1, the input n-tuples $\vec{\xi}$ are mapped correspondingly onto the 2^n corners of a $2 \times 2 \times \ldots \times 2$ cube centered on the origin of a Euclidean n-space. For a given f, those corners (or vertices) for which $f(\vec{\xi}) = 1$, are called 1-vertices; if $f(\vec{\xi}) = 0$, the vertex is a 0-vertex. An (n + 1)-tuple $a_o, a_1, \ldots, a_n$ of real numbers is a realization of f when the hyperplane

$$a_o + a_1 x_1 + \ldots + a_n x_n = 0$$

separates the cube so that 0-vertices lie on one side, 1-vertices on the other; when such a hyperplane exists, f is a threshold function. (Note: We still use 0 and 1 for outputs.)

In order that we can treat the threshold in the same manner as other weights, and so that the hyperplane will pass symmetrically through the origin, we add a new dimension and variable x_o; when $x_o = +1$ we define the new function to agree with our original function, when $x_o = -1$, we define the new function to agree with the dual of the original. (This is the self-dualization idea of [Goto-Takahasi].)

Now: An appropriate normal form for the equation of such a hyperplane is

$$x_o \cos \alpha_o + x_1 \cos \alpha_1 + x_2 \cos \alpha_2 + \ldots + x_n \cos \alpha_n = 0,$$

where the α_i are direction angles between a normal to the plane and the corresponding coordinate axes. We will relate direction angles to area on an n-sphere, and then area on the n-sphere to the $m(f_{x_i})$, by straightforward geometric arguments, sketched in the following.

Suppose we pass an origin-centered (n + 1)-sphere of radius $\sqrt{(n+1)}$ through the 2^{n+1} vertices of the "cube" which we have defined in E^{n+1}. (See figure, next page.) For concreteness, let us consider now a particular coordinate (say x) which we consider "up". (We should speak of an x_i; "i" is dropped for convenience. We want to find $a = \cos \alpha$ for this x.) All the other axes define a hyperplane, which we call "horizontal". If we pass hyperplanes parallel to this one, at a distance 1 "above" and 1 "below", we have isolated the regions where x = + 1 and x = - 1 respectively -- this is where f_x and $f_{\bar{x}}$ are represented. We will consider only f_x below; by our construction, $f_{\bar{x}}$ is just its dual. Within the n-dimensional region containing f_x, the original (n+1)-sphere defines an n-sphere by intersection. Furthermore, let us imagine our separating hyperplane passed through the figure; it will divide the n-sphere into two parts (corresponding to 0-vertices and 1-vertices). Now, since the 2^n vertices are spread evenly over the surface of the n-sphere, the ratio $m(\bar{f}_x)/m(f_x)$ is an estimate of the ratio of areas cutoff by the separating hyperplane. For greater convenience, we define the ratio

$$r = \frac{(\text{Area on 1-vertex side in upper n-sphere}) \; -1/2 \; (\text{Area of n-sphere})}{1/2 \; (\text{Area of n-sphere})}$$

$$\approx \frac{m(f_x) - 2^{n-1}}{2^{n-1}} \; .$$

(r will have the same sign as the final weight; r = 0 when f is insensitive to x.)

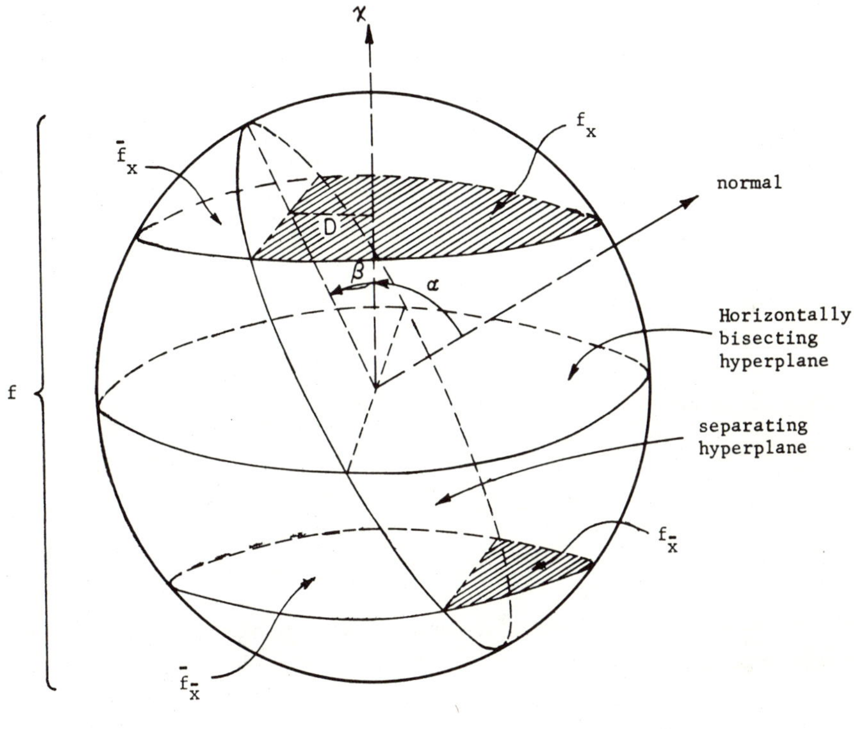

We assume that r is known by counting (or sampling) vertices; we see next that this ratio determines the distance, D, which separates the separating hyperplane (as induced in the upper n-sphere) from the origin (of the upper n-sphere). With a bit of trigonometry, it can be seen that

$$dr = \frac{2\omega_{n-1}(\sqrt{n-D^2})^{n-2}}{\omega_n \; (\sqrt{n})^{n-1}} \cdot \frac{\sqrt{n}\; dD}{\sqrt{n-D^2}}$$

(where ω_n is the area of the unit n-sphere) so

$$\frac{dD}{dr} = \frac{\sqrt{n}\,\omega_n}{2\,\omega_{n-1}} \left(1 - \frac{D^2}{n}\right)^{\frac{3-n}{2}} .$$

Set

$$k = \frac{\sqrt{n}\,\omega_n}{2\,\omega_{n-1}} .$$

Initial conditions are that r = 0 when D = 0 (and r = 1 when D = $\sqrt{n}$).

But if we know D (in terms of r), then we can determine the angle β between the separating hyperplane in (n+1)-space, and the x - axis -- we have a right triangle with adjacent side 1, opposite side D. And the direction angle α is the complement of β, so

$$a = \cos\alpha = \sin\beta = \frac{D}{\sqrt{1+D^2}} = \frac{\text{sign (D)}}{\left(\frac{1}{D^2} + 1\right)^{1/2}}$$

(We drop the "sign (D)", but in practice it is used, of course, to assign the sign!) Solving for D:

$$D^2 = \frac{a^2}{1-a^2} .$$

Now we can calculate

$$\frac{da}{dr} = \frac{da}{dD}\frac{dD}{dr} = (D^2 + 1)^{-3/2} \cdot k\left(1 - \frac{D^2}{n}\right)^{\frac{3-n}{2}}$$

$$= k(1 - a^2)^{n/2} \left(1 - \frac{n+1}{n} a^2\right)^{\frac{3-n}{2}}$$

(after substituting and rearranging). Noting that a = r = 0 at D = 0, we calculate an expansion for a around r = 0:

$$a = kr - k^3\left(2 + \frac{3}{n}\right)\frac{r^3}{6} + k^5\left(22 + \frac{54}{n} + \frac{4s}{n^2}\right)\frac{r^5}{120} - \cdots$$

The constant

$$k = \frac{\sqrt{n}\,\omega_n}{2\,\omega_{n-1}} = \sqrt{n}\,\frac{2\,\pi^{n/2}}{\Gamma\left(\frac{n}{2}\right)} \Bigg/ 2 \cdot \frac{2\,\pi^{\frac{n-1}{2}}}{\Gamma\left(\frac{n-1}{2}\right)} = \frac{\sqrt{n\,\pi}\,\Gamma\left(\frac{n-1}{2}\right)}{2\,\Gamma\left(\frac{n}{2}\right)},$$

$k \to \sqrt{\frac{\pi}{2}}$ as $n \to \infty$ (Wallis' Theorem).

If we take out the dummy x_o and divide all weights by $k \cdot 2^{-n}$, we obtain (setting $k^2(2 + 3/n)/6 = \lambda$)

$$a_i = [m(f_{x_i}) - m(f_{\bar{x}_i})] - \lambda\, [m(f_{x_i}) - m(f_{\bar{x}_i})]^3 + \ldots$$

and threshold

$$T' = [2^{n-1} - m(f)] - \lambda\, [2^{n-1} - m(f)]^3 + \ldots$$

This threshold is for a ± 1 system; using a standard rule, the threshold for a (0, 1) system (as defined in the introduction) is then

$$T = 1/2\ (T' + a_1 + a_2 + \ldots + a_n).$$

Experience in the application of these rules has been very good: Often the first approximation, $a_i = m(f_{x_i}) - m(f_{\bar{x}_i})$ and $T' = 2^{n-1} - m(f)$, realizes given threshold functions. For all functions tried (including a complicated ten-argument example), it was easy to find a λ so that the second approximations worked; the values were very close to the predicted λ's. Randomized experiments on a computer are planned to check the general worth of the second approximation, to determine the variation of λ from function to function for a given n, and to determine a good value of λ as a function of n. (λ = .0008 worked nicely for n = 7, λ = .00001 for n = 10.)

An important note: Chow [Chow-2], along with other theoretically very interesting results, has shown that the signs and relative magnitudes of the a_i assigned by the first approximation $a_i = m(f_{x_i}) - m(f_{\bar{x}_i})$ are always correct.

Comparison and Comments

Theorem: The Bayes approach produces a set of weights worse than does the first geometric approximation, described above.

Proof: Assume that the weights should all be positive -- if they aren't, suitable complementations make them so. It is clear from experience with the first approximation, and follows from the fact that a better approximation subtracts a cubic term from the first, that the first approximation gives exaggeratedly high first estimates to the larger a_i; in other words, for $a_i > a_j$, the ratio

$$\frac{m(f_{x_i}) - m(f_{\bar{x}_i})}{m(f_{x_j}) - m(f_{\bar{x}_j})}$$

is too high (for the best chance of realization). Let us abbreviate, putting $m_i = m(f_{x_i})$, and m = m(f). Now we will show that the Bayesian weights

$$a_i = \log \frac{m_i/m}{1-m_i/m} = \log \frac{m_i}{m-m_i}$$

are worse yet, because for $m_i > m_j$,

$$\frac{\log \frac{m_i}{m-m_i}}{\log \frac{m_j}{m-m_j}} > \frac{m_i - (m-m_i)}{m_j - (m-m_j)} = \frac{m_i - m/2}{m_j - m/2}$$

which is already too large. We know that $0 \leq m_j < m_i \leq m$, and we drop the equality possibilities, where the Bayes weights blow up. Furthermore, because of the positivity assumption (and [Chow-2], for instance), $m(f_{x_j}) > m(f_{\bar{x}_j})$, i.e. $m_j > m-m_j$, so $m_j > m/2$. Putting $y = \frac{m_i}{m}$ and $x = \frac{m_j}{m}$, we want then to prove: For $1/2 < x < y < 1$,

$$\frac{\log \frac{y}{1-y}}{\log \frac{x}{1-x}} > \frac{y - 1/2}{x - 1/2} \; .$$

Since $\log \frac{x}{1-x} > 0$ and $x - 1/2 > 0$, we need only show that the function

$$g(x,y) = (x-1/2) \log \frac{y}{1-y} - (y-1/2) \log \frac{x}{1-x}$$

is positive in the range R: $1/2 < x < y < 1$. But

$$\frac{\partial g}{\partial y} = (x-1/2) \cdot \frac{1-y}{y} \cdot \left[\frac{1}{1-y} + \frac{y}{(1-y)^2}\right] - \log \frac{x}{1-x}$$

$$= \frac{(x-1/2)}{y(1-y)} - \log \frac{x}{1-x}$$

and

$$\frac{\partial}{\partial x} \frac{\partial g}{\partial y} = \frac{1}{y(1-y)} - \frac{1}{x(1-x)} = \frac{(y-x)(y+x-1)}{y(1-y)x(1-x)}$$

which is positive in R. And

$$\left.\frac{\partial g}{\partial y}\right]_{x=1/2} = 0,$$

(the left boundary of R), so $\frac{\partial g}{\partial y}$ is positive in R. (There are no discontinuities.) But

$$g(x,x) = 0,$$

(The lower boundary of R), so g is positive in R (again no discontinuities), as we wanted to show. Thus the ratio of larger weights to smaller weights is greater in the Bayesian approach than in the first geometric approximation, where it is already too high.

END OF PROOF.

We have shown that the Bayesian approach is poor for the synthesis of threshold functions, assuming equiprobable inputs and complete specification. It should be clear that neither of these are important in geometric synthesis, however: Probabilities of inputs play no role, and the areas can be estimated from samples, when the function is incompletely specified. (Use a weighting density function so that closely packed sample points have their proper effect relative to sparsely packed ones.). Whether the Bayesian approach is inferior to the geometric in the case of non-threshold functions, has not been investigated. (Here probabilities mean something -- the problem is to minimize the probability of error, say, when a threshold function is used as an approximation.) I would guess that it still is.

As an example of these ideas, consider the function expressed by

$$A[B(C+D+E)+CD(E+F)+(C+D)EF]+BCD(E+F),$$

which has (minimum integral) realization

7, 6, 4, 4, 3, 2; Threshold 16.

The weights generated by the Bayesian approach are

$$\log \frac{19}{3}, \log \frac{17}{5}, \log \frac{15}{7}, \log \frac{15}{7}, \log \frac{14}{8}, \log \frac{13}{9}$$

or (dividing through by .08)

10.04, 6.66, 4.15, 4.15, 3.04, 2.00 .

With these weights, at best 62 out of the 64 vertices can be separated properly (threshold 19.2). Note the characteristic manner in which higher weights are exaggerated, as compared with the minimal realization.

The first geometric approximation is

19-3, 17-5, 15-7, 15-7, 14-8, 13-9, Threshold 32

or (dividing by 2)

8, 6, 4, 4, 3, 2, Threshold 16.

This realization also fails on two vertices; if optimization by varying the threshold is allowed, the same weights, with threshold 17, fails only on one vertex. Any (positive) λ up to .004 will, in the second geometric approximation, give a realization of the original function; the theoretically calculated value of .0034 works fine.

A final comment: The iterative synthesis of Mattson* apparently begins with our first geometric approximation as initial trial (although no rigorous basis is suggested).

* R. L. Mattson, "A Self-Organizing Binary System," PROC EJCC, pp. 212-217, December 1959.

Mattson's idea is to optimize on one weight (or the threshold) at a time. As with the Bayesian approach, however, threshold functions will usually not be realized. Jack Sklansky, of RCA Laboratories, raised this issue by constructing a "pathological" plane which almost realizes A(B+C), but which cannot be transformed to realization by changing any one coefficient. The example discussed above was subsequently chosen to illustrate that even with a very good initial try (in fact the try which I believe Mattson intended), namely

8, 6, 4, 4, 3, 2, Threshold 6

(in the ± 1 system), which misses only the 1-vertex

$$\bar{A}BCD\bar{E}F: \quad -8+6+4+4-3+2 = 5 < 6,$$

Mattson's iteration won't converge: If a change in some weight is to improve the realization, it will clearly have to be a decrease in the weight a of A, an increase in b or c or d, a decrease in e, an increase in f, or a decrease in T. But a decrease in a loses the 1-vertices $AB\bar{C}\bar{D}E\bar{F}$, $A\bar{B}C\bar{D}EF$, and $A\bar{B}\bar{C}DEF$ at the same time it gains $\bar{A}BCD\bar{E}F$ -- this is no progress. Similarly increasing b loses 1-vertex $A\bar{B}C\bar{D}EF$ and $A\bar{B}\bar{C}DEF$ and "gains" 0-vertex $AB\bar{C}\bar{D}\bar{E}F$; increasing c loses $AB\bar{C}\bar{D}E\bar{F}$ and "gains" $A\bar{B}CD\bar{E}\bar{F}$; d symmetrically; decreasing e loses $AB\bar{C}\bar{D}E\bar{F}$, $A\bar{B}C\bar{D}EF$, and $A\bar{B}\bar{C}DEF$; increasing f loses $AB\bar{C}\bar{D}E\bar{F}$ and "gains" $A\bar{B}CD\bar{E}\bar{F}$; decreasing T "gains" $AB\bar{C}\bar{D}\bar{E}F$ and $A\bar{B}CD\bar{E}\bar{F}$. Thus a combination of changes will be needed to effect a realization by iteration; the "hill" being climbed requires a more subtle approach. This is strong reason for considering more direct methods, as is outlined above.

The main conclusion of this section is: If we decide in a recognition problem to try to use a threshold decision function, then switching theoretic methods for synthesizing the function are preferable to the conventional Bayesian approach.

SURVEY OF THRESHOLD LOGIC

The discussion above is intended to interest investigators of artificial intelligence in a relevant area of switching theory -- threshold logic. We will outline here the relevant areas of threshold logic, and suggest some open problems whose solutions would be significant in artificial intelligence.

Most of the threshold logic literature deals with one or more of the following three areas: Conditions which functions must satisfy to be threshold functions, algorithms for determining the existence and nature of realizations, and methods (heuristic) for synthesizing networks built from threshold gates, often, in particular, from three-input majority gates (AB+AC+BC). In the following we discuss the large body of simple transformations and other properties known, then the necessary conditions, one-element test-synthesis, network synthesis, and finally the more important miscellaneous results, (See

[Winder-3] for an earlier survey.)

Simple Properties

The following are typical simple facts about threshold functions:

1.) Realizing weights and threshold are not unique.

2.) All threshold functions can be realized with integral weights and threshold.

3.) Any pair of (unequal) numbers (i.e. 0 and 1, -1 and +1, etc.) can be used as the numerical equivalents of the switching variables in order to define threshold functions. (The same weights can be used in the different systems; the appropriate thresholds are easily calculated.)

4.) Given a threshold function f, functions derived from f by permuting or complementing arguments, or by dualizing or complementing f, or any combination of these, are also threshold functions. (Again, appropriate transformation rules are easy to define.)

A general treatment of these, and most of the topics mentioned below, can be found in the papers [Elgot], [Gabelman-1], [Muroga-1,4], and [Winder-1,4]. These are relatively comprehensive papers, with much duplication of the basic material. [Coates-Lewis] also covers a wide range of material, but with a specific slant towards the test-synthesis problem.

Necessary Conditions

The simplest condition which all threshold functions must meet is unateness*, discussed originally in [McNaughton] and [Paull-McCluskey]. [Paull-McCluskey], [Winder-1], and [Muroga-1] generalize this condition, obtaining an infinite family of necessary conditions: 1-monotonicity (equivalent to unateness), 2-monotonicity, etc. A function satisfying all of these conditions is completely monotonic. [Winder-1,4] give the most complete treatment of these ideas, including an important function due to E. F. Moore of Bell Laboratories -- a twelve-argument function which is completely monotonic, but is not a threshold function.

Because complete monotonicity fails to characterize threshold functions, this idea in turn is generalized in various ways in [Elgot] and [Gabelman-1]. [Winder-2,4] discusses these generalizations further, settling some questions left open in [Elgot] and [Elgot-Muroga], and concentrating on a second infinite family of necessary conditions: 2-asummability (equivalent to complete monotonicity), 3-asummability, etc. A function 2-asummability

* A function is unate when it can be expressed by a Boolean expression in which each variable appears uniformly: everywhere with negation, or everywhere without.

satisfying all of these conditions is proved in [Elgot] to be a threshold function. This necessary and sufficient condition was published about the same time in [Chow-1]. It is discussed in terms of convex sets in [Highleyman] and [Gabelman-2]. (See a more detailed survey of this subject in a review by this author to appear in October's IRE TEC.)

These various necessary conditions have obvious importance in artificial intelligence. Even for sparsely specified functions (where most inputs don't have outputs specified) of many arguments, functions can often be shown to be non-threshold functions by simple observations. More work is needed, however, to adapt the ideas more specifically to the case of sparse specification, many inputs.

Test-Synthesis

The question: "Is a given function a threshold function, and if it is, what weight and threshold assignments realize it?" is easily seen to be equivalent to the consistency and solution of a certain system of linear inequalities I, on the weights and threshold as "unknowns" -- [McNaughton]. If the function has n arguments, I contains 2^n inequalities. The theory of k-monotonicities can be used to reduce this system to manageable proportions -- in various forms, most of the papers to be mentioned in this section make use of ideas equivalent to at least 1-monotonicity, and often 2-monotonicity. The problem of the equivalence of these reduced systems I' with the original is discussed in [Winder-1,4]. Many different methods of solution for I' have been proposed. Algebraic solution, which involves successive elimination of unknowns and yields a specification of all solutions, is discussed in [Elgot] and [Winder-1,4].

The important idea of solving I' by linear programming is discussed in [Minnick], [Stram-1], [Muroga-1], and [Einhorn]. Integers are usually obtained under a condition that their sum (absolute values) be minimum; by a technical device, integer programming has been avoidable except for some specially constructed examples of E. F. Moore and [Winder-2,4] (thus settling the other open problem of [Elgot-Muroga]). A game theoretic approach to the solution of I' is discussed in [Akers-1]. Both the linear programming and game theoretic approaches produce just one realization, or else prove that there are none.

The procedure of [Coates-Lewis] and [Coates-Kirchner-Lewis] is a specialized algorithm which algebraically produces a single solution, or proves that there are none. A geometric, heuristic procedure is described in [Stram-1,2]. In [Dadda-1,2] methods suitable for small n are given. In [Varshavskii-1] a fallacious procedure is summarized.

The question of obtaining minimal integral realizations (the sum of absolute values of weights and threshold minimized) is very nicely solved in [Gabelman-1]; the procedure is refined and rigorously established in [Winder-4]. Synthesis when the function is incompletely specified is treated in [Winder-1,4] (algebraically, with not too many inputs unspecified) and in [Singleton] (by matrices, with not too many inputs specified). The intermediate problem has obvious importance in artificial intelligence and in character recognition; the ideas described in the first part of this paper may provide a start in this direction.

All methods discussed above (except those of the first part of the paper) are switching theory oriented, in the sense that they work exactly, and are not feasible when the number of arguments becomes large (over 20, say). It is likely that artificial intelligence motivations will soon be producing some useful results for large n (and for largely unspecified functions).

Networks

The question of synthesizing a given function in a network of threshold gates is a typically difficult switching theoretic problem. (A single threshold gate realizes a threshold function; a network of threshold gates corresponds to a composition of threshold functions.) It has been considered under various constraints: In computer design applications, tolerance considerations drastically limit the number of inputs that can be allowed. [Muroga-3] is a general discussion of this; [Muroga-4] goes into important details. There are several papers on synthesis by networks of three-input majority gates (AB+AC+BC), the simplest threshold functions beyond the conventional NOT, OR, AND, and their variants. The methods can be divided according to the means of function representation: Working algebraically, [Lindaman-1,2], [Cohn-Lindaman], and [Akers-2] discuss various transformations, analogous to the ordinary Boolean transformations, which may be helpful in synthesis. [Winder-4] gives an axiomatic treatment which may be more useful in this context than that of [Cohn-Lindaman]. A geometric approach is described in [Miiller-Winder], and results on all four-argument functions are reported in [Winder-5]. [Akers-3] employs truth tables in interesting fashion.

The synthesis of a specific class of functions -- symmetric functions -- has been treated in [Muroga-1], [Minnick], and [Kautz].

A geometric approach to the unrestricted problem is described in [Winder-2,4], where the question of determining whether a given function can be realized using just two threshold gates is answered. An algebraic method, where constraints on the magnitude of the threshold can be made conveniently, is given in [Lewis-Coates]. [Varshavskii-2] summarizes an interesting construction, and gives a startling (but false, see below) "theorem" that a function of n arguments can always be realized in a network of n+1 threshold gates. Many of the one-element test-synthesis procedures discussed above go on, when a function is shown to be non-threshold, to produce a network in heuristic fashion.

Typically, several fragmentary functions are OR'ed together. A heuristic modification of linear programming is used in [Minnick] to produce a table of network realizations for all (classes of) 4-argument functions.

The work in network synthesis is just beginning, and so far is restrained to very small n (less than 10). Perhaps the most promising approach for the (heuristic) design of large-n two-level networks (several "upper-level" gates feeding a single "output gate", as in the Perceptron, etc.) lies in the methods of [Winder-2,4], where failures of the k-monotonicity tests are used to specify appropriate upper-level gates -- i.e. each upper gate "rectifies" certain inconsistencies in the desired function, so that the output gate can make the final decision as a threshold function. (Incidentally, the conjecture that the output gate can always be taken as a simple many-input majority gate, still yielding optimal networks, can be disproved by counter example.)

Other Major Subjects

The parameters of [Chow-2] have been discussed in the first half of the paper. Besides their practical use, the paper cited opens up a theoretically very interesting possibility that threshold functions may be characterizable by their parameters (the $m(f_{x_i})$ and $m(f)$).

A large number of "functional properties" of threshold functions, dealing with various combinations of functions, chains of functions obtained by varying threshold, duality relations, classification by prime implicants, and similar ideas, are treated in [Muroga-1,2,5], [Elgot], and [Gabelman-1]. These ideas are rather of theoretical than practical interest, and at present don't appear to have much bearing on artificial intelligence.

R_n, the number of threshold functions of n arguments, has been shown to be bounded above ([Muroga-1] [Winder-1,4], [Cameron]) and below ([Goto-Takahasi], [Muroga-1, 5]) as follows:

$$2^{0.33n^2} < R_n < 2^{n^2} \ll 2^{2^n} \qquad (n > 1),$$

where 2^{2^n} is the total number of switching functions of n arguments. Thus threshold functions become a vanishingly small proportion of all functions, as n increases. [This suggests that the often-used idea of randomly chosen upper-level threshold gates in a two-level network is rather likely to require the output gate to realize a non-threshold function. A rational procedure, such as that mentioned in the section on networks, is much more likely to work with fewer upper-level gates. In particular, tentative ideas indicate that the output gate, not the upper-level gates, should be partially specified at the outset (for instance, the weights' signs, and possibly their relative absolute magnitudes, might be determined on a heuristic or random basis); then existing methods, as mentioned above, can be used to specify appropriate upper-level gates (and the output gate), even for very sparsely specified, many-input functions. (Modifications for iterative synthesis would be required.) As noted earlier, the best networks are obtained by allowing the output gate to be as complicated as is needed.] In [Cameron] it is shown, using the upper bound, that networks to realize given n-argument functions will for most functions require exponentially many threshold gates -- something like $2^{n/3}$. Bounds on the size of integral weights that will be required for some functions are found in [Myhill-Kautz] and [Muroga-5].

The classification and enumeration of classes, for threshold functions, has been studied in [Winder-1,4] and [Muroga-1]. Tables listing representatives of all six-argument threshold functions, with minimum integral realizations, are to be found in [Winder-4] and [Muroga-6]. A more efficient classification scheme has recently been described in [Goto-Takahasi]; relevant results are in [Muroga-5].

Two variants of threshold logic are discussed in [Ercoli-Mercurio] and [Hotz].

ACKNOWLEDGEMENTS

I would like to make thankful acknowledgement of the encouragement and advice of Saul Amarel. From his understanding of the field of artificial intelligence have come the ideas which motivated the first section of this paper; his original support of my studies of threshold logic also made possible the second section. Saul Amarel and Saul Levy caught several mistakes and made valuable comments on the first draft of this paper.

REFERENCES

Only English-language papers commercially available are listed below. Almost all papers on threshold logic not covered by them are Lockheed (Missiles and Space Division) Technical Notes and Reports, authored by D. T. Perkins, D. G. Willis, E. A. Whitmore, Sze-Tsen Hu, and probably others. Also, at a Lockheed Symposium in February 1962, Willis gave a paper "Minimum Weights for Threshold Switches", and E. Goto a paper "Threshold, Majority and Bilateral Switching Devices" -- the latter seems to be subsumed by [Goto-Takahasi]. Papers in Italian, Japanese, and Russian don't appear to contain material not covered by the references below.

The "[R62-33]", etc. give the number of a review of the cited paper, in the IRETEC (IRE Transactions on Electronic Computers). "SCTLD" is the Proceedings of the Annual Symposia on Switching Circuit Theory and Logical Design; the 1960 and 1961 proceedings are Publication S-134 of the AIEE, the 1962 proceedings are Publication S-141.

S. B. Akers, [1] "Threshold Logic and Two-Person, Zero-Sum Games," SCTLD (1961) pp.27-33, September 1961.

__________, [2] "On the Algebraic Manipulation of Majority Logic," IRE Transactions on Electronic Computers, Vol. EC-10, No. 4, p. 779, December 1961.

__________, [3] "Synthesis of Combinational Logic Using Three-Input Majority Gates" SCTLD (1962), pp. 149-157, September 1962.

S. H. Cameron, "An Estimate of the Complexity Requisite in a Universal Decision Network," Bionics Symposium, WADD Report 60-600, pp. 197-212, December 1960.

C. K. Chow, [1] "Boolean Functions Realizable with Single Threshold Devices," Proc. IRE, Vol. 39, pp. 370-371, January 1961.

__________, [2] "On the Characterization of Threshold Functions," SCTLD (1961), pp. 34-38, September 1961. [R62-33].

C. L. Coates, R. B. Kirchner, P. M. Lewis II, "A Simplified Procedure for the Realization of Linearly-Separable Switching Functions", IRE Transactions on Electronic Computers, Vol. EC-11, pp. 447-458, August 1962.

C. L. Coates and P. M. Lewis II, "Linearly Separable Switching Functions," Journal of the Franklin Institute, Vol. 272, pp. 360-410, November 1961.

M. Cohn and R. Lindaman, "Axiomatic Majority-Decision Logic," IRE Transactions on Electronic Computers, Vol. EC-10, pp. 17-21, March 1961. (See also correspondence in IRETEC of September 1961, pg. 530.) [R61-85].

L. Dadda, [1] "Synthesis of Threshold Logic Combinatorial Networks," Alta Frequenza, n.3, Vol. XXX, pp. 224-28E-35E-231, 1961. [R61-86]

________, [2] "Synthesis of Threshold Switching Networks by Map Methods," (Abstract) Proceedings of the IFIP Congress 62, to be published by North Holland, Conference: Munich, August 1962.

S. N. Einhorn, "The Use of the Simplex Algorithm in the Mechanization of Boolean Switching Functions by Means of Magnetic Cores," IRE Transactions on Electronic Computers, Vol. EC-10, No. 4, pp. 615-622, December 1961. (See also correspondence in IRETEC of August 1962, pg. 573).

C. C. Elgot, "Truth Functions Realizable by Single Threshold Organs," SCTLD (1960), pp. 225-245, September 1961, and AIEE Conference Paper 60-1311, October 1960, revised November 1960.

C. C. Elgot, S. Muroga, "Two Open Problems on Threshold Logic," SCTLD (1961), pg. 166, September 1961.

P. Ercoli, L. Mercurio, "Threshold Logic with one or more than one Threshold," Proceedings of the IFIP Congress 62, to be published by North Holland, Conference: Munich, August 1962.

I. J. Gabelman, [1] "The Functional Behavior of Majority (Threshold) Elements," Doctoral Dissertation for Syracuse University, Electrical Engineering Department. Available through University Microfilms. June 1961.

I. J. Gabelman, [2] "A Note on the Realization of Boolean Functions Using a Single Threshold Element," Proc IRE, Vol. 50, No. 2, pp. 225-226, February 1962.

E. Goto, H. Takahasi, "Some Theorems Useful in Threshold Logic for Enumerating Boolean Functions," Proceeding of the IFIP Congress 62, to be published by North Holland. Conference: Munich, August 1962.

W. H. Highleyman, "A Note on Linear Separation," IRE Transactions on Electronic Computers, Vol. EC-10, No. 4, pp. 777-778, December 1961.

G. Hotz, "Digital Filters of Threshold Elements", Proceedings of the IFIP Congress 62, to be published by North Holland. Conference: Munich, August 1962.

W. H. Kautz, "The Realization of Symmetric Switching Functions with Linear-Input Logical Elements," IRE Transactions on Electronic Computers, Vol. EC-10, No. 3, pp. 371-378, September 1961. [R62-2]

P. M. Lewis II, C. L. Coates, "A Realization Procedure for Threshold Gate Networks," SCTLD (1962), pp. 159-168, September 1962.

R. Lindaman, [1] "A New Concept in Computing," Proc. IRE, Vol. 48, p. 257, February 1960.

__________, [2] "A Theorem for Deriving Majority-Logic Networks within an Augmented Boolean Algebra," IRE Transactions on Electronic Computers, Vol. EC-9, pp. 338-342, September 1960.

R. McNaughton, "Unate Truth Functions," IRE Transactions on Electronic Computers, Vol. EC-10, pp. 1-6, March 1961, and previously available as Technical Report No. 4, Applied Mathematics and Statistics Laboratory, Stanford University, October 1957. [R61-85]

S. Muroga, I. Toda, and S. Takasu, [1] "Theory of Majority Decision Elements," Journal of the Franklin Institute, Vol. 271, pp. 376-418, May 1961.

__________, [2] "Functional Forms of Majority Functions and a Necessary and Sufficient Condition for their Realizability," SCTLD (1961), pp. 39-46, September 1961. [R62-35]

__________, [3] "Restrictions in Synthesis of a Network with Majority Elements," Proc. IRE, Vol. 49, p. 1455, September 1961.

__________, [4] "Majority Logic and Problems of Probabilistic Behavior," Self Organizing Systems 1962, pp. 243-281, Spartan Books, 1962, (Proceedings of Conference May 1962)

__________, [5] "Generation of Self-Dual Threshold Functions and Lower Bounds of the Number of Threshold Functions and a Maximum Weight," SCTLD (1962), pp. 169-184, September 1962.

__________, I. Toda, M. Kondo, [6] "Majority Decision Functions of up to Six Variables", to appear in the Journal of Math. of Comp., October 1962, (Published in Japanese in 1959 and 1960).

H. S. Miiller and R. O. Winder, "Majority Logic Synthesis by Geometric Methods," IRE Transactions on Electronic Computers, pp. 89-90, February 1962.

R. C. Minnick, "Linear-Input Logic," IRE Transactions on Electronic Computers, Vol. EC-10, pp. 6-16, March 1961; essential ideas delivered at the sixth Annual Symposium on Computers and Data Processing of the Denver Research Institute, July 1959 [R61-85]

J. Myhill and W. H. Kautz, "On the Size of Weights Required for Linear-Input Switching Functions," IRE Transactions on Electronic Computers, Vol. EC-10, pp. 288-290, June 1961.

M. C. Paull and E. J. McCluskey, Jr., "Boolean Functions Realizable with Single Threshold Devices," Proc. IRE, Vol. 48, pp. 1335-1337, July 1960.

R. C. Singleton, "A Test for Linear Separability as Applied to Self-Organizing Machines," Self Organizing Systems 1962, pp-503-524, Spartan Books, 1962 (Proceedings of the Conference, May 1962).

O. B. Stram, [1] "Arbitrary Boolean Functions of N Variables Realizable in Terms of Threshold Devices," Proc IRE, Vol. 49, pp. 210-220, January 1961. [R61-85][R62-76]

__________, [2] "The Profile Technique for the Design of Threshold Device Logic," SCTLD (1961), pp. 47-54,[R62-76].

V. I. Varshavskii, [1] "Functional Possibilities and Synthesis of Threshold Elements," Soviet Physics Doklady, Vol. 6, No. 8, pp. 678-680, February 1962.

__________, [2] "On the Complexity of Networks of Depth Two Formulated From Threshold Elements," Soviet Physics Doklady, Vol. 6, No. 8, pp. 683-685, February 1962.

R. O. Winder, [1] "Single Stage Threshold Logic," SCTLD (1960), pp. 321-332, September 1961, and AIEE Conference Paper 60-1261, October 1960.

__________, [2] "More About Threshold Logic," SCTLD (1961), pp. 55-64, September 1961. [R62-31]

__________, [3] "Some Recent Papers in Threshold Logic," Proc IRE, Vol. 49, p. 1100, June 1961.

__________, [4] "Threshold Logic," Doctoral Dissertation for the Mathematics Department of Princeton University. (This paper incorporates the material of [Winder-1] and [Winder-2].) Available through University Microfilms or directly from the author. May 1962.

__________, [5] "Networks of Threshold Gates," (abstract) Proceedings of the IFIP Congress 62, to be published by North Holland. Conference: Munich, August 1962.

Reprinted from *IEEE Trans. on Electron. Comput.*, **EC-14,** No. 5, 1965, pp. 683–688

An Algorithm for Linear Inequalities and its Applications

3

Y-C. HO, SENIOR MEMBER, IEEE, AND R. L. KASHYAP

***Abstract*—An exponentially convergent and finite algorithm is presented for the determination of the solution α of the linear inequalities $A\alpha>0$ for a given matrix A, or for determining the nonexistence of solution for $A\alpha>0$. This result is useful in threshold-switching theory and in pattern classification problems. Experiments indicate extremely rapid convergence of the method.**

I. Introduction

A FUNDAMENTAL PROBLEM in pattern classification, threshold switching theory, and mathematical programming is to find the m-vector α such that $A\alpha>0$ where A is a given $N\times m$ matrix with $N>m$. There are essentially three approaches to the solution of this problem.

1) Linear programming (LP)—The problem is treated as that of finding a feasible solution to an LP problem with an artificially created cost vector.
2) The fixed increment method [1]—Starting with any trial vector $\alpha(0)$, we add to it successively different rows of A according to whether or not a given constraint is satisfied.
3) The relaxation method [2]—This is similar to the fixed increment method except that the amount of a given row added is proportional to the amount the corresponding constraint is violated.

There are some other minor variants and extensions of these approaches. They are discussed in [3]. All the approaches are characterized by fairly long convergence time and by the difficulty in obtaining good estimates for convergence rate. We shall present an algorithm which is exponentially convergent and finite, and which produces, as a by-product, a test for nonseparability.

II. Notation

Lower case Greek or Roman letters denote column vectors. Subscripts indicate the components of the corresponding vectors. Upper case letters denote matrices. The derivative of a scaler J with respect to a column vector α will be a column vector denoted by

$$\frac{\partial J}{\partial \alpha} \text{ whose } i\text{th component } \left(\frac{\partial J}{\partial \alpha}\right)_i \triangleq \frac{\partial J}{\partial \alpha_i}.$$

Scalar will be specifically noted. The expression $x>0$ means $x_i\geq 0$ for all i; $x\geq 0$ means that $x_i\geq 0$ for all i and that x possesses *at least* one positive component, i.e., $x\geq 0 \Rightarrow x\neq 0$. Similarly, $x\leq 0$ is defined. $|x|$ is a vector defined by relation $(|x|)_i=|x_i|$. Further, lower case letters like i, j in parentheses denote iteration number. For example, $x(i)$ denotes the vector x on ith iteration. Finally, the positive semi-definiteness of matrix A is denoted by $A\geqq 0$. Superscript T means transpose of a vector or matrix.

Manuscript received December 11, 1964; revised June 8, 1965. This work was supported in part by the Joint Services Electronics Program under Contract Nonr-1866(16), and by the Division of Engineering and Applied Physics, Harvard University.

The authors are with the Division of Engineering and Applied Physics, Harvard University, Cambridge, Mass.

III. Restatement of the Problem

It is clear that the fundamental problem in Section I can be restated as

$$\begin{cases}\text{Find } \alpha(m\text{-vector}) \text{ and } \beta(N\text{-vector})\\ \text{such that } A\alpha=\beta \text{ and } \beta>0.\end{cases}$$

But this problem is further equivalent to

$$\begin{cases}\text{Find } \alpha \text{ and } \beta>0 \text{ such that}\\ J=\|A\alpha-\beta\|^2 \text{ is minimized.}\end{cases}$$

Thus, the original problem has been converted to an optimization problem to which gradient method of computation [4] is applicable. We shall see later on that the introduction of the vector β as *additional* optimization variables plays a crucial part in the convergence rate of the algorithm without any appreciable increase in computational complexities.

IV. The Algorithm

It is well known that the gradient of J with respect to α and β is

$$\frac{\partial J}{\partial \alpha} = A^T(A\alpha-\beta) \tag{1}$$

$$\frac{\partial J}{\partial \beta} = (\beta - A\alpha). \tag{2}$$

Since α is not constrained, $\partial J/\partial\alpha=0$ implies

$$\alpha = (A^TA)^{\sharp}A^T\beta \triangleq A^{\sharp}\beta. \tag{3}$$

$A^{\sharp}$ is the generalized inverse of A [6]. If A is of maximal rank, then $(A^TA)^{\sharp}=(A^TA)^{-1}$. On the other hand, $\beta>0$ dictates a descent procedure[1] of the follow-

[1] Another descent formula is

$$\delta\beta(i) \sim \begin{cases}[A\alpha(i)-\beta(i)]_j \text{ if } [A\alpha(i)-\beta(i)]_j\geqq 0\\ \text{Max}\,[-\beta_j(i)+\epsilon, \{A\alpha(i)-\beta(i)\}_j], \text{ if } [A\alpha(i)-\beta(i)]_j\leqq 0 \text{ and } \epsilon>0.\end{cases}$$

However (4) is used for mathematical simplicity in the proof of convergence.

ing type, with i denoting iteration number:

$$\beta(i+1) = \beta(i) + \delta\beta(i)$$

$$\delta\beta_j(i) \sim \begin{cases} (A\alpha(i) - \beta(i))_j & \text{if } (A\alpha(i) - \beta(i))_j > 0 \\ 0 & \text{if } (A\alpha(i) - \beta(i))_j \leqq 0 \end{cases} \tag{4}$$

or

$$\delta\beta(i) = \rho[A\alpha(i) - \beta(i) + |A\alpha(i) - \beta(i)|]$$

where $\rho > 0$ is a scalar positive constant to be determined later. Writing

$$\alpha(i+1) = A^{\#}\beta(i+1) = A^{\#}[\beta(i) + \delta\beta(i)]$$

we immediately obtain the *algorithm*

$$\begin{cases} \alpha(0) = A^{\#}\beta(0), \quad \beta(0) > 0, \quad \text{but otherwise arbitrary} \\ y(i) = A\alpha(i) - \beta(i) \\ \alpha(i+1) = \alpha(i) + \rho A^{\#}[y(i) + |y(i)|] \\ \beta(i+1) = \beta(i) + \rho[y(i) + |y(i)|]. \end{cases} \tag{5}$$

In words, the algorithm consists of the following alternate steps,

1) For a fixed β, a vector α is determined such that it constitutes a least square fit.
2) For a fixed α, allow β to change in the direction of steepest descent, subject to the condition $\beta > 0$.

This algorithm converges exponentially to the solution, if one exists, in a finite number of steps. Further, this algorithm can be used to test the inconsistency of a set of inequalities. In other words, we have the

Proposition

Consider the set of inequalities (6) and the algorithm (5) to solve these inequalities,

$$A\alpha > 0 \tag{6}$$

Let $V(y(i)) = \|y(i)\|^2$.

1) If (6) is *consistent*, then

a) $\lim_{i\to\infty} V(y(i)) = 0$ implying convergence to a solution in an infinite number of steps.

b) $\Delta V(y(i)) \stackrel{\Delta}{=} V(y(i+1)) - V(y(i)) < -\lambda_0 V(y(i))$, $\lambda_0 > 0$ showing exponential convergence.

c) A solution is obtained in a finite number of steps.

2) If (6) is *inconsistent*, then there exists a positive integer i^* such that

$$\begin{aligned} \Delta V(y(i)) &< -\lambda_0 V(y(i)) && \text{if } i < i^* \\ &= 0 && i \geq i^* \\ y(i) &\nleq 0 && i < i^* \\ y(i) &= y(i^*) \leq 0 && i \geq i^* \\ \left.\begin{aligned} \alpha(i) &= \alpha(i^*) \\ \beta(i) &= \beta(i^*) \end{aligned}\right\} & && i \geq i^*. \end{aligned}$$

In other words, the occurrence of a nonpositive vector $y(i)$ at any stage terminates the algorithm and indicates the inconsistency of (6).

Before proving this theorem, a lemma will be stated and proved. This lemma is nothing but a rigorous statement of a heuristic fact that in a least square fit with a consistent set of equations, all the components of the error vector cannot have the same sign.

Lemma

Consider the inequalities (6), and the algorithm (5) to solve it. Then

1) $y(i) \ngeq 0$ for any i

2) If (6) is consistent, then

$$y(i) \nleq 0 \quad \text{for any } i.$$

Proof of Lemma

Part 1): The proof will be given by establishing a contradiction.

Let

$$y(i) \geq 0 \quad \text{for some } i.$$

Then

$$y^T(i)\beta(i) > 0 \quad \text{since} \quad \beta(i) > 0.$$

But

$$y(i) \stackrel{\Delta}{=} A\alpha(i) - \beta(i) = (AA^{\#} - I)\beta(i).$$

Hence

$$y^T(i)\beta(i) = \beta^T(i)(AA^{\#} - I)\beta(i) \leq 0,$$

since

$$(AA^{\#} - I) \leq 0.$$

This is a contradiction.

Part 2): Again assume that (6) is consistent and the existence of $y(i) \leq 0$ for some i. Consistency of (6) implies the existence of an α^* and $\beta^* > 0$ such that

$$A\alpha^* = \beta^* > 0.$$

Therefore

$$y^T(i)\beta^* < 0. \tag{7}$$

But for any $y(i)$

$$\begin{aligned} A^T y(i) &= A^T[AA^{\#} - I]\beta(i) \\ &= [(A^T A)(A^T A)^{\#} A^T - A^T]\beta(i) = 0 \end{aligned}$$

by the theory of generalized inverse [6]

$$A^T y(i) = 0 \Rightarrow (\alpha^*)^T A^T y(i) = 0 \Rightarrow y^T(i)\beta^* = 0.$$

This contradicts (7).

Proof of the Proposition

Algorithm (5) can be rewritten as a recursive relation in $y(i)$

$$y(i+1) = y(i) + \rho(AA^{\#} - I)(y(i) + |y(i)|). \quad (8)$$

Part 1: $V(y(i)) = \|y(i)\|^2 > 0 \ \forall y(i) \neq 0$

$$\Delta V(y(i)) \triangleq V(y(i+1)) - V(y(i))$$
$$= 2\rho y^T(i)(AA^{\#} - I)(y(i) + |y(i)|) + \rho^2\|y(i) + |y(i)|\|^2(I - AA^{\#}). \quad (9)$$

Equation (9) can be simplified by noting that

$$AA^{\#}y(i) \triangleq AA^{\#}(AA^{\#} - I)\beta(i) = 0$$

and

$$(y(i) + |y(i)|)^T(y(i) - |y(i)|) = 0.$$

Thus

$$\Delta V(y(i)) = -\|y(i) + |y(i)\|^2 \{\rho^2 AA^{\#} + (\rho - \rho^2)I\}.$$

For

$$0 < \rho < 1, \quad [\rho^2 AA^{\#} + (\rho - \rho^2)I] \geqq 0$$
$$\Delta V(y(i)) \leqq 0 \qquad \forall y(i)$$
$$\Delta V(y(i)) = 0 \text{ if and only if } y(i) = 0 \text{ or } y(i) \leq 0.$$

By the lemma,

$$y(i) \nleq 0.$$

Therefore,

$$\Delta V(y(i)) < 0 \quad \forall y(i) \neq 0$$
$$= 0 \quad \text{if } y(i) = 0.$$

By Lyapunov's stability theorem for discrete systems, (8) is globally asymptotically stable.

Therefore,

$$\lim_{i \to \infty} \|y(i)\|^2 = 0,$$

which is Proposition 1a.

To prove exponential convergence, we observe that

$$y(i) + |y(i)| = C(i)y(i).$$

$C(i)$ is a diagonal matrix with

$$C_{jj}(i) = 2 \quad \text{if } y_j(i) \geqq 0$$
$$= 0 \quad \text{if } y_j(i) < 0$$
$$\Delta V(y(i)) < 0 \Rightarrow \Delta V(y(i)) < -\lambda_0 V(y(i))$$

where

$0 < \lambda_0 =$ minimum non-zero eigenvalue of the matrix

$$C(i)\{\rho^2 AA^{\#} + (\rho - \rho^2)I\}C(i).$$

This implies exponential convergence.

To prove convergence in a finite number of steps, we note that β is a nondecreasing vector.

Let

$$[\beta(0)]^T = [1, 1, \cdots]; \quad \beta(i) \geqq \beta(0) \quad \text{for any } i$$

since

$$A\alpha(i) \triangleq \beta(i) + y(i), \quad |y(i)| < 1 \Rightarrow A\alpha(i) > 0.$$

But

$$V(y(i)) \leq 1 \Rightarrow |y(i)| < 1.$$

Since

$V(y)$ converges to zero in infinite time, it must converge to the sphere $V(y) = 1$ in finite time.

Part 2: As in Part 1), we prove that

$$\Delta V(y(i)) \triangleq V(y(i+1)) - V(y(i)) \leq 0.$$

Since $y(i)$ and hence $V(y(i))$ cannot become zero for any i, there must exist a value of i, say i^*, such that

$$\Delta V(y(i)) < 0 \quad \text{for } i < i^*$$
$$= 0 \quad \text{for } i = i^*$$
$$\Delta V(y(i^*)) = 0 \quad \text{if either} \quad y(i^*) = 0 \quad \text{or} \quad y(i^*) \leq 0.$$

Since

$$y(i^*) \neq 0, \quad \text{this implies} \quad y(i^*) \leq 0.$$

Equation (8) implies that $y(i) = y(i^*) \leq 0$ for $\forall i \geq i^*$.

Consequently, we have

$$\left.\begin{array}{l} \Delta V(y(i)) = 0 \\ \alpha(i) = \alpha(i^*) \\ \beta(i) = \beta(i^*) \end{array}\right\} \forall i \geqq i^*.$$

Further, the convergence of y from $y(o)$ to $y(i^*)$ is exponential.

Remarks

1) The condition $0 < \rho \leqq 1$ is only a sufficient condition of convergence. It is not necessary. The convergence rate could be further improved by varying ρ at every stage.

2) In pattern classification problems, the solution obtained by applying this algorithm has an interesting statistical interpretation. Consider for simplicity only the zeroth iteration of the algorithm. Let $n_a = n_b$ and $\beta^T(0) = (1, 1 \cdots 1)$.

Let the two classes that are to be separated be A and B.

Let

$$\text{Class } A = \{x_A^{(1)}, x_B^{(2)}, \cdots x_A^{(n_a)}\}$$
$$\text{Class } B = \{x_B^{(1)}, x_B^{(2)}, \cdots x_B^{(n_b)}\}.$$

Then

$$\text{matrix } A = \begin{bmatrix} x_A^{(1)} \\ x_A^{(n_a)} \\ -x_B^{(1)} \\ -x_B^{(n_b)} \end{bmatrix}.$$

In pattern classification problems, we have to find a solution (if one exists) of the inequalities $A\alpha > 0$. Let us apply the algorithm to solve these inequalities.

Let

$$\mu_A = \frac{1}{n_a}\sum_{i=1}^{n_a} x_A^{(i)} = \text{sample mean of Class } A$$

$$\mu_B = \frac{1}{n_b}\sum_{i=1}^{n_b} x_B^{(i)} = \text{sample of mean of Class } B$$

$$\textstyle\sum_A = \frac{1}{n_a}\sum_i (x_A^{(i)} - \mu_A)(x_A^{(i)} - \mu_A)^T$$

$$= \text{sample covariance of Class } A$$

$$\textstyle\sum_B = \frac{1}{n_b}\sum_i (x_B^{(i)} - \mu_B)(x_B^{(i)} - \mu_B)^T$$

$$= \text{sample covariance of Class } B$$

We can express the solution α obtained by the algorithm in the following manner:

$$\alpha = k(\textstyle\sum_A + \sum_B)^{-1}(\mu_A - \mu_B), \quad k > 0. \tag{10}$$

This maximizes the function J

$$J = \frac{\{\alpha^T(\mu_A - \mu_B)\}^2}{\alpha^T(\sum_A + \sum_B)\alpha}.$$

In other words, if we consider the two clusters of the projection points of the pattern vectors of the two classes on the hyperplane with normal α, then α given by (10) maximizes the "distance" between the clusters of the two classes and minimizes the "spread" of the cluster of each of the two classes. The details are given in [7].

V. Comparison with Other Approaches

Suppose we fix vector β at $\beta^T(0) = [1, \cdots 1]$. Then roughly speaking, fixed increment procedure can be written as[2]

$$\alpha(i+1) = \alpha(i) + \rho A^T\{\text{sgn}\,[\,|\,A\alpha(i) - \beta(0)\,|\,] - \text{sgn}\,[A\alpha(i) - \beta(0)]\} \tag{11}$$

and the relaxation procedure as[2]

$$\alpha(i+1) = \alpha(i) + \rho A^T\{\,|\,A\alpha(i) - \beta(0)\,| - [A\alpha(i) - \beta(0)]\}. \tag{12}$$

This is in contrast with our algorithm which can be rewritten as

$$\begin{cases} \alpha(i+1) = \alpha(i) + \rho(A^TA)^{-1}\{\,|\,A\alpha(i) - \beta(i)\,| - [A\alpha(i) - \beta(i)]\} \\ \beta(i+1) = \beta(i) + \rho\{\,|\,A\alpha(i) - \beta(i)\,| + [A\alpha(i) - \beta(i)]\}. \end{cases}$$

The main difference is the presence of $(A^TA)^{-1}$ and the use of β as a variable instead of fixed vector. The inversion of A^TA need only be done *once per problem* and is of dimension m which is usually small. Furthermore, it is also known that $(A^TA)^{-1}$ can be computed recursively as new rows of A are added [5]. Thus, the additional computational burden on the proposed algorithm is minimal.

We might also note that the algorithm (13) can be rewritten so that the rows of A can be processed sequentially. In view of this and the recursive generation of $(A^TA)^{-1}$, the so-called "zero memory" restriction appearing in perception-type problems ([1], [3]) is satisfied by our algorithm except for the fact that the matrix $(A^TA)^{-1}$ has to be stored.

VI. Experimental Results with Switching Problems and Conclusions

In this section, we will apply the algorithm to the solution of switching problems. On account of the special nature of these problems, there is a significant decrease in the amount of computations required to obtain the solution.

In a switching problem with m-variables, one is concerned with the vertices of a m-cube, each one of which may be assigned to only one of two Classes A and B. It is required to find a separating hyperplane between the two classes, if one exists. The switching problem which possesses a separating hyperplane is known as a linearly separable problem. There is no easy test in the literature for determining the nonseparability of a problem. Our algorithm gives the separating hyperplane, if one exists, and acts as a test for nonseparability as well.

Let us associate a $(m+1)$ vector x with every vertex. Let

$$x^T = (x_0, x_1, \cdots, x_m).$$

The component $x_0 = +1$ always. The components $x_1, \cdots, x_m$ are the coordinates of the vertex assumed to be a point in m-dimensional space. In particular, let us assume that the values of the components x_i be only ± 1.

Let

$$\text{Class } A = \{x_A^{(1)}, \cdots x_A^{(n_a)}\}, \quad \#(A) = n_a$$
$$\text{Class } B = \{x_B^{(1)}, \cdots x_B^{(n_b)}\}, \quad \#(B) = n_b$$
$$N \triangleq n_a + n_b = 2^m.$$

We want to find a $(m+1)$ vector α such that

$$\alpha^T x_A^{(i)} > 0 \qquad i = 1, \cdots, n_a$$
$$\alpha^T x_B^{(i)} < 0 \qquad i = 1, \cdots, n_b.$$

Let us rewrite (15) in a compact form.

$$A \triangleq \begin{bmatrix} x_A^{(1)} \\ \cdot \\ \cdot \\ x_A^{(n_a)} \\ -x_B^{(1)} \\ -x_B^{(n_b)} \end{bmatrix}.$$

[2] Equations (11) and (12) represent our interpretations of the algorithms which are mentioned in a different language in [1] and [2], respectively.

Then (15) can be rewritten as (16),

$$A\alpha > 0. \tag{16}$$

If a separating hyperplane does not exist for the problem, (16) will be inconsistent.

We proceed to the solution of (16) by our algorithm. We note, first of all, that [12]

$$A^T A = (2^m)I.$$

Therefore the algorithm simplifies to

$$\begin{cases} \alpha(0) = \dfrac{1}{2^m} A^T\beta(0); \quad \beta(0) > 0, \quad \text{otherwise arbitrary} \\ y(i) = A\alpha(i) - \beta(i) \\ \alpha(i+1) = \alpha(i) + \rho A^T[y(i) + |y(i)|] \\ \beta(i+1) = \beta(i) + \rho[y(i) + |y(i)|] \end{cases}, \quad 0 < \rho \leq 1. \tag{17}$$

Let us choose $\beta^T(0) = [1, 1, \cdots, 1]$.

Then the zeroth iteration solution $\alpha(0)$ has an elegant statistical interpretation. If we ignore the component $\alpha_0(o)$, then it represents the vector joining the tips of the simple mean vector of Classes A, and B, i.e., If

$$\mu_A \stackrel{\Delta}{=} \frac{1}{n_a}\sum_{i=1}^{n_a} x_A^{(i)} = \text{sample mean of Class } A$$

$$\mu_B \stackrel{\Delta}{=} \frac{1}{n_b}\sum_{i=1}^{n_b} x_B^{(i)} = \text{sample mean of Class } B$$

then

$$\begin{bmatrix} \alpha_1(0) \\ \alpha_m(0) \end{bmatrix} \sim \begin{bmatrix} (\mu_A)_1 \\ (\mu_A)_m \end{bmatrix} - \begin{bmatrix} (\mu_B)_1 \\ (\mu_B)_m \end{bmatrix}.$$

Hence, it is not surprising to note that in many threshold problems, $\alpha(0)$ itself is the normal to the separating hyperplane. Further, the components of the vector $\alpha(0)$ are the same as the so-called Chow Parameters [8] which were found from heuristic considerations.

Moreover, in many nonseparable problems, the vector $y(0)$ will be nonpositive showing the nonseparability of the problem on the zeroth iteration.

We will present here three examples. In these examples the vertices of the cube will be identified by the decimal equivalent of the binary number associated with it.

Example 1: This is the 8-variable treated by Sheng [10]. The solution is obtained on zeroth iteration by our algorithm.

Class $A = \{0$ to 46, 48 to 50, 52, 56, 64 to 78, 80 to 82, 84, 88, 96, 128 to 138, 140, 144 to 146, 148$\}$

Class $B = \{47$, 51, 53 to 55, 57 to 63, 79, 83, 85 to 87, 89 to 95, 97 to 127, 139, 141, 147, 169 to 255$\}$

$n_a = 89, \quad n_b = 167$

$\beta^T(0) = [1, 1, \cdots, 1]$

$\alpha^T(0) = \{-0.304, -0.445, -0.367, -0.367, -0.227, -0.132, -0.101, -0.101, -0.101\}.$

Example 2: This is a 4-variable separable problem for which the solution is obtained on the first iteration.

Class $A = \{7, 9 \text{ to } 15\}, \quad n_a = 8$

Class $B = \{0 \text{ to } 6, 8\}, \quad n_b = 8$

$\beta^T(o) = [1, \cdots 1]$

$\alpha^T(o) = [0, 0.75, 0.25, 0.25, 0.25]$

$y^T(o) = [-1, -0.5, -0.5, 0, -0.5, 0, 0, 0.5, 0.5, 0, 0, -0.5, 0\ 0, -0.5, -1$

$\beta^T(1) = \beta^T(0) + \rho\{y(0) + |y(0)|\}^T = [1, 1, 1, 1, 1, 1, 1, 2, 2, 1, 1, 1, 1, 1, 1, 1], \quad \rho = 1$

$\alpha(1) = \alpha(0) + \rho A^T\{y(0) + |y(0)|\}$

$\alpha^T(1) = [0, 0.875, 0.375, 0.375, 0.375]$

$\alpha(1)$ is the desired solution.

This solution is to be contrasted with that of Dertouzos [9] which involves the solution of 5 cubic equations.

Example 3: This is a 4-variable nonseparable problem. This is problem 132 in Minnick's paper [11].

$A = \{0, 1, 2, 4, 7, 9, 14\} \quad n_a = 7$

$B = \{3, 5, 6, 8, 10 \text{ to } 13, 15\} \quad n_b = 9$

$\beta^T(o) = \{1, \cdots 1\}$

$\alpha^T(o) = \frac{1}{8}[-1, -3, -1, -1, -1]$

$y^T(o) = \frac{1}{8}[-3, -5, -5, -5, -9, -11, -13, -9, -9, -9, -7, -5, -3, -5, -3, -1]$

$y(0)$ is the nonpositive vector showing the nonseparability of the problem.

In addition, the algorithm has been applied to the following.

1) All 3-variable separable switching problems.
2) All 4-variable separable switching problems.
3) A number of switching problems with variables equal to 5, 6, 7, 8 successively.
4) One case of 24 randomly generated (1, 0) patterns in 16 variables.

In all except two of the above examples, the algorithm converges to a solution in *zero* iteration, i.e., $\alpha(0)$ represents a solution, the exceptions being one case 4) which took two iterations, and one case of 2) which took one iteration.

Further, in every one of many typical 4-variable nonseparable switching problems, the condition that error vector $y \leq 0$ was reached in no more than one iteration, indicating their nonlinear separability.

These experimental results are highly encouraging and indicate useful application of the algorithm to many current problems of interest in pattern classification, switching theory, and other related areas [7].

ACKNOWLEDGMENT

The authors would like to acknowledge the various suggestions of a reviewer, which were incorporated in the paper, and which improved its presentation.

REFERENCES

[1] A. Novikoff, "On convergence proofs for perceptrons," *1963 Proc. Symp. on Math. Theory of Automata*, vol. XII, pp. 615–622.
[2] S. Agmon, "The relaxation method for linear inequalities," *Canad. J. Math.*, vol. 6, pp. 382–392, 1954.
[3] C. H. Mays, "Effect of adaptation parameters on convergence time and tolerance for adaptive threshold elements," *IEEE Trans. on Electronic Computers*, vol. EC-13, pp. 465–468, August 1964. (See also Stanford Electronic Lab. Rept. SEL-63-027 TR 1557-1, April 1963.)
[4] Y. C. Ho and P. Brentani, "On computing optimal control with inequality constraints," *SIAM J. on Control*, series A, vol. 1, pp. 319–347, 1963.
[5] E. Bodewig, *Matrix Calculus*, New York: Interscience, 1956, p. 30.
[6] R. Penrose, "On the generalized inverse of a matrix," *1955 Proc. Cambridge Philosoph. Soc.*, pp. 406–413.
[7] Y. C. Ho, A. Arcese, R. L. Kashyap, and C. C. Blaydon, "Experiments in pattern classification," Cruft Lab., Havard University, Cambridge, Mass., Rept. 472, June 1965.
[8] C. K. Chow, "On the characterization of threshold functions," *Switching Circuit Theory and Logical Design*, AIEE Publ. S-134, pp. 34–38, September 1961.
[9] M. L. Dertouzos, "An approach to single threshold elements synthesis," *IEEE Trans. on Electronic Computers*, vol. EC-13, pp. 519–528, October 1964.
[10] C. L. Sheng, "A method for testing and realization of threshold functions," *IEEE Trans. on Electronic Computers*, vol. EC-13, pp. 232–239, June 1964.
[11] R. C. Minnick, "Linear-input logic," *IRE Trans. on Electronic Computers*, vol. EC-10, pp. 6–16, March 1961.
[12] J. L. Walsh, "A closed set of normal orthogonal functions," *Am. J. Math.*, vol. 45, pp. 5–24, January 1923.

Reprinted from *Self-Organizing Systems 1962*, M. C. Yovitts et al. (eds.), 1962, pp. 503–524

4

A TEST FOR LINEAR SEPARABILITY AS APPLIED TO SELF-ORGANIZING MACHINES*

Richard C. Singleton
Stanford Research Institute
Menlo Park, California

INTRODUCTION

The concept of linear separability arises in the analysis of threshold logic elements. These elements are widely used in self-organizing machines as the basis for machine learning [1,2,3].

An n-input threshold logic element (see Figure 1) is a device which gives a binary [4] response, i.e., an output of r = 1 or r = 0, to an n-dimensional binary input vector s according to the rule

$$r = \begin{cases} 1 & \text{if } \sum_{i=1}^{n} s_i w_i > w_{n+1} \quad \text{and} \\ 0 & \text{if } \sum_{i=1}^{n} s_i w_i < w_{n+1} \quad , \end{cases}$$

where w is an $(n+1)$-dimensional vector of weights [5]. The weights are variable, partially variable, or fixed, according to the application of the threshold logic element. The reader familiar with Rosenblatt's 3-layer α-perceptron [1] will note that his A-units are threshold logic elements with fixed weights; his R-unit is a threshold logic element with weights variable through training and with binary input vectors s derived from the A-unit responses for the various stimuli.

*The work reported here was sponsored partially by the U. S. Army Signal Supply Agency (Contract DA-36-039-SC-78343) and partially by the Office of Naval Research [Contract Nonr 3438(00)].

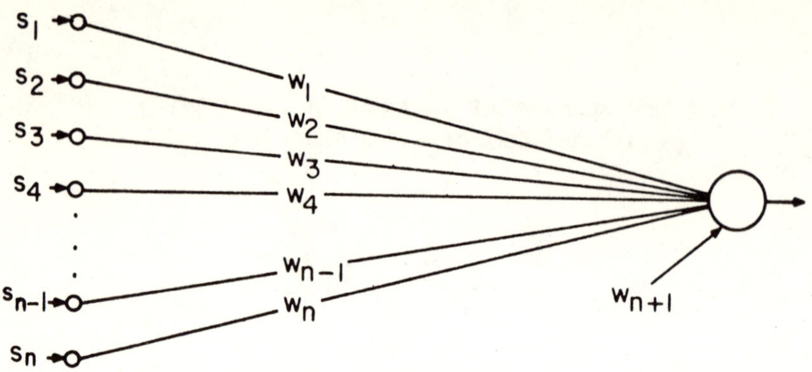

Figure 1. Threshold Logic Element.

The n-dimensional binary input vectors s to a threshold logic element may be viewed as vertices of the unit n-cube, and the equation

$$\sum_{i=1}^{n} z_i \, w_i = w_{n+1}$$

as an (n-1)-dimensional hyperplane in the same space as the cube. Any such hyperplane passing through the cube and touching no vertices divides the vertices of the cube into two classes. By varying the weight vector w, the hyperplane may be given any desired normal direction and distance from the origin of the cube; in machine learning, this weight adjustment results from the training process. Here it will be assumed that all weights, including the threshold level w_{n+1}, are variable.

If the input vectors s fall in two non-overlapping classes, a threshold unit response $r = 1$ for one class and $r = 0$ for the other class is possible if and only if the two sets of vertices of the unit n-cube corresponding to the input vectors can be separated with an (n-1)-dimensional hyperplane, i.e., if the two sets of vertices are linearly separable. Not all assignments of the vertices of the unit n-cube are linearly separable; for $n = 2$, the assignment in Figure 2a is not separable by a line, while that in Figure 2b is separable by a line. For large n, the proportion of all possible assignments of the full 2^n vertices which are linearly separable is very small. However, in self-organizing machine problems, typically only a very small proportion of the 2^n possible input patterns are represented in the training sequence; thus the likelihood of linear separability of two arbitrary sets of vertices may be high.

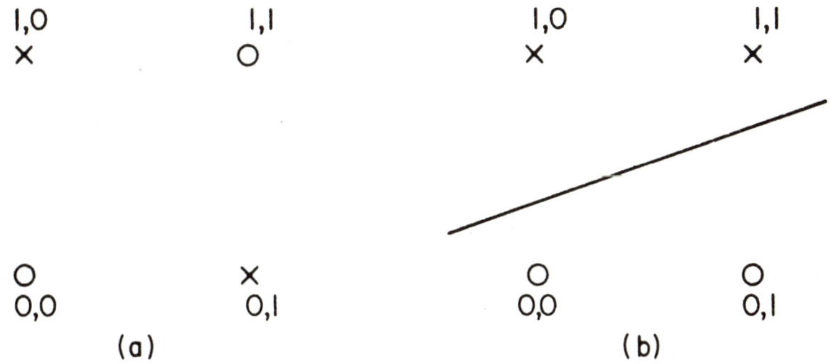

Figure 2. Examples of Non-Separable and Separable Problems for n = 2.

For the purpose of testing for linear separability, vertices not associated with patterns in the training sequences are considered as "don't care" vertices. This paper gives a method for testing for linear separability which is particularly suited to handling problems with numerous don't care vertices.

LINEAR SEPARABILITY

A vertex of the unit n-cube can be represented as an n-dimensional vector s, with components $s_i = 1$ or 0. Two subsets $\mathcal{T}$ and $\mathcal{F}$ of vertices, containing a total of $m \leqq 2^n$ vertices, are linearly separable if and only if there exists an $(n + 1)$-dimensional vector w, with components w_i, such that

$$\sum_{i=1}^{n} s_i w_i > w_{n+1} \quad \text{if } s \in \mathcal{T} \text{ and}$$

$$< w_{n+1} \quad \text{if } s \in \mathcal{F} .$$

These relations can be expressed in a simple matrix form through use of an $(n + 1)$-by-m matrix B constructed as follows: the n-dimensional vertex vectors are listed as the columns of a matrix, a final $n+1^{st}$ row of minus ones is appended to the matrix, and then every column corresponding to a vertex in $\mathcal{F}$ has all of its elements multiplied by -1. The problem is then linearly separable if and only if there exists an $(n+1)$-dimensional vector w whose dot product with each of the m column vectors of B is strictly greater than zero. The definition of linear separability can now be restated as:

Def. Two subsets of vertices of the unit cube are linearly separable if and only if there exists a vector w such that

$B^t w > 0$, where the matrix B associated with the two subsets of vertices is constructed in the manner described above. If such a vector w exists, the set of n-dimensional points r such that

$$\sum_{i=1}^{n} r_i w_i = w_{n+1}$$

form a separating hyperplane.

NOTATION AND PREVIOUS RESULTS

Lower case letters without subscripts denote either scalars or column vectors; the usage is stated each time a new variable is introduced. Lower case letters with subscripts denote elements of vectors. Upper case letters denote matrices.

Def. If x is a vector, the expressions $x = 0$, $x > 0$, $x \geqq 0$, and $x \leqq 0$ mean that the indicated relationship holds for every element of x. The expression $x \neq 0$ means that x is not equal to the zero vector. The notation (x, y) denotes the inner product of x and y, i.e., $\Sigma x_i y_i$.

Lemma 1. (Minimax Theorem.) For any matrix A, there exists a scalar value v and vectors $x \geqq 0$ and $y \geqq 0$, with $\Sigma x_i = \Sigma y_i = 1$, such that $A^t x \geqq V$ and $Ay \leqq V$, where V is a vector, all of whose components are v. Furthermore, there is no vector x', $\sum_i x_i' = 1$, such that $A^t x' > V$ or vector y', $\sum_i y_i' = 1$, such that $Ay' < V$.

Proof. A number of authors have given proofs of this important theorem of von Neumann's. Gale [6] presents an algebraic proof that relates well to the concepts developed here.

The following lemma is a special case of a more general theorem proved by Gale [6], and is equivalent to a result shown in recent notes by both Highleyman [7] and Gabelman [8].

Lemma 2. For a given matrix B, either there exists a vector w such that $B^t w > 0$ or a vector $z \geqq 0$, $z \neq 0$, such that $Bz = 0$, but not both.

Proof. Form from B and its negative the matrix $C = \left(\frac{B}{-B}\right)$. The existence of a vector w such that $B^t w > 0$ is equivalent to the existence of a vector $x \geqq 0$ such that $C^t x > 0$. Also, for a vector $z \geqq 0$, $z \neq 0$, the conditions $Bz = 0$, $Cz = 0$, and $Cz \leqq 0$ are equivalent. However, as a consequence of lemma 1, either there exists a vector $x \geqq 0$ such that $C^t x > 0$ or a vector $z \geqq 0$, $z \neq 0$, such that $Cz \leqq 0$, but not both.

If the matrix B of lemma 2 is the matrix associated with a separability problem, then the m-by-$2(n+1)$ matrix C^t used in the proof can be viewed as the payoff matrix of a two-person, zero-sum game. If the value of this game is zero, there exists a vector $z \geqq 0$, $z \neq 0$, such that $Cz \leqq 0$, and the original problem is not separable. If the value is greater than zero, there exists a vector $x \geqq 0$ such that $C^t x > 0$, and the original problem is separable [9]. A linear programming formulation for solution of this game is minimize Σx_i subject to $C^t x \geq 1$ and $x \geq 0$; the sum of the absolute magnitudes of the weights is minimized and the game value is $1/\Sigma x_i$. As compared to the method described in the next section, this method of testing for linear separability has several disadvantages. The payoff matrix used here is larger, a game or linear programming solution is always required, and for nonseparable problems an exact calculation of the game value is necessary.

The following lemma is due to Rosenblatt [1]. A number of proofs have been given, including a recent contribution by Novikoff [10]. The proof here is algebraic and contains some simplifications over previous proofs of this type.

Lemma 3. (Perceptron Convergence Theorem.) Suppose there exists a vector w such that $B^t w > 0$. Form a sequence $\{x_j\}$ of vectors of integers, with $x_o = 0$, according to the rule

$$x_j = \begin{cases} x_{j-1} + e_k & \text{if } e_k^t B^t Bx_{j-1} \leq 0 \text{ for some } k, \text{ or} \\ x_{j-1} & \text{if } B^t Bx_{j-1} > 0, \end{cases}$$

where e_k is a vector with a *one* in the kth position and *zeros* elsewhere. Then $B^t Bx_{j-1} > 0$ for all

$$j > \frac{(w,w) \max_i (B^t B)_{ii}}{\left[\min_i (B^t w)_i\right]^2},$$

i.e., the iterative process converges in a finite number of steps to a weight vector Bx such that $B^t B > 0$.

Proof. Suppose $B^t w > 0$ and $e_k^t B^t Bx_{j-1} \leq 0$ for some k. It will be shown that this implies

$$j \leq \frac{(w,w) \max_i (B^t B)_{ii}}{\left[\min_i (B^t w)_i\right]^2}.$$

First,

$$(w, Bx_j) = (B^t w, x_j) \geq j \min_i (B^t w)_i > 0 .$$

By the Schwarz inequality,

$$(w, Bx_j)^2 \leq (w,w)\ (Bx_j, Bx_j)\ .$$

Then

$$\begin{aligned}(Bx_j, Bx_j) - (Bx_{j-1}, Bx_{j-1}) &= 2\,(Be_k, Bx_{j-1}) + (Be_k, Be_k)\\ &= 2\, e_k^t\, B^t\, Bx_{j-1} + e_k^t\, B^t\, Be_k\\ &\leq e_k^t\, B^t\, Be_k \leq \max_i\, (B^t\, B)_{ii}\end{aligned}$$

Thus

$$(Bx_j, Bx_j) \leq j\ \max_i\, (B^t B)_{ii}$$

Combining results,

$$j^2 \left[\min_i\, (B^t\, w)_i\right]^2 \leq j\,(w,w)\, \max_i\, (B^t\, B)_{ii}\ , \quad \text{or}$$

$$j \leq \frac{(w,w)\, \max_i\, (B^t\, B)_{ii}}{\left[\min_i\, (B^t\, w)_i\right]^2}\ .$$

In the above proof, an initial weight vector of zero is assumed. This assumption is easily removed. If the initial weight vector is w_o, a correction to the x vector takes place only if $e_k^t\, B^t\, (Bx_{j-1} + w_o) \leq 0$ for some k; then $B^t\, (Bx_{j-1} + w_o) > 0$ for all

$$j > \frac{(w,w)\left[\max_i\, (B^t\, B)_{ii} - 2\min_i\, (B^t\, w_o)_i\right]}{\left[\min_i\, (B^t\, w_i)\right]^2}\ .$$

If the m-by-m matrix $B^t\, B$ is viewed as the payoff matrix of a game, the game value will be positive if the original problem is linearly separable and zero if the original problem is not separable. Since $B^t\, B$ is non-negative semidefinite [11], the game value cannot be negative. The iterative construction used in the above proof can be used to test for linear separability; however, unless an $x \geq 0$, $x \neq 0$ is found such that $B^t\, Bx = 0$, in which case the original problem is not separable, the process terminates only if the original problem is linearly separable [12]. A possible formulation as an integer linear programming problem is to minimize Σx_i subject to $B^t Bx \geq 1$ and $x \geq 0$. If a basic feasible solution exists, the problem is linearly separable. If x^* is an optimum solution, then $1/\Sigma x_i^*$ is the value of the game and Σx_i^* gives the minimum number of corrections to teach a set of separating weights according to the rule of lemma 3; thus for any teaching sequence, the number of corrections $\sum_i x_i$ is bounded by

$$\sum_i x_i^* \leq \sum_i x_i \leq (Bx^*, Bx^*) \max_i (B^t B)_{ii} \quad .$$

A problem is said to be in positive form if there exists a vector $w \geq 0$, such that $B^t w > 0$; in this case, the matrix B^t can be used directly as the payoff matrix of a game. Again, the original problem is not separable if the value is zero and separable if the value is greater than zero. Several authors [13,14, 15,16,17] have proposed linear separability tests of this type for problems in positive form. A linear programming formulation for this problem is minimize

$$\sum_{i=1}^{n} w_i \ ,$$

subject to $B^t w \geq 1$ and $w \geq 0$; this minimizes the sum of the weights, not including the threshold w_{n+1}. If it is known that at least one weight, say w_j, must be $\leq$ all other weights for every separating plane for the problem, as is true if all 2^n vertices are specified [18], then w_j can be minimized to minimize the maximum weight; integer linear programming may be used if integer weights are desired. While separable problems with all 2^n vertices specified can readily be transformed to positive form [19], no simple method of doing so is known for the case in which fewer than the complete set of vertices are specified. In the latter case, the condition that for no $t \in \mathcal{T}$ and $f \in \mathcal{F}$ does the relation $t \leq f$ hold is no longer sufficient to guarantee that a problem is in positive form. For example, the problem $\mathcal{T} = \{(0, 1, 1, 0, 0, 1), (0, 0, 0, 1, 1, 0)\}$ and $\mathcal{F} = \{(1, 1, 0, 0, 1, 1), (0, 0, 1, 1, 0, 0), (0, 0, 0, 0, 1, 1)\}$ has no inclusions in either direction, but can be separated only by weight vectors with both positive and negative weights. The new test described below has the advantage of handling problems which are not in positive form.

TEST FOR LINEAR SEPARABILITY

The matrix B can be reduced by row operations and column permutations to the form

$$\mathrm{TBP} = \begin{pmatrix} \mathrm{I} & \mathrm{A} \\ 0 & 0 \end{pmatrix},$$

where T is a non-singular transformation matrix, P is a permutation matrix, and I is an identity matrix; the final rows of zeros occur only if there are linear dependencies among the row vectors of B. Although it is always possible to carry out this reduction, the matrix A is not unique, but depends on the transformations used. In general, the reduction of B is done by forming the identity matrix I one element at a time, using the allowed row operations and column permutations; the transformation matrix T can be constructed simultaneously by applying the same row operations to an $(n+1)$-by-$(n+1)$ identity matrix. As a special case, if the zero vertex and all vertices at distance one from the origin are included in one class or the other, the reduction of B to the form (I:A) can be done by adding the sum of the first n rows to the $n+1^{st}$ row, then rearranging rows and columns and reversing row signs if needed.

The following theorem shows that the question of linear separability can be resolved by examination of the matrix A.

Theorem: For a given matrix B, and a matrix A constructed from B by pre-multiplication by a non-singular transformation matrix T and post-multiplication by a permutation matrix P, such that

$$\mathrm{TBP} = \begin{pmatrix} \mathrm{I} & \mathrm{A} \\ 0 & 0 \end{pmatrix},$$

(i) There exists a vector w such that $\mathrm{B^t\, w} > 0$ if and only if there exists a vector $\mathrm{x} \geqq 0$ such that $\mathrm{A^t\, x} > 0$,

(ii) There exists a vector $\mathrm{z} \geqq 0$, $\mathrm{z} \neq 0$, such that $\mathrm{Bz} = 0$ if and only if there exists a vector $\mathrm{y} \geqq 0$, $\mathrm{y} \neq 0$, such that $\mathrm{Ay} \leqq 0$, and

(iii) Either there exists a vector $\mathrm{x} \geqq 0$ such that $\mathrm{A^t\, x} > 0$ or a vector $\mathrm{y} \geqq 0$, $\mathrm{y} \neq 0$, such that $\mathrm{Ay} \leqq 0$, but not both.

Proof:

(i) Suppose there exists a vector w such that $\mathrm{B^t\, w} > 0$. Then since P is a permutation matrix, $\mathrm{P^t\, B^t\, w} > 0$. Thus

$$P^t B^t T^t (T^t)^{-1} w = \begin{pmatrix} I & 0 \\ A^t & 0 \end{pmatrix} w' > 0 ,$$

where $w' = (T^t)^{-1} w$. If the matrix product $P^t B^t T^t$ contains any columns of zeros, they and the corresponding elements of w' are deleted, leaving

$$\begin{pmatrix} I \\ A^t \end{pmatrix} x > 0 .$$

Thus $x \geqq 0$ and $A^t x > 0$.

(ii) Suppose there exists a vector $z \geqq 0$, $z \neq 0$, such that $Bz = 0$. Then

$$TBP P^{-1} z = \begin{pmatrix} I & A \\ 0 & 0 \end{pmatrix} y' = 0 ,$$

where $y' = P^{-1} z \geqq 0$, $y' \neq 0$. Then, partitioning y' into $y' = \begin{pmatrix} y'' \\ y \end{pmatrix}$, $Iy'' + Ay = 0$, and thus $y \geqq 0$, $y \neq 0$, and $Ay \leqq 0$.

(iii) Conclusion (iii) is a consequence of lemma 1, the minimax theorem. Then if there exists a vector $x \geqq 0$ such that $A^t x > 0$, there exists no vector $y \geqq 0$, $y \neq 0$, such that $Ay \leqq 0$, and thus no vector $z \geqq 0$, $z \neq 0$, such that $Bz = 0$, and thus, by lemma 2 there exists a vector w such that $B^t w > 0$. Similarly if there exists a vector $y \geqq 0$, $y \neq 0$, such that $Ay \leqq 0$, there exists no vector $x \geqq 0$ such that $A^t x > 0$, and thus no vector w such that $B^t w > 0$, and thus by lemma 2 there exists a vector $z \geqq 0$, $z \neq 0$, such that $Bz = 0$.

Remark: Given a vector $x \geqq 0$ such that $A^t x > 0$, there exists a vector $x' > 0$ such that $A^t x' > 0$; x' can be formed by adding a small positive quantity ϵ to each component of x, where

$$0 < \epsilon < \frac{\min_i (A^t x)_i}{\left| \min_i \sum_i a_{ij} \right|} .$$

The vector x' can be extended to dimension $n+1$ by appending zeros, if needed. Then $w = T^t x'$ satisfies $B^t w > 0$.

The proposed test for linear separability is based on an examination of the matrix A. If there exists a vector $x \geqq 0$ such that $A^t x > 0$, the original problem is linearly separable; and if there exists a vector $y \geqq 0$, $y \neq 0$, such that $Ay \leqq 0$, the problem is not separable. One of these two mutually exclusive conditions must always hold, and the problem now is to determine which one does. A possible method of doing this is to treat the matrix A^t as the payoff matrix of a game; if the value of the game is >0, the original problem is linearly separable, and if the value of the game is $\leqq 0$ the original problem is not separable. The value of this game can be found by linear programming methods, or can be approximated arbitrarily closely from above and below by the iterative game solution technique of fictitious play. Since it is only necessary to know the region in which the value lies, the latter method will in a finite number of iterations answer the question of whether or not the original problem is linearly separable, except possibly for a game whose value is exactly zero. For a description of this method, see Luce and Raiffa [20] or Akers [14]. If the original problem is linearly separable, solution of the game can yield a vector $x > 0$ such that $A^t x > 0$; then if the transformation T has been constructed during the reduction of B, the equation of a separating hyperplane can be readily obtained. A possible linear programming formulation is minimize Σx_i subject to $A^t x \geq 1$ and $x \geq 1$; if x^* is a solution to this problem, $w = T^t x^*$ is a solution for the weight vector. The components of the weight vector may be bounded by adding constraints in the linear programming solution. For example, if $\underline{w} \leq w \leq \overline{w}$, then the constraints $T^t x \geq \underline{w}$ and $T^t x \leq \overline{w}$ are added.

It should be noted that it is actually not necessary to obtain an identity sub-matrix I during the reduction of B. In place of I, any diagonal sub-matrix with positive elements will suffice. Thus, the reduction may conveniently be carried out using integer arithmetic, and round-off problems avoided. With this modification, the value of the game will remain > 0 or ≤ 0 as before.

After completion of the process of obtaining the matrix A from B, if any column of A has no positive element, then the original problem is not separable, since a vector y with a unity element corresponding to that column, and with all other elements zero, will satisfy $Ay \leq 0$. If the sum of any subset of the columns is non-positive, the original problem for similar reasons is not separable.

If any column of A is greater than or equal in every element to a non-negative sum of other columns, it can be eliminated. If the value of the game was > 0 before the deletion it will remain > 0, and if ≤ 0, it will remain ≤ 0. This step is an extension of the standard game solution step of deleting dominated strategies. The process here might be termed deletion of "weakly dominated" strategies. Similarly, any column of A with all non-negative elements can be deleted, as long as at least one element in the column is $\geq$ the corresponding element in the "identity" portion of $(I \vdots A)$.

We have applied this method in a computer test for linear separability, using the method of fictitious play for the game solution. A number of problems have been run, with dimension up to n = 32. Frequently, the question of separability has been answered without the need for solving the game. Only once has the iterative solution method failed to converge; since at the time the solution was stopped the value was known to lie between -0.0064 and 0.0010, it is conjectured that the value was exactly zero. It should be possible to resolve a case of this type with an exact linear programming solution.

If only the separability question is of interest, and the equation of the separating hyperplane is not needed, further simplifications in the method are possible. First, the transformation T need not be constructed during the reduction of B. Second, if any row of B becomes all non-negative or all non-positive during the reduction, every column in which the row has a non-zero entry may be deleted, then the remaining row of zeros deleted. If all columns are deleted in this way, the problem is separable. Third, if any row of A is less than or equal to a non-negative sum of other rows, it can be deleted. And finally, although to obtain a separating hyperplane it is necessary to find a strictly positive vector x that $A^t x > 0$, to show separability it is only necessary to find a non-negative vector x such that $A^t x > 0$.

Example 1: Consider the following B matrix, representing a 4-dimensional problem with 7 vertices in one class and 9 in the other:

$$B = \begin{pmatrix} 0 & 1 & 0 & 0 & 0 & 1 & 1 & 1 & 0 & 0 & 0 & -1 & 1 & 1 & 0 & -1 \\ 0 & 0 & -1 & 0 & 0 & 1 & 0 & 0 & -1 & -1 & 0 & -1 & 1 & 0 & -1 & -1 \\ 0 & 0 & 0 & -1 & 0 & 0 & 1 & 0 & -1 & 0 & -1 & -1 & 0 & 1 & -1 & -1 \\ 0 & 0 & 0 & 0 & -1 & 0 & 0 & 1 & 0 & -1 & -1 & 0 & 1 & 1 & -1 & -1 \\ -1 & -1 & 1 & 1 & 1 & -1 & -1 & -1 & 1 & 1 & 1 & 1 & -1 & -1 & 1 & 1 \end{pmatrix}.$$

If the final row is moved to the top of the matrix, and the sum of the other 4 rows added to it, the result is

$$\begin{pmatrix} -1 & 0 & 0 & 0 & 0 & 1 & 1 & 1 & -1 & -1 & -1 & -2 & 2 & 2 & -2 & -3 \\ 0 & 1 & 0 & 0 & 0 & 1 & 1 & 1 & 0 & 0 & 0 & -1 & 1 & 1 & 0 & -1 \\ 0 & 0 & -1 & 0 & 0 & 1 & 0 & 0 & -1 & -1 & 0 & -1 & 1 & 0 & -1 & -1 \\ 0 & 0 & 0 & -1 & 0 & 0 & 1 & 0 & -1 & 0 & -1 & -1 & 0 & 1 & -1 & -1 \\ 0 & 0 & 0 & 0 & -1 & 0 & 0 & 1 & 0 & -1 & -1 & 0 & 1 & 1 & -1 & -1 \end{pmatrix},$$

and changing the sign of the first and the last three rows gives

$$(I\vdots A) = \begin{pmatrix} 1 & 0 & 0 & 0 & 0 & -1 & -1 & -1 & 1 & 1 & 1 & 2 & -2 & -2 & 2 & 3 \\ 0 & 1 & 0 & 0 & 0 & 1 & 1 & 1 & 0 & 0 & 0 & -1 & 1 & 1 & 0 & -1 \\ 0 & 0 & 1 & 0 & 0 & -1 & 0 & 0 & 1 & 1 & 0 & 1 & -1 & 0 & 1 & 1 \\ 0 & 0 & 0 & 1 & 0 & 0 & -1 & 0 & 1 & 0 & 1 & 1 & 0 & -1 & 1 & 1 \\ 0 & 0 & 0 & 0 & 1 & 0 & 0 & -1 & 0 & 1 & 1 & 0 & -1 & -1 & 1 & 1 \end{pmatrix};$$

the transformation used is

$$T = \begin{pmatrix} -1 & -1 & -1 & -1 & -1 \\ 1 & 0 & 0 & 0 & 0 \\ 0 & -1 & 0 & 0 & 0 \\ 0 & 0 & -1 & 0 & 0 \\ 0 & 0 & 0 & -1 & 0 \end{pmatrix}.$$

The 6th and 8th columns can be deleted since they are both ≧ the 13th column, the 7th column can be deleted since it is ≧ the 14th column, and the 15th and 16th columns can be deleted since they are ≧ the 12th column. Similarly, the 9th and 11th columns can be deleted since they are ≧ the sum of the 12th and 13th columns, and the 10th column deleted since it is ≧ the sum of the 12th and 14th columns. This gives the reduced A matrix

$$A = \begin{pmatrix} 2 & -2 & -2 \\ -1 & 1 & 1 \\ 1 & -1 & 0 \\ 1 & 0 & -1 \\ 0 & -1 & -1 \end{pmatrix}.$$

The vector

$$x = \begin{pmatrix} 0 \\ 3 \\ 2 \\ 2 \\ 0 \end{pmatrix}$$

satisfies the condition $A^t x > 0$, and thus the problem is linearly separable; this vector was obtained by fictitious play. The zeros in the first and last positions of x reflect the fact that the first and last rows of A can be deleted if only the separability question is of interest; the first row is $\leq$ twice the 4th, and the last row is $\leq$ the 4th.

By starting the fictitious play with an x vector of all *ones*, the result

$$x = \begin{pmatrix} 1 \\ 7 \\ 3 \\ 3 \\ 1 \end{pmatrix}$$

is obtained. This solution is shown in Figure 3. The solution is started by adding the five columns of A^t to give the first column on the right. Then the row of A^t corresponding to the minimum of this column is entered below. The column of A^t

2	-1	1	1	0	3	2	1	0	-1^x	-2^x	-3^x	-2^x	-1^x	0^x	1
-2	1	-1	0	-1	-3^x	-2	-1^x	0	1	2	3	2	2	1	1
-2_x	1_x	0_x	-1_x	-1_x	-3	-2^x	-1	0^x	1	2	3	3	2	2	1
-2	1^x	-1	0	-1											
-4	2^x	-1	-1	-2											
-6	3^x	-2	-1	-3											
-8	4^x	-2	-2	-4											
-6	3^x	-1	-1	-4											
-4	2^x	0	0	-4											
-2	1	1^x	1	-4											
0	0	2	2^x	-4											
2	-1	3^x	3	-4											
4	-2	4	4^x	-4											

Figure 3. Example of Solution by Fictitious Play.

corresponding to the maximum of the row below is then added to the first column on the right to form the second. The row of A^t corresponding to the minimum of this column is added to the first row below to form the second. This process continued until either the column on the right is all > 0, in which case the problem is linearly separable and the x vector is obtained by adding up the number of times each column of A^t has been added to obtain this column, or until the row below is all ≤ 0, in which case the problem is not separable. The method of handling ties is optional; in this example, ties are taken in rotation, starting from the next previous correction. Multiplication of the solution vector x by T^t gives

$$w = T^t x = \begin{pmatrix} 6 \\ -4 \\ -4 \\ -2 \\ -1 \end{pmatrix};$$

thus

$$6z_1 - 4z_2 - 4z_3 - 2z_4 = -1$$

is the equation of a separating hyperplane for the problem.

Example 2: If only the separability question is of interest, it is sometimes possible to form a row of all non-negative or non-positive entries at an early stage and simplify the test process. Starting with the B matrix of the previous example, if the first row is subtracted from both the second and third rows, they become all non-positive. If this is done and all rows but the first are negated, the matrix

$$\begin{array}{c} \begin{pmatrix} 0 & 1 & 0 & 0 & 0 & 1 & 1 & 1 & 0 & 0 & 0 & -1 & 1 & 1 & 0 & -1 \\ 0 & 1 & 1 & 0 & 0 & 0 & 1 & 1 & 1 & 1 & 0 & 0 & 0 & 1 & 1 & 0 \\ 0 & 1 & 0 & 1 & 0 & 1 & 0 & 1 & 1 & 0 & 1 & 0 & 1 & 0 & 1 & 0 \\ 0 & 0 & 0 & 0 & 1 & 0 & 0 & -1 & 0 & 1 & 1 & 0 & -1 & -1 & 1 & 1 \\ 1 & 1 & -1 & -1 & -1 & 1 & 1 & 1 & -1 & -1 & -1 & -1 & 1 & 1 & -1 & -1 \end{pmatrix} \begin{matrix} \\ x \\ x \\ \\ \\ \end{matrix} \\ \begin{matrix} & x & x & x & & x & x & x & x & x & x & & x & x & x & \end{matrix} \end{array}$$

is obtained. The rows and columns marked with x's can then be deleted giving

$$\begin{pmatrix} 0 & 0 & -1 & -1 \\ 0 & 1 & 0 & 1 \\ 1 & -1 & -1 & -1 \end{pmatrix} \begin{matrix} x \\ x \\ \\ \end{matrix}$$

$$\begin{matrix} & x & x & x \end{matrix}$$

The rows and columns in this matrix marked with x's can then be deleted, leaving a single *one* which can also be deleted. Since the matrix vanishes, the only solution $z \geq 0$ to $Bz = 0$ is $z = 0$, and thus the problem is linearly separable.

The solution in example 2 suggests a modification in the linear separability test and the procedure for finding a separating hyperplane if one exists. Using the same row operations and column permutations as before, the objective is to form from *B* a transformed matrix TPB, all of whose entries are non-negative integers. If this is possible, then the original problem is linearly separable, and an *x* vector of all *ones* leads to a weight vector $w = T^t x$ which satisfies $B^t w \geq 1$. The general plan is to work toward forming a row with all non-negative entries, by addition, subtraction, and negation of rows. When such a row is formed, it is shifted to the bottom of the array and all columns in which this row has non-zero entries are shifted to the right side of the array. The reduction then continues on the remaining rows and columns, however applying all row operations to the full row. If the matrix is finally reduced in this way to a single residual row with non-negative entries in those columns still under consideration, then all remaining negative entries in the full matrix can be deleted by row additions. Working back, taking the columns in the same groupings as when set aside, negative entries in the first row in the column group corresponding to the second row are eliminated by adding a suitable multiple of the second row to the first. Or if the first row is all positive in that column group, the largest integer multiple of the second row possible, without introducing negative entries in the first row in this column group, is subtracted from the first row. The remaining rows are used in turn in the same fashion, and on completion all rows are non-negative and the matrix is minimum in the sense that no row may be subtracted from another without introducing negative entries.

A possible systematic procedure for carrying out the reduction is to begin by negating the final row so as to make all columns non-negative or non-positive. If the number of non-positive columns exceeds the number of non-negative columns, the entire matrix is then negated. Then the non-negative columns are grouped on the left by permutation. The plan then is to enlarge the non-negative portion of the matrix by adding columns one at a time from the remaining group, watching while doing so for non-negative rows which may be formed in the process. First, any row subtractions possible without creating negative entries in the non-negative portion of the matrix are made. If any non-negative rows are formed, they are shifted as described above, and the portion of the array under consideration reduced in size. And if any non-negative columns are created, they are shifted to the left. Then a column from the right with one or more positive entries is brought into the non-negative portion of the array by row additions. This process continues until the remaining portion of the array is all non-negative or until the remaining columns have no positive entries. If the latter happens, the problem can be shown to be non-separable if the non-negative portion of the remaining array has columns with single non-zero entries to correspond to one of the non-positive columns. Otherwise, the remaining portion of the array is converted to the (I:A) form and a game solution used as in the original formulation of the method. The separability question is resolved without reference to the rows and columns set aside due to rows becoming all non-negative. If the problem is linearly separable and a weight vector $x \geq 1$ such that $A^t x \geq 1$ is constructed, it can easily be extended to length $n + 1$ by appending positive integers of sufficient magnitude such that $P^t B^t T^t x \geq 1$ for the full matrix.

This modified method has been used with success in hand computation of a number of examples. In each separable case, a full matrix of non-negative entries was obtained. The following two examples may clarify the steps of the modified method.

Example 3: Using the same initial B matrix as in examples 1 and 2, the matrix is transformed to

$$\begin{pmatrix}
1 & -1 & 1 & 1 & -1 & -1 & -1 & -1 & 1 & -1 & 1 & 1 & -1 & -1 & 1 & -1 \\
0 & 1 & 0 & -1 & 0 & 1 & 0 & 1 & 0 & 0 & 0 & -1 & 0 & 1 & -1 & 1 \\
0 & 0 & 1 & 1 & 0 & 0 & -1 & -1 & 0 & -1 & 0 & 0 & -1 & -1 & 0 & -1 \\
0 & 0 & 0 & 0 & 1 & 1 & 1 & 1 & 0 & 0 & -1 & 0 & 1 & 0 & -1 & 1 \\
0 & 0 & 0 & 0 & 0 & 0 & 0 & 0 & 1 & 1 & 1 & 1 & 1 & 1 & 1 & 1
\end{pmatrix},$$

where the successive reductions in size of the remaining matrix during reduction are indicated by dashed lines; the row transformation used is

$$\begin{pmatrix} 0 & 0 & 0 & 0 & -1 \\ 0 & 0 & 0 & -1 & 0 \\ 0 & 1 & 0 & 0 & 0 \\ 0 & 0 & -1 & 0 & 0 \\ 1 & -1 & 0 & 0 & 0 \end{pmatrix}.$$

(The column permutations used are not recorded, as this information is not used later.) Then by row additions, the matrix

$$\begin{pmatrix} \underline{1} & 0 & 1 & 0 & 0 & 1 & 0 & 1 & 2 & 0 & 1 & 1 & 1 & 1 & 0 & 2 \\ 0 & \underline{1} & 1 & 0 & 1 & 2 & 0 & 1 & 2 & 1 & 1 & 1 & 2 & 2 & 0 & 3 \\ 0 & 0 & 1 & \underline{1} & 1 & 1 & 0 & 0 & 1 & 0 & 0 & 1 & 1 & 0 & 0 & 1 \\ 0 & 0 & 0 & 0 & 1 & 1 & \underline{1} & 1 & 1 & 1 & 0 & 1 & 2 & 1 & 0 & 2 \\ 0 & 0 & 0 & 0 & 0 & 0 & 0 & 0 & 1 & 1 & 1 & 1 & 1 & 1 & \underline{1} & 1 \end{pmatrix}$$

is obtained, the complete row transformation being

$$T = \begin{pmatrix} 1 & -1 & -1 & -1 & -1 \\ 2 & -1 & -1 & -1 & 0 \\ 1 & 0 & -1 & 0 & 0 \\ 1 & -1 & -1 & 0 & 0 \\ 1 & -1 & 0 & 0 & 0 \end{pmatrix}.$$

The underlined entries in the transformed matrix stand alone in columns, and thus the matrix can be transformed, if desired, by column permutations to

$$(I \vdots A) = \begin{pmatrix} 1 & 0 & 0 & 0 & 0 & 1 & 0 & 1 & 1 & 2 & 0 & 1 & 1 & 1 & 1 & 2 \\ 0 & 1 & 0 & 0 & 0 & 1 & 1 & 2 & 1 & 2 & 1 & 1 & 1 & 2 & 2 & 3 \\ 0 & 0 & 1 & 0 & 0 & 1 & 1 & 1 & 0 & 1 & 0 & 0 & 1 & 1 & 0 & 1 \\ 0 & 0 & 0 & 1 & 0 & 0 & 1 & 1 & 1 & 1 & 1 & 0 & 1 & 2 & 1 & 2 \\ 0 & 0 & 0 & 0 & 1 & 0 & 0 & 0 & 0 & 1 & 1 & 1 & 1 & 1 & 1 & 1 \end{pmatrix}.$$

Using a x vector of all ones, the separating weight vector

$$w = T^t x = \begin{pmatrix} 6 \\ -4 \\ -4 \\ -2 \\ -1 \end{pmatrix}$$

is obtained, the same result found in example 1. Since the entries in each column of T have the same sign, the weight magnitudes cannot be reduced by further row additions on the matrix (I:A).

Example 4: Starting with the matrix

$$B = \begin{pmatrix} 0 & 1 & 0 & 0 & 0 & -1 & -1 & -1 & 0 & 0 & 0 & -1 & -1 & -1 & 0 & -1 \\ 0 & 0 & 1 & 0 & 0 & -1 & 0 & 0 & -1 & 1 & 0 & -1 & -1 & 0 & -1 & -1 \\ 0 & 0 & 0 & 1 & 0 & 0 & -1 & 0 & -1 & 0 & 1 & -1 & 0 & -1 & -1 & -1 \\ 0 & 0 & 0 & 0 & 1 & 0 & 0 & -1 & 0 & 1 & 1 & 0 & -1 & -1 & -1 & -1 \\ -1 & -1 & -1 & -1 & -1 & 1 & 1 & 1 & 1 & -1 & -1 & 1 & 1 & 1 & 1 & 1 \end{pmatrix},$$

the matrix

$$\begin{pmatrix} 1 & -1 & 0 & 0 & -1 & 0 & -1 & 0 & 0 & 0 & 0 & -1 & 0 & -1 & -1 & -1 \\ 0 & 1 & 0 & -1 & 0 & 0 & 1 & 1 & 0 & 0 & -1 & 0 & -1 & 0 & 1 & 1 \\ 0 & 0 & 1 & 1 & 0 & -1 & 0 & -1 & 0 & 0 & 0 & -1 & 0 & -1 & -1 & -1 \\ 0 & 0 & 0 & 0 & 1 & 1 & 1 & 1 & 0 & -1 & 0 & 0 & -1 & 1 & 0 & 1 \\ 0 & 0 & 0 & 0 & 0 & 0 & 0 & 0 & 1 & 1 & 1 & 1 & 1 & 1 & 1 & 1 \end{pmatrix}$$

is obtained by using column permutations and the row transformation

$$\begin{pmatrix} 1 & 0 & 0 & 0 & 0 \\ 0 & 0 & 0 & -1 & 0 \\ 0 & 1 & 0 & 0 & 0 \\ 0 & 0 & -1 & 0 & 0 \\ -1 & -1 & 0 & 0 & -1 \end{pmatrix}.$$

After elimination of negative entries by row additions, the matrix becomes

$$\mathrm{TBP} = \begin{pmatrix} \underline{1} & 0 & 1 & 0 & 0 & 0 & 1 & 1 & 2 & 1 & 1 & 0 & 0 & 1 & 1 & 2 \\ 0 & \underline{1} & 1 & 0 & 1 & 0 & 2 & 1 & 2 & 1 & 1 & 1 & 0 & 2 & 2 & 3 \\ 0 & 0 & 1 & \underline{1} & 1 & 0 & 1 & 0 & 1 & 0 & 1 & 0 & 0 & 1 & 0 & 1 \\ 0 & 0 & 0 & 0 & 1 & \underline{1} & 1 & 1 & 1 & 0 & 1 & 1 & 0 & 2 & 1 & 2 \\ 0 & 0 & 0 & 0 & 0 & 0 & 0 & 0 & 1 & 1 & 1 & 1 & \underline{1} & 1 & 1 & 1 \end{pmatrix},$$

where

$$T = \begin{pmatrix} -1 & -1 & -1 & -1 & -2 \\ -2 & -1 & -1 & -1 & -2 \\ -1 & 0 & -1 & 0 & -1 \\ -1 & -1 & -1 & 0 & -1 \\ -1 & -1 & 0 & 0 & -1 \end{pmatrix}.$$

Using an x vector of all *ones*, the separating weight vector

$$w = T^t x = \begin{pmatrix} -6 \\ -4 \\ -4 \\ -2 \\ -7 \end{pmatrix}$$

is obtained. Since the entries in each column of T have the same sign, the weight magnitudes cannot be reduced by further row additions on the matrix TBP.

ACKNOWLEDGMENT

The author wishes to thank C. A. Rosen, A. E. Brain, G. E. Forsen, and N. J. Nilsson for numerous discussions of the problem of determining linear separability in the case in which there are many "don't care" vertices; this problem arose in research on self-organizing machines. William Kautz gave many suggestions which aided in the development of this test, and provided the author with general background on linearly separable truth functions. The proof of lemma 3 resulted from a joint attempt by the author and A. Novikoff to find simpler proofs for the perceptron convergence theorem.

REFERENCES AND NOTES

1. Frank Rosenblatt, "Principles of Neurodynamics: Perceptrons and the Theory of Brain Mechanisms," Spartan Books, Washington, D. C., 1961.
2. J. K. Hawkins, "Self-Organizing Systems—A Review and Commentary," Proceedings of the IRE, V. 49, pp. 31-48; January 1961.
3. A. E. Brain, N. J. Nilsson, R. C. Singleton, and C. P. Bourne, "Graphical Data Processing Research Study and Experimental Investigation: Report No. 6," prepared by Stanford Research Institute, Menlo Park, California, for the U. S. Army Signal Research and Development Laboratory, Fort Monmouth, New Jersey, Contract DA-36-039-SC-78343, December 1961 (ASTIA No. AD-265314).
4. Binary vectors are assumed here to be composed of *ones* and *zeros*. However, all of the results of this paper hold without modification if the ± 1 representation for binary vectors is used instead.
5. An alternative definition of a threshold logic element replaces $<$ by $\leq$ in the second line of the output response rule; this definition is not used here, as it adds unnecessary complexity to the mathematical formulation of the problem. The difference in definition is only important when studying the question of minimizing weights.
6. David Gale, "The Basic Theorems of Real Linear Equations, Inequalities, Linear Programming, and Game Theory," Naval Research Logistics Quarterly, V. 3, No. 3, pp. 193-200; September 1956.
7. W. H. Highleyman, "A Note on Linear Separation," *IRE Trans. on Electronic Computers* (correspondence), V. EC-10, pp. 777-778; December, 1961.
8. Irving J. Gabelman, "A Note on the Realization of Boolean Functions Using a Single Threshold Element," Proc. IRE (correspondence), V. 50, pp. 225-226; February, 1962.
9. Minnick uses a linear programming formulation similar to this to find separating hyperplanes. See Robert C. Minnick, "Linear-Input Logic," *IRE Trans. on Electronic Computers*, V. EC-10, pp. 6-16; March, 1961.

10. A. Novikoff, "On Convergence Proofs for Perceptrons," Symposium on Mathematical Theory of Automata, Polytechnic Institute of Brooklyn, April 1962 (Proceedings in Press).
11. P. R. Halmos, "Finite Dimensional Vector Spaces," 2nd edition, D. Van Nostrand Co., Inc., Princeton, New Jersey, 1958; p. 140.
12. Before developing the test described in the next section, we used this procedure in a computer program;

$$\min_i (B^t Bx)_i / \Sigma x_i ,$$

a lower bound on the value of the game, was observed during the running of the program, and cases which did not appear to be converging to a positive value were stopped and considered not separable or difficult to separate (i.e., difficult to teach). The ±1 representation for binary vectors appeared to lead to faster convergence than the 0, 1 representation; this should be studied further, since the same choice of representation is available in actual construction of self-organizing machines. Several training sequences were used in the computer program. The one which seemed to work best was to correct for the pattern giving the largest error; i.e., after making a correction, the minimum element of $B^t Bx$ was found and the correction made by adding the corresponding column of $B^t B$ to $B^t Bx$. In case of ties, the first tied pattern in rotation from the previous correction was used.
13. R. McNaughton, "Unate Truth Functions," *IRE Trans. on Electronic Computers,* V. EC-10, pp. 1-6; March, 1961.
14. S. B. Akers, Jr., "Threshold Logic and Two-Person, Zero-Sum Games," in *Proc. of the Second Annual Symposium on Switching Circuit Theory and Logical Design,* pp. 27-33, American Institute of Electrical Engineers, New York; September, 1961.
15. S. Muroga, I. Toda, and S. Takasu, "Theory of Majority Decision Elements," Journal of the Franklin Institute, V. 271, pp. 376-418; May, 1961. Their approach is similar to that of Minnick (Reference 9 above); however, they take advantage of simplifications which can be made when a function is in positive form. See the footnote on p. 402 of their paper.
16. Irving J. Gabelman, "The Synthesis of Boolean Functions Using a Single Threshold Unit," Report No. RADC-TDR-62-99, Rome Air Development Center, Griffiss Air Force Base, New York, March 1962.

17. V. I. Varshavskii, "Functional Possibilities and the Synthesis of Threshold Elements," Doklady Akademii Nauk, SSSR, V. 139(5), pp. 1071-4, 1961 (in Russian).
18. Muroga, Toda, and Takasu, op. cit. (Reference 15), show that the weights can be ordered when all 2^n vertices are specified.
19. Muroga, Toda, and Tokasu, op. cit. (Reference 15).
20. R. D. Luce and Howard Raiffa, *Games and Decisions*, John Wiley and Sons, Inc., New York; 1957.

Reprinted from *Psychological Rev.*, **65**, No. 6, 1958, pp. 386–408

THE PERCEPTRON: A PROBABILISTIC MODEL FOR INFORMATION STORAGE AND ORGANIZATION IN THE BRAIN [1]

5

F. ROSENBLATT

Cornell Aeronautical Laboratory

If we are eventually to understand the capability of higher organisms for perceptual recognition, generalization, recall, and thinking, we must first have answers to three fundamental questions:

1. How is information about the physical world sensed, or detected, by the biological system?
2. In what form is information stored, or remembered?
3. How does information contained in storage, or in memory, influence recognition and behavior?

The first of these questions is in the province of sensory physiology, and is the only one for which appreciable understanding has been achieved. This article will be concerned primarily with the second and third questions, which are still subject to a vast amount of speculation, and where the few relevant facts currently supplied by neurophysiology have not yet been integrated into an acceptable theory.

With regard to the second question, two alternative positions have been maintained. The first suggests that storage of sensory information is in the form of coded representations or images, with some sort of one-to-one mapping between the sensory stimulus and the stored pattern. According to this hypothesis, if one understood the code or "wiring diagram" of the nervous system, one should, in principle, be able to discover exactly what an organism remembers by reconstructing the original sensory patterns from the "memory traces" which they have left, much as we might develop a photographic negative, or translate the pattern of electrical charges in the "memory" of a digital computer. This hypothesis is appealing in its simplicity and ready intelligibility, and a large family of theoretical brain models has been developed around the idea of a coded, representational memory (**2**, **3**, **9**, **14**). The alternative approach, which stems from the tradition of British empiricism, hazards the guess that the images of stimuli may never really be recorded at all, and that the central nervous system simply acts as an intricate switching network, where retention takes the form of new connections, or pathways, between centers of activity. In many of the more recent developments of this position (Hebb's "cell assembly," and Hull's "cortical anticipatory goal response," for example) the "responses" which are associated to stimuli may be entirely contained within the CNS itself. In this case the response represents an "idea" rather than an action. The important feature of this approach is that there is never any simple mapping of the stimulus into memory, according to some code which would permit its later reconstruction. Whatever in-

[1] The development of this theory has been carried out at the Cornell Aeronautical Laboratory, Inc., under the sponsorship of the Office of Naval Research, Contract Nonr-2381(00). This article is primarily an adaptation of material reported in Ref. 15, which constitutes the first full report on the program.

formation is retained must somehow be stored as a *preference for a particular response;* i.e., the information is contained in *connections* or *associations* rather than topographic representations. (The term *response*, for the remainder of this presentation, should be understood to mean any distinguishable state of the organism, which may or may not involve externally detectable muscular activity. The activation of some nucleus of cells in the central nervous system, for example, can constitute a response, according to this definition.)

Corresponding to these two positions on the method of information retention, there exist two hypotheses with regard to the third question, the manner in which stored information exerts its influence on current activity. The "coded memory theorists" are forced to conclude that recognition of any stimulus involves the matching or systematic comparison of the contents of storage with incoming sensory patterns, in order to determine whether the current stimulus has been seen before, and to determine the appropriate response from the organism. The theorists in the empiricist tradition, on the other hand, have essentially combined the answer to the third question with their answer to the second: since the stored information takes the form of new connections, or transmission channels in the nervous system (or the creation of conditions which are functionally equivalent to new connections), it follows that the new stimuli will make use of these new pathways which have been created, automatically activating the appropriate response without requiring any separate process for their recognition or identification.

The theory to be presented here takes the empiricist, or "connectionist" position with regard to these questions. The theory has been developed for a hypothetical nervous system, or machine, called a *perceptron*. The perceptron is designed to illustrate some of the fundamental properties of intelligent systems in general, without becoming too deeply enmeshed in the special, and frequently unknown, conditions which hold for particular biological organisms. The analogy between the perceptron and biological systems should be readily apparent to the reader.

During the last few decades, the development of symbolic logic, digital computers, and switching theory has impressed many theorists with the functional similarity between a neuron and the simple on-off units of which computers are constructed, and has provided the analytical methods necessary for representing highly complex logical functions in terms of such elements. The result has been a profusion of brain models which amount simply to logical contrivances for performing particular algorithms (representing "recall," stimulus comparison, transformation, and various kinds of analysis) in response to sequences of stimuli—e.g., Rashevsky (**14**), McCulloch (**10**), McCulloch & Pitts (**11**), Culbertson (**2**), Kleene (**8**), and Minsky (**13**). A relatively small number of theorists, like Ashby (**1**) and von Neumann (**17**, **18**), have been concerned with the problems of how an imperfect neural network, containing many random connections, can be made to perform reliably those functions which might be represented by idealized wiring diagrams. Unfortunately, the language of symbolic logic and Boolean algebra is less well suited for such investigations. The need for a suitable language for the mathematical analysis of events in systems where only the gross organization can be characterized, and the precise structure is unknown, has led the author to formulate the current model in terms of probability theory rather than symbolic logic.

The theorists referred to above were chiefly concerned with the question of how such functions as perception and recall might be achieved by a deterministic physical system of any sort, rather than how this is actually done by the brain. The models which have been produced all fail in some important respects (absence of equipotentiality, lack of neuroeconomy, excessive specificity of connections and synchronization requirements, unrealistic specificity of stimuli sufficient for cell firing, postulation of variables or functional features with no known neurological correlates, etc.) to correspond to a biological system. The proponents of this line of approach have maintained that, once it has been shown how a physical system of any variety might be made to perceive and recognize stimuli, or perform other brainlike functions, it would require only a refinement or modification of existing principles to understand the working of a more realistic nervous system, and to eliminate the shortcomings mentioned above. The writer takes the position, on the other hand, that these shortcomings are such that a mere refinement or improvement of the principles already suggested can never account for biological intelligence; a *difference in principle* is clearly indicated. The theory of statistical separability (Cf. **15**), which is to be summarized here, appears to offer a solution in principle to all of these difficulties.

Those theorists—Hebb (**7**), Milner (**12**), Eccles (**4**), Hayek (**6**)—who have been more directly concerned with the biological nervous system and its activity in a natural environment, rather than with formally analogous machines, have generally been less exact in their formulations and far from rigorous in their analysis, so that it is frequently hard to assess whether or not the systems that they describe could actually work in a realistic nervous system, and what the necessary and sufficient conditions might be. Here again, the lack of an analytic language comparable in proficiency to the Boolean algebra of the network analysts has been one of the main obstacles. The contributions of this group should perhaps be considered as suggestions of what to look for and investigate, rather than as finished theoretical systems in their own right. Seen from this viewpoint, the most suggestive work, from the standpoint of the following theory, is that of Hebb and Hayek.

The position, elaborated by Hebb (**7**), Hayek (**6**), Uttley (**16**), and Ashby (**1**), in particular, upon which the theory of the perceptron is based, can be summarized by the following assumptions:

1. The physical connections of the nervous system which are involved in learning and recognition are not identical from one organism to another. At birth, the construction of the most important networks is largely random, subject to a minimum number of genetic constraints.
2. The original system of connected cells is capable of a certain amount of plasticity; after a period of neural activity, the probability that a stimulus applied to one set of cells will cause a response in some other set is likely to change, due to some relatively long-lasting changes in the neurons themselves.
3. Through exposure to a large sample of stimuli, those which are most "similar" (in some sense which must be defined in terms of the particular physical system) will tend

to form pathways to the same sets of responding cells. Those which are markedly "dissimilar" will tend to develop connections to different sets of responding cells.

4. The application of positive and/or negative reinforcement (or stimuli which serve this function) may facilitate or hinder whatever formation of connections is currently in progress.

5. *Similarity*, in such a system, is represented at some level of the nervous system by a tendency of similar stimuli to activate the same sets of cells. Similarity is not a necessary attribute of particular formal or geometrical classes of stimuli, but depends on the physical organization of the perceiving system, an organization which evolves through interaction with a given environment. The structure of the system, as well as the ecology of the stimulus-environment, will affect, and will largely determine, the classes of "things" into which the perceptual world is divided.

THE ORGANIZATION OF A PERCEPTRON

The organization of a typical photo-perceptron (a perceptron responding to optical patterns as stimuli) is shown in Fig. 1. The rules of its organization are as follows:

1. Stimuli impinge on a retina of sensory units (S-points), which are assumed to respond on an all-or-nothing basis, in some models, or with a pulse amplitude or frequency proportional to the stimulus intensity, in other models. In the models considered here, an all-or-nothing response will be assumed.

2. Impulses are transmitted to a set of association cells (A-units) in a "projection area" (A_I). This projection area may be omitted in some models, where the retina is connected directly to the association area (A_{II}).

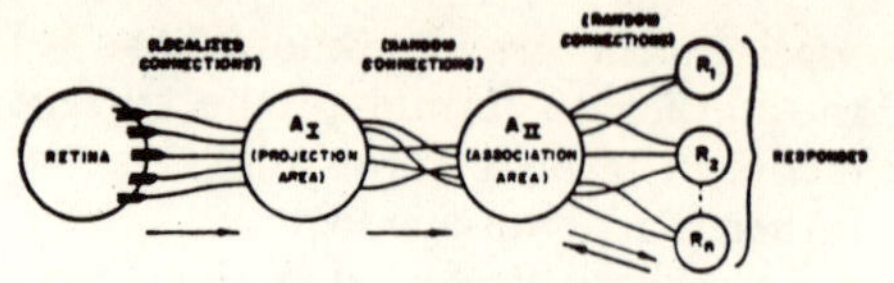

FIG. 1. Organization of a perceptron.

The cells in the projection area each receive a number of connections from the sensory points. The set of S-points transmitting impulses to a particular A-unit will be called the *origin points* of that A-unit. These origin points may be either *excitatory* or *inhibitory* in their effect on the A-unit. If the algebraic sum of excitatory and inhibitory impulse intensities is equal to or greater than the threshold (θ) of the A-unit, then the A-unit fires, again on an all-or-nothing basis (or, in some models, which will not be considered here, with a frequency which depends on the net value of the impulses received). The origin points of the A-units in the projection area tend to be clustered or focalized, about some central point, corresponding to each A-unit. The number of origin points falls off exponentially as the retinal distance from the central point for the A-unit in question increases. (Such a distribution seems to be supported by physiological evidence, and serves an important functional purpose in contour detection.)

3. Between the projection area and the association area (A_{II}), connections are assumed to be random. That is, each A-unit in the A_{II} set receives some number of fibers from origin points in the A_I set, but these origin points are scattered at random throughout the projection area. Apart from their connection distribution, the A_{II} units are identical with the A_I units, and respond under similar conditions.

4. The "responses," R_1, R_2, . . . , R_n are cells (or sets of cells) which

respond in much the same fashion as the A-units. Each response has a typically large number of origin points located at random in the A_{II} set. The set of A-units transmitting impulses to a particular response will be called the source-set for that response. (The source-set of a response is identical to its set of origin points in the A-system.) The arrows in Fig. 1 indicate the direction of transmission through the network. Note that up to A_{II} all connections are forward, and there is no feedback. When we come to the last set of connections, between A_{II} and the R-units, connections are established in both directions. The rule governing feedback connections, in most models of the perceptron, can be either of the following alternatives:

(*a*) Each response has excitatory feedback connections to the cells in its own source-set, or

(*b*) Each response has inhibitory feedback connections to the complement of its own source-set (i.e., it tends to prohibit activity in any association cells which do not transmit to it).

The first of these rules seems more plausible anatomically, since the R-units might be located in the same cortical area as their respective source-sets, making mutual excitation between the R-units and the A-units of the appropriate source-set highly probable. The alternative rule (*b*) leads to a more readily analyzed system, however, and will therefore be assumed for most of the systems to be evaluated here.

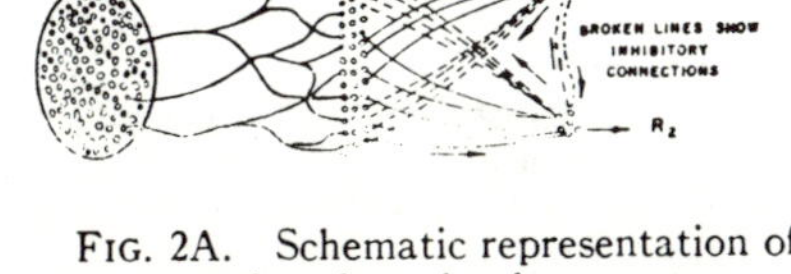

FIG. 2A. Schematic representation of connections in a simple perceptron.

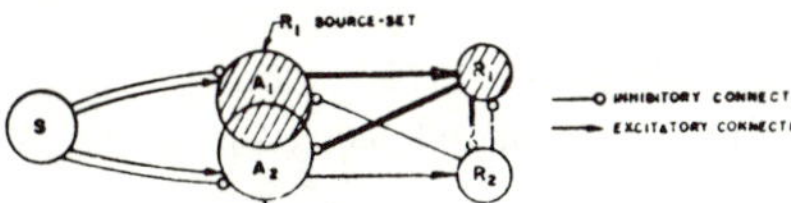

FIG. 2B. Venn diagram of the same perceptron (shading shows active sets for R_1 response).

Figure 2 shows the organization of a simplified perceptron, which affords a convenient entry into the theory of statistical separability. After the theory has been developed for this simplified model, we will be in a better position to discuss the advantages of the system in Fig. 1. The feedback connections shown in Fig. 2 are inhibitory, and go to the complement of the source-set for the response from which they originate; consequently, this system is organized according to Rule *b*, above. The system shown here has only three stages, the first association stage having been eliminated. Each A-unit has a set of randomly located origin points in the retina. Such a system will form similarity concepts on the basis of *coincident areas* of stimuli, rather than by the similarity of contours or outlines. While such a system is at a disadvantage in many discrimination experiments, its capability is still quite impressive, as will be demonstrated presently. The system shown in Fig. 2 has only two responses, but there is clearly no limit on the number that might be included.

The responses in a system organized in this fashion are mutually exclusive. If R_1 occurs, it will tend to inhibit R_2, and will also inhibit the source-set for R_2. Likewise, if R_2 should occur, it will tend to inhibit R_1. If the total impulse received from all the A-units in one source-set is stronger or more frequent than the impulse received by the alternative (antagonistic) response, then the first response will tend to gain an advantage over the other, and will be the one which occurs. If such a system is to be capable of learning, then it must be possible to modify the A-units or their connections in such a way that stimuli of one class will tend to evoke a stronger impulse in the R_1 source-set than in the R_2 source-set, while stimuli of another (dissimilar) class will tend to evoke a stronger impulse in the R_2 source-set than in the R_1 source-set.

It will be assumed that the impulses delivered by each A-unit can be characterized by a value, V, which may be an amplitude, frequency, latency, or probability of completing transmission. If an A-unit has a high value, then all of its output impulses are considered to be more effective, more potent, or more likely to arrive at their endbulbs than impulses from an A-unit with a lower value. The value of an A-unit is considered to be a fairly stable characteristic, probably depending on the metabolic condition of the cell and the cell membrane, but it is not absolutely constant. It is assumed that, in general, periods of activity tend to increase a cell's value, while the value may decay (in some models) with inactivity. The most interesting models are those in which cells are assumed to compete for metabolic materials, the more active cells gaining at the expense of the less active cells. In such a system, if there is no activity, all cells will tend to remain in a relatively constant condition, and (regardless of activity) the net value of the system, taken in

TABLE 1

COMPARISON OF LOGICAL CHARACTERISTICS OF α, β, AND γ SYSTEMS

	α-System (Uncompensated Gain System)	β-System (Constant Feed System)	γ-System (Parasitic Gain System)
Total value-gain of source set per reinforcement	N_{a_r}	K	0
ΔV for A-units active for 1 unit of time	+1	K/N_{a_r}	+1
ΔV for inactive A-units outside of dominant set	0	K/N_{A_r}	0
ΔV for inactive A-units of dominant set	0	0	$\frac{-N_{a_r}}{N_{A_r}-N_{a_r}}$
Mean value of A-system	Increases with number of reinforcements	Increases with time	Constant
Difference between mean values of source-sets	Proportional to differences of reinforcement frequency $(n_{s_{r_1}}-n_{s_{r_2}})$	0	0

Note: In the β and γ systems, the total value-change for any A-unit will be the sum of the ΔV's for all source-sets of which it is a member.

N_{a_r} = Number of active units in source-set
N_{A_r} = Total number of units in source-set
$n_{s_{r_j}}$ = Number of stimuli associated to response r_j
K = Arbitrary constant

its entirety, will remain constant at all times. Three types of systems, which differ in their value dynamics, have been investigated quantitatively. Their principal logical features are compared in Table 1. In the alpha system, an active cell simply gains an increment of value for every impulse, and holds this gain indefinitely. In the beta system, each source-set is allowed a certain constant rate of gain, the increments being apportioned among the cells of the source-set in proportion to their activity. In the gamma system, active cells gain in value at the expense of the inactive cells of their source-set, so that the total value of a source-set is always constant.

For purposes of analysis, it is convenient to distinguish two phases in the response of the system to a stimulus (Fig. 3). In the *predominant phase*, some proportion of A-units (represented by solid dots in the figure) responds to the stimulus, but the R-units are still inactive. This phase is transient, and quickly gives way to the *postdominant phase*, in which one of the responses becomes active, inhibiting activity in the complement of its own source-set, and thus preventing the occurrence of any alternative response. The response which happens to become dominant is initially random, but if the A-units are reinforced (i.e., if the active units are allowed to gain in value), then when the same stimulus is presented again at a later time, the same response will have a stronger tendency to recur, and learning can be said to have taken place.

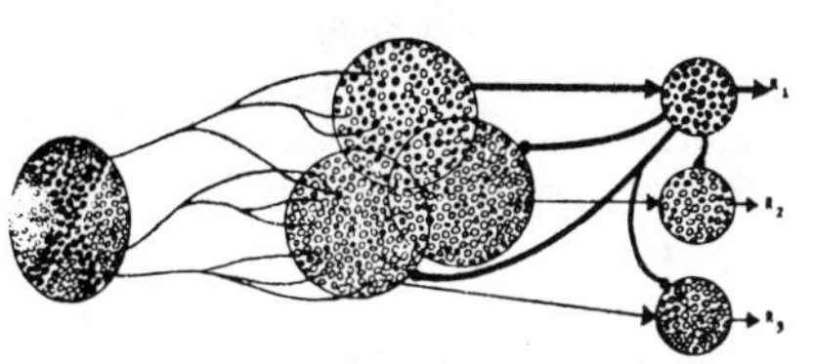

FIG. 3A. Predominant phase. Inhibitory connections are not shown. Solid black units are active.

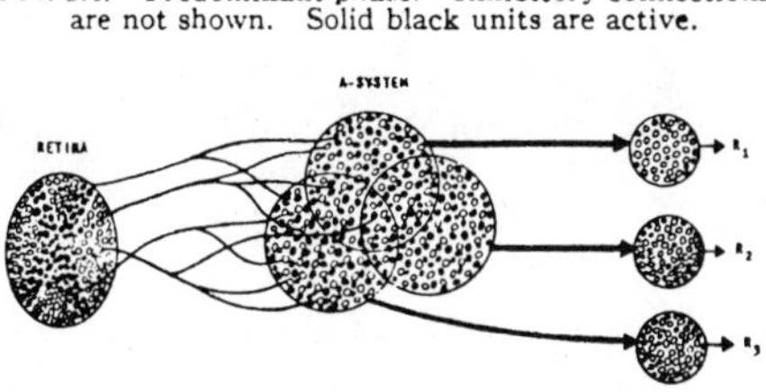

FIG. 3B. Postdominant phase. Dominant subset suppresses rival sets. Inhibitory connections shown only for R_1.

FIG 3. Phases of response to a stimulus.

ANALYSIS OF THE PREDOMINANT PHASE

The perceptrons considered here will always assume a fixed threshold, θ, for the activation of the A-units. Such a system will be called a *fixed-threshold model*, in contrast to a *continuous transducer model*, where the response of the A-unit is some continuous function of the impinging stimulus energy.

In order to predict the learning curves of a fixed-threshold perceptron, two variables have been found to be of primary importance. They are defined as follows:

P_a = the expected proportion of A-units activated by a stimulus of a given size,

P_c = the conditional probability that an A-unit which responds to a given stimulus, S_1, will also respond to another given stimulus, S_2.

It can be shown (Rosenblatt, **15**) that as the size of the retina is increased, the number of S-points (N_s) quickly ceases to be a significant parameter, and the values of P_a and P_c approach the value that they would have for a retina with infinitely many points. For a large retina, therefore, the equations are as follows:

$$P_a = \sum_{e=\theta}^{x} \sum_{i=\theta}^{\min(y,\, e-\theta)} P(e,i) \qquad (1)$$

where

$$P(e,i) = \binom{x}{e} R^e(1 - R)^{x-e} \times \binom{y}{i} R^i(1 - R)^{y-i}$$

and

R = proportion of S-points activated by the stimulus
x = number of excitatory connections to each A-unit
y = number of inhibitory connections to each A-unit
θ = threshold of A-units.

(The quantities e and i are the excitatory and inhibitory components of the excitation received by the A-unit from the stimulus. If the algebraic sum $\alpha = e + i$ is equal to or greater than θ, the A-unit is assumed to respond.)

$$P_c = \frac{1}{P_a} \sum_{e=\theta}^{x} \sum_{i=e-\theta}^{y} \sum_{l_e=0}^{e} \sum_{l_i=0}^{i} \sum_{g_e=0}^{x-e} \sum_{g_i=0}^{y-i} P(e,i,l_e,l_i,g_e,g_i) \quad (2)$$

$$(e - i - l_e + l_i + g_e - g_i \geq \theta)$$

where

$$P(e,i,l_e,l_i,g_e,g_i) = \binom{x}{e} R^e(1 - R)^{x-e} \times \binom{y}{i} R^i(1 - R)^{y-i} \times \binom{e}{l_e} L^{l_e}(1 - L)^{e-l_e} \times \binom{i}{l_i} L^{l_i}(1 - L)^{i-l_i} \times \binom{x-e}{g_e} G^{g_e}(1 - G)^{x-e-g_e} \times \binom{y-i}{g_i} G^{g_i}(1 - G)^{y-i-g_i}$$

and

L = proportion of the S-points illuminated by the first stimulus, S_1, which are not illuminated by S_2
G = proportion of the residual S-set (left over from the first stimulus) which is included in the second stimulus (S_2).

The quantities R, L, and G specify the two stimuli and their retinal overlap. l_e and l_i are, respectively, the numbers of excitatory and inhibitory origin points "lost" by the A-unit when stimulus S_1 is replaced by S_2; g_e and g_i are the numbers of excitatory and inhibitory origin points "gained" when stimulus S_1 is replaced by S_2. The summations in Equation 2 are between the limits indicated, subject to the side condition $e - i - l_e + l_i + g_e - g_i \geq \theta$.

Some of the most important characteristics of P_a are illustrated in Fig. 4, which shows P_a as a function of the retinal area illuminated (R). Note that P_a can be reduced in magnitude by either increasing the threshold, θ, or by increasing the proportion of inhibitory connections (y). A comparison of Fig. 4b and 4c shows that if the excitation is about equal to the inhibition, the curves for P_a as a function of R are flattened out, so that there is little variation in P_a for stimuli of different sizes. This fact is of great importance for systems which require P_a to be close to an optimum value in order to perform properly.

The behavior of P_c is illustrated in Fig. 5 and 6. The curves in Fig. 5 can be compared with those for P_a in Fig. 4. Note that as the threshold is increased, there is an even sharper reduction in the value of P_c than was the case with P_a. P_c also decreases as the proportion of inhibitory connections increases, as does P_a. Fig. 5, which is

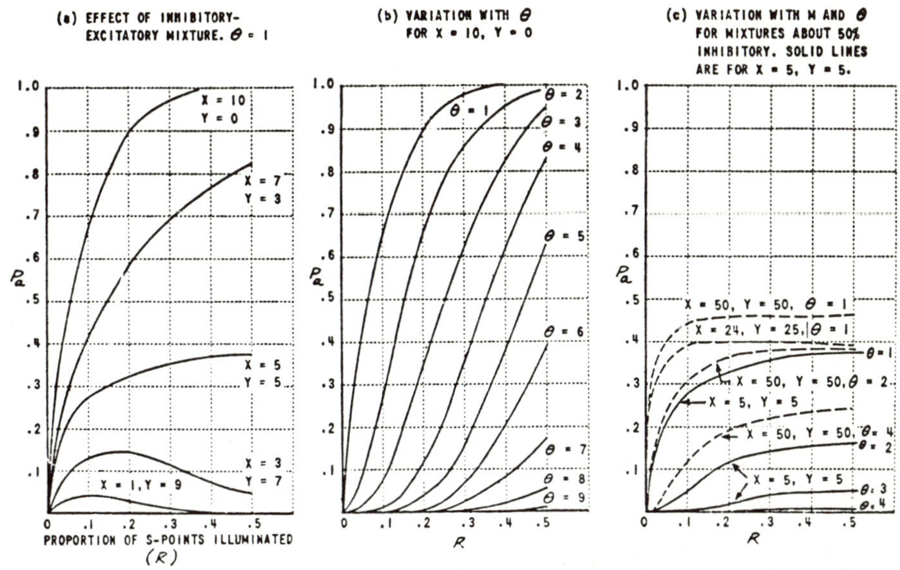

FIG. 4. P_a as function of retinal area illuminated.

calculated for nonoverlapping stimuli, illustrates the fact that P_c remains greater than zero even when the stimuli are completely disjunct, and illuminate no retinal points in common. In Fig. 6, the effect of varying amounts of overlap between the stimuli is shown. In all cases, the value of P_c goes to unity as the stimuli approach perfect identity. For smaller stimuli (broken line curves), the value of P_c is lower than for large stimuli. Similarly, the value is less for high thresholds than for low thresholds. The minimum value of P_c will be equal to

$$P_{c_{min}} = (1 - L)^x(1 - G)^y. \quad (3)$$

In Fig. 6, $P_{c_{min}}$ corresponds to the curve for $\theta = 10$. Note that under these conditions the probability that the A-unit responds to both stimuli (P_c) is practically zero, except for stimuli which are quite close to identity. This condition can be of considerable help in discrimination learning.

MATHEMATICAL ANALYSIS OF LEARNING IN THE PERCEPTRON

The response of the perceptron in the predominant phase, where some fraction of the A-units (scattered throughout the system) responds to the stimulus, quickly gives way to the postdominant response, in which activity is limited to a single source-set, the other sets being suppressed. Two possible systems have been studied for the determination of the "dominant" response, in the postdominant phase. In one (the mean-discriminating system, or μ-system), the response whose inputs have the greatest mean value responds first, gaining a slight advantage over the others, so that it quickly becomes dominant. In the second case (the sum-discriminating system, or Σ-system), the response whose inputs have the greatest net value gains an advantage. In most cases, systems which respond to mean values have an advantage over systems which respond to sums, since the means are

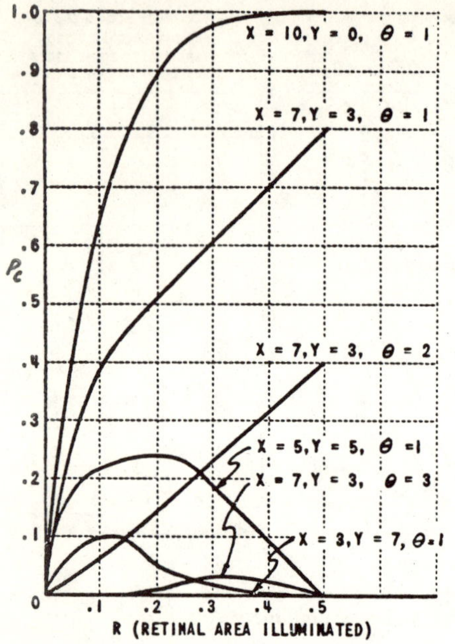

FIG. 5. P_c as a function of R, for nonoverlapping stimuli.

less influenced by random variations in P_a from one source-set to another. In the case of the γ-system (see Table 1), however, the performance of the μ-system and Σ-system become identical.

We have indicated that the perceptron is expected to learn, or to form associations, as a result of the changes in value that occur as a result of the activity of the association cells. In evaluating this learning, one of two types of hypothetical experiments can be considered. In the first case, the perceptron is exposed to some series of stimulus patterns (which might be presented in random positions on the retina) and is "forced" to give the desired response in each case. (This forcing of responses is assumed to be a prerogative of the experimenter. In experiments intended to evaluate trial-and-error learning, with more sophisticated perceptrons, the experimenter does not force the system to respond in the desired fashion, but merely applies positive reinforcement when the response happens to be correct, and negative reinforcement when the response is wrong.) In evaluating the learning which has taken place during this "learning series," the perceptron is assumed to be "frozen" in its current condition, no further value changes being allowed, and the same series of stimuli is presented again in precisely the same fashion, so that the stimuli fall on identical positions on the retina. The probability that the perceptron will show a bias towards the "correct" response (the one which has been previously reinforced during the learning series) in preference to any given alternative response is called P_r, the probability of correct choice of response between two alternatives.

In the second type of experiment, a learning series is presented exactly as before, but instead of evaluating the perceptron's performance using the same series of stimuli which were shown before, a new series is presented, in which stimuli may be drawn from the same *classes* that were previ-

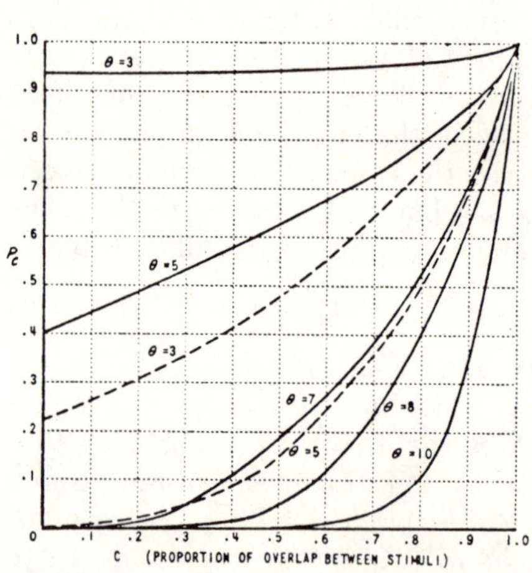

FIG. 6. P_c as a function of C. $X = 10$, $Y = 0$. Solid lines: R = .5; broken lines: R = .2.

ously experienced, but are not necessarily identical. This new test series is assumed to be composed of stimuli projected onto random retinal positions, which are chosen independently of the positions selected for the learning series. The stimuli of the test series may also differ in size or rotational position from the stimuli which were previously experienced. In this case, we are interested in the probability that the perceptron will give the correct response for the *class* of stimuli which is represented, regardless of whether the particular stimulus has been seen before or not. This probability is called P_g, the probability of correct generalization. As with P_r, P_g is actually the probability that a bias will be found in favor of the proper response rather than any one alternative; only one pair of responses at a time is considered, and the fact that the response bias is correct in one pair does not mean that there may not be other pairs in which the bias favors the wrong response. The probability that the correct response will be preferred over *all* alternatives is designated P_R or P_G.

In all cases investigated, a single general equation gives a close approximation to P_r and P_g, if the appropriate constants are substituted. This equation is of the form:

$$P = P(N_{a_r} > 0)\cdot\phi(Z) \qquad (4)$$

where

$$P(N_{a_r} > 0) = 1 - (1 - P_a)^{N_e}$$

$\phi(Z)$ = normal curve integral from $-\infty$ to Z

and

$$Z = \frac{c_1 n_{s_r} + c_2}{\sqrt{c_3 n_{s_r}^2 + c_4 n_{s_r}}}.$$

If R_1 is the "correct" response, and R_2 is the alternative response under consideration, Equation 4 is the probability that R_1 will be preferred over R_2 after n_{s_r} stimuli have been shown for each of the two responses, during the learning period. N_e is the number of "effective" A-units in each source-set; that is, the number of A-units in either source-set which are not connected in common to both responses. Those units which are connected in common contribute equally to both sides of the value balance, and consequently do not affect the net bias towards one response or the other. N_{a_r} is the number of active units in a source-set, which respond to the test stimulus, $S_t \cdot P(N_{a_r} > 0)$ is the probability that at least one of the N_e effective units in the source-set of the correct response (designated, by convention, as the R_1 response) will be activated by the test stimulus, S_t.

In the case of P_g, the constant c_2 is always equal to zero, the other three constants being the same as for P_r. The values of the four constants depend on the parameters of the physical nerve net (the perceptron) and also on the organization of the stimulus environment.

The simplest cases to analyze are those in which the perceptron is shown stimuli drawn from an "ideal environment," consisting of randomly placed points of illumination, where there is no attempt to classify stimuli according to intrinsic similarity. Thus, in a typical learning experiment, we might show the perceptron 1,000 stimuli made up of random collections of illuminated retinal points, and we might arbitrarily reinforce R_1 as the "correct" response for the first 500 of these, and R_2 for the remaining 500. This environment is "ideal" only in the sense that we speak of an ideal gas in physics; it is a convenient artifact for purposes of analysis, and does not lead to the best performance from the perceptron. In the ideal environment situation, the constant c_1 is always equal to zero, so that, in the case of P_g (where c_2 is also zero), the value of Z will be zero, and P_g can never be any better than the random expectation of 0.5. The evaluation of P_r for these conditions, however, throws some interesting light on the differences between the alpha, beta, and gamma systems (Table 1).

First consider the alpha system, which has the simplest dynamics of the three. In this system, whenever an A-unit is active for one unit of time, it gains one unit of value. We will assume an experiment, initially, in which N_{s_r} (the number of stimuli associated to each response) is constant for all responses. In this case, for the sum system,

$$\left.\begin{aligned} c_1 &= 0 \\ c_2 &= (1 - P_a)N_e \\ c_3 &= 2P_a\omega \\ c_4 &\approx 0 \end{aligned}\right\} \qquad (5)$$

where ω = the fraction of responses connected to each A-unit. If the source-sets are disjunct, $\omega = 1/N_R$, where N_R is the number of responses in the system. For the μ-system,

$$\left.\begin{aligned} c_1 &= 0 \\ c_2 &= (1 - P_a)N_e \\ c_3 &= 0 \\ c_4 &= 2\omega \end{aligned}\right\} \qquad (6)$$

The reduction of c_3 to zero gives the μ-system a definite advantage over the Σ-system. Typical learning curves for these systems are compared in Fig. 7 and 8. Figure 9 shows the effect of variations in P_a upon the performance of the system.

If n_{s_r}, instead of being fixed, is treated as a random variable, so that the number of stimuli associated to each response is drawn separately from some distribution, then the per-

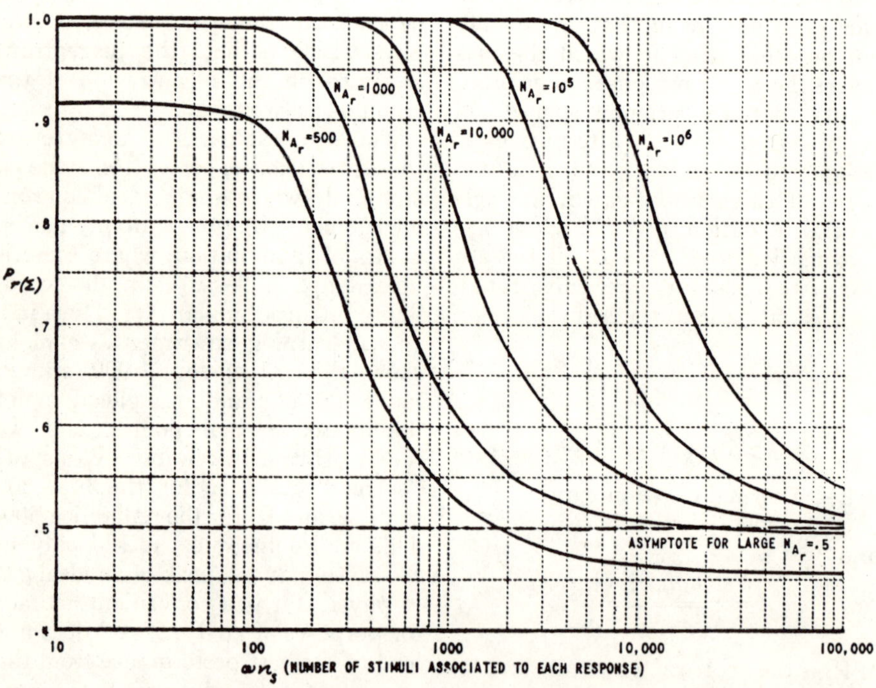

FIG. 7. $P_r(\Sigma)$ as function of ωn_s, for discrete subsets. ($\omega_e = 0$, $P_a = .005$. Ideal environment assumed.)

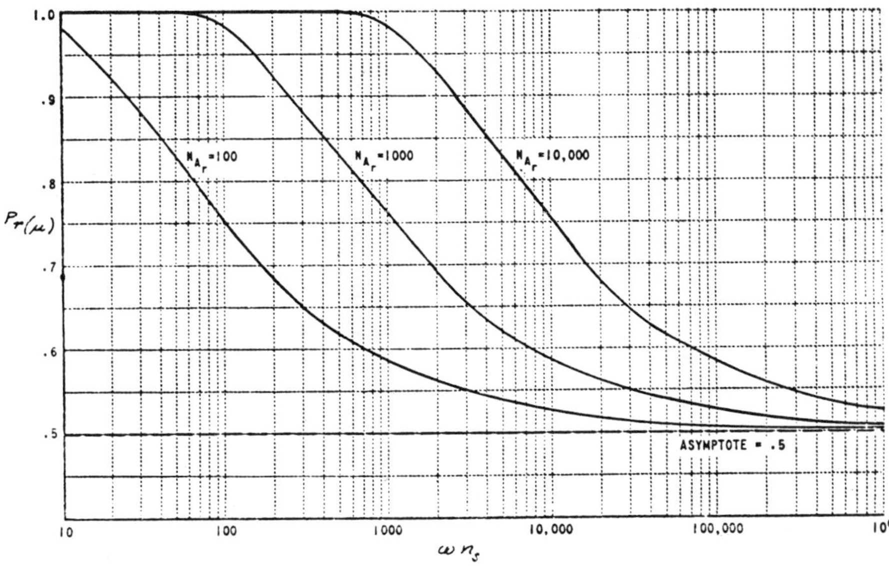

FIG. 8. $P_{r(\mu)}$ as function of ωn_s. (For $P_a = .07$, $\omega_c = 0$. Ideal environment assumed.)

formance of the α-system is considerably poorer than the above equations indicate. Under these conditions, the constants for the μ-system are

$$\left.\begin{aligned} c_1 &= 0 \\ c_2 &= 1 - P_a \\ c_3 &= 2P_a^2q^2\left[\frac{(\omega N_R - 1)^2}{N_R - 2} + 1\right] \\ c_4 &= \frac{2(1 - P_a)N_R}{(1 - \omega_c)N_A} \end{aligned}\right\} \quad (7)$$

where

q = ratio of $\sigma_{n_{s_r}}$ to $\bar{n}_{s_r}$
N_R = number of responses in the system
N_A = number of A-units in the system
ω_c = proportion of A-units common to R_1 and R_2.

For this equation (and any others in which n_{s_r} is treated as a random variable), it is necessary to define n_{s_r} in Equation 4 as the expected value of this variable, over the set of all responses.

For the β-system, there is an even greater deficit in performance, due to the fact that the net value continues to grow regardless of what happens to the system. The large net values of the subsets activated by a stimulus tend to amplify small statistical differences, causing an unreliable performance. The constants in this case (again for the μ-system) are

$$\left.\begin{aligned} c_1 &= 0 \\ c_2 &= (1 - P_a)N_e \\ c_3 &= 2(P_aN_eq\omega N_R^2)^2 \\ c_4 &= 2(1 - P_a)\omega N_RN_e \end{aligned}\right\} \quad (8)$$

In both the alpha and beta systems, performance will be poorer for the sum-discriminating model than for the mean-discriminating case. In the gamma-system, however, it can be shown that $P_{r(\Sigma)} = P_{r(\mu)}$; i.e., it makes no difference in performance whether the Σ-system or μ-system is used. Moreover, the constants for the γ-system, with variable n_{s_r}, are identical to the constants for the alpha μ-sys-

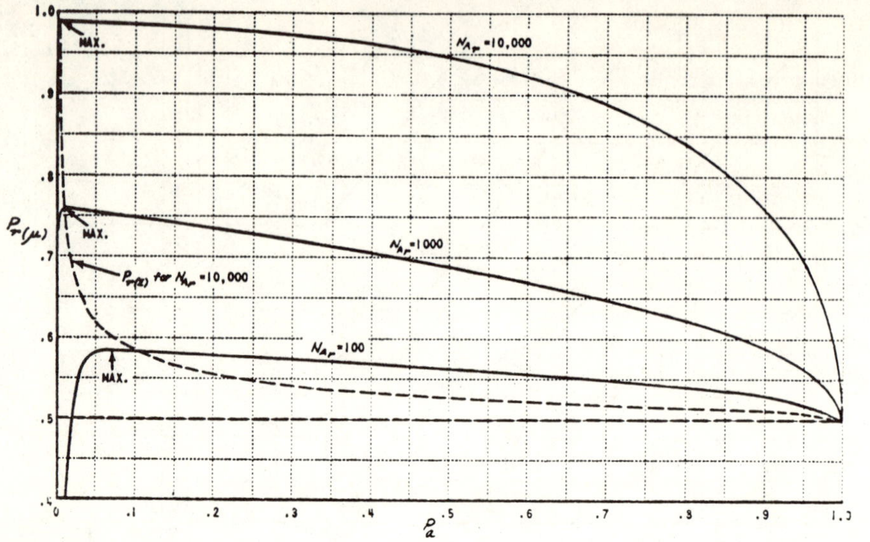

FIG. 9. $P_{r(\mu)}$ as function of P_a. (For n_{s_r} = 1,000, ω_c = 0. Ideal environment assumed.)

tem, with n_{s_r} fixed (Equation 6). The performance of the three systems is compared in Fig. 10, which clearly demonstrates the advantage of the γ-system.

Let us now replace the "ideal en-

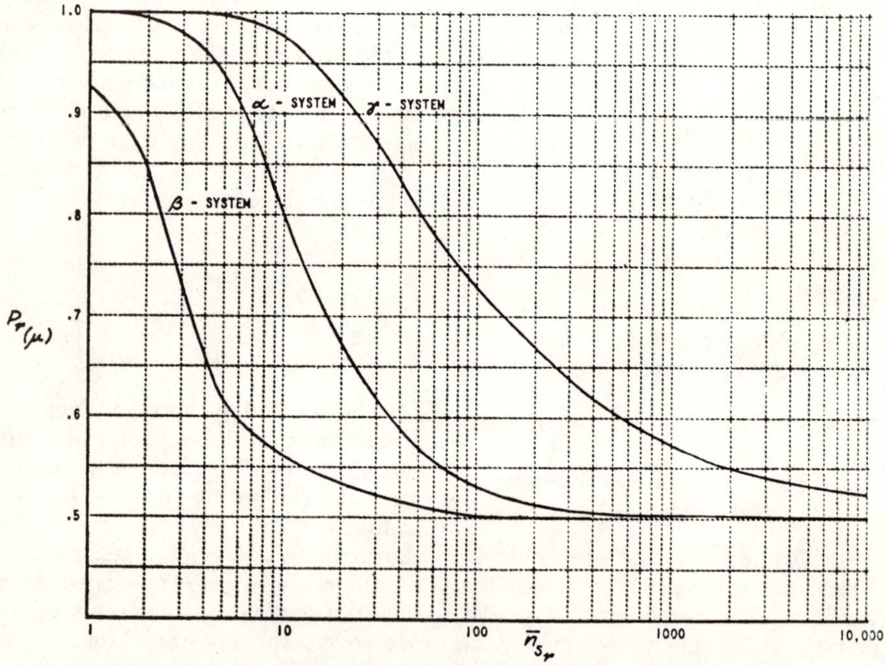

FIG. 10. Comparison of α, β, and γ systems, for variable n_{s_r} (N_R = 100, $\sigma_{n_{rs}}$ = .5$\bar{n}_{s_r}$, N_A = 10,000, P_a = .07, ω = .2).

vironment" assumptions with a model for a "differentiated environment," in which several distinguishable classes of stimuli are present (such as squares, circles, and triangles, or the letters of the alphabet). If we then design an experiment in which the stimuli associated to each response are drawn from a different class, then the learning curves of the perceptron are drastically altered. The most important difference is that the constant c_1 (the coefficient of n_{s_r} in the numerator of Z) is no longer equal to zero, so that Equation 4 now has a nonrandom asymptote. Moreover, in the form for P_g (the probability of correct generalization), where $c_2 = 0$, the quantity Z remains greater than zero, and P_g actually approaches the same asymptote as P_r. Thus the equation for the perceptron's performance after infinite experience with each class of stimuli is identical for P_r and P_g:

$$P_{r\infty} = P_{g\infty} = [1 - (1 - P_a)^{N_e}] \times \phi\left(\frac{c_1}{\sqrt{c_3}}\right) \qquad (9)$$

This means that *in the limit it makes no difference whether the perceptron has seen a particular test stimulus before or not; if the stimuli are drawn from a differentiated environment, the performance will be equally good in either case.*

In order to evaluate the performance of the system in a differentiated environment, it is necessary to define the quantity $P_{c\alpha\beta}$. This quantity is interpreted as the expected value of P_c between pairs of stimuli drawn at random from classes α and β. In particular, P_{c11} is the expected value of P_c between members of the same class, and P_{c12} is the expected value of P_c between an S_1 stimulus drawn from Class 1 and an S_2 stimulus drawn from Class 2. P_{c1x} is the expected value of P_c between members of Class 1 and stimuli drawn at random from all other classes in the environment.

If $P_{c11} > P_a > P_{c12}$, the limiting performance of the perceptron ($P_{g\infty}$) will be better than chance, and learning of some response, R_1, as the proper "generalization response" for members of Class 1 should eventually occur. If the above inequality is not met, then improvement over chance performance may not occur, and the Class 2 response is likely to occur instead. It can be shown (15) that for most simple geometrical forms, which we ordinarily regard as "similar," the required inequality can be met, if the parameters of the system are properly chosen.

The equation for P_r, for the sum-discriminating version of an α-perceptron, in a differentiated environment where n_{s_r} is fixed for all responses, will have the following expressions for the four coefficients:

$$\left.\begin{aligned}
c_1 &= P_a N_e (P_{c11} - P_{c12}) \\
c_2 &= P_a N_e (1 - P_{c11}) \\
c_3 &= \sum_{r=1,2} P_a (1 - P_a) N_e \\
&\quad \times [P_{c\,1r}^2 + \sigma_3^2(P_{c1r}) \\
&\quad + \sigma_j^2(P_{c1r}) + (\omega N_R - 1)^2 \\
&\quad \times (P_{c1x} + \sigma_s^2(P_{c1x}) \\
&\quad + \sigma_j^2(P_{crx})) + 2(\omega N_R - 1) \\
&\quad (P_{c1r} P_{c1x})] + P_a^2 N_e^2 \\
&\quad \times [\sigma_s^2(P_{c1r}) + (\omega N_R - 1)^2 \\
&\quad \times \sigma_s^2(P_{c1x}) + 2(\omega N_R - 1)\epsilon] \\
c_4 &= \sum_{r=1,2} P_a N_e [P_{c1r} - P_{c1r}^2 \\
&\quad - \sigma_s^2(P_{c1r}) - \sigma_j^2(P_{c1r}) \\
&\quad + (\omega N_R - 1)(P_{c1x} - P_{c1x}^2 \\
&\qquad - \sigma_j^2(P_{c1x}))]
\end{aligned}\right\} \qquad (10)$$

where

$\sigma_s^2(P_{c1r})$ and $\sigma_s^2(P_{c1x})$ represent the variance of P_{c1r} and P_{c1x} measured over the set of possible test stimuli, S_t, and

$\sigma_j^2(P_{c1_r})$ and $\sigma_j^2(P_{c1_x})$ represent the variance of P_{c1_r} and P_{c1_x} measured over the set of all A-units, a_j.

ϵ = covariance of $P_{c1_r}P_{c1_x}$, which is assumed to be negligible.

The variances which appear in these expressions have not yielded, thus far, to a precise analysis, and can be treated as empirical variables to be determined for the classes of stimuli in question. If the sigma is set equal to half the expected value of the variable, in each case, a conservative estimate can be obtained. When the stimuli of a given class are all of the same shape, and uniformly distributed over the retina, the subscript s variances are equal to zero. $P_{g(\Sigma)}$ will be represented by the same set of coefficients, except for c_2, which is equal to zero, as usual.

For the mean-discriminating system, the coefficients are:

$$\left.\begin{aligned}
c_1 &= (P_{c11} - P_{c12}) \\
c_2 &= (1 - P_{c11}) \\
c_3 &= \sum_{r=1,2}\left[\frac{1}{P_a(N_e-1)} - \frac{1}{N_e-1}\right] \\
&\quad \times[\sigma_j^2(P_{c1_r}) + (\omega N_R - 1)^2 \\
&\quad \times \sigma_j^2(P_{c1_x})] + [\sigma_s^2(P_{c1_r}) \\
&\qquad + (\omega N_R - 1)^2 \sigma_s^2(P_{c1_x})] \\
c_4 &= \sum_{r=1,2} \frac{1}{P_a N_e}[P_{c1_r} - P_{c1_r}^2 \\
&\quad - \sigma_s^2(P_{c1_r}) - \sigma_j^2(P_{c1_r}) \\
&\quad + (\omega N_R - 1)(P_{c1_x} - P_{c1_x}^2 \\
&\qquad - \sigma_s^2(P_{c1_x}) - \sigma_j^2(P_{c1_x}))]
\end{aligned}\right\} \quad (11)$$

Some covariance terms, which are considered negligible, have been omitted here.

A set of typical learning curves for the differentiated environment model is shown in Fig. 11, for the mean-discriminating system. The parameters are based on measurements for a

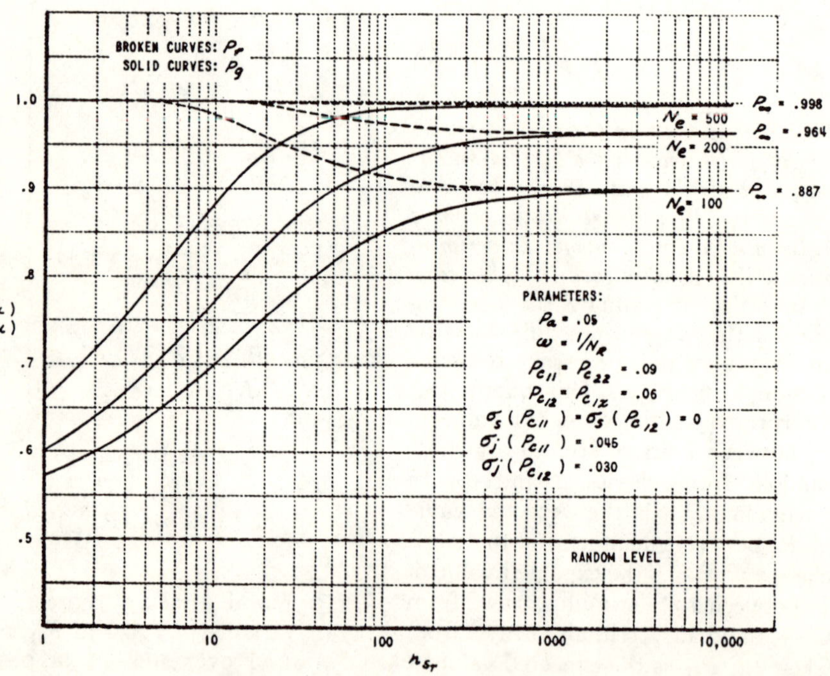

FIG. 11. P_r and P_g as function of n_{s_r}. Parameters based on square-circle discrimination.

square-circle discrimination problem. Note that the curves for P_r and P_g both approach the same asymptotes, as predicted. The values of these asymptotes can be obtained by substituting the proper coefficients in Equation 9. As the number of association cells in the system increases, the asymptotic learning limit rapidly approaches unity, so that for a system of several thousand cells, the errors in performance should be negligible on a problem as simple as the one illustrated here.

As the number of responses in the system increases, the performance becomes progressively poorer, if every response is made mutually exclusive of all alternatives. One method of avoiding this deterioration (described in detail in Rosenblatt, **15**) is through the binary coding of responses. In this case, instead of representing 100 different stimulus patterns by 100 distinct, mutually exclusive responses, a limited number of discriminating features is found, each of which can be independently recognized as being present or absent, and consequently can be represented by a single pair of mutually exclusive responses. Given an ideal set of binary characteristics (such as dark, light; tall, short; straight, curved; etc.), 100 stimulus classes could be distinguished by the proper configuration of only seven response pairs. In a further modification of the system, a single response is capable of denoting by its activity or inactivity the presence or absence of each binary characteristic. The efficiency of such coding depends on the number of independently recognizable "earmarks" that can be found to differentiate stimuli. If the stimulus can be identified only in its entirety and is not amenable to such analysis, then ultimately a separate binary response pair, or bit, is required to denote the presence or absence of each stimulus class (e.g., "dog" or "not dog"), and nothing has been gained over a system where all responses are mutually exclusive.

Bivalent Systems

In all of the systems analyzed up to this point, the increments of value gained by an active A-unit, as a result of reinforcement or experience, have always been *positive*, in the sense that an active unit has always *gained* in its power to activate the responses to which it is connected. In the gamma-system, it is true that some units lose value, but these are always the *inactive units*, the active ones gaining in proportion to their rate of activity. In a *bivalent system*, two types of reinforcement are possible (positive and negative), and an active unit may either gain or lose in value, depending on the momentary state of affairs in the system. If the positive and negative reinforcement can be controlled by the application of external stimuli, they become essentially equivalent to "reward" and "punishment," and can be used in this sense by the experimenter. Under these conditions, a perceptron appears to be capable of trial-and-error learning. A bivalent system need not necessarily involve the application of reward and punishment, however. If a binary-coded response system is so organized that there is a single response or response-pair to represent each "bit," or stimulus characteristic that is learned, with positive feedback to its own source-set if the response is "on," and negative feedback (in the sense that active A-units will lose rather than gain in value) if the response is "off," then the system is still bivalent in its characteristics. Such a bivalent system is particularly efficient in reducing some of the bias effects (preference for the wrong response due to greater size or frequency of its associated stimuli) which plague the alternative systems.

Several forms of bivalent systems have been considered (**15**, Chap. VII). The most efficient of these has the following logical characteristics.

If the system is under a state of positive reinforcement, then a positive ΔV is added to the values of all active A-units in the source-sets of "on" responses, while a negative ΔV is added to the active units in the source-sets of "off" responses. If the system is currently under negative reinforcement, then a negative ΔV is added to all active units in the source-set of an "on" response, and a positive ΔV is added to active units in an "off" source-set. If the source-sets are disjunct (which is essential for this system to work properly), the equation for a bivalent γ-system has the same coefficients as the monovalent α-system, for the μ-case (Equation 11).

The performance curves for this system are shown in Fig. 12, where the asymptotic generalization probability attainable by the system is plotted for the same stimulus parameters that were used in Fig. 11. This is the probability that all bits in an n-bit response pattern will be correct. Clearly, if a majority of correct responses is sufficient to identify a stimulus correctly, the performance will be better than these curves indicate.

In a form of bivalent system which utilizes more plausible biological assumptions, A-units may be either excitatory or inhibitory in their effect on connected responses. A positive ΔV in this system corresponds to the incrementing of an excitatory unit, while a negative ΔV corresponds to the incrementing of an inhibitory unit. Such a system performs similarly to the one considered above, but can be shown to be less efficient.

Bivalent systems similar to those illustrated in Fig. 12 have been simulated in detail in a series of experiments with the IBM 704 computer at the Cornell Aeronautical Laboratory. The results have borne out the theory in all of its main predictions, and will be reported separately at a later time.

Improved Perceptrons and Spontaneous Organization

The quantitative analysis of perceptron performance in the preceding sections has omitted any consideration of *time* as a stimulus dimension. A perceptron which has no capability for temporal pattern recognition is referred to as a "momentary stimulus perceptron." It can be shown (**15**) that the same principles of statistical separability will permit the perceptron to distinguish velocities, sound sequences, etc., provided the stimuli leave some temporarily persistent trace, such as an altered threshold,

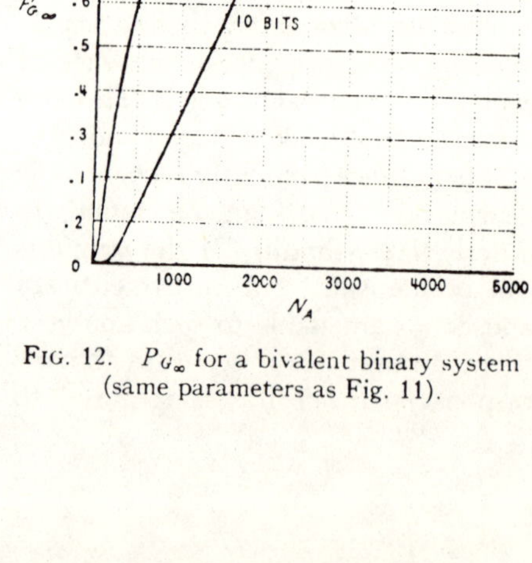

FIG. 12. P_{G_∞} for a bivalent binary system (same parameters as Fig. 11).

which causes the activity in the A-system at time t to depend to some degree on the activity at time $t - 1$.

It has also been assumed that the origin points of A-units are completely random. It can be shown that by a suitable organization of origin points, in which the spatial distribution is constrained (as in the projection area origins shown in Fig. 1), the A-units will become particularly sensitive to the location of contours, and performance will be improved.

In a recent development, which we hope to report in detail in the near future, it has been proven that if the values of the A-units are allowed to decay at a rate proportional to their magnitude, a striking new property emerges: the perceptron becomes capable of "spontaneous" concept formation. That is to say, if the system is exposed to a random series of stimuli from two "dissimilar" classes, and all of its responses are automatically reinforced without any regard to whether they are "right" or "wrong," the system will tend towards a stable terminal condition in which (for each binary response) the response will be "1" for members of one stimulus class, and "0" for members of the other class; i.e., the perceptron will spontaneously recognize the difference between the two classes. This phenomenon has been successfully demonstrated in simulation experiments, with the 704 computer.

A perceptron, even with a single logical level of A-units and response units, can be shown to have a number of interesting properties in the field of selective recall and selective attention. These properties generally depend on the intersection of the source sets for different responses, and are elsewhere discussed in detail (**15**). By combining audio and photo inputs, it is possible to associate sounds, or auditory "names" to visual objects, and to get the perceptron to perform such selective responses as are designated by the command "Name the object on the left," or "Name the color of this stimulus."

The question may well be raised at this point of where the perceptron's capabilities actually stop. We have seen that the system described is sufficient for pattern recognition, associative learning, and such cognitive sets as are necessary for selective attention and selective recall. The system appears to be potentially capable of temporal pattern recognition, as well as spatial recognition, involving any sensory modality or combination of modalities. It can be shown that with proper reinforcement it will be capable of trial-and-error learning, and can learn to emit ordered sequences of responses, provided its own responses are fed back through sensory channels.

Does this mean that the perceptron is capable, without further modification in principle, of such higher order functions as are involved in human speech, communication, and thinking? Actually, the limit of the perceptron's capabilities seems to lie in the area of relative judgment, and the abstraction of relationships. In its "symbolic behavior," the perceptron shows some striking similarities to Goldstein's brain-damaged patients (**5**). Responses to definite, concrete stimuli can be learned, even when the proper response calls for the recognition of a number of simultaneous qualifying conditions (such as naming the color if the stimulus is on the left, the shape if it is on the right). As soon as the response calls for the recognition of a relationship between stimuli (such as "Name the object left of the square." or "Indicate the pattern that appeared before the circle."), however, the problem generally becomes excessively difficult for the perceptron. Statistical separability alone does not provide a sufficient basis for higher order abstraction. Some system, more advanced in principle than the perceptron, seems to be required at this point.

CONCLUSIONS AND EVALUATION

The main conclusions of the theoretical study of the perceptron can be summarized as follows:

1. In an environment of random stimuli, a system consisting of randomly connected units, subject to the parametric constraints discussed above, can learn to associate specific responses to specific stimuli. Even if many stimuli are associated to each response, they can still be recognized with a better-than-chance probability, although they may resemble one another closely and may activate many of the same sensory inputs to the system.
2. In such an "ideal environment," the probability of a correct response diminishes towards its original random level as the number of stimuli learned increases.
3. In such an environment, no basis for generalization exists.
4. In a "differentiated environment," where each response is associated to a distinct class of mutually correlated, or "similar" stimuli, the probability that a learned association of some specific stimulus will be correctly retained typically approaches a better-than-chance asymptote as the number of stimuli learned by the system increases. This asymptote can be made arbitrarily close to unity by increasing the number of association cells in the system.
5. In the differentiated environment, the probability that a stimulus *which has not been seen before* will be correctly recognized and associated to its appropriate class (the probability of correct generalization) approaches the same asymptote as the probability of a correct response to a previously reinforced stimulus. This asymptote will be better than chance if the inequality $P_{c12} < P_a < P_{c11}$ is met, for the stimulus classes in question.
6. The performance of the system can be improved by the use of a contour-sensitive projection area, and by the use of a binary response system, in which each response, or "bit," corresponds to some independent feature or attribute of the stimulus.
7. Trial-and-error learning is possible in bivalent reinforcement systems.
8. Temporal organizations of both stimulus patterns and responses can be learned by a system which uses only an extension of the original principles of statistical separability, without introducing any major complications in the organization of the system.
9. The memory of the perceptron is *distributed*, in the sense that any association may make use of a large proportion of the cells in the system, and the removal of a portion of the association system would not have an appreciable effect on the performance of any one discrimination or association, but would begin to show up as a general deficit in *all* learned associations.
10. Simple cognitive sets, selective recall, and spontaneous recognition of the classes present in a given environment are possible. The recognition of relationships in space and time, however, seems to represent a limit to the perceptron's ability to form cognitive abstractions.

Psychologists, and learning theorists in particular, may now ask: "What has the present theory accomplished, beyond what has already been done in the quantitative theories of Hull, Bush and Mosteller, etc., or physiological theories such as Hebb's?" The present theory is still too primitive, of course, to be considered as a full-fledged rival of existing theories of human learning. Nonetheless, as a first approximation, its chief accomplishment might be stated as follows:

For a given mode of organization (α, β, or γ; Σ or μ; monovalent or bivalent) the fundamental phenomena of *learning, perceptual discrimination, and generalization can be predicted entirely from six basic physical parameters*, namely:

- x: the number of excitatory connections per A-unit,
- y: the number of inhibitory connections per A-unit,
- θ: the expected threshold of an A-unit,
- ω: the proportion of R-units to which an A-unit is connected,
- N_A: the number of A-units in the system, and
- N_R: the number of R-units in the system.

N_s (the number of sensory units) becomes important if it is very small. It is assumed that the system begins with all units in a uniform state of value; otherwise the initial value distribution would also be required. *Each of the above parameters is a clearly defined physical variable, which is measurable in its own right, independently of the behavioral and perceptual phenomena which we are trying to predict.*

As a direct consequence of its foundation on physical variables, the present system goes far beyond existing learning and behavior theories in three main points: parsimony, verifiability, and explanatory power and generality. Let us consider each of these points in turn.

1. *Parsimony.* Essentially all of the basic variables and laws used in this system are already present in the structure of physical and biological science, so that we have found it necessary to postulate only one hypothetical variable (or construct) which we have called V, the "value" of an association cell; this is a variable which must conform to certain functional characteristics which can clearly be stated, and which is assumed to have a potentially measurable physical correlate.

2. *Verifiability.* Previous quantitative learning theories, apparently without exception, have had one important characteristic in common: they have all been based on measurements of *behavior*, in specified situations, using these measurements (after theoretical manipulation) to predict *behavior* in other situations. Such a procedure, in the last analysis, amounts to a process of curve fitting and extrapolation, in the hope that the constants which describe one set of curves will hold good for other curves in other situations. While such extrapolation is not necessarily circular, in the strict sense, it shares many of the logical difficulties of circularity, particularly when used as an "explanation" of behavior. Such extrapolation is difficult to justify in a new situation, and it has been shown that if the basic constants and parameters are to be derived anew for any situation in which they break down empirically (such as change from white rats to humans), then the basic "theory" is essentially irrefutable, just as any successful curve-fitting equation is irrefutable. It has, in fact, been widely conceded by psychologists that there is little point in trying to "disprove" any of the major learning theories in use today, since by extension, or a change in parameters, they

have all proved capable of adapting to any specific empirical data. This is epitomized in the increasingly common attitude that a choice of theoretical model is mostly a matter of personal aesthetic preference or prejudice, each scientist being entitled to a favorite model of his own. In considering this approach, one is reminded of a remark attributed to Kistiakowsky, that "given seven parameters, I could fit an elephant." This is clearly *not* the case with a system in which the independent variables, or parameters, can be measured *independently* of the predicted behavior. In such a system, it is not possible to "force" a fit to empirical data, if the parameters in current use should lead to improper results. In the current theory, a failure to fit a curve in a new situation would be a clear indication that either the theory or the empirical measurements are wrong. Consequently, if such a theory *does* hold up for repeated tests, we can be considerably more confident of its validity and of its generality than in the case of a theory which must be hand-tailored to meet each situation.

3. *Explanatory power and generality.* The present theory, being derived from basic physical variables, is not specific to any one organism or learning situation. It can be generalized in principle to cover any form of behavior in any system for which the physical parameters are known. A theory of learning. constructed on these foundations, should be considerably more powerful than any which has previously been proposed. It would not only tell us what behavior might occur in any known organism, but would permit the *synthesis* of behaving systems, to meet special requirements. Other learning theories tend to become increasingly qualitative as they are generalized. Thus a set of equations describing the effects of reward on T-maze learning in a white rat reduces simply to a statement that rewarded behavior tends to occur with increasing probability, when we attempt to generalize it from any species and any situation. The theory which has been presented here loses none of its precision through generality.

The theory proposed by Donald Hebb (7) attempts to avoid these difficulties of behavior-based models by showing how psychological functioning might be derived from neurophysiological theory. In his attempt to achieve this, Hebb's philosophy of approach seems close to our own, and his work has been a source of inspiration for much of what has been proposed here. Hebb, however, has never actually achieved a model by which behavior (or any psychological data) can be *predicted* from the physiological system. His physiology is more a suggestion as to the *sort* of organic substrate which might underlie behavior, and an attempt to show the plausibility of a bridge between biophysics and psychology.

The present theory represents the first actual completion of such a bridge. Through the use of the equations in the preceding sections, it is possible to predict learning curves from neurological variables, and likewise, to predict neurological variables from learning curves. How well this bridge stands up to repeated crossings remains to be seen. In the meantime, the theory reported here clearly demonstrates the feasibility and fruitfulness of a quantitative statistical approach to the organization of cognitive systems. By the study of systems such as the perceptron, it is hoped that those fundamental laws of organization which are common to all information handling systems, machines and men included, may eventually be understood.

REFERENCES

1. ASHBY, W. R. *Design for a brain.* New York: Wiley, 1952.
2. CULBERTSON, J. T. *Consciousness and behavior.* Dubuque, Iowa: Wm. C. Brown, 1950.
3. CULBERTSON, J. T. Some uneconomical robots. In C. E. Shannon & J. McCarthy (Eds.), *Automata studies.* Princeton: Princeton Univer. Press, 1956. Pp. 99–116.
4. ECCLES, J. C. *The neurophysiological basis of mind.* Oxford: Clarendon, 1953.
5. GOLDSTEIN, K. *Human nature in the light of psychopathology.* Cambridge: Harvard Univer. Press, 1940.
6. HAYEK, F. A. *The sensory order.* Chicago: Univer. Chicago Press, 1952.
7. HEBB, D. O. *The organization of behavior.* New York: Wiley, 1949.
8. KLEENE, S. C. Representation of events in nerve nets and finite automata. In C. E. Shannon & J. McCarthy (Eds.), *Automata studies.* Princeton: Princeton Univer. Press, 1956. Pp. 3–41.
9. KÖHLER, W. Relational determination in perception. In L. A. Jeffress (Ed.), *Cerebral mechanisms in behavior.* New York: Wiley, 1951. Pp. 200–243.
10. MCCULLOCH, W. S. Why the mind is in the head. In L. A. Jeffress (Ed.), *Cerebral mechanisms in behavior.* New York: Wiley, 1951. Pp. 42–111.
11. MCCULLOCH, W. S., & PITTS, W. A logical calculus of the ideas immanent in nervous activity. *Bull. math. Biophysics*, 1943, **5**, 115–133.
12. MILNER, P. M. The cell assembly: Mark II. *Psychol. Rev.*, 1957, **64**, 242–252.
13. MINSKY, M. L. Some universal elements for finite automata. In C. E. Shannon & J. McCarthy (Eds.), *Automata studies.* Princeton: Princeton Univer. Press, 1956. Pp. 117–128.
14. RASHEVSKY, N. *Mathematical biophysics.* Chicago: Univer. Chicago Press, 1938.
15. ROSENBLATT, F. *The perceptron: A theory of statistical separability in cognitive systems.* Buffalo: Cornell Aeronautical Laboratory, Inc. Rep. No. VG-1196-G-1, 1958.
16. UTTLEY, A. M. Conditional probability machines and conditioned reflexes. In C. E. Shannon & J. McCarthy (Eds.), *Automata studies.* Princeton: Princeton Univer. Press, 1956. Pp. 253–275.
17. VON NEUMANN, J. The general and logical theory of automata. In L. A. Jeffress (Ed.), *Cerebral mechanisms in behavior.* New York: Wiley, 1951. Pp. 1–41.
18. VON NEUMANN, J. Probabilistic logics and the synthesis of reliable organisms from unreliable components. In C. E. Shannon & J. McCarthy (Eds.), *Automata studies.* Princeton: Princeton Univer. Press, 1956. Pp. 43–98.

(Received April 23, 1958)

Statistical Classifiers

II

Editor's Comments on Papers 6, 7, and 8

6 **Chow:** *An Optimum Character Recognition System Using Decision Functions*

7 **Abramson and Braverman:** *Learning to Recognize Patterns in a Random Environment*

8 **Sebestyen:** *Pattern Recognition by an Adaptive Process of Sample Set Construction*

Although the assumption of nonoverlapping class regions in feature space is acceptable in many cases, there are many other cases where the classes are best described by overlapping probability densities of the pattern classes. Examples of such cases occur in weather prediction and medical diagnosis, where a single feature can occur in more than one class.

It is interesting to note that the training procedures developed for nonoverlapping class regions, such as Rosenblatt's error-correcting procedure [Ros-2], for example, do not, as a rule, approach either minimal-error decisions asymptotically or even approximations of such decisions. Consequently, special classification techniques were developed, based on statistical models of the feature vectors.

This part presents three papers that describe some of the most important of these techniques. The first paper, by C. K. Chow [Chow-1], introduces the use of decision theory and likelihoods as tools for optimum classification. Later, others extended the concept of "likelihoods" to "discriminant functions" for classification machines [Nil].

The second paper, by Abramson and Braverman [Abr], extends the decision-theoretic techniques of optimum classification to take into account the finiteness of the number of observed feature vectors (i.e., the finiteness of the sample size). Using Bayes' theory, the authors of this paper show how to find the effect of each new sample on the best estimate on the mean of a gaussian distribution, assuming that the mean was initially unknown. Although this paper is restricted to gaussian densities of the feature vectors, it pointed the way to more general approaches to parametric estimation of the class densities.

The third paper, by Sebestyen [Seb-2], describes an effective method for accounting for finite sample sizes when the class densities are of a general form. Here a training procedure generates an approximation to the actual probability densities of each class. The approximation consists of a sum of multivariate gaussian densities, all with different means.

Reprinted from *IRE Trans. Electron. Comput.*, **EC-6,** No. 4, 1957, pp. 247–254

6

An Optimum Character Recognition System Using Decision Functions*

C. K. CHOW†

Summary—The character recognition problem, usually resulting from characters being corrupted by printing deterioration and/or inherent noise of the devices, is considered from the viewpoint of statistical decision theory. The optimization consists of minimizing the expected risk for a weight function which is preassigned to measure the consequences of system decisions. As an alternative, minimization of the error rate for a given rejection rate is used as the criterion. The optimum recognition is thus obtained.

The optimum system consists of a conditional-probability densisities computer; character channels, one for each character; a rejection channel; and a comparison network. Its precise structure and and ultimate performance depend essentially upon the signals and noise structure.

Explicit examples for an additive Gaussian noise and a "cosine" noise are presented. Finally, an error-free recognition system and a possible criterion to measure the character style and deterioration are presented.

* Manuscript received by the PGEC, June 3, 1957.

† Burroughs, Corp., Paoli, Pa.

Introduction

CHARACTER recognition has been receiving considerable attention as the result of the phenomenal growth of office automation and the need for translating human language into machine language.[1,2] Broadly speaking, the character printed in conventional form and size on the document (checks, etc.) is first converted to electrical signals, and sufficient information is then extracted from the latter. The purpose of the recognition system is based on the observed data and on *a priori* knowledge of the signal and noise structure

[1] K. R. Eldredge, F. J. Kamphoefner, and P. H. Wendt, "Automatic input for business data processing system," *Proc. Eastern Joint Computer Conf.*, pp. 69–73; December 11, 1956.

[2] E. C. Greanias and Y. M. Hill, "Considerations in the design of character recognition devices," 1957 IRE National Convention Record, pt 4, vol. 5 pp. 119–126.

to identify which of the possible characters is present, or to reject if the data are ambiguous.

The over-all performance of the recognition system depends not only upon itself, but also upon the number of characters to be recognized, the character style, and noise statistics. In this paper the character style and noise statistics are assumed given and adequate, and the purpose of the paper is to obtain an optimum recognition system. For convenience, the recognition problem is considered one of statistical inference, so that useful results in decision theory can be applied.[3-5] To accomplish this, the notion of risk is employed and proper weights are assigned to various types of error, rejection, and correct recognition to measure the consequences of decisions. This results in an optimum system which minimizes the expected (average) risk function and includes a possible alternate system with a minimum error rate. The results reveal the explicit structure of an optimum system which is determined by the *a priori* noise statistics, the signal structure, and the preassigned weights.

System Approach to the Problem

One practical application of a character recognition system for business documents is to read arabic numerals and selected symbols printed in magnetic ink. A method[1] for achieving this is shown in Fig. 1. The character is first passed through the field of a permanent magnet where it is magnetized in a given direction before being scanned by the read head. From the read head, the printed character is converted into an electrical signal corresponding to the differentiation of the plane area of the character. The function of the recognition system is to examine the amplitude-time signal obtained by the read head and to decide which of the possible characters is being recognized.

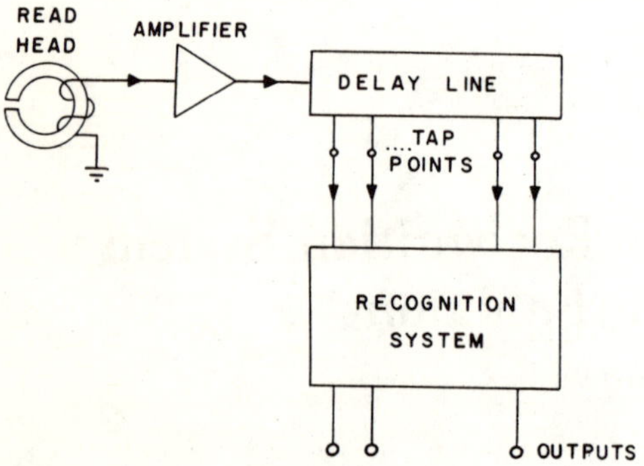

Fig. 1—A recognition system.

It is convenient, at times, to deal with the sampled data rather than the continuous time waveforms. By the sampling theory, if the number of samples is sufficiently large, little information carried by the continuous signal is lost. As shown in Fig. 1, the signal from the read head is first amplified and then fed into a tapped delay line. This serves as a means for sampling and acts as a temporary storage device to convert the series information into parallel information. Although not essential, sampled data are used in the following discussion.

Let the vector $v=(v_1, v_2, \cdots v_s)$ (subscript s being the number of samples) denote voltages on the taps of the delay line at the instant of sampling. (See Appendix I for the meaning of the Symbols.) The vector $a_i=(a_{i1}, a_{i2}, \cdots, a_{is})$ denotes the true sampled signal associated with the ith character where $i=1, 2, \cdots, c$, c being the number of possible characters to be recognized. The vector v constitutes the input to the recognition system. It is assumed that the characters are distinct, *i.e.*, all a_i's are different.

In a simple form, the recognition system may consist of c separate channels, one for each character. Each channel obtains a weighted sum of v_i's, with properly chosen weights, b_{ij}. The output of the ith channel is

$$X_i(v) = \sum_{j=1}^{s} b_{ij}v_j \tag{1}$$

This operation may be realized by a summing amplifier and possibly with some inverters to provide negative weights, if required. One possible set of weights is:

$$b_{ij} = \frac{a_{ij}}{\left[\sum_{j=1}^{s} a_{ij}^2\right]^{1/2}}. \tag{2}$$

The recognition system is known as a correlation network when the weights are defined by (2).

If the printing is perfect, and the reading devices are noiseless, the observed data v will be identical to one of the a_i's and therefore, it can easily be shown that the right channel of the correlation network has the largest (algebraic) output. Consequently, the recognition system identifies the character with absolute accuracy by the channel having the highest output. However, in practice, there are always, to some degree, deteriorations in printing and inherent noise in the devices. Therefore, the observed data v generally will not be identical to any of the a_i's. In view of this, ambiguities arise which may result in possible misrecognition. To safeguard against the occurrence of error, the recognition system should have provisions for examining the degree of ambiguity and making rejects when required. This function can be achieved in various ways; *e.g.*, whenever the next highest output of the correlation network exceeds some preassigned fraction of the highest output, the system will reject, otherwise the system

[3] A. Wald, "Statistical Decision Functions," John Wiley & Sons, Inc., New York, N. Y., 1950.

[4] D. Van Meter and D. Middleton, "Modern statistical approaches to reception in communication theory," IRE Trans., vol. PGIT-4, pp. 119–145; September, 1954.

[5] D. Middleton and D. Van Meter, "On optimum multiple-alternative detection of signals in noise," IRE Trans., vol. IT-1, pp. 1–9; September, 1955.

identifies the character by the channel having the highest output.

The system described above merely represents one of many possible recognition systems and is not necessarily optimum. A basic problem in the design of recognition systems is to evaluate the system performance in the presence of printing deterioration and inherent noise and to obtain an optimum system. Optimum performance depends primarily upon the character style and permissible deterioration. Greanias and Hill in a recent paper[2] describe the effects of character style and printing deterioration on the character recognition problem from the viewpoint of matching the character with an ideal character and further propose definitions for character quality and style factors. In this paper, the discussion is confined to the problem of obtaining an optimum recognition system for a given set of adequately styled characters and known statistics of character deterioration. The recognition problem is considered to be that of testing multiple hypotheses in the statistical inference. Consequently, the design and evaluation of a recognition system is comparable to a statistical test. Results of decision theory can be applied.[3-5].

In order to judge the relative merit of recognition systems, some criterion of evaluating system performance must be established. The error rate of the system for a given rejection rate is used as the performance criterion for cases where no distinction is made among misrecognitions. Cases may arise where different misrecognitions have different consequences; *e.g.*, the registering of a four as an asterisk may not be as serious an error as registering it as a nine. The criterion of minimum error rate is then no longer appropriate. Instead, the criterion of minimum risk[3] is employed. Proper weights are assigned to measure the consequences of errors, rejections, and correct recognitions. These weights indicate the loss incurred by the system for every possible decision. The loss, which should be regarded as negative utility, may actually represent loss in dollars or unit of utility in measuring the consequence of the system decision. The over-all performance of the system is judged by its expected (or average) risk.

In the following discussion, an optimum system which minimizes the expected risk is derived, and a system having minimum error rate is obtained. Examples are presented for illustration purposes. An error-free system and a possible criterion for judging character style and deterioration are also presented.

The Expected Risk

The vector $a_i=(a_{i1}, a_{i2}, \cdots, a_{is})$ in the s-dimensional space denotes the true sampled signal associated with the ith character ($i=1, 2, \cdots, c$), where c and s are respectively, the number of possible characters to be recognized and the number of samples. Let $p=(p_1, p_2, \cdots, p_c)$ be the *a priori* distribution of characters (p_i is the *a priori* probability that the ith character occurs). Then, evidently,

$$\sum_{i=1}^{c} p_i = 1, \qquad p_i > 0. \tag{3}$$

The received data are denoted by a s-components vector $v=(v_1, v_2, \cdots, v_s)$. It is the signal corrupted by factors such as the deterioration of printing and inherent noise of the devices. *A priori* noise statistics and the manner in which various signals and noise are combined determine precisely the conditional probability density $F(v|a_i)$ of the observed data v when a_i is the incoming signal.

The space of decisions available to the recognition system consists of $c+1$ possible decisions $d_0, d_1, d_2, \cdots, d_c$. The quantity $d_i(i\neq 0)$ is the decision that the ith character is present while d_0 is the decision for reject. A basic problem in statistical decision theory is the selection of a proper decision rule δ. The rule is expressed as a vector function of the data v, namely, $\delta(v)=(\delta(d_0|v), \delta(d_1|v), \delta(d_2|v) \cdots \delta(d_c|v))$ with $c+1$ components, and satisfies the restriction that:

$$\sum_{i=0}^{c} \delta(d_i | v) = 1 \qquad \text{for all } v, \tag{4}$$

and

$$\delta(d_i | v) \geq 0 \qquad \text{for all } i \text{ and } v. \tag{5}$$

The quantity $\delta(d_i|v)$ is the probability that, for a given observed data v, the decision d_i will be made.

In order to judge the relative merits of the decision rules it is necessary to assign the weight function $W(a_i, d_j)$. This is a function of a_i and d_j, which is the loss incurred by the system if the decision d_j is made when a_i is the true signal. This measure of consequence for various d_j under various a_i is a datum of the problem and is given in advance. Let the weight function be:

$$W(a_i, d_j) = w_{ij} \qquad \begin{matrix} i = 1, 2 \cdots c \\ j = 0, 1, 2 \cdots c, \end{matrix} \tag{6}$$

where $w_{ii}(i\neq 0)$ is the weight of correct recognition of the ith character; $w_{ij}(i\neq j\neq 0)$ is the weight of misreading the ith character as the jth one, and $w_{i0}(i\neq 0)$ is the weight of rejecting the ith characters. Therefore, it is required that

$$w_{ij} > w_{i0} > w_{ii} \qquad (i \neq j \neq 0). \tag{7}$$

Usually, w_{ij} is much larger than w_{i0} since the most serious consideration in design of a character recognition system is the occurrence of undetected errors.

In general, w_{ij}'s may all differ, so that various misrecognitions, rejections, and correct recognitions can be properly weighted. The expected risk for any decision rule δ is

$$R(p, \delta) = \sum_{i=1}^{c}\sum_{j=0}^{c} \int_V \delta(d_j | v) p_i w_{ij} F(v | a_i) dv, \tag{8}$$

with integration over the entire observation space V.

The Minimum Risk System

The problem is then to choose a decision rule to minimize the average risk. By using (4), and since $\int_V F(v|a_i)dv=1$ for all i, (8) may be written as:

$$R(p, \delta) = R_0(p) + R_1(p, \delta), \tag{9}$$

where

$$R_0 = \sum_{i=1}^{c} p_i w_{i0}, \tag{10}$$

$$R_1 = \int_V \sum_{j=0}^{c} \delta(d_j \mid v) Z_j(v) dv, \tag{11}$$

and

$$Z_j(v) = \begin{cases} \sum_{i=1}^{c} (w_{ij} - w_{i0}) p_i F(v \mid a_i); \; j = 1, 2 \cdots c \\ 0 \qquad \text{for } j = 0. \end{cases} \tag{12}$$

The symbol R_0 will express the expected risk when rejection is made for all recognition and R_1 is that part of R which may be adjusted through the choice of δ. Evidently

$$R_1(p, \delta) \geq \int_V \min_j [Z_j(v)] dv, \tag{13}$$

and the equality sign holds if, and only if, the decision rule is chosen as:

$$\delta^*(d_k \mid v) = 1, \qquad \delta^*(d_j \mid v) = 0 \quad \text{for all } j \neq k \tag{14}$$

whenever

$$\min_j [Z_j(v)] = Z_k(v). \tag{15}$$

This is the optimum decision rule δ^* (the Bayes strategy) which minimizes the expected risk and is nonrandomized since its components are either zero or one. Therefore, R_1 for this decision rule is always nonpositive, and its expected risk (the Bayes risk) is no greater than R_0. The expected risk for the optimum decision rule, δ^*, is

$$R(p, \delta^*) = \sum_{i=1}^{c} p_i w_{i0} + \int_V \min_j [Z_j(v)] dv. \tag{16}$$

Eqs. (14) and (15) reveal that the optimum system for character recognition consists of a computer which evaluates $F(v|a_i)$'s; $(i=1, 2, \cdots, c)$ for an observed data v; computes the various $Z_j(v)$ $(j=1, 2, \cdots, c)$; examines and compares these $Z_j(v)$ $(j=0, 1, 2, \cdots, c)$; selects the smallest (algebraically) one, say $Z_k(v)$; and finally makes the decision d_k [having the same subscript as $Z_k(v)$]. Of course, this method of setting up the computing procedures is not unique; *e.g.*, any ordering-preserving transformation may be used. In any event, the system must be equivalent to the above.

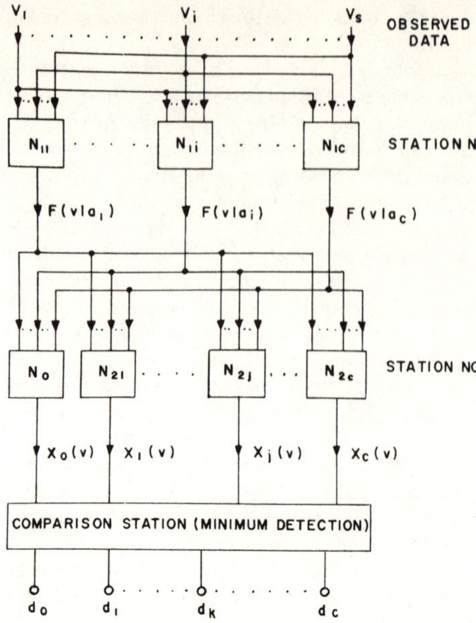

Fig. 2—Functional diagram of an optimum system.

The functional diagram of the optimum system is shown in Fig. 2. Station No. 1 consists of c similar component networks. Each network receives the observed data $v=(v_1, v_2, \cdots, v_s)$ and computes the corresponding conditional probability density $F(v|a_i)$ as its output. This operation depends only upon the *a priori* knowledge of signal and noise structure and on the observed data v; it does not depend upon the weight function $W(a_i, d_j)$ or on *a priori* probability distribution of signals, p.

The outputs of station No. 1 are fed to station No. 2, which consists of c character channels $N_{2j}(j\neq 0)$, and one rejection channel, N_0. They perform the linear operation of weighting each input and then the summing of all weighted inputs. The weights are $p_i w_{ij}$'s and $p_i w_{i0}$'s. The output of the rejection channel is

$$X_0(v) = \sum_{i=1}^{c} w_{i0} p_i F(v \mid a_i), \tag{17}$$

while the outputs of character channels are

$$X_j(v) = \sum_{i=1}^{c} w_{ij} p_i F(v \mid a_i) \quad (j = 1, 2 \cdots c). \tag{18}$$

The comparison station receives X's from station No. 2, examines all its inputs, and makes decision by selecting the algebraically smallest of the $c+1$ X's. If the rejection channel has the smallest one, the system rejects. If one of the character channels has the smallest output (say $X_k(v)$, $(k\neq 0)$) then the system recognizes the signal as the kth character.

Since $X_j(v)$ $(j=0, 1, \cdots, c)$ is equal to $Z_j(v)+X_0(v)$, this system makes decisions in accordance with δ^* as defined by (14) and (15), and thus minimizing the expected risk.

Probabilities of Error and Rejection

The expected risk provides a means for evaluating the performance of a recognition system. At times, it may be desirable to compute the probabilities of error, rejection, and correct recognition as an auxiliary set of merit figures. They are obtained for any decision rule δ as follows:

The probability of correct recognition is:

$$P_c(\delta) = \int_V \sum_{i=1}^{c} \delta(d_i \mid v) p_i F(v \mid a_i) dv; \tag{19}$$

the probability of rejection, or rejection rate, is:

$$P_r(\delta) = \int_V \delta(d_0 \mid v) \sum_{i=1}^{c} p_i F(v \mid a_i) dv; \tag{20}$$

and the probability of misrecognition, or error rate, is:

$$P_e(\delta) = 1 - P_c - P_r. \tag{21}$$

Eqs. (19)–(21) result directly from the fact that $\int_V \delta(d_0 \mid v) F(v \mid a_i) dv$ and $\int_V \delta(d_i \mid v) F(v \mid a_i) dv$ are, respectively, the conditional probabilities of rejection of the ith character and correct recognition of the ith character.

Criterion of Minimum Error Rate

Cases may arise in which the criterion of judging the system performance is the magnitude of its error rate for a given rejection rate. In using this criterion, the optimum recognition system is the one which, for a given rejection rate, α, has a minimum error rate. The optimum decision rule is obtained as: (See Appendix II for proof.)

$$\delta^{**}(d_k \mid v) = 1 \qquad (k \neq 0) \tag{22}$$

whenever

$$p_k F(v \mid a_k) \geq p_j F(v \mid a_j) \qquad \text{for all } j \neq k \text{, and}$$

$$p_k F(v \mid a_k) \geq \beta \sum_{i=1}^{c} p_i F(v \mid a_i), \tag{23}$$

and

$$\delta^{**}(d_0 \mid v) = 1, \tag{24}$$

whenever

$$\beta \sum_{i=1}^{c} p_i F(v \mid a_i) > p_j F(v \mid a_j) \quad \text{for all } j (j = 1, 2 \cdots c), \tag{25}$$

where $\beta(0 \leq \beta \leq 1)$ is a nonnegative constant determined by the condition that $P_r(\delta^{**}) = \alpha$; namely,

$$\int_V \delta^{**}(d_0 \mid v) \sum_{i=1}^{c} p_i F(v \mid a_i) dv = \alpha. \tag{26}$$

The constant β increases with increasing α, and $P_e(\delta^{**})$ and $P_c(\delta^{**})$ are monotonic decreasing functions of α.

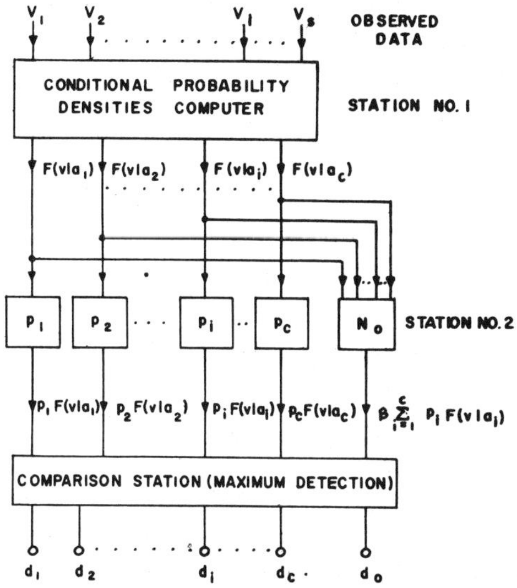

Fig. 3—Functional diagram of the system having the minimum error rate.

The change in the constant β provides a control over the error-reject ratio.

The optimum rule δ^{**} provides the basis for the functional diagram of the system of minimum error rate as shown in Fig. 3. The first station is identical to that of the minimum risk system (see Fig. 2) which computes the conditional probability densities $F(v \mid a_i)$'s.

The second station for this system is somewhat similar to that shown in the functional diagram for the minimum risk system (see Fig. 2). The c-character channels perform the weighting operation and have $p_i F(v \mid a_i)$ as outputs. The rejection channel, N_0, performs the operation of weighting and summing and has $\beta \sum_{i=1}^{c} p_i F(v \mid a_i)$ as its output. All of these $c+1$ outputs are nonnegative. The comparison station then examines these outputs and selects the largest. If the output of the rejection channel is the largest, the system rejects; otherwise the system will identify the character by the channel having the largest output.

It can be shown that the system depicted in Fig. 2 reduces to the system shown in Fig. 3 when β is replaced by $(w_m - w_r)/(w_m - w_c)$, and the following weight function is used.

$$W(a_i, d_j) = \begin{cases} w_c & \text{for } i = j \neq 0 \\ w_r & \text{for } i \neq 0, j = 0. \\ w_m & \text{for } i \neq j \neq 0. \end{cases} \tag{27}$$

Examples

1) As an illustration, consider a condition where the signals and noise are additive, and the noise has independent normal distribution. To be explicit, the probability density function of the noise of the jth component of the ith character is taken as:

$$\frac{1}{\sqrt{2\pi}\sigma_{ij}} \exp\left\{-\frac{(v_j - a_{ij})^2}{2\sigma_{ij}^2}\right\}, \tag{28}$$

where $v_j - a_{ij}$ is the noise and σ_{ij}^2 is the given variance.

The conditional probability density $F(v|a_i)$, under the assumption that noise is statistically independent, is

$$F(v \mid a_i) = \frac{\exp\left\{-\sum_{j=1}^{s} \frac{(v_j - a_{ij})^2}{2\sigma_{ij}^2}\right\}}{(2\pi)^{s/2} \prod_{j=1}^{s} \sigma_{ij}}. \tag{29}$$

Therefore, the last expression dictates the precise structure of station No. 1 for the optimum system. Each component circuit performs the operations of taking differences, squaring, weighting, summing, and taking exponential. This station is common for a minimum risk or minimum error rate system. The structures of the second station and comparison station are indicated in Figs. 2 and 3.

2) In this example, the signal and noise structure are such that the conditional probability density for a given length, $|v|$, of v is directly proportional to the cosine of the angle θ between vectors v and a_i for $|\theta| < \pi/2$ and is zero elsewhere, and that the distributions of $|v|$ for given a_i are identical for all i.[6] [It is denoted as $f(|v|)$.] In other words, $F(v|a_i)$ can be written as

$$\begin{aligned} F(v \mid a_i) &= \rho f(\mid v \mid) \frac{a_i \cdot v}{\mid a_i \mid \cdot \mid v \mid} && \text{for } a_i \cdot v > 0 \\ &= 0 && \text{elsewhere,} \end{aligned} \tag{30}$$

where ρ is a constant independent of i and is determined by the fact that $\int_V F(v|a_i)dv = 1$, and $a_i \cdot v$ denotes the scalar product of vectors a_i and v.

An inspection of the optimum decision rule (δ^* or δ^{**}) reveals that the system remains optimum if the first station is to compute $T[F(v|a_i)]$ instead of $F(v|a_i)$, where T is defined as

$$T(v \mid a_i) = \frac{\mid v \mid}{\rho f(\mid v \mid)} F(v \mid a_i)$$

$$= \begin{cases} \dfrac{a_i}{\mid a_i \mid} \cdot v = \sum_{j=1}^{s} b_{ij} v_j & \text{for } a_i \cdot v > 0 \\ 0 & \text{for } a_i \cdot v \leq 0, \end{cases} \tag{31}$$

where b_{ij}'s are constants [see (2)]. This operation can be easily realized. Each component of the first station is simply a correlation network followed by a half-wave rectifying circuit. The circuit passes the positive output of the correlation network unaltered and converts its negative output into zero.

The above results also indicate that the recognition system described in the second section of this paper is not optimum for the particular signal and noise structure as given in examples 1 or 2.

[6] This particular signal and noise structure was suggested by the author's colleague, I. M. Sheaffer, Jr., Burroughs Corp., Paoli, Pa.

Error-Free System

For convenience, let V_i denote the set (or region) of all possible observation v when the ith character is present, and let $\tilde{V}_i$ be the largest subset of V_i so that $\tilde{V}_i$'s are nonoverlapping. If noise distributions are so truncated and the signal vectors a_i's are so placed that all $\tilde{V}_i$'s are nonempty, then an error-free system for character recognition does exist. Evidently for any observed data v belonging to $\tilde{V}_k$, only $F(v|a_k)$ is nonzero while all others are zero; the character can then be identified with certainty. On the other hand, if the data v do not belong to any one of the $\tilde{V}_i$'s, then more than one of the $F(v|a_i)$'s will be nonzero. This results in the data being ambiguous for recognition purpose, and an error-free system will reject. Symbolically, the error-free decision rule is:

$$\delta(d_k \mid v) = 1 \quad \text{if } F(v \mid a_k) > 0$$

and

$$F(v \mid a_i) = 0 \quad \text{for all } i \neq k, \tag{32}$$

and

$$\delta(d_0 \mid v) = 1, \quad \text{otherwise,}$$

the rejection rate is determined by the probability measures of $\tilde{V}_i$'s, namely $\int_{\tilde{V}_i} F(v|a_i)dv$. The latter is determined by the character style and allowable deterioration. The character style may be considered ideal and the control over the printing perfect, if the resultant $\int_{\tilde{V}_i} F(v|a_i)dv$ is unity for all i, and all characters with allowable deterioration can then be recognized with neither an error nor reject. In this sense, the probability measures of $\tilde{V}_i$'s may be used to evaluate the combined quality of the character style and printing.

Conclusion

The decision theory has been successfully applied to the problem of character recognition. By employing the concept of risk, differences in consequences for various decisions have been taken into consideration. A rejection channel has been introduced to examine the degree of ambiguity of input signal and make rejections when necessary.

As developed, the structure and performance of an optimum system depend upon the signal and noise statistics; therefore, *a priori* knowledge of these statistics is required. Usually, a realistic estimate of noise statistics is not easy to obtain. However, it is sincerely felt that the requirement for high grade performance in character recognition warrants the expenditures in this direction.

Quite often an optimum system may prove to be too expensive for mechanization. Nevertheless, the results presented in this paper are considered useful in that they provide insight into the recognition problem and furnish an ideal system, which actual recognition circuitry may be patterned after.

Although it is recognized as being beyond the scope of this paper, it is worth mentioning that one practical approach to the over-all problem would be to design adequately the character style and to control properly the printing process so that a reliable system would not be too far fetched or difficult to ultimately realize.

Appendix I.

List of Symbols

$a_i=(a_{i1}, a_{i2}, \cdots, a_{is})$, s-dimensional vector associated with the ith character, $(i=1, 2, \cdots, c)$.
$a_{ij}=j$th sample of the signal of the ith character.
$|a_i|=(\sum_{j=1}^{s} a_{ij}^2)^{1/2}$, the length of vector a_i.
c = number of characters.
d_0 = decision that rejection be made.
d_j = decision that the signal is the jth character $(j=1, 2, \cdots, c)$.
$f(|v|)$ = probability density of the length of v.
$F(v|a_i)$ = conditional probability density for the observed data v when a_i is the incoming signal.
i, j, k = indexes.
N_{1i} = a network of station No. 1, $i=1, 2, \cdots, c$.
N_{2i} = a network of station No. 2, $i=1, 2, \cdots, c$.
N_0 = the network of rejection channel.
P_c = probability of correct recognition.
P_r = probability of rejection (rejection rate).
P_e = probability of misrecognition (error rate).
p_i = *a priori* probability that the ith character occurs, $(i=1, 2, \cdots, c)$.
$p=(p_1, p_2, \cdots, p_c)$.
$R(p, \delta)$ = expected risk of the system; $R=R_0+R_1$.
$R_0(p)$ = expected risk of the system when rejection is made for all recognition.
$R_1(p, \delta)$ = part of R which is dependent upon δ.
s = number of samples.
T = functional transformation.
V = s-dimension observation space.
V_i = set of all v when the ith character is present.
$\tilde{V}_i$ = largest subset of V_i such that $\tilde{V}_i \cap \tilde{V}_j=0$ for all $j\neq i$.
$v=(v_1, v_2, \cdots, v_s)$, a vector in V.
$|v|=(\sum_{i=1}^{s} v_i^2)^{1/2}$, the length of vector v.
vi = ith component of the observed data v.
$W(a_i, d_j)$ = weight function.
$w_{ij}=W(a_i, d_j)$.
w_c, w_r, w_m = weights.
$x_i(v)$ = output of the ith channel.
α = permissible rejection rate.
β = constant.
$\delta(v)$ = decision rule, $\delta=[\delta(d_0|v), \delta(d_1|v) \cdots \delta(d_c|v)]$.
$\delta^*(v)$ = optimum decision rule which minimizes the expected risk.
$\delta^{**}(v)$ = optimum decision rule which minimizes the error rate.
θ = angle.
ρ = a normalizing constant.
σ_{ij}^2 = statistical variance of noise.

Appendix II.

To Prove That δ^{**} Has a Minimum Error Rate for a Given Rejection Rate

Without loss of generality, it is assumed that the absolute probability density of the occurrence of v, namely, $\sum_{i=1}^{c} p_iF(v|a_i)$ is nonzero over the entire observation space V. Otherwise, the set over which $\sum_{i=1}^{c} p_iF(v|a_i)$ is zero is first deleted.

Let $m(v)$ be the subscript such that

$$\max_i [p_iF(v \mid a_i)] = p_mF(v \mid a_m) \tag{33}$$

and let $\delta^1(v)$ be any arbitrary decision rule having the same rejection rate as δ^{**}. It is to be proved that $P_e(\delta^1)\geq P_e(\delta^{**})$.

For every $\delta^1(v)$, a decision rule $\delta^2(v)$ can be constructed as follows:

For every v,

$$\begin{aligned} \delta^2(d_0 \mid v) &= \delta^1(d_0 \mid v) \\ \delta^2(d_m \mid v) &= 1 - \delta^1(d_0 \mid v) = \sum_{i=1}^{c} \delta^1(d_i \mid v) \\ \delta^2(d_i \mid v) &= 0 \quad \text{for all } i \neq 0 \neq m. \end{aligned} \tag{34}$$

Evidently,

$$P_r(\delta^2) = P_r(\delta^1) = \alpha, \tag{35}$$

and

$$\begin{aligned} P_c(\delta^1) &= \int_V \sum_{i=1}^{c} \delta^1(d_i \mid v)p_iF(v \mid a_i)dv \\ &\leq \int_V \sum_{i=1}^{c} \delta^1(d_i \mid v)p_mF(v \mid a_m)dv \\ &= \int_V \delta^2(d_m \mid v)p_mF(v \mid a_m)dv \\ &= P_c(\delta^2). \end{aligned} \tag{36}$$

It follows from (35) and (36) that

$$P_e(\delta^2) \leq P_e(\delta^1). \tag{37}$$

That is, δ^2 is better than δ^1 (or at least as good) in the sense that for the same rejection rate δ^2 has an error rate smaller than, or equal to, that of δ^1.

The next step is to show that $P_e(\delta^{**})\leq P_e(\delta^2)$. As shown in (22) ad (23), the decision rule δ^{**} partitions the observation space V into two nonintersecting regions, V_0^{**} and $V-V_0^{**}$, so that for every $v\epsilon V_0^{**}$

$$p_mF(v \mid a_m) < \beta \sum_{i=1}^{c} p_iF(v \mid a_i) \tag{38a}$$

$$\delta^{**}(d_0 | v) = 1, \tag{38b}$$

and for every $v \in V - V_0^{**}$

$$p_m F(v \mid a_m) \geq \beta \sum_{i=1}^{c} p_i F(v \mid a_i) \quad (39a)$$

$$\delta^{**}(d_m \mid v) = 1. \quad (39b)$$

Let V_0^2 be the largest subspace of V such that $\delta^2(d_0|v)$ is nonzero for all v belonging to V_0^2. V_0^2 is not properly contained in V_0^{**}. This follows readily from the condition that $P_r(\delta^{**}) = P_r(\delta^2)$. The latter may be written as:

$$\int_{V_0^{**}-V_0^{**}\cap V_0^2} \sum_{i=1}^{c} p_i F(v \mid a_i) dv + \int_{V_0^{**}\cap V_0^2} [1 - \delta^2(d_0 \mid v)] \sum_{i=1}^{c} p_i F(v \mid a_i) dv = \int_{V_0^2-V_0^{**}\cap V_0^2} \delta^2(d_0 \mid v) \sum_{i=1}^{c} p_i F(v \mid a_i) dv. \quad (40)$$

Substitution of (38) and (39) in (40) gives:

$$\int_{V_0^{**}-V_0^{**}\cap V_0^2} p_m F(v \mid a_m) dv + \int_{V_0^{**}\cap V_0^2} [1 - \delta^2(d_0 \mid v)] p_m F(v \mid a_m) dv \leq \int_{V_0^2-V_0^{**}\cap V_0^2} \delta^2(d_0 \mid v) p_m F(v \mid a_m) dv. \quad (41)$$

The equality sign prevails if, and only if, $p_m F(v|a_m)$ is equal to $\beta \sum_{i=1}^{c} p_i F(v|a_i)$ throughout the region $V_0^{**} \cup V_0^2$.

The probabilities of correct recognition of δ^{**} and δ^2 may be written respectively as:

$$P_c(\delta^{**}) = \int_{V-V_0^{**}} p_m F(v \mid a_m) dv = \int_{V-(V_0^{**}\cup V_0^2)} p_m F(v \mid a_m) dv + \int_{V_0^2-V_0^{**}\cap V_0^2} p_m F(v \mid a_m) dv, \quad (42a)$$

$$P_c(\delta^2) = \int_V \sum_{i=1}^{c} \delta^2(d_i \mid v) p_i F(v \mid a_i) dv = \int_{V-(V_0^{**}\cup V_0^2)} p_m F(v \mid a_m) dv + \int_{V_0^{**}-V_0^{**}\cap V_0^2} p_m F(v \mid a_m) dv + \int_{V_0^{**}\cap V_0^2} \delta^2(d_m \mid v) p_m F(v \mid a_m) dv + \int_{V_0^2-V_0^{**}\cap V_0^2} \delta^2(d_m \mid v) p_m F(v \mid a_m) dv. \quad (42b)$$

In accordance with (42), (41) is equivalent to $P_e(\delta^{**}) \leq P_e(\delta^2)$. Proof that $P_e(\delta^{**}) \leq \delta P_e(\delta^1)$ is thus completed.

Acknowledgment

This paper is based upon research performed in the Electromechanisms Department of the Burroughs Corporation Research Center at Paoli, Pa. The author wishes to thank his colleagues and Department Manager, G. A. Baird for their encouragement and assistance relative to this paper. The permission of the Burroughs Corporation for release of the material presented here is also acknowledged.

Reprinted from *IRE Trans. Inform. Theory,* **IT–8,** No. 5, 1962, pp. S58–S63

7

LEARNING TO RECOGNIZE PATTERNS IN A RANDOM ENVIRONMENT

N. Abramson
Stanford Electronics Laboratory
Stanford, California

D. Braverman
California Institute of Technology
Pasadena, California

Summary

This paper deals with the optimal use of a sequence of prior observations in order to recognize patterns. The class of pattern recognition problems which we treat is completely general in that the results may be applied to patterns of a visual, aural or electromagnetic origin. We show that the use of prior observations for pattern recognition may be described as a process of learning the statistical characteristics of the patterns involved. The mathematical description of the learning process is analyzed in order to obtain optimal (i.e., minimum probability of error) solutions to various types of pattern recognition problems. These solutions to the mathematical problem are then interpreted in terms of the systems implementation they imply. The optimum systems are shown to consist of banks of generalized correlators. Under assumption of independent measurements, the optimum systems reduce to a class of systems which function by reinforcing desired responses.

I. Introduction

The problem of automatic pattern recognition may profitably be subdivided into two subsidiary problems--what to measure and how to process the measurements. The first of these problems is undoubtedly the harder to deal with in a quantitative fashion. Our concern here will be the second problem--how to process a set of measurements once that set has been decided upon.

Any measurement, or set of measurements, on an object we wish to recognize can be reduced to a finite set of numbers by well known sampling techniques. Accordingly we write an arbitrary set of measurements $x_1, x_2, \cdots, x_d$, as a column vector X, and interpret X as a point in a d dimensional space. If we must recognize the measurements X as belonging to one of c possible classes, say $\omega_1, \omega_2, \cdots, \omega_c$, pattern recognition is equivalent to a partitioning of the space of all possible measurements into c subspaces. We note parenthetically that one of the classes (or equivalently one of the subspaces) may correspond to a "rejection" subclass, indicating that recognition of X cannot be achieved with some required degree of reliability.

It is clear that recognition of membership in a class can only be effected on the basis of differences in the characteristics of the c classes. We express these differences by assuming the vector measurement X is drawn from one of c populations described by the (perhaps unknown) conditional densities $P(X|\omega_1), P(X|\omega_2), \cdots, P(X|\omega_c)$. It is important to emphasize we do <u>not</u> necessarily assume that the $P(X|\omega_i)$ are known a priori. In fact we shall see that the heart of a realistic model of pattern recognition is the ability to <u>learn</u> properties of the $P(X|\omega_i)$ by observing <u>past</u> samples drawn from the same statistical population.

Before proceeding to the more realistic model of <u>unknown</u> conditional densities $P(X|\omega_i)$, it would be well to review some simple facts about pattern recognition when $P(X|\omega_i)$ is known. For simplicity we take the a priori probabilities of the c classes to be equal. Then the probability of misrecognition will be minimized[1] if we decide the measurement X is a sample of class $\hat{\omega}$ where

$$P(X|\hat{\omega}) \geq P(X|\omega_j) \qquad \text{all } \omega_j . \tag{1}$$

Since the choice of $\hat{\omega}$ is determined by the maximum of the c quantities $P(X|\omega_i)$, one may just as easily compute an arbitrary monotonic function of the conditional densities $P(X|\omega_i)$ and select $\hat{\omega}$ by determining the maximum of these new quantities. We call any such monotonic function a <u>likelihood</u>, and write it as $L(X|\omega_i)$. Then (1) becomes

$$L(X|\hat{\omega}) \geq L(X|\omega_j) \qquad \text{all } \omega_j . \tag{2}$$

We may draw a block diagram of the prototype pattern recognition system as shown below

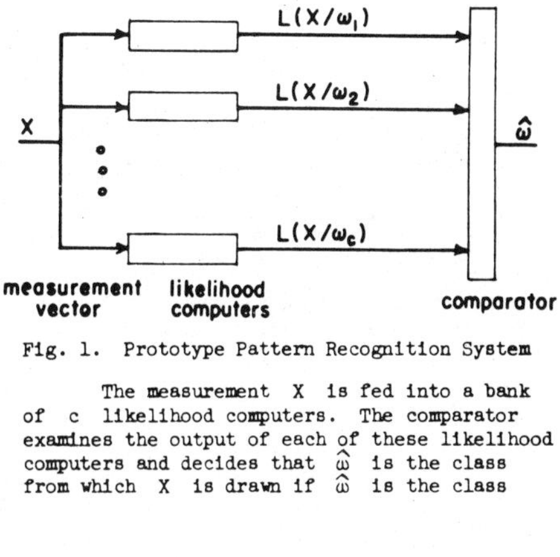

Fig. 1. Prototype Pattern Recognition System

The measurement X is fed into a bank of c likelihood computers. The comparator examines the output of each of these likelihood computers and decides that $\hat{\omega}$ is the class from which X is drawn if $\hat{\omega}$ is the class corresponding to the likelihood computer with the greatest output. These considerations allow us to concentrate our attention on the design of the individual likelihood computers; the remainder of the paper will treat this problem.

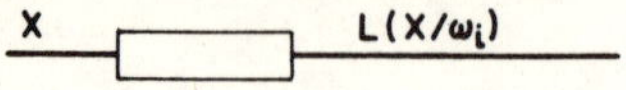

Fig. 2. Likelihood Computer

The recognition system described implies the systems designer has available a complete statistical description of the various classes to be recognized. We have already noted that this assumption is not realistic in most pattern recognition problems. It is appropriate therefore to consider methods of relaxing the assumptions leading to the system of Figures 1 and 2. The assumptions will be relaxed by allowing the conditional density $P(X|\omega_i)$ (or equivalently the likelihood $L(X|\omega_i)$) to change on the basis of observations of sample measurements. These measurements are called <u>learning measurements</u> and are denoted by the vectors $X_1, X_2, \cdots, X_k$. We start with an initial density of X, $P(X|\omega_i)$. After observing the first learning measurement, X_1, we describe the density of X by $P(X|\omega_i, X_1)$; after a second learning observation, by $P(X|\omega_i, X_1, X_2)$, etc. Since the class ω_i is to be understood throughout the rest of this paper, we omit ω_i when writing the above succession of conditional densities. The learning process for class ω_i is then given by

$$P(X) \to P(X|X_1) \to P(X|X_1,X_2) \cdots \to P(X|X_1,X_2,\cdots,X_k) \tag{3}$$

or, in terms of the likelihood

$$L(X) \to L(X|X_1) \to L(X|X_1,X_2) \cdots \to L(X|X_1,X_2,\cdots,X_k) \tag{4}$$

In order to develop (3) and (4) further it is convenient to assume that learning measurements from one class do not provide information about the statistical structure of other classes. That is, if Y_1 is a learning measurement from class $\omega_j \neq \omega_i$, we assume

$$\begin{aligned} P(X|Y_1) &= P(X) \\ P(X|X_1,Y_1) &= P(X|X_1) \\ &\text{etc.} \end{aligned} \tag{5}$$

We may therefore take the learning measurements $X_1, X_2, \cdots, X_k$ to be k learning measurements <u>from class ω_i</u>. As learning measurements from class ω_i arrive in the system we alter the likelihood computer for class ω_i as indicated by (4) in order to classify the next measurement, X.

II. The Likelihood Computer

For a more detailed view of the structure of the likelihood computer it is necessary to assume a particular form for the initial density $P(X)$. We assume the vector measurement X is adequately represented as a sample from a normal population with mean vector M and covariance matrix K. This is written

$$p(X) \sim N(M,K) \tag{6}$$

It is <u>not</u> necessary to assume that M and K are <u>known</u> for each class ω_i. In fact, in order to allow the possibility of learning we can assume <u>the parameters M and K are themselves random variables</u>. There are two possible interpretations of this assumption. The first is that there exists a "true" mean and covariance but we express our ignorance about them by assuming densities over the allowable values. This approach may be compared with an equivalent approach in the radar range estimation problem where an a priori density over the set of possible ranges is postulated even though there exists some true target range. A more fashionable view is that there exists an ensemble of normal densities, that one of these is chosen according to a probability measure over the ensemble, and that X is then chosen from this normal density.

When the mean and covariance are known (i.e., degenerate random variables) the structure of the likelihood computer is easily found. In this case

$$P(X) = [(2\pi)^d|K|]^{-1/2}\exp[-\tfrac{1}{2}(X-M)_t K^{-1}(X-M)] \tag{7}$$

where the subscript t denotes the transpose of a vector. A useful monotonic function of this density is

$$\ln P(X) = -\tfrac{1}{2}\ln[(2\pi)^d|K|] - \tfrac{1}{2}(X-M)_t K^{-1}(X-M) \tag{8}$$

Quantities not depending upon X in (8) may be absorbed into the comparator (Fig. 1) so that the likelihood is

$$L(X) = X_t K^{-1} M - \tfrac{1}{2} X_t K^{-1} X \tag{9}$$

The likelihood calculation consists of linear and quadratic data processing on the measurement X. Assume the covariance matrix is non-singular. Then K^{-1} is positive definite and can be written[2] $K^{-1} = K^{-1/2}_t K^{-1/2}$.

$$L(X) = (K^{-1/2}X)_t(K^{-1/2}M) - \tfrac{1}{2}(K^{-1/2}X)_t(K^{-1/2}X) \tag{10}$$

The matrix operation $K^{-1/2}$ on the measurement X or on the known mean M can be interpreted [3]as a linear <u>bleaching filter</u> which serves to whiten the variations about the mean. The linear term of (10) can be interpreted as a correlation of the bleached input measurement with the bleached mean vector; the quadratic term of (10) can be interpreted as an energy measurement on the bleached input.

The likelihood computer may be synthesized in a number of other ways depending upon how we choose to rearrange and interpret the terms of (9). For example, various forms of matched filter implementations are possible together with different forms of correlation and energy detection systems.[4,5]

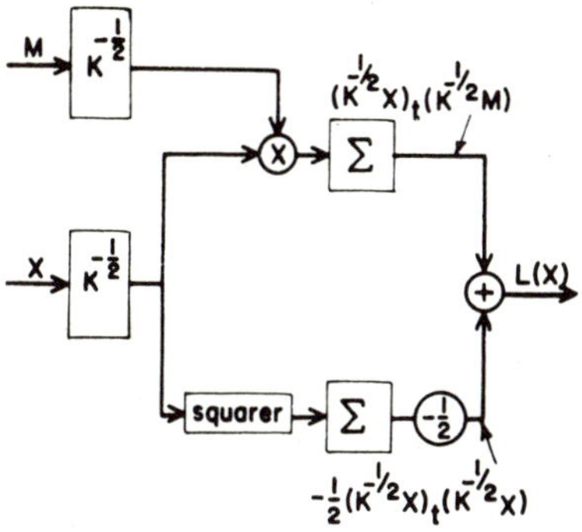

Fig. 3. Likelihood Computer for Known Mean and Covariance.

III. The Learning Process

Next consider the case where the mean vector M is itself a random variable. This is a more realistic assumption in most pattern recognition problems. Let M have a normal distribution* with mean vector μ and covariance matrix ϕ .

$$M \sim N(\mu,\phi) \tag{11}$$

In sections IV and V we investigate two cases when the mean M is normally distributed. The present discussion of the structure of the likelihood computer is directly applicable to these situations.

In order to find the distribution of X when the mean M is normally distributed as in (11) we might average the distribution of (6) over all values of the random mean, M . A simpler method is to note that X may be written as the sum of a random mean M and an independent noise N

$$X = M + N \tag{12}$$

where N is a normal vector with zero mean and covariance K ,

$$N \sim N(0,K) \ . \tag{13}$$

Thus X must also be normal with mean equal to the sum of the means and covariance equal to the sum of the covariances,

$$X \sim N(\mu,K + \phi) \ . \tag{14}$$

Equation (14) expresses a most significant result. It says if we determine that the mean of our normal measurements is a random variable, normally distributed as in (11), the measurement can be treated as a sample from a normal population with mean μ and covariance $K + \phi$. Loosely speaking, it says if we do not know the mean exactly we should use our "best guess" of the mean (i.e., μ) as if it were the exact mean and increase the covariance matrix (from K to $K + \phi$) to account for our uncertainty in the mean.

*We indicate means and covariances of the measurement X by Roman letters, while those of M are denoted by Greek letters.

The likelihood computer for this situation is structurally identical to that of Fig. 3 if we replace M by μ and K by $K + \phi$. As we now show, however, there are important differences in the likelihood computer using μ and $K + \phi$ and the computer of Fig. 3. These differences stem from the fact that μ and ϕ can be functions of the learning measurements.

The evolution of μ and ϕ as we acquire new learning measurements allows us to realize the learning process of (4). Before acquiring any learning measurements we assume $P(M)$, the initial density of M , is normal with mean μ_o and covariance matrix ϕ_o . After obtaining the first learning measurement we use Bayes law to find the new, conditional distribution of M .

$$P(M|X_1) = \frac{P(X_1|M)\ P(M)}{P(X_1)} \tag{15}$$

The terms involving M on the right side of (15) are

$$\exp[-\tfrac{1}{2}(X_1-M)_t K^{-1}(X_1-M)]\exp[-\tfrac{1}{2}(M-\mu_o)\phi_o^{-1}(M-\mu_o)] . \tag{16}$$

We can complete the square[6] in (16) to obtain

$$\exp[-\tfrac{1}{2}(M-\mu_1)_t\ \phi_1^{-1}(M-\mu_1)] \ , \tag{17}$$

where

$$\mu_o = K(\phi_o + K)^{-1}\ \mu_o + \phi_o(\phi_o + K)^{-1}X_1 \tag{18a}$$

$$\phi_1 = K(\phi_o + K)^{-1}\ \phi_o \tag{18b}$$

are the mean and covariance of the a posteriori density.

After taking another learning measurement X_2 we may use an induction argument to obtain a new a posteriori density $P(M|X_2,X_1)$ starting from $P(M|X_1)$. The new density will also be normal and the new mean and covariance may be calculated from (18). The normal density (for $P(M)$) reproduces itself as we obtain new learning observations. Under the assumption of normal statistics, the learning process of (4) reduces to a learning process on the parameters μ and ϕ , i.e.,

$$\mu_o \to \mu_1 \to \mu_2 \cdots \to \mu_k \tag{19a}$$

$$\phi_o \to \phi_1 \to \phi_2 \cdots \to \phi_k \ . \tag{19b}$$

Since only the parameters of the density change with the acquisition of learning measurements, only the parameters of the learning system, and not its form, are affected by learning measurements. We therefore call the system an adaptive correlator.

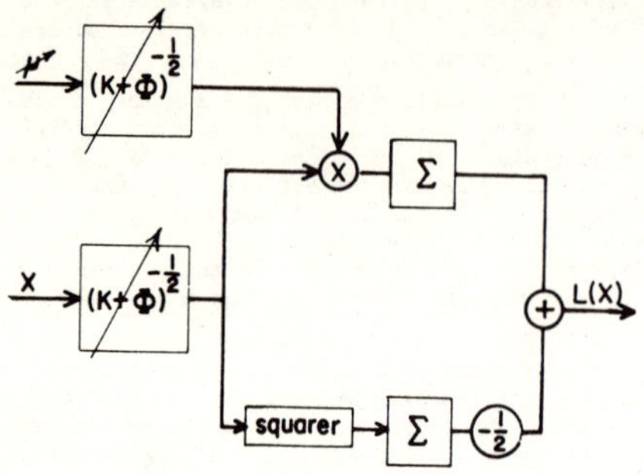

Fig. 4. Adaptive Correlator Likelihood Computer

It is also possible[7] to give arguments for a self-reproducing density on the covariance K . However, we have not yet been able to find a ready interpretation for these arguments in terms of the optimum recognition system.

IV. Locking on to a Pattern

To illustrate the approach discussed above consider the case where M , the unknown mean of class ω_1 , does not change as we acquire learning measurements. We assume the initial density of M is $N(\mu_o, \phi_o)$. In pattern recognition terminology this problem corresponds to a recognition of unknown perfect patterns immersed in a random environment. Using induction on (18) we calculated the conditional mean and covariance of M after k learning measurements, $X_1, X_2, \cdots, X_k$. Let the sample mean be

$$\langle X \rangle = \frac{1}{k} \sum_{i=1}^{k} X_i \qquad (20)$$

then

$$\mu_k = (k^{-1}K)(\phi_o + k^{-1}K)^{-1}\mu_o + \phi_o(\phi_o + k^{-1}K)^{-1}\langle X \rangle \qquad (21a)$$

$$\phi_k = (k^{-1}K)(\phi_o + k^{-1}K)^{-1}\phi_o \qquad (21b)$$

Equation (21) shows μ_k is a weighted average of the a priori mean and the sample mean. The nature of this mixture is seen more easily in the special case where

$$\phi_o = \frac{1}{\alpha} K \qquad (22)$$

where α is some positive constant. Then (21) becomes

$$\mu_k = \frac{\alpha}{k+\alpha}\,\mu_o + \frac{k}{k+\alpha}\langle X \rangle \qquad (23a)$$

$$\phi_k = \frac{1}{k+\alpha} K \qquad (23b)$$

When the covariance of M is large ($\alpha \ll 1$) the conditional mean μ_k weights the initial mean μ_o lightly; and the sample mean heavily. When the covariance of M is small ($\alpha \gg 1$) the conditional mean tends to retain its initial value of μ_o even if the sample mean differs a great deal from μ_o . Accordingly, the constant α is termed the dogmatism of the pattern class.

Returning to the more general equation (21), we see that as k increases the system locks onto the unknown pattern, that is, μ_k approaches $\langle X \rangle$ and ϕ_k approaches 0 . The adaptive correlator learns the true mean and the system reverts to that of Fig. 3.

V. Tracking Wandering Patterns

Another case of interest in pattern recognition is the tracking of a wandering pattern. For example, in automatic word recognition problems, we might use the results of Section 4 to lock onto word patterns as spoken by a single speaker. If the speaker is changed we might expect the statistics of the various words to alter slightly. In this section we discuss the problem of tracking slowly varying statistics in a random environment.

As before, we assume k vector learning measurements $X_1, X_2, \cdots, X_k$ and a vector to be classified, X . The X_j are taken to be the sum of M_j , a mean depending upon j and a noise N_j

$$X_j = M_j + N_j \; . \qquad (24)$$

The noise vectors from measurement to measurement are assumed independent while the M_j are related by the recursion relation

$$M_j = aM_{j-1} + \Delta_{j-1} \; , \qquad (25)$$

where a is a constant scalar ($0 < a < 1$) and Δ_j is a normal vector, also independent from measurement to measurement. Let Δ_j have mean 0 and covariance ϕ_Δ . As in Section 4, the problem is one of computing the conditional mean and covariance of M ,

$$\mu_k = E[M_{k+1} | X_k, X_{k-1}, \cdots, X_1] \qquad (26a)$$

$$\phi_k = \mathrm{cov}[M_{k+1} | X_k, X_{k-1}, \cdots, X_1] \qquad (26b)$$

In appendix A we show

$$\mu_k = K(\phi_{k-1} + K)^{-1} a\mu_{k-1} + \phi_{k-1}(\phi_{k-1} + K)^{-1} aX_k \qquad (27a)$$

$$\phi_k = a^2 K(\phi_{k-1} + K)^{-1}\phi_{k-1} + \phi_\Delta \qquad (27b)$$

If M_j is a stationary, vector valued random process we must have

$$\phi_\Delta = (1 - a^2)\, \phi_o \quad . \tag{28}$$

We are interested in the steady state behavior of μ_k and ϕ_k. For large k, $\phi_k \approx \phi_{k-1}$, and we may solve (27b) for ϕ_k. When the mean is slowly varying $(a \approx 1)$ this solution is

$$\phi_k \approx [\phi_\Delta K^{-1}]^{1/2} K \tag{29}$$

Using (29) in (27a) and expanding $[I + (\phi_\Delta K^{-1})^{\frac{1}{2}}]^{-1}$ in a Neumann series[8] we get

$$\mu_k \approx [I - (\phi_\Delta K^{-1})^{1/2}]\mu_{k-1} + (\phi_\Delta K^{-1})^{1/2} X_k \tag{30}$$

Equation (30) shows the new mean μ_k is a mixture of the old mean and the new observation. Again an example will serve to bring out the significance of the results. Assume

$$\phi_\Delta = \beta^2 K \tag{31}$$

where β^2 is a constant. We call β^2 the <u>drift-to-noise ratio</u>. In this case (29) and (30) become

$$\phi_k = \beta K \tag{32}$$

$$\mu_k = (1 - \beta)\mu_{k-1} + \beta X_k \tag{33}$$

We track the pattern by adding βX_k onto an attenuated version of the previous estimate of the pattern. In this manner we follow the slowly varying pattern as new learning measurements arrive.

VI. Binary Recognition

The material of the last three sections dealt with pattern recognition when the input measurement might belong to one of c possible classes. Several pattern recognition systems built recently have restricted the number of possible classes to two; others have employed a combination of b binary decisions to obtain separation into 2^b classes. It is therefore of some interest to investigate our model when c, the number of classes, is set equal to two.

For simplicity we examine only the case of fixed unknown mean, treated in Section IV. We assume the initial distribution of the mean M for each of our two classes is $N(0, \frac{1}{\alpha} K)$ where α is the dogmatism, defined in (22). Finally we assume $K = \sigma^2 I$ where σ^2 is some constant and I is the identity matrix. If $X_1, X_2, \cdots, X_k$ are k learning observations from class ω_i and $Y_1, Y_2, \cdots Y_k$ are k learning observations from class ω_j, then for large k, the two likelihoods are

$$L^{(i)}(X) = \frac{1}{\sigma^2} X_t < X > \tag{34a}$$

$$L^{(j)}(X) = \frac{1}{\sigma^2} X_t < Y > \tag{34b}$$

where

$$< X > = \frac{1}{k} \sum_{i=1}^{k} X_i \quad \text{and} \quad < Y > = \frac{1}{k} \sum_{j=1}^{k} Y_j \tag{35}$$

The comparator compares $L^{(i)}(X) - \frac{1}{2\sigma^2} <X>_t <X>$ with $L^{(j)}(X) - \frac{1}{2\sigma^2} <Y>_t <Y>$ and selects the larger of these quantities. An equivalent procedure is to compute $L^{(i)}(X) - L^{(j)}(X)$ and compare this difference of likelihoods with a threshold $\frac{1}{2\sigma^2}(<X>_t <X> - <Y>_t <Y>)$.

We see that an optimum system for the recognition of two patterns requires a variable weighting of the input data, according to $<X> - <Y>$, and a variable threshold proportional to $(<X>_t <X> - <Y>_t <Y>)$. This discussion suggests that a simplified, non-optimum binary recognition system might compare the difference $L^{(i)}(X) - L^{(j)}(X)$ with a <u>fixed</u> threshold set at zero.

$$k\sigma^2[L^{(i)}(X) - L^{(j)}(X)] = X_t[\sum_{i=1}^{k} X_i - \sum_{j=1}^{k} Y_j] \tag{36}$$

The sub-optimum, binary recognition system with fixed threshold set at 0, obtained from (36), is shown in Figure 5.

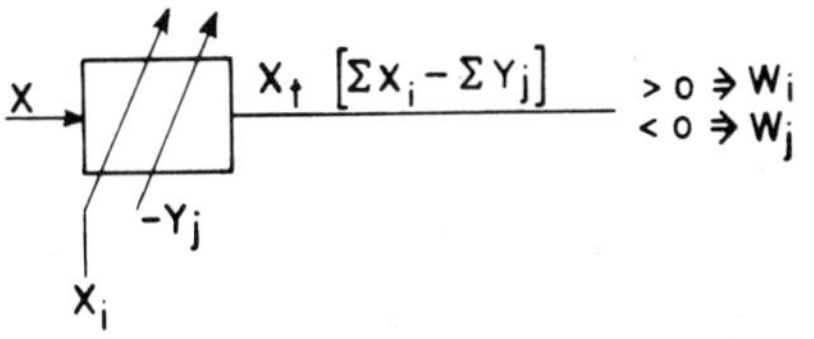

Fig. 5. A Sub-Optimum Binary Recognition System

Learning measurements from class ω_i are used to bias a set of weights in one direction while learning measurements from class ω_j bias the same weights in an opposite direction. As a result the pattern $[\sum X_i - \sum Y_j]$ is constructed and used to correlate with an input X. A threshold setting on the output makes the final decision. The simplest system employing a variable threshold which has been constructed along these lines appears to be ADALINE[9], although a number of variations[10,11] are possible.

Appendix A

In this appendix we calculate

$$\mu_k = E[M_{k+1} | X_k, X_{k-1}, \cdots, X_1] \tag{A-1}$$

$$\phi_k = \mathrm{cov}[M_{k+1} | X_k, X_{k-1}, \cdots, X_1] \tag{A-2}$$

where the quantities involved are defined in Section V. Let us define

$$\mu' = E[M_k | X_k, X_{k-1}, \cdots, X_1] \quad \text{(A-3)}$$

$$\phi' = \text{cov}[M_k | X_k, X_{k-1}, \cdots, X_2] \quad . \quad \text{(A-4)}$$

Since

$$M_{k+1} = aM_k + \Delta_k \quad \text{(A-5)}$$

we have

$$\mu_k = a\mu' \quad \text{(A-6)}$$

$$\phi_k = a^2\phi' + \phi_\Delta \quad . \quad \text{(A-7)}$$

Now to find μ' and ϕ' we use (15) and (18) by identifying the a priori density $P(M)$ in (15) with $P(M_k | X_{k-1}, X_{k-2}, \cdots, X_1)$ and $P(X_1|M)$ in (15) with $P(X_k|M_k)$. Then

$$\mu' = K(\phi_{k-1} + K)^{-1} \mu_{k-1} + \phi_{k-1}(\phi_{k-1} + K)^{-1} X_k \quad \text{(A-8)}$$

$$\phi' = K(\phi_{k-1} + K)^{-1} \phi_{k-1} \quad \text{(A-9)}$$

and the solution follows immediately from (A-6) and (A-7).

Acknowledgement

Some of the work reported in this paper was performed by one of the authors (N.A.) as a consultant for ITT Federal Laboratories, Palo Alto, a division of International Telephone and Telegraph Corp.

References

1. Braverman, D., Learning Filters for Optimum Pattern Recognition, Trans. I.R.E., PGIT-8, July 1962.

2. Guillemin, E., The Mathematics of Circuit Analysis, John Wiley and Sons, Inc., New York, N.Y., 1949.

3. Kailath, T., Correlation Detection of Signals Perturbed by a Random Channel, Trans. I.R.E., PGIT-6, June 1960.

4. Kailath, T., Communication via Randomly Varying Channels, Dept. of Electrical Engineering, Mass. Inst. of Technology, Cambridge, Mass; May 1961.

5. Middleton, D., An Introduction to Statistical Communication Theory, McGraw Hill Inc., New York, 1960.

6. Abramson, N., Learning in Pattern Recognition, First Technical Note, AF30(602)-2278, ITT Federal Laboratories, Palo Alto.

7. Raiffa H. and Schlaifer, Applied Statistical Decision Theory, Division of Research, Harvard Business School, Harvard University, Boston, Mass., 1961, pp.318-321.

8. Riesz, F. and Nagy, B., Functional Analysis Frederick Ungar Co., New York, 1955.

9. Widrow, B., and Hoff, M., Adaptive Switching Circuits, Tech. Report No. 1553-1, Stanford Electronics Laboratories, Stanford, Calif., June 30, 1960.

10. Rosenblatt, F., The Perceptron; A Theory of Statistical Separability in Cognitive Systems, Report No. VG1196-G-1, Cornell Aeronautical Laboratory, Buffalo, N.Y.

11. Uffelman, M., Conflex I - A Conditional Reflex System, 1962 I.R.E. Convention Record, Session 20.

Reprinted from *IRE Trans. Inform. Theory,* **IT–8,** No. 5, 1962, pp. S82–S91

8

PATTERN RECOGNITION BY AN ADAPTIVE PROCESS OF SAMPLE SET CONSTRUCTION

George S. Sebestyen
Litton Systems, Inc.
Waltham, Massachusetts

Summary

A pattern recognition technique is described in which a parametric representation of input signals or stimuli is employed. An input is considered as a vector, while the stimulus class is a multivariate process in the vector space. An adaptive sample set construction technique is described through which the conditional joint probability density of a class is approximated by the sum of Gaussian densities. The mean of each such density is an adaptively chosen "typical" sample of the class, and the set of samples so chosen are contained in the region of the space in which samples of the class are most populous. The decision process using the typical samples partitions the space into regions that envelop the chosen samples of a class. Arbitrary shaped and multiply connected regions can be constructed in this way, and multimodal probability densities can be approximated with a computationally simple procedure. Decision making on an incomplete set of parameters and on multiple observations of the input stimulus are discussed. This technique was successfully applied to the automatic recognition of speaker identity regardless of the spoken test. Experimental results are given.

Introduction

The common starting point of all pattern recognition techniques is a parametric representation of the physical world. Visual images are represented by the intensities of cells in a two-dimensional field, band-limited electrical signals by the magnitudes of samples taken at the Nyquist rate, and human speech signals by the numerical values of a set of its distinctive features. In a representation of this type, an input signal or stimulus is described by the set of numerical values obtained when quantitative measurements are made on a set of its attributes. Attributes or parameters can be thought of as coordinates of a vector, and input stimuli can be considered as points in a finite dimensional vector space. Alternatively an input stimulus may be regarded as a member function of a multivariate random process which corresponds to the stimulus class. A single speech sound uttered by a specific talker is an example of an input stimulus, while continuous speech by the talker in question is the stimulus class which altogether too often is a random process.

In addition to providing a parametric representation of the physical world, pattern recognition techniques must perform two basic functions. First, they must provide a means for characterizing classes from a small number of their members, and then, they must recognize a new input stimulus and classify it as a member of one of several classes. Machine learning, the automatic accomplishment of the first of these functions, requires partitioning the vector space into regions so that each region should contain mostly members of a single class. The regions so constructed characterize the classes. The second function, that of classifying new inputs, consists of the determination of the region of the vector space in which the new input is contained. Different pattern recognition techniques differ from one another chiefly in the manner in which they construct regions from a finite set of points and in the limitations on the type of regions they are able to construct. The block diagram shown in Fig. 1 illustrates a general pattern recognition system that exhibits all of the functions discussed above. The parameter extractor is used to represent the machine's environment as a vector in an N-dimensional vector space, machine learning is employed to determine, from sample inputs, the best method of partitioning the space into different decision regions, and the decision device, which implements the regions designed through machine learning, evaluates new input stimuli and classifies them according to the region in which they are contained.

Many of the current techniques of machine learning and decision making have been motivated by biological models. Other techniques that have been developed were motivated by probabilistic decision making but were restricted even in their theoretical execution by considerations of equipment complexity. We thus have techniques that approximate likelihood ratio computers, but usually only under the most elementary assumptions about the stimulus class probability densities. Most of the resulting machines are linear,

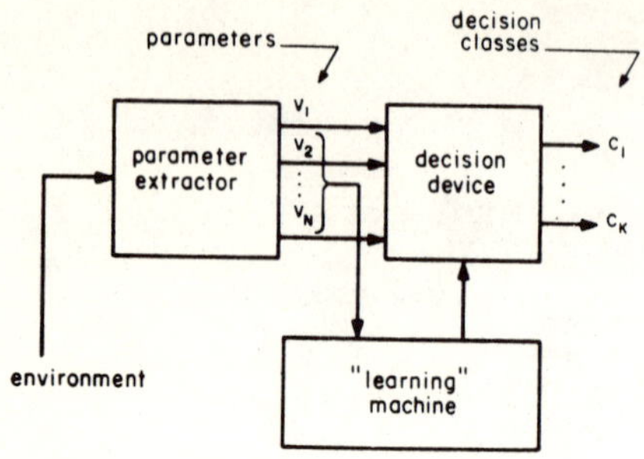

Fig. 1
General pattern recognition system

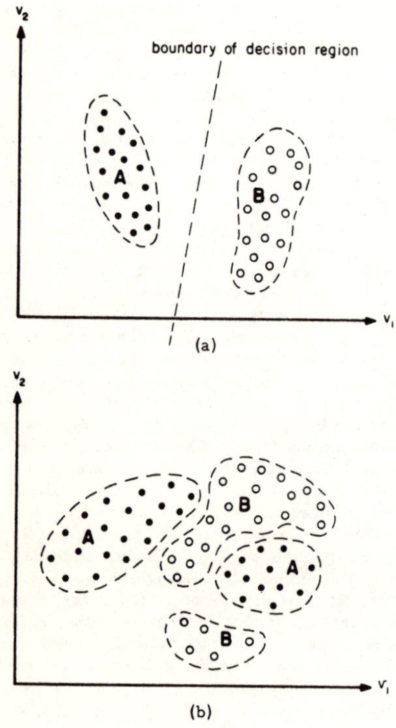

Fig. 2
Different distributions of two classes

employing only linear discriminants, i.e. correlations with stored reference vectors or comparisons of weighted combinations of the parameters. Hyperplanes are used to partition the space of measurable input parameters to separate members of one stimulus class from those of another. Combinations of these linear techniques with logical rules, of course, can construct boundaries to quite complex distributions. These methods are useful if classes are contained in disjointed, well-separated, simply-connected regions of the space, and they can even be made optimum (in the sense that the probability of decision errors can be minimized) under certain special circumstances. If two classes are Gaussian processes with equal covariance matrices, for instance, a hyperplane that partitions the space can discriminate optimally between members of the two classes.

In many practical problems, such as the speaker recognition problem to be described later, the classes are not linearly separable (not separable by hyperplanes) and their members are not contained in disjointed simply-connected regions of the space of observable parameters. In these cases a better approximation of likelihood ratio computation is required than that provided by linear discriminants. This is illustrated in Fig. 2 where members of the different classes are contained in regions labeled A and B. These classes are linearly separable in Fig. 2a but not in the more complex distribution shown in Fig. 2b.

Approximation of Likelihood Ratio Computation

From the point of view of maximizing the probability of correct decision, the a posteriori probability of each of the stimulus classes must be evaluated, and the boundaries of the decision regions must be determined on the basis of a comparison of these probabilities. Without loss of generality, this is stated by (1) for the case where we wish to decide whether or not the observed vector $v = v_1, v_2, \ldots, v_N$ is more likely a member of stimulus class A than of B.

$$\text{Decide } v = v_1 \ldots v_N \in A, \text{ if } \frac{P(A \mid v_1 \ldots v_N)}{P(B \mid v_1 \ldots v_N)} > 1 \quad (1)$$

By the usual manipulations this decision rule can be expressed in terms of the conditional joint probability densities and the a priori probabilities of the classes A and B, as in (2).

Even if the a priori probabilities are unknown, as is the case in many practical applications, the functional form of the decision rule

S 83

remains unchanged. The likelihood ratio (ratio of conditional joint probability densities) is to be compared with a constant as shown in (3).

$$\frac{P(A \mid v_1 \ldots v_N)}{P(B \mid v_1 \ldots v_N)} = \frac{p(v_1 \ldots v_N \mid A)\, P(A)}{p(v_1 \ldots v_N \mid B)\, P(B)} \gtrless 1 \qquad (2)$$

$$\ell(v_1 \ldots v_N) = \frac{p(v_1 \ldots v_N \mid A)}{p(v_1 \ldots v_N \mid B)} \gtrless \frac{P(B)}{P(A)} = C \qquad (3)$$

The boundary between the region where v is classified a member of A and the region where it is classified B is the locus where the ratio of the two densities equals C. Thus the region of the space within which inputs are classified as members of a specific class is the region in which the density of members of that class exceeds by C the density of members of any other class.

Unfortunately the densities are usually unknown and classes are known to the decision maker only through a finite number of their samples. From knowledge of the correct decision at only a finite number of points, machine learning in pattern recognition attempts to define a decision for each point of the vector space. A computational procedure has already been developed to generate a generalized nonlinear discriminant that minimizes the expected error, while it defines a decision at every point of the space from knowledge of finite samples only.[1,2] The computational complexity of such a technique, however, limits its practical usefulness.

In many instances, particularly in applications where learning in real time is an important requirement, approximations to the probability densities of class populations by non-analytic means may be desired. The adaptive process of sample set construction described in this paper approximates the probability density of a class by a surface constructed from a set of "typical" samples of the class chosen from among those encountered while learning. The "typical" samples cover, more or less uniformly, the region of the space in which members of the class have been observed. The density in the neighborhood of the "typical" points is sampled, and a function that interpolates between the values of the probability density at each of these neighborhoods is used to approximate the probability density of the class, and hence, the decisions at all other points of the space.

It is readily appreciated that there are a large number of different ways in which the method of obtaining "typical" samples and interpolation functions can be postulated, the choice depending on the properties desired of the solution. Some of these have already been considered.[2] The specific method described here has been motivated, on the one hand, by the requirement that, as each new sample is introduced, the choice of selected samples be updated without requiring the storage or recall of all previous given inputs, and, on the other hand, by requiring ease of computations in decision making on incomplete sets of observations.

Approximation of a Probability Density

Let us consider the given sample population of a class to be represented by the union of normally distributed subpopulations, where each of the latter can be represented by its mean and covariance matrix. This is illustrated in Fig. 3, where the region occupied by members of class A is approximated by the union of circles representing equiprobable contours of Gaussian processes. For simplicity, these are shown to have equal variances in all directions and are assumed to have uncorrelated variables.

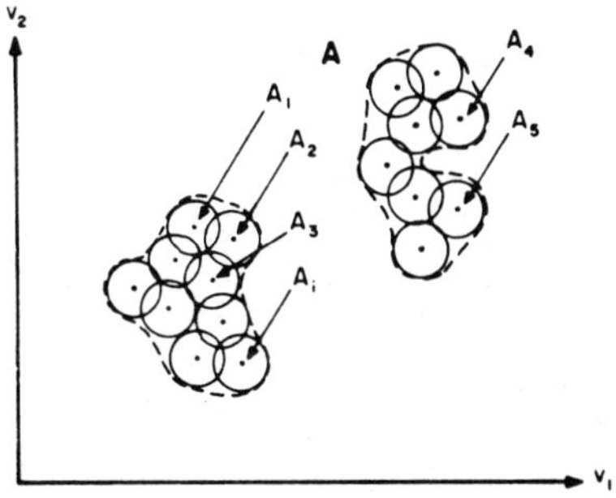

Fig. 3
Class A, the union of Gaussian processes

The decision that the vector v be termed a member of A rather than B can be written as in (4). In this equation the basic decision, "given the set of observations described by the vector v, is A more likely than B?" is transformed into the evaluation and comparison of sums of joint probability densities. K_A and K_B are the number of A and B subclasses, v is a vector of N dimensions, and $p(v \mid A_i)$ is the conditional probability density of subclass A_i. This is expressed in (5), where $m_n(A_i)$ is the n-th coordinate of the mean of the A_i subpopulation.

Decide $v \epsilon A$, if $\frac{P(A|v)}{P(B|v)} > 1$, where

$$\frac{P(A|v)}{P(B|v)} = \frac{p(v|A)P(A)}{p(v|B)P(B)} = \frac{\sum_{i=1}^{K_A} P(A_i)\,p(v|A_i)}{\sum_{j=1}^{K_B} P(B_j)\,p(v|B_j)} \qquad (4)$$

$$p(v|A_i) = \frac{1}{(\sqrt{2\pi}\,\sigma)^N} \exp\left(-\frac{1}{2\sigma^2}\sum_{n=1}^{N}[v_n - m_n(A_i)]^2\right) \qquad (5)$$

Since the a priori probability of Class A_i is proportional to M_i, the number of samples observed in the heighborhood of $m_n(A_i)$, the decision rule can be written as in (6), where the constant C is the ratio of the costs of the two kinds of decision errors (false alarm and false dismissal).

Decide $v \epsilon A$, if

$$\sum_{i=1}^{K_A} M_i \exp\left(-\frac{1}{2\sigma^2}\sum_{n=1}^{N}[v_n - m_n(A_i)]^2\right)$$

$$> C\sum_{j=1}^{K_B} M_j \exp\left(-\frac{1}{2\sigma^2}\sum_{n=1}^{N}[v_n - m_n(B_j)]^2\right) \qquad (6)$$

Fig. 4 illustrates in one dimension the manner in which the sum of Gaussian densities approximates an arbitrary but slowly varying probability density.

In the decision rule given in (6), all but a few terms are essentially zero. If the input vector v is near the mean of subclass A_i - that is, if v is near the center of the i-th circle in Fig. 3 - then only those terms that have means near $m(A_i)$ contribute significantly to the left hand side of the inequality. The numerical value of the left hand side of (6) is a measure of the number of samples of A near v, weighted according to their distances from v. The comparison of the measures of the numbers of A and B samples near v is a qualitative approximation of the likelihood ratio computation.

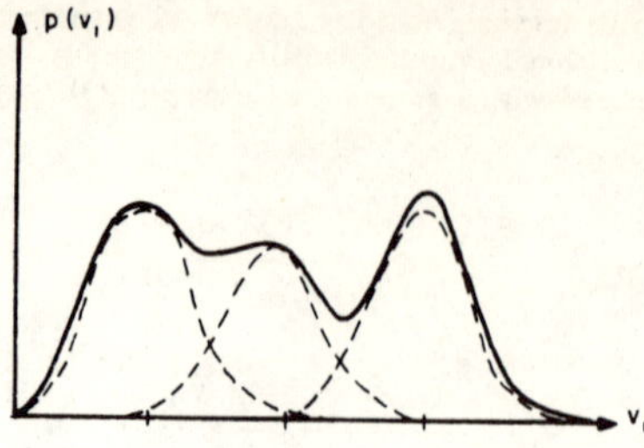

Fig. 4
Approximation of a probability density

Adaptive Sample Set Construction

The selection of the set of points $m(A_i)$ and $m(B_j)$, the means of the A and B subpopulations, can be approximated by a step-by-step adaptive procedure. The optimum choice of subclass means is not guaranteed by this procedure, but its usefulness is evidenced by its simplicity and by low error probabilities obtained in a number of practical problems.

Assuming that the memory of the system is empty at the start of the procedure, let us consider the construction of the sample set, step-by-step, as a set of labeled members of class A and B are introduced sequentially. When the first input is introduced, assuming it is a member of A, it is assigned to subclass A_1 and is assumed to be its mean. The sample is stored as $m(A_1)$ and the number of observed samples in the neighborhood of $m(A_1)$, M_1, is set equal to one.

The second input (assume that it also belongs to A) is now introduced. If this sample is within an as yet arbitrary threshold distance, T, of $m(A_1)$, it is assigned to A_1, $m(A_1)$ is updated by recomputing the mean of the two samples of A_1, and M_1 is set equal to two. If, on the other hand, the second input is not within a distance T of $m(A_1)$, it is assigned to A_2 and is assumed to be its mean, $m(A_2)$. It is then put in storage together with M_2, the number of occurrences of A_2. At this stage M_2 equals one.

This procedure is continued as additional vectors are introduced. A known sample of class A is compared with each of the stored synthetic samples, $m(A_i)$ to determine the one nearest the input vector. If the minimum distance between v and the stored $m(A_i)$ samples is less than T, v is assigned to A_i, $m(A_i)$ is updated, and M_i is increased by one. If the distance between v and the nearest stored sample exceeds T, a new subclass of A is created and v is assumed its mean. Samples of other classes are processed similarly.

With the sample set constructed in this way, the probability density of a class can be approximated by the sum of Gaussian densities. The mean of each such density is a "typical" sample of the class and the set of samples so chosen cover the region of the space in which the known samples of the class are contained. The magnitude of the threshold T is generally on the order of σ, while both are determined on the basis of limitations imposed on the number of stored subpopulation means. The larger T, the fewer stored samples will cover the region of the space in which the population of a class is contained.

Classification Based on Multiple and Incomplete Observations

The practical application of adaptive sample set construction, to be described later, departs in two respects from the usual problems in pattern recognition: a) decision making can be based on the repeated observation of a set of parameters, and b) not all measured parameters are available during each observation. Decision making in each of these cases is discussed next.

Decisions Based on Incomplete Observations

The problem of decision making has been treated as the problem of comparing the probability densities of N statistically dependent parameters on the input. In many practical instances, however, all N parameters are not always measurable. Some of the parameters (say L of them) maybe missing either because of malfunction of L instruments or because of reasons otherwise beyond our control. It can be shown that the optimum decision based on N-L variables is based on the N-L variate marginal probability densities.[2] The resulting decision rule (assuming, without loss of generality, that the last L parameters are missing) is given in (7). Following the steps already taken in (1) through (4), we obtain (8) and (9). In (9) the probability density of the N-L observed variables is expressed by substituting the Gaussian form from (5). Because of the independence of the variables in (5), the marginal densities appearing in (8) can be obtained by inspection.

$$\text{Decide } v_1 \dots v_{N-L} \in A, \text{ if } \frac{P(A \mid v_1 \dots v_{N-L})}{P(B \mid v_1 \dots v_{N-L})} > 1 \tag{7}$$

$$\frac{P(A \mid v_1 \dots v_{N-L})}{P(B \mid v_1 \dots v_{N-L})} = \frac{\sum_{i=1}^{K_A} P(A_i)\, p(v_1 \dots v_{N-L} \mid A_i)}{\sum_{j=1}^{K_B} P(B_j)\, p(v_1 \dots v_{N-L} \mid B_j)} \tag{8}$$

$$\frac{P(A \mid v_1 \dots v_{N-L})}{P(B \mid v_1 \dots v_{N-L})} = \frac{\sum_{i=1}^{K_A} P(A_i) \exp\left(-\frac{1}{2\sigma^2} \sum_{n=1}^{N-L} [v_n - m_n(A_i)]^2\right)}{\sum_{j=1}^{K_B} P(B_j) \exp\left(-\frac{1}{2\sigma^2} \sum_{n=1}^{N-L} [v_n - m_n(B_j)]^2\right)} \tag{9}$$

Since $P(A_i)$ is proportional to M_i, the decision rule can be written in a form directly comparable to (6), the rule used when all N parameters can be observed. A comparison of (10), the rule applicable when decisions must be based on incomplete observations, with (6) reveals the nature and the simplicity of the change that must be made on the decision rule if a subset of the parameters is missing. The contribution to the quadratic form of the terms corresponding to the missing parameters must be ignored. It should be noted that even if the variances associated with each parameter and each subpopulation were different, the decision rule applicable when decisions must be based on incomplete observations would be only slightly more complicated.

Decide $v \in A$, if

$$\sum_{i=1}^{K_A} M_i \exp\left(-\frac{1}{2\sigma^2} \sum_{n=1}^{N-L} [v_n - m_n(A_i)]^2\right) > C \sum_{j=1}^{K_B} M_j \exp\left(-\frac{1}{2\sigma^2} \sum_{n=1}^{N-L} [v_n - m_n(B_j)]^2\right) \tag{10}$$

S 86

Decisions Based on Multiple Observations

If a classification decision can be based on the cumulative evidence collected from r repeated observations, the probability of correct recognition can usually be increased over that obtained with decisions based on a single look. This is an inportant fact in speaker recognition where it will result in the recognition of the speaker with a certainty that increases with the length of time the speaker is under observation.

If $v_k = v_{k1}, v_{k2}, \ldots, v_{kN}$ represents the set of N parameter values measured during the k-th observation, and if the different observations are statistically independent, the optimum procedure for deciding whether or not the set of r observations of the N parameters is more likely caused by a stimulus from class A or by one from class B is given by (11). Note that v_k, in this equation, represents the set of N parameter measurements during the k-th look. It does not represent the k-th parameter value of an observation (i. e., v_k is a vector quantity).

Decide that the vectors $v_1 \ldots v_r \in A$, if

$$\frac{P(A)}{P(B)} \frac{\prod_{k=1}^{r} p(v_{k1} \ldots v_{kN} | A)}{\prod_{k=1}^{r} p(v_{k1} \ldots v_{kN} | B)} = \frac{P(A)}{P(B)} \prod_{k=1}^{r} \ell(v_k) > 1 \qquad (11)$$

The decision based on multiple observations is thus based on the product of likelihood ratios computed at each of the r observation instances.

The reduction of the probability of error resulting from decisions based on multiple observations can now be computed if the likelihood ratio of each observation is known. The relationship between the error probability and the likelihood ratio of a specific observation is given in (12), while the error probability based on r specific observations is expressed in terms of the likelihood ratio of each observation in (13). The result is derived in Reference 3 and is briefly summarized in the Appendix.

$$P(\text{error}|v_k) = \frac{1}{1 + \left[\frac{P(B)}{P(A)} \ell(v_k)\right]}, \quad \text{for } \ell(v_k) > \frac{P(B)}{P(A)} \qquad (12)$$

$$P(\text{error} | v_1 \ldots v_r) = \frac{1}{1 + \left[\frac{P(B)}{P(A)} \prod_{k=1}^{r} \ell(v_k)\right]}, \quad \text{for } \prod_{k=1}^{r} \ell(v_k) > \frac{P(B)}{P(A)} \qquad (13)$$

In the above expressions, if the stated condition on the likelihood ratio does not hold, in (12) and (13) the inverse of the expression in the square bracket must be used.

By denoting $P(\text{error} | v_k) = P_k$, to simplify the notation, and solving for $\ell(v_k)$ in (12), the expression in (14) is obtained.

$$\ell(v_k) = \frac{P(A)}{P(B)} \left(\frac{1 - P_k}{P_k} \right) \qquad (14)$$

By substituting (14) into (13), the probability of error based on r observations is expressible in (15) in terms of the probability of error of the specific observations. To simplify the notation, the probability of error based on the r observations is denoted by P_r.

$$P_r = \frac{\prod_{k=1}^{r} P_k}{\prod_{k=1}^{r} P_k + \left[\frac{P(A)}{P(B)}\right]^{r-1} \prod_{k=1}^{r} (1-P_k)} \qquad (15)$$

In the special case where each likelihood ratio has the same value and P(A) = P(B), the probability of error resulting from r observations is expressible in terms of the probability of error resulting from a single observation, P_1. The relationship is given in (16) and is plotted in Fig. 5 for several values of P_1. For a single observation error probability of 0. 4, eleven observations are required before an error rate less than 1 percent is obtained. If the single observation error probability is 0. 3, only six observations are required, while an error probability of 0. 2 on single observations requires only four observations for the achievement of a less than 1 percent error rate.

$$P_r = \frac{P_1^r}{P_1^r + (1 - P_1)^r} \qquad (16)$$

In general, of course, the likelihood ratios of different observations are not equal, and the above simple formula cannot be used to predict the probability of error as a function of the number of observations. Yet, this formula gives some insight into the potential improvement achievable through multiple observations.

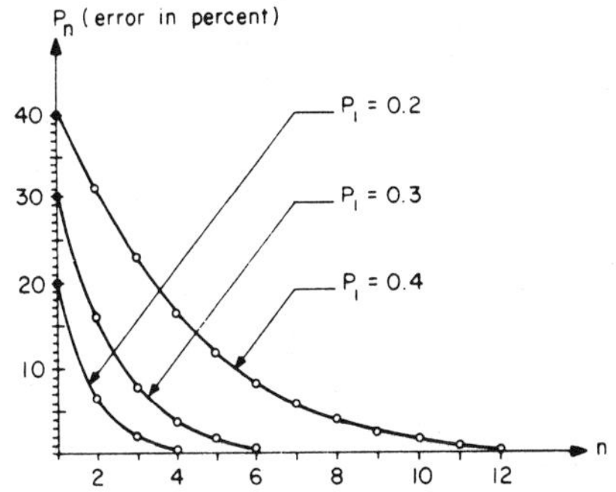

Fig. 5
Error probabilities as a function of the number of independent observations

Speaker Recognition

The above-described adaptive process of sample set construction was applied to the problem of designing a machine for the recognition of any one of a large number of speakers, regardless of the text they spoke. The problem to be solved was the design of a machine that could examine tape recordings of speech by many different speakers, learn the characteristics of each of the speakers, and then use this knowledge to recognize any one of the selected talkers, regardless of the spoken text. In an alternate mode of operation the machine was used to learn the characteristics of a specific speaker from tape recorded samples of his speech. The machine was then required to detect the desired speaker when he spoke again.

The first mode of operation required the machine to test the multiple hypothesis leading to a decision regarding the identity (among a finite number of speakers) of the talker presently speaking. In the second mode of operation, the machine was required to test the simple hypothesis leading to a determination of whether the present talker is the selected speaker or not.

Characterization of Speech Sounds

For the purpose of clarifying the illustration about to begin, we must very briefly review the human speech generating mechanism. As a rough approximation, humans are said to utter voiced and unvoiced sounds. Voiced sounds include most of the vowels, while unvoiced sounds contain most consonants. During the utterance of voiced sounds, the human speech generating mechanism can be approximated by the block diagram of Fig. 6. Although a number of slightly different models of speech exist, for purposes of the present illustration this model will suffice. It consists of a generator of approximately triangular shaped pulses feeding several band-pass filters with center frequencies variable over somewhat overlapping ranges. The pulse repetition frequency, commonly called pitch frequency, is largely responsible for the pitch of the human voice, while variations in the tuned frequencies and amplitudes of the four resonant circuits serve to form the various vowel sounds we utter. For this reason, the four resonant frequencies are called formant frequencies. During the utterance of unvoiced sounds, a different model, employing a noise generator must be used.

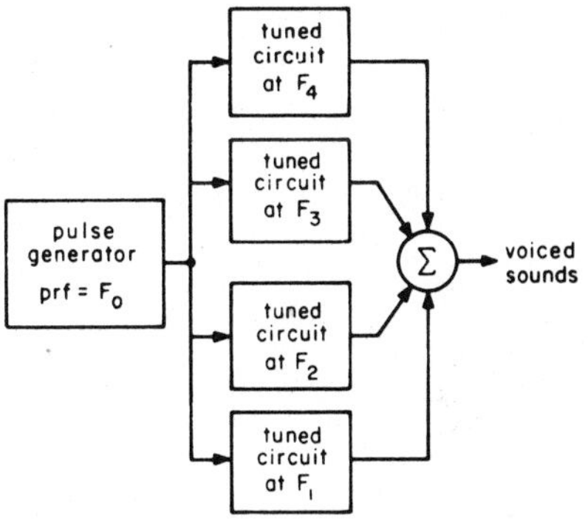

Fig. 6
Model for generating "voiced" sounds

It is evident, from the preceding, that human speech can be characterized parametrically (at least during the utterance of vowel sounds) by the sequence of instantaneous values that the network variables assume as a function of time. Such parametric descriptions of human speech have formed the bases of many investigations throughout the last twenty years or so. It is also evident that if speech can be characterized parametrically, so can the characteristics that account for the speaker's identity. To be sure useful parameters in addition to those already described may have to be added.

For purposes of speaker recognition it was postulated that sounds uttered by one speaker (as characterized by a suitable parametric description) are not identical, most of the time, to sounds uttered by another. Anatomical and other differences assure the discriminability of speakers. In the four-dimensional space of the four formant frequencies, for example, it was postulated that different speakers would have different probability densities. The library of sounds from which one speaker draws while speaking, differs from that from which other speakers draw. Minor differences in the sound probability densities can be exploited to identify the speaker.

Human speech was represented parametrically by the instantaneous and simultaneous observation of a set of 13 speech parameters. In the 13-dimensional space, continuous speech by a given talker can be thought of as a point moving as a function of time and generally occupying a multiply connected region of the space. Other talkers occupy largely overlapping but not identical regions of the space. The speech parameters employed in this study consisted of the four formant frequencies (locations of four local maxima of the instantaneous sound spectrum), the instantaneous sound intensity, the pitch frequency, and time derivatives of these six parameters. In addition to these twelve speech parameters, a binary parameter indicating whether the sound is voiced or unvoiced was also used. The latter was used more for switching purposes than as a speech parameter. In view of the results of a number of independent experiments corroborating the observed fact that speaker recognition capability rests primarily in the characteristics of the voiced sounds, unvoiced sounds and their characteristics were ignored in all speaker recognition experiments. The purpose of including time derivatives of the six basic speech parameters studied was to represent short time history and characteristics of speech mannerisms.

It is only fair to say that during the speaker recognition study several other speech parameters, not dependent on the spectrum, but dependent on long term observations, were found useful. The duty cycle of voiced to unvoiced intervals of speech, for example, was such a speech parameter. For the purposes of this paper, and for the achievement of sufficiently low speaker recognition error rates, however, the characterization of human speech by the above 13 speech parameters proved adequate.

A brief review of the nature of human speech characterized by means of formant frequencies may be interesting. Researchers have found that a different region corresponds to each voiced sound in the four-dimensional formant frequency space and that these regions are fairly disjointed. That is to say, only a modest overlap exists between the regions containing different vowel sounds. Thus the probability density of vowel sounds uttered by a speaker is expected to contain many modes. Sounds produced by a specific speaker are expected to lie in a multiply connected domain. Sounds uttered by another speaker are also expected to lie in a multiply connected domain with considerable overlap between the domains of the two speakers. This is a typical situation where we would expect linear discriminants, best fitting Gaussian probability densities, or hyperplanes to <u>fail</u> to separate sounds of different speakers. A glance at Fig. 7 illustrates the distribution of speech sounds in the two-dimensional linear manifold consisting of the first and second formant frequencies. This figure shows the distribution of

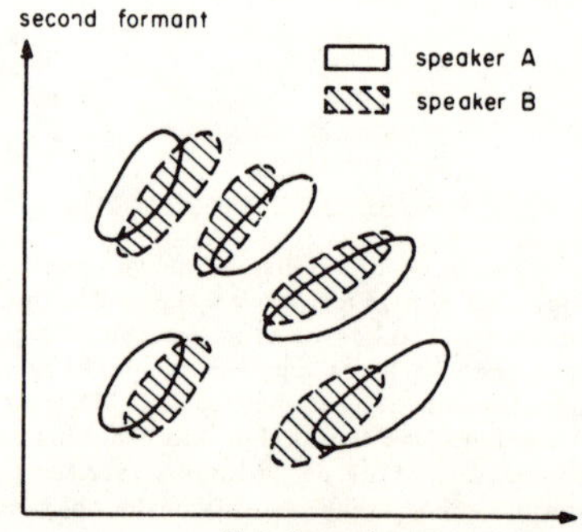

Fig. 7
Sound distributions of two speakers

speech sounds of two different speakers. The union of the solid regions indicate the region of the two-dimensional space in which sounds uttered by one speaker were contained while the shaded multiply connected region indicated with the dotted lines represents the boundary within which representations of vowel sounds of another

S 89

speaker were contained. The slight speaker to speaker differences in the location and shape of these regions are exploited by the adaptive process of sample set construction described above.

Experimental Procedures

As a result of simple experiments, coupled with intuition based on everyday experience, a few seconds of speech was found sufficient to "learn" a new speaker's voice characteristics. Therefore three phonetically balanced sentences, totaling approximately 18 seconds of speech, were recorded as spoken by each of 20 speakers including males and females. About half of the total of approximately 360 seconds of speech was voiced; the rest was silent or unvoiced.

Samples of the 13 speech parameters were taken at a rate of 50 samples per second. The typical results quoted in this paper were obtained on 11 of the 20 speakers, yielding a total of 5, 176 sampling instances and 67, 288 parameter readings. This data required 10, 353 punched cards for computer input.

Formant frequency measurements were obtained from sonagrams of the recorded speech by simulating a "peak-picking" formant tracking vocoder. The other speech parameters were obtained from a multichannel oscillograph recorder used to record instantaneous frequency, speech amplitude, the voiced-unvoiced binary waveform, and a 50 cps synchronizing clock frequency.

An IBM 7090 digital computer was programmed to perform the computations discussed in the preceding sections of this paper. Decision making on an incomplete set of parameters and on repeated observations of the set of parameter values was included in the computer program.

Incomplete sets of parameters are observed when the formant tracking vocoder fails to track a formant, either because less than four formants exist at the given instant of time, or because the instrument erroneously indicates a formant frequency value outside its permissible range. The first sampling instant after the onset of voicing is another common source of incomplete sets of parameter values. In this case the formant derivatives lie outside the acceptable range of values since the formant measurements rise from zero to a high value in a single sampling interval. On the punched cards an appropriate code indicated a parameter value missing for one of the above mentioned reasons.

The set of 13 speech parameter values represent the speaker's voice at only a single instant of time. Since usually several seconds of listening is permitted before the speaker's identity must be recognized, decision making can be based on multiple observations of the set of parameter values. Statistical independence of the observations is assured by taking samples only every 0. 2 second. In the English language this assures that successive observations originate from different syllables.

Results

Many automatic speaker recognition experiments were conducted involving a large number of different combinations of speakers and speech parameters.[4] The results of three different typical experiments are described below.

Experiment 1. In one of the first experiments, speaker recognition was learned from two phonetically balanced sentences spoken by each of two male speakers. With the aid of the technique already described, the characteristics of the two speakers were "learned" by the adaptive construction of their sample sets. Using the decision rule given in (6) or (10) and (11), the more probable of the two speakers (A or B) was determined from the utterance of a third sentence by each. The results of this experiment are tabulated in Fig. 8, and are included here because they demonstrate the improvement in performance resulting from an increase in the number of observations on which a decision is based. It is worthwhile to note that computations were performed by the computer at approximately 2-3 times real time.

Percent error in recognizing speaker	Decision was made in		
	20 msec	1 sec	2 sec
A	40. 2 %	31. 2%	21. 5%
B	4. 4%	1. 1%	0 %
Percent error	27. 3 %	15. 8%	10. 6%

Fig. 8
Error rates in Experiment 1

Experiment 2. Substantially the same experiment described above was performed on a collection of 11 speakers represented by more parameters. When decisions were based on 1 second of speech, no speaker recognition errors were made by the computer.

Experiment 3. In this experiment the probability density of a single "desired" speaker was approximated by the technique already described. Sounds contained in two sentences of the speaker were used in the approximation. The computer then determined a threshold value so that, 90% of the 1 second speech segments from the two sentences would yield above-threshold values of the decision variable. The decision variable is the product of the specific values of the probability density observed during 1 second of speech and sampled 5 times per second. Thus, on the sounds available to the computer for the characterization of the speaker's voice, 90% correct detection would be obtained after 1 second observation time.

The computer was then required to make the binary choice of declaring 1 second speech segments as originating from the desired speaker or from someone else. Of the approximately 75 seconds of speech by a number of other speakers, the computer decisions were in error 7% of the time. The probability of false alarm was thus 7%. It is interesting to note that when *new text* by the desired speaker was processed by the computer, 97% correct detection was achieved.

Conclusion

A simply-computed procedure is described for fitting a smooth function to a set of samples drawn from a random process having an arbitrary probability density. The procedure can be updated easily as new samples of the process are introduced, and it lends itself readily to optimum decision making even when an arbitrary combination of the parameters representing samples are missing.

Appendix

If A and B are mutually exclusive causes of the observation v_k, the optimum decision rule is given by (17).

$$\text{Decide } v_k \in A, \text{ if } P(A \mid v_k) > P(B \mid v_k) \qquad (17)$$

If the inequality holds in the direction indicated for a specific observation v_k, and we decide that the cause is A, the probability of being in error is $P(B \mid v_k)$. The probability of error is $P(A \mid v_k)$ if the inequality is reversed for the specific observation. Thus the probability of error is given by (18).

$$P(\text{error} \mid v_k) = \min\left[P(A \mid v_k),\ P(B \mid v_k)\right] \qquad (18)$$

By using the two equalities given by (19) and (20), the probability of error can be expressed in terms of the likelihood ratio, as in (21).

$$\frac{P(A \mid v_k)}{P(B \mid v_k)} = \frac{P(B)}{P(A)}\,\ell(v_k) \qquad (19)$$

$$P(A \mid v_k) + P(B \mid v_k) = 1 \qquad (20)$$

$$P(B \mid v_k) = P(\text{error} \mid v_k)$$

$$= \frac{1}{1 + \left[\frac{P(B)}{P(A)}\,\ell(v_k)\right]}, \quad \text{for } \ell(v_k) > \frac{P(B)}{P(A)} \qquad (21)$$

References

1. Sebestyen, G. S., "Classification Decisions in Pattern Recognition", Technical Report 381, M. I. T.; April 25, 1960.

2. ——————, "Decision Making Processes in Pattern Recognition", The Macmillan Company; 1962.

3. Nuttall, A. H., "Error Probabilities Conditioned on Specific Observations", Litton Internal Memorandum; December 20, 1961.

4. Litton Systems, Inc., "Voice Identification Study", Final Report on Contract No. AF30(602)-2499; 1962.

Feature Selection and Reduction

III

Editor's Comments on Papers 9 Through 12

9 **Marill and Green:** *On the Effectiveness of Receptors in Recognition Systems*

10 **Kailath:** *The Divergence and Bhattacharyya Distance Measures in Signal Selection*

11 **Watanabe:** *Karhunen–Loève Expansion and Factor Analysis. Theoretical Remarks and Applications*

12 **Chien and Fu:** *A Modified Sequential Recognition Machine Using Time-Varying Stopping Boundaries*

In most applications of recognition technology, the dimensionality of feature space tends to be very large, the number of dimensions typically ranging from 20 to 200. This great dimensionality is a major cause of the cost and practical limitations of recognition technology. Consequently, the choice of features and the reduction of the dimensionality of the feature space are important engineering problems. The available techniques for overcoming these problems fall into the following two categories: (1) selection of a "best" subset of features from a large initial set, taking into account both the cost of extracting each feature and the effectiveness of each feature in the classification process, and (2) transforming the feature space into a "reduced" feature space that has fewer coordinates than the original feature space with little reduction in the effectiveness of the recognizer.

One may envision these two categories of techniques as decomposing the feature extractor of Fig. 1 (page 1) into two or three components. One of these components is a device that transforms the "filtered data" of Fig. 1 into raw features. We refer to this as a *raw feature extractor.*

Another of these components is a *feature transformer* or *feature reducer,* which transforms each feature vector so that the dimensionality of the transformed feature space is smaller than that of the original feature space. In some cases the reducer also arranges the transformed features in their order of effectiveness for the classification process. In these cases the reducer also acts as a *feature orderer.*

Making the dimensionality, d, of the reduced feature space as small as possible is usually advantageous when the cost of the classifier depends heavily on the dimensionality of the feature vector. Such a situation may arise when the classifier stores a fixed number of prototype vectors for comparison against the reduced feature vector. This form of classifier must incorporate a number of storage elements that is linearly proportional to d. The reduction in the cost of the classifier resulting from the reduction in the dimensionality of the feature space must, of course, be balanced against the cost of the feature reducer.

The third component is a *feature selector,* which selects a subset of the features for the measurement process. The selector may operate on the outputs of either the raw feature extractor or the feature reducer. Applying a selection process to the raw feature extractor (or the feature reducer) is advantageous whenever the cost of extracting raw features (or reduced features) is significant.

The first two papers of this part, those by Marill and Green [Mar] and Kailath [Kai], develop distance measures that are useful in feature selection and feature ordering. The third paper, by Watanabe [Wat], describes how the Karhunen–Loève expansion may be used in feature reduction. (This expansion may also be used for feature ordering, by arranging the eigenvalues of the expansion in descending order.) The last paper, by Chien and Fu [Chi], describes a procedure for choosing features sequentially. By using a technique for feature ordering (such as the Karhunen–Loève expansion) it is possible to effectively combine sequential selection and feature reduction [Fu].

Reprinted from *IEEE Trans. Inform. Theory*, **IT-9**, No. 1, 1963, pp. 11–17

9

On the Effectiveness of Receptors in Recognition Systems*

T. MARILL†, MEMBER, IRE, AND D. M. GREEN‡

Summary—In the type of recognition system under discussion, the physical sample to be recognized is first subjected to a battery of *tests*; on the basis of the test results, the sample is then assigned to one of a number of prespecified categories.

The theory of how test results should be combined to yield an optimal assignment has been discussed in an earlier paper. Here, attention is focused on the tests themselves. At present, we usually measure the effectiveness of a set of tests empirically, *i.e.*, by determining the percentage of correct recognitions made by some recognition device which uses these tests. In this paper, we discuss some of the theoretical problems encountered in trying to determine a more formal measure of the effectiveness of a set of tests; a measure which might be a practical substitute for the empirical evaluation. Specifically, the following question is considered: What constitutes an effective set of tests, and how is this effectiveness dependent on the correlations among, and the properties of, the individual tests in the set?

Specific suggestions are considered for the case in which the test results are normally distributed, but arbitrarily correlated. The discussion is supported by the results of experiments dealing with automatic recognition of hand-printed characters.

* Received December 17, 1961; revised manuscript received, April 10, 1962. This research has been sponsored by Electronics Research Directorate, AFCRL, under Contract AF 19(604)-6632 and AF 19(628)-227.

† Bolt Beranek and Newman Inc., Cambridge, Mass.
‡ Bolt Beranek and Newman Inc., Cambridge, Mass., and Massachusetts Institute of Technology, Cambridge, Mass.

Introduction

We cannot hope, in this introduction, to do justice to the many papers, ideas and techniques that have been contributed to the young but already large field of automatic recognition. An extensive bibliography is given by Minsky [13]. Interesting discussions have been given by Bledsoe and Browning [2], Bomba [3], Doyle [5], Grimsdale, *et al.*, [6], Harmon [7], Hawkins [8], Highleyman [9], Minsky [14], Rosenblatt [15], Selfridge [17], Sherman [18], Uhr and Vossler [20] and Unger [21].

The present discussion applies to a specific type of recognition model, namely, the type that derives from, or is related to, *statistical classification theory* (Anderson [1]). Models of this type have been investigated with a certain degree of success by Chow [4], Marill and Green [12], Sebestyen [16], Smith and Klem [19] and Welch and Wimpress [22]. These models are of the following sort (see Fig. 1): In the first stage of the process, the input (a pattern, or object, or event) is subjected to a battery of *tests*, each of which generates a number. The term "receptor" is applied to the part of the system that performs this first stage of processing. The output of

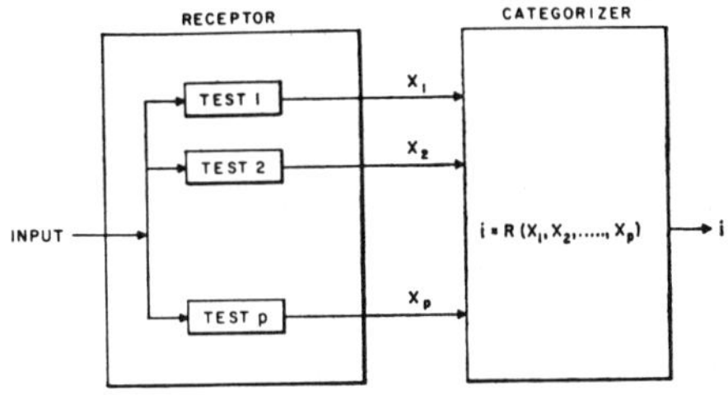

Fig. 1—Schematic representation of a recognition system.

the receptor may be represented as a p-dimensional column vector

$$\mathbf{X} = \begin{bmatrix} X_1 \\ X_2 \\ \vdots \\ X_p \end{bmatrix},$$

where p is the number of tests, and the ith component X_i is the output of the ith test. As an aid to intuition, we may find it useful to think of each test as measuring some property of the input; accordingly we speak of the various X_i as measurements, and of $\mathbf{X}$ as a measurement vector.

In the second stage of the process, the measurement vector is assigned by a decision procedure to one of a finite number of categories. The term "categorizer" is applied to the part of the system that performs this second stage of processing. The output of the categorizer may be represented as an integer $i = 1, 2, \cdots, m$, under the convention that output j is to mean that the categorizer has assigned the input to the jth of the m permissible categories.

The theory of optimal categorizers has been discussed by the authors in an earlier paper [12]. Here, our concern will be with the first stage of the process, the receptor. Insofar as the present theoretical formulation is concerned, there is no limit to the effectiveness of a receptor in a given situation. There is, therefore, no theory of the "optimal" receptor to match the theory of the optimal categorizer. What we shall attempt to do is to understand what is meant by the effectiveness of a set of tests and how this effectiveness depends on the properties of the individual tests and their interrelations. We shall not be concerned with what appears to be the much more difficult problem of how an effective set of tests actually may be discovered.

Geometric Interpretation: Criterion of Effectiveness

A receptor consisting of p tests may be thought of as mapping each input into a point of a p-dimensional space. Corresponding to each input category there exists, then, a set of points in the space. Since we wish to consider each category as having potentially infinitely many members, and since we place no restriction on the range of the output of any test, points from any category may fall anywhere in the space. It is fruitful, therefore, to think of each category as generating a certain *density* of points at each location in the space, or, in other words, to think of the (multivariate) probability density function corresponding to each category. Now, it is quite clear that if the mapping generated by the tests is such that, at each location in the space, the density due to category i is equal to the density due to category j, then *no* categorizer will be able to discriminate between these two categories. The tests that generate these separate mappings are then ineffective. On the other hand, if, by this mapping, category i generates a high density in one region of the space while category j generates a high density in a quite different region, then it should be possible to discriminate between these two categories, and the tests are said to be effective.

Roughly speaking, then, we may say that a set of tests generates a probability density corresponding to each input category, and that the ability of the tests to discriminate between two given categories depends upon the "distance" between the densities. We wish to consider, therefore, the formulation of such a "distance" measure in terms of the parameters of the densities involved. This distance will then reflect the effectiveness of the tests.

We must first ask what requirements we wish such a measure of effectiveness to fulfill. There is, it would seem, only one sensible criterion: *the measure must reflect the error probability of the recognition system incorporating the tests in question.* To put it more specifically: let ρ be a set of tests which maps input category i into probability density p_i ($i = 1, \cdots, m$); let P be a recognition system having ρ as receptor, and let e_{ij} be the probability that P will make an error in discriminating between category i and j (assuming these two categories to be *a priori* equally likely). We then assert that the relevant measure must be so formulated that the "distance" between p_i and p_j is large or small accordingly as e_{ij} is small or large.

Even this does not pin down the requirements sufficiently. The effectiveness of a recognition system depends, after all, not only on the tests used, but also on the adequacy of the decision-logic, or categorizer. Hence, the error probability e_{ij} is undefined so long as the categorizer is undefined. This difficulty may be circumvented in a theoretically satisfactory manner by agreeing that the categorizer in question be *optimal* with respect to ρ (in the sense of [12]).

In this view, then, the theory of the receptor is intertwined with the theory of the optimal categorizer. This implies that the former theory will be tractable only in those areas in which there is available an explicit formulation for the latter. Such a formulation was given in [12], following Anderson [1], for the special case in which the probability densities are normal. Accordingly, the discussion given below is also restricted to that case.

Normal Variables and Equal Covariance Matrices

Assume that we are dealing with a receptor which, for any i, maps inputs of category i into the (multivariate) normal density with mean $\mathbf{\mu}_i$ and with covariance matrix[1] $\mathbf{V}$. (This matrix being the same for all categories.) Thus, when the input is from category i, the measurement vector $\mathbf{X}$ has density (Anderson [1]):

$$p_i(\mathbf{X}) = \frac{1}{(2\pi)^{p/2}|\mathbf{V}|^{1/2}} \exp\left[-\tfrac{1}{2}(\mathbf{X}-\mathbf{\mu}_i)'\mathbf{V}^{-1}(\mathbf{X}-\mathbf{\mu}_i)\right].$$

Consider the quantity α_{ij} defined for two densities p_i and p_j as follows (Mahalanobis [11]):

$$\alpha_{ij} = (\mathbf{\mu}_i - \mathbf{\mu}_j)'\mathbf{V}^{-1}(\mathbf{\mu}_i - \mathbf{\mu}_j). \tag{1}$$

If $\mathbf{V}$ is the identity matrix, then α_{ij} represents the squared distance between the means of p_i and p_j. If $\mathbf{V}$ is not the identity, α_{ij} still has some aspects of a distance:

1) $\alpha_{ij} > 0$, $i \neq j$, $\mathbf{V}$ being positive definite
2) $\alpha_{ii} = 0$
3) $\alpha_{ij} = \alpha_{ji}$.

We wish to determine the relation between the quantity α_{ij} and the probability of error.

Let the random vector $\mathbf{X}$ have one or the other of two probability densities, p_i or p_j, accordingly as the input is from category i or j. The random variable defined by

$$L(\mathbf{X}) = \frac{p_i(\mathbf{X})}{p_j(\mathbf{X})} \tag{2}$$

is the likelihood ratio of the vector $\mathbf{X}$. Note that $L(\mathbf{X})$ is a scalar quantity.

If we consider that $\mathbf{X}$ has one or the other of two normal distributions, the one having mean $\mathbf{\mu}_i$ and covariance matrix $\mathbf{V}$, the other having mean $\mathbf{\mu}_2$ and the same covariance matrix, then the logarithm of the likelihood ratio is

$$\begin{aligned} u_{ij} &= \log_e L(\mathbf{X}) \\ &= \mathbf{X}'\mathbf{V}^{-1}(\mathbf{\mu}_i - \mathbf{\mu}_j) - \tfrac{1}{2}(\mathbf{\mu}_i + \mathbf{\mu}_j)'\mathbf{V}^{-1}(\mathbf{\mu}_i - \mathbf{\mu}_j). \end{aligned} \tag{3}$$

As was seen in [12], the optimal categorizer for the case of normal variables and equal covariance matrices calculates the functions u_{ij}. If a decision is to be made between category i and category j, it decides for the former if u_{ij} is positive, and for the latter if u_{ij} is negative (assuming that categories i and j are equally probable). Hence, the probability of error is given by

$$\begin{aligned} e_{ij} &= \tfrac{1}{2}\Pr(u_{ij} > 0 \mid \text{category } j) \\ &\quad + \tfrac{1}{2}\Pr(u_{ij} < 0 \mid \text{category } i). \end{aligned}$$

It is readily shown[2] that in this case the error probability is given by the following quantity (note the quantity α_{ij} in the lower limit of integration):

$$e_{ij} = \int_{\frac{1}{2}\sqrt{\alpha_{ij}}}^{\infty} \frac{1}{\sqrt{2\pi}} \exp\left[-\tfrac{1}{2}y^2\right] dy.$$

Hence, the probability of error e_{ij} is a monotonically decreasing function of α_{ij}. We notice that the function which relates the "distance" α_{ij} to the error probability e_{ij} is the univariate normal distribution with zero mean and unit variance. The effectiveness with which a receptor discriminates between categories i and j may thus be identified with the number α_{ij}, in the case of normal variables and equal covariance matrices.

The following interesting question may be raised: let ρ, consisting of tests $t_1, \cdots, t_p$, have effectiveness α_{ij} for discriminating between category i and j; how is this effectiveness changed if a new test t_{p+1} is added to the set? The answer to this question can be obtained directly from the definition of α_{ij}. The result is as follows:

Let $t_1, \cdots, t_p$ have effectiveness α_{ij}. Let t_{p+1} be a new test whose output has mean m_i or m_j accordingly as the input is from category i or j, and variance σ^2 in either case. Moreover, let γ be the vector of covariances that obtain between the output of t_{p+1} and the output of each of the other tests (*i.e.*, let the kth component of γ be the covariance between t_k and t_{p+1}). Then if α_{ij}^* is the effectiveness of the augmented set $t_1, \cdots, t_p, t_{p+1}$, we have that

$$\alpha_{ij}^* - \alpha_{ij} = \frac{[(m_i - m_j) - (\mathbf{\mu}_i - \mathbf{\mu}_j)'\mathbf{V}^{-1}\gamma]^2}{\sigma^2 - \gamma'\mathbf{V}^{-1}\gamma}.$$

This quantity is the incremental effectiveness due to the addition of t_{p+1}. Note that when the output of t_{p+1} is uncorrelated with the output of the other tests, *i.e.*, when γ is the zero vector, then the incremental effectiveness is $(m_i - m_j)^2/\sigma^2$, which is precisely the effectiveness of test t_{p+1} alone. In general, however, the increment is seen to depend on the interrelations of all the tests in a fairly complex manner.

The Divergence

We should like to gain some intuitive appreciation of the quantity α_{ij} and to generalize this quantity to other cases, particularly to the case of normal variables with unequal covariance matrices.

[1] $\mathbf{V}$ is taken to be a positive definite (symmetric) matrix of order $p \times p$, $\mathbf{x}$ and $\mathbf{\mu}_i$ are taken to be column matrices of order $p \times 1$. The inverse of a matrix $\mathbf{A}$ is indicated by $\mathbf{A}^{-1}$, the transpose by $\mathbf{A}'$, the determinant by $|\mathbf{A}|$, and the trace (*i.e.*, the sum of the diagonal elements) by tr $\mathbf{A}$.

[2] Anderson [1], p. 135.

Consider again the logarithm of the likelihood ratio for the case of normal variables with equal covariance matrices, as given by (3). On the assumption that the input is from category i, the expected value of u_{ij} is

$$E[u_{ij}|i] = \mathbf{\mu}_i'\mathbf{V}^{-1}(\mathbf{\mu}_i - \mathbf{\mu}_j) - \tfrac{1}{2}(\mathbf{\mu}_i + \mathbf{\mu}_j)'\mathbf{V}^{-1}(\mathbf{\mu}_i - \mathbf{\mu}_j)$$
$$= \tfrac{1}{2}(\mathbf{\mu}_i - \mathbf{\mu}_j)'\mathbf{V}^{-1}(\mathbf{\mu}_i - \mathbf{\mu}_j). \quad (4)$$

Whereas, if the input is from category j, the corresponding value is

$$E[u_{ij}|j] = -\tfrac{1}{2}(\mathbf{\mu}_i - \mathbf{\mu}_j)'\mathbf{V}^{-1}(\mathbf{\mu}_i - \mathbf{\mu}_j). \quad (5)$$

Subtracting (5) from (4), we have

$$E[u_{ij}|i] - E[u_{ij}|j] = (\mathbf{\mu}_i - \mathbf{\mu}_j)\mathbf{V}^{-1}(\mathbf{\mu}_i - \mathbf{\mu}_j) = \alpha_{ij}.$$

Hence, we see that α_{ij} can be interpreted as the difference between the two expected values of the log likelihood ratio of $\mathbf{X}$, for the particular case of normally distributed variables with equal covariance matrices. A generalization of α_{ij} to the case of arbitrary distributions may be expressed by

$$E[\log L(\mathbf{X})\ |i] - E[\log L(\mathbf{X})|\ j] \quad (6)$$

where $L(\mathbf{X})$ is defined by (2) for arbitrary densities p_i and p_j.

It has recently been argued by Kullback [10] that the quantity defined by (6) is indeed an appropriate "distance" between *arbitrary* distributions. This quantity (which is given very general definition by Kullback) is asserted to be "a measure of the difficulty of discriminating" between two distributions,[3] and given the name "divergence."

Divergence is a quantity defined for pairs of probability distributions or densities. In the context of recognition systems, such a pair of distributions comes into being as a result of applying a set of tests to two categories of inputs. We will write

$$\text{Div}\ \ (i, j \mid t_1, \cdots, t_p)$$

to represent the divergence between the two distributions that are generated when tests $t_1, \cdots, t_p$ are applied to the members of categories i and j.

Certain properties of divergence may be noted (see [10] for a more rigorous setting, and for proofs).

1) $\text{Div}\ (i, j \mid t_1, \cdots, t_p) > 0, i \neq j$
2) $\text{Div}\ (i, i \mid t_1, \cdots, t_p) = 0$
3) $\text{Div}\ (i, j \mid t_1, \cdots, t_p) = \text{Div}\ (j, i \mid t_1, \cdots, t_p)$
4) Divergence is additive for independent tests. That is, if, regardless of whether the input is from category i or j, $t_1, \cdots, t_p$ have statistically independent outputs, then

$$\text{Div}\ (i, j \mid t_1, \ldots, t_p) = \sum_{k=1}^{p} \text{Div}\ (i, j \mid t_k).$$

5) Adding new tests to a set of tests never decreases the divergence; *i.e.*,

$$\text{Div}\ (i, j \mid t_1, \ldots, t_p) \leq \text{Div}\ (i, j \mid t_1, \ldots, t_p, t_{p+1}).$$

[3] Kullback [10], p. 6.

NORMAL VARIABLES AND UNEQUAL COVARIANCE MATRICES

Consider now the case in which the receptor maps the input categories into normal densities, no further restrictions being imposed. Thus, as in the case of normal variables with equal covariance matrices, we allow that the outputs of the tests be arbitrarily intercorrelated; here we allow further that the system of intercorrelations be different for inputs belonging to different categories.

Let p_i be the normal density with mean $\mathbf{\mu}_i$ and covariance matrix $\mathbf{V}_i$ and let p_j be the normal density with mean $\mathbf{\mu}_j$ and covariance matrix $\mathbf{V}_j$. The divergence for this case[4] is given by

$$\text{Div}\ (i, j \mid t_1, \cdots, t_p) = \tfrac{1}{2}\,\text{tr}(\mathbf{V}_i - \mathbf{V}_j)(\mathbf{V}_j^{-1} - \mathbf{V}_i^{-1}) + \tfrac{1}{2}\,\text{tr}(\mathbf{V}_i^{-1} + \mathbf{V}_j^{-1})(\mathbf{\mu}_i - \mathbf{\mu}_j)(\mathbf{\mu}_i - \mathbf{\mu}_j)'. \quad (7)$$

Notice that if we set $\mathbf{V}_i = \mathbf{V}_j$, we obtain

$$\text{Div}\ (i, j \mid t_1, \cdots, t_p) = \alpha_{ij}.$$

While there is in the present instance no simple function that relates divergence to the probability of error, certain bounds may be set. Thus, an examination[5] of the univariate case yields the bounds indicated in Fig. 2. For a given value of divergence, the probability of correct recognition (*i.e.*, one minus the probability of error) is constrained to lie between the two indicated curves. The upper curve, it may be noted, also gives the exact relation between probability of correct recognition and divergence for the multivariate normal case with equal covariance matrices.

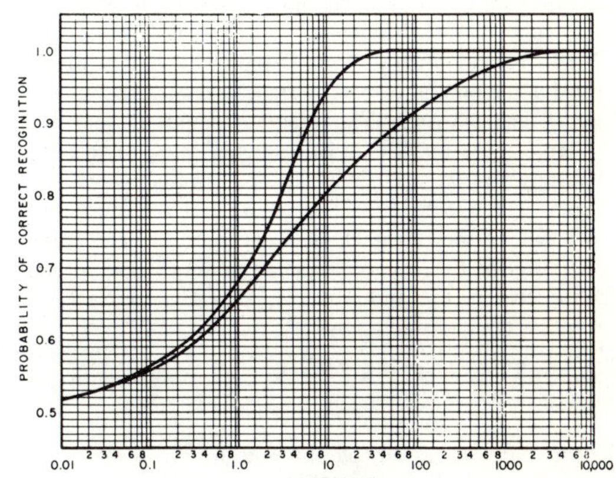

Fig. 2—Upper and lower bounds on probability of correct recognition as a function of divergence, for normal variables with unequal covariance matrices. Upper curve also represents the exact relation for normal variables with equal covariance matrices. Lower curve determined from univariate case.

[4] Kullback [10], p. 190.
[5] Performed with the aid of a Monte-Carlo-type computer program.

Some Experimental Results

Motivated by the preceding considerations, several experiments were performed. The raw data for these experiments were obtained by asking subjects to print the letters A, B, C and D by hand. Each of 40 subjects produced five examples of each of the four letters. Our entire sample, then, consisted of 800 individual characters. Each character was printed within a two-inch square.

Our tests consisted of determining the distance, along predetermined paths, from the edge of the square field to the edge of the character. These tests were performed by hand. Specifically, a grid of intersecting lines was overlaid on each character. The ith test ($i = 1, \cdots, 8$) consisted of determining the distance, along the ith line segment, from the edge of the field to the edge of the character.[6] Thus, each character yielded a vector of eight measurements. The entire sample, therefore, produced 800 vectors of eight measurements each. The four letters A, B, C and D represent the four input categories used in these experiments.

Two programs for the LGP-30 computer were prepared in connection with these experiments. The first program was used for computing the divergence, based on a specific set of tests, between specified input categories. Thus, for example, this program could be used to calculate Div $(A, C \mid t_1, t_3, t_5)$, *i.e.*, to calculate the divergence between categories A and C as based on the first, third and fifth tests.

The divergence is calculated by this program in accordance with (7) (normal variables, unequal covariance matrices). The program demands the following quantities as inputs: the two "full" (8×1) mean vectors for the two categories in question, the two "full" (8×8) covariance matrices for the same categories and an indication of which particular tests the divergence is to be based on.

The second program was designed to be an optimal categorizer for the case of normal variables and unequal covariance matrices. The program could be set up to assign any vector $\mathbf{X}$ of p components ($p \leq 8$) to one of m categories ($m \leq 4$), given the appropriate m covariance matrices $\mathbf{V}_i$ (each of order $p \times p$) and the appropriate m mean vectors $\boldsymbol{\mu}_i$ (each of order $p \times 1$). The rule of operation of this program was as follows:[7] assign vector $\mathbf{X}$ to category k if and only if $l_k(\mathbf{X})$ is the largest of the m quantities $l_i(\mathbf{X})$ given by

$$l_i(\mathbf{X}) = -(\mathbf{X} - \boldsymbol{\mu}_i)'\mathbf{V}_i^{-1}(\mathbf{X} - \boldsymbol{\mu}_i) - \log_e |\mathbf{V}_i| \qquad i = 1, \cdots, m.$$

The covariances among the outputs of all eight tests were computed separately for each of the four categories, the resulting matrices being given in Table I(A–D). The corresponding four mean vectors are given in Table II.

[6] This method of analysis of characters is identical to that used in [12], which may be consulted for further details and illustrations.

[7] This rule is equivalent to, but computationally much simpler than, the one given in [12] for the case of normal variables and unequal covariance matrices.

TABLE I-A

Covariance Matrix for Letter A Based on Eight Tests

1.034	1.281	0.351	−0.293	0.098	0.301	0.141	1.336
	1.967	0.664	−0.219	0.259	0.556	0.276	2.094
		7.138	1.192	2.726	1.116	0.678	2.097
			2.269	1.367	0.146	0.201	−0.308
				5.727	1.280	0.933	2.107
					2.941	1.949	2.197
						1.577	1.229
							6.606

TABLE I-B

Covariance Matrix for Letter B Based on Eight Tests

4.792	4.417	4.244	2.406	1.798	0.790	0.785	2.993
	5.074	4.636	2.798	1.824	0.639	0.644	2.799
		5.428	3.224	2.111	0.903	1.131	2.943
			5.287	3.006	1.326	1.897	2.648
				3.574	2.229	2.471	1.915
					4.008	2.405	1.106
						4.507	1.727
							3.972

TABLE I-C

Covariance Matrix for Letter C Based on Eight Tests

1.638	2.153	1.482	1.695	−0.557	−2.443	−0.710	1.983
	3.596	2.461	2.436	−0.591	−3.711	−0.493	2.434
		2.500	2.834	−0.665	−2.621	0.248	1.738
			4.704	−0.629	−2.913	0.576	2.471
				19.000	0.896	8.622	−0.254
					5.856	1.357	−2.915
						20.800	−0.622
							3.214

TABLE I-D

Covariance Matrix for Letter D Based on Eight Tests

5.116	4.736	4.058	1.821	1.109	1.289	1.029	2.232
	5.684	4.523	2.311	1.273	1.328	1.151	2.425
		6.117	2.525	1.321	1.501	1.274	2.191
			4.432	2.481	2.179	1.080	1.784
				2.134	2.325	1.017	1.030
					4.099	2.019	1.803
						1.872	2.081
							3.806

TABLE II

Mean Measurement-Vectors Based on Eight Tests

μ'_A =	[7.825	6.750	5.835	8.525	6.615	7.065	7.865	4.435]
μ'_B =	[5.760	5.715	5.705	4.150	6.225	6.960	6.750	3.910]
μ'_C =	[6.610	5.060	5.980	3.975	9.020	14.685	10.640	4.175]
μ'_D =	[6.120	6.285	5.850	4.365	6.340	4.675	6.260	4.440]

Experiment 1

This experiment dealt with the discrimination between the letters A and B. First, various "effective" subsets of the set of eight tests were generated, by the following method: Calculate the divergence for the 8 possible subsets consisting of 7 tests each. Pick the subset yielding the largest divergence. Now, starting with the set of 7 tests already picked, calculate the divergence for the 7 possible

TABLE III

Discrimination of A vs B: Divergence and Observed Percent of Correct Recognition for Various Sets of Tests

	Divergence	Percent Correct Recognition
All Tests	Div $(A, B \mid t_1, t_2, t_3, t_4, t_5, t_6, t_7, t_8) = 36.1$	Pr $(C) = 97.25\%$
Effective Subsets	Div $(A, B \mid t_1, t_2, t_3, t_4, t_5, t_6, t_7) = 33.1$	
	Div $(A, B \mid t_1, t_2, t_3, t_4, t_6, t_7) = 29.8$	Pr $(C) = 95.75\%$
	Div $(A, B \mid t_1, t_2, t_4, t_6, t_7) = 25.2$	
	Div $(A, B \mid t_1, t_2, t_4, t_7) = 19.9$	Pr $(C) = 93.5\ \%$
	Div $(A, B \mid t_1, t_2, t_4) = 19.0$	
	Div $(A, B \mid t_1, t_4) = 11.9$	Pr $(C) = 91.5\ \%$
	Div $(A, B \mid t_4) = 6.53$	Pr $(C) = 89.75\%$
Ineffective Subsets	Div $(A, B \mid t_1, t_2, t_3, t_5, t_6, t_7, t_8) = 21.2$	
	Div $(A, B \mid t_2, t_3, t_5, t_6, t_7, t_8) = 12.7$	
	Div $(A, B \mid t_2, t_3, t_5, t_6, t_8) = 5.01$	
	Div $(A, B \mid t_3, t_5, t_6, t_8) = 1.40$	Pr $(C) = 62\ \%$
	Div $(A, B \mid t_3, t_5, t_6) = 0.582$	
	Div $(A, B \mid t_3, t_6) = 0.099$	Pr $(C) = 58.75\%$
	Div $(A, B \mid t_3) = 0.041$	Pr $(C) = 54.75\%$
Individual Tests	Div $(A, B \mid t_1) = 3.93$	
	Div $(A, B \mid t_2) = 0.861$	
	Div $(A, B \mid t_3) = 0.041$	Pr $(C) = 54.75\%$
	Div $(A, B \mid t_4) = 6.53$	Pr $(C) = 89.75\%$
	Div $(A, B \mid t_5) = 0.148$	
	Div $(A, B \mid t_6) = 0.051$	
	Div $(A, B \mid t_7) = 1.14$	
	Div $(A, B \mid t_8) = 0.188$	

subsets consisting of 6 tests each. Pick the subset yielding the highest divergence; etc. In this manner, effective subsets of 7, 6, $\cdots$, 1 tests were obtained (see Table III).

Next, "ineffective" subsets of the set of 8 tests were generated by the following complementary method: Calculate the divergence for the 8 subsets of 7 tests each. Pick the subset yielding the *smallest* divergence. Now, starting with the set of 7 tests already picked, calculate the divergence for the 7 subsets of 6 tests each. Pick the subset yeilding the smallest divergence; etc. In this manner, ineffective subsets consisting of 7, 6, $\cdots$, 1 tests were obtained (see Table III).

For purposes of comparison, the divergence for each of the eight individual tests were also calculated (see Table III).

In the second phase of the experiment, eight of the selected sets of tests were each coupled, so to speak, to a categorizer, and each of the eight systems so formed was given the task of recognizing 200 samples of the letter A and 200 of the letter B.[8] The percentage of samples correctly recognized is given in the right side of Table III. The results, plotted in graphic form, are given in Fig. 3. The solid curves of Fig. 3 are those of Fig. 2.

[8] The particular choice of these eight sets was dictated by a desire to economize on computer time while still covering the total available range of divergences. The original plan called for obtaining the per cent correct recognition for the set consisting of all eight tests and for both the "effective" and "ineffective" sets consisting of 6, 4, 2 and 1 tests. This plan was carried out with the exception that the "ineffective" set of six tests was omitted, since its divergence nearly duplicated that of another set which had already been run (the "effective" set of two tests).

Experiment 2

In the preceding experiment the nature of the discrimination, A vs B, was held constant, and the receptor of the system was varied. In the present experiment, the receptor consisting of tests 4 and 6 was used throughout, and the discrimination was varied. All six possible two-fold discriminations among the four letters were investigated: A vs B, A vs C, A vs D, B vs C, B vs D and C vs D. The results are plotted in Fig. 4, each point being based on 400 samples.

Experiment 3

As a matter of general interest, although not directly related to the preceding discussion, the categorization program was set up for the four-fold discrimination: A vs B vs C vs D, based (as in Experiment 2) on tests 4 and 6. Two hundred samples of each letter were used. The results are given in Table IV.

Discussion

Several aspects of these results may be noted. Experiment 1 shows that, for any number n, the set of n tests having high divergence yields higher percentage of correct recognition than the set of n tests having low divergence. In fact, the rank ordering of various sets of tests by divergence is equal to their rank ordering by percentage of correct recognition.

From the graphic representations of Figs. 3–4, we see that the points, except at the low end of the graph where sampling error may be expected to be greater, fall within the curves of Fig. 2. For the type of situation under

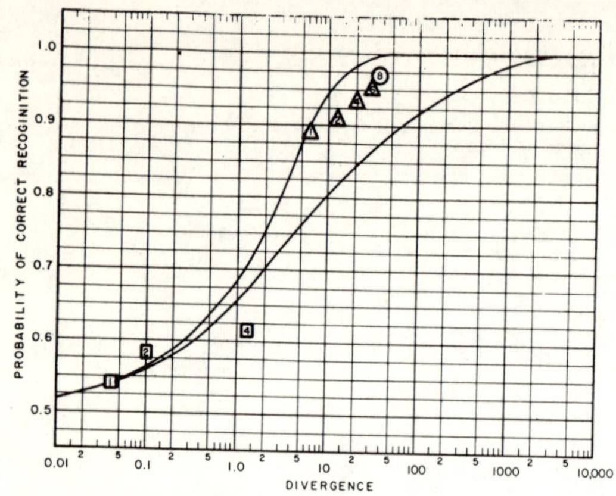

Fig. 3—Discrimination of A vs B. Observed probability of correct recognition as a function of divergence, for eight receptors investigated in Experiment 1. The solid curves are those of Fig. 2. The triangular and square points represent, respectively, so-called "effective" and "ineffective" subsets. The number within the points indicate the number of tests used in the discrimination.

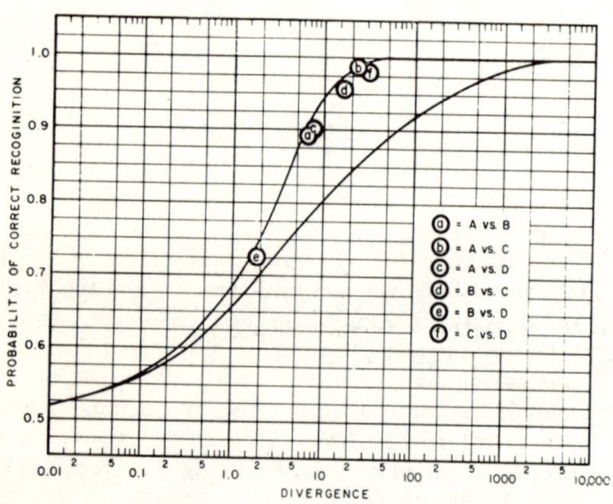

Fig. 4—Discrimination using a receptor consisting of tests 4 and 6. Observed probability of correct recognition as a function of divergence, for the six two-fold discriminations investigated in Experiment 2. Solid curves are those in Fig. 2.

TABLE IV

Results of Experiment 3: Four-Fold Discrimination, Using Tests 4 and 6

		INPUT				
		A	*B*	*C*	*D*	
OUTPUT	*A*	184	27	1	30	242
	B	9	117	7	41	174
	C	0	7	189	0	196
	D	7	49	3	129	188
		200	200	200	200	800

discussion, then, these curves may be used to make approximate predictions of the ability of a set of tests to discriminate between given categories. Thus, for example, we may predict on the basis of divergence measurements that tests 4 and 6 are adequate for the discrimination of C vs D, but quite unsatisfactory for the discrimination of B vs D. Fig. 4 shows that this prediction is borne out.[9]

References

[1] T. W. Anderson, "Introduction to Multivariate Statistical Analysis," John Wiley and Sons, Inc., New York, N. Y., 1958.

[2] W. W. Bledsoe and I. Browning, "Pattern recognition and reading by machine," *Proc. Eastern Joint Conf.*, pp. 225–232; December, 1959.

[3] J. S. Bomba, "Aplha-numeric character recognition using local operations," *Proc. Eastern Joint Conf.*, pp. 218–224; December, 1959.

[4] C. K. Chow, "Optimum character recognition system using decision functions," 1957 IRE WESCON Convention Record, pt. 4, pp. 121–129. Also in IRE Trans. on Electronic Computers, vol. EC-6, pp. 247–254; December, 1957.

[5] W. Doyle, "Recognition of sloppy hand-printed characters," *Proc. Western Joint Computer Conf.*, pp. 133–142; May, 1960.

[6] R. L. Grimsdale, F. H. Summer, C. J. Tunis and T. Kilburn, "A system for the automatic recognition of patterns," Proc. IEE, vol. 106, pt. B, March, 1959.

[7] L. D. Harmon, "A line-drawing recognizer," *Proc. Western Joint Computer Conf.*, pp. 351–364; May, 1960.

[8] J. K. Hawkins, "Self-organizing systems—a review and commentary," Proc. IRE, pp. 31–48; January, 1961.

[9] W. H. Highleyman, "An analog method for character recognition," IRE Trans. on Electronic Computers, vol. EC-10, p. 502–512; September, 1961.

[10] S. Kullback, "Information Theory and Statistics," John Wiley and Sons, Inc., New York, N. Y., 1959.

[11] P. C. Mahalanobis, "On the generalized distance in statistics," *Proc. Nat'l. Inst. Sci. India*, vol. 12, pp. 49–55; 1936.

[12] T. Marill and D. M. Green, "Statistical recognition functions and the design of pattern recognizers," IRE Trans. on Electronic Computers, vol. EC-9, pp. 472–477; December, 1960.

[13] M. Minsky, "A selected descriptor-indexed bibliography to the literature on artificial intelligence," IRE Trans. on Human Factors in Electronics, vol. HFE-2, pp. 39–56; March, 1961.

[14] M. Minsky, "Steps toward artificial intelligence," Proc. IRE, vol. 49, pp. 8–30; January, 1961.

[15] F. Rosenblatt, "The perceptron: a probabilistic model for information storage and organization in the brain," *Psychol. Rev.*, vol. 65, pp. 386–407; November, 1958.

[16] G. S. Sebestyen, "Recognition of membership in classes," IRE Trans. on Information Theory, vol. IT-7, pp. 44–50; January, 1961.

[17] O. G. Selfridge, "Pandemonium: A paradigm for learning," *Proc. Symp. on Mechanisation of Thought Processes*, H.M.S.O., London, England, pp. 511–529; 1959.

[18] H. Sherman, "A quasi-topological method for machine recognition of line patterns," *Proc. Internatl. Conf. on Information Processing (ICIP)*, UNESCO House, Paris, France, pp. 232–238; 1959.

[19] Smith, J. E. Keith, and L. Klem, "Vowel recognition using a multiple discriminant function," *J. Acoust. Soc. Am.*, vol. 33, p. 358; March, 1961.

[20] L. Uhr and C. Vossler, "A pattern recognition program that generates, evaluates, and adjusts its own operators, *Proc. Western Joint Computer Conf.*, Los Angeles, Calif., pp. 555–561; May 9–11, 1961.

[21] S. H. Unger, "Pattern detection and recognition," Proc. IRE, vol. 47, pp. 1737–1752; October, 1959.

[22] P. D. Welch, and R. S. Wimpress, "Two multivariate statistical computer programs and their application to the vowel recognition problem," *J. Acoust. Soc. Am.*, vol. 33, pp. 426–434; April, 1961.

[9] It may also be of interest to observe in Table III that, of the eight possible subsets consisting of a single test, the method for picking "effective" subsets did indeed pick the one having the highest divergence, while the method for picking "ineffective" subsets did indeed pick the one with the lowest divergence. Unfortunately, situations can be devised in which this will not be the case. It may be conjectured that such situations are of a pathological sort; the matter is far from clear, however.

Reprinted from *IEEE Trans. Commun. Tech.*, **COM–15,** No. 1, 1967, pp. 52–60

The Divergence and Bhattacharyya Distance Measures in Signal Selection

10

THOMAS KAILATH, MEMBER, IEEE

REFERENCE: Kailath, T.: THE DIVERGENCE AND BHATTACHARYYA DISTANCE MEASURES IN SIGNAL SELECTION,[1] Stanford University, Stanford, Calif., and Stanford Research Institute, Menlo Park, Calif. Rec'd 4/6/66; revised 10/14/66. Paper 19TP67-906. IEEE TRANS. ON COMMUNICATION TECHNOLOGY, 15-1, February 1967, pp. 52–60.

ABSTRACT: Minimization of the error probability to determine optimum signals is often difficult to carry out. Consequently, several suboptimum performance measures that are easier than the error probability to evaluate and manipulate have been studied. In this partly tutorial paper, we compare the properties of an often used measure, the divergence, with a new measure that we have called the Bhattacharyya distance. This new distance measure is often easier to evaluate than the divergence. In the problems we have worked, it gives results that are at least as good as, and are often better, than those given by the divergence.

***KEYWORDS:* Communication Theory, Detection, Digital Signals, Fading, Matched Filters, Signal-to-Noise Ratio.**

IN PROBLEMS of communication and radar, the optimum signals are those that minimize the probability of error. However, in many cases, direct minimization of the probability of error so as to determine an optimum signal set is often impossible. This may be because an explicit analytical expression for the error probability is too difficult to find, or even if it can be found, the expression may be too complicated for analytical or numerical minimization. Therefore, it is useful to search for signal selection criteria that may be weaker than the error probability but that are easier to evaluate and manipulate. Maximizing a *deflection ratio* or a *signal-to-noise* (*SNR*) is an example of such a weaker criterion—in general, maximizing the SNR may not lead to the minimum error probability, but the SNR may still be used because it is easier to analyze and does provide some guidance in many cases. In the search for suitable criteria, the notion of a *distance* between two probability distributions is quite useful. The two distributions will be the distributions of the observations in a binary hypothesis testing situation and the further *apart* we can make these distributions, hopefully the smaller will be the probability of mistaking one for the other. Therefore, various distance measures have been studied as simpler substitutes for the error probability.

What we would like for such distance measures is a property of the following type: if the distance between the two distributions is greater for a signal set α than for a signal set β, then the error probability for set α is always less than the error probability for set β. This is too much to hope for—we shall only be able to find *weaker* relations between distance measures and the probability of error.

In statistics, the use of such distance measures has a long history beginning with the work of Pearson (as quoted in Tildesley [1]). Two widely used distance measures in statistics are the D^2-statistic of Mahalanobis [2], [3] and the linear discriminant function introduced by Fisher [4]. These measures are discussed in detail in many statistical texts, e.g., Anderson [5] or Rao [6]. With the advent in 1948 of Shannon's information theory, the divergence, a measure closely related to Shannon's logarithmic measure of information, has become popular, though it had first been proposed before Shannon's work by Jeffreys [7]. Several properties and applications of the divergence are noted in Kullback [8].

In the engineering literature the divergence has recently been applied to several problems with varying degrees of success (as seen in Marill and Green [9], Grettenberg [10], Hingorani [11], and others). In this paper, we propose another criterion for signal selection based on a statistic first introduced in a statistical context[2] by Bhattacharyya [12]. In the various signal selection problems we have considered so far, the Bhattacharyya distance has turned out to give better results than the divergence. Therefore, it seems like a useful measure to study.

It should be pointed out that the Bhattacharyya distance is actually a special case of a more general distance measure introduced by Chernoff [15]. This measure, which will be discussed briefly in Section III, is in general *closer* to the error probability than the Bhattacharyya distance. On the other hand, it is usually not as easy to evaluate as the Bhattacharyya distance, which, for this reason, will be preferred in this paper.

We shall first briefly review some of the properties of the divergence and of the Bhattacharyya distance and shall then compare the two measures in various ways.

We shall confine ourselves largely to two-hypothesis problems. The two hypotheses will be denoted h_i, $i = 1,2$; and we shall set $p_i(x)dx$ = probability of the observation x when hypotheses h_i is true. The observation x will, for simplicity be taken as an N-component vector. [The concepts can be extended to the case of continuous-time observations (See Section IV).]

The likelihood ratio

$$L(x) = \frac{p_1(x)}{p_2(x)}$$

[1] This work was supported by AFOSR Contract AF 49(638)1517, by Tri-Service Nonr 225(83), and by DA 36-039SC-90859 at S.R.I.

[2] Another early and well-known statistical application of this statistic was made by Kakutani [13], who notes an earlier appearance in a nonstatistical problem (Hellinger [14]). Therefore, the names Hellinger and Kakutani are often associated with the Bhattacharyya statistic.

will play a prominent part in our discussions. In fact, both the divergence and the Bhattacharyya distance are convex functionals of the likelihood ratio.

I. The Divergence and the Bhattacharyya Distance

The divergence was first introduced by Jeffreys [7], [16]. It is defined as the difference in the mean values of the log-likelihood ratio under the two hypotheses

$$J = E_1[\ln L(x)] - E_2[\ln L(x)] \tag{1}$$

where

$$E_i[\ln L(x)] = \int [\ln L(x)] p_i(x) dx, \; i = 1,2. \tag{2}$$

These expectations of $\ln L(x)$ are often called the Kullback-Leibler (K-L) numbers (Kullback and Leibler [17] and written

$$I(1, 2) = E_1[\ln L(x)], I(2, 1) = -E_2[\ln L(x)]. \tag{3}$$

In general

$$I(1, 2) \neq I(2, 1). \tag{4}$$

The divergence is a symmetrized form of the K-L numbers

$$J = I(1, 2) + I(2, 1). \tag{5}$$

We shall calculate J for several examples in Section II. The divergence satisfies all the postulates for a metric (distance) except the triangle inequality. That is we have $J(1, 2) = J(2, 1)$, $J(1, 2) \geq 0$ with equality only when $p_1 = p_2$ but $J(1, 2) + J(2, 3)$ may be less than $J(1, 3)$. This last statement can be checked by taking p_1, p_2, p_3 to be normal distributions with means zero and variances 1, 4, and 5.

Several other properties of the divergence—its additivity for independent observations, its behavior under transformations, relations to channel capacity, etc.,—and various applications to classification and hypothesis testing are given in Kullback [8].

For the present paper, we are interested in a property of the divergence that is related to signal selection. If we have two signal sets—or more generally, two sets of parameters for the densities $p_i(x)$, $i = 1,2$—say α and β, we can *order* (or rank) them by means of the divergence. That is, we can say the signal set α is better than the signal set β if $J(\alpha)$, the divergence between p_1 and p_2 for parameters α is larger than $J(\beta)$. In communications and radar, the phrase "signal set α is better than set β" generally means "the error probability (or more generally, the Bayes' risk) is less for signal set α than it is for signal set β." Now the error probability depends on the total distribution (and hence all the moments) of the likelihood ratio while the divergence depends only upon the first moments (mean values) of the likelihood ratio. Therefore, in general, if $J(\alpha) > J(\beta)$ [i.e., α is better than β under the divergence criterion] it will not be true that $P_e(\alpha) < P_e(\beta)$. Consequently, the following theorem of Karlin and Bradt [18] is quite surprising.

If $J(\alpha) > J(\beta)$, there exists a set of prior probabilities $\pi = (\pi_1, \pi_2)$ for the two hypotheses, for which

$$P_e(\alpha, \pi) < P_e(\beta, \pi).^3 \tag{6}$$

This is an interesting result, but it would be much more so if we could assert something more than just existence about the *good* set of prior probabilities. Unfortunately, this is hard to do. Nevertheless, Karlin and Bradt's result encouraged Grettenberg [10] to apply the divergence criterion to several signal selection problems. He was followed by several others.

Before discussing these signal selection problems, let us introduce the Bhattacharyya distance. We first define the Bhattacharyya coefficient for two densities $p_i(x)$ by

$$\rho = \text{Bhattacharyya coefficient} = \int \sqrt{p_1(x) p_2(x)}\, dx. \tag{7}$$

Clearly ρ lies between zero and unity. We can associate several distance measures with this coefficient. The one we shall use will be[4]

$$B = \text{the Bhattacharyya distance} = -\ln \rho. \tag{8}$$

Clearly $0 \leq B \leq \infty$. It can be shown that B need not obey the triangle inequality (consider normal populations with means zero and variances 1, 4, and 5). (But $\sqrt{1 - \rho}$ does obey the triangle inequality.) We shall evaluate B for several distributions in Sections II and III.

The Bhattacharyya distance has many interesting properties, some of which we shall discuss later, but what led us to investigate its application to signal selection was the fact that B has the property discovered by Karlin and Bradt for the divergence.

If for two sets of system parameters α and β, we have $B(\alpha) > B(\beta)$ or equivalently $\rho(\alpha) < \rho(\beta)$, then there exists a set

$$\pi = (\pi_1, \pi_2) \tag{9}$$

of prior probabilities for which $P_e(\alpha, \pi) < P_e(\beta, \pi)$.

This result, as well as the earlier one of Karlin and Bradt for the divergence, follows easily from a theorem proved by Blackwell [19] and attributed by him to unpublished work by H. Bohnenblust, L. Shapley, and S. Sherman. We have

Theorem (Blackwell)[5]

$P_e(\alpha, \pi)$ will be less than or equal to $P_e(\beta, \pi)$ for all π if and only if

$$E_\alpha[\psi(L_\alpha) | h^{(2)}] \leq E_\beta[\psi(L_\beta) | h^{(2)}] \tag{10}$$

for all continuous concave functions $\psi(L)$. $\{E_\alpha[\psi(L_\alpha)|h^{(2)}]$ is the expectation of $\psi(L_\alpha)$ under the hypothesis $h^{(2)}$.$\}$

[3] $P_e(\alpha, \pi)$ is the error probability with parameter set α and prior probabilities II.

[4] Another possibility is the quantity $\sqrt{1-\rho}$.

[5] We note incidentally that this theorem is attributed to Karlin and Bradt by Grettenberg (cf. Theorem 1 of Grettenberg [10]), whereas Grettenberg's Theorem 2 should in fact have been credited to Karlin and Bradt.

The proof of (9) is now simple. We note that $\sqrt{L}$ is a concave function of L and that

$$\rho(\alpha) = \int \sqrt{p_1(x, \alpha)p_2(x,\alpha)}\,dx$$
$$= \int \sqrt{\frac{p_1(x, \alpha)}{p_2(x, \alpha)}}\, p_2(x, \alpha)dx = E_\alpha[\sqrt{L_\alpha}|h^{(2)}]. \quad (11)$$

Similarly

$$\rho(\beta) = E_\beta[\sqrt{L_\beta}|h^{(2)}].$$

But then $\rho(\beta) < \rho(\alpha)$ implies $E_\beta[\sqrt{L_\beta}|h^{(2)}]\, E_\alpha[\sqrt{L_\alpha}|h^{(2)}]$, which contradicts (10). Therefore, Blackwell's theorem shows that if $\rho(\beta) < \rho(\alpha)$, then $P_e(\alpha, \pi)$ cannot be strictly smaller than $P_e(\beta, \pi)$ for all π, which is just the result (9).

II. Some Applications to Signal Selection

Grettenberg [10] used the comparison property (6) of the divergence J as a rationale for using J as a tool for signal selection. We have found that the Bhattacharyya distance B has a similar property (9) and this leads us to compare J and B as tools for signal selection. We shall consider three examples originally studied by the divergence method—two were treated by Grettenberg [10] and one by Reiffen and Sherman [20].

A. Gaussian Processes with Unequal Mean Value Functions

The detection problem is to choose between the two hypotheses

$$h_1: x(t) = m_1(t) + n(t),\ h_2: x(t) = m_2(t) + n(t),\ t\epsilon T$$

where $m_1(t)$ and $m_2(t)$ are known functions of time, $n(t)$ is a sample function of a zero mean Gaussian process with covariance function $R(t, s)$, and $x(t)$ is the observation on the basis of which we are to decide whether h_1 or h_2 is true. For simplicity, we shall assume that the noise is white, with

$$R(t, s) = \frac{N_0}{2}\delta(t - s)$$

and that the signals $m_i(t)$, $i = 1,2$ have equal energies

$$\int_T m_i^2(t)dt = E,\ i = 1,2 \quad (12)$$

and a correlation coefficient μ defined by

$$\int_T m_1(t)m_2(t)dt = E\mu. \quad (13)$$

Now some computation will show that

$$B = \frac{1}{8}J = \frac{1}{8}\frac{2E}{N_0}(1 - \mu) \quad (14)$$

so that both the Bhattacharyya distance B and the divergence J are maximized by choosing the signals $m_i(t)$, $i = 1,2$ to be antipodal, viz., such that

$$m_1(t) = -m_2(t) \text{ or } \mu = -1. \quad (15)$$

It is well-known that this choice of signals is in fact the one that minimizes the error probability for all prior probabilities II, so that in this problem both the divergence and the Bhattacharyya distance signal selection criteria yield signals that are in fact also optimum on an error probability basis. This happy coincidence is unfortunately not universal, as the next example shows.

B. Gaussian Processes with Unequal Covariance Functions

The problem is the following: one of two signals $m_i(t)$, $i = 1,2$ each of energy E/L

$$\int_T m_i^2(t)dt = E/L,\ i = 1,2 \quad (16)$$

is transmitted over L channels in each of which the signal is perturbed multiplicatively by α_k and additively by $n_k(t)$, so that the received signals are

$$h^{(i)}: x_k(t) = \alpha_k m_2(t) + n_k(t),\ k = 1,\ldots,L,\ i = 1,2.^6 \quad (17)$$

We shall assume that the $\{\alpha_k\}$ are independent identically distributed Gaussian random variables with

$$E[\alpha_k] = 0,\ E[\alpha_k\alpha_j] = \sigma^2\delta_{kj},\ k, j = 1,\ldots,L. \quad (18)$$

The additive noises will be assumed to be Gaussian, independent, identically distributed with

$$E[n_k(t)] = 0,\ E[n_k(t)n_j(s)] = \left[\frac{N_o}{2}\delta(t - s)\right]\delta_{kj} \quad (19)$$

and independent of the random variables $[\alpha_k]$

$$E[\alpha_k n_j(t)] = 0,\ k, j = 1,\ldots,L. \quad (20)$$

The signal selection problem in the above is the following: if we had just a single link, there is a large probability that the transmitted signal will be drastically weakened by the multiplicative noise assuming a low value. To combat this loss of signal, which is usually called the loss due to *fading*, a classical solution (1923–1927) is to use a number of links to provide *diversity*. If we use a number of links with independent multiplicative noises, the probability that the signal will be simultaneously reduced on all links can be made quite small. It would therefore seem desirable to use as many diversity links as possible. However, another factor has to be taken into account. The total signal energy is usually constrained, say to E, and therefore, the more links we use the less will be the available signal energy per link. If too many links are used, the signal energy per link may be so small that the resulting greater degradation in the performance of each link cannot be compensated for by the diversity gain provided by the use of the larger number of links. There should therefore be an optimum number of links to use for a given total signal energy E.

Let us now see what results the use of the divergence and Bhattacharyya measures yield. First for the diver-

[6] In the communication problem, it is physically most reasonable to take α_k, $x_k(t)$, $m_i(t)$ and $n_k(t)$ to be the complex envelopes of the corresponding real (narrowband) signals. For comparison with the earlier results of Pierce [21] and Grettenberg [10], we shall make this assumption here. However B and J can be calculated and optimized whether or not the signals are narrowband.

gence, some computation shows that, if (for simplicity) we make the additional assumption that the signals are orthogonal, viz.,

$$\int_0^T m_1(t)m_2(t)dt = 0 \qquad (21)$$

then the divergence is

$$J = \frac{R^2}{R + L}, R = 2E\sigma^2/N_o. \qquad (22)$$

And clearly for a fixed E, this is maximized by setting $L = 1$, that is by putting all the energy in a single link. However, our previous discussion indicates that this is not a very reasonable thing to do when R is large. And in fact, by the use of certain bounding techniques and by numerical evaluation, Pierce [21] found the optimum number of links as a function of the SNR, $R = 2E\sigma^2/N_o$, for the case of equal prior probabilities. Pierce showed that for low SNR $R \ll 1$ the use of a single link is optimum but that for large SNR, $R \gg 1$, the optimum number of links is given (to a very good approximation) by the remarkably simple formula[7]

$$L_{\text{opt}} = [R/3] \qquad (23)$$

where $[x]$ means "the greatest integer less than or equal to x." We conclude from this that in Grettenberg's words ([10], p. 275), "the range of source statistics for which the maximum divergence code has a lower error probability than a different code does not always include the equiprobable case." We should repeat that the Karlin-Bradt theorem (6) tells us that the maximum divergence solution ($L = 1$) must be best, no matter how large the SNR is, for some set of prior probabilities. Unfortunately, the theorem gives us no information about this *good* set of prior probabilities and in many problems it might be that this set is highly skewed [π_1 = unity] and therefore highly improbable.

The Bhattacharyya distance in this problem can be calculated to be

$$\rho = e^{-B} = \left(1 + \frac{R}{L}\right)^L \bigg/ \left(1 + \frac{R}{2L}\right)^{2L}, R = \frac{2E\sigma^2}{N_o}.$$

Differentiation shows that B is maximum when

$$x^2/(x+1)(x+2) = \ln\{(x^2 + 4x + 4)/4x + 4\}, x = R/L$$

and computer solution of this equation yields

$$L_{\text{opt}} = R/3.07$$

which is the same as the solution (23) found by Pierce [21] from the exact expression for P_e, which incidentally is

$$P_e = \frac{1}{(2 + R/L)^L} \sum_{k=0}^{L-1} \binom{L - 1 + k}{k} \left(\frac{1 + R/L}{2 + R/L}\right)^k.$$

[7] Grettenberg ([10], p. 275) claims erroneously that the error probability for this case decreases monotonically with L, so that the best choice is $L = \infty$.

It can be shown [see discussion after (49)] that asymptotically the Bhattacharyya distance essentially determines the error probability in the sense that

$$\lim_{P_e \to 0} P_e = c \cdot e^{-B}, c = \text{a constant}.$$

Thus for the (zero-mean) Gaussian signal in Gaussian noise problem, the Bhattacharyya distance yields better results (at least for the situation of most interest in communication problems where $\pi_1 \doteq \pi_2$) than the divergence.

Gaussian processes with different means and covariance yield similar results—the divergence and Bhattacharyya distance criteria yield similar results at low SNR,[8] but at high SNR they give different solutions, with the divergence solution being poorer (at least for $\pi_1 \doteq \pi_2$).

However, as a last example, we treat a problem in which the two criteria again yield similar results.

C. Poisson Processes with Unequal Mean Value Functions

The detection problem is to choose between two Poisson processes whose mean value functions are

$$m^{(k)}(t) = \lambda_i^{(k)} + \lambda_o, (i-1)\Delta \le t \le i\Delta,$$
$$i = 1, \ldots N, k = 1,2 \qquad (24)$$

where the observation interval T has been divided into N intervals of length Δ, $N\Delta = T$. The $\{\lambda_i^{(k)}\}$ are determined by our choice of signals. We constrain this choice by

$$\lambda_i^{(k)} \ge 0, \Sigma\Delta(\lambda_i^{(1)} + \lambda_i^{(2)}) = 2E. \qquad (25)$$

The observation is the sequence $\{n_i\}$ of the number of events (photon arrivals at a photon detector) occurring in the several intervals; the number of events in the ith interval is Poisson distributed with

$$P^{(k)}\{n_i \text{ events in } (i-1)\Delta \le t \le i\Delta\}$$
$$= \frac{[(\lambda_i^{(k)} + \lambda_o)\Delta]^{n_i}}{n_i!} e^{-\Delta}(\lambda_i^{(k)} + \lambda_o).^9 \qquad (26)$$

The numbers of events in disjoint intervals are assumed to be independently distributed. For this problem, the divergence J, and Bhattacharyya distance B can be shown to be

$$J = \sum_1^N (\lambda_i^{(1)} + \lambda_o) \ln\left[\frac{\lambda_i^{(1)} + \lambda_o}{\lambda_i^{(2)} + \lambda_o}\right] +$$
$$\sum_1^N (\lambda_i^{(2)} + \lambda_o) \ln\left[\frac{\lambda_i^{(2)} + \lambda_o}{\lambda_i^{(1)} + \lambda_o}\right]. \qquad (27)$$

$$B = 2\sum_1^N [\sqrt{\lambda_i^{(1)} + \lambda_o} - \sqrt{\lambda_i^{(2)} + \lambda_o}]^2. \qquad (28)$$

Let us first determine the choice of signals (i.e., of the $\lambda_i^{(k)}$) that maximizes J. A first step is clearly to make

$$\lambda_i^{(k)} = 0 \text{ when } \lambda_i^{(j)} \ne 0, j \ne k \qquad (29)$$

[8] It is easy to check in this problem that at low SNR, $J \doteq 8B$. [At all SNR, we shall show cf. (72), that for Gaussian densities $J \ge 8B$.]

[9] For convenience, we shall henceforth take $\Delta = 1$.

i.e., to make the signals *orthogonal* in a certain sense. However, the divergence can be increased still further. Thus, let us define a sequence

$$q_i = \lambda_i^{(1)} \text{ if } \lambda_i^{(2)} = 0, \lambda_i^{(1)} \geq 0. \tag{30}$$

The constraint (25) now is $\sum_1^N q_i = 2E$ and the divergence is

(31)

$$\frac{1}{\lambda_o} J = \sum \frac{q_i}{\lambda_o} \ln\left(\frac{q_i}{\lambda_o} + 1\right), \sum q_i = 2E. \tag{32}$$

A stationary point for the expression in (32) is easily found by the use of Lagrange multipliers to be

$$q_i = 2E/N, i = 1,\ldots,N.$$

However, this stationary point is a minimum rather than a maximum. We can show that J is a convex function of the q_i so that the maximum of J will occur at any extreme point.

$$q_i = 2E \text{ for some } i, q_i = 0, i \neq j. \tag{33}$$

Therefore, an optimum choice of signals (based on the divergence criterion) is

$$\{\lambda_i^{(1)}\} = \{2E, 0,\ldots,0\}, \{\lambda_i^{(2)}\} = \{0, 0,\ldots,0\} \tag{34}$$

or any permutation of (44).

As we shall now show, maximization of B yields the same result. With formula (28) for B in mind, we note that

$$\left[\sqrt{\lambda_i^{(1)} + \lambda_o} - \sqrt{\lambda_i^{(2)} + \lambda_o}\right]^2$$

$$= (\lambda^{(1)} + \lambda_o)\left[1 - \sqrt{\frac{\lambda_i^{(1)} + \lambda_o}{\lambda_i^{(2)} + \lambda_o}}\right]^2 \leq$$

$$(\lambda_i^{(1)} + \lambda_o)\left[1 - \sqrt{\frac{\lambda_o}{\lambda_i^{(1)} + \lambda_o}}\right]^2 \tag{35}$$

with equality if and only if $\lambda_i^{(2)} = 0$. The argument can be repeated with $\lambda^{(1)}$ in place of $\lambda^{(2)}$. Therefore, for a maximum of B, we must set

$$\lambda_i^{(k)} = 0 \text{ if } \lambda_i^{(j)} > 0, j \neq k. \tag{36}$$

This is also one of the conditions necessary for the maximization of the divergence J. Therefore, as in (30), let us define a sequence

$$q_i = \begin{cases} \lambda_i^{(1)} \text{ if } \lambda_i^{(2)} = 0, \lambda_i^{(1)} \geq 0 \\ \lambda_i^{(2)} \text{ if } \lambda_i^{(1)} = 0, \lambda_i^{(2)} \geq 0 \end{cases} \tag{37}$$

with this the Bhattacharyya distance (28) can be written

$$B = 2\sum_1^N [\sqrt{q_i + \lambda_o} - \sqrt{\lambda_o}]^2, \sum_1^N q_i = 2E \tag{38}$$

and we have

$$B \leq 2\left[\sum_1^N \sqrt{q_i + \lambda_o} - \sqrt{\lambda_o}\right]^2 \tag{39}$$

with equality if and only if all the terms in the sum (38) save one, say $\sqrt{q_i + \lambda_o} - \sqrt{\lambda_o}$, are equal to zero. Therefore an optimum choice of signals (based on the Bhattacharyya distance criterion) is

$$\{\lambda_i^{(1)}\} = \{2E, 0,\ldots,0\}, \{\lambda_i^{(2)}\} = \{0, 0,\ldots,0\} \tag{40}$$

or any permutation thereof.

Thus the optimum signals under the divergence and Bhattacharyya distance criteria are the same. Some computer studies by Blumenthal (Stanford University) indicate that sharp pulse-like signals of the form (34) or (40) also minimize the error probability (for equally likely signals). We should point out that Reiffen and Sherman [20] suggested the optimality of signals like (34) or (40) at low SNR[10] by using essentially the divergence criterion. Abend [22] proved that similar signals maximized a suitably defined SNR at all signal levels.

III. Some Further Properties of B and J

In the last section, we have shown in several problems that the Bhattacharyya distance is a good measure for signal selection. In this section, we shall present some additional properties of B, and pursue the comparison with the divergence J a little further. This section is largely a compilation of several results culled from the statistical literature. We begin with a convenient geometric interpretation of B or, actually, $\rho = e^{-B}$.

Geometric Interpretation

Bhattacharyya [12] proposed that the numbers $\{\sqrt{p_i(x)}$, all allowable x, $i = 1,2\}$, be regarded as the direction-cosines of two vectors in the space of x. Alternatively, we can regard them as defining two points on the unit sphere (since $\int p_i(x)dx = 1$, $i = 1,2$) of x. The Bhattacharyya coefficient ρ can be regarded as the cosine of the angle between these two vectors, i.e., $\rho = \cos \Delta$, Δ = angle between the lines with direction cosines

$$\{\sqrt{p_i(x)}\}. \tag{41}$$

The angle Δ must clearly be between 0 and $\pi/2$ and therefore $0 \leq \rho \leq 1$. It is now natural to also consider the distance, say $\eth$, between the two points $\{\sqrt{p_i(x)}, i = 1,2\}$ on the unit sphere

$$\eth \triangleq \int [\sqrt{p_1(x)} - \sqrt{p_2(x)}]^2 dx. \tag{42}$$

Clearly

$$\eth = 4 \sin^2 \frac{\epsilon}{2} = 2(1 - \cos \Delta) = 2(1 - \rho). \tag{43}$$

The distance $\eth$ occurs in the work of Jeffreys [7], [16].

The Kolmogorov Variational Distance

Another distance measure closely related to ρ is the *variational* distance of Kolmogorov (see Adhikari and Joshi [23], p. 71); this is defined as

$$K(\pi) = \frac{1}{2}\int |\pi_1 p_1(x) - \pi_2 p_2(x)| dx \tag{44}$$

[10] At low SNR all proposed measures of distance seem to coincide.

where π_1 and π_2 are the prior probabilities of the hypotheses h_1 and h_2. Kraft [24] has obtained certain important inequalities between ρ and $K(\pi)$. His inequalities (extended to the case $\pi_1 \neq \pi_2$) are

$$\sqrt{1 - 4\pi_1\pi_2\rho^2} \geq 2K(\pi) \geq [1 - 2\sqrt{\pi_1\pi_2}\rho]. \quad (45)$$

The first inequality follows via Schwarz's inequality from

$$[\int|\pi_1 p_1 - \pi_2 p_2|dx]^2 \leq \int|\sqrt{\pi_1 p_1} - \sqrt{\pi_2 p_2}|^2 dx. \times |\sqrt{\pi_1 p_1} + \sqrt{\pi_2 p_2}|^2 dx = [1 - 2\sqrt{\pi_1\pi_2}\rho][1 + 2\sqrt{\pi_1\pi_2}\rho].$$

The second inequality follows from

$$\int|\pi_1 p_1 - \pi_2 p_2|dx \geq \int|\sqrt{\pi_1 p_1} - \sqrt{\pi_2 p_2}|^2 dx = 1 - 2\sqrt{\pi_1\pi_2}\rho.$$

There is another useful way of writing $K(\pi)$. A standard argument in analysis shows that

$$K(\pi) = \max_A |\pi_1 Pr\{x\epsilon A|h_1\} - \pi_2 Pr\{x\epsilon A|h_1\}| \quad (46)$$

where the maximum is taken over all sets A in the space of x. This form for $K(\pi)$ shows that it is closely related to the (optimum) probability of error. For, if we define $A_i = \{x|h_i$ is chosen when x is received$\}$

$$\begin{aligned} P_e &= \min_{A_1}\left\{\pi_1 \int_{A_2} p_1(x)dx + \pi_2 \int_{A_1} p_2(x)dx\right\} \\ &= \pi_1 - \max_{A_1}\left\{\left|\int_{A_1} \pi_1 p_1(x) - \pi_2 p_2(x)dx\right|\right\} \\ &= \pi_1 - \max_{A_1}|Pr\{x\epsilon A_1|h_1\} \equiv \pi_2 Pr\{x\epsilon A_1|h_2\}| \\ &= \pi_1 - K(\pi). \end{aligned} \quad (47)$$

Upper and Lower Bounds on Error Probability

Combining (47) and the relations (45), we note that

$$2\pi_1 - \sqrt{1 - 4\pi_1\pi_2\rho^2} \leq 2P_e = 2\pi_1 - 2K(\pi) \leq 2\pi_1 - 1 + 2\sqrt{\pi_1\pi_2}\rho. \quad (48)$$

If $\pi_1 = \pi_2 = 1/2$, this becomes

$$\frac{1}{4}\rho^2 \leq \frac{1}{2}(1 - \sqrt{1 - \rho^2}) \leq P_e \leq \frac{1}{2}\cdot\rho.^{11} \quad (49)$$

The bounds (49) are not entirely satisfactory. As $\rho \to 0$ (low P_e) the difference between the upper and lower bounds tends to zero but their ratio tends to infinity. However, in an important special case the upper bound is *exponentially* best, i.e.,

$$\ln P_e \doteq -\ln \rho = B \text{ for } P_e \to 0.$$

This happens under the following circumstances (Chernoff [15]):

1) The components X_i of the observation $X' = X_1, \ldots, X_N$ are independent and identically distributed

2) $\int [p_1(x)]^{1-t}[p_2(x)]^t dx$ is symmetric in t

3) N is large.

We shall not prove this result here. We should note that similar results are encountered in the study of error probability bounds for discrete-memoryless-channels (Gallager [25]). The upper bound in (49) appears to be good even in some cases where the conditions just given are not met (see e.g., Example B in the last section), but no general statement seems to be possible.

The Divergence and Error Probability

The upper bound on P_e in terms of ρ is quite useful. No similar bound in terms of the divergence J appears to be generally true. However by using an inequality between ρ and J we can obtain a crude lower bound on P_e in terms of J. The basic inequalities (apparently first derived by Hoeffding and Wolfowitz [26]) are

$$2B = -\ln \rho \leq I(1, 2) \text{ and } 2B \leq I(2,1) \quad (50)$$

where $I(1, 2)$ and $I(2, 1)$ are the Kullback-Leibler(K-L) numbers defined earlier [cf. (2)-(3)]. From (50), we get

$$4B \leq J \text{ or } \rho \geq \exp -(J/4). \quad (51)$$

The proofs of (50) follow via Jensen's equality

$$-\frac{1}{2}I(1, 2) = \int p_1(x) \ln \sqrt{\frac{p_2(x)}{p_1(x)}}\, dx = E_1\left[\ln \sqrt{\frac{p_2(x)}{p_1(x)}}\right] \leq \ln [E_1(\sqrt{p_2(X)/p_1(X)})] = \ln \rho.$$

A crude lower bound on P_e now follows from (49) and (51)

$$P_e \geq \rho^2/8 \geq \frac{1}{8}e^{-J/2}. \quad (52)$$

Of course, in particular cases, e.g., when $p_1(\cdot)$ and $p_2(\cdot)$ are Gaussian, we can obtain tighter relations between ρ and J than are provided by (51). We shall note some of these special relations when we give explicit formulas for B and J below. To close the present discussion of error bounds, we note that the divergence and the K-L numbers are quite useful in providing lower bounds on the conditional error probabilities. These follow from two formulas given by Kullback [8].

$$I(1, 2) \geq P_{e1} \ln\left(\frac{P_{e1}}{1 - P_{e2}}\right) + (1 - P_{e1}) \ln\left(\frac{1 - P_{e1}}{P_{e2}}\right) \quad (53)$$

and

$$I(2, 1) \geq P_{e2} \ln\left(\frac{P_{e2}}{1 - P_{e1}}\right) + (1 - P_{e2}) \ln\left(\frac{1 - P_{e2}}{P_{e1}}\right). \quad (54)$$

Note that for a fixed value of $P_{e1}\{P_{e2}\}$, (53), $\{(54)\}$ provides a lower bound on $P_{e2}\{P_{e1}\}$. The RHS in (53) and (54)

[11] If we assume $\pi_1 = \pi_2$ when in fact they are not, we can only increase the probability of error. Hence, the upper bound in (49) is true for any (π_1, π_2).

have interesting interpretations—they are the values of $I(1, 2)$ and $I(2, 1)$ for binomial distributions with parameters P_{e1} and $(1 - P_{e2})$. Tables for the calculations in (53) and (54) are given by Kullback [8], (see pp. 74–75 and pp. 378–379).

As with the Bhattacharyya distance, the bounds provided by (53)-(54) are *exponentially optimum* under certain conditions. Thus if $x' = \underbrace{x_1, \ldots, x_N}$ where the x_i, $i = 1, \ldots N$ are independent and identically distributed, it has been shown that

$$\text{for any value of } P_e^{(1)}, \lim_{N\to\infty} -\frac{\ln P_e^{(2)}}{N} = I(1, 2)$$

where

$$I(1, 2) = \int p_1(x) \ln \left[\frac{p_1(x)}{p_2(x)}\right] dx.$$

A similar statement holds with 1 and 2 interchanged. These results were first given by Stein (unpublished); a proof appears in Kullback [8], pp. 74–77. (See also Chernoff [27]). Daly [28] has applied these results to some problems of radar signal design.

Relation of ρ to Fisher's Information

In problems of parameter estimation, we usually have not just two but a continuum of hypotheses. For such problems, a special information measure, introduced by Fisher in 1925, has been used in the statistical literature, see, e.g., Kullback [8], p. 26. It turns out that the Bhattacharyya distance and the divergence reduce to the Fisher information in estimation problems. To show this, we now let $p(x|\theta)$ = a probability density function depending upon a real-valued parameter θ, $0 \le \theta \le 1$, say. Then returning to our geometric picture, (41), we can calculate

$$\cos \delta s = \int \sqrt{p(x|\theta)p(x|\theta + \delta\theta)}dx$$

$$\doteq 1 - \frac{(\delta\theta)^2}{8}\int_{-\infty}^{\infty} \frac{[\dot{p}(x|\theta)]^2}{p(x|\theta)}dx \quad (55)$$

where $\dot{p}(x|\theta) = (d/dx)\dot{p}(x|\theta)$ and δs = actual length between the points with direction cosiness

$$\sqrt{p(x|\theta)} \text{ and } \sqrt{p(x|\theta + \delta\theta)}. \quad (56)$$

In the limit as δs and $\delta\theta$ tend to zero we get

$$\left(\frac{ds}{d\theta}\right)^2 = \frac{1}{4}\int_{-\infty}^{\infty} \frac{[\dot{p}(x|\theta)]^2}{p(x|\theta)}dx$$

$$= -\frac{1}{4}\int_{-\infty}^{\infty} p(x|\theta)\left[\frac{\partial^2}{\partial\theta^2}\ln p(x|\theta)\right]d\theta$$

$$\triangleq \frac{1}{4} \text{ (the Fisher measure of information).} \quad (57)$$

This derivation is due to Bhattacharyya [12]. A similar calculation for the divergence[12] can be found in Kullback [8], p. 55. The somewhat unexpected appearance of the Fisher information in certain singular detection problems has recently been noted by Shepp [29].

Explicit Formulas for B and J

We can calculate B explicitly for a large class of distributions—the exponential family. Before giving the general formula we list a few important special cases.

Multinomial Distributions

If $p_1(x) = \sum_{j=1}^{N} p_j^{(i)}\delta(x - j)$, then B

$$= -\ln\left[\sum_1^N \sqrt{p_j^{(1)}p_j^{(2)}}\right]. \quad (58)$$

Poisson Distributions

If $p_i(x) = e^{-m_i}\cdot\frac{(m_i)^n}{n!}\delta(x - n)$, then

$$B = \frac{1}{2}(\sqrt{m_1} - \sqrt{m_2})^2. \quad (59)$$

Univariate Gaussian Distributions

If $p_i(x) = N(m_1, \sigma_1)$, then

$$B = \frac{1}{4}\frac{(m_1 - m_2)^2}{\sigma_1^2 + \sigma_2^2} + \frac{1}{2}\ln\left\{\frac{\sigma_1^2 + \sigma_2^2}{2\sigma_1\sigma_2}\right\}. \quad (60)$$

Multivariate Gaussian Distributions

If $p_i(x) = N(m_i, R_i)$, then

$$B = \frac{1}{8}(m_1 - m_2)'R^{-1}(m_1 - m_2) + \frac{1}{2}\ln\left(\frac{\det R}{\sqrt{\det R_1 \cdot \det R_2}}\right) \quad (61)$$

where

$$2R = R_1 + R_2. \quad (62)$$

Huzurbazar [30] has calculated B for exponential densities.

Exponential Densities

Let $p_i(x)$

$$= d(x)b(h_i)\exp\left[\sum_{j=1}^{r} V_j(h_i)U_j(x)\right], i = 1,2. \quad (63)$$

The $V_j(h_i)$ are independent functions of h_i, or more precisely, of the V parameters of the density $p_i(\cdot)$. Since the $b(h_i)$ also depend upon h_i, we can express the $b(h_i)$ in terms of the $V_j(h_i)$ as

$$b(h_i) = g\{[V_j(h_i)]\}. \quad (64)$$

[Note: g depends on the h_i only through the $V_j(h_i)$, $j = 1, \ldots r$]. Then the Bhattacharyya distance is

$$B = -\ln\rho, \rho = \frac{\sqrt{b(h_j)b(h_i)}}{g\left(\left\{\frac{1}{2}V_j(h_1) + \frac{1}{2}V_j(h_2)\right\}\right)}. \quad (65)$$

[12] A variety of distance measure seem to have a similar property for small variations.

The Divergence

Huzurbazar [30] also calculates the divergence J for the exponential densities

$$J = \sum_{j=1}^{r} [V_j(h_2) - V_j(h_1)][E_2 V_j(x) - E_1 V_j(x)] \quad (66)$$

where

$$J = -\sum_{j=1}^{r} \sum_{k=1}^{r} \frac{\partial^2}{\partial V_j \partial V_k} \times \{V_j(h_2) - V_j(h_1)\}\{V_k(h_2) - V_k(h_1)\}. \quad (67)$$

We give one special case because of its importance.

If $p_i(x) = N(m_i, R_i)$, then

$$I(1, 2) = \frac{1}{2} \ln \frac{\det R_2}{\det R_1} + \frac{1}{2} tr\, R_1[R_2^{-1} - R_1^{-1}] + \frac{1}{2} tr\, R_2^{-1}[m_1 - m_2][m_1 - m_2]' \quad (68)$$

and

$$J(1, 2) = \frac{1}{2} tr[R_1 - R_2][R_2^{-1} - R_1^{-1}] + \frac{1}{2} tr[R_1^{-1} + R_2^{-1}][m_1 - m_2][m_1 - m_2]'. \quad (69)$$

If the covariances are equal, say, $R_1 = R_2 = R$, we have

$$2I(1, 2) = J = tr\, R^{-1}[m_1 - m_2][m_1 - m_2]'.^{13} \quad (70)$$

We note that the Bhattacharyya distance in this case is

$$B = \frac{J}{8}. \quad (71)$$

Whether or not $R_1 = R_2$, we can establish the inequality [which is better by a factor of two than the general inequality (51)]

$$J \geq 8B. \quad (72)$$

The simplest proof of (72) is obtained by considering the case $R_1 = \Lambda$, a diagonal matrix with entries λ_i, $i = 1, \ldots N$ and $R_2 = I$, the identity matrix. (The general case can be obtained from this by using a nonsingular matrix to simultaneously diagonalize R_1 and R_2.) Then from (67) and (75) we will have, after some algebra,

$$8B - J = 2\sum \ln(1 + \lambda_i)^2/4\lambda_i - \sum(\lambda_i - 1)^2/2\lambda_i.$$

But from the inequality $\ln(1 + \lambda) < \lambda$, we have

$$\ln(1 + \lambda)^2/4\lambda = \ln(1 + [(\lambda - 1)^2)/4\lambda]) \leq (\lambda - 1)^2/4\lambda \quad (73)$$

so that, using this for each λ_i, we get

$$8B - J \leq 0.$$

Differential Equations for B and J

Recently there has been interest (Schweppe [31], Schweppe and Athans [32]), in applying the techniques of control theory to signal design. To do this, it is convenient to obtain differential equations (in continuous-time) for the performance criterion. Schweppe has used B and J for these criteria and obtained differential equations for them when the signal and noise process are projections of Gaussian-Markov processes. The detailed formulas are too complicated to reproduce here, but they can be found in Schweppe [31]. However, we may note that for Gaussian processes with unequal covariances the differential equations for J are so much more complicated than the equations for B that Schweppe does not put down the equations for J. To quote him, "readers who subscribe to the theory that 'the best answer is the simplest answer' may decide that the Bhattacharyya distance is superior to the divergence."

[13] This is the famous Mahalanobis D^2-statistic.

IV. Further Applications and Extensions to Continuous-Time

The Bhattacharyya distance has found several applications in classical statistics (see, e.g., the papers by Matusita [33], Hannan [34], Rao [35]. A recent application is by Stein [36], p. 17. Stein's result is that the increase in the Bayes risk in a decision problem when an incorrect prior distribution, say π', is used on the hypotheses is bounded (under sufficient regularity conditions) by a constant times the Bhattacharyya distance between π' and the true prior distribution π. (This result also extends to prior distributions on unknown parameters.)

We have treated only the two-hypothesis case. In the M-hypothesis case, it appears that the average Bhattacharyya distance

$$\bar{B} = \sum_{i,j}^{M} \pi^{(i)}\pi^{(j)} \int_{-\infty}^{\infty} \sqrt{p_i(x)p_j(x)}\, dx$$

would be a suitable measure for signal selection. This average measure will have the same *minimax* property discussed by Grettenberg [10] for the average divergence. Furthermore it appears (cf. Gallager [25]), (87)) that, for low P_e, $\bar{B}$ essentially determines the error probability, P_e, in the M-hypothesis case.

We close with some comments on the continuous-time case. The usual method of solving continuous-time problems is to start with an approximate discrete-time problem and then obtain the final answer as a limit of the solution to the discrete-time problem. The same procedure works here with one modification. If we set $X(t_i) = x_i$, $i = 1, \ldots N$, then the Bhattacharyya distance when observations are restricted to $\{t_i, i = 1, \ldots N\}$ is

$$B_N = -\ln \int \sqrt{p_{1N}(x)p_{2N}(x)}\,dx \quad (74)$$

where

$p_{iN}(x)$ — probability density function of the N random variables $x(t_i)$, $i = 1, \ldots N$. (75)

As $N \to \infty$, $\lim_{N\to\infty} p_{iN}(x)$ is generally not defined. However, the ratios

$$\lim_{N\to\infty} q_{iN}(x) = \lim_{N\to\infty} \frac{p_{iN}(x)}{p_{1N}(x) + p_{2N}(x)} \quad (76)$$

will be well behaved (if the sets $\{t_i\}$ are monotone increasing) as $N \to \infty$. Therefore, in the continuous-time case we should define B as

$$B = -\ln \rho, \text{ where } \rho = \lim_{N\to\infty} \int \sqrt{q_{1N}(x)q_{2N}(x)}\,dx. \quad (77)$$

Similar arguments can be used to define J in the continuous-time case. With this modification, all the relations and properties that we have obtained in Sections II and III will hold also for the case of continuous-time observations. The relations

$$\frac{1}{8}\rho^2 \le P_e \le \frac{1}{2}\rho \quad (78)$$

provide a simple criterion for singular detection, i.e., being able to discriminate between two processes with arbitrarily low error probability. We see that a sufficient condition, first noted by Kraft [24], for (extreme) singular detection is that $\rho = 0$. The Bhattacharyya distance can also be used to provide a simple proof of a result of Hajek [37] that the detection problem for two *Gaussian* processes for which the divergence $J = \infty$ is singular. The proof follows essentially from the fact that in the Gaussian case we can supplement the lower bound (51) on $J (J \ge 4B)$ by an upper bound on J of the form $J \le (\text{constant})\cdot B$. This and some other aspects of the interplay between B and J in questions of singular detection will be discussed in a separate note.

References

[1] Tildesley, "A first study of the Burmese skull," *Biometrika*, vol. 13, pp. 176–262, 1921.
[2] P. C. Mahalanobis, "Analysis of race mixture in Bengal," *J. Asiat. Soc. (India)*, vol. 23, pp. 301–310, 1925.
[3] ——"On the generalized distance in statistics," *Proc. Nat'l Inst. Sci. (India)*, vol. 12, pp. 49–55, 1936.
[4] R. A. Fisher, "The use of multiple measurements in taxonomic problems," *Ann. Eugencis*, vol. 7, pp. 179–188, 1936; *Contributions to Mathematical Statistics*. New York: Wiley, 1950.
[5] T. W. Anderson, *An Introduction to Multivariate Statistical Analysis*. New York: Wiley, 1958.
[6] C. R. Rao, *Advanced Statistical Methods in the Estimation of Statistical Parameters*. New York: Wiley, 1952.
[7] H. Jeffreys, "An invariant form for the prior probability in estimation problems," *Proc. Roy. Soc. A.*, vol. 186, pp. 453–461, 1946.
[8] S. Kullback, *Information Theory and Statistics*. New York: Wiley, 1959.
[9] T. Marill and D. M. Green, "On the effectiveness of receptors in recognition systems," *IEEE Trans. on Information Theory*, vol. IT-9, pp. 11–17, January 1963.
[10] T. L. Grettenberg, "Signal selection in communication and radar systems," *IEEE Trans. on Information Theory*, vol. IT-9, pp. 265–275, October 1963.
[11] G. P. Hingorani and J. C. Hancock, "A transmitted reference system for communication in random or unknown channels, *IEEE Trans. on Communication Technology*, vol. COM-13, pp. 293–301, September 1965.
[12] A. Bhattacharyya, "On a measure of divergence between two statistical populations defined by their probability distributions," *Bull. Calcutta Math. Soc.*, vol. 35, pp. 99–109, 1943.
[13] S. Kakutani, "On equivalence of infinite product measures," *Ann. Math. Stat.*, vol. 49, pp. 214–224, 1948.
[14] E. Hellinger, "Neue begrundung der theorie quadrātischer formen von unendlichvielen verānderlichen," *J. für die Reine und angew. Math.*, vol. 36, pp. 210–271, 1909.
[15] H. Chernoff, "A measure of asymptotic efficiency for tests of a hypothesis based on a sum of observations," *Ann. Math. Stat.*, vol. 23, pp. 493–507, 1952.
[16] H. Jeffreys, *Theory of Probability*. Oxford University Press, 1948.
[17] S. Kullback and R. A. Leibler, "On information and sufficiency," *Ann. Math. Stat.*, vol. 22, pp. 79–86, 1951.
[18] S. Karlin and R. N. Bradt, "On the design and comparison of dichotomous experiments," *Ann. Math. Stat.*, vol. 27, pp. 390–409, 1956.
[19] D. Blackwell, "Comparison of experiments," *Proc. Second Berkeley Symp. on Probability and Statistics*. Berkeley, Calif.: University of California Press, vol. 1, pp. 93–102, 1951.
[20] B. Reiffen and H. Sherman, "An optimum demodulator for Poisson processes: photon source detectors," *Proc. IEEE*, vol. 51, pp. 1316–1320, October 1963.
[21] J. N. Pierce, "Theoretical limitations of frequency and time diversity for fading binary transmissions, *IRE Trans. on Communications Systems (Corres.)*, vol. CS-9, pp. 186–187, June 1961.
[22] K. Abend, "Optimum photon detection," *IEEE Trans. on Information Theory*, vol. IT-12, pp. 64–65, January 1966.
[23] B. P. Adhikari and D. D. Joshi, "Distance discrimation et resume exhaustif," *Publs. Inst. Statist.*, vol. 5, pp. 57–74, 1956.
[24] C. H. Kraft, "Some conditions for consistency and uniform consistency of statistical procedures," University of California Publications in Statistics, 1955.
[25] R. G. Gallager, "A simple derivation of the coding theorem and some applications," *IEEE Trans. on Information Theory*, vol. IT-11, pp. 3–18, January 1965.
[26] W. Hoeffding and J. Wolfowitz, "Distinguishability of sets of distributions," *Ann. Math. Stat.*, vol. 29, pp. 700–718, 1958.
[27] H. Chernoff, "Large-sample theory: parametric case," *Ann. Math. Stat.*, vol. 27, pp. 1–22, 1956.
[28] R. F. Daly, "Signal design for efficient detection in randomly dispersive media," SRI Tech. Rept. on Project 186531-144, 1965.
[29] L. A. Shepp, "Distinguishing a sequence of random variables from a translate of itself," *Ann. Math. Stat.*, vol. 36, pp. 1107–1112, 1965.
[30] V. S. Huzurbazar, "Exact forms of some invariants for distributions admitting sufficient statistics," *Biometrika*, vol. 42, pp. 533–537, 1955.
[31] F. Schweppe, "On the distance between Gaussian processes: the state space approach," *Information and Control*, 1967.
[32] F. Schweppe and M. Athans, "On the design of optimal modulation schemes via control-theoretic concepts I: formulation," to be published.
[33] K. Matusita, "Decision rules, based on the distance for problems of fit, two samples and estimation," *Ann. Math. Stat.*, vol. 26, pp. 631–640, 1955.
[34] J. Hannan, "Consistency of maximum likelihood estimation of discrete distributions," in *Contributions to Probability and Statistics*, I. Olkin, Ed. Stanford, Calif.: Stanford University Press, 1960.
[35] C. R. Rao, "Asymptotic efficiency and limiting information," *Proc. Fourth Berkeley Symp. on Probability and Statistics*. Berkeley, Calif.: University of California Press, vol. 1, pp. 531–545, 1961.
[36] C. Stein "Approximation of improper prior measures by prior probability measures," Department of Statistics, Stanford University, Stanford, Calif., Tech. Rept. 12, 1964.
[37] J. Hajek, "On a property of normal distribution of any stochastic process" (in Russian), *Czech. Math. J.*, vol. 83, pp. 610–618, 1958; a translation appears in "Selected Translations" in *Math. Statistics and Probability*, vol. 1, pp. 245–252.

Thomas Kailath (S'57–M'62) was born in Poona, India, on June 7, 1935. He received the B.E. degree from the College of Engineering, Poona, in 1956, and the M.S. and Ph.D. degrees in electrical engineering from Massachusetts Institute of Technology, Cambridge, in 1959 and 1961, respectively.

He worked at the Jet Propulsion Laboratories in Pasadena, Calif., until December, 1962. Since then he has been at Stanford University, Calif., where he is Associate Professor of Electrical Engineering. He is a consultant for several industrial companies and is also editor of the Prentice-Hall series in Information Theory.

He is a member of IMS, AMS, MAA, URSI, and Sigma Xi.

Reprinted from *Trans. Fourth Prague Conf. Inform. Theory, Statist. Decision Functions, and Random Processes,* Prague, 1965, pp. 635–660

KARHUNEN-LOÈVE EXPANSION AND FACTOR ANALYSIS THEORETICAL REMARKS AND APPLICATIONS *

11

SATOSI WATANABE

NEW HAVEN

ABSTRACT

The Karhunen-Loève expansion is shown to be a powerful tool in information compression for the purpose of pattern recognition. Two mathematical theorems are proven, establishing not only the well-known error-minimizing property, but also the entropy-minimizing property of the K—L-expansion. An example of application of the method in speech recognition is adduced. An identical mathematical structure is pointed out in the K—L-method and in factor analysis, and some suggestions will be made to reduce the over-abundance of arbitrariness inherent in the factor analysis.

1. INTRODUCTION

The purpose of the present paper is threefold: (1) To provide theoretical grounds for the K–L-expansion as a tool of "pre-selection" of variables in classification problems. (2) To present some results of an application of the K–L-expansion

* The present paper contains results obtained in three different projects: (1) A project at IBM Research Center sponsored in part by the Aerospace Medical Research Laboratories, Aerospace Medical Division, Air Force Systems Command, United States Air Force; (2) A project at Yale University sponsored in part by the Decision Science Laboratory, Electronics Systems Division, Air Force Systems Command, United States Air Force; (3) A project at Dunlap and Associates, Inc., sponsored in part by the latter-named agency. The author acted as the chief investigator in the first two projects and as a consultant in the third project.

to a speech recognition problem. (3) To point out an identical mathematical structure in the $K-L$-expansion and the factor analysis method, offering opportunities for the user of either method to profit from the technique developed in connection with the other method.

It is assumed that we are given a large number of objects with known "properties". The properties of an object may be described in the simplest case by a binary vector of which each component specifies whether or not the object satisfies a certain predicate. The properties of an object may also be represented by an n-dimensional vector whose components can take any value from a continuous range. Each component may then be considered as one of the variables describing the objects. Further, an object can be described by a function defined in a continuous domain of the argument variable. The case where the objects are continuous signals in time is an example of this type. This case is a generalization of the earlier case in which the number of components (n) has become continuously many. The binary vector case may be considered a special case of the continuously-valued n-vector case, and this latter may be considered a special case of the case of continuous functions. However, on the other hand, this last case can be reduced to the binary case if the value of the function is bounded and is subject to an intrinsic finite imprecision and if it is measured at a finite number of sampling points.

The kind of tasks to which we intend to apply the present consideration is either a problem of "clustering" or a problem of "recognition" [1]. (We are not discussing these problems directly in the present paper.) In a problem of clustering, we are required to classify the points representing the objects into more than one class according to the "similarity" between objects. In a problem of recognition, we are first shown "paradigms" which are a limited number of sample objects whose "classes" are given to us together with their properties. We are then required to classify the new-comers imitating the examples set by these paradigms.

In either category of problems, no unique solution can be expected if all possible predicates or variables are assumed to have equal importance in determining the similarity or distance between objects. In the case of binary vectors, the Theorem of the Ugly Duckling [2] exposes this ambiguity most dramatically: If we decide to measure the similarity between two objects by the number of logically possible predicates shared by them simultaneously, we come to a disturbing consequence that any pair of two objects (say, a duckling and a swan) are as similar to each other as any other pair of two objects (say, two swans). The situation is essentially the same in the case of continuously-valued vectors or in that of functions. The existence of classes of objects (which is possible only if some pairs of objects are more similar than some others) therefore presupposes the non-uniform importance of predicates or variables. For this reason the problem of clustering and recognition often reduces to a problem of weighting given variables.

The weighting of predicates and variables can, however, have different origins and can be executed at different stages. In the case of recognitive problems as defined above, a special "posterior" process of weighting of variables is called for in order to bring out as conspicuously as possible the class distinction indicated by the paradigms. In contrast to this posterior weighting which depends on the additional information carried by the assigned classification of the paradigms, there can be a preliminary weighting of variables which depend only on the statistical structure of the collection of objects when the notion of distance is already defined. This kind of pre-weighting or pre-selection of variables becomes obviously justifiable when, for example, a certain variable has the same value for all the objects in the collection. (This value can be made equal to zero by shifting the origin of the variable.) Such a variable is unimportant and can be eliminated from the list of variables. Those variables which take widely different values for various members of the collection are important ones, carrying more information regarding distinction of members. Omission of variables which have small weights in this process of pre-weighting will result in "information compression". We should understand the terms, pre-selection of variables and information compression, in this sense when we use them in connection with the K – L-expansion in this paper. At the end of Section 4, we shall see that another aspect of information compression, viz., that of elimination of redundancy ensues from this approach.

The K – L-expansion is usually known as one which minimizes the average error committed by taking only a finite number of terms in the infinite series of an expansion when a given collection of functions is to be expressed as series in terms of some complete set of orthogonal functions. (See Section 3 for a more rigorous characterization.) We shall point out that the K – L-expansion can also be characterized as one which minimizes the entropy defined in terms of the average squared coefficients of an expansion. These two characteristic features show that the K – L-expansion is the most efficient tool of information compression for a collection of continuously-valued functions. A continuously-valued function of a continuous domain contains, in general, doubly infinite information. By expanding, however, such a function in terms of a complete set of orthogonal base functions, we can at least reduce the number of variables from a continuous infinity to an enumerable infinity, provided the original domain is finite. Further, we should notice that not all the base functions will have the same weight or importance in the expansions; some of them will receive large coefficients in great many members of the collection and some of them will perhaps not be used at all. The degree of evenness of the distribution of importance among base functions in this sense is expressed by the above mentioned entropy. In other words, to say that this entropy is small in the case of K – L-expansion amounts to saying, in somewhat loose use of language, that the importance in the above sense is concentrated heavily on very few base functions in this case. In fact, the error-minimizing property of the K – L-expansion points to the same fact, because if the distribution of importance is very uneven, neglect of less important terms would not cause appreciable errors.

The K – L-expansion has been conceived, as explained in the above paragraph, in the framework of curves in a continuous domain. But if we use the method on a digital computer, we have to take sample values of the curve at certain intervals, hence the curve becomes represented by a discrete set of sample values, i.e., by a vector. Similarly, the base functions will be replaced by coordinate vectors. We shall explain the theory for the continuous case first, and then add remarks regarding the necessary modification for the case of vectors. This vector analogue of the K–L-expansion is characterized as the best coordinate system for information compression.

We shall show by way of illustration the results obtained by the vector version of the K–L-expansion applied to a speech recognition problem. In this case, two coordinare axes are practically sufficient to distinguish the characteristic power spectra of ten different vowels.

The third purpose of this report is to point out that the method of K–L-expansion known and used mainly among electrical engineers and the method of factor analysis developed and applied mostly by psychologists can be brought to a problem of an identical mathematical structure. Recognition of this basic identity, as well as a study of the differences in usage, interpretation, application, and modification between these two methods will be beneficial to users of either method. In particular, comparison with the K–L-expansion will permit one to restrict, to some extent, the well-known abundance of arbitrariness inherent in the method of factor analysis.

The method of factor analysis grew out of a natural desire to attribute correlation among many (n) observed random variables to the fact that they are linearly dependent on fewer (m) hidden common random variables which are mutually uncorrelated. Since it is in general impossible to consider each observed random variable to depend solely on the m common random variables, the observed random variable is allowed to depend also on a "specific" random variable. In the literature on factor analysis, it is sometimes neglected to emphasize the following point, but it has always been the tacitly understood goal to make the number (m) of hidden common random variables as small as possible and to minimize this dependence on the specific variable, a goal which can be achived only on compromise. In some sense, the common variables are considered to be the "causes" and the observed variables are considered to be the "effects", and it is customary that a scientific effort is regarded as successful when many effects are explained by few causes.

In other words, the factor analysis can be considered as having an aspect of information compression, because correlation means redundancy, and reduction of many redundant variables to fewer redundancy-free variables is a task of information compression. This suggests that there could be some analogy between the K–L-expansion and factor analysis. Indeed in both cases, we are dealing with a linear expansion and the aim of the expansion is to compress the information into fewer and more important variables.

It was aimed in this introductory section to indicate, without mathematical formulae, the different origins as well as the intrinsic similarity underlying the two methods. We have now to leave this section since no verbal explanation without mathematics is possible any longer for our further explanation. After a few sections presenting a mathematical description of the two methods, the concluding section will explain the true common ground of the two methods in mathematically-defined terms. We can anticipate and summarize the conclusion by saying that the common ground is found in the idea of diagonalization of correlation matrix which Karl Pearson [3] proposed in 1901, i.e., long before either the Karhunen-Loève method or the factor analysis became a practical tool of scientists and engineers. It is true that Pearson's method of principal axes had to wait for the advent of electronic computers to become really practicable and versatile. However, it is none the less anticlimactic indeed if we have to conclude our review of the two modern methods of applied mathematics by discovering the essence of both methods to have already been suggested in a paper more than three generations old.

2. OPTIMAL COORDINATE SYSTEM FOR INFORMATION COMPRESSION

We consider an ensemble of a large number N of similar objects, of which $Nw^{(\alpha)}$, $\alpha = 1, 2, \ldots, v$ belong to type α, whereby the relative frequency $w^{(\alpha)}$ satisfies the probability axioms:

$$w^{(\alpha)} \geqq 0 , \quad \sum_{\alpha=1}^{v} w^{(\alpha)} = 1 .$$

Since we usually only consider the limiting case $N \to \infty$, we can make abstraction of the number N, and use only $\{w^{(\alpha)}\}$, $\alpha = 1, 2, \ldots, v$ to describe the statistical structure of the ensemble. We assume that each type specified by a value of the index α is represented by a complex square-integrable function $f^{(\alpha)}(\xi)$ in a real domain $a \leqq \xi \leqq b$, which we normalize by

$$\int_a^b |f^{(\alpha)}(\xi)|^2 \, \mathrm{d}\xi = 1 . \tag{2.1}$$

Let $\{\psi_i(\xi)\}$, $i = 1, 2, \ldots$, be a complete set of orthogonal and normalized base functions defined in the domain $[a, b]$,

$$\int_a^b \psi_i^*(\xi) \, \psi_j(\xi) \, \mathrm{d}\xi = \delta_{ij} , \tag{2.2}$$

so that any function $f^{(\alpha)}(\xi)$ can be expanded as

$$f^{(\alpha)}(\xi) = \sum_{i=1}^{\infty} x_i^{(\alpha)} \, \psi_i(\xi) \tag{2.3}$$

with

$$x_i^{(\alpha)} = \int_a^b \psi_i^*(\xi) f^{(\alpha)}(\xi)\, d\xi\,. \tag{2.4}$$

The asterisk means the complex conjugate. The normalization (2.1) results in

$$\sum_{i=1}^{\infty} |x_i^{(\alpha)}|^2 = 1\,. \tag{2.5}$$

Substitution of (2.4) in (2.3) results in

$$f^{(\alpha)}(\xi) = \int_a^b f^{(\alpha)}(\eta) \left[\sum_{i=1}^{\infty} \psi_i^*(\eta)\, \psi_i(\xi)\right] d\eta\,, \tag{2.6}$$

showing, in view of the completeness of the function set, the inverse orthogonality and inverse normalization (the Parseval relations):

$$\sum_{i=1}^{\infty} \psi_i^*(\xi)\, \psi_i(\eta) = \delta(\xi - \eta) \tag{2.7}$$

where δ is Dirac's delta function.

The ensemble is now fully specified by two sets $\{f^{(\alpha)}(\xi)\}$ and $\{w^{(\alpha)}\}$, $\alpha = 1, 2, \ldots, \nu$, or alternatively by two sets $\{x_i^{(\alpha)}\}$ and $\{w^{(\alpha)}\}$. The reason why the expression of the same information requires in one case a continuous parameter ξ while in another only a discrete parameter i lies of course in the fact that we are supposed, in the second case, to know the function set $\{\psi_i(\xi)\}$ to which the $x_i^{(\alpha)}$ refer. For a given ensemble of objects, the set of values $\{x_i^{(\alpha)}\}$ depends on the "coordinate system" $\{\psi_i(\xi)\}$. When we speak of an optimization in connection with the K–L-expansion, we mean varying the coordinate system $\{\psi_i(\xi)\}$ in such a way that the components $\{x_i^{(\alpha)}\}$ satisfy a certain condition which we shall presently introduce.

In the case where the objects are represented by n-component vectors $\{v^{(\alpha)}\}$ instead of continuous functions $\{f^{(\alpha)}(\xi)\}$, we can skip the set $\{f^{(\alpha)}\}$ in the above description and start from the set $\{x_i^{(\alpha)}\}$ where $x_i^{(\alpha)}$ is to be considered as the i-th component of the vector $v^{(\alpha)}$ in a coordinate system $\{\psi_i\}$, where ψ_i is no longer a function, but is to be regarded as a coordinate vector. To treat the vector case simultaneously with the function case, one needs only to remember that the index i in the following runs from 1 to n in the former case, while it runs from 1 to ∞ in the latter case.

The distance D between two functions, $f^{(\alpha)}(\xi)$ and $f^{(\beta)}(\xi)$, is assumed to be defined as the non-negative real number D determined by

$$[D(\alpha, \beta)]^2 = \int_a^b |f^{(\alpha)}(\xi) - f^{(\beta)}(\xi)|^2\, d\xi = \tag{2.8}$$

$$= 2 - \int_a^b [f^{(\alpha)*}(\xi) f^{(\beta)}(\xi) + f^{(\beta)*}(\xi) f^{(\alpha)}(\xi)]\, d\xi \tag{2.9}$$

which, in terms of the components, becomes

$$[D(\alpha, \beta)]^2 = \sum_i |x_i^{(\alpha)} - x_i^{(\beta)}|^2 = \tag{2.10}$$

$$= 2 - \sum_i [x_i^{(\alpha)*} x_i^{(\beta)} + x_i^{(\beta)*} x_i^{(\alpha)}] . \tag{2.11}$$

If the average (with respect to i) of $x_i^{(\alpha)}$ and that of $x_i^{(\beta)}$ are zero, the second term in (2.11) acquires the meaning of "correlation" in the case of real numbers. Hence, Eq. (2.11) can be interpreted as meaning that the larger the correlation the smaller the distance, which is intuitively satisfactory.

The important fact about the concept of distance is that it is invariant for a unitary transformation. This means that if we use another coordinate system $\{\varphi_j\}$ instead of $\{\psi_i\}$, the form of the expression of the distance remains unchanged. If $y_j^{(\alpha)}$ is the component of $f^{(\alpha)}$ (or $v^{(\alpha)}$) in the $\{\varphi_j\}$ coordinate system, then it will be related to $x_i^{(\alpha)}$ by a linear relation

$$y_j^{(\alpha)} = \sum_i (j|U|\, i)\, x_j^{(\alpha)} \tag{2.12}$$

and

$$x_i^{(\alpha)} = \sum_j (i|U^{-1}|\, j)\, y_j^{(\alpha)} \tag{2.13}$$

where the double-indexed coefficients or matrices $(j|U|\, i)$ and $(i|U^{-1}|\, j)$ will satisfy

$$(i|\overline{U}|\, j) = (i|U^{-1}|\, j) \quad \text{for all } i, j . \tag{2.14}$$

The U and the inverse U^{-1} are obviously related by

$$\sum_j (i|\, U^{-1}|\, j)\,(j|U|\, k) = \delta_{ik} , \quad \sum_i (j|U|\, i)\,(i|U^{-1}|\, k) = \delta_{jk} \tag{2.15}$$

$\overline{U}$ is defined as the "hermitian conjugate" of U, i.e.,

$$(i|\overline{U}|\, j) = (j|U|\, i)^* . \tag{2.16}$$

The unitarity condition (2.14) can be easily derived, with the help of (2.2) and (2.7), from

$$(j|U|\, i) = \int_a^b \varphi_j^*(\xi)\, \psi_i(\xi)\, \mathrm{d}\xi \tag{2.17}$$

and

$$(i|U^{-1}|\, j) = \int_a^b \psi_i^*(\xi)\, \varphi_j(\xi)\, \mathrm{d}\xi . \tag{2.18}$$

The relations (2.17) and (2.18) can be proved immediately from (2.12) and (2.13) by the use of

$$\sum_i x_i^{(\alpha)}\, \psi_i(\xi) = \sum y_j^{(\alpha)}\, \varphi_j(\xi) \tag{2.19}$$

which is obtained by equating (2.3) with the corresponding expression in the $\{\varphi_j\}$ coordinate system. Note that Eq. (2.19) is valid for any function $f^{(\alpha)}(\xi)$.

The passage from the representation in terms of ξ to that in terms of i, expressed by (2.3) and (2.4), can also be considered as a unitary transformation:

$$x_i^{(\alpha)} = \int_a^b (i|V|\,\xi)\, f^{(\alpha)}(\xi)\, d\xi \tag{2.20}$$

and

$$f^{(\alpha)}(\xi) = \sum_i (\xi|V^{-1}|\, i)\, x_i^{(\alpha)} \tag{2.21}$$

with

$$(\xi|V^{-1}|\, i) = (\xi|\bar{V}|\, i) = \psi_i(\xi) \tag{2.22}$$

and

$$(i|V|\,\xi) = \psi_i^*(\xi)\,. \tag{2.23}$$

The magnitude $x_i^{(\alpha)}$, or more conveniently, the squared magnitude $|x_i^{(\alpha)}|^2$ of the coefficient for ψ_i in the expansion of $f^{(\alpha)}$ (2.3) can be considered as a good measure of the extent to which the coordinate vector ψ_i is useful in representing the given function $f^{(\alpha)}$. Those coordinate vectors ψ_i whose coefficients are small in magnitude in (2.3) can be ignored without altering $f^{(\alpha)}$ appreciably. Therefore, its average in the ensemble

$$\varrho_i = \sum_{\alpha=1}^{n} w^{(\alpha)} |x_i^{(\alpha)}|^2 \tag{2.24}$$

can be considered as the measure of importance of ψ_i when we represent the ensemble of objects by the coordinate system $\{\psi_i\}$. The convenience of ϱ_i thus defined for this purpose stems from the fact that it is a probability measure defined on $\{\psi_i\}$ satisfying

$$\varrho_i \geqq 0\,, \quad \sum_i \varrho_i = 1\,. \tag{2.25}$$

For a given ensemble of objects, $\{f^{(\alpha)}\}$, $\{w^{(\alpha)}\}$, the values of the ϱ's vary depending on the choice of the orthogonal coordinate system $\{\psi_i\}$. From the point of view of information compression, it is desirable that the ϱ's are concentrated on a few components instead of being widely spread over many components. To formulate mathematically this idea, it would be convenient to introduce the entropy function in terms of the ϱ's.

$$S(\{\psi_i\}) = -\sum_i \varrho_i \log \varrho_i \tag{2.26}$$

which depends, other than $\{\psi_i\}$, also on $\{f^{(\alpha)}\}$, $\{w^{(\alpha)}\}$, but these two latter sets are kept unchanged in the present discussion. The desirable choice of the coordinate system $\{\psi_i\}$ will then be characterized as one that minimizes S. If there is more than one such optimal coordinate system, we need to select any one of them. If $\{\Theta_j\}$ is one such optimal coordinate system, we shall have

$$S(\{\Theta_j\}) = \operatorname*{Min}_{\{\psi_i\}} S(\{\psi_i\}). \tag{2.27}$$

3. ENTROPY-MINIMIZING PROPERTY OF THE KARHUNEN-LOÈVE COORDINATE SYSTEM

One of the key results reported in this paper is the following theorem.

THEOREM 3.1. *A coordinate system is optimal in the sense of* (2.27) *if, and only if, it is a Karhunen-Loève coordinate system.*

To prove this theorem, we have to explain first what the K–L-expansion and K–L-coordinate systems are [5]. A complex function with two real argument variables ξ, ξ' is called autocorrelation function for a given ensemble $\{w^{(\alpha)}\}$, $\{f^{(\alpha)}(\xi)\}$ when it is given by

$$(\xi|G|\,\xi') = \sum_\alpha w^{(\alpha)} f^{(\alpha)}(\xi) f^{(\alpha)*}(\xi'). \tag{3.1}$$

This quantity can be considered also as a matrix with two continuous indices ξ and ξ'. From the standpoint that one can pass from the ξ-representation to i-representation by a unitary transformation, $(\xi|V^{-1}|\,i)$, of (2.22), it is natural to consider

$$(i|G|\,i') = \sum_\alpha w^{(\alpha)}\, x_i^{(\alpha)} x_{i'}^{(\alpha)*} \tag{3.2}$$

as the same matrix G, expressed only in reference to another coordinate system, $\{\psi_i(\xi)\}$, since the expression (3.1) and the expression (3.2) are connected by

$$(i|G|\,i') = \int_a^b d\xi \int_a^b d\xi' (i|V|\xi)\,(\xi|G|\,\xi')\,(\xi'|V^{-1}|\,i'), \tag{3.3}$$

$$(\xi|G|\,\xi') = \sum_i \sum_{i'} (\xi|V^{-1}|\,i)\,(i|G|\,i')\,(i'|V|\,\xi'). \tag{3.4}$$

By the same token, the matrix elements of G in the $\{\varphi_j\}$-coordinate system are related to those in the $\{\psi_i\}$-coordinate system by the unitary transformation U of (2.12). No matter what coordinate system is used, the matrix is hermitian:

$$G = \bar{G}, \tag{3.5}$$

meaning that the complex conjugate of a matrix element of G with a given column label and a given row label, is equal to the element with the column and row labels interchanged. This entails that the diagonal elements of G are real numbers. Further, the expression (3.1) or (3.2) shows that the diagonal elements are non-negative. One should note that the ϱ's in the $\{\psi_i\}$-coordinate system of the last section are nothing but the diagonal elements of G in that coordinate system:

$$\varrho_i = (i|G|\,i) \geqq 0\,. \tag{3.6}$$

Then, the normalization $\sum \varrho_i = 1$ becomes simply

$$\text{trace } G = 1 \tag{3.7}$$

where trace means the diagonal sum. A physicist reader will notice that G is a density matrix, as far as its mathematical properties are concerned [4].

We define a special function system $\{\Theta_k(\xi)\}$ as the set of eigen-functions of G, i.e.

$$\int_a^b (\xi|G|\,\xi')\,\Theta_k(\xi')\,\mathrm{d}\xi' = \lambda_k\,\Theta_k(\xi)\,. \tag{3.8}$$

If the original set of functions $\{f^{(\alpha)}(\xi)\}$, $\alpha = 1, 2, \ldots, \nu$, contains μ linearly independent functions, there will be μ non-zero eigen-values λ_k, $k = 1, 2, \ldots, \mu$, counting an r-ple eigen-value as r separate eigen-values. In the case of degeneracy ($r \geqq 2$), only an r-dimensional space is determined in which the eigen-functions are not uniquely defined, but we assume, for the present, that within this freedom we have chosen a μ-dimensional coordinate system. In order to make the function set $\{\Theta_k(\xi)\}$ complete, we have to add an infinite number of functions, which are mutually orthogonal and orthogonal to the original μ functions. Formally, these new functions are the eigen-functions of G corresponding to the infinitely degenerate eigen-value $\lambda = 0$. This ambiguity regarding the eigen-functions coresponding to this eigen-value does not interfere, however, with the practical use of the $\{\Theta_k(\xi)\}$ coordinate system, because, as we shall presently see, the functions corresponding to the eigen-value zero will never be used in the mathematical treatment of the ensemble we are discussing. For this reason, we assume the function set $\{\Theta_k(\xi)\}$ to be complete, without specifying the eigen-functions beyond the first μ of them.

In the case where the data are not functions $f^{(\alpha)}(\xi)$ but vectors $v^{(\alpha)}$ whose components are $x_i^{(\alpha)}$ in the ψ_i system, we should start from the discrete equivalent of (3.8), viz.

$$\sum_{i'} (i|G|\,i')\,t_{i'}^{(k)} = \lambda_k t_i^{(k)} \tag{3.9}$$

where $t_i^{(k)}$ is the i-th component of the vector Θ_k in the coordinate system $\{\psi_i\}$. If the original ensemble $\{v^{(\alpha)}\}$ $\alpha = 1, 2, \ldots, \nu$ contains μ linearly independent vectors, and if μ is smaller than n (the number of dimensions of the space or equivalently the number of components of the vectors), then the equation (3.9) will determine only μ coordinates. The remaining $n - \mu$ coordinates need not be specified for practical purposes. On the other hand μ can never be larger than n.

The expansion of any function $f^{(\alpha)}(\xi)$ in terms of the set of the orthogonal and normalized eigen-functions $\{\Theta_k(\xi)\}$,

$$f^{(\alpha)}(\xi) = \sum_k c_k^{(\alpha)} \Theta_k(\xi), \quad c_k^{(\alpha)} = \int_a^b \Theta_k^*(\xi) f^{(\alpha)}(\xi) \, \mathrm{d}\xi \tag{3.10}$$

or equivalently

$$x_i^{(\alpha)} = \sum_k c_k^{(\alpha)} t_i^{(k)} \quad \text{for all } i, \quad c_k^{(\alpha)} = \sum_i t_i^{(k)*} x_i^{(\alpha)} \tag{3.11}$$

is called Karhunen-Loève expansion of $f^{(\alpha)}(\xi)$ or of $v^{(\alpha)}$. The coordinate system $\{\Theta_k(\xi)\}$ is a Karhunen-Loève coordinate system (the indefinite article is used because of the ambiguity due to degeneracy) determined by the ensemble $\{w^{(\alpha)}\}$, $\{f^{(\alpha)}(\xi)\}$. As far as Theorem 3.1 is concerned, this definition is sufficient, but for the purpose of Theorem 4.1 which will be introduced shortly, it is convenient to arrange the functions (vectors) Θ_k in such a way that the series of inequalities

$$\lambda_1 \geqq \lambda_2 \geqq \ldots \geqq \lambda_{k-1} \geqq \lambda_k \geqq \ldots \tag{3.12}$$

holds.

If we write the matrix elements of G in a Karhunen-Loève coordinate system, we shall have, according to (3.2),

$$(k|G|\, k') = \sum_\alpha w^{(\alpha)} c_k^{(\alpha)} c_{k'}^{(\alpha)*} \tag{3.13}$$

where $c_k^{(\alpha)}$ is given by (3.10) or (3.11). By the use of the definition (3.8), and the orthogonality and normalization of $\{\Theta_k\}$, we can show by (3.13) that G is diagonal in the $\{\Theta_k\}$ coordinate systems and the diagonal elements become the λ's.

$$(k|G|\, k') = \lambda_k \delta_{kk'} \,. \tag{3.14}$$

The λ's are nothing but the ϱ's in the K–L-coordinate system. The λ's in the $\{\Theta_k\}$ system and the ϱ's in any other coordinate system $\{\psi_i\}$ are related by the unitary transformation V between these two systems,

$$(i|G|\, i') = \sum_k \sum_k (i|U|\, k)\,(k|G|\, k')\,(k'|U^{-1}|\, i') \tag{3.15}$$

with

$$(i|U|\, k) = t_i^{(k)} = \int_a^b \psi_i^*(\xi)\, \Theta_k(\xi)\, \mathrm{d}\xi \,. \tag{3.16}$$

Since G is diagonal in the k-representation, (3.15) reduces for $i = i'$ to

(3.17) $$\varrho_i = \sum_k A_{ik}\lambda_k$$

with

(3.18) $$A_{ik} = t_i^{(k)} t_i^{(k)*} = |(i|U|\,k)|^2 .$$

The unitarity of U results obviously in the double stochasticity of A_{ik}

(3.19) $$\sum_i A_{ik} = \sum_k A_{ik} = 1\,, \quad A_{ik} \geqq 0\,.$$

Note:

$$|(i|U|\,k)|^2 = (i|U|\,k)\,(k|\bar{U}|\,i) = (i|U|\,k)\,(k|U^{-1}|\,i)\,.$$

Now, the "if" part of Theorem 3.1 becomes a direct corollary of the well-known simplest version of the H-Theorem:

LEMMA 3.1. *If two probability distributions* λ_k, $k = 1, 2, \ldots,$ *and* ϱ_i, $i = 1, 2, \ldots$ *are related by* (3.17) *with a doubly stochastic matrix* (3.19), *then*

(3.20) $$-\sum_k \lambda_k \log \lambda_k \leqq -\sum_i \varrho_i \log \varrho_i\,.$$

The "only-if" part of Theorem 3.1 can be proven with a sharpened version of the H-Theorem as explained in Appendix 1.

4. ERROR-MINIMIZING PROPERTY OF THE KARHUNEN-LOÈVE EXPANSION

As far as the function set $\{\psi_i(\xi)\}$ is complete, any function of reasonable behavior can be expressed by an infinite series as in (2.3) without committing error. But, if we use only a finite number, say, m, of terms in this series we of course commit some errors in expressing the function. In the case of n-component vectors, the errors are, in general, inevitable if $m < n$. The mean squared errors of this kind for a given m in the ensemble of objects $\{w^{(\alpha)}\}$, $\{f^{(\alpha)}\}$ is

(4.1) $$E(\{\psi_i\}, m) = \sum_\alpha w^{(\alpha)} \int_a^b |f^{(\alpha)}(\xi) - \sum_{i=1}^m x_i^{(\alpha)}\, \psi_i(\xi)|^2 \, d\xi =$$

(4.2) $$= \sum_\alpha w^{(\alpha)} \sum_{i=m+1} |x_i^{(\alpha)}|^2 =$$

(4.3) $$= 1 - \sum_{i=1}^m \varrho_i$$

where $x_i^{(\alpha)}$ is given by

$$x_i^{(\alpha)} = \int_a^b \psi_i^*(\xi) f^{(\alpha)}(\xi)\, \mathrm{d}\xi \tag{4.4}$$

as in (2.4). In the case of n-dimensional vectors, we should consider $x_i^{(\alpha)}$ as their components in a coordinate system which can be later varied.

It is customary to characterize the K–L-expansion as the error-minimizing one in the following sense.

THEOREM 4.1. *The K–L-coordinate system* $\{\Theta_k\}$ *defined by* (3.8) *with the additional condition* (3.12) *is such that*

$$E(\{\Theta_k\}, m) = \operatorname*{Min}_{\{\psi_i\}} E(\{\psi_i\}, m) \tag{4.5}$$

for every integer $m > 0$. ($m < n$ *in a vector case.*)

One may perhaps suspect that when m is given, one can better approximate an $f^{(\alpha)}(\xi)$ by $\psi_1(\xi), \psi_2(\xi), \ldots, \psi_m(\xi)$ using coefficients $x_i^{(\alpha)\prime}$ which are different from those $x_i^{(\alpha)}$ given by (4.4). But, it is easy to see that this is not the case because

$$\int_a^b |f^{(\alpha)}(\xi) - \sum_{i=1}^m x_i^{(\alpha)\prime} \psi_i(\xi)|^2 \,\mathrm{d}\xi = \sum_{i=1}^m |x_i^{(\alpha)} - x_i^{(\alpha)\prime}|^2 + \sum_{i=m+1} |x_i^{(\alpha)}|^2 . \tag{4.6}$$

In view of the fact that the ϱ's become the λ's in the Θ-system, Theorem 4.1 must be, in virtue of (4.3), equivalent to:

THEOREM 4.2. *If two probability distributions* λ_k, $k = 1, 2, \ldots$ *and* ϱ_i, $i = 1, 2, \ldots$, *are related by* (3.17) *with a doubly stochastic matrix* (3.19) *and if the labeling of* λ_k *is in a descending order in the sense of* (3.12), *then*

$$\sum_{k=1}^m \lambda_k \geqq \sum_{i=1}^m \varrho_i \tag{4.7}$$

for any given integer $m > 0$.

I conjectured without proof the validity of Theorem 4.2 and told Professor Shizuo Kakutani about it, who thereupon immediately provided me with a proof, which I shall reproduce in Appendix 2 in my own language. There could be a simpler proof, but Kakutani's proof is intuitively clear and very instructive.

When I explained Theorem 3.1 and Theorem 4.2 to my student, Jay Luck, he came up with a theorem which proves the consequence of Theorem 3.1 from the consequence of Theorem 4.2.

THEOREM 4.3. *If two probability distributions λ_k, $k = 1, 2, \ldots$ and ϱ_i, $i = 1, 2, \ldots$ are such that*

$$\lambda_{k-1} \geqq \lambda_k, \quad \varrho_{i-1} \geqq \varrho_i \text{ for all } k \text{ and all } i \tag{4.8}$$

and

$$\sum_{k=1}^{m} \lambda_k \geqq \sum_{i=1}^{m} \varrho_i \tag{4.9}$$

for every integer $m > 0$, then

$$-\sum_k \lambda_k \log \lambda_k \leqq -\sum_i \varrho_i \log \varrho_i \tag{4.10}$$

with the equality holding in (4.10) *if, and only if,*

$$\sum_{k=1}^{m} \lambda_k = \sum_{i=1}^{m} \varrho_i \tag{4.11}$$

for every integer $m > 0$. (The summation in (4.10) runs up to n or to ∞.)

A proof to this theorem is given in Appendix 3. This theorem combined with Theorem 4.2 thus provides a proof of Theorem 3.1 without the help of the H-Theorem.

It may be noted that Eqs. (3.13) and (3.14) in the real case can be interpreted as showing that the K–L-coefficients c_k's with different k's are statistically uncorrelated if α is regarded as specifying a particular value and $w^{(\alpha)}$ as the statistical weight of occurrence of this value. This provides another argument for using the K–L-coefficients as variables to represent economically the members of the ensemble. It would be desirable, from the viewpoint that information compression means elimination of redundancy, to use variables which are statistically independent, but in the absence of such variables, statistically uncorrelated variables may be the next best. Further, if each of the c_i's has a Gaussian distribution, they become statistically independent.

As a practical advice, it may be added that for the purpose of discrimination it is advisable to subtract the average function $\sum_\alpha w^{(\alpha)} f^{(\alpha)}(x)$ from each function $f^{(\alpha)}(x)$ before applying the K–L-method, for if this average is not zero, the first eigen-function tends to represent this average function which has no discriminating power.

5. APPLICATION OF THE K–L-METHOD TO THE POWER-SPECTRUM OF ENGLISH VOWELS

Figure 1 represents results obtained by applying the K–L-method to the deviation from the average of the power-spectra (obtained by 36 bandpass filters) of twelve different vowels (i, I, ε, a, e, o, ʌ, u, U, ɔ, ə, æ) spoken by 19 different persons (male and female). Each record is a 36-component vector. The center-frequencies of the filters range from 100 to 10,000 cycles per second and their bandwidths from 50 to 1,200 cycles per second. Figure 1 represents 12 × 19 points in the space defined by "longitude" $\tan^{-1}(c_2/c_1)$ and "latitude" $\tan^{-1}[(c_3/\sqrt{(c_1^2 + c_2^2)})]$, where c_1, c_2, and c_3 are the first, second and third K–L-coefficients as defined in (3.10) or (3.11).

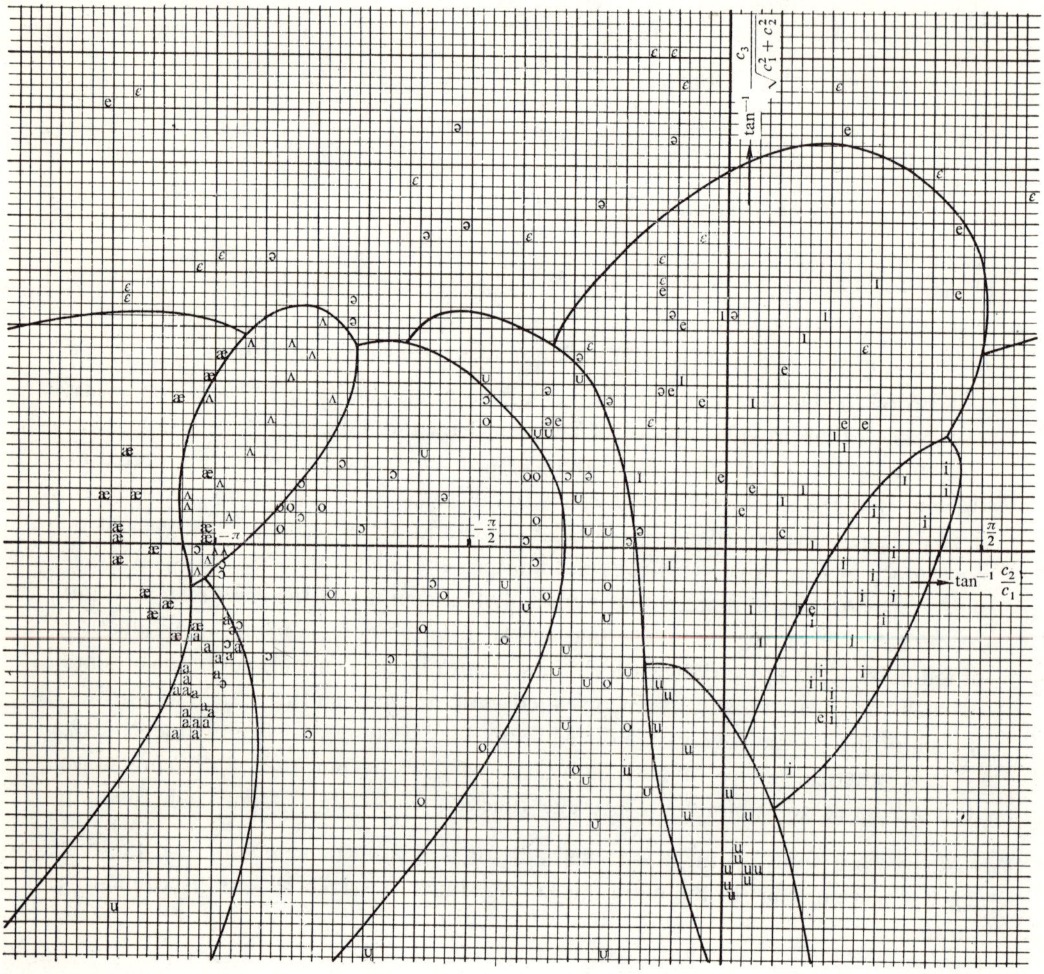

Fig. 1.

The subscript α in this case identifies each of the 12 × 19 points. Figure 1 shows also a rough determination of 9 disjoint regions, purposely tolerating intrusion of some "alien" element in each territory in order to avoid excessive gerrimandering. These zones have been drawn by a human hand to facilitate inspection. The *o* and ɔ occupy a common region, and this may lie in the nature of things. The distinction between I and e is so small that a confusion of these two may be forgiven at this stage of the game. The most troublesome one is ə (er, ir, or ur in the usual spelling) which intrudes different regions. However, the histogram of Figure 2, which represents the distribution along c_4, shows that the ə forms almost a separate island in the c_4 space. It is to be expected from the beginning that considerable overlapping of regions is inevitable in speech recognition. We should probably be surprised that the extent of overlapping is not more than seen on Figure 1. The determination of zones and location of a newly arriving signal in one of the ready-made zones could be done by the customary decision function method on a computer. A better result may be expected if we make smaller meshes than these nine zones and apply the Bayesian decision method.

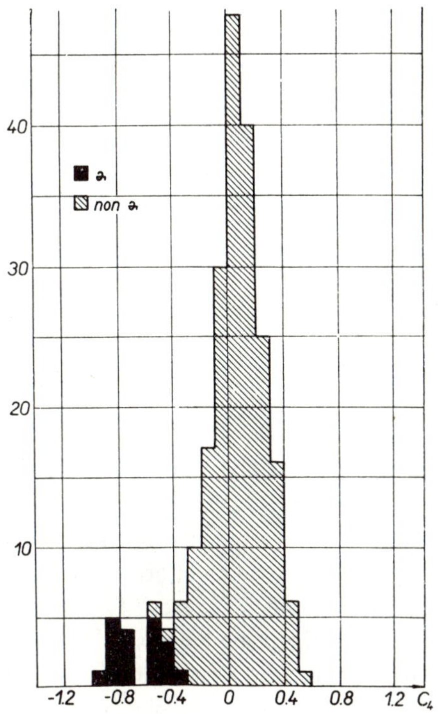

Fig. 2.

6. FACTOR ANALYSIS

Without any pejorative connotation, one may perhaps state that the method of factor analysis is laden with divergencies and complications due partly to historical accidents and partly to personal likings of the large number of researchers in the field. As a result, the brief schematized account of factor analysis given below may not be regarded as a standard version of the method by many researchers (see, for instance, [6] and [7] for classical description of factor analysis). But since the purpose of the present paper is, in a sense, to introduce another modified version of factor analysis which will be explained in the next section, it really does not matter where we start.

For the purpose of this section, we are going to introduce various notations entirely anew. Hence, it is advisable to forget, for the time being, the meanings we attached to various symbols and letters in the foregoing sections.

We consider n real random variables, x_i, $i = 1, 2, \ldots, n$ which may be in general mutually correlated. We assume that if we would make observations of these random variables in the entire population of corresponding systems, we would obtain a set of values $(x_1^{(\alpha)}, \ldots, x_n^{(\alpha)})$ $\alpha = 1, 2, \ldots, \nu$, with relative frequences $\gamma^{(\alpha)}$. We agree that we take the origin of each x_i so that its average becomes 0.

$$(6.1) \qquad \langle x_i^{(\alpha)} \rangle_\alpha = \sum_{\alpha=1}^{\nu} \gamma^{(\alpha)} x_i^{(\alpha)} = 0 .$$

Similarly, we use a suitable scaling so that its standard deviations become unity

$$(6.2) \qquad \langle x_i^{(\alpha)2} \rangle_\alpha = \sum_{\alpha=1}^{\nu} \gamma^{(\alpha)} x_i^{(\alpha)2} = 1 .$$

The central idea of factor analysis is to consider the existing correlation among the x's as stemming from a relatively small number of common variables on which the x's are linearly dependent. Thus, the task of the analysis starts with writing the random variables x_i as

$$(6.3) \qquad x_i = \sum_{j=1}^{m} a_{ij} y_j + b_i z_i , \quad i = 1, 2, \ldots, n$$

with

$$(6.4) \qquad m \leqq n$$

where the y's are the hidden common variables (which are called "factors"), and the z's are introduced as a necessary compromise because the variation of x_i cannot be entirely attributed to the common factors. At this stage, we can already point out the basic dilemma underlying the factor analysis, namely in an effort to attribute the multifariousness of the apparent data (x_i) to fewer hidden "causes" (y_j) we are forced to introduce more new variables than we had at the beginning ($m + n$ versus n variables). The enormous degree of arbitrariness brought into the problem by this fact is partially eliminated by the requirement that all the $m + n$ variables (y_j and z_i) be statistically uncorrelated. Yet, arbitrariness is a characteristic feature, if not a necessary evil, inherent in the method of factor analysis. It is of course possible to utilize this arbitrariness to enhance in some sense the "effectiveness" of factor analysis. In this connection, it should be kept in mind that the factorization would become more "effective" by using as small a number as possible as the integer m and by making the magnitudes of the b's above as small as possible.

It is customary to introduce the standardizing conditions

$$(6.5) \qquad \begin{aligned} \langle y_j^{(\alpha)} \rangle_\alpha &= 0 , \quad \langle y_j^{(\alpha)} \rangle_\alpha^2 = 1 , \\ \langle z_i^{(\alpha)} \rangle_\alpha &= 0 , \quad \langle z_i^{(\alpha)} \rangle_\alpha^2 = 1 \end{aligned}$$

as well as the assumptions of uncorrelatedness

$$(6.6) \qquad \begin{aligned} &\langle y_j^{(\alpha)} \cdot y_k^{(\alpha)} \rangle_\alpha = 0 , \quad j \neq k , \quad j, k = 1, 2, \ldots, m , \\ &\langle y_j^{(\alpha)} \cdot z_i^{(\alpha)} \rangle_\alpha = 0 , \quad j = 1, 2, \ldots, m , \quad i = 1, 2, \ldots, n \end{aligned}$$

where the superscript (α) indicates the "data values" of the random variables in the same sense as $x_i^{(\alpha)}$ was the data value of the random variable x_i. These two conditions can be regarded also as the conditions of normalization and orthogonality.

The interesting part of the problem is that the search for the common factors y's can be based on the observed correlations among the x's instead of the values of the x's themselves. From (6.3), (6.5) and (6.6) we obtain

$$r_{ij} = \langle x_i^{(\alpha)} x_j^{(\alpha)} \rangle_\alpha = \sum_{k=1}^{m} a_{ik} a_{jk} + \delta_{ij} b_i^2 \,. \tag{6.7}$$

In particular, for $i = j$, we have

$$r_{ii} = \langle x_i^{(\alpha)2} \rangle_\alpha = a_i^2 + b_i^2 = 1 \tag{6.8}$$

with

$$a_i^2 = \sum_{j=1}^{m} a_{ij}^2 \tag{6.9}$$

where a_i^2 is called "communality" of x_i and measures the degree to which the variable x_i can be attributed to the common factors. The total communality $\sum_{i=1}^{m} a_i^2$ is the degree, so to speak, of factorization of the entire problem.

The above mentioned arbitrariness manifests itself in three ways: arbitrariness in value of m, arbitrariness in the values of the a_i's, and arbitrariness in the choice of the new variables y's for a given set of values of m and the a_i's. It is intuitively easy to expect that for a given n and r_{ij} a sufficiently large number of m will make the "factorization" (6.3) always possible. There exists an algebraic theorem which gives the number N of independent conditions imposed on the adjusted correlation

$$\sigma_{ij} = r_{ij} - \delta_{ij} b_i^2 = \sum_{k=1}^{m} a_{ik} a_{jk} \tag{6.10}$$

as a function of n and m so that factorization (6.3) is possible, $N = \binom{n - m + 1}{2}$.

If N is equal to or less than n (the number of the a's), factorization is possible for a given arbitrary correlation matrix r_{ij}, provided we adjust suitably the communalities a_i. The third arbitrariness mentioned above resides in the fact that if a set of y_j's is a solution of (6.3) with (6.6), we can apply any orthogonal transformation to this set of variables to obtain another set of y's satisfying all the requirements.

The so-called principal-factor solution is the oldest in the sense that the idea was already proposed by Karl Pearson in 1901 ([3], [8], [9], [10]) long before the problem of factor analysis was formulated, and the newest in the sense that it became practicable only after the advent of electronic computers. The major portion of what we learn as an integral part of factor analysis is something which happened during the in-between time and has lost usefulness considerably by now.

Consider a rotation among the y's which were introduced in (6.3). The result would be a linear transformation among the a_{ij} in such a way that the communalities of the x_i, $\sum_{j=1}^{m} a_{ij}^2 = a_i^2$, remain unchanged. The term a_{ij}^2 can be considered as the contribution to the communality of variable x_i from the common factor y_j, while the sum $\sum_{i=1}^{m} a_{ij}^2$, is the contribution of the factor y_j to the total communality. If we aim at discovering those important common factors which are greatly responsible for the behavior of the observed variables, it is natural to set up the problem so as first to find the y_j which maximizes $\sum_{i=1}^{m} a_{ij}^2$, and the next to find y_j which has the next largest value of $\sum_{i=1}^{m} a_{ij}^2$, etc. It can be shown that this strategy amounts to finding eigen-vectors of σ_{ij} in the descending order of the eigen-values. Since the total communality $\sum_{i=1}^{n} \sum_{j=1}^{m} a_{ij}^2$ is the trace of the matrix σ_{ij}, we have to stop the process when the sum of the eigen-values has become just the trace of the matrix. The remaining eigen-values will be degenerate eigen-values zero.

The psychologists are not usually satisfied with these optimum axes on the ground that they do not represent intuitively meaningful quantities. They apply again an orthogonal or even oblique transformation within this space subtended by the y's until the axes satisfy a certain set of criteria. Some of the often used criteria which have originally had intuitive reason for their adoption, can be formulated analytically, yet nobody can claim the "necessity" of such criteria. (These criteria are sometimes called principles of simple structure.)

7. KARHUNEN-LOÈVE EXPANSION AND FACTOR ANALYSIS

The Karhunen-Loève expansion was originally conceived in the framework of square-integrable functions in a continuous domain. But if we once expand such functions, in terms of a complete set of orthogonal functions, each function can be expressed by a vector with an enumerable number of components. If we use the Fourier expansion and ignore high frequencies, then the number of components becomes finite. In other words, if we take a finite number of sampling points, as we are bound to do in handling continuous functions on a computer, each curve can be represented by a vec'or with a finite number of components. The finiteness of the number of components makes the comparison with the factor analysis immediate.

If we make correspondence between the vector representation of objects in the Karhunen-Loève method and the observed value set of variables in factor analysis, we notice that a close analogy emerges between the two methods; in fact, the essential part of both methods resides in diagonalization of its corresponding matrices G and σ. If we ignore the z's in (6.3), then σ becomes r, and r has essentially the same definition as G. Compare (3.2) and (6.7). The difference, as we shall explain presently, seems to suggest a possible improvement in the methodology of factor analysis, although how much practical gain can be achieved is not easy to predict. There are other minor differences which can be eliminated easily. Examples: in K – L, we have $\sum_{i=1}^{n} x_i x_i = 1$ (2.5) while in factor analysis we have $\langle \sum_{i=1}^{n} x_i x_i \rangle = n$ (6.2). This is a matter of normalization. In the K – L method, it is not required but is found useful for the purpose of pattern recognition to substract the average vector so that $\sum_{\alpha} x_i^{(\alpha)} w^{(\alpha)} = 0$, which corresponds to Eq. (6.1).

The basic methodological weakness of factor analysis is to be found in the artificial distinction between the specific variables z_i and the common factor y_j. Each factor y_j contributes to variable x_i to the extent quantitatively expressible by $\tau_{ij} = a_{ij}^2 / \sum_{i=1}^{n} a_{ij}^2$. Some factor y_j may have a widely spread contribution, i.e., a large value of $S_j = -\sum_{i=1} \tau_{ij} \log \tau_{ij}$ and some factor may have a sharply concentrated contribution, i.e., a small value of S_j. The specific variable z_i is just an idealized case of the entropy S_j zero. By rotation among the y_j axes, the entropy value of each y axis varies and can in some cases approach zero, i.e., such a y is nothing essentially different from a z. Hence there is no necessary reason to separate out the z's from the y's.

An alternative way to express the same point is to consider the matrix σ_{ij} which is an by n symmetrical matrix. Hence, it could determine in principle n eigen-vectors. The reason why the above-described method stops at m eigen-vectors is that the diagonal elements are reduced so as to give room for the b's, i.e., for the z's; but these extra dimensions preserved for the z's must correspond to the $n - m$ dimensional subspace corresponding to the degenerate eigen-value zero in this space. Hence, there is no justification to apportion again a full n-dimensional subspace to the-z's.

This suggests that it would be very logical to assume that the space subtended by the y's and the z's is just n-dimensional as in the case of K – L-expansion, and not $(n + m)$ dimensional as often assumed in the factor analysis. Then, we do not need to separate the y's and z's. As a consequence, the distinction between the matrix r_{ij} and σ_{ij} also disappears. An important by-product of this point of view is that one need no longer use the guess work (as often done in the factor analysis) in determining the appropriate values for the communalities a_j^2 (which in turn determines the m). We just diagonalize the observed estimate of the r_{ij}. The distinction between the y's and z's becomes then a matter of degree; more precisely, it depends on the extent to which an y_j reaches out its influence over many x's. The entropy S_j is a good measure of this degree, and may be called the "reach" of a common variable. A common variable of small reach is a specific variable.

This modifications eliminates the main cause of abundant arbitrariness in the factor analysis, or more precisely it eliminates the first two of the three kinds of arbitrariness mentioned in the last section. The third arbitrariness, namely an arbitrary rotation among the discovered y's could be retained in our modified version of factor analysis, and be applied to a limited number of y's which correspond to large eigen-values and whose "reaches" are sufficiently large. However, the distinction between acceptable factors and inacceptable factors according to some ad hoc criteria is, in my opinion, somewhat wanton, and is comparable to saying that the variable "linear polarization" is acceptable but the variable "elliptical polarization" is inacceptable in optics. (This example is not a metaphor; it stems from the same mathematical structure.) The factor which has the largest eigen-value, for instance, has a special distinction of its own, and need not be watered down by mixing with some less conspicuous factors to become "acceptable".

In conclusion, we should like to submit that the "unique" approach of the K−L method can certainly be applied to any factor analysis problem, and it will definitely streamline this method, getting rid of many unimportant complications peculiar to this tradition-laden discipline. This, of course, is not meant to preclude useful mathematical devices contrived specially for individual problems.

Appendix 1. PROOF OF THEOREM 3.1 FOR A DEGENERATE CASE

The "if" part of Theorem 3.1 was proved in Section 3. The "only-if" part of the theorem means that an optimal coordinate system is bound to be a K−L-coordinate system. In other words, if $\{\Theta_k\}$ and $\{\psi_i\}$ are such that the equality holds in (3.20), then $\{\psi_i\}$ must be another K−L-coordinate system, which is equally allowed due to degeneracy of the G matrix. To prove this, we invoke a detailed version of the simple H-Theorem which supplements Lemma 3.1. [1].

LEMMA A. 1.1. *Equality in* (3.20) *holds if, and only if, the λ_k's whose indices belong to a "terminally connected" family have the same value.*

DEFINITION. Two indices k and l are said to be "terminally connected" (a term borrowed from a consideration of Markov chains, hence it may sound a little awkward here) if there exists a chain of indices $(k, \ldots, m, n, \ldots, l)$ in which each pair of consecutive indices, say, m and n, are such that there is, at least, one index i which satisfies both $A_{im} \neq 0$ and $A_{in} \neq 0$. A family of terminally connected indices is such that any two members of the family are terminally connected and a member and a non-member of the family are not terminally connected.

Applying this idea to our problem, let us assume that λ_k and ϱ_i are such that equality in (3.20) holds. The lemma then tells us that if Θ_k and Θ_l belong to a terminally connected family, then λ_k and λ_l must be equal. Hence, each non-degenerate eigen-function Θ_k constitutes a family with only one member. On the other hand, more than one eigen-function corresponding to a multiple eigen-value may constitute a terminally connected family. Now, $A_{ik} = 0$ means that Θ_k and ψ_i are orthogonal and $A_{ik} \neq 0$ means that they have mutually non-vanishing projections. Hence, if a subspace subtended by a certain number, say, d, of Θ's is also subtended by $d\ \psi$'s in such a way that no subspace of lesser dimension within it is shared by Θ's and ψ's, then, and only then, the $d\ \Theta$'s are "terminally connected". From this we conclude that $\{\Theta_k\}$ and $\{\psi_i\}$ yield the same entropy value if, and only if, they are systems of eigen-functions of the same matrix G and they differ only through the arbitrariness allowed by the degeneracy of the eigen-values.

Appendix 2. PROOF OF THEOREM 4.2

The following proof of Theorem 4.2 was given orally to me by Professor S. Kakutani.

LEMMA A. 2.1. *For any given integer m and for a given doubly-stochastic matrix A_{ij} $(i, j = 1, 2, \ldots, \infty)$, there exists another doubly-stochastic matrix B_{ij}, such that $B_{ij} = 0$ for $i > m$ or $j > m$ and $B_{ij} \geqq A_{ij}$ for $1 \leqq i \leqq m$ and $1 \leqq j \leqq m$.*

Proof. Let D denote the class of $m \times m$ matrices with non-negative elements C_{ij} $(i, j = 1, 2, \ldots, m)$ which satisfy $\sigma_j = \sum_{i=1}^{m} C_{ij} \leqq 1$ and $\sigma_i = \sum_{j=1}^{m} C_{ij} \leqq 1$. A row (column) whose row-sum σ_i (column-sum σ_j) is less than unity is said to be deficient. The total number δ of deficient rows and columns is called the degree of deficiency. The degree zero, $\delta = 0$, means that the $m \times m$ matrix is doubly stochastic. A simple fact to note about the deficient rows and columns is that if there is one or more deficient rows (columns) then there is, at least, one deficient column (row). This can be seen easily if one notices that the sum of all row-sums is equal to the sum of all column-sums; $\sum_{i=1}^{m} \sigma_i = \sum_{j=1}^{m} \sigma_j$. We shall now prove the following statement by induction with respect to δ. If $\|C_{ij}\|$ is a matrix belonging to D and has degree of deficiency δ, then there exists another matrix $\|C'_{ij}\|$ belonging to D with degree $\delta - 1$ or $\delta - 2$ such that $C'_{ij} \geqq C_{ij}$. Among δ deficient row-sums and column-sums of $\|C_{ij}\|$, let the row-sum σ_k be (one of) the largest. (The argument goes exactly the same way when a column-sum is the largest.) Due to the above mentioned fact, there is, at least, one column, say, the l-th, which is deficient since there is a deficient row $\sigma_k < 1$. Increase the element C_{kl} until its k-th row becomes non-deficient. This will not make the l-th column larger than unity. The matrix thus obtained will be denoted $\|C'_{ij}\|$. This matrix $\|C'_{ij}\|$ differs from $\|C_{ij}\|$ only by one element at the intersection of the k-th row and the l-th column, and $C'_{kl} > C_{kl}$, hence we can write in general $C'_{ij} \geqq C_{ij}$ $(i, j = 1, 2, \ldots, m)$. The degree of deficiency of $\|C'_{ij}\|$ will be either $\delta - 1$ or $\delta - 2$ according as $\sigma_k > \sigma_l$ or $\sigma_k = \sigma_l$. The case $\sigma_k < \sigma_l$ is excluded since σ_k is the largest non-unity sum. We can continue this process until the degree of deficiency is two, and then these two deficient rows will be eliminated by one stroke. (The case $\delta = 1$ cannot happen.) Coming back to the statement of the lemma, let the matrix $\|A'_{ij}\|$ be defined as an $m \times m$ matrix such that $A'_{ij} = A_{ij}$ for $1 \leqq i \leqq m$ and $1 \leqq j \leqq m$. Then, this $\|A'_{ij}\|$ is a member of D, and the above proof shows that there exists a non-deficient (doubly-stochastic) matrix $\|B'_{ij}\|$ belonging to D such that $B'_{ij} \geqq A'_{ij} = A_{ij}$ for $1 \leqq i \leqq m$, $1 \leqq j \leqq m$. The B_{ij} of the lemma can be defined by $B_{ij} = B'_{ij}$ for $1 \leqq i \leqq m$, $1 \leqq j \leqq m$ and $B_{ij} = 0$ otherwise. This completes the proof of the lemma.

Proof of Theorem 4.2. Let ε_{ij} $(i, j = 1, 2, \ldots, m)$ be defined by

$$B_{ij} = A_{ij} + \varepsilon_{ij} \tag{A.2.1}$$

where A_{ij} and B_{ij}, $(i, j = 1, 2, \ldots, \infty)$ are related as in Lemma A.2.1. $\varepsilon_{ij} \geqq 0$ due to Lemma A.2.1. Since the matrices A_{ij} and B_{ij} are doubly-stochastic, we have

$$\sum_{j=1}^{m} \varepsilon_{ij} = \sum_{j=m+1}^{\infty} A_{ij}. \tag{A.2.2}$$

We have then

$$\begin{aligned}
\sum_{j=1}^{m} \lambda_j &= \sum_{i=1}^{m} \sum_{j=1}^{m} B_{ij}\lambda_j && \left(\text{since } \sum_{i=1}^{m} B_{ij} = 1\right) \\
&\geqq \sum_{i=1}^{m} \sum_{j=1}^{m} A_{ij}\lambda_j + \sum_{i=1}^{m} \sum_{j=1}^{m} \varepsilon_{ij}\lambda_{m+1} && \text{(due to (3.12) and (A.2.1) and Lemma A.2.1.)} \\
&\geqq \sum_{i=1}^{m} \sum_{j=1}^{m} A_{ij}\lambda_j + \sum_{i=1}^{m} \sum_{j=m+1}^{\infty} A_{ij}\lambda_j && \text{(due to (3.12) and (A.2.2))} \\
&= \sum_{i=1}^{m} \varrho_i && \text{(due to (3.17))}.
\end{aligned}$$

This completes the proof.

Appendix 3. A PROOF TO THEOREM 4.3

Consider the entropy S defined by the probability distribution p_i, $i = 1, 2, \ldots$,

$$S = -\sum_{i=1}^{\infty} p_i \log p_i \tag{A.3.1}$$

under the condition that

$$p_i \geqq p_{i+1} \quad (i = 1, 2, \ldots)\,. \tag{A.3.2}$$

Introducing a new set of variables

$$\sigma_r = \sum_{i=1}^{r} p_i \tag{A.3.3}$$

we can rewrite S as

$$S = -\sum_{r=1}^{\infty} (\sigma_r - \sigma_{r-1}) \log (\sigma_r - \sigma_{r-1}) \tag{A.3.4}$$

with the obvious provisions that

$$\sigma_0 = 0\,, \quad \lim_{r\to\infty} \sigma_r = 1 \tag{A.3.5}$$

and

$$\sigma_{r+1} - \sigma_r \geqq 0 \quad (r = 1, 2, \ldots)\,. \tag{A.3.6}$$

The additional condition (A.3.2) is now rewritten as

$$\sigma_{r+1} - 2\sigma_r + \sigma_{r-1} \leqq 0 \quad (r = 1, 2, \ldots)\,. \tag{A.3.7}$$

Now the partial derivatives of S with respect to σ_r is

$$\frac{\partial S}{\partial \sigma_r} = \log \frac{\sigma_{r+1} - \sigma_r}{\sigma_r - \sigma_{r-1}}\,. \tag{A.3.8}$$

The condition (A.3.7) shows that

$$\frac{\partial S}{\partial \sigma_r} \leqq 0 \tag{A.3.9}$$

in the domain allowed by (A.3.6). Suppose we are given two probability distributions $\{p_i\}$ and $\{p_i'\}$, or equivalently $\{\sigma_r\}$ and $\{\sigma_r'\}$, both obeying (A.3.2) or equivalently (A.3.7) such that

$$\sigma_r \geqq \sigma_r' \qquad r = 1, 2, \ldots \tag{A.3.10}$$

These two probability distributions (two points in the σ-space) can be connected continuously by a straight line which lies entirely within the allowed domain. This is because each of the conditions (A.3.6) and (A.3.7) means that one side of a hyperplane is allowed. Then, our result (A.3.9) entails that

$$S(\{\sigma_r\}) \leqq S(\{\sigma_r'\})\,. \tag{A.3.11}$$

In order for the equality to hold in (A.3.11), we must have, for each r, either (A) $\partial S/\partial\sigma_r = 0$ all along the path, or (B) $\sigma_r = \sigma'_r$. The former case (A) implies $p_{r+1} = p_r$ and $p'_{r+1} = p'_r$. Suppose $\sigma_1 = \sigma'_1$, $\sigma_2 = \sigma'_2, \ldots, \sigma_{r-1} = \sigma'_{r-1}$, and $\sigma_r \neq \sigma'_r$ (which implies $p_r \neq p'_r$). Then, (A) must hold for r and $\sigma_{r+1} \neq \sigma'_{r+1}$, because $\sigma_{r+1} = \sigma_{r-1} + 2p_r$ and $\sigma'_{r+1} = \sigma'_{r-1} + 2p'_r$. Hence, option (A) must continue to hold for all larger values of r. This in turn means that $p_r = p_{r+1} = p_{r+2} = \ldots$ as well as $p'_r = p'_{r+1} = p'_{r+2} = \ldots$ Since $p_r \neq p'_r$ for a value of r, one of them must be non-zero and this would imply either $\sum_{i=0}^{\infty} p_{r+i} = \infty$, or $\sum_{i=0}^{\infty} p'_{r+1} = \infty$. This is impossible, hence, we have to adopt option (B) for all r. This means that the equality in (A.3.11) holds if, and only if, $\sigma_r = \sigma'_r$ for all r.

ACKNOWLEDGMENT

Part of the results reported in Sections 1 through Section 5, in particular, the experiments reported in Section 5, were partly supported by Research Contract AF33(657)-11 347. The contents of Sections 6 and 7 were obtained partly under Research Contract AF19(628)-4303. Additional results which made the present comprehensive report possible were obtained partly under Research Contract AF19(628)-4804. The excellent programming job on IBM 1094, which made the experiment of Section 5 possible, was done by Joseph Harry of IBM Research Center. The raw data used by this experiment was generously provided by R. Bakis of IBM Research Center. After the author decided to try the present method on a speech recognition problem, it came to his attention that Kramer and Mathews [11] had tried a similar method on the coding problem with vocoders. An interesting fact is that Kramer and Mathews came to this idea through a consideration quite different from the K – L-method, and that the name of K – L-method is not mentioned even a single time in their paper. R. Bakis [12] independently, but later than these two authors, also tried a similar method to a problem of speech recognition. The present author is inclined to believe that had their results been as encouraging as ours they would have followed through their initial attempts and would have made our experiment of Section 5 unnecessary. The author would also like to thank Eugene Wong [13] who initially attracted his attention to the K – L-method in general.

REFERENCES

[1] S. Watanabe: *Knowing and Guessing* (New York, John Wiley, in preparation).

[2] S. Watanabe: *Une explication mathématique du classement d'objets*, in Information and Prediction in Science, editors: Bernays and Dockx (New York, Academic Press, 1965).

[3] K. Pearson: *On Lines and Planes of Closest Fit to Systems of Points in Space.* Philos. Mag. 6 (1901), p. 559.

[4] P. A. M. Dirac: *The Principles of Quantum Mechanics* (Cambridge University Press, 1930).

[5] M. Loève: *Probability Theory*, 3rd ed. (Princeton, Van Nostrand, 1963).

[6] Harry H. Harman: *Modern Factor Analysis* (University of Chicago Press, 1960).

[7] L. L. Thurstone: *Multiple Factor Analysis* (University of Chicago Press, 1947).

[8] H. Hotelling: *Analysis of Complex Statistical Variables into Principal Components*, Journal Exp. Psy. 24, 1933, p. 417 and p. 498.

[9] T. L. Kelly: *Essential Traits of Mental Life*, Harvard Study in Education 26 (Harvard University Press, 1935), p. 146.

[10] T. W. Anderson: *An Introduction to Multivariate Statistical Analysis* (New York, John Wiley, 1958).

[11] H. P. Kramer, M. V. Mathews: *A Linear Coding for Transmitting a Set of Correlated Signals*, IRE Trans. IT-2, 1956, p. 41.

[12] R. Bakis: *Some Observations Concerning the Number of Filters Needed for Speech Analysis*, Research Memorandum PR 13, AR 31, February 17, 1960 (IBM internal publication).

[13] E. Wong: *Vector Stochastic Processes in Problems of Communication Theory*, Thesis, Princeton University, May, 1959.

YALE UNIVERSITY

Reprinted from *IEEE Trans. Inform. Theory,* **12,** No. 2, 1966, pp. 206–214

A Modified Sequential Recognition Machine Using Time-Varying Stopping Boundaries

12

Y. T. CHIEN AND K. S. FU, MEMBER, IEEE

Abstract—The problem of optimally terminating the sequential recognition procedure at a finite time prespecined by the designer is considered. The application arises, in practice, when the receptor (feature extraction) part of a sequential recognition machine has only a finite number of suitable features available to the categorizer (decision) part, or the cost of taking observation is found too high as the recognition process exceeds a certain time limit. In either case, the urgency to terminate the recognition procedure becomes greater when the available measurements are to be exhausted. The problem is studied by considering time-varying stopping boundaries for the sequential procedure such that by a preassigned length of time, the acceptance and rejection regions meet and, therefore, one of the pattern classes has to be accepted as the terminal decision. The idea of varying the stopping rules as a function of time enables us to investigate the behavior of a modified sequential test as compared to the standard Wald test with constant stopping boundaries. Computer simulation of English character recognition using the modified sequential test procedure indicates very satisfactory results.

I. Introduction

Recent studies in the design of pattern recognition machines [1]–[6] have resulted in a sequential decision model that appears extraordinarily attractive when optimum performance (minimized misrecognition and average observation time) or learning property is desired.

Essentially, this model considers, by use of testing hypotheses in statistical inference, the process of recognizing patterns in random environment. The model makes use of the optimum character of Wald's sequential probability ratio test (SPRT) in the testing of one hypothesis (pattern class) against another. The standard Wald test requires two parallel boundaries with which the likelihood ratio, computed at each observation instant, is compared; the crossing of each of the boundaries is associated with the acceptance of one of the two hypotheses. Following Wald's sequential analysis, it has been shown [4], [11] that a recognition machine, using the sequential probability ratio test, has an optimum character for two hypothesized pattern classes; i.e., there is no other procedure with at least as low error probabilities and with smaller length of average observation time than the sequential recognition procedure. One difficulty with this procedure, however, is that for most cases the length of the observation time up to termination is a random variable which, in general, is unbounded and has a positive probability of being greater than any constant. Since it is impractical to allow an arbitrarily long time to terminate the procedure, one is frequently interested in setting an upper limit for the observation time at which the system is bound to make a terminal decision.

In this paper, we consider the problem of optimally terminating the sequential test procedure at a finite time which is preassigned by the designer. The application arises, in practice, when the receptor part of a recognition machine has only a finite number of suitable features available to the categorizer (discrete observation), or the cost of taking observation is found too high as the recognition process exceeds a certain time limit (continuous observation). In either case, the urgency to terminate the procedure becomes greater when the available observations are to be exhausted. The problem is studied by considering time-varying stopping boundaries for the sequential procedure such that by a preassigned length of time the acceptance and rejection regions meet and, therefore, one of the pattern classes has to be accepted as the terminal decision. The idea of varying the stopping rules as a function of time enables us to investigate the behavior of a modified sequential test as compared to the standard Wald test with constant stopping boundaries.

II. Sequential Decision Procedure with Time-Varying Boundaries

Formulation of the Modified SPRT

The truncation of the sequential probability ratio test at a given time can occur, if it is to occur, in different ways: 1) it may be abrupt, as may be used in the standard Wald test where no change of test procedure is introduced until the instant of truncation,[1] or 2) it may be gradual, i.e., where the test procedure is modified at each time instant so that the stopping boundaries monotonically converge [1], [2]. In the following, a general formulation of the modified sequential probability ratio test, which includes the standard Wald test as a special case, is presented. Continuous time parameter is adopted for reasons that will become clear in later discussion.

Let $\{X_1(t), t \geq 0\}$ and $\{X_2(t), t \geq 0\}$ be two different stochastic processes, corresponding to two pattern classes subject to a random environment (due to noise, distor-

This work was supported by National Science Foundation Grant GP-2183.

The authors are with Purdue University, Lafayette, Ind.

[1] This truncation procedure is inefficient because if the logarithm of the probability ratio is large and the time of observation is near truncation value, a small amount of additional observation will not, in general, permit much chance of rejecting either hypothesis whatever the observation may be.

tion, etc.) The decision-maker (categorizer) observes continuously, beginning at $t = 0$, a process $\{X(t), t \geq 0\}$ (in the observation space) which is either $\{X_1(t)\}$ or $\{X_2(t)\}$, and wishes to decide, as soon as possible, whether $\{X(t)\}$ is $\{X_1(t)\}$ or $\{X_2(t)\}$ (that is, which one of the two classes is the true one being observed). "As soon as possible" means the following: let t_T be the time when the decision-maker reaches a terminal decision (called termination time). In general, t_T is a random variable and need not be constant. Let $E_i(t_T)$ denote the expected value of t_T when $\{X(t)\} = \{X_i(t)\}$, $i = 1, 2$. Let α_i, $i = 1, 2$ be two positive constants, $\alpha_1 + \alpha_2 < 1$. Subject to the requirement that the probability of an incorrect decision when $\{X(t)\} = \{X_i(t)\}$ be at most α_i, the problem is to give a procedure for deciding between $\{X_1(t)\}$ and $\{X_2(t)\}$ such that $E_i(t)$ is a minimum for $i = 1, 2$. This is simply the same formulation for stochastic processes with continuous time parameter as that originally given by Wald for stochastic process with a discrete time parameter. In this study, we shall limit ourselves to the recognition problems whose associated stochastic processes satisfy the following condition [1]. For every $t \geq 0$, $X(t)$ is a sufficient statistic for the process; that is, the conditional distribution of the random function $X(\tau)$, $0 \leq \tau \leq t$, given $X(t)$, for every t, is, with probability one the same for the processes $\{X_1(t)\}$ and $\{X_2(t)\}$.

In order to describe the sequential test procedure, let us suppose that, for every t and $X(t)$, both $X_1(t)$ and $X_2(t)$ have probability density functions $P_1(X(t))$ and $P_2(X(t))$, respectively. Let the likelihood ratio be denoted by

$$L(X(t)) = \frac{P_2(X(t))}{P_1(X(t))}$$

and let

$$\Lambda(X(t)) = \log L(X(t)).$$

Now, the modified sequential probability ratio test can be generally stated as follows. Let $g_1(t)$ and $g_2(t)$ be either constants, or monotonically nondecreasing and nonincreasing functions of t, respectively. The decision-maker continues observing $\{X(t)\}$ as long as the likelihood ratio $L(X(t))$ lies between $e^{g_1(t)}$ and $e^{g_2(t)}$; that is, the process of forming $L(X(t))$ continues as long as

$$e^{g_1(t)} \leq L(X(t)) \leq e^{g_2(t)} \qquad t \geq 0. \tag{1}$$

As soon as $L(X(t)) \leq e^{g_1(t)}$, stop observing $\{X(t)\}$ and decide $\{X(t)\} = \{X_1(t)\}$; namely, pattern class one is accepted. As soon as $L(X(t)) \geq e^{g_2(t)}$, stop observing $\{X(t)\}$ and decide $\{X(t)\} = \{X_2(t)\}$; that is, pattern class two is accepted.

In this formulation, we have essentially derived a modified version of sequential probability ratio test with continuous time parameter, which includes the standard Wald test with discrete parameter as a special case (i.e., $g_1(t)$ and $g_2(t)$ are constants, and t is considered to belong to some non-negative integer set $I = \{0, 1, 2, \cdots, \}$). The fact that, in general, $g_1(t)$ and $g_2(t)$ can be made functions of the observation time t enables us to design a sequential test procedure for the decision-maker such that the expected termination time of reaching a decision and the probability of misrecognition may be controlled in advance.

A Class of Convergent Stopping Boundaries[2]

Consider a simple class of modified sequential probability ratio test in which the functions $g_1(t)$ and $g_2(t)$,[3] introduced above, are polynomials in t. Specifically, let

$$g_1(t) = -b'(1 - t/T)^{r_1} \qquad 0 \leq t \leq T \tag{2}$$
$$g_2(t) = a'(1 - t/T)^{r_2}$$
$$0 < r_1, r_2 \leq 1 \quad \text{and} \quad a' > 0,\ b' > 0$$

where T is the preassigned observation time at which the test is truncated and the decision-maker is forced to reach a terminal decision; namely, stop observing $\{X(t)\}$ and decide either $\{X(t)\} = \{X_1(t)\}$ or $\{X(t)\} = \{X_2(t)\}$. The graph of $g_1(t)$ and $g_2(t)$ as functions of time is shown in Fig. 1.

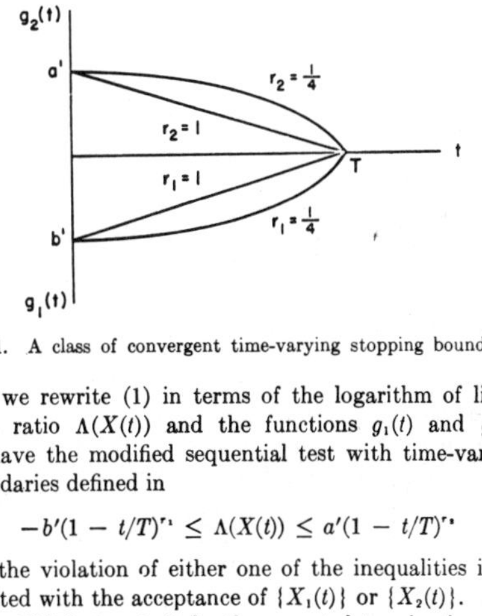

Fig. 1. A class of convergent time-varying stopping boundaries.

If we rewrite (1) in terms of the logarithm of likelihood ratio $\Lambda(X(t))$ and the functions $g_1(t)$ and $g_2(t)$, we have the modified sequential test with time-varying boundaries defined in

$$-b'(1 - t/T)^{r_1} \leq \Lambda(X(t)) \leq a'(1 - t/T)^{r_2} \tag{3}$$

and the violation of either one of the inequalities is associated with the acceptance of $\{X_1(t)\}$ or $\{X_2(t)\}$.

Let $E_i'(t_T)$, $i = 1, 2$, be the expected termination time for the modified test defined in (3), conditioned by the fact that the sample function being observed belongs to the stochastic process $\{X_i(t)\}$, $i = 1, 2$; and let α_i', $i = 1, 2$, be the error of the first and second kind, respectively, upon the termination of the test. We make the following two observations.

[2] A similar discussion in the case of discrete observation may be found in [2].
[3] In this and the following equations, a prime indicates a quantity's association with the modified sequential test.

1) The modified sequential test reduces to the standard Wald test with continuous time parameter as $T \to \infty$, where $a' = \log A$ and $b' = -\log B$ with $A = (1 - \alpha_2/\alpha_1)$ and $B = (\alpha_2/1 - \alpha_1)$. (The assumption of neglecting the excess over the boundaries is no longer needed and the relations are strict equalities, since this excess is zero, with probability one, in the case of continuous time parameter).

2) $-r_1 b'/T$ and $r_2 a'/T$ are the derivatives of $g_1(t)$ and $g_2(t)$, respectively, at $t = 0$; they characterize the slope of the boundaries and therefore determine the rate of convergence to time T when the test is to be truncated.

With the assumption that the random variables observed in the stochastic process $\{\Lambda(X(t))\}$ are identically distributed, and with the establishment of symmetry relationship on the conditional distribution of termination time (stated and proved in Appendix I), it is possible to derive approximate relations of $E_i'(t_T)$ and α_i', $i = 1, 2$, for the modified test (Appendix II). Here we shall simply summarize the results (4), (5) and display how they can be applied to the design of pattern recognition machine in achieving a better performance. Using the notations defined above we have

$$E_2'(t_T) \geq \frac{a'}{E_2(\Lambda) + \dfrac{a' r_2}{T}} \tag{4}$$

$$\alpha_1' = e^{-a'}\left[1 + \frac{a'^2 r_2}{T E_2(\Lambda) + a' r_2}\right] \tag{5}$$

where a', r_2, and T are design parameters defined as before, and $E_2(\Lambda)$ is the conditional expected value of $\Lambda(X(t)) = \log\,[P_2(X(t))/P_1(X(t))]$ which is constant by the assumption made in the derivation. (See Appendix II.) Similar equations may be obtained when $\{X_1(t)\}$ is the true process being observed, by replacing a by $-b'$, α_1' by α_2', and $E_2'(t_T)$ by $E_1'(t_T)$.

In order to compare these results with those in the standard Wald test, consider the Wald test with $g_1(t) = -b$ and $g_2(t) = a$. If α_1 and α_2 are very small and if $a = a'$, $b = b'$, i.e., the boundaries of the Wald test and the modified test begin ($t = 0$) at the same point, then (4) and (5) can be rewritten in the following form.

$$E_2'(t_T) \geq \frac{E_2(t_T)}{1 + \dfrac{r_2}{T} E_2(t_T)} \tag{4'}$$

$$\alpha_1' = \alpha_1\left[1 + \frac{a r_2 E_2(t_T)}{T + r_2 E_2(t_T)}\right] \tag{5'}$$

where $E_2(t_T)$ is the conditional expected value of t_T for Wald test. From (4') and (5'), it is important to observe the following implications.

1) $\dfrac{E_2(t_T)}{1 + r_2} < E_2'(t_T) \leq E_2(t_T)$.

This is to say that, because of the convergent property of the time-varying boundaries, the modified sequential test has a shorter expected length of experiment. The degree of improvement in the expected length is controlled by the design parameter r_2.

2) α_1' is greater than α_1. This result is to be expected due to the optimality of the Wald test.

3) If it is desired in application that error probability α_1' be set equal to α_1, then from (5)

$$\alpha_1' = \alpha_1 = e^{-a'}\left[1 + \frac{a'^2 r_2}{T E_2(\Lambda) + a' r_2}\right].$$

Since $\alpha_1 = e^{-a}$ for a Wald test with $g_2(t) = a$, we have

$$e^{-a'}\left[1 + \frac{a'^2 r_2}{T E_2(\Lambda) + a' r_2}\right] = e^{-a}$$

$$\frac{e^{-a}}{e^{-a'}} > 1 \to e^{a'} > e^{a} \to a' > a.$$

In other words, if it is desired that the same error probabilities be achieved in both tests, the boundaries of the modified test should begin at a higher value than that in the Wald test. This relation is graphically shown in Fig. 2.

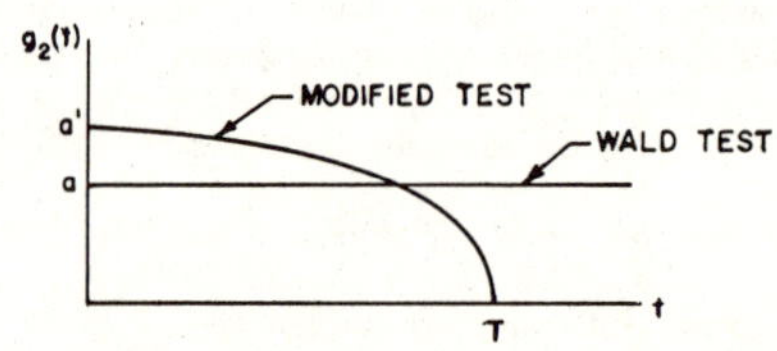

Fig. 2. Graphical relation showing the upper boundary of the modified test and that of the Wald test for obtaining the same error probabilities.

With regard to these implied results, it becomes clear that by properly constructing the time-varying boundaries for the sequential recognition procedure, the following purposes will be accomplished: 1) the recognition procedure always terminates by a preassigned observation time, 2) the expected length of termination time is controllable and shorter in comparison with the procedure with fixed boundaries, while 3) it is possible by adjusting the starting boundaries to achieve the error probabilities as low as those in the Wald test.

Procedure of Modified GSPRT

Generally speaking, the principle of constructing the time-varying boundaries for optimum stopping rule also applies to the generalized sequential ratio test (GSPRT) [4], [10] when the number of pattern classes in recognition is more than two. In order to describe the procedure, let us suppose that $\{X_i(t),\ t \geq 0\}$ $(i = 1, 2, \cdots, m)$ be the hypothesized stochastic process associated with the ith pattern class whose probability density function is $P_i(X(t))$. The decision-maker continuously observes a stochastic process $\{X(t),\ t \geq 0\}$ and decides, as soon as possible, to accept one of the m stochastic processes as the true hypothesis being observed, that is, to accept $\{X(t)\} = \{X_i(t)\}$. In a modified GSPRT based on rejection criterion,[4] the generalized sequential probability ratio for each pattern class is computed upon the observation of $X(t)$, at time instant t,

$$\Lambda_i(X(t)) = \frac{P_i(X(t))}{\left[\prod_{j=1}^{m} P_j(X(t))\right]^{1/m}} \qquad i = 1, 2, \cdots, m \qquad (6)$$

and is compared with the stopping boundaries $g_i(t)$ $(i = 1, 2, \cdots, m)$. As soon as $\Lambda_i(X(t)) \le g_i(t)$, the ith hypothesis is dropped from consideration, and the number of hypotheses m is reduced by one for the next computation. The process of forming the likelihood ratio continues until there is only one hypothesis retained, whose associated pattern class would then be accepted. Note that the stopping boundaries $g_i(t)$ $(i = 1, 2, \cdots, m)$ are, in general, functions of time and need not be identical. In fact, the spirit of the modified GSPRT relies on the optimum construction of these functions such that all the hypotheses but one are dropped from consideration by a preassigned time T. As a result of the construction of a specified class of stopping boundaries, it remains to determine the error probabilities and expected termination time in terms of the design parameters (such as T, etc.) Following the work of Reed [10], the modified GSPRT defined above may be viewed as a special Markov process with continuous time parameter. Analysing the probability aspects of the modified GSPRT can be considered as analyzing the probability aspects of the corresponding Markov process. We shall not attempt the analytic investigation in this aspect here, for the optimum properties of GSPRT are not as yet completely known. In Section III, an algorithmic construction of the boundaries will be given, and the experimental results will be used to illustrate how the desirable performance resulting from the modified SPRT may also be achieved in the modified GSPRT.

III. Illustrative Examples and Simulation Results

As examples of the scheme described in Section II, several recognition tasks were carried out. The problem consisted in recognizing the handwritten English characters a, b, and c. Sixty samples of each character were processed in establishing the necessary information for the construction of suitable mathematical models. The samples were obtained by asking subjects to write the characters within a two-inch diameter circle. Typical samples thus obtained are shown in Fig. 3.

In presenting the character samples for recognition, measurements were made on each sample as follows.

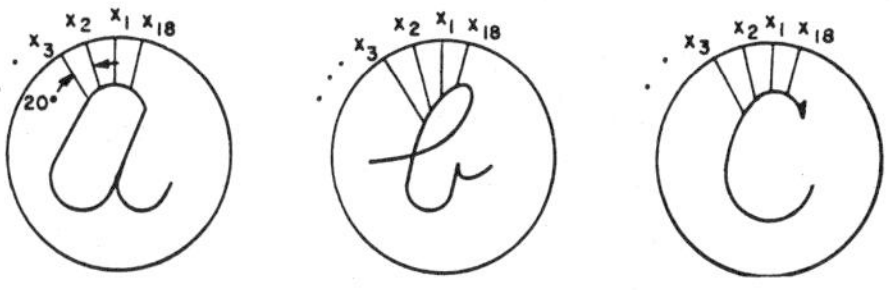

Fig. 3. Typical samples of characters a, b, and c for Examples 1 and 2.

Eighteen distances were measured, along a predetermined path from the periphery of the circle to the edge of the character. Each sample to be recognized was then represented by a sequence of eighteen numbers denoted by an observation vector $X = (X_1, X_2, \cdots, X_{18})$ in the observation space. Note that the process of discretizing the observations in our examples is simply for the purpose of their being easily simulated on a digital computer, under the situation that our results apply without any modification to stochastic processes with a discrete time parameter. In Example 1, we assume that the observation vector X is taken from a multivariate normal process where the dependence among all the components of the vector is considered. The case of Markovian dependent observations is investigated in Example 2. Since the way that the measurements were made was arbitrarily chosen, we shall not try to justify the validity of these assumptions on the process observed. Instead, the superiority of one model to the other will be judged merely by the experimental results obtained from practical recognitions.

Example 1: Assumption of Multivariate Normal Observation[5]

We here assume that $P_i^k(X)$, $i = 1, 2, 3$, represent the multivariate normal densities at the kth stage for characters a, b, and c, respectively, where X is a k-vector denoting the successive observation of $(X_1, X_2, \cdots, X_k)$, $k \le 18$. This is the case when the observation time belongs to a set $[1, 2, \cdots, 18]$, and the recognition procedure terminates in no more than 18 observations. Specifically, we have

$$P_i^k(X) = \frac{1}{(2\pi)^{k/2} |\Sigma|^{1/2}} \exp\left[-\tfrac{1}{2}(X - m_i)^t \Sigma^{-1} (X - m_i)\right]$$

where m_i is the mean vector (with k components) for class i, Σ is the $k \times k$ common covariance matrix for all classes, and the superscript "t" indicates the matrix transpose operation. Both Σ and m_i's are estimated from the samples described previously.

Case 1: Binary Classification of Characters a and b Using Modified SPRT. In this case, $i = 1, 2$. The logarithm of likelihood ratio computed at kth stage is

[4] A GSPRT based on REJECTION (ACCEPTANCE) criterion is a test rejecting (accepting) subsets of the original set of hypotheses until the subset retained (accepted) consisting of a single element.

[5] The normal assumption for the measurement distribution in character recognition has been studied by many authors [7], [8].

$$\Lambda(k) = X'\Sigma^{-1}(m_2 - m_1) - \tfrac{1}{2}(m_2 + m_1)'\Sigma^{-1}(m_2 - m_1).$$

The lower stopping boundary for the modified SPRT is chosen as

$$g_1(k) = -b'(1 - k/18) \qquad k = 1, \cdots, 18$$

and the upper stopping boundary is

$$g_2(k) = a'(1 - k/18) \qquad k = 1, \cdots, 18$$

where a' and $-b'$ are the starting boundaries adjusted in such a way that various levels of error probabilities and expected (average) number of observations were obtained. The result is shown in Fig. 4, in which the trading relationship between error and recognition time (expected number of observations) is demonstrated. On the same plot, the corresponding curve for the standard Wald test (by setting constant boundaries of various levels) is shown for the purpose of comparison. It is noted that while the same power of classification between two characters may be achieved, the modified SPRT has shown its capability of saving recognition time up to 40 percent for small error probability.

Case 2: Multiclassification of Characters a, b, and c Using Modified GSPRT. In this case, $i = 1, 2, 3$. The generalized likelihood ratio computed at kth stage for each class is

$$\Lambda_i(k) = \frac{P_i^k(X)}{\left[\prod_{j=1}^{m} P_j^k(X)\right]^{1/m}} \qquad i = 1, 2, 3$$

where m may assume the value 1, 2, or 3, depending on the number of pattern classes under consideration at each stage. Following Case 1, an algorithmic way of constructing the convergent stopping boundaries is as follows. Let

$$g_i(k) = -G'(1 - k/18)$$

where

$$G' > 0, \qquad i = 1, 2, 3 \quad k = 1, 2, \cdots, 18.$$

The procedure of the modified GSPRT is to drop ith class from consideration at the kth observation if $\Lambda_i(k) \leq g_i(k)$. As soon as there is only one class left not satisfying the inequality, this class is accepted as the true character. In Fig. 5, the relationship between error and recognition time is obtained by setting different values for the starting boundary G'. The corresponding result for GSPRT is also shown. It is important to observe that by properly constructing the time-varying boundaries, a better performance of shortening the recognition time may also be achieved in modified GSPRT without sacrificing the specification in error probability.

Example 2: Assumption of Markovian Observation

Consider the successive observation of $X = (X_1, X_2, \cdots, X_{18})$ for each input sample (character a or b) forming a Markov Chain. Let the state space $E = (E_1, E_2, \cdots, E_{10})$ where the E_i's are ten possible values of distance measurements, as described before (i.e., $E_1 = 1$, $E_2 = 2$, etc; any measurements with value beyond ten were truncated to be ten). The transition probability matrices $P_l = [p_l(i, j)]$, $l = 1, 2$, corresponding to character a or b are defined as follows.

$$p_l(i, j) = Pr(X_k = E_j \mid X_{k-1} = E_i) \qquad i, j = 1, 2, \cdots, 10$$

equals the conditional probability that the kth observation belongs to state E_j, given that the $(k - 1)$th observation belongs to state E_i.

It is assumed that the Markov chain is ergodic, and that the transition probability matrices are known a priori (estimated from the given samples; see Fig. 7 for the flow diagrams). Then, the modified SPRT is to compute the likelihood ratio $L(k)$ at the kth observation

$$L(k) = \frac{P_2(X)}{P_1(X)} = \frac{P_2(X_1, X_2, \cdots, X_k)}{P_1(X_1, X_2, \cdots, X_k)}$$

$$= \frac{P_2(X_1)P_2(X_2/X_1)P_2(X_3/X_2) \cdots P_2(X_k/X_{k-1})}{P_1(X_1)P_1(X_2/X_1)P_1(X_3/X_2) \cdots P_1(X_k/X_{k-1})}$$

by Markov property.
Taking the logarithm of $L(k)$ we have

$$\Lambda(k) = \sum_{r=2}^{k} \log P_2(X_r/X_{r-1}) - \sum_{r=2}^{k} \log P_1(X_r/X_{r-1})$$

$$= n_{ij} \log \frac{p_2(i, j)}{p_1(i, j)} \qquad i, j = 1, 2, \cdots, 10$$

for sufficiently large number of observations, n_{ij} is the number of transitions from state E_i to state E_j, and $\sum_{i,j} n_{ij} = k - 1$ = total number of transition at the kth observation. By employing the same time-varying boundaries chosen in Case 1 of Example 1, $\Lambda(k)$ is computed and decision is made upon the crossing of either boundary. A set of curves showing the relationship between error and expected number of observations for both tests is presented in Fig. 6.

Two additional results of this example may be mentioned here. 1) It is seen that in the Markovian-dependent model, only the transition probabilities $P_l(i, j)$ and the number of transitions n_{ij} are needed in performing the sequential test; complex computation of matrix operations is therefore avoided and computer time is greatly reduced. 2) In comparing Fig. 6 with Fig. 4, a consistent reduction of expected number of observations is seen. It appears that Markov dependence among the measurements may be a much more valid approximation to the physical situation of character recognition.

For the procedure of estimation and recognition for Example 2, see Fig. 7.

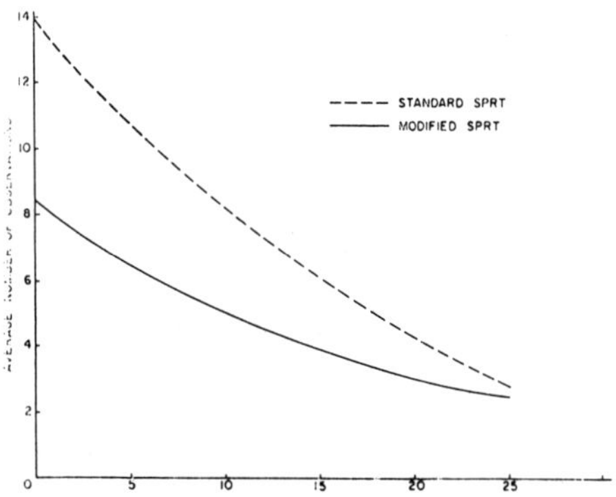

Fig. 4. Performance curves—recognition of characters a and b (normal model).

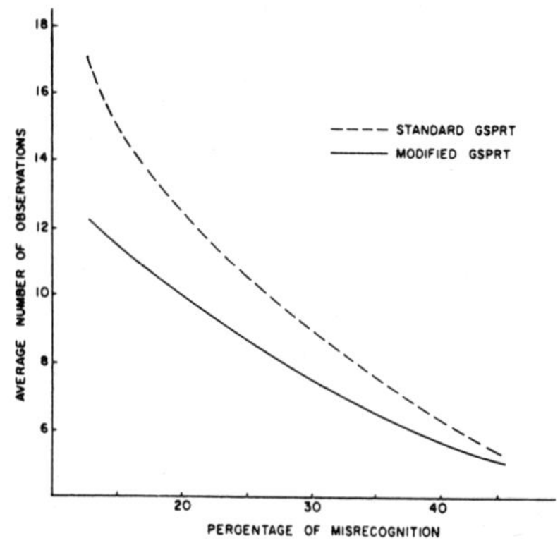

Fig. 5. Performance curves—recognition of characters a, b, and c (normal model).

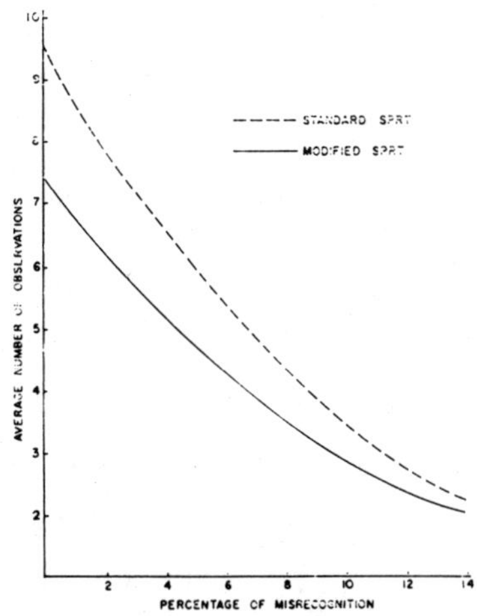

Fig. 6. Performance curves—recognition of characters a and b (Markovian model).

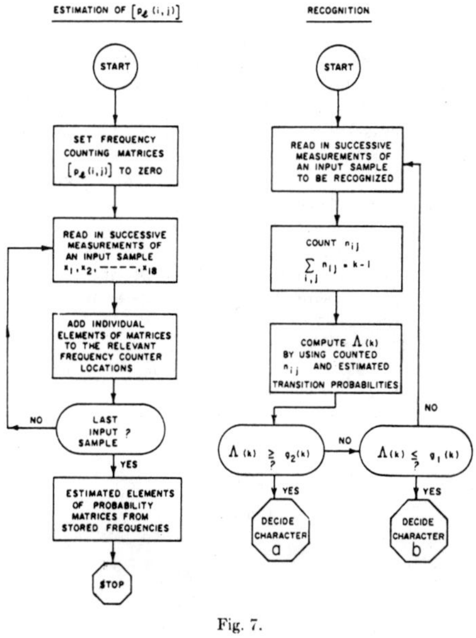

Fig. 7.

IV. Conclusions

The SPRT has been reformulated in terms of continuous time parameter which includes the standard Wald test as a special case. The modified SPRT and GSPRT with time-varying stopping boundaries have been found capable of reducing the average recognition time in a sequential recognition machine, and making possible the termination of the recognition procedure by a predetermined time. Both these features are essential to the design of a practical and efficient machine. Although independent observations were assumed in the derivation of error probabilities and expected termination time, the employment of multivariate normal and Markovian dependent models in the simulated examples has nevertheless shown the desirable performance as expected.

Appendix I

The following lemmas and corollaries will be needed in deriving the expected termination time and error probabilities for the modified sequential test. Similar statements and proofs in the case of discrete observation may be found in [2]. We shall state and prove them in terms of continuous time parameter so that some of the approximated relations due to Wald should become exact with probability one. (Note: the single and double asterisks indicate the condition that the lower and upper boundaries, respectively, are violated.)

Let $U_1^*(t_T)$ and $U_2^*(t_T)$ be the probability measures, corresponding to the stochastic process $\{X_1(t),\ t \geq 0\}$ and $\{X_2(t),\ t \geq 0\}$, of the set of sample functions $X(t)$, $t \geq 0$, which cause the lower inequality in (1) to be violated for the first time at the observation time t_T. And, let $U_1^{**}(t_T)$ and $U_2^{**}(t_T)$ be the corresponding probability measures with the violation of upper inequality in (1).

Let $f_i^*(t_T)$ $(i = 1, 2)$ be the conditional probability measure that the sequential test terminates at the observation time t_T given that $\{X_i(t),\ t \geq 0\}$ $(i = 1, 2)$ is the true stochastic process being observed, and that the lower inequality is violated. Corresponding conditional probability measure $f_i^{**}(t_T)$, $i = 1, 2$ for the violation of upper inequality is similarly defined.

Let $E_i^*(t_T)$ and $E_i^{**}(t_T)$ $(i = 1, 2)$ be the corresponding conditional expectations based on the above conditional probability measures.

Lemma 1

$$f_i^*(t_T) = \frac{U_i^*(t_T)}{\int_0^\infty U_i^*(\tau)\, d\tau} \qquad i = 1, 2$$

$$f_i^{**}(t_T) = \frac{U_i^{**}(t_T)}{\int_0^\infty U_i^{**}(\tau)\, d\tau}.$$

Proof: Let A be the event that the sequential test terminates at the observation time t_T, and let B be the event that the test procedure exceeds the upper boundary when $\{X_2(t),\ t \geq 0\}$ is the true process being observed. Then

$$P_r(B) = \int_0^\infty U_2^{**}(\tau)\, d\tau.$$

We have $P_r(A \cap B) = U_2^{**}(t_T)$. Therefore,

$$f_2^{**}(t_T) = P_r(A/B) = P_r(A \cap B)/P_r(B) = \frac{U_2^{**}(t_T)}{\int_0^\infty U_2^{**}(\tau)\, d\tau}.$$

other parts of the lemma can be proved in exactly the same manner.

Lemma 2

Consider the Wald test with continuous time parameter (the assumption of neglecting the excess over the boundaries is no longer needed, since the excess is zero with probability one) which leads to the acceptance of $\{X_2(t)\}$. We have

$$f_1^{**}(t_T) = f_2^{**}(t_T) \quad \text{for} \quad t_T > 0.$$

Similarly, in the case when $\{X_1(t)\}$ is accepted,

$$f_1^*(t_T) = f_2^*(t_T) \quad \text{for} \quad t_T > 0.$$

Proof: Let $X(t)$, $0 \leq t \leq t_T$ be the sample function which leads to the acceptance of $\{X_2(t)\}$ at the observation time t_T; then from (1), we have

$$\frac{P_2(X(t_T))}{P_1(X(t_T))} = e^{g_2(t_T)} \text{ with probability one}$$

or

$$P_2(X(t_T)) = e^{g_2(t_T)} P_1(X(t_T)).$$

Let $\Omega_{X(t_T)}$ be the set of all sample functions for which the above equality holds, conditioned by the fact that (1) was satisfied for all $t < t_T$; then,

$$\int_{\Omega_{X(t_T)}} P_2(X(t_T))dX(t_T) = e^{g_2(t_T)} \int_{\Omega_{X(t_T)}} P_1(X(t_T))dX(t_T).$$

According to our definitions, this equation has the following equivalent statement,

$$U_2^{**}(t_T) = e^{g_2(t_T)} U_1^{**}(t_T).$$

Noting that, in the Wald test with continuous time parameter,

$$e^{g_2(t_T)} = A = \frac{1 - \alpha_2}{\alpha_1}$$

with probability one, we have

$$U_2^{**}(t_T) = \frac{1 - \alpha_2}{\alpha_1} U_1^{**}(t_T). \tag{7}$$

Furthermore,

$$\int_0^\infty U_2^{**}(t_T)\,dt_T = 1 - \alpha_2$$

and

$$\int_0^\infty U_1^{**}(t_T)\,dt_T = \alpha_1.$$

By Lemma 1,

$$f_2^{**}(t_T) = \frac{U_2^{**}(t_T)}{1-\alpha_2}$$

and

$$f_1^{**}(t_T) = \frac{U_1^{**}(t_T)}{\alpha_1}.$$

Substituting back into (7) we have

$$(1-\alpha_2)f_2^{**}(t_T) = \frac{1-\alpha_2}{\alpha_1}\alpha_1 f_1^{**}(t_T)$$

which is

$$f_2^{**}(t_T) = f_1^{**}(t_T).$$

The other part of the lemma can be similarly proved.

Corollary 2.1

In a Wald test with continuous time parameter, the conditional moments of the termination time t_T, if they exist, are all equal, i.e.,

$$E_1^{**}(t_T^r) = E_2^{**}(t_T^r)$$

$$E_1^{*}(t_T^r) = E_2^{*}(t_T^r).$$

Proof: Immediately follows from the application of Lemma 2.

Corollary 2.2

For the general sequential test defined in (1), the following relations are true:

$$E_1^{**}(e^{g_2(t_T)}) = \frac{1-\alpha_2}{\alpha_1} \tag{8}$$

$$E_2^{**}(e^{-g_2(t_T)}) = \frac{\alpha_1}{1-\alpha_2} \tag{9}$$

$$E_1^{**}(e^{g_2(t_T)})E_2^{**}(e^{-g_2(t_T)}) = 1. \tag{10}$$

Proof: To prove (8) we note

$$U_2^{**}(t_T) = e^{g_2(t_T)}U_1^{**}(t_T).$$

Hence

$$E_1^{**}(e^{g_2(t_T)}) = \int_0^\infty e^{g_2(t_T)}f_1^{**}(t_T)\,dt_T$$

$$= \int_0^\infty \frac{U_2^{**}(t_T)}{U_1^{**}(t_T)}\cdot\frac{U_1^{**}(t_T)}{\alpha_1}\,dt_T$$

$$= \frac{1}{\alpha_1}\int_0^\infty U_2^{**}(t_T)\,dt_T = \frac{1-\alpha_2}{\alpha_1}.$$

The proof of (9) is similar, and (10) follows from the application of (8) and (9).

Appendix II

This appendix covers the derivation of the expected value of termination time t_T and error probabilities for the Modified sequential test.

In this derivation we need a theorem concerning Wald's equation with continuous time parameter, which is stated and proved as follows.

Theorem

Let $\{\Lambda(t), t \geq 0\}$ be a stochastic process whose expected value exists and is equal to $E(\Lambda)$. Let $\{Z(t_T); t_T \geq 0\}$ be another stochastic process where $Z(t_T) = \int_0^{t_T}\Lambda(t)\,dt$ and t_T is a random variable whose $E(t_T)$ exits. If t_T and $\Lambda(t)$, for all t, are statistically independent, i.e., $p(t_T, \Lambda(t)) = P(t_T)P(\Lambda(t))$, then $E[Z(t_T)] = E[t_T]E[\Lambda]$ if the expected value is finite.

Proof:

$$E[Z(t_T)] = \int_{\Omega_{\Lambda(t)}}\int_{\Omega_{t_T}}\int_0^{t_T}\Lambda(t)\,dt\,P(t_T, \Lambda(t))\,dt_T\,d\Lambda(t)$$

$$= \int_{\Omega_{\Lambda(t)}}\int_{\Omega_{t_T}}\int_0^{t_T}\Lambda(t)\,dt\,P(t_T)P(\Lambda(t))\,dt_T\,d\Lambda(t).$$

Since the expected value is assumed to be finite, we apply Fubini's theorem and the above integral becomes

$$= \int_{\Omega_{t_T}}\int_0^{t_T}\int_{\Omega_{\Lambda(t)}}\Lambda(t)P(\Lambda(t))\,d\Lambda(t)P(t_T)\,dt\,dt_T$$

$$= \int_{\Omega_{t_T}}\int_0^{t_T}E[\Lambda]P(t_T)\,dt\,dt_T$$

$$= E[\Lambda]\int_{\Omega_{t_T}}t_TP(t_T)\,dt_T = E[t_T]E[\Lambda]. \qquad \text{Q.E.D.}$$

Now, let $E_i'(t_T)$ $(i = 1, 2)$ be the conditional expected value of termination time t_T for the modified test. Let $\alpha_i'(i = 1, 2)$ be the error of the first and second kind. Assuming the α''s are small such that $1 - \alpha_1' \approx 1$ and $1 - \alpha_2' \approx 1$, we have

$$E_2'(t_T) = E_2'^{*}(t_T)\alpha_2' + E_2'^{**}(t_T)(1-\alpha_2') \approx E_2'^{**}(t_T).$$

Using the above theorem and following the path of Bussgang's [2] derivation

$$E_2'\left[\int_0^{t_T}\Lambda(t)\,dt\right] = E_2'(t_T)E_2'(\Lambda) \approx E_2'^{**}(t_T)E_2(\Lambda)$$

where

$$\Lambda = \log L(X(t)) = \log \frac{P_2(X(t))}{P_1(X(t))}$$

and

$$E_2'\left[\int_0^{t_T} \Lambda(t)\,dt\right] = \alpha_2' E_2'^*\left[-b'\left(1 - \frac{t_T}{T}\right)^{r_1}\right] + (1 - \alpha_1')E_2'^{**}\left[a'\left(1 - \frac{t_T}{T}\right)^{r_2}\right] \approx E_2'^{**}[a'(1 - t_T/T)^{r_2}].$$

Letting $u = t_T/T$ and equating the two foregoing equations,

$$E_2'^{**}(t_T)E_2(\Lambda) \approx E_2'^{**}[a'(1 - u)^{r_2}].$$

By expanding $(1 - u)^{r_2}$ and neglecting all the conditional moments of u higher than the first we have

$$E_2'^{**}(t_T) \geq \frac{a'}{E_2(\Lambda) + \dfrac{a'r_2}{T}}. \tag{4}$$

To obtain the error probability α_1' for the modified test, we use Corollary 2.2(9) in Appendix I with $g_2(t_T) = a'(1 - u)^{r_2}$.

$$E_2'^{**}[e^{-a'(1-u)^{r_2}}] = \frac{\alpha_1'}{1 - \alpha_2'}.$$

Again we assume small error probabilities and neglect higher orders of u.

$$E_2'^{**}[e^{-a'(1-r_2u)}] \approx \alpha_1'.$$

Using the first-order approximation for the exponential term and substituting (4) (with equality sign), we have

$$\alpha_1' \approx e^{-a'}\left[1 + \frac{a'^2 r_2}{TE_2(\Lambda) + a'r_2}\right]. \tag{5}$$

Finally, consider the standard Wald test with upper boundary e^a and lower boundary e^{-b}. If the errors are small, then following Wald's [11] derivation

$$E_2(t_T) \approx \frac{a}{E_2(\Lambda)} \quad \text{and} \quad e^{-a} = \frac{\alpha_1}{1 - \alpha_2} \approx \alpha_1.$$

Suppose $a = a'$, i.e., the boundaries of the Wald test and the modified test begin at the same point, then

$$E_2'(t_T) \approx E_2'^{**}(t_T) \geq \frac{a'}{E_2(\Lambda) + \dfrac{a'r_2}{T}} = \frac{E_2(t_T)}{1 + \dfrac{r_2}{T}E_2(t_T)} \tag{4'}$$

and

$$\alpha_1' = \alpha_1\left[1 + \frac{ar_2E_2(t_T)}{T + r_2E_2(t_T)}\right]. \tag{5'}$$

References

[1] T. W. Anderson, "A modification of the sequential probability ratio test to reduce the sample size," *Ann. Math. Stat.*, vol. 31, March 1960.

[2] J. J. Bussgang and M. B. Marcus, "Truncated sequential hypothesis tests," Memorandum, Rm-4268-APRA, The Rand Corp., November 1964.

[3] A. Dvoretzky, J. Kiefer, and J. Wolfowitz, "Sequential decision problems for processes with continuous time parameter. Testing Hypotheses," *Ann. Math. Stat.*, vol. 24, pp. 87–93, June 1953.

[4] K. S. Fu, "A sequential decision model for optimum recognition," in *Biological Prototypes and Synthetic System*. vol. 1, 1962.

[5] K. S. Fu and C. H. Chen, "Learning in sequential decision approach to pattern recognition," Internat'l Conf. on Microwaves, Circuit Theory and Information Theory, Tokyo, Japan, 1964.

[6] K. S. Fu and C. H. Chen, "Sequential decisions, pattern recognition, and machine learning," Tech. Rept. TR-EE65-6, School of Elec. Engrg., Purdue University, Lafayette, Ind., April 1965.

[7] K. S. Fu and J. A. Lebo, "On the selection of decision criteria and the estimation of probabilities in pattern recognition," Tech. Rept. TR-EE64-16, School of Elec. Engrg., Purdue University, Lafayette, Ind. September 1964.

[8] T. Marill and D. M. Green, "Statistical recognition functions and the design of pattern recognizers," *IRE Trans. on Electronic Computers*, vol. EC-9, pp. 472–477, December 1960.

[9] R. M. Phataford, "Large sample sequential analysis of Markovian observations," *J. Indiana Stat. Ass.*, 1963.

[10] F. C. Reed, "A sequential multi-decision procedure," *Proc. Symp. On Decision Theory and Application to Electronic Equipment Development*, USAF Development Center, Rome, N. Y., April 1960.

[11] A. Wald, *Sequential Analysis*. New York: Wiley, 1947.

Automata, Linguistics, and Heuristics

IV

Editor's Comments on Papers 13 Through 17

"Switching circuits" and "Turing machines" are the predecessors of today's "automata." (By an automaton we mean a formal mathematical model of information processing.) The subjects of automata, linguistics, heuristic processing, pattern recognition, and learning have been closely intertwined. This section presents a selection of introductory and basic papers on this subject.

A switching circuit is a network of devices, each of which operates on or stores a finite (usually very small) amount of binary information. A switching circuit is usually represented as a finite set of states, a finite set of input and output terminals, a finite set of input and output symbols, and a finite set of rules for moving from the present state to the next state. Each of these rules depends only on the present inputs, present outputs, and present state. The motion among the states determines the sequence of output symbols.

It was Turing's basic thesis that the use of an infinite tape as a "scratch-paper" memory in conjunction with a finite switching circuit could implement any information-processing task that is computable (i.e., that can be computed by any correctly working digital computer). This combination of an infinite tape and a finite switching circuit is known today as a *Turing machine.* The theory of automata is concerned with the relation between information-processing tasks and the various modifications and restrictions of Turing machines.

Beginning in 1956, Chomsky and his successors developed a fascinating connection between linguistic structures and automata. In particular, Chomsky invented "phrase-structured language" and "generative grammar." Later, Rabin and Scott [Rab] showed that a device which parses sentences of a phrase-structured language must, in general, be of the same complexity as a Turing machine. [A *language*, in Chomsky's sense, is any set of finite sentences (or strings) of symbols, where the symbols are taken from a finite alphabet. Each of these strings is a *sentence*.] Parsing a string may be viewed as a form of pattern detection, since the parsing process classifies the string as either a member or a nonmember of the language under consideration. The possibility of extending the notion of a sentence to line drawings and other pictures was proposed by Narasimhan in 1962 [Nar-1]. Since then many papers have appeared on the use of this approach for the design of recognition machines.

Chomsky's classic paper on phrase-structured languages [Chom] is the first selection in this part. In the second paper, Kirsch [Kir] describes how a generative grammar may be used for analyzing geometric figures and English prose. In the next paper, Narasimhan describes the results of using generative grammars for analyzing bubble chamber photographs and hand-printed English characters [Nar-2].

The use of special languages as a tool for the development of recognition machines was thrust in another important direction by Newell and Simon and their collaborators. The next selection is their first major paper on this subject [New]. It demonstrates the information-processing power of a *list language*—i.e., a special language for operating on a hierarchy of lists—and *heuristic processing*. Newell and Simon's heuristic processing has the following significant features: (1) the descriptions of the elements of the list are relatively simple, with few or no formal relationships among the descriptions (thus a mathematics for the descriptions of sentences in mathematical proofs did not arise from this paper); (2) it uses the notion of "hypothesize and test" (i.e., it generates a hypothesis or guess concerning a subset of the problem, and tests the hypothesis by examining its consequences); and (3) there is no formal guarantee of the effectiveness of a heuristic process. Confidence in their heuristic techniques has to be established by extensive empirical observations. These features of heuristic processing are the results of an attempt to imitate the manner in which human beings solve complex problems, such as the discovery and recognition of mathematical proofs.

Simultaneously with the development of linguistic structures and the theory of automata as models of recognition and problem solving, mathematical psychologists, mathematicians, and engineers used Markov chains and probabilistic automata as models of simple forms of learning [Bus, Est, Kem, Paz, Sk1-3]. (Probabilistic automata are automata whose operating rules determine the probability of moving from the present state to the various possible next states. Such automata reduce to Markov chains [Kem] when the inputs are constant or statistically independent.) It is not surprising, therefore, that such models have been proposed for the study of simple trainable recognizers. A paper by Sklansky [Sk1-3], the last in this part, is one of the early papers taking this point of view.

Reprinted from *IRE Trans. Inform. Theory,* **IT-2,** No. 3, 1956, pp. 113-124

13

THREE MODELS FOR THE DESCRIPTION OF LANGUAGE*

Noam Chomsky
Department of Modern Languages and Research Laboratory of Electronics
Massachusetts Institute of Technology
Cambridge, Massachusetts

Abstract

We investigate several conceptions of linguistic structure to determine whether or not they can provide simple and "revealing" grammars that generate all of the sentences of English and only these. We find that no finite-state Markov process that produces symbols with transition from state to state can serve as an English grammar. Furthermore, the particular subclass of such processes that produce n-order statistical approximations to English do not come closer, with increasing n, to matching the output of an English grammar. We formalize the notions of "phrase structure" and show that this gives us a method for describing language which is essentially more powerful, though still representable as a rather elementary type of finite-state process. Nevertheless, it is successful only when limited to a small subset of simple sentences. We study the formal properties of a set of grammatical transformations that carry sentences with phrase structure into new sentences with derived phrase structure, showing that transformational grammars are processes of the same elementary type as phrase-structure grammars; that the grammar of English is materially simplified if phrase structure description is limited to a kernel of simple sentences from which all other sentences are constructed by repeated transformations; and that this view of linguistic structure gives a certain insight into the use and understanding of language.

1. Introduction

There are two central problems in the descriptive study of language. One primary concern of the linguist is to discover simple and "revealing" grammars for natural languages. At the same time, by studying the properties of such successful grammars and clarifying the basic conceptions that underlie them, he hopes to arrive at a general theory of linguistic structure. We shall examine certain features of these related inquiries.

The grammar of a language can be viewed as a theory of the structure of this language. Any scientific theory is based on a certain finite set of observations and, by establishing general laws stated in terms of certain hypothetical constructs, it attempts to account for these observations, to show how they are interrelated, and to predict an indefinite number of new phenomena. A mathematical theory has the additional property that predictions follow rigorously from the body of theory. Similarly, a grammar is based on a finite number of observed sentences (the linguist's corpus) and it "projects" this set to an infinite set of grammatical sentences by establishing general "laws" (grammatical rules) framed in terms of such hypothetical constructs as the particular phonemes, words, phrases, and so on, of the language under analysis. A properly formulated grammar should determine unambiguously the set of grammatical sentences.

General linguistic theory can be viewed as a metatheory which is concerned with the problem of how to choose such a grammar in the case of each particular language on the basis of a finite corpus of sentences. In particular, it will consider and attempt to explicate the relation between the set of grammatical sentences and the set of observed sentences. In other words, linguistic theory attempts to explain the ability of a speaker to produce and understand new sentences, and to reject as ungrammatical other new sequences, on the basis of his limited linguistic experience.

Suppose that for many languages there are certain clear cases of grammatical sentences and certain clear cases of ungrammatical sequences, e.g., (1) and (2), respectively, in English.

(1) John ate a sandwich
(2) Sandwich a ate John.

In this case, we can test the adequacy of a proposed linguistic theory by determining, for each language, whether or not the clear cases are handled properly by the grammars constructed in accordance with this theory. For example, if a large corpus of English does not happen to contain either (1) or (2), we ask whether the grammar that is determined for this corpus will project the corpus to include (1) and exclude (2). Even though such clear cases may provide only a weak test of adequacy for the grammar of a given language taken in isolation, they provide a very strong test for any general linguistic theory and for the set of grammars to which it leads, since we insist that in the case of each language the clear cases be handled properly in a fixed and predetermined manner. We can take certain steps towards the construction of an operational characterization of "grammatical sentence" that will provide us with the clear cases required to set the task of linguistics significantly.

*This work was supported in part by the Army (Signal Corps), the Air Force (Office of Scientific Research, Air Research and Development Command), and the Navy (Office of Naval Research), and in part by a grant from Eastman Kodak Company.

Observe, for example, that (1) will be read by an English speaker with the normal intonation of a sentence of the corpus, while (2) will be read with a falling intonation on each word, as will any sequence of unrelated words. Other distinguishing criteria of the same sort can be described.

Before we can hope to provide a satisfactory account of the general relation between observed sentences and grammatical sentences, we must learn a great deal more about the formal properties of each of these sets. This paper is concerned with the formal structure of the set of grammatical sentences. We shall limit ourselves to English, and shall assume intuitive knowledge of English sentences and nonsentences. We then ask what sort of linguistic theory is required as a basis for an English grammar that will describe the set of English sentences in an interesting and satisfactory manner.

The first step in the linguistic analysis of a language is to provide a finite system of representation for its sentences. We shall assume that this step has been carried out, and we shall deal with languages only in phonemic or alphabetic transcription. By a _language_, then, we shall mean a set (finite or infinite) of sentences, each of finite length, all constructed from a finite alphabet of symbols. If A is an alphabet, we shall say that anything formed by concatenating the symbols of A is a _string_ in A. By a _grammar_ of the language L we mean a device of some sort that produces all of the strings that are sentences of L and only these.

No matter how we ultimately decide to construct linguistic theory, we shall surely require that the grammar of any language must be finite. It follows that only a countable set of grammars is made available by any linguistic theory; hence that uncountably many languages, in our general sense, are literally not describable in terms of the conception of linguistic structure provided by any particular theory. Given a proposed theory of linguistic structure, then, it is always appropriate to ask the following question:

(3) Are there interesting languages that are simply outside the range of description of the proposed type?

In particular, we shall ask whether English is such a language. If it is, then the proposed conception of linguistic structure must be judged inadequate. If the answer to (3) is negative, we go on to ask such questions as the following:

(4) Can we construct reasonably simple grammars for all interesting languages?

(5) Are such grammars "revealing" in the sense that the syntactic structure that they exhibit can support semantic analysis, can provide insight into the use and understanding of language, etc.?

We shall first examine various conceptions of linguistic structure in terms of the possibility and complexity of description (questions (3), (4)). Then, in § 6, we shall briefly consider the same theories in terms of (5), and shall see that we are independently led to the same conclusions as to relative adequacy for the purposes of linguistics.

2. Finite State Markov Processes.

2.1 The most elementary grammars which, with a finite amount of apparatus, will generate an infinite number of sentences, are those based on a familiar conception of language as a particularly simple type of information source, namely, a finite-state Markov process.[1] Specifically, we define a _finite-state grammar_ G as a system with a finite number of states $S_o, \ldots, S_q$, a set $A = \{a_{ijk} \mid 0 \leq i, j \leq q;\ 1 \leq k \leq N_{ij}$ for each $i, j\}$ of transition symbols, and a set $C = \{(S_i, S_j)\}$ of certain pairs of states of G that are said to be _connected_. As the system moves from state S_i to S_j, it produces a symbol $a_{ijk} \epsilon A$. Suppose that

(6) $S_{\alpha_1}, \ldots, S_{\alpha_m}$

is a sequence of states of G with $\alpha_1 = \alpha_m = 0$, and $(S_{\alpha_i}, S_{\alpha_{i+1}}) \epsilon C$ for each $i < m$. As the system moves from S_{α_i} to $S_{\alpha_{i+1}}$ it produces the symbol

(7) $a_{\alpha_i \alpha_{i+1} k}$

for some $k \leq N_{\alpha_i \alpha_{i+1}}$. Using the arch $\frown$ to signify concatenation,[2] we say that the sequence (6) generates all sentences

(8) $a_{\alpha_1 \alpha_2 k_1} \frown a_{\alpha_2 \alpha_3 k_2} \frown \ldots \frown a_{\alpha_{m-1} \alpha_m k_{m-1}}$

for all appropriate choices of k_i (i.e., for $k_i \leq N_{\alpha_i \alpha_{i+1}}$). The language L_G containing all and only such sentences is called the language _generated_ by G.

Thus, to produce a sentence of L_G we set the system G in the initial state S_o and we run through a sequence of connected states, ending again with S_o, and producing one of the associated transition symbols of A with each transition from one state to the next. We say that a language L is a _finite-state language_ if L is the set of sentences generated by some finite-state grammar G.

2.2. Suppose that we take the set A of transition symbols to be the set of English phonemes. We can attempt to construct a finite state grammar G which will generate every string of English phonemes which is a grammatical sentence of English, and only such strings. It is immediately evident that the task of constructing a finite-state grammar for English can be considerably simplified if we take A as the set of English morphemes[3] or words, and construct G so that it will generate exactly the grammatical strings of these units. We can then complete the grammar by giving a finite set of rules that give the phonemic spelling of each word or morpheme in each context in which it occurs. We shall consider briefly the status of such rules in § 4.1 and § 5.3.

Before inquiring directly into the problem of constructing a finite-state grammar for English morpheme or word sequences, let us investigate the absolute limits of the set of finite-state languages. Suppose that A is the alphabet of a language L, that $a_1,\dots,a_n$ are symbols of this alphabet, and that $S=a_1{}^\frown\dots{}^\frown a_n$ is a sentence of L. We say that S has an (i, j)-<u>dependency</u> with respect to L if and only if the following conditions are met:

(9)(i) $1 \le i < j \le n$

(ii) there are symbols $b_i, b_j \epsilon A$ with the property that S_1 is not a sentence of L, and S_2 is a sentence of L, where S_1 is formed from S by replacing the ith symbol of S (namely, a_i) by b_i, and S_2 is formed from S_1 by replacing the jth symbol of S_1 (namely, a_j) by b_j.

In other words, S has an (i,j)-dependency with respect to L if replacement of the ith symbol a_i of S by b_i ($b_i \neq a_i$) requires a corresponding replacement of the jth symbol a_j of S by b_j ($b_j \neq a_j$) for the resulting string to belong to L.

We say that $D=\left\{(\alpha_1,\beta_1),\dots,(\alpha_m,\beta_m)\right\}$ is a <u>dependency set</u> for S in L if and only if the following conditions are met:

(10)(i) For $1 \le i \le m$, S has an (α_i,β_i)-dependency with respect to L

(ii) for each i, j, $\alpha_i < \beta_j$

(iii) for each i, j such that $i \neq j$, $\alpha_i \neq \alpha_j$ and $\beta_i \neq \beta_j$.

Thus, in a dependency set for S in L every two dependencies are distinct in both terms and each "determining" element in S precedes all "determined" elements, where we picture a_{α_i} as determining the choice of a_{β_i}.

Evidently, if S has an m-termed dependency set in L, at least 2^m states are necessary in the finite-state grammar that generates the language L.

This observation enables us to state a necessary condition for finite-state languages.

(11) Suppose that L is a finite-state language. Then there is an m such that no sentence S of L has a dependency set of more than m terms in L.

With this condition in mind, we can easily construct many nonfinite-state languages. For example, the languages L_1, L_2, L_3 described in (12) are not describable by any finite-state grammar.

(12)(i) L_1 contains $a^\frown b$, $a^\frown a^\frown b^\frown b$, $a^\frown a^\frown a^\frown b^\frown b^\frown b,\dots$, and in general, all sentences consisting of n occurrences of a followed by exactly n occurrences of b, and only these;

(ii) L_2 contains $a^\frown a$, $b^\frown b$, $a^\frown b^\frown b^\frown a$, $b^\frown a^\frown a^\frown b$, $a^\frown a^\frown b^\frown b^\frown a^\frown a,\dots$, and in general, all "mirror-image" sentences consisting of a string X followed by X in reverse, and only these;

(iii) L_3 contains $a^\frown a$, $b^\frown b$, $a^\frown b^\frown a^\frown b$, $b^\frown a^\frown b^\frown a$, $a^\frown a^\frown b^\frown a^\frown a^\frown b,\dots$, and in general, all sentences consisting of a string X followed by the identical string X, and only these.

In L_2, for example, for any m we can find a sentence with a dependency set $D_m=\left\{(1,2m),(2,2m-1),\dots,(m,m+1)\right\}$.[4]

2.3. Turning now to English, we find that there are infinite sets of sentences that have dependency sets with more than any fixed number of terms. For example, let $S_1, S_2,\dots$ be declarative sentences. Then the following are all English sentences:

(13)(i) If S_1, then S_2.

(ii) Either S_3, or S_4.

(iii) The man who said that S_5, is arriving today.

These sentences have dependencies between "if"-"then", "either"-"or", "man"-"is". But we can choose S_1, S_3, S_5 which appear between the interdependent words, as (13i), (13ii), or (13iii) themselves. Proceeding to construct sentences in this way we arrive at subparts of English with just the mirror image properties of the languages L_1 and L_2 of (12). Consequently, English fails condition (11). English is not a finite-state language, and we are forced to reject the theory of language under discussion as failing condition (3).

We might avoid this consequence by an arbitrary decree that there is a finite upper limit to sentence length in English. This would serve no useful purpose, however. The point is that there are processes of sentence formation that this elementary model for language is intrinsically incapable of handling. If no finite limit is set for the operation of these processes, we can prove the literal inapplicability of this model. If the processes have a limit, then the construction of a finite-state grammar will not be literally impossible (since a list is a trivial finite-state grammar), but this grammar will be so complex as to be of little use or interest. Below, we shall study a model for grammars that can handle mirror-image languages. The extra power of such a model in the infinite case is reflected in the fact that it is much more useful and revealing if an upper limit is set. In general, the assumption that languages are infinite is made for the purpose of simplifying the description.[5] If a grammar has no recursive steps (closed loops, in the model discussed above) it will be prohibitively complex- - it will, in fact, turn out to be little better than a list of strings or of morpheme class sequences in the case of natural languages. If it does have recursive devices, it will produce infinitely many sentences.

2.4 Although we have found that no finite-state Markov process that produces sentences from left to right can serve as an English grammar, we might inquire into the possibility of constructing a sequence of such devices that, in some nontrivial way, come closer and closer to matching the output of a satisfactory English grammar. Suppose, for example, that for fixed n we construct a finite-state grammar in the following manner: one state of the grammar is associated with each sequence of English words of length n and the probability that the word X will be produced when the system is in the state S_i is equal to the conditional probability of X, given the sequence of n words which defines S_i. The output of such grammar is customarily called an n+1st order approximation to English. Evidently, as n increases, the output of such grammars will come to look more and more like English, since longer and longer sequences have a high probability of being taken directly from the sample of English in which the probabilities were determined. This fact has occasionally led to the suggestion that a theory of linguistic structure might be fashioned on such a model.

Whatever the other interest of statistical approximation in this sense may be, it is clear that it can shed no light on the problems of grammar. There is no general relation between the frequency of a string (or its component parts) and its grammaticalness. We can see this most clearly by considering such strings as

(14) colorless green ideas sleep furiously

which is a grammatical sentence, even though it is fair to assume that no pair of its words may ever have occurred together in the past. Notice that a speaker of English will read (14) with the ordinary intonation pattern of an English sentence, while he will read the equally unfamiliar string

(15) furiously sleep ideas green colorless

with a falling intonation on each word, as in the case of any ungrammatical string. Thus (14) differs from (15) exactly as (1) differs from (2); our tentative operational criterion for grammaticalness supports our intuitive feeling that (14) is a grammatical sentence and that (15) is not. We might state the problem of grammar, in part, as that of explaining and reconstructing the ability of an English speaker to recognize (1), (14), etc., as grammatical, while rejecting (2), (15), etc. But no order of approximation model can distinguish (14) from (15) (or an indefinite number of similar pairs). As n increases, an nth order approximation to English will exclude (as more and more improbable) an ever-increasing number of grammatical sentences, while it still contains vast numbers of completely ungrammatical strings.[6] We are forced to conclude that there is apparently no significant approach to the problems of grammar in this direction.

Notice that although for every n, a process of n-order approximation can be represented as a finite-state Markov process, the converse is not true. For example, consider the three-state process with (S_o,S_1), (S_1,S_1), (S_1,S_o), (S_o,S_2), (S_2,S_2), (S_2,S_o) as its only connected states, and with a, b, a, c, b, c as the respective transition symbols. This process can be represented by the following state diagram:

(16) 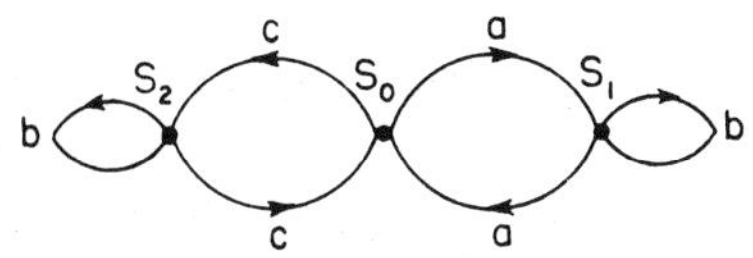

This process can produce the sentences $a^\frown a$, $a^\frown b^\frown a$, $a^\frown b^\frown b^\frown a$, $a^\frown b^\frown b^\frown b^\frown a$,..., $c^\frown c$, $c^\frown b^\frown c$, $c^\frown b^\frown b^\frown c$, $c^\frown b^\frown b^\frown b^\frown c$,..., but not $a^\frown b^\frown b^\frown c$, $c^\frown b^\frown b^\frown a$, etc. The generated language has sentences with dependencies of any finite length.

In § 2.4 we argued that there is no significant correlation between order of approximation and grammaticalness. If we order the strings of a given length in terms of order of approximation to English, we shall find both grammatical and ungrammatical strings scattered throughout the list, from top to bottom. Hence the notion of statistical approximation appears to be irrelevant to grammar. In § 2.3 we pointed out that a much broader class of processes, namely, all finite-state Markov processes that produce transition symbols, does not include an English grammar. That is, if we construct a finite-state grammar that produces only English sentences, we know that it will fail to produce an infinite number of these sentences; in particular, it will fail to produce an infinite number of true sentences, false sentences, reasonable questions that could be intelligibly asked, and the like. Below, we shall investigate a still broader class of processes that might provide us with an English grammar.

3. Phrase Structure.

3.1. Customarily, syntactic description is given in terms of what is called "immediate constituent analysis." In description of this sort the words of a sentence are grouped into phrases, these are grouped into smaller constituent phrases and so on, until the ultimate constituents (generally morphemes[3]) are reached. These phrases are then classified as noun phrases (NP), verb phrases (VP), etc. For example, the sentence (17) might be analyzed as in the accompanying diagram.

(17)

the man	took	the book
NP	Verb	NP
	VP	
Sentence		

Evidently, description of sentences in such terms permits considerable simplification over the word-by-word model, since the composition of a complex class of expressions such as NP can be stated just once in the grammar, and this class can be used as a building block at various points in the construction of sentences. We now ask what form of grammar corresponds to this conception of linguistic structure.

3.2. A phrase-structure grammar is defined by a finite vocabulary (alphabet) V_P, a finite set Σ of initial strings in V_P, and a finite set F of rules of the form: $X \rightarrow Y$, where X and Y are strings in V_P. Each such rule is interpreted as the instruction: rewrite X as Y. For reasons that will appear directly, we require that in each such $[\Sigma, F]$ grammar

$$(18) \quad \Sigma : \Sigma_1, \ldots, \Sigma_n$$

$$F: \quad X_1 \rightarrow Y_1 \quad \vdots \quad X_m \rightarrow Y_m$$

Y_i is formed from X_i by the replacement of a single symbol of X_i by some string. Neither the replaced symbol nor the replacing string may be the identity element U of footnote 4.

Given the $[\Sigma, F]$ grammar (18), we say that:

(19)(i) a string β follows from a string α if $\alpha = Z^\frown X_i{}^\frown W$ and $\beta = Z^\frown Y_i{}^\frown W$, for some $i \leq m$;[7]

(ii) a derivation of the string S_t is a sequence $D = (S_1, \ldots, S_t)$ of strings, where $S_1 \in \Sigma$ and for each $i < t$, S_{i+1} follows from S_i;

(iii) a string S is derivable from (18) if there is a derivation of S in terms of (18);

(iv) a derivation of S_t is terminated if there is no string that follows from S_t;

(v) a string S_t is a terminal string if it is the last line of a terminated derivation.

A derivation is thus roughly analogous to a proof, with Σ taken as the axiom system and F as the rules of inference. We say that L is a derivable language if L is the set of strings that are derivable from some $[\Sigma, F]$ grammar, and we say that L is a terminal language if it is the set of terminal strings from some system $[\Sigma, F]$.

In every interesting case there will be a terminal vocabulary V_T ($V_T \subset V_P$) that exactly characterizes the terminal strings, in the sense that every terminal string is a string in V_T and no symbol of V_T is rewritten in any of the rules of F. In such a case we can interpret the terminal strings as constituting the language under analysis (with V_T as its vocabulary), and the derivations of these strings as providing their phrase structure.

3.3. As a simple example of a system of the form (18), consider the following small part of English grammar:

(20) Σ : #⌒Sentence⌒#
F: Sentence → NP⌒VP
VP → Verb⌒NP
NP → the⌒man, the⌒book
Verb → took

Among the derivations from (20) we have, in particular:

(21) D_1: #⌒Sentence⌒#
#⌒NP⌒VP⌒#
#⌒NP⌒Verb⌒NP⌒#
#⌒the⌒man⌒Verb⌒NP⌒#
#⌒the⌒man⌒Verb⌒the⌒book⌒#
#⌒the⌒man⌒took⌒the⌒book⌒#

D_2: #⌒Sentence⌒#
#⌒NP⌒VP⌒#
#⌒the⌒man⌒VP⌒#
#⌒the⌒man⌒Verb⌒NP⌒#
#⌒the⌒man⌒took⌒NP⌒#
#⌒the⌒man⌒took⌒the⌒book⌒#

These derivations are evidently equivalent; they differ only in the order in which the rules are applied. We can represent this equivalence graphically by constructing diagrams that correspond, in an obvious way, to derivations. Both D_1 and D_2 reduce to the diagram:

(22)

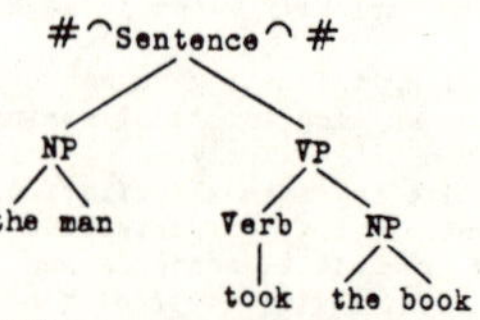

The diagram (22) gives the phrase structure of the terminal sentence "the man took the book," just as in (17). In general, given a derivation D of a string S, we say that a substring s of S is an X if in the diagram corresponding to D, s is traceable back to a single node, and this node is labelled X. Thus given D_1 or D_2, corresponding to (22), we say that "the⌒man" is an NP, "took⌒the⌒book" is a VP, "the⌒book" is an NP, "the⌒man⌒took⌒the⌒book" is a Sentence. "man⌒took," however, is not a phrase of this

117

string at all, since it is not traceable back to any node.

When we attempt to construct the simplest possible $[\Sigma, F]$ grammar for English we find that certain sentences automatically receive non-equivalent derivations. Along with (20), the grammar of English will certainly have to contain such rules as

(23) Verb → are⁀flying
Verb → are
NP → they
NP → planes
NP → flying⁀planes

in order to account for such sentences as "they are flying - a plane" (NP-Verb-NP), "(flying) planes - are - noisy" (NP-Verb-Adjective), etc. But this set of rules provides us with two non-equivalent derivations of the sentence "they are flying planes", reducing to the diagrams:

(24) 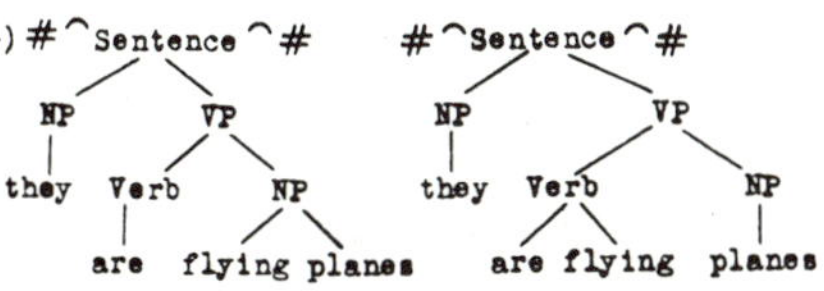

Hence this sentence will have two phrase structures assigned to it; it can be analyzed as "they - are - flying planes" or "they - are flying - planes." And in fact, this sentence is ambiguous in just this way; we can understand it as meaning that "those specks on the horizon - are - flying planes" or "those pilots - are flying - planes." When the simplest grammar automatically provides nonequivalent derivations for some sentence, we say that we have a case of <u>constructional</u> <u>homonymity</u>, and we can suggest this formal property as an explanation for the semantic ambiguity of the sentence in question. In §1 we posed the requirement that grammars offer insight into the use and understanding of language (cf.(5)). One way to test the adequacy of a grammar is by determining whether or not the cases of constructional homonymity are actually cases of semantic ambiguity, as in (24) We return to this important problem in § 6.

In (20)-(24) the element # indicated sentence (later, word) boundary. It can be taken as an element of the terminal vocabulary V_T discussed in the final paragraph of § 3.2.

3.4. These segments of English grammar are much oversimplified in several respects. For one thing, each rule of (20) and (23) has only a single symbol on the left, although we placed no such limitation on $[\Sigma, F]$ grammars in § 3.2. A rule of the form

(25) Z⁀X⁀W → Z⁀Y⁀W

indicates that X can be rewritten as Y only in the context Z--W. It can easily be shown that the grammar will be much simplified if we permit such rules. In § 3.2 we required that in such a rule as (25), X must be a single symbol. This ensures that a phrase-structure diagram will be constructible from any derivation. The grammar can also be simplified very greatly if we order the rules and require that they be applied in sequence (beginning again with the first rule after applying the final rule of the sequence), and if we distinguish between <u>obligatory</u> rules which must be applied when we reach them in the sequence and <u>optional</u> rules which may or may not be applied. These revisions do not modify the generative power of the grammar, although they lead to considerable simplification.

It seems reasonable to require for significance some guarantee that the grammar will actually generate a large number of sentences in a limited amount of time; more specifically, that it be impossible to run through the sequence of rules vacuously (applying no rule) unless the last line of the derivation under construction is a terminal string. We can meet this requirement by posing certain conditions on the occurrence of obligatory rules in the sequence of rules. We define a <u>proper</u> <u>grammar</u> as a system $[\Sigma, Q]$, where Σ is a set of initial strings and Q a sequence of rules $X_i \to Y_i$ as in (18), with the additional condition that for each i there must be at least one j such that $X_j = X_i$ and $X_j \to Y_j$ is an obligatory rule. Thus, each left-hand term of the rules of (18) must appear in at least one obligatory rule. This is the weakest simple condition that guarantees that a nonterminated derivation must advance at least one step every time we run through the rules. It provides that if X_i can be rewritten as one of $Y_{i_1}, \ldots, Y_{i_k}$ then at least one of these rewritings must take place. However, proper grammars are essentially different from $[\Sigma, F]$ grammars. Let D(G) be the set of derivations producible from a phrase structure grammar G, whether proper or not. Let $D_F = \{D(G) \mid G$ a $[\Sigma, F]$ grammar$\}$ and $D_Q = \{D(G) \mid G$ a proper grammar$\}$. Then

(26). D_F and D_Q are incomparable; i.e., $D_F \not\subset D_Q$ and $D_Q \not\subset D_F$.

That is, there are systems of phrase structure that can be described by $[\Sigma, F]$ grammars but not by proper grammars, and others that can be described by proper grammars but not by $[\Sigma, F]$ grammars.

3.5. We have defined three types of language: finite-state languages (in §2.1), derivable and terminal languages (in §3.2). These are related in the following way:

(27)(i) every finite-state language is a terminal language, but not conversely;
(ii) every derivable language is a terminal language, but not conversely;
(iii) there are derivable, nonfinite-state languages and finite-state, nonderivable languages.

Suppose that L_G is a finite-state language

with the finite-state grammar G as in § 2.1. We construct a [Σ ,F] grammar in the following manner: $\Sigma = \{S_o\}$; F contains a rule of the form (28i) for each i,j,k such that $(S_i,S_j)\epsilon C$, $j \neq 0$, and $k \leq N_{ij}$; F contains a rule of the form (28ii) for each i,k such that $(S_i,S_o)\epsilon C$ and $k \leq N_{io}$.

(28)(i) $S_i \rightarrow a_{ijk} \frown S_j$

(ii) $S_i \rightarrow a_{iok}$

Clearly, the terminal language from this [Σ ,F] grammar will be exactly L_G, establishing the first part of (27i).

In § 2.2 we found that L_1, L_2 and L_3 of (12) were not finite-state languages. L_1 and L_2, however, are terminal languages. For L_1, e.g., we have the [Σ ,F] grammar

(29) Σ : Z
F : $Z \rightarrow a \frown b$
$Z \rightarrow a \frown Z \frown b$

This establishes (27i).

Suppose that L_4 is a derivable language with the vocabulary $V_P = \{a_1,\ldots,a_n\}$. Suppose that we add to the grammar of L_4 a finite set of rules $a_i \rightarrow b_i$, where the b_i's are not in V_P and are all distinct. Then this new grammar gives a terminal language which is simply a notational variant of L_4. Thus every derivable language is also terminal.

As an example of a terminal, nonderivable language consider the language L_5 containing just the strings

(30) $a \frown b$, $c \frown a \frown b \frown d$, $c \frown c \frown a \frown b \frown d \frown d$, $c \frown c \frown c \frown a \frown b \frown d \frown d \frown d$,...

An infinite derivable language must contain an infinite set of strings that can be arranged in a sequence $S_1,S_2,\ldots$ in such a way that for some rule $X \rightarrow Y$, S_i follows from S_{i-1} by application of this rule, for each $i>1$. And Y in this rule must be formed from X by replacement of a single symbol of X by a string (cf. (18)). This is evidently impossible in the case of L_5. This language is, however, the terminal language given by the following grammar:

(31) Σ : Z
F : $Z \rightarrow a \frown b$
$Z \rightarrow c \frown Z \frown d$

An example of a finite-state, nonderivable language is the language L_6 containing all and only the strings consisting of 2n or 3n occurrences of a, for n=1,2,.... Language L_1 of (12) is a derivable, nonfinite-state language, with the initial string $a \frown b$ and the rule: $a \frown b \rightarrow a \frown a \frown b \frown b$.

The major import of Theorem (27) is that description in terms of phrase structure is essentially more powerful (not just simpler) than description in terms of the finite-state grammars that produce sentences from left to right. In § 2.3 we found that English is literally beyond the bounds of these grammars because of mirror-image properties that it shares with L_1 and L_2 of (12). We have just seen, however, that L_1 is a terminal language and the same is true of L_2. Hence, the considerations that led us to reject the finite-state model do not similarly lead us to reject the more powerful phrase-structure model.

Note that the latter is more abstract than the finite-state model in the sense that symbols that are not included in the vocabulary of a language enter into the description of this language. In the terms of § 3.2, V_P properly includes V_T. Thus in the case of (29), we describe L_1 in terms of an element Z which is not in L_1; and in the case of (20)-(24), we introduce such symbols as Sentence, NP, VP, etc., which are not words of English, into the description of English structure.

3.6. We can interpret a [Σ ,F] grammar of the form (18) as a rather elementary finite-state process in the following way. Consider a system that has a finite number of states $S_o,\ldots,S_q$. When in state S_o, it can produce any of the strings of Σ , thereby moving into a new state. Its state at any point is determined by the subset of elements of $X_1,\ldots,X_m$ contained as substrings in the last produced string, and it moves to a new state by applying one of the rules to this string, thus producing a new string. The system returns to state S_o with the production of a terminal string. This system thus produces derivations, in the sense of § 3.2. The process is determined at any point by its present state and by the last string that has been produced, and there is a finite upper bound on the amount of inspection of this string that is necessary before the process can continue, producing a new string that differs in one of a finite number of ways from its last output.

It is not difficult to construct languages that are beyond the range of description of [Σ ,F] grammars. In fact, the language L_3 of (12iii) is evidently not a terminal language. I do not know whether English is actually a terminal language or whether there are other actual languages that are literally beyond the bounds of phrase structure description. Hence I see no way to disqualify this theory of linguistic structure on the basis of consideration (3). When we turn to the question of the complexity of description (cf. (4)), however, we find that there are ample grounds for the conclusion that this theory of linguistic structure is fundamentally inadequate. We shall now investigate a few of the problems

119

that arise when we attempt to extend (20) to a full-scale grammar of English.

4. Inadequacies of Phrase-Structure Grammar

4.1. In (20) we considered only one way of developing the element Verb, namely, as "took". But even with the verb stem fixed there are a great many other forms that could appear in the context "the man -- the book," e.g., "takes," "has taken," "has been taking," "is taking," "has been taken," "will be taking," and so on. A direct description of this set of elements would be fairly complex, because of the heavy dependencies among them (e.g., "has taken" but not "has taking," "is being taken" but not "is being taking," etc.). We can, in fact, give a very simple analysis of "Verb" as a sequence of independent elements, but only by selecting as elements certain discontinuous strings. For example, in the phrase "has been taking" we can separate out the discontinuous elements "has..en," "be..ing," and "take", and we can then say that these elements combine freely. Following this course systematically, we replace the last rule in (20) by

(32) (i) Verb → Auxiliary⌢V
(ii) V → take, eat,...
(iii) Auxiliary → C(M)(have⌢en) (be⌢ing) (be⌢en)
(iv) M → will, can, shall, may, must
(v) C → past, present

The notations in (32iii) are to be interpreted as follows: in developing "Auxiliary" in a derivation we must choose the unparenthesized element C, and we may choose zero or more of the parenthesized elements, in the order given. Thus, in continuing the derivation D_1 of (21) below line five, we might proceed as follows:

(33) #⌢the⌢man⌢Verb⌢the⌢book⌢#
[from D_1 of (21)]
#⌢the⌢man⌢Auxiliary⌢V⌢the⌢book⌢#
[(32i)]
#⌢the⌢man⌢Auxiliary⌢take⌢the⌢book⌢#
[(32ii)]
#⌢the⌢man⌢C⌢have⌢en⌢be⌢ing⌢take⌢the⌢book⌢#
[(32iii), choosing the elements C, have⌢en, and be⌢ing]
#⌢the⌢man⌢past⌢have⌢en⌢be⌢ing⌢take⌢the⌢book⌢#
[(32v)]

Suppose that we define the class Af as containing the affixes "en", "ing", and the C's; and the class v as including all V's, M's, "have", and "be." We can then convert the last line of (33) into a properly ordered sequence of morphemes by the following rule:

(34) Af⌢v → v⌢Af⌢#

Applying this rule to each of the three Af⌢v sequences in the last line of (33), we derive

(35) #⌢the⌢man⌢have⌢past⌢#⌢be⌢en⌢#⌢take⌢ing⌢#⌢the⌢book⌢#.

In the first paragraph of § 2.2 we mentioned that a grammar will contain a set of rules (called morphophonemic rules) which convert strings of morphemes into strings of phonemes. In the morphophonemics of English, we shall have such rules as the following (we use conventional, rather than phonemic orthography):

(36) have⌢past → had
be⌢en → been
take⌢ing → taking
will⌢past → would
can⌢past → could
M⌢present → M
walk⌢past → walked
take⌢past → took
etc.

Applying the morphophonemic rules to (35) we derive the sentence:

(37) the man had been taking the book.

Similarly, with one major exception to be discussed below (and several minor ones that we shall overlook here), the rules (32), (34) will give all the other forms of the verb in declarative sentences, and only these forms.

This very simple analysis, however, goes beyond the bounds of [Σ,F] grammars in several respects. The rule (34), although it is quite simple, cannot be incorporated within a [Σ,F] grammar, which has no place for discontinuous elements. Furthermore, to apply the rule (34) to the last line of (33) we must know that "take" is a V, hence, a v. In other words, in order to apply this rule it is necessary to inspect more than just the string to which the rule applies; it is necessary to know some of the constituent structure of this string, or equivalently (cf. § 3.3), to inspect certain earlier lines in its derivation. Since (34) requires knowledge of the 'history of derivation' of a string, it violates the elementary property of [Σ,F] grammars discussed in § 3.6.

4.2. The fact that this simple analysis of the verb phrase as a sequence of independently chosen units goes beyond the bounds of [Σ,F] grammars, suggests that such grammars are too limited to give a true picture of linguistic structure. Further study of the verb phrase lends additional support to this conclusion. There is one major limitation on the independence of the elements introduced in (32). If we choose an intransitive verb (e.g., "come," "occur," etc.) as V in (32), we cannot select be⌢en as an auxiliary. We cannot have such phrases as "John has been come," "John is occurred," and the like. Furthermore, the element be⌢en cannot be chosen independently of the context of the phrase "Verb." If we have the element "Verb" in the context "the man -- the food," we are constrained not to select be⁀en in applying (32), although we are free to choose any other element of (32). That is, we can have "the man is eating the food," "the man would have been eating the food," etc., but not "the man is eaten the food," "the man would have been eaten the food," etc. On the other hand, if the context of the phrase "Verb" is, e.g., "the food -- by the man," we are <u>required</u> to select be⁀en. We can have "the food is eaten by the man," but not "the food is eating by the man," etc. In short, we find that the element be⁀en enters into a detailed network of restrictions which distinguish it from all the other elements introduced in the analysis of "Verb" in (32). This complex and unique behavior of be⁀en suggests that it would be desirable to exclude it from (32) and to introduce passives into the grammar in some other way.

There is, in fact, a very simple way to incorporate sentences with be⁀en (i.e., passives) into the grammar. Notice that for every active sentence such as "the man ate the food" we have a corresponding passive "the food was eaten by the man" and conversely. Suppose then that we drop the element be⁀en from (32iii), and then add to the grammar the following rule:

(38) If S is a sentence of the form NP_1-Auxiliary-V-NP_2, then the corresponding string of the form NP_2-Auxiliary⁀be⁀en-V-by⁀NP_1 is also a sentence.

For example, if "the man - past - eat the food" (NP_1-Auxiliary-V-NP_2) is a sentence, then "the food - past be en - eat - by the man" (NP_2-Auxiliary⁀be⁀en-V-by⁀NP_1) is also a sentence. Rules (34) and (36) would convert the first of these into "the man ate the food" and the second into "the food was eaten by the man."

The advantages of this analysis of passives are unmistakable. Since the element be⁀en has been dropped from (32) it is no longer necessary to qualify (32) with the complex of restrictions discussed above. The fact that be⁀en can occur only with transitive verbs, that it is excluded in the context "the man -- the food" and that it is required in the context "the food -- by the man," is now, in each case, an automatic consequence of the analysis we have just given.

A rule of the form (38), however, is well beyond the limits of phrase-structure grammars. Like (34), it rearranges the elements of the string to which it applies, and it requires considerable information about the constituent structure of this string. When we carry the detailed study of English syntax further, we find that there are many other cases in which the grammar can be simplified if the $[\Sigma, F]$ system is supplemented by rules of the same general form as (38). Let us call each such rule a <u>grammatical transformation</u>. As our third model for the description of linguistic structure, we now consider briefly the formal properties of a transformational grammar that can be adjoined to the $[\Sigma, F]$ grammar of phrase structure.[8]

<u>5. Transformational Grammar.</u>

5.1. Each grammatical transformation T will essentially be a rule that converts every sentence with a given constituent structure into a new sentence with derived constituent structure. The transform and its derived structure must be related in a fixed and constant way to the structure of the transformed string, for each T. We can characterize T by stating, in structural terms, the domain of strings to which it applies and the change that it effects on any such string.

Let us suppose in the following discussion that we have a $[\Sigma, F]$ grammar with a vocabulary V_P and a terminal vocabulary $V_T \subset V_P$, as in § 3.2.

In § 3.3 we showed that a $[\Sigma, F]$ grammar permits the derivation of terminal strings, and we pointed out that in general a given terminal string will have several equivalent derivations. Two derivations were said to be equivalent if they reduce to the same diagram of the form (22), etc.[9] Suppose that $D_1, \ldots, D_n$ constitute a maximal set of equivalent derivations of a terminal string S. Then we define a <u>phrase marker</u> of S as the set of strings that occur as lines in the derivations $D_1, \ldots, D_n$. A string will have more than one phrase marker if and only if it has nonequivalent derivations (cf. (24)).

Suppose that K is a phrase marker of S. We say that

(39) (S,K) is <u>analyzable</u> into $(X_1, \ldots, X_n)$ if and only if there are strings $s_1, \ldots, s_n$ such that

(i) $S = s_1 ⁀ \ldots ⁀ s_n$

(ii) for each $i \leq n$, K contains the string $s_1 ⁀ \ldots ⁀ s_{i-1} ⁀ X_i ⁀ s_{i+1} ⁀ \ldots ⁀ s_n$

(40) In this case, s_i is an X_i in S with respect to K.[10]

The relation defined in (40) is exactly the relation "is a" defined in § 3.3; i.e., s_i is an X_i in the sense of (40) if and only if s_i is a substring of S which is traceable back to a single node of the diagram of the form (22), etc., and this node is labelled X_i.

The notion of analyzability defined above allows us to specify precisely the domain of application of any transformation. We associate with each transformation a restricting class R defined as follows:

(41) R is a <u>restricting class</u> if and only if for some r,m, R is the set of sequences:

$$X_1^1, \ldots, X_r^1$$

$$\vdots$$

$$X_1^m, \ldots, X_r^m$$

where X_i^j is a string in the vocabulary V_P, for each i,j. We then say that a string S with the phrase marker K belongs to the domain of the transformation

T if the restricting class R associated with T contains a sequence $(X_1^j, \ldots, X_r^j)$ into which (S,K) is analyzable. The domain of a transformation is thus a set of ordered pairs (S,K) of a string S and a phrase marker K of S. A transformation may be applicable to S with one phrase marker, but not with a second phrase marker, in the case of a string S with ambiguous constituent structure.

In particular, the passive transformation described in (38) has associated with it a restricting class R_p containing just one sequence:

(42) $R_p = \{(NP, \text{Auxiliary}, V, NP)\}$.

This transformation can thus be applied to any string that is analyzable into an NP followed by an Auxiliary followed by a V followed by an NP. For example, it can be applied to the string (43) analyzed into substrings $s_1, \ldots, s_4$ in accordance with the dashes.

(43) the man - past - eat - the food.

5.2. In this way, we can describe in structural terms the set of strings (with phrase markers) to which any transformation applies. We must now specify the structural change that a transformation effects on any string in its domain. An <u>elementary transformation</u> t is defined by the following property:

(44) for each pair of integers n,r $(n \leq r)$, there is a unique sequence of integers $(a_0, a_1, \ldots, a_k)$ and a unique sequence of strings in V_P $(Z_1, \ldots, Z_{k+1})$ such that (i) $a_0 = 0$; $k \geq 0$; $1 \leq a_j \leq r$ for $1 \leq j \leq k$; $Y_0 = U$[11]

(ii) for each $Y_1, \ldots, Y_r$,

$t(Y_1, \ldots, Y_n; Y_n, \ldots, Y_r) = Y_{a_0}{}^\frown Z_1{}^\frown Y_{a_1}{}^\frown Z_2{}^\frown Y_{a_2}{}^\frown \ldots {}^\frown Y_{a_k}{}^\frown Z_{k+1}$:

Thus t can be understood as converting the occurrence of Y_n in the context

(45) $Y_1{}^\frown \ldots {}^\frown Y_{n-1}{}^\frown - - {}^\frown Y_{n+1}{}^\frown \ldots {}^\frown Y_r$

into a certain string $Y_{a_0}{}^\frown Z_1{}^\frown \ldots {}^\frown Y_{a_k}{}^\frown Z_{k+1}$ which is unique, given the sequence of terms $(Y_1, \ldots, Y_r)$ into which $Y_1{}^\frown \ldots {}^\frown Y_r$ is subdivided. t carries the string $Y_1 - \ldots - Y_r$ into a new string $W_1 - \ldots - W_r$ which is related in a fixed way to $Y_1 - \ldots - Y_r$. More precisely, we associate with t the derived transformation t*:

(46) t* is the <u>derived transformation</u> of t if and only if for all $Y_1, \ldots, Y_r$, $t^*(Y_1, \ldots, Y_r) = W_1{}^\frown \ldots {}^\frown W_r$, where $W_n = t(Y_1, \ldots, Y_n; Y_n, \ldots, Y_r)$ for each $n \leq r$.

We now associate with each transformation T an elementary transformation t. For example, with the passive transformation (38) we associate the elementary transformation t_p defined as follows:

(47) $t_p(Y_1; Y_1, \ldots, Y_4) = Y_4$
$t_p(Y_1, Y_2; Y_2, Y_3, Y_4) = Y_2{}^\frown be^\frown en$
$t_p(Y_1, Y_2, Y_3; Y_3, Y_4) = Y_3$
$t_p(Y_1, \ldots, Y_4; Y_4) = by^\frown Y_1$
$t_p(Y_1, \ldots, Y_n; Y_n, \ldots, Y_r) = Y_n$ for all $n \leq r \neq 4$.

The derived transformation t_p^* thus has the following effect:

(48)(i) $t_p^*(Y_1, \ldots, Y_4) = Y_1 - Y_2{}^\frown be^\frown en - Y_3 - by^\frown Y_1$

(ii) t_p^*(the⁀man, past, eat, the⁀food) = the⁀food - past⁀be⁀en - eat - by⁀the⁀man.

The rules (34),(36) carry the right-hand side of (48ii) into "the food was eaten by the man," just as they carry (43) into the corresponding active "the man ate the food."

The pair (R_p, t_p) as in (42),(47) completely characterizes the passive transformation as described in (38). R_p tells us to which strings this transformation applies (given the phrase markers of these strings) and how to subdivide these strings in order to apply the transformation, and t_p tells us what structural change to effect on the subdivided string.

A grammatical transformation is specified completely by a restricting class R and an elementary transformation t, each of which is finitely characterizable, as in the case of the passive. It is not difficult to define rigorously the manner of this specification, along the lines sketched above. To complete the development of transformational grammar it is necessary to show how a transformation automatically assigns a derived phrase marker to each transform and to generalize to transformations on sets of strings. (These and related topics are treated in reference [3].) A transformation will then carry a string S with a phrase marker K (or a set of such pairs) into a string S' with a derived phrase marker K'.

5.3. From these considerations we are led to a picture of grammars as possessing a tripartite structure. Corresponding to the phrase structure analysis we have a sequence of rules of the form X→Y, e.g., (20), (23), (32). Following this we have a sequence of transformational rules such as (34) and (38). Finally, we have a sequence of morphophonemic rules such as (36), again of the form X→Y. To generate a sentence from such a grammar we construct an extended derivation beginning with an initial string of the phrase structure grammar, e.g., #⁀Sentence⁀#, as in (20). We then run through the rules of phrase structure, producing a terminal string. We then apply certain transformations, giving a string of morphemes in the correct order, perhaps quite a different string from the original terminal string. Application of the morphophonemic rules converts this into a string of phonemes. We might run through the phrase structure grammar several times and then apply a generalized transformation to the resulting set of terminal strings.

In § 3.4 we noted that it is advantageous to order the rules of phrase structure into a sequence, and to distinguish obligatory from optional rules. The same is true of the transformational part of the grammar. In § 4 we discussed the transformation (34), which converts a sequence affix-verb into the sequence verb-affix, and the passive transformation (38). Notice that (34) must be applied in every extended derivation, or the result will not be a grammatical sentence. Rule (34), then, is an obligatory transformation. The passive transformation, however, may or may not be applied; either way we have a sentence. The passive is thus an optional transformation. This distinction between optional and obligatory transformations leads us to distinguish between two classes of sentences of the language. We have, on the one hand, a kernel of basic sentences that are derived from the terminal strings of the phrase-structure grammar by application of only obligatory transformations. We then have a set of derived sentences that are generated by applying optional transformations to the strings underlying kernel sentences.

When we actually carry out a detailed study of English structure, we find that the grammar can be greatly simplified if we limit the kernel to a very small set of simple, active, declarative sentences (in fact, probably a finite set) such as "the man ate the food," etc. We then derive questions, passives, sentences with conjunction, sentences with compound noun phrases (e.g., "proving that theorem was difficult," with the NP "proving that theorem"),[12] etc., by transformations. Since the result of a transformation is a sentence with derived constituent structure, transformations can be compounded, and we can form questions from passives (e.g., "was the food eaten by the man"), etc. The actual sentences of real life are usually not kernel sentences, but rather complicated transforms of these. We find, however, that the transformations are, by and large, meaning-preserving, so that we can view the kernel sentences underlying a given sentence as being, in some sense, the elementary "content elements" in terms of which the actual transform is "understood." We discuss this problem briefly in § 6, more extensively in references [1], [2].

In § 3.6 we pointed out that a grammar of phrase structure is a rather elementary type of finite-state process that is determined at each point by its present state and a bounded amount of its last output. We discovered in § 4 that this limitation is too severe, and that the grammar can be simplified by adding transformational rules that take into account a certain amount of constituent structure (i.e., a certain history of derivation). However, each transformation is still finitely characterizable (cf. §§ 5.1-2), and the finite restricting class (41) associated with a transformation indicates how much information about a string is needed in order to apply this transformation. The grammar can therefore still be regarded as an elementary finite-state process of the type corresponding to phrase structure. There is still a bound, for each grammar, on how much of the past output must be inspected in order for the process of derivation to continue, even though more than just the last output (the last line of the derivation) must be known.

6. Explanatory Power of Linguistic Theories

We have thus far considered the relative adequacy of theories of linguistic structure only in terms of such essentially formal criteria as simplicity. In § 1 we suggested that there are other relevant considerations of adequacy for such theories. We can ask (cf.(5)) whether or not the syntactic structure revealed by these theories provides insight into the use and understanding of language. We can barely touch on this problem here, but even this brief discussion will suggest that this criterion provides the same order of relative adequacy for the three models we have considered.

If the grammar of a language is to provide insight into the way the language is understood, it must be true, in particular, that if a sentence is ambiguous (understood in more than one way), then this sentence is provided with alternative analyses by the grammar. In other words, if a certain sentence S is ambiguous, we can test the adequacy of a given linguistic theory by asking whether or not the simplest grammar constructible in terms of this theory for the language in question automatically provides distinct ways of generating the sentence S. It is instructive to compare the Markov process, phrase-structure, and transformational models in the light of this test.

In § 3.3 we pointed out that the simplest $[\Sigma, F]$ grammar for English happens to provide nonequivalent derivations for the sentence "they are flying planes," which is, in fact, ambiguous. This reasoning does not appear to carry over for finite-state grammars, however. That is, there is no obvious motivation for assigning two different paths to this ambiguous sentence in any finite-state grammar that might be proposed for a part of English. Such examples of constructional homonymity (there are many others) constitute independent evidence for the superiority of the phrase-structure model over finite-state grammars.

Further investigation of English brings to light examples that are not easily explained in terms of phrase structure. Consider the phrase

(49) the shooting of the hunters.

We can understand this phrase with "hunters" as the subject, analogously to (50), or as the object, analogously to (51).

(50) the growling of lions

(51) the raising of flowers.

Phrases (50) and (51), however, are not similarly ambiguous. Yet in terms of phrase structure, each of these phrases is represented as: the - $V^\frown$ing - of$^\frown$NP.

Careful analysis of English shows that we can simplify the grammar if we strike the phrases (49)-(51) out of the kernel and reintroduce them transformationally by a transformation T_1 that carries such sentences as "lions growl" into (50), and a transformation T_2 that carries such sentences as "they raise flowers" into (51). T_1 and T_2 will be similar to the nominalizing transformation described in fn.12, when they are correctly constructed. But both "hunters shoot" and "they shoot the hunters" are kernel sentences; and application of T_1 to the former and T_2 to the latter yields the result (49). Hence (49) has two distinct transformational origins. It is a case of constructional homonymity on the transformational level. The ambiguity of the grammatical relation in (49) is a consequence of the fact that the relation of "shoot" to "hunters" differs in the two underlying kernel sentences. We do not have this ambiguity in the case of (50), (51), since neither "they growl lions" nor "flowers raise" is a grammatical kernel sentence.

There are many other examples of the same general kind (cf. [1],[2]), and to my mind, they provide quite convincing evidence not only for the greater adequacy of the transformational conception of linguistic structure, but also for the view expressed in §5.4 that transformational analysis enables us to reduce partially the problem of explaining how we understand a sentence to that of explaining how we understand a kernel sentence.

In summary, then, we picture a language as having a small, possibly finite kernel of basic sentences with phrase structure in the sense of §3, along with a set of transformations which can be applied to kernel sentences or to earlier transforms to produce new and more complicated sentences from elementary components. We have seen certain indications that this approach may enable us to reduce the immense complexity of actual language to manageable proportions and, in addition, that it may provide considerable insight into the actual use and understanding of language.

Footnotes

1. Cf. [7]. Finite-state grammars can be represented graphically by state diagrams, as in [7], p.15f.

2. See [6], Appendix 2, for an axiomatization of concatenation algebras.

3. By 'morphemes' we refer to the smallest grammatically functioning elements of the language, e.g., "boy", "run", "ing" in "running", "s" in "books", etc.

4. In the case of L_1, b_j of (9ii) can be taken as an identity element U which has the property that for all X, $U^\frown X = X^\frown U = X$. Then D_m will also be a dependency set for a sentence of length 2m in L_1.

5. Note that a grammar must reflect and explain the ability of a speaker to produce and understand new sentences which may be much longer than any he has previously heard.

6. Thus we can always find sequences of n+1 words whose first n words and last n words may occur, but not in the same sentence (e.g. replace "is" by "are" in (13iii), and choose S_5 of any required length).

7. Z or W may be the identity element U (cf. fn.4) in this case. Note that since we limited (18) so as to exclude U from figuring significantly on either the right- or the left-hand side of a rule of F, and since we required that only a single symbol of the left-hand side may be replaced in any rule, it follows that Y_i must be at least as long as X_i. Thus we have a simple decision procedure for derivability and terminality in the sense of (19iii), (19v).

8. See [3] for a detailed development of an algebra of transformations for linguistic description and an account of transformational grammar. For further application of this type of description to linguistic material, see [1], [2], and from a somewhat different point of view, [4].

9. It is not difficult to give a rigorous definition of the equivalence relation in question, though this is fairly tedious.

10. The notion "is a" should actually be relativized further to a given occurrence of s_i in S. We can define an occurrence of s_i in S as an ordered pair (s_i, X), where X is an initial substring of S, and s_i is a final substring of X. Cf. [5], p.297.

11. Where U is the identity, as in fn. 4.

12. Notice that this sentence requires a generalized transformation that operates on a pair of strings with their phrase markers. Thus we have a transformation that converts S_1, S_2 of the forms NP-VP_1, it-VP_2, respectively, into the string: ing$^\frown VP_1$ - VP_2. It converts S_1= "they - prove that theorem", S_2= "it - was difficult" into "ing prove that theorem - was difficult," which by (34) becomes "proving that theorem was difficult." Cf. [1], [3] for details.

Bibliography

[1] Chomsky, N., The Logical Structure of Linguistic Theory (mimeographed).

[2] Chomsky, N., Syntactic Structures, to be published by Mouton & Co., 'S-Gravenhage, Netherlands.

[3] Chomsky, N., Transformational Analysis, Ph. D. Dissertation, University of Pennsylvania, June, 1955.

[4] Harris, Z.S., Discourse Analysis, Language 28,1 (1952).

[5] Quine, W.V., Mathematical Logic, revised edition, Harvard University Press., Cambridge, 1951.

[6] Rosenbloom, P., Elements of Mathematical Logic, Dover, New York, 1950

[7] Shannon & Weaver, The Mathematical Theory of Communication, University of Illinois Press, Urbana, 1949.

Reprinted from *IEEE Trans. Electron. Comput.*, **EC–13,** No. 4, 1964, pp. 363–376

14

Computer Interpretation of English Text and Picture Patterns

RUSSELL A. KIRSCH, MEMBER, IEEE

***Summary*—This paper considers a class of information sources consisting of text and pictures. The text is English language text appearing in scientific and technical documents. The picture sources are the largely schematic pictures that occur in the same class of documents. However, the discussion is broadened slightly to include other picture sources. For a tiny fragment of English, the paper shows how the syntactic structure of text may be described, and then goes on to suggest that a similar analysis may be performed on the class of pictures under study. The description of these two kinds of information sources with a single class of descriptive techniques is suggested as an alternative to the synthetic approach in which artificial languages are specified and then learned and used. The major reason for doing syntactical analysis of such sources discussed here is that several information processing operations, amounting to the interpretation of the information sources looked upon as languages, can be done by the technique of syntax direction which uses the results of syntactic analysis to mediate subsequent processes for manipulating the information tokens. The paper concludes with an illustration of an algorithm for matching the sentences given by a simple grammar against the class of simple pictures which these sentences purport to describe.**

I. A Class of Information Sources

IN THIS PAPER we shall consider as a single class of information sources that which is usually considered to be two or perhaps more disjoint classes of information for information processing purposes. To exemplify this class of information sources, the information content of formal scientific and technical documents may be considered, even though in the present pre-systematic state of affairs, we have no means of quantitatively and precisely speaking of the information content of documents (except in the communication theoretic sense which shall not be of concern here). It is, nevertheless, intuitively plausible that two kinds of information sources be recognized, *viz.*, the textual matter of the documents (this paper shall be restricted to a consideration only of English text) and the pictorial matter. The text includes, but is not restricted to, sequences of English sentences. Text is also understood here to include the quasi-textual matter contained in the format of documents and also contained in captions, labels, and the like.

The pictorial information includes, but again is not restricted to, the stylized schematic information that occurs in diagrams and drawings. With the pictorial matter also it is desirable to include information of a format nature where the information bearing function is served by the juxtaposition of information symbols in two dimensions rather than by linear concatenation as in text.

A degree of overlap is seen here between text and pictures that suggests a first reason for not disjoining these two sources but instead attempting to treat them by uniform methods. It is certainly clear that most pictorial matter in formal scientific documents contains text within it, but if the converse (that text is also pictorial in nature) is not clear to the reader, he need only consider the fairly elaborate instructions necessary to enable several people key-punching nominally clear text to observe consistent conventions [1].

One reason such key-punching instructions must necessarily be fairly elaborate is that the key puncher must translate from a basically pictorial two dimensional source into the sort of linear string representation which characterizes text input for most computer processing purposes. One is thus led to the view that text as it occurs in technical documents is a special case of a pictorial source, admittedly with some very special properties derived from its parent, spoken language.

The inseparability of text and pictures is indicated still further by the fact that they perform much the same functions within documents Take the example of a document containing an electrical circuit diagram and some text which describes it. Questions may be asked and answered either on the basis of the diagrams or the text or both. One may be a paraphrase for the other. Indeed, in such documents as U. S. patents, the paraphrase is a most thoroughgoing one with the circuit diagrams that occur largely reproduced in the form of textual descriptions.

Now, although it might be possible to marshal many arguments to demonstrate the inseparability of natural language text and pictures (at least in technical documents), no important consequences would follow from this observation were it not for the significant fact that these two kinds of information sources can probably be handled with very similar techniques. From the standpoint of computer information processing, the important fact about natural language text and pictures is that they both have a syntactic structure which is capable of being described to a machine and of being used for purposes of interpreting the information within a data processing system. The problem of how to describe the syntactic structure of text and pictures and

Manuscript received March 13, 1964. The work in this paper was supported in part by grant GN-107 from the National Science Foundation.

The author is with the National Bureau of Standards, Washington, D. C.

how to use this syntactic description in interpreting the text and pictures will be the main concern of this paper.

In studying the syntax of these languages, we shall be concerned with identifying in the language the primitive symbols whose internal structure need not be considered. We shall then be mostly interested in the rules of arrangement of these primitive symbols that allow certain arrangements and disallow others, and that allow new language objects to be constructed from previously constructed ones.

We will be concerned with the semantics of these languages to the extent that we will consider how the syntactic descriptions of language objects may be interpreted. A syntactical system is interpreted when it is used to denote or refer to objects outside of itself [2]. We shall, however, speak of interpretation in a somewhat wider sense whenever we invoke the syntactic description of arrays of words and other symbols to perform manipulations on the arrays.

II. The Approach of Syntactical Description

In order to see how the syntax of a language may be exhibited, let us consider as examples a traditional grammar book which describes the purported grammar of English, the syntactical specification of a programming language like ALGOL, and the description given by a logician of the rules of formation for a logical language. The grammar books attempts to record the results of an empirical investigation into an existing spoken language. That the grammar book fails to describe the language as it is spoken (or even formally written), results from the normative approach usually taken in grammar books to the description of "correct" usage. The traditional grammar book fails to be descriptive and substitutes normative, prescribed usage in its place. In the case of ALGOL, prescription and usage must agree. If one ignores the possibility of minor errors in the construction of ALGOL algorithms on the part of users of the language, it is found that the formal definition of the language coincides very closely with the language as it is used. We say closely rather than completely because the ALGOL specifications do contain some informal comments regarding statements in the language. It is by no means difficult to observe the informal restrictions thus specified notwithstanding the fact that the restrictions are to an extent outside of the formal specification of the language [3]. In the third example, the language that the logician constructs is usually a comparatively simple language whose syntax is completely and precisely specified.

In making the above comparison between traditional grammar-books on the one hand and descriptions of formal languages on the other, our purpose has been to prepare for the suggestion that it would not be out of place to demand of descriptions of natural languages such as English, those very qualities of exhaustiveness and precision that we demand of descriptions of artificial languages such as ALGOL [4].

To describe and formalize a previously unformalized natural language may seem like an unnecessarily difficult task, particularly when there is the possibility of creating a special purpose artificial language and formalizing its description instead. If our task is, for example, to provide a computer with a programming language in which algebraic manipulations may be described, then an admittedly unattractive candidate for this language is a formalization of natural English. The demonstrated success of such artificial languages as ALGOL argues against the use of natural languages in such specialized contexts.

There are other contexts, however, in which the use of an artificial language is precluded for other reasons and where, if communication with a machine is at all to be possible by automatic techniques, the descriptive approach to an already existing language must necessarily be taken. Wherever there are archives of records and documents primarily intended for human use and where the cost of manual interpretation and preprocessing for machine purposes is prohibitive, there we find a language source that requires a descriptive approach to the archives. The world's technical literature is, and very likely will continue to be, a case in point insofar as the possibility of using anything other than natural language for communication between scientists seems remote. If such literature is also to be manipulated by machine, one is thus led to investigate the possibility of providing a precise description of a natural language to a machine. If that should prove possible, one would then wish to explore the possibility of providing such a machine with procedures for interpreting the language in terms of the functions which the language is capable of performing.

Let us first try to decide what it is about English language text that can be described to a machine. Whatever description we give to a machine, it must agree with the observed fact that English text consists of certain units which for the moment shall be undefined, and a set of allowable arrangements of these units. Not all units can occur in all places in text. From a formal analysis of English text, we would expect to get a formally-defined unit in terms of arrangements of which sentences may best be described. However, in this informal discussion, no harm will be done by resorting to an informally-defined unit, and one, moreover, which has little to do with whatever formal units a complete analysis might define. Our informally-defined unit will be called the "word," and it shall correspond to the native speaker's (reader's) informal notion. Using this intuitive unit, then, one may consider the "word" to be the basic unit of English text. Having done so, we will take the syntactical investigation of the properties of English text to be an investigation into the allowable arrangements in text of English "words." The weakest acceptable goal of such an investigation would be to produce an algorithm which, when given any sequence of English "words," would determine whether or not that sequence was an

English "sentence," where, again, we accept the judgments of English-speakers as specifying what "sentences" are. This algorithm would then provide a decision procedure for sentencehood applied to sequences of English words.

There is evidence, however, to give hope that a more difficult and stronger goal is both achievable and desirable. This goal of syntactic analysis would be not only to provide a decision procedure for sentencehood, but, in addition, to so classify words and sequences of English words that those which are intersubstitutable are similarly classified. Those sequences of English words which are intersubstitutable would be said to belong to the same syntactic category. Syntactic analysis would then assign words to syntactic categories and sequences of syntactic categories to other, not necessarily different, syntactic categories in turn, in such a way that for any sequence, if it is a sentence of the language, there will be a syntactic analysis assigned to certain subsequences in it and an analysis to the whole sequence which assigns it to the category of sentence. What we have outlined here is the procedure of immediate constituent analysis [5].

English text has syntactic structure notwithstanding several important problems which have been largely glossed over here. To mention them briefly, there is the question of the choice of a suitable analysis technique, immediate constituent analysis being only one. The identification of the primitive units at any one level of analysis is itself a difficult problem that we have alluded to. So is the problem of delimiting language. Many sentences are questionable grammatically, and assigning them degrees of grammaticalness is a difficult job. The difficulty of these and related problems may be taken as a partial explanation for the fact that there does not exist any complete syntactic analysis of English text. For certain very narrowly delimited segments of the language, complete syntactical descriptions or grammars exist. So do broad sketches of what a grammar for the whole of the language might look like [6].

But it is suggested above that the same arguments with suitable changes can also be applied to the analysis of pictorial images such as those which occur in technical documents. The case here is somewhat more difficult to make because there does not exist any tradition in analyzing pictorial images. By comparison, the tradition of linguistic analysis is highly developed with its modern descriptive version for the analysis of spoken utterances, at least, and also to some extent, of printed text.

In order to establish the thesis that pictures of certain kinds have a syntactic structure capable of being described to a machine, let us subclassify pictorial sources into three kinds. A prototype of the first kind will be the diagrams and schematics that occur in documents; examples are electrical circuit diagrams, chemical structure diagrams, and flow charts. The second class of pictorial sources will consist of synthesized images which purport to be representational and thus include sketches and drawings, especially mechanical drawings. The last class of pictorial sources will be photographs of natural objects, but this class goes beyond the scope of this paper.

In the first class of pictorial sources, the diagrams and schematics, it is fairly clear that the set of primitive symbols should be chosen from among that set for which we have character-recognition techniques currently in existence [7]. Thus in an electrical circuit diagram, it is quite reasonable to locate and identify capacitor, resistor, and inductance symbols and the many other symbols that occur, as well as the English letters which label them, by the use of character-recognition techniques of the kind that have already been developed. Let us call these symbols so recognizable the "characters" in the schematic sources. We immediately recognize, however, that the identification of the specific characters in a circuit diagram falls far short of the identification of all the significant information in the diagram. Of considerable importance, even more so than the recognition of the characters themselves, is the recognition of the way in which they are connected by lines and related to each other by juxtaposition. This interconnection of the characters is the syntactical structure of the diagram, and one would expect that the information content of a diagrammatic source would be conveyed as much by the syntactic structure as by the characters within the diagram. It is fairly evident, furtheremore, that the syntactic structure does exist and has the usual properties of a syntactically structured language, *viz.*, that there are allowable as well as disallowed juxtapositions of the primitive symbols.

For the second class of picture sources, the drawings and representations, the existence of a syntactic structuring is not quite so evident as it is for schematics. The question has recently been studied, perhaps not surprisingly, by an art historian, Gombrich [8]. He is concerned with graphic art in its many forms, in particular, drawing and sketching. What is important for our purposes is the conclusion that he draws: "Everything points to the conclusion that the phrase 'the language of art' is more than a loose metaphor, that even to describe the visible world in images we need a developed system of schemata." Gombrich's schemata are what we refer to as rules of syntax, and the point that he develops through his whole study is that the syntactic structure of graphic art, in particular representational art (thereby including drawings and sketches), is determined largely by a set of syntactic rules.

There is a common argument against the possibility of producing a syntactical description of pictorial sources or of English text, for that matter. The argument is to the effect that such languages are essentially complex. They have no simple syntactical description except one that only very loosely approximates the languages as they occur in practice. If these languages are exceedingly complex (and there is every reason to believe that they are) the argument concludes that it is unlikely that people will be able to understand the structure of such languages or be able to understand their syntactical description except as users of the languages. However, enough is known about how to write extremely large computer programs that the mere fact of complexity of a language being described should not in itself preclude any attempts to describe it to a machine because it may have a simple syntactical description when the correct tools are used in describing it. Even if its syntactical characterization is complex in the sense of being very large, that still does not preclude the possibility that the language can be so segmented that each of the segments has a sufficiently simple syntactic description to prove tractable. Some light is shed on syntactical description in this fashion by the study of the so-called sequential languages [9]. These languages have the useful property that their syntactic description can be built up in an hierarchical fashion from the primitives which compose the language. From these considerations we are led to the conclusion that complexity in a language and in its syntactical description need not rule out the possibility of providing such a description to a computer for subsequent interpretation, at least in limited areas of application.

III. Techniques for Syntactical Description

It has been argued thus far that information sources occurring in technical documents can profitably be looked upon as languages whose syntaxes are amenable to precise and exhaustive description of a computer. Of course it is one thing to recognize the existence of a language and to infer the existence of its grammar, and quite another matter to exhibit the grammar. It is, therefore, important that we investigate the techniques that are available for doing syntactic description of the textual and pictorial languages existing in documents in order to get an indication of how likely it is that these techniques will prove sufficient for describing the languages with which we are concerned.

Bobrow has surveyed the existing computer programs for syntactic analysis of English printed text [10]. Our purpose here will be to consider one or two such techniques in somewhat greater detail. In the next section, it will be shown how a particular technique, that of the use of context-free grammars, permits an effective interpretation of the languages so described.

If we compare different grammars for the same language as, for example grammars of English text, we find a substantial disagreement as to the kind of analysis assigned by the grammars to the text. Even where the agreement exists on what the corpus shall be, the analyses assigned to that corpus very often differ. This difference in analyses may be attributed to the difference in the linguistic intuitions of the linguists who write the grammars. It may also be attributed to differences in the dialects being accounted for. But the most important reason for differences is that the purposes of performing a syntactical analysis might differ from one case to the next. We can mention several different purposes served by a syntactic analysis of a language for any pair of which the syntactic analyses necessary to accomplish the purposes are likely to differ. For example, in performing mechanical translation in attempting to do auto extracting [11], in attempting automatically to paraphrase [12], in attempting to do automatic indexing and finally, in attempting to do automatic question answering [13], all from natural language text, it is likely that the syntactic analysis necessary to achieve the purpose will be quite specialized.

There are a few ways in which a syntactic description (of an underlying language which is to be interpreted for machine processing purposes) may be embedded in a larger system. One kind of syntactic description is implicit in the part of the system that does syntactic analysis. Thus, in the Kuno and Oettinger [14] syntactic analyzer, an underlying descriptive theory of the language is implicit in the analyzer and can indeed be resurrected and put in explicit form, although this is unnecessary for the intended purposes of syntactic analysis. Or in the discourse generator of Simmons, Klein, and McConlogue [15], the dependency analysis and their so-called transitivity rule have implicit in them a syntactic description of the underlying language.

In the applications that are of interest here, what is being described in a descriptive language is itself a very large natural language whose description necessarily is an open-ended task. The empirical problem then is to determine what descriptive languages can be used in describing natural languages like English text or schematic pictures. There are several different types of descriptive languages which serve as candidates, and we wish briefly to compare some properties of these different kinds of descriptive languages within which syntactic theories of, *e.g.*, English text can be formulated.

The first possible descriptive language is a natural language, perhaps the natural language that is itself being described. We must reject this out of hand because of the unformalized state of the natural language. Thus, to describe English syntax in English is, in the present state of the art, useless to a machine. Paradoxically though, one result of achieving a syntactic description of English might be to permit a suitable formalization of a sufficiently large fragment of English that the product might be used for describing English itself. This initial bootstrapping step has yet to be taken.

When we come to the formalized programming languages as candidates for use in describing the structure of English text, we run into a paradoxical difficulty that the most powerful languages are the least useful. To explore this difficulty, let us consider the restricted task of describing the structure of English text in some suitable programming language by writing a program which is capable of systematically exhibiting all and only the English text that has occurred in some corpus plus a linguist's extrapolation thereof. If our task is thus restricted, the ideal candidate would, of course, be such a programming language as is convenient to use, easy to learn, and for which efficient object language can be compiled, etc. But, as a matter of fact, the task of producing a description of a natural language is not so restricted as we have assumed. To see this, let us assume that we had written a program P_1 which, when provided with a list of all English words [16], could in some systematic sense list a set of all and only the English sentences $\{S\}$ occurring in some corpus and in a reasonable infinite extrapolation therefrom [34]. To actually run P_1 and allow it to produce $\{S\}$ serves no useful purpose. The real purpose of writing P_1 is to use it as one of the inputs to another program P_2 which is capable of analyzing the sentences in $\{S\}$. The way the P_2 would operate is that it would accept as input S_i, a sequence of words, and also P_1. Then P_2 would furnish as output $P_1(S_i)$, the trace of P_1 in one possible process of its producing S_i, or an indication if no such process exists. Thus, P_1, in conjunction with the analyzing program P_2, produces the set of analyses $\{P_1(S)\}$ for the language $\{S\}$. But what happens if P_1 is written in some powerful programming language of a general purpose nature? The peculiar fact is that *in general* no such P_2 can be written unless we know *a priori* that P_1 has some limiting restrictions built into it which have the effect of making it a program in a much less powerful programming language than the one in which it would otherwise have been written.

It is important to realize that our argument (which is of a recursive function theoretic nature) [17] about the impossibility of constructing P_2 depends essentially upon the stipulation that P_2 be a *uniform* analyzing program, *i.e.*, one which works over a wide class of P_1's which are themselves programs in a general purpose programming language. To see why this stipulation is made, notice that if the S_i in $\{S\}$ are sentences of a natural language like English; then the task of writing P_1 is substantially an open ended one, perhaps never capable of definitive completion. P_2, on the other hand, need by no means necessarily be an elaborate program. Examples of some kinds of P_2's which one might want to construct are syntactic analyzers which calculate $P_1(S_i)$, or ambiguity testers which determine if there is a unique such $P_1(S_i)$ or grammar equivalence testers which determine of a P_1 and a P_1' whether for all S_i, $P_1(S_i)$ corresponds to $P_1'(S_i)$. In all these cases, if no restrictions are placed upon P_1 other than that it be a program in say FAP or IPL-V or machine language for just about any computer, then none of these different kinds of P_2's are constructable.

The way out of this impasse is, as was suggested above, to restrict P_1 to be a descriptive syntactic theory within a language of much less computing power than the conventional computing languages we are accustomed to using. As an example of a P_1 so restricted, we have the syntactic description of ALGOL. Large parts (but not all) of ALGOL are described by a P_1 which is in the Backus normal form (or a context-free phrase structure language). That the context-free phrase structure languages are incapable of being used as meta-languages to describe object languages of some very simple types is well known [18]. However, this very restriction of the ALGOL syntax to be largely context-free phrase structure in form is what enables syntactic analyzers for ALGOL to be written, even if we allow the possibility that ALGOL will be expanded, so long as the indicated restriction remains satisfied.

Of the many possible models available for descriptive analysis of a language, the one that we elect to use here is the context-free (or so-called "simple") phrase structure language, sometimes called immediate constituent analysis.

The choice of this model for syntactic description of a tiny fragment of English in this paper is dictated largely by expository considerations. Much probably unnecessary controversy exists over the question of what meta-language is appropriate for the description of English. Many models have been suggested [19] [20] and the suitability of the various models for describing different corpora has been heatedly discussed in the literature.

Two of the candidate models, the phrase structure language and the finite state language, are both represented interestingly enough by the same example that is offered in Fig. 1. Here a grammar is presented for a tiny fragment of English consisting of simple declarative sentences about circles, triangles, squares, and polygons, their color, size, and relative positions. The notation used for this context-free or phrase-structure grammar is similar to the Backus normal form [21] but for subsequent application purposes, the notation is modified sightly. To interpret the notation of this example, consider rule 1. This rule indicates that a syntactic category called SENT, which of course denotes "sentence," can be replaced by the concatenation, denoted by the plus symbol, of SUBJ with PRED. In other words, every sentence has a subject followed by a predicate in this simple grammar. Mnemonic symbols are chosen for purposes of clarity. Then, the expansion of the category SUBJ is obtained by choosing either of two alternatives, given in rules 2 and 3, *viz.*, the word "a" followed by the syntactic category NHEADSG or alternatively the word "each" followed by the syntactic category NHEADSG. By continuing to exercise choices among those available, ultimately a sequence of English words will be produced which purportedly constitutes an English sentence. For those familiar with Backus normal form, we indicate below how rules 39

1.	SENT	=	SUBJ + PRED
2.	SUBJ	=	a + NHEADSG
3.		=	each + NHEADSG
4.	NHEADSG	=	NOUN
5.		=	PREMOD + NOUN
6.		=	NOUN + POSTMOD
7.		=	PREMOD + NOUN + POSTMOD
8.	PREMOD	=	ADJS
9.		=	ADJ1 + ADJ2
10.	ADJS	=	ADJ1
11.		=	ADJ2
12.-15.	ADJ1	=	big, large, little, small
16.-17.	ADJ2	=	black, white
18.-20a.	NOUN	=	circle, triangle, square, polygon
21.	POSTMOD	=	UNLIM + COM
22.		=	COM
23.		=	LIM + ADJS
24.	UNLIM	=	REL + is + not
25.		=	REL + is
26.		=	not
27.	LIM	=	REL + is + not
28.		=	REL + is
29.-30.	REL	=	that, which
31.	COM	=	PREP1 + the + LOC
32.		=	RELPHR
33.	PREP1	=	on, at
34.-37.	LOC	=	right, left, top, bottom
38.	RELPHR	=	INTROD + NPHRZ
39.	INTROD	=	PREP1 + the + LOC + of
40.		=	PREP2
41.		=	COMPADJ + than
42.-44.	PREP2	=	in, below, above
45.-48.	COMPADJ	=	bigger, littler, larger, smaller
49.	NPHRZ	=	a + NHEADSG
50.		=	each + NHEADSG
51.	PRED	=	is + COMNA
52.		=	is + not + COMNA
53.	COMNA	=	COM
54.		=	a + NHEADSG

Fig. 1—A grammar for a small fragment of English.

through 41 would be written in that format.

⟨INTROD⟩ = ::⟨PREP1⟩ / the ⟨LOC⟩ of
⟨PREP2⟩ / ⟨COMPADJ⟩ than.

Of the infinite number of distinct sentences producible by this grammar, we list below a few typical examples.

1) Each polygon smaller than a black triangle is a square.
2) A big black polygon which is on the left is a triangle.
3) Each triangle that is not in a circle below each square is larger than a polygon which is at the top.

In this grammar, although we have used the context-free phrase structure mechanism, and notwithstanding the fact that this mechanism is capable of syntactically describing languages which are not describable by the so-called finite state grammars, it turns out, nevertheless, to be an accidental fact that the particular grammar that we present is weakly equivalent to a finite state grammar. The reader may, if he wishes, construct a state graph [22] for this grammar by treating words as output and the left to right sequence of unexpanded syntactic categories at any one time as the name of the state in the finite state process for producing the sentence. Such a diagram will turn out to have a finite number of states in it; in fact, it has 79 states. This is, of course, an accident of the peculiarly small language we have chosen to describe with this grammar. In fact, with the addition of one particular rule to the grammar, it becomes impossible to produce a finite state diagram for the modified language. The single rule is shown below.

INTROD = between + a + NPHRZ + and.

The self-embedding introduced by this additional rule makes the language no longer finite state.

As a final illustration of how our simple grammar works, we show in Fig. 2 a tree diagram for the first of the sentences mentioned above as it is produced by or analyzed with respect to the grammar shown in Fig. 1.

In discussing the techniques that are available for syntactic description of a natural language, our illustrations and discussion thus far have been confined to the one dimensional languages. The reason for this is that all of the study which has been devoted thus far to properties of metalanguages for syntactic description has been directed toward the linear, that is one dimensional, languages. For the two dimensional languages, what we want to be able to do is to articulate the two dimensional structure of images in such a way that the well-formed sub-parts of a picture will be assigned to syntactic categories in very much the way that well-formed sub-strings in a sentence grammar are assigned to suitable syntactic categories. Before that can be done, however (and it shall not be done in this paper), it is necessary to solve several problems. It shall be satisfactory here merely to mention some problems which must be solved for the two dimensional case before any satisfactory grammar or syntactic description of an important pictorial source can be written.

The first problem is how to generalize the notion of juxtaposition, which in one dimension reduces to concatenation. The arrangement of words within a sentence in text is apparently entirely describable in terms of the one dimensional notion of concatenation. However, for pictorial sources, quite evidently concatenation must be replaced by at least one two-dimensional notion and perhaps several such operating simultaneously.

As a class of pictorial sources, consider electrical circuit diagrams. Several kinds of juxtaposition can be

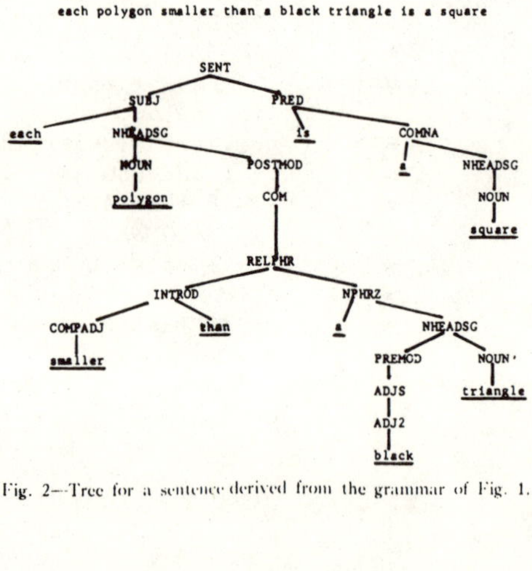

Fig. 2—Tree for a sentence derived from the grammar of Fig. 1.

suggested that will probably be useful for circuit diagrams. First there is a juxtaposition of proximity independent of direction. This is the kind of juxtaposition that relates a resistor symbol to the letter that acts as its label and that is generally used for labelling purposes. A second quite different kind of juxtapostion in two dimensions for circuit diagrams is that which denotes electrical connection between symbols. A third is superimposition. In circuit diagrams, for example, superimposition holds between the symbols for, say, a capacitor and the arrow which denotes variability. A still different kind of juxtaposition in circuit diagrams is left-to-right and sometimes top-to-bottom juxtaposition which usually indicates input-output relations in circuit diagrams. There are other (some quite unusual) kinds of juxtaposition that occur in circuit diagrams.

A possible solution to the choice of a metalanguage in which to represent the syntactic structure of such schematic sources is implicit in a suggestion made by Minsky [23]. His functional notation would be used for denoting the syntactic structure of circuit diagrams by invoking a set of specialized predicates each of which is used to denote a special kind of juxtaposition that exists in a schematic drawing between the symbols that it relates. Unfortunately, it is not yet possible with such a solution to the two dimensional representation problem to produce a syntactic theory having the clarity of a generative grammar such as was exhibited above for English text. The reason for this difficulty is that with several different kinds of functions denoting position in circuit diagrams, there occur conflicts between them, and the rules for resolving these conflicts to produce a diagram whose syntactic description is given are not evident. Thus, the main problem in developing two dimensional grammars is to get a good generalization of the notion of one dimensional concatenation.

Among the other problems that must be solved, there is the problem of how to do syntactic analysis. The scanning of a one dimensional sentence from left to right is a good heuristic and there are others that make a parser or syntactic analyzer efficient. No such simple correspondence suggests itself for circuit diagrams or some of the other pictorial sources.

Another problem is the identification of the primitive symbols or what we call characters. Probably the simplest way to solve that problem is to define those symbols as primitive which are recognizable by suitable character recognition equipment. A final problem in developing a two dimensional grammar is the problem of displaying the results of a syntactic analysis. The tree representation is a convenient two dimensional form for displaying the results of one dimensional syntactic analysis. Perhaps some suitable three dimensional representaion is necessary to display the results of syntactically analyzing two dimensional pictorial sources.

Although there has been no study of two dimensional languages for syntactic description of two dimensional sources, it may be suggestive to see what one might look like. In Fig. 3 is shown a simple two dimensional grammar for a class of pictures consisting of 45° right triangles drawn in the plane which has been divided into unit squares. The alphabet consists of the symbols, V, H, W, L, I, B, R, and the blank symbol. The grammar consists of the ten production rules shown in Fig. 3. If these rules are applied starting with the single symbol, V, as in the left side of production 1, and if the rules are applied an arbitrary number of times in an arbitrary order until no rule applied, then a terminal array of symbols will be obtained which is in the form of a triangle as shown in Fig. 3. There are an infinite number of such triangles obtainable but what is important about our example is that in each such triangle, the symbols which denote it constitute a syntactic analysis of the triangle, the right angle being marked with an R, the two remaining vertices with letters V and W, the hypotenuse letters H, the base with letters B, the other leg with letters L, and the interior points of the triangle with letters I. For such a simple pictorial source as these triangles, the syntactic analysis is self-evident and the mechanism that we exhibit is sufficient to do the analysis of the triangle. It is not clear, however, how to extend the implicit underlying model used here to other pictorial sources of greater interest and importance. This example may suggest some, however.

Although no studies have been reported in the literature of the underlying languages to be used for syntactic description of pictorial sources, there have nevertheless been several successful attempts to describe certain pictorial sources without an explicit underlying model. Eden [24] has shown successfully how cursive handwriting may be described as a language in which certain primitive strokes are juxtaposed according to rules which he makes explicit to form cursive handwriting. The pictorial source here may be considered to be an example of the class that we called "synthetic representations." Grimsdale, *et al.* [25] studied the syntactic structure of hand printed block letters for character recognition purposes. Narasimhan [26] has applied the technique of syntactic description to photographs taken in hydrogen bubble chambers of particle tracks. Finally, in the Sketchpad system of Sutherland [27], there is implicit the syntactic description of the class of drawings consisting of straight lines and circular arcs. In none of these examples, however, has any systematic attempt been made to construct a language for syntactic description and in that language to describe the pictorial sources being processed. As has been suggested above, further study of the underlying languages is needed before such a syntactic description may conveniently be constructed.

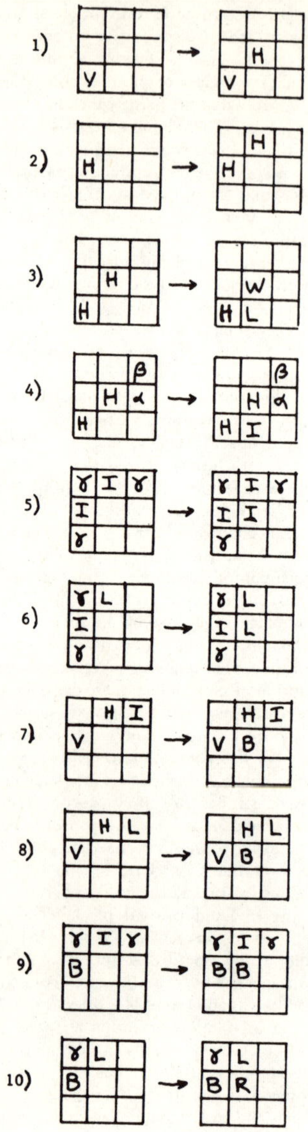

In these productions:

- α is any member of {L, I}
- β is any member of {H, W}
- γ is any member of {V, H, W, L, I, B, R, blank}, i.e., any symbol, including the blank

In each production, the Greek letters stand for the same symbol on both sides of the production although in #5, 6, 9, γ may have different values in different positions.

An example of a triangle derivation:

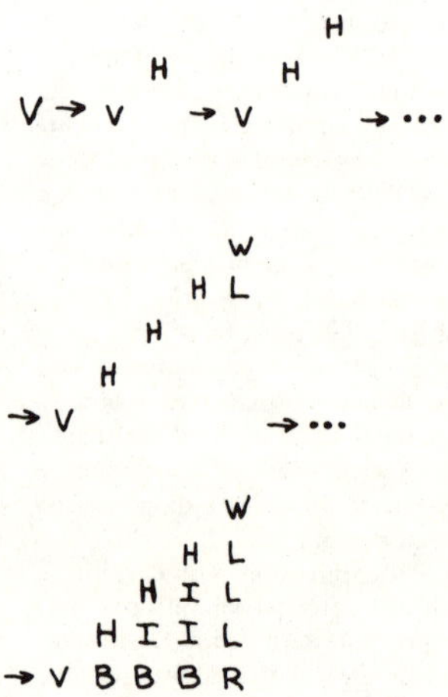

Fig. 3—A two-dimensional grammar for triangles.

IV. Syntax-Directed Interpretation of English Sentences

The two preceding sections have attempted to show that text and pictures may be syntactically described to make explicit some of the implicit properties of such information, and have discussed some techniques that may profitably be used in exhibiting such a syntactic description and in analyzing information sources with respect to such syntactic descriptions. Syntactic analysis, however, from the point of view of this paper, is not an end in itself but an important and probably essential intermediate step in other information processing operations. This section will consider one class of such information processing operations in which the results of a syntactic analysis of English text are used to provide to a machine a certain kind of "understanding" of the English sentences in the text.

The operations that will be performed here upon the syntactically analyzed sentences amount to an interpretation of these sentences. The notion interpretation is used here in a manner roughly analogous to the way it is used in logic. Objects are given in a syntactic metalanguage which, in this case, consists of the syntactically analyzed English sentences. Then, with these objects, or certain ones of them, are associated objects of a different system which need not even be a language. The objects associated with the syntactic objects are their interpretation. Operations upon the objects are also associated with corresponding operations on their interpretations. This process of associating the syntactic and operations on them with the objects and operations of another system will be referred to as interpreting them.

The kind of interpretation in mind here is fairly common in the so-called syntax directed compilers. In such compilers, first there is obtained the syntactic analysis of the input string and then this syntactic analysis is used to produce machine code. The process of producing the machine code from syntactically analyzed input strings is an interpretation process (on objects only in this case) in the sense that the term is used here.

It will appear below that several kinds of information processing operations may be looked upon as instances of interpretation of syntactically analyzed information sources where the syntactic analysis directs the nature of the interpretation operation. Thus, such processes may be called "syntax directed interpretation."

To see in detail how the process of syntax directed interpretation for English sentences, in particular, may be accomplished, the problem of translation into a logical language will be considered in some detail. It is desired to see how a set of English sentences, in particular those given by the grammar in Fig. 1, may be so translated into a logical language representation that it becomes possible by mechanical procedures to determine of the given sentences whether or not they are correct descriptions of simple pictures which they purport to describe. This shall be accomplished by the syntax directed interpretation of the syntactically analyzed English sentences interpreted in a language which is very much like a first order predicate or functional calculus. The well-formed formulae (WFF) of the logical language will consist of predicates or functions denoted by mnemonic strings of letters and arguments shown inside of parentheses. There will be allowed the logical connectives of conjunction shown by the symbol & and implication shown by the symbol $\supset$. Two quantifiers will be allowed, the existential quantifier denoted by ⫯, and the universal quantifier denoted by $\forall$. The tilde ($\sim$) will denote negation.

Fig. 4 shows the rules for interpreting the syntactically analyzed sentences generated by the grammar of Fig. 1. Corresponding to each syntactic replacement rule in the grammar for English sentences of Fig. 1, there is an interpretation rule with an identical number given in Fig. 4. The interpretation rule tells how to transform WFF's of the logical language corresponding to each operation performed upon the syntactic categories of the English language sentences. This process can be illustrated by reference to both Figs. 2 and 5.

In Fig. 2 a particular English sentence producible by the grammar is shown, "each polygon smaller than a black triangle is a square." In the process of producing this sentence according to the syntactic analysis given in the tree diagram of Fig. 2, there are 21 replacement steps to produce the final sentence. In the first step, the syntactic category SENT is replaced by SUBJ followed by PRED. In the next step, SUBJ is expanded into the word "each" followed by NHEADSG, etc. For each of these steps in the syntactic construction of the sentence, there is a corresponding step illustrated in Fig. 5 for the production of the logical translation of this sentence. In step number 1, corresponding to the syntactic category SENT, there is written first the well-formed formula symbol WFF of the logical language. Then when syntax rule number 1 is used to expand SENT correspondingly, interpretation rule number 1 is used to expand WFF to the well-formed formula PRED(SUBJ) which is shown in line 2 of Fig. 5.

The next syntax expansion rule used to produce the given sentence is rule number 3 of the syntax, and corresponding to it, rule number 3 of the interpretation requires that the well-formed formula in line 2 be written in the form shown in line 3 of Fig. 5. If this process is continued, at each step performing an interpretation operation corresponding to the identically numbered syntactic operation, there will be produced, at the end, two objects; the first object is a sentence with its syntactic analysis, and the second is the logical translation of that sentence. The logical translation of the given sentence is shown in line 21 of Fig. 5. It is thus found that the translation of the sentence, "each polygon smaller than a black triangle is a square," is the well-formed formula

$\forall x((\text{pgn}(x)\ \&\ ⫯y(\text{smr}(x, y)\ \&\ \text{bk}(y)\ \&\ \text{tri}(y))) \supset (\text{sq}(x)))$.

1.	WFF	→	PRED (SUBJ)
2.	PRED(SUBJ)	→	∃x (PRED(x) & NHEADSG(x)) where x is a previously unused variable
3.		→	∀x ((NHEADSG(x)) ⊃ (PRED(x))) where x is a previously unused variable
4.	NHEADSG(x)	→	NOUN(x)
5.		→	PREMOD(x) & NOUN(x)
6.		→	NOUN(x) & POSTMOD(x)
7.		→	PREMOD(x) & NOUN(x) & POSTMOD(x)
8.	PREMOD(x)	→	ADJS(x)
9.		→	ADJ1(x) & ADJ2(x)
10.	ADJS(x)	→	ADJ1(x)
11.		→	ADJ2(x)
12.-15.	ADJ1(x)	→	bg(x), lg(x), lt(x), sm(x) respectively
16.-17.	ADJ2(x)	→	bk(x), wt(x)
18.-20a.	NOUN(x)	→	cir(x), tri(x), sq(x), pgn(x) respectively
21.	POSTMOD(x)	→	UNLIMCOM(x)
22.		→	COM(x)
23.		→	LIMADJS(x)
24.	UNLIMCOM(x)	→	~(COM(x))
25.		→	COM(x)
26.		→	~(COM(x))
27.	LIMADJS(x)	→	~(ADJS(x))
28.		→	ADJS(x)
29.-30.			No operation
31.	COM(x)	→	LOC(x) LOC is a unary predicate here
32.		→	RELPHR(x)
33.			No operation
34.	LOC(x)	→	rt (x) if LOC is a unary predicate
	LOC(x,y)	→	rt(x,y) if LOC is a binary predicate
35.	LOC(x)	→	lf(x) if LOC is a unary predicate
	LOC(x,y)	→	lf(xy) if LOC is a binary predicate
36.-37.			Same as 34 and 35 for top(x), top(x,y), bot(x), and bot(x,y) respectively
38.	RELPHR(x)	→	INTROD(x,NPHRZ) i.e., the unary predicate RELPHR becomes a binary predicate INTROD
39.	INTROD(x,NPHRZ)	→	LOC(x,NPHRZ) LOC is a binary predicate here
40.		→	PREP2(x,NPHRZ)
41.		→	COMPADJ(x,NPHRZ)
42.-44.	PREP2(x,NPHRZ)	→	in(x,NPHRZ), bel(x,NPHRZ), abv(x,NPHRZ) respectively
45.-48.	COMPADJ(x,NPHRZ)	→	bgr(x,NPHRZ), ltr(x,NPHRZ), lgr(x,NPHRZ), smr(x,NPHRZ) respectively
49.	Φ(x,NPHRZ)	→	∃y(Φ(x,y) & NHEADSG(y)) where Φ is any binary predicate having NPHRZ as an argument and Φ(x,y) is the result of substituting any previously unused variable, y, for the occurence of NPHRZ.
50.		→	∀y((NHEADSG(y)) ⊃ (Φ(x,y))) Same as for 49
51.	PRED(x)	→	COMNA(x)
52.		→	~(COMNA(x))
53.	COMNA(x)	→	COM(x)
54.		→	NHEADSG(x)

Fig. 4—Interpretation rules for Fig. 1 grammar.

A similar process may be carried out for any sentence of the infinite number of sentences that can be generated from the grammar of Fig. 1. For each such sentence, there is a logical translation and it is obtained by carrying out the process given in Fig. 4.

The reason for obtaining the logical translation of such sentences is that from the logical translation it is very easy to determine whether the given sentences are true or false descriptions of patterns that they purport to describe. Let us consider how one might determine for the sentence of our example whether it is a correct description of a picture. For the given picture, one would first have to determine what the syntactically well-formed objects are in the simple pictures which the sentences of our grammar can describe. These syntactically well-formed objects would be what we have once called "blobs," that is, disjoint objects in the picture [28]. The variables denoted by x, y, z, etc., in our logical language will range over the blobs in the picture. Then a character-recognition process would determine for any arbitrary blob whether it had the property of being a polygon or of being black or of being a triangle or of being a square, each of which is denoted, respectively, in our logical language by the symbols pgn, bk, tri, sq. A simple subroutine could determine of two such blobs, x and y, whether x is smaller than y, *e.g.*, in area, in which case the logical predicate smr(x, y) would be true for x and y. Finally, to determine of the whole logical expression whether it is true for a given picture, it is necessary to find out by a search program whether for every object x, if the character recognizer says that it is a polygon and there is an object y such that x is smaller than y, and the character recognizer says that y is black and that y is a triangle, then, in such case, the character recognizer says that x is a square. If this is the case, then indeed the logical expression given in line 21 of Fig. 5 is satisfied by the given picture and one may say that the original sentence is a correct (partial) description of the given picture.

The reader may wish to test his own implicit character-recognition procedure on the three pictures of Fig. 6 and verify that the original sentence, the logical translation of which is given in Fig. 5, is a true description of the first two pictures in Fig. 6 and not a true description of the third.

This example has illustrated how the truth-functional evaluation of simple sentences as descriptions of simple pictures may be mechanically accomplished. The truth-functional properties that are assigned to the English sentences are actually properties of the logical language WFF's into which the sentences have been translated. If the sentences in the logic language are intuitively acceptable interpretations of the original English sentences, then to that extent the truth-functional evaluation of the logical sentences is a corresponding truth-functional evaluation of the original English sentences. For other purposes, different logical languages or perhaps no logical language at all is needed. If one's purpose were to do question answering, the different types of questions might require processing operations of logically distinct types. Thus, for answering yes-no types of questions, a mechanism virtually identical to the one illustrated here would be sufficient. For answering the wh-type questions (those introduced by "which," "what," "when," etc.), one would use a logical language in which properties other than truth-functional ones could be evaluated, that is, in which the values of certain functions would be objects or the names of objects within the picture.

An attractive alternative to the use of logical languages suggests itself in the possibility of using the language of the syntactically analyzed English sentence as the logical language itself. The reason for using a logical

```
1.   WFF
2.   PRED(SUBJ)
3.   ∀x((NHEADSG(x)) ⊃ (PRED(x)))
4.   ∀x((NOUN(x) & POSTMOD(x)) ⊃ (PRED(x)))
 :
7.   ∀x((pgn(x) & RELPHR(x)) ⊃ (PRED(x)))
8.   ∀x((pgn(x) & INTROD(x,NPHRZ)) ⊃ (PRED(x)))
 .
10.  ∀x((pgn(x) & smr(x,NPHRZ)) ⊃ (PRED(x)))
11.  ∀x((pgn(x) & ∃y(smr(x,y) & NHEADSG(y))) ⊃ (PRED(x)))
12.  ∀x((pgn(x) & ∃y(smr(x,y) & PREMOD(y) & NOUN(y))) ⊃ (PRED(x)))
 :
20.  ∀x((pgn(x) & ∃y(smr(x,y) & bk(y) & tri(y))) ⊃ (NOUN(x)))
21.  ∀x((pgn(x) & ∃y(smr(x,y) & bk(y) & tri(y))) ⊃ (sq(x)))
```

Fig. 5—Steps in developing a WFF translation for the sentence of Fig. 2.

Picture 1)

Description is true for the picture

Picture 2)

Description is (vacuously) true for the picture

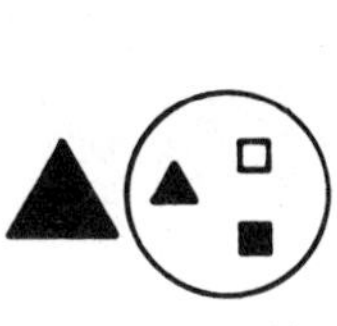

Picture 3)

Description is false for the picture

Fig. 6—Three pictures for testing the logical translation shown in Fig. 5.

language is that the logical properties of it are usually well understood. However, to use a logical language necessitates a translation into that language. The alternative of using the language of the syntactically analyzed source sentences requires that if one were interested in performing such processes as inference, question answering, or truth-functional evaluation, then these processing operations would have to be reformulated in terms of the language used for the syntactic analysis of the English sentences. This possibility, however, will not be further explored here.

V. Syntax-Directed Interpretation in Other Applications

In the example discussed in Section IV, a syntax-directed interpretation process was used to match syntactically analyzed sentences against syntactically analyzed pictures, although, admittedly, syntactic analysis of the pictures was relatively trivial. The process of syntax-directed interpretation, however, has many other applications which we wish briefly to mention in this section.

The first application is to the process of performing inference on natural language text which can clearly be done to the extent that text can be translated into a logical language as we illustrated in the simple example of the previous section. The inference in turn corresponds to a natural-language inference. This possibility of performing inference has been a main concern of symbolic logic for a long time. What is apparently new, however, is the possibility of making use of an exhaustive syntactic analysis as the input which can direct the process of translation into a logical language. The language which is used for representing the syntactically-analyzed sentences can itself serve as a logical language in terms of which rules of inference may be constructed. This possibility does not seem to have been explored previously.

Another application of syntax-directed interpretation is encoding of text for storage and transmission. The usual procedures for encoding text make use of letter frequencies, or letter pair, or in some cases, higher order *n* tuples of letters, or perhaps words and their corresponding frequencies. Here the probability distribution used for designing a code is based on observed statistics of various corpora. A different possibility, however, would be based upon a probability distribution that comes directly out of a grammar for the underlying language.

Suppose that in the grammar of Fig. 1, each of the alternative choices made in the process of generating a sentence were assumed to be equally likely. This assumption would induce a probability distribution on the sentences produced which would have the desirable property of usually associating low probabilities with longer sentences and higher probabilities with shorter sentences. Thus, the sentence used for an example in Fig. 2 would have a probability of $2^{-22} \cdot 3^{-2}$ or approximately 2^{-26}. A Huffman code based on this probability distribution (described in Fano [29]) would thus represent the sentence "each polygon smaller than a black triangle is a square," with a 26-bit sequence.

There are applications of the syntax-directed interpretation process to the problem of inductive inference. A technique such as the one described immediately above for assigning probabilities to sentences can similarly be used to assign probabilities to the events described by such sentences. Then when one wishes to assign probabilities to alternative hypotheses about a particular universe of discourse (pictures in our simple case above), the probabilities that are assigned to the hypotheses are the probabilities assigned to the sentences that denote these hypotheses.

For complex languages like English, this approach to inductive inference offers an interesting alternative to the one suggested by Carnap and Bar-Hillel [30] and the one suggested by Kochen [31].

Syntax directed interpretation for pictorial sources is an important possibility for investigation. The first instance of syntax directed interpretation is in the encoding of pictures for storage and transmission purposes. The usual approach to picture encoding makes use of picture statistics such as run-length statistics and the design of matching codes for these statistics. Code compressions up to about 10 to 1 have been achieved by such techniques. However, for certain pictorial sources like schematic diagrams, the explicit syntactic analysis of such diagrams and then the use of syntax directed coding techniques would very likely lead to a considerable further code compression for storage or transmission purposes. Thus, for an electrical circuit diagram, the list of the names of the circuit components (the primitive symbols) and the list of the syntactic relations that hold among them would be, for most purposes, a sufficient characterization of the diagrams to serve the purposes of reproducing them. We would estimate that if an exhaustive grammar of electrical circuit diagrams were to be written, then the encoding or transmission of such diagrams as information sources could be done with a code compression of perhaps 100 to 1 or 1 decimal order of magnitude greater than can be achieved with statistical coding techniques [32].

Another pictorial language which could lend itself to syntax directed interpretation is the language of chemical structure diagrams. Much attention has been devoted to techniques for going from such diagrams by manual procedures to linear ciphers, and some effort has been devoted to machine manipulation of some of these ciphers [33]. There seems further to be the possibility of providing a syntactical characterization of chemical structure diagrams as pictorial sources and the possibility of manipulating these diagrams as the codes which represent chemical compounds rather than their linear cipher representations.

VI. Conclusion

In this paper, an attempt has been made to show that the class of information sources occurring in technical and scientific documents which contain text and pictures can be uniformly treated as languages. They are languages in the strong sense that descriptive theories of these languages can be exhibited by means of computer processing techniques that are available or with some extensions of these techniques. Such descriptive theories for these languages can provide to machines an effective partial substitute for the cultural environment in which human beings ordinarily encounter the languages. With such descriptive theories of text and picture sources, a machine can analyze individual information items at a purely syntactic (formal) level. It appears that if the descriptive theory goes deep into the structure of the underlying language, then the corresponding syntactic analysis made by a machine can lead, through the process of syntax direction, to an interpretation of these languages by entirely automatic procedures. It is tempting to identify these interpretation operations with the informal notion of "understanding." The methods of syntax directed interpretation for natural languages described here will appear attractive to those who wish to provide machines with the very elaborate structural details that are known and can be discovered about natural languages.

Acknowledgment

Many of the ideas in this paper arose in discussions with the author's colleagues to whom credit is gratefully given: S. Cappell, D. Cohen, A. J. Goldman, R. W. Hsu, E. Jones, J. Randolf, B. K. Rankin III, W. A. Sillars and W. C. Watt. Rankin and Randolf wrote grammars similar to those of Figs. 1 and 3 and Sillars wrote a translation algorithm similar to that of Fig. 4. Finally, to Mrs. Arlene V. Ruhl who did all the output work, special thanks are extended.

Bibliography

[1] S. M. Newman, R. W. Swanson, and K. Knowlton, "A Notation System for Transliterating Technical and Scientific Texts for Use in Data Processing Systems," U. S. Patent Office, Washington, D. C., Research and Dev. Rept., No. 15; May 22, 1959.

[2] R. Carnap, "Introduction to Symbolic Logic and Its Applications," Dover Publications, Inc., New York, N. Y., Ch. B, Sec. 20; 1958.

[3] R. W. Floyd, "On the Non-existence of a phrase structure grammar for ALGOL 60," *Commun. ACM*, vol. 5 pp. 483–484; September, 1962.

[4] Z. S. Harris, "String Analysis of Sentence Structure," N. V. Mouton and Company, The Hague, The Netherlands; 1962.

[5] R. S. Wells, "Immediate Constituents," *Language*, vol. 23, pp. 81–117; April–June, 1947.

[6] N. Chomsky, "Syntactic Structures," N. V. Mouton and Company, The Hague, The Netherlands; 1957.

[7] M. E. Stevens, "Automatic Character Recognition: A State-of-the-Art Report," National Bureau of Standards, Washington, D. C., Tech. Note 112, PB 161613; May, 1961.

[8] E. H. Gombrich, "Art and Illusion," Pantheon, New York, N. Y.; 1960.

[9] S. Ginsburg and H. G. Rice, "Two Families of Languages Related to ALGOL," System Development Corp., Santa Monica, Calif., Rept. No. TM-578; July, 1961, and *J. ACM*, p. 350, March, 1962.

[10] D. G. Bobrow, "Syntactic Analysis of English by Computer—A Survey," Proc. Fall Joint Computer Conf., vol. 24, pp. 365–387; 1963.

[11] H. P. Edmundson and R. E. Wyllys, "Automatic abstracting and indexing, survey and recommendations," *Commun. ACM*, vol. 4, pp. 226–234; May, 1961.

[12] S. Klein, "Some Experiments Performed with an Automatic Paraphraser," System Development Corp., Santa Monica, Calif.; 1963.

[13] E. A. Feigenbaum and J. Feldman, "Computers and Thought," McGraw-Hill Book Co., New York, N. Y.; 1963. (See the chapters by R. K. Lindsay and B. F. Green Jr., pp. 207–223.)

[14] S. Kuno and A. G. Oettinger, "Syntactic Structure and Ambiguity of English," *Proc. Fall Joint Computer Conf.*, pp. 397–418; 1963.

[15] R. F. Simmons, S. Klein and K. McConlogue, "Co-occurrence and Dependency Logic for Answering English Questions," Systems Development Corp., Santa Monica, Calif., SP-1155, pp. 1–29; April 3, 1963.

[16] A. F. Brown, "Normal and Reverse English Word List," University of Pennsylvania Press, Philadelphia, Pa.; January, 1963.

[17] M. Davis, "Computability and Unsolvability," McGraw-Hill Book Co., Inc., New York, N. Y.; 1958.

[18] R. W. Floyd, "The Syntax of Programming Languages—A Survey," this issue, page 346.

[19] N. Chomsky, "Formal Properties of Grammars," in "Handbook of Mathematical Psychology," vol. 2, R. R. Bush, E. H. Galanter, and R. D. Luce, eds., John Wiley and Sons, Inc., New York, N. Y.; 1962.

[20] V. H. Yngve, "A Model and an Hypothesis for Language Structure," *Proc. American Philsophical Soc.*, vol. 104, pp. 444–466; October, 1960.

[21] J. W. Backus, "The Syntax and Semantics of the Proposed International Algebraic Language—Zurich ACM-GAMM Conference," *Proc. Internat'l Conf. on Information Processing*, pp. 125–132; June, 1959.

[22] R. F. McNaughton and H. Yamada, "Regular Expressions and State Graphs for Automata," IRE Trans. on Electronic Computers, vol. EC-9, pp. 39–47; March, 1960.

[23] M. L. Minsky, "Steps Toward Artificial Intelligence," Proc. IRE, vol. 49, pp. 8–30; January, 1961.

[24] M. Eden, "On the Formalization of Handwriting," in "Structure of Language and Its Mathematical Aspect," American Mathematical Society, Providence, R. I., pp. 83–88; 1961.

[25] R. L. Grinsdale, *et al.*, "A System for the Automatic Recognition of Patterns," *Proc. IEE*, vol. 106, Pt. B, pp. 210–221; March, 1959.

[26] R. Narasimhan, "Syntactic Description of Pictures and Gestalt Phenomena of Visual Perception," Digital Computer Laboratory, University of Illinois, Urbana; July 25, 1963.

[27] I. E. Sutherland, "Sketchpad, A Man-Machine Graphical Communication System," *Proc. SJCC*, vol. 23, pp. 329–346; 1963.

[28] R. A. Kirsch, L. Cahn, L. C. Ray, and G. H. Urban, "Experiments in Processing Pictorial Information with a Digital Computer," *Proc. EJCC*, pp. 221–229; December, 1957.

[29] R. M. Fano, "Transmission of Information," Mass. Inst. Tech. Press, Cambridge, Mass., 1961. (see pp. 75ff.)

[30] R. Carnap and Y. Bar-Hillel, "An Outline of a Theory of Semantic Information," Research Lab. of Electronics, Mass. Inst. of Tech., Cambridge, Mass., Tech. Rept. No. 247; October 27, 1952.

[31] M. Kochen, "An Experimental Program for the Selection of 'Disjunctive Hypotheses'," *Proc. WJCC*, vol. 19, pp. 571–578; May 1961.

[32] Cherry, C., M. H. Kubba, D. E. Pearson, and M. P. Barton, "An Experimental Study of the Possible Bandwidth Compression of Visual Image Signals," Proc. IRE, vol. 51, pp. 1507–1517; November, 1963.

[33] L. C. Ray and R. A. Kirsch, "Finding Chemical Records by Digital Computers," *Science*, vol. 126, pp. 814–189; October 25, 1957.

[34] P. Ziff, "Semantic Analysis," Cornell University Press, Ithaca, N. Y.; 1960. (See esp. Section 21 and discussion of Ziff's "E**.")

15

Syntax-Directed Interpretation of Classes of Pictures

R. Narasimhan

Tata Institute of Fundamental Research, Bombay, India

A descriptive scheme for classes of pictures based on labeling techniques using parallel processing algorithms was proposed by the author some years ago. Since then much work has been done in applying this to bubble chamber pictures. The parallel processing simulator, originally written for an IBM 7094 system, has now been rewritten for a CDC 3600 system. This paper describes briefly the structure of syntactic descriptive models by considering their specific application to bubble chamber pictures. How the description generated in this phase can be embedded in a larger "conversation" program is explained by means of a certain specific example that has been worked out. A partial generative grammar for "handwritten" English letters is given, as are also a few computer-generated outputs using this grammar and the parallel processing simulator mentioned earlier.

Presented at an ACM Programming Languages and Pragmatics Conference, San Dimas, California, August, 1965.

1. Introduction

Recent active interest in the area of graphic data-based "conversation programs"[1] has pointed up the urgent need for sophisticated picture processing models in a convincing manner. Kirsch [2] has very ably argued that "from the point of view of computer information processing, the important fact about natural language text and pictures is that both have a syntactic structure which is capable of being described to a machine and of being used for purposes of interpreting the information within a data processing system." "The problem of how to describe the syntactic structure of text and pictures and how to use the syntactic description in interpreting the text and pictures" has been tackled in a certain specific way by Kirsch and his coworkers. (For other references, see [9].)

[1] See [9] for a good survey of work accomplished and in progress in this area, as well as in the general field of "English question-answer" programs.

For over three years now the author has been actively engaged in investigating the possibilities of syntax-directed interpretation of classes of pictures.[2] The immediate problem that was tackled was the development of a computer program for the automatic scanning[3] of bubble chamber negatives. One was fortunate, in a certain basic sense, that one's first introduction to picture processing was through bubble chamber pictures and not alphanumeric characters. For it became clear from the very beginning that an appeal to most of the existing pattern recognition models would not only not work, but the models themselves were basically inadequate. These models are based on the categorization of images as belonging to one or another of a finite set of prototypes. Bubble chamber picture scanning defines a context for visual data processing and pattern recognition in which the concepts "prototypes" and "images" become virtually meaningless.

It was clear very soon that what was needed to cope with the problem on hand was a descriptive scheme in terms of which the structural features of individual bubble chamber pictures could be efficiently described and talked about. Pattern recognition is only one aspect of the much more fundamental problem of analysis and description of *classes* of patterns (or equivalently, *classes* of pictures). The aim of any adequate recognition procedure should be not merely to arrive at a "yes," "no," "don't know" decision but to produce a structured description of the input picture. The author has argued elsewhere [3] at some length that no processing model could hope to accomplish this in a satisfactory way unless it has built into it, in some sense, a generative grammar for the class of patterns it is set up to analyze and recognize.

For the bubble chamber scanning program we worked out a processing model, called the syntactic model, and a programming language, called the parallel processing language, in which picture processing algorithms based on the above model could be designed and described [4]. An interpreter for this language was designed for the University of Illinois IBM 7094-1401 system [10], and using this a very wide variety of picture processing algorithms was investigated. A first version of a scanning program, BUBBLE SCAN I, based on this model and using the above programming language was successfully completed [5]. Later, the structure of a "conversation" program, BUBBLE TALK, for use in the context of bubble chamber pictures was worked out in considerable detail [7]. Most of this work, except for two papers, exists as yet only in the form of internal technical reports.

Outlined briefly in Section 2 of this paper are the syntactic model and the processing details, with specific reference to bubble chamber pictures. In Section 3 the environment in which the "conversation" program is intended to function is described and it is indicated how the program is set up to make use of the syntactic details generated by the parallel processor.

The interpreter for the parallel processing language has been rewritten for the CDC 3600 computer system and named COMPAX. In Section 4 a generative grammar for a subset of "handprinted" letters of the English alphabet is described and a few computer-generated specimens using COMPAX and this generative grammar are exhibited.

Appendix I contains a summary of the features incorporated in COMPAX and its basic specifications.

2. Syntactic Model and Labeling Schemata

For the sake of definiteness let us confine ourselves to black-white pictures.[4] A picture is a finite, two-dimensional array of points (say, a square array of size $N \times N$ points), each point having one of two values, viz., black, white. Every such assignment of one of the values, black/white, to each of the N^2 points of the array constitutes a particular picture. We now assume that there is a well-defined process (i.e., a generative mechanism) which generates a class of such pictures.[5] The problem is to formulate descriptive schemata associated with classes of pictures such that, given a picture belonging to a stated class, one can generate a description of that picture. The description, needless to say, must be of a type (i.e., must consist of statements) which would fit into a normal discourse concerning that particular class of pictures.

The syntactic model is a metatheoretic model set up to furnish a uniform framework within which descriptive models for specific classes of pictures could be designed. The statement of the syntactic model amounts to this: given a picture belonging to a well-defined class, the proposal is to generate the types of descriptive statements as indicated earlier on the basis of the assignment of a hierarchic system of labels to the points making up the picture. The labels assigned form a hierarchy[6] in the following sense: the procedure for labeling divides into a

[2] The author began research on picture processing models during a stay in the Digital Computer Laboratory, University of Illinois between 1961 and 1964. Professor B. H. McCormick was the Principal Investigator of the research project (described in the text) with which the author was associated and which was supported in part by the US Atomic Energy Commission. Several graduate and undergraduate student assistants made active contributions to the work on which the main part of this paper is based. Their names appear in the literature at the end of this paper.

[3] "Scanning" in the terminology of the bubble chamber physicists is concerned with the visual inspection of the myriads (literally!) of photographs resulting from an experimental setup in order to separate out those which contain "interesting" particle track configurations and discard the rest. Traditionally this operation has been performed by trained human scanners who are guided in this work by the sketches of the "interesting" configurations, together with appropriate marginal comments, supplied to them by the physicists who set up and perform the experiments.

[4] All our label generation techniques will apply equally well, in fact will apply better, to pictures involving multiple grey scales. For a treatment of classes of pictures of this type, see [6].

[5] The bubble chamber experimental setup is such a process. Some other processes which generate familiar classes of pictures are: people handprinting alphanumeric letters; a setup that generates biological slides (say, of blood smears); and so forth.

[6] Strictly speaking, they form a partial-ordering.

series of well-defined steps or levels. At each level, the labeled outputs from the lower levels serve as inputs to the current level of labeling. What particular labels are assigned at each level would, of course, depend on the class of pictures being, or sought to be described. But, in general, the labels would belong to two broad groups: names of object types (in other words, names of syntactic categories or phrase names), and attribute values of objects (belonging to named object types) occurring in the picture. The set of object types and attributes would form an essential part of the vocabulary of descriptive statements sought to be generated. As such they would carry in themselves, implicitly, a characterization of the class of pictures for the purpose of the discourse.

To illustrate how the proposed scheme would work in an actual application, let us consider the class of bubble chamber pictures and the system of labels as incorporated in BUBBLE SCAN, the version of the scanning program referred to in the introduction.

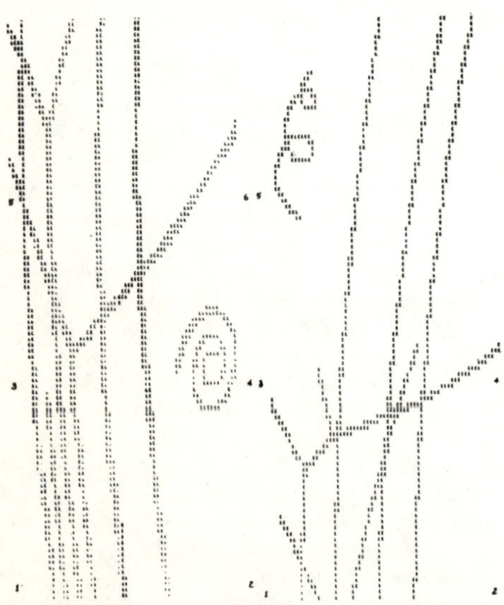

FIG. 1. Parts of two bubble chamber pictures

Figure 1 shows parts of two bubble chamber pictures. Typically, the sort of descriptions the physicist who deals with this class of pictures is interested in is: what kinds of particle tracks are present in the picture? is a given configuration of tracks (i.e., a physical event of interest) present in the picture? etc. He usually describes a picture by making statements of the form: these are beam tracks; here is a spiral; there is a vertex with two prongs; etc. The set of objects and attributes the syntactic model has to cope with is thus determined by the types of descriptive statements, such as those above, which are required to be generated.

In the scanning program a hierarchy of object types are made use of, each with a set of admissible attributes. An *attribute* is a function defined over the object types. A set of admissible attributes must be given whenever a new object type is defined. Given an occurrence of a particular object type in a picture and an admissible attribute for that object type, computing the value of the attribute for that occurrence of the object type consists in evaluating the function which the attribute denotes with that occurrence of the object type as its argument.

The *primitive* object type is the POINT (of the $N \times N$ array). Two permissible attributes are: **grey scale** (black/white, in our case), and **coordinates** (X, Y-coordinates). New object types are defined as compositions of known object types with specific constraints on their attribute values. At the first level, connected sets of (black) points are composed into line elements (referred to as ROAD SEGMENTS) having locally one of four directional orientations. This orientation **label** is thus an attribute of road segments and can assume one of four values: N (north-south), E (east-west), A (right-diagonal), B (left-diagonal).

At the next level, the nodes where the road segments intersect are defined as MULTI (i.e., connected sets of points with multiple labels). Permissible attributes for these are: **direction numbers** (whose values specify the directions along which the road segments leave a node; it is easily verified that there are eight possible values of these); **angle** (whose values specify the angle between the road segments incident on a node); **wall** (whose values specify whether the node lies on a wall of the bubble chamber or not, and if so which wall). TERMINALS are open end points of road segments. The object types MULTI and TERMINAL together constitute the object type BASIC SET. Based upon the associated direction numbers, the object type MULTI is further categorized into BEND, CROSSOVER and VERTEX.

At the next level, a TRACK is defined as a string of road segments with certain constraints on the end conditions and the occurrences of basic sets on it; for instance, a track could have a bend or a crossover occurring inside it but not a terminal or a vertex; the end points of a track must be terminals or vertices; and so on. Two permissible attributes of tracks are **length** and **curvature**. Depending on the values of these attributes and other end conditions, tracks are further categorized into BEAM TRACKS, PRONGS, etc.

Finally, at the highest level, an EVENT of a particular type is defined as a vertex (or a set of vertices) with associated tracks having certain specified attribute values.

Table I lists the object types with their admissible attributes that BUBBLE SCAN is set up to handle. In Table II are given the ranges of the respective attributes. The details of the processing algorithms used in the generation of the hierarchic system of description labels (i.e., names of object types and values of specific admissible attributes) can be found in [1]. Most of these algorithms

TABLE I. Object Types With Attributes and Functions on Attributes Incorporated in Bubble Scan

R \ A	1	2	3	4	5	6	7	8	9	10	11	12	13
1	1	1	1	0	0	0	1	1	1	1	1	0	1
2	1	1	1	0	0	0	1	1	1	1	1	0	1
3	1	1	1	0	0	0	1	1	1	1	1	0	1
4	1	1	1	0	0	1	1	1	1	1	1	1	1
5	1	1	1	0	0	1	1	1	1	1	1	1	1
6	1	1	1	0	0	1	1	1	1	1	1	1	1
7	0	0	0	1	1	0	0	0	0	0	0	0	0

OBJECTS	ATTRIBUTES	FUNCTIONS ON ATTRIBUTES
R=1 Terminal	A=1 Coordinates	A=8 Specified labels
2 Multi	2 Labels	9 Specified direction numbers.
3 Basic Set	3 Direction Numbers	10 Number of labels
4 Bend	4 Length	11 Number of direction numbers.
5 Crossover	5 Curvature	12 Specified Angle.
6 Vertex	6 Angle	13 Specified Walls
7 Track	7 Wall	

TABLE II. Admissible Values of Attributes and Functions on Attributes Included in Table I

NUMBER	NAME	ADMISSIBLE VALUES
1	Coordinates	(X,Y), Window $1 \leqslant X, Y \leqslant 32$, $1 \leqslant \text{Window} \leqslant 10^3$
2	Labels	Any Subset of {A, B, N, E}
3	Direction Numbers	Any Subset of {1, 2, 3, 4, 5, 6, 7, 8}
4	Length	Any positive integer
5	Curvature	Any integer with sign + or −
6	Angle	(a,b) where $a \in \{<, =, >\}$ & $b \in \{45, 90, 135\}$
7	Wall	L, R, T, B ie, Left, Right, Top, Bottom
8	Specified Labels	Any Subset of {A, B, N, E}
9	Specified Direction Numbers	Any Subset of {1, 2, 3, 4, 5, 6, 7, 8}
10	Number of Labels	1, 2, 3, or 4
11	Number of Direction Numbers	1, 2, 3, 4, 5, 6, 7 or 8
12	Specified Angle	(a,b) where $a \in \{<, \leqslant, =, \geqslant, >\}$ & $b \in \{45, 90, 135\}$
13	Specified Wall	(a,b) where $a \in \{L, R, T, B\}$ & $b \in$ {Picture, Window}

are written in the parallel processing language referred to earlier.

3. "Conversation" Environment of BUBBLE TALK

In Section 2 a certain processing model was considered for the identification of the syntactic categories and their attribute values were given a picture belonging to a stated class of pictures. The details of the model were explained in terms of a specific, implemented version intended to deal with the class of bubble chamber pictures. However, the original problem we started out with requires a processing scheme that generates descriptive **statements** concerning the pictures under investigation. In this section, this aspect of the problem is considered. Again, it is done in terms of a program called BUBBLE TALK, that was designed for online conversation in the context of bubble chamber pictures.

Figure 2 shows in schematic the operational environment in which BUBBLE TALK would function. It will be seen that the operator has the facility to communicate with the program both by means of statements typed on a console typewriter and by the use of a light-pen on a CRT display tube. The light-pen is intended not only for pointing to features (objects, etc.) in the display but, ultimately, for inputting information to the program by means of sketches drawn on the display tube together with appropriate marginal comments (either typed in or written on the display screen).

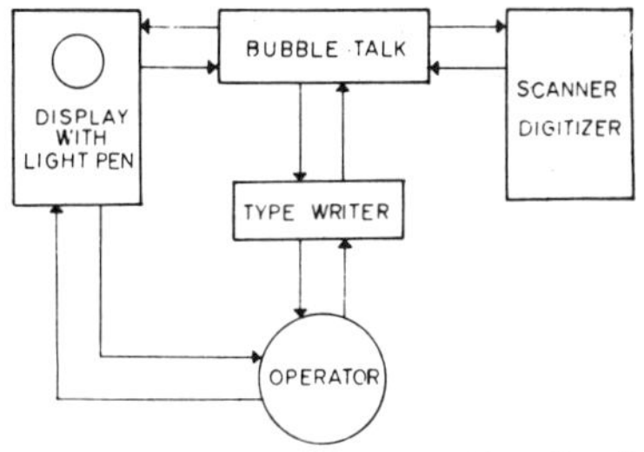

Fig. 2. Operational environment of bubble talk: schematic

Typically, the operator might ask questions pertaining to the existence of certain object types in the input picture (or a specified portion of the picture), or pertaining to an attribute of a named object of a certain type; or he could issue a command to compute the value of a certain attribute of a named object, or to display a specified part of the input picture, or to locate and display a part having certain attributes, or to perform certain library routines on the display, and so on. The ultimate sophistication aimed for is, of course, the ability to conduct the conversation in an extended language in which pictorial sketches are embedded in linguistic statements in an integral manner. Specifically, as it is done with human scanners, the operator should be able to instruct the program to look for the occurrence of an event described by means of a sketch with suitable marginal comments.

Needless to say, BUBBLE TALK is nowhere near the sophistication implied by the above requirement. But it is intended to serve as a framework within which algorithms capable of carrying out the above task can be developed in stages, tested on actual data, modified, refined, edited, and so on.

In its present version, motivated by practical expediency, the linguistic interface has been somewhat artificially simplified. The result has been the reduction of the syntax analysis part to a rather trivial level. However, the significant aspect of a system such as BUBBLE TALK is not either the language interface or the picture interface in isolation, but the way the pragmatics of the coupling between the two interfaces is taken care of. This aspect is considered very briefly as exemplified in BUBBLE TALK.

Conversation in BUBBLE TALK is conducted by means of statements each of which belongs to one of a fixed, finite set of statement types. Although the actual format of a statement varies from type to type, the basic syntax is roughly the same for all types. Each statement consists of a string of phrases: the first phrase is the "command" phrase which identifies the statement type. The phrases that follow are the "argument" phrases. Each statement type is distinguished by the particular phrase types that can occur as arguments and by the order of these phrases as they occur in the statement.

It is to be pointed out that a command could be declarative, indicative, imperative, or question-type. The statement types thus refer to certain computable function schemata whose parameters (i.e., variables, or arguments) are specific phrase types. The phrase types refer to (or, in their turn, are computable functions having as their arguments) the object types, attributes, and attribute values pertaining to the class of pictures under discussion.

Thus a statement, if declarative, makes certain assertions about the underlying labels that are the results of the computations on the input picture. If the statement is a question, then, it defines a certain function on a set of the computed labels (for the input picture). The output of the function as evaluated using the computed labels is the answer. And analogously for the other statement types.

In the current version of the program, the responses again are stereotyped and belong to a fixed, finite set of statement formats. Working out the structure of a program that would synthesize natural language sentences relevant to the pragmatics of a given context is really a problem of fundamental importance and, so far as we know, has not been adequately tackled by anyone.[7]

4. A Generative Grammar for a Subset of English Letters

Kirsch has argued [2] that one of the main problems to be solved before "a satisfactory grammar or syntactic description of an important pictorial source can be written" is a suitable generalization to the two-dimensional case of the notion of juxtaposition, or composition, which in the linear case reduces to concatenation. In this section is outlined one possible solution that is applicable to a wide class of pictures composed of line-like elements. The bubble chamber pictures belong to this category. However, to demonstrate the scope of the processing techniques based on the parallel processing language, a distinctly different class of pictures is considered, viz., "hand-printed" English letters, and a generative grammar for a subset of these letters is exhibited.

Figure 3 shows the terminal vocabulary of the grammar. Their names are referred to here as word-names. The set of rewriting rules is shown in Table 3. The metalinguistic notations should be self-explanatory.

Each element of the vocabulary (word, as well as phrase) has associated with it a distinct set of vertices. This set could be null, of course. Where it is not null, the individual vertices are identified by the ordinals: 1, 2, 3, etc. These are shown for the words in Figure 3.[8] The vertex set forms an integral part of the definition of a phrase or word. The vertices are the points where a word/phrase can be linked to another word/phrase to form a phrase. The vertex set of the resulting phrase is

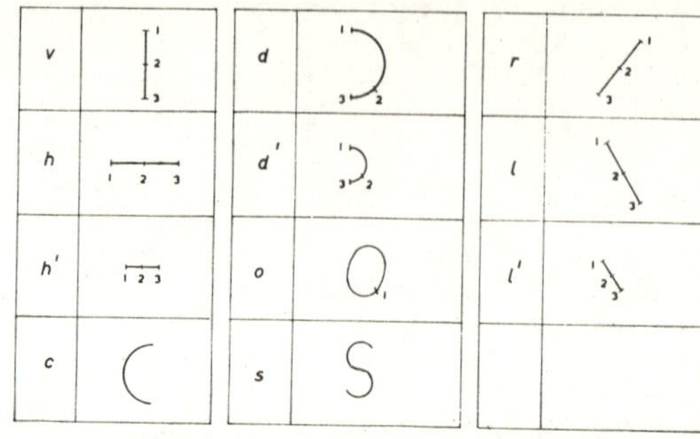

FIG. 3. Terminal vocabulary of a partial grammar for english letters.

TABLE III. LIST OF REWRITING RULES FOR A PARTIAL GRAMMAR FOR ENGLISH LETTERS

```
LETER          →  |A|B|C|D|E|F|H|I|L|N|O|P|Q|R|S|T|V|X|Z|

A              →  INVE·h (11,23;) | INVH·h (11,23;)
INVE(1,2)      →  r·l (11;2;2) | r·v (11;2;2) | v·l (11;2;2)
INVH (1,2)     →  SGMMA·l (31:1:2)
SGMMA(1,2,3)   →  r·h' (11;2,3;3)
B              →  PE·d' (11,23;)
PE(1,2,3)      →  v·d' (11,23;2,3:2) | r·d' (11,23;2,3;2)
C              →  c
D              →  v·d (11,33;) | r·d (11,33;)
E              →  BRKET·h (11;) | BRKET. h' (11;)
BRKET(1)       →  GMMA·h (21;1) | GMMA·h' (21;1)
                  SGMMA·h' (21;1) | ELL·h (11;2)
GMMA(1,2)      →  v·h (11;2,3;)| r·h (11;2,3;)| v·h'(11;2,3;)| r·h'(11;2,3;)
ELL (1,2)      →  v·h (31;1,2;)| r·h (31;1,2;) | v·h'(31;1,2;) | r·h' (31;1,2;)
F              →  GMMA·h (11;) |GMMA·h' (11;) | SGMMA·h'(11;)| AITCH·h(11;)
H              →  AITCH·v (32;) | AITCH·r (32;)
AITCH (1,2,3)  →  v·h (21;1,3;3) | v·h'(21:1,3;3) | r·h (21;1,3;3) | r·h'(21;1,3;3
I              →  TEE·h'(12;) | v | r
TEE (1)        →  v·h (12;3) | v·h' (12;3) | r·h (12;3) | r·h' (12;3)
L              →  ELL
N              →  ENN·v (13;) | ENN·r (13;)
ENN (1)        →  v·l (11;;3) | r·l (11;;3)
O              →  o
P              →  PE
Q              →  o·l' (12;) | o·l' (11;)
R              →  PE·l'(31;) | PE·l'(11;)
S              →  s
T              →  TEE
V              →  l·r (33;) | v·r (33;) | l·v (33;)
X              →  r·l (22;) | v·l (22;) | v.r (22;)
Z              →  SEVEN·h (11;)| SEVEN·h'(11;)
SEVEN (1)      →  h·r (31;;3) | h'·r (31;;3)
```

REVISIONS IN PROOF. Line 10 should read:

E → BRKET·h(11;) | BRKET·h′(11;) | EFF·h(11;) | EFF·h′(11;)

Add the following line to the table:

EFF(1) → GMMA·h(11; 2) | GMMA·h′(11; 2) | SGMMA·h′(11; 2) | AITCH·h(11; 2)

---

[7] It will be evident from the description given above that there are some similarities between BUBBLE TALK and the picture language machine (PLM) developed at the US National Bureau of Standards by R. A. Kirsch and his colleagues [9]. The linguistic interface in PLM is much more sophisticated than is the case in BUBBLE TALK, but the picture interface is much less so. Since PLM restricts itself to a "conversation" consisting of truth functional statements, the responses are a simple "yes" or "no."

given by a subset of the sum of the vertex sets of its component phrases.

The rewriting rules must, then, specify the following information: assuming binary composition without loss of generality, each rule must specify which two phrases are composed; which vertices of the first are linked to which ones of the second; the correspondence between the vertices of the resulting phrase and those of its component phrases.

In the list of rewriting rules given in Table III, the following notational convention has been used. The vertex set of the defined phrase is shown as an ordinal list immediately following the phrase name. On the right-hand side, the phrase (and/or word) names are given as an ordered pair, followed by an ordinal pair sequence and two ordinal sequences. The symbol ";" is used as a sequence delimiter. The ordinal pairs define the vertex linkages of the component phrases. The two ordinal sequences establish the correspondences between the vertex set of the defined phrase and those of the defining phrases.

As an illustration, consider the rewriting rule:

$$\text{SGMMA } (1, 2, 3) \rightarrow r \cdot h' \ (11; 2, 3; 3).$$

This means, the phrase SGMMA is composed of the words r and h' by linking together vertex 1 of each of them. SGMMA has three vertices: the first corresponds to vertex 2 of r, the second to vertex 3 of r, and the third to vertex 3 of h'.

The following diagrams show three possible derivations of the letter E according to the grammar rules of Table III.

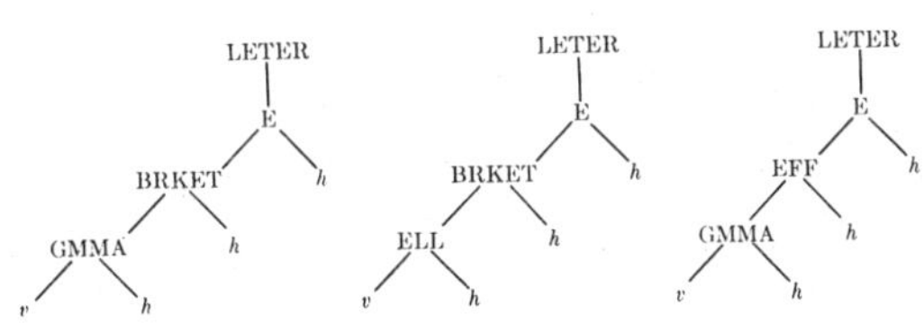

Writing p-name for phrase-name and w-name for word-name, it is readily seen that the grammar given is really a finite state grammar all of whose rules have one or the other of the following two simple forms:

(1) p-name → p-name·w-name
(2) p-name → w-name·w-name

Because of these facts, computer simulation of a letter

FIG. 4. Computer generated letters

generator using the above grammar is a comparatively straightforward programming task. Such a program, making use of COMPAX, has been written for the CDC 3600 system at the Tata Institute of Fundamental Research, Bombay.[9] In Figure 4 is shown a computer-generated letter using the above program.

5. Concluding Remarks

In this paper, a specific metatheoretic model for the analysis and description of classes of pictures has been considered. A particular class of processing procedures, termed parallel processing algorithms, has been referred to, and it has been shown how, in terms of labeling schemata based on these techniques, appropriate descriptive statements concerning specific pictures belonging to a given class can be generated. The power and scope of the model and the parallel processing techniques has been illustrated by considering in some detail two different classes of pictures: bubble chamber pictures, and "hand-printed" letters of the English alphabet.

The unifying factor in all the above has been the view that adequate descriptive schemes that can cope with the analysis of classes of pictures should also prove to be naturally embeddable in larger systems within which conversation, in some version of a natural language, can be conducted about pictures belonging to these classes. Syntax-directed interpretation of pictures meets this adequacy criterion in a satisfactory way, as has been seen in this paper. But, in the author's opinion, the much more fundamental significance of syntax-directed picture processing models lies in the possibility they offer for constructing a theory of a "General Problem Solver" that can deal with linguistic data and pictorial (or visual) data in an integrated and uniform manner. One cannot emphasize

[8] The terminal "vocabulary" actually consists of a set of primitive functions whose names are the word-names. The outputs of these functions are classes of pictures: a typical representative of the class is shown against each word-name. Thus a word-name denotes an equivalence class and the vertex set is a characteristic of the equivalence class.

Strictly speaking, one should associate with these primitive functions input parameters which signify attributes of the generated outputs (e.g., length, curvature, etc.). By this means one could delete from the vocabulary h', l', d', and subsume them in h, l, d, thus rendering the whole grammar much more natural.

[9] The design and the actual coding of the program was done by V. S. N. Reddy.

too strongly that working out an adequate metatheory for "problem solving behavior" is really the basic problem of artificial intelligence, and it still remains very much an open problem.

Acknowledgment. It is a pleasure to acknowledge the assistance of G. N. Phatak for all the typing work, and of V. S. Patil for the figure work and lettering.

APPENDIX I. COMPAX

1. Preliminaries

COMPAX is the name of a parallel processing simulator that has been designed and coded for the CDC 3600 system at the Tata Institute of Fundamental Research, Bombay [8]. In writing COMPAX, full advantage has been taken of the already existing simulator PAX for the IBM 7094 system at the University of Illinois [10]. In this appendix, a brief description of COMPAX and the special features incorporated in it is given.

The pseudo-machine simulated by COMPAX consists of five units:

(1) The *plane memory* is a stack of 51 planes, each plane consisting of a 96 × 96 array. Sometimes this memory is visualised as consisting of 9216 Z-words (or columns) of 51 bits each.

(2) A *conventional memory* used for storing COMPAX code, 3600 code, direction lists, coordinate pairs, and similar information.

(3) *Logical units* capable of performing operations on planes such as shifting, thresholding, various set-theoretic operations, and index arithmetic operations.

(4) A *control unit* which interprets the COMPAX code, as well as the 3600 code and carries out the processing defined by them.

(5) An *I/O device* for transmitting digitized, pictorial information (i.e., planar, array of bits) and an additional output device for transmitting ancillary information.

The 51 planes of the plane-memory are designated by symbolic names $P_0, P_1, \cdots, P_{50}$. Plane names enter as arguments in COMPAX instructions. For mnemonic purposes the programmer can assign and use "arbitrary" identifiers as names of planes.

Although the parallel processing instructions themselves treat an entire plane (96 × 96 array) as a single operand, it is sometimes necessary to refer to and operate on individual points of a specified plane. The points are referred to by their coordinates. The lower left bit has the coordinates (0, 0), and the upper right, (95, 95). A coordinate pair can be stored in a single location of the conventional memory.

There are 8 immediate neighbors to every point in a plane. These are individually identified by 8 direction numbers: $d = 1, 2, \cdots, 8$. The 1-neighbor is the East-neighbor, and the numbering runs counterclockwise. $d = 0$ denotes the point itself (i.e., the self).

A direction list, *DL*, is a list of direction numbers, and specifies a subset of the immediate neighbors. A direction list enters into a COMPAX instruction much as a parameter does in a conventional instruction. A *DL* can be assigned and identified by a symbolic name.

The simulator has 25 built-in registers *IR*1, *IR*2, $\cdots$, *IR*25, for counting and indexing purposes. The first 7 of these can be used for indexing, i.e., the modification of an instruction argument at execution time.

2. Instruction Set

The list given below does not include all the instructions. In particular, the I/O instructions have been omitted. An asterisk (*) on the operand denotes that it can be index modified. (The asterisk is omitted in all explanations for convenience.) For a more formal description of the instructions, one should consult [4].

1. *BOOLOP* (P_1*, P_2*, P_3*, *TYPE*, *BAR*)
   TYPE = *CLEAR*/*EQUAL*/*AND*/*OR*/*EXOR*
   The several outcomes are as follows:
   P_1 = all 0's / all 1's
   $P_1 = P_2 / \bar{P}_2$
   $P_1 = P_2 \wedge P_3 / P_2 \wedge \bar{P}_3$
   $P_1 = P_2 \vee P_3 / P_2 \vee \bar{P}_3$
   $P_1 = P_1 \oplus P_3 / P_2 \oplus \bar{P}_3$
2. *WRITE* (P*, X*, Y*)
   The X,Y-bit of plane P is set to 1.
3. *RENAME* (P*, *NAME*)
   Plane P is assigned the name *NAME*.
4. *LISTXY* (P*, *NAME*, N*)
   Starting from the memory location *NAME*, a list of coordinate pairs of the points in P having the value 1 is stored. N is the maximum length of the list.
5. *READ Z* (*NAME*, X*, Y*, B*, *LIST**, N, *OP*)
   Read Z-word corresponding to the coordinate pair (X, Y). The planes included in the Z-word are specified by *LIST* (≤ 48). The Z-word is stored in location *NAME* starting from its Bth bit (mod 48).
6. *MARK* (*DL**, P_1*, P_2*, P_3*)
   For each point p in P_2 having the value 1, consider p_d, its d-neighbor for some d contained in the direction list *DL*. If P_3 is specified, then the point p_d in P_1 is set to 1 provided p_d is 1 in P_3. If P_3 is not specified, p_d is set to 1 in P_1 unconditionally.
7. *CONNECT* (*DL**, P_1*, P_2*, P_3*)
   A point p in P_1 is set to 1 provided the following holds: there exists a sequence of points $p_0, p_1, \cdots, p_n$, such that p_0 in P_2 has the value 1, $p_n = p$, all the p_i ($1 \leq i \leq n$) in P_3 have the value 1, and for each i ($1 \leq i \leq n$), p_i is a d-neighbor of p_{i-1} for some d included in the direction list *DL*.
   If *DL* contains only one direction number (or a conjugate pair, e.g., 15, 37, etc.), then the p_i form a straight line or a "chain."
8. *TMARK* (*DL**, P_1*, P_2*, P_3*, *REL*, N*)
   A point p in P_1 is set to 1 provided p in P_2 is 1 and the number of d-neighbors specified by *DL* of p in P_3 having the value 1 satisfies the relation *REL* to N.

   $$REL = < \mid \leqslant \mid = \mid \geqslant \mid >$$
   $$N \geq 0 \text{ is an integer}$$
9. *TCHAIN* (*DL**, P_1*, P_2*, P_3*, *REL*, N)
   A point p in P_1 is set 1 provided there is a sequence of points p_i ($0 \leq i \leq m$) such that p_0 in P_2 has the value 1; p_i ($1 \leq i < m$) in P_3 have the value 1; p_m in P_3 has the value 0; each p_i is a *DL*-neighbor of p_{i-1}, and m has the relation *REL* to N, as in (8). *DL* is a direction list consisting of a single d.
10. *BOOFUN* (P_1*, P_2*, P_3*, *FUNCTION*)
    A point p in P_1 is set to 0 if it has the value 0 in P_2. Otherwise, it is set to the value of the Boolean *FUNCTION* at the point p in P_3. *FUNCTION* is specified in the sum of products form, and the variables are the direction numbers: 0, 1, 2, $\cdots$, 8.
11. *INDEX* (*TYPE*, N, K)
    TYPE = *SET*/*DECREM*/*INCR*/*TRANS*
    The several outcomes are as follows:
    Set *IRK* = N
    Decrement *IRK* by N
    Increment *IRK* by N
    Transfer *IRK* to *IRN*
12. *JUMP* (*TYPE*, *NAME*, C, *TEST*)
    TYPE = *UC*/*NULL*/*NONULL*/*ZERO*/*NOZERO*/*LESS*/*EXACT*/*MORE*/*LINK*/*RETURN*
    NAME identifies a COMPAX instruction
    TEST identifies a plane or an index register $C < 2^{15}$

The several outcomes are as follows:

JUMP unconditionally to *NAME*
JUMP to *NAME* if *TEST* contains all 0's
JUMP to *NAME* unless *TEST* contains all 0's
JUMP to *NAME* if $(IRK) = 0/(IRK) \neq 0$ / $(IRK) < C$ / $(IRK) = C/(IRK) > C$
JUMP to *NAME* after planting link in *IRK*
Return *JUMP* to *(IRK)*

COMPASS, the assembly language of the 3600 system, forms a subset of COMPAX, so that a programmer can interleave COMPAX code with COMPASS code.

An experimental CRT display has been connected to the 3600 system for online visual display of a 64 × 64 segment of any plane.

REFERENCES

1. BOND, W. D., RICE, R. K., AND WIEGEL, R. BUBBLE SCAN I, Parts I, II, III, IV. Digital Computer Lab. File Nos. 590, 594, 585, 606; U. of Illinois, Urbana, Ill., 1964.
2. KIRSCH, R. A. Computer interpretation of English text and picture patterns. *Trans. IEEE EC 13* (Aug. 1964), 363–376.
3. NARASIMHAN, R. A linguistic approach to pattern recognition. Digital Computer Lab. Rep. No. 121, U. of Illinois, Urbana, Ill., 1962.
4. ——. Labeling schemata and syntactic descriptions of pictures. *Inf. Contr.* 7 (1964), 151–179.
5. ——. BUBBLE SCAN. Digital Computer Lab. Rep. No. 167, U. of Illinois, 1964.
6. —— AND FORNANGO, J. P. Some further experiments in the parallel processing of pictures. Digital Computer Lab. *Trans. IEEE EC 13* (Dec. 1964).
7. ——, WITSKEN, J. R., AND JOHNSON, H. BUBBLE TALK. Digital Computer Lab. File No. 604, U. of Illinois, 1964.
8. REDDY, V. S. N. COMPAX, users' manual. Computer Group, Tata Inst. of Fundamental Research, Bombay-5, 1965.
9. SIMMONS, R. F. Answering English questions by computer: a survey. *Comm. ACM* 8 (1965), 53–69.
10. STEIN, J. H. Users' manual for PAX. Digital Computer Lab Rep. No. 147, U. of Illinois, 1964.

Reprinted from *IRE Trans. Inform. Theory*, **IT-2,** No. 3, 1956, pp. 61–79

16

THE LOGIC THEORY MACHINE A COMPLEX INFORMATION PROCESSING SYSTEM

Allen Newell and Herbert A. Simon[1]
The RAND Corporation, Santa Monica, Calif.
and the Carnegie Institute of Technology,
Pittsburgh, Pa.

Abstract

In this paper we describe a complex information processing system, which we call the logic theory machine, that is capable of discovering proofs for theorems in symbolic logic. This system, in contrast to the systematic algorithms that are ordinarily employed in computation, relies heavily on heuristic methods similar to those that have been observed in human problem solving activity. The specification is written in a formal language, of the nature of a pseudo-code, that is suitable for coding for digital computers. However, the present paper is concerned exclusively with specification of the system, and not with its realization in a computer.

The logic theory machine is part of a program of research to understand complex information processing systems by specifying and synthesizing a substantial variety of such systems for empirical study.

Introduction

In this paper we shall report some results of a research program directed toward the analysis and understanding of complex information processing systems. The concept of an information processing system is already fairly clear and will be made precise in Section I, below. The term 'complex' is not so easily disposed of; but it is the crucial distinguishing characteristic of the class of systems with which we are concerned.

We may identify certain characteristics of a system that make it complex:

1. There is a large number of different kinds of processes, all of which are important, although not necessarily essential, to the performance of the total system;

2. The uses of the processes are not fixed and invariable, but are highly contingent upon the outcomes of previous processes and on information received from the environment;

3. The same processes are used in many different contexts to accomplish similar functions towards different ends, and this often results in organizations of processes that are hierarchical, iterative, and recursive in nature.

Complexity is to be distinguished sharply from amount of processing. Most current computing programs for high speed digital computers would not be classified as complex according to the above criteria, even though they may involve a vast amount of processing. In general they call for the systematic use of a small number of relatively simple subroutines that are only slightly dependent on conditions. In order to distinguish such systematic computational processes from the processes we regard as complex, we shall call the former <u>algorithms</u>, the latter <u>heuristic methods</u>. The appropriateness of these terms will become clearer as we proceed.

One tactic for exploring the domain of complex systems is to synthesize some and study their structure and behavior empirically. This paper provides an explicit specification for a particular complex information processing system --a system that is capable of discovering proofs for theorems in elementary symbolic logic. We will call the system the <u>logic theorist</u> (LT), and the language in which it is specified the <u>logic language</u> (LL). This system is of interest for a number of reasons. First, it satisfies the criteria of complexity we have listed above. Second, it is not so large but that it can be hand simulated (barely). Third, the tasks it can perform are well-known human problem solving tasks--it is a genuine problem solving system. Fourth, there are available algorithms, and a realization of at least one of these algorithms (the Kalin-Burkhart machine),[2] that can perform these same tasks; hence, the logic theorist provides a contrast between algorithmic and heuristic approaches in performing the same problem solving tasks.

The task of this paper, then, is to specify LT with sufficient rigor to establish precisely the complete set of processes involved and exactly how they interact. This is a lengthy and somewhat arduous undertaking but one that the authors feel is required in the present state of knowledge. As a result, the paper largely abstains both from comment on the more general significance of the ideas and techniques introduced, and from relating these to contemporary work.[3]

The plan of the paper is to give, in Section I, a description of the language, LL, in which LT

[1] The authors are indebted to Mr. J.C.Shaw of the RAND Corporation, who has been their partner in many aspects of this enterprise and particularly in undertaking to realize the logic theorist in a computer—work that will be reported in subsequent papers.

[2] See B. V. Bowden[1]

[3] We should like to make general acknowledgment of our indebtedness for many of the ideas incorporated in LL and LT to two areas of vigorous contemporary research activity: (1) to research on automatic programming of digital computers, for the approach to the construction of LL; and (2) to research on human problem solving, for the basic structure of the program of LT. In addition we should like to record a specific indebtedness to the work of O.G.Selfridge and G.P.Dinneen on pattern recognition, which clarified many basic conceptual issues in the specification and realization of complex information processes.

will be specified. In Section II there is given a verbal description of LT, which is closely enough tied in to the formal program to motivate most of the latter. Finally, in Section III, the program is given in full detail.

I

Language for Information Processing Systems

The two major technical problems that have to be solved in studying information processing systems by means of synthesis may be called the specification problem and the realization problem. To study all but the simplest of such systems, it is necessary to make a complete and precise statement of their characteristics. This statement, or specification, must be sufficiently complete to determine the behavior of the system once the initial and boundary conditions are given. An example, familiar to mathematicians, is a system specified by n first order differential equations in n variables.

Once the specification has been given, a second problem is to find or construct a physical system that will behave in the manner specified. This can be a trivial or an insurmountable task. For example, it is relatively easy to find electrical circuitry that will behave like a system of linear differential equations; it is rather difficult to represent by circuitry most kinds of nonlinear systems. We will call the problem of finding or constructing the physical system the realization problem, and the particular physical system that is used the realization.[4]

Although this paper is concerned exclusively with the specification problem, the form of language chosen is dictated also by the requirements of realization. Since an important technique for studying the behavior of complex systems is to realize them and to study their time paths empirically under a range of initial and boundary conditions, they must be specified in terms that make this realization relatively easy.

The high speed digital computer is a physical system that can realize almost any information processing system and our research is oriented toward using it. Its limitations are in overall speed and memory, rather than in the complexity of the processes it can realize. The machine code of the computer is the language in which a system must ultimately be specified if it is to be realized by a computer. Conversely, however, once the system is correctly specified in machine code, the realization problem is essentially solved; for the computer can accept these specifications, and will behave like the system specified.

The machine code, although suitable for communicating with the computer, is not at all suitable for human thinking or communication about complex systems. For these purposes, we need a language that is more comprehensible (to humans), but one that can still be interpreted by the computer by means of a suitable program. Technically, such a language is known as a pseudo-code or interpretive language. Hence the two problems of specification and realization of an information processing system are subsumed under the single task of describing the system in an appropriate pseudo-code.

This paper is concerned solely with specifying the system of LT. The particular language, LL exhibited here has not been coded for a computer. However, one very similar to it, which is less convenient for exposition, is in the process of being coded and will be the subject of later papers. Here, no further mention will be made of the relation of the logic language to computers.

The terms of the language that are undefined--its primitives--determine implicitly a set of information processes that are to be regarded as elementary and not reducible, within the language, to simpler processes. The more complex processes are to be specified by suitable combinations of these elementary processes. Generally speaking, the elementary processes in LL are of the nature of information processes: that is, their inputs and outputs are comprised of symbolized information.

Information Processing Systems: Basic Terms

An information processing system, IPS, consists of a set of memories and a set of information processes, IP's. The memories form the inputs and outputs for the information processes. A memory is a place that holds information over time in the form of symbols. The symbols function as information entirely by virtue of their capacity for making the IP's act differentially. The IP's are, mathematically speaking, functions from the input memories and their contents to the symbols in the output memories. The set of elementary IP's is defined explicitly, and through these definitions all relevant characteristics of symbols and memories are specified.

Particular systems can be constructed from the memories and processes of an IPS that behave in a determinate way once the initial information in the memories is given (initial conditions), along with whatever external information is stored in the memories during the course of the system's operation (boundary conditions). Each such particular system we call a program, IPP. Thus an IPS defines a whole class of particular IPP's, and conversely, an IPP consists of an IPS together with a set of rules that determines when the several information processes will occur. The logic language is an IPS; the logic theorist is an IPP. Many variations of LT could be constructed with the same IPS.

Symbolic Logic

The logic language handles information referring to expressions in the sentential calculus and their properties. This paper assumes some

---

[4] We prefer "realization" to "simulation," for the latter implies that what is being imitated is another physical system. Since the specification is an abstract set of characteristics, not a physical system, it is not correct to speak of "simulating" the specification.

familiarity with elementary symbolic logic,[5] and only a resume of the notation will be given.

The sentential calculus deals with variables, p, q, ..., A, B, ..., a, b, ..., which are usually interpreted to mean sentences. These variables are combined into expressions by means of connectives. The primitive connectives of Whitehead and Russell (and ours) are "not" (-) and "or" (v). In this paper we shall have occasion to use only one other connective: "implies" (→), which is defined by:[6]

1.01 p → q =def -p v q (Read: (p implies q) is equivalent by definition to (not-p or q).)

Coding

A logic expression, X, is represented in the IPS by a set of elements, E, one corresponding to each variable and to each connective (excluding the punctuation dots and negation symbols) in the logic expression. Each element holds a number of symbols that refer to the various properties of the element. (Note that the term "element" and not the term "symbol" is used in this paper to refer to the variables and connectives in logic expressions. Symbols denote properties of elements, and to each element there correspond a number of symbols.) An example will show what is meant by these terms.[7] Consider the expression 1.7:

1.7 -p .→. q v -p ((not-p) implies (q or not-p))

The entire sequence is the expression, X(1.7). It consists of the elements -p, →, q, v, -p. The expression may be written in "tree" form, as follows, where the rectangles indicate the elements:

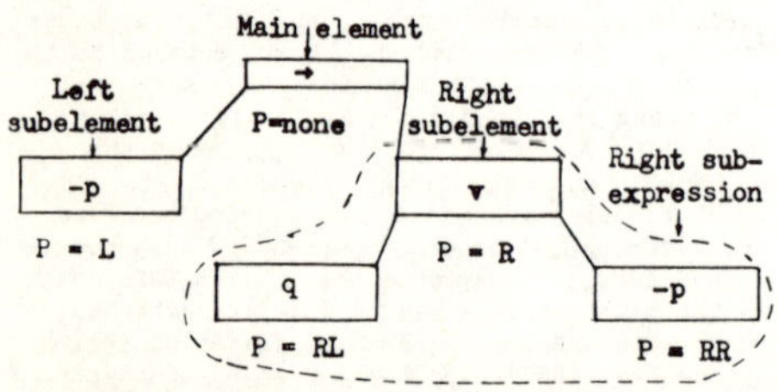

The main connective at the top is called the main element, EM (1.7). The other elements are reached through a series of Left and Right branches from the main element. With each element there is associated a subexpression, namely, the subtree of which that element is the top element.

The symbols in each element provide the following information, which will be explained more fully as we proceed.

Symbol

- G The number of negation signs (-) before the expression. In the figure above, two elements--those containing the variable p--have G = 1; all the rest have G = 0. If a negation applies to a whole expression it appears in the element associated with that expression.
- V Whether the element is a variable or not.
- F Whether the element is free, i.e., available for substitution. This is relevant only if E is a variable.
- C The connective (v or →). This is relevant only if E is not a variable.
- N The name of the variable or expression. In X(1.7), there are variables named "p" and "q".
- P The position of the element in the tree. This is represented by a sequence of L's and R's, counting branches from the main element. In the figure, the P for each element is shown beneath the element.
- A The location of the whole expression (not the element) in storage memory.
- U Whether the element is to be viewed as a unit or not. The term "unit" will be explained later.

The eight symbols defined above characterize completely each element and the expression in which it occurs. For many purposes, however, it is convenient to define additional symbols ("descriptive symbols") that correspond to interesting or important properties of expressions. In LL, three such descriptive symbols, represented as small positive integers, are defined. These are:

- H The number of variable places in an expression. Thus X(1.7) has three variable places: P = L, RL, and RR; hence, H(1.7) = 3.
- J The number of distinct variables (i.e., distinct names) in the expression, ignoring negation signs. Since X(1.7) contains the names "p" and "q", J(1.7) = 2.
- K The number of levels in the expression. The number of levels corresponds to one plus the maximum number of letters in P for any element in the expression. Hence, K(1.7) = 3.

Memory Structure

There are two kinds of memories, working memories and storage memories. The major distinction —that all information to be processed must be

---

[5] For definiteness, we have used the system of A.N. Whitehead and Bertrand Russell.[3] An introduction sufficient for our purposes will be found in D. Hilbert and W. Ackermann.[2]

[6] For ease of reference, we shall use the numbers employed by Whitehead and Russell to identify particular propositions and definitions, only omitting the asterisk (*) that they insert in front of the number.

[7] We follow Whitehead and Russell in using dots in place of parentheses as punctuation. It is unnecessary here to give exact rules for numbers of punctuation dots.

brought in from the storage memories to the working memories and then returned—will be brought out clearly when we define the elementary IP's. Structurally, the working memories hold single elements, E, with additional spaces for the symbols H, J, and K. Hence, we can picture a working memory unit as:

W: [E] — [H] -- [J] — [K]

The storage memories consist of lists. A list holds either a whole logic expression or some set of elements generated during a process, such as a set of elements having certain properties. Each list of logic expressions has a location, symbolized by A. The elements are placed in the list in arbitrary order, since the information in each element is sufficient to locate it unequivocally in the tree of the logic expression. (The ordering of the list is used only to carry out searches.) For example, X(1.7) might be listed in the storage memory thus:

A (1.7): [q,RL] → [-p,L] → [v,R] → [→,none] → [-p,RR]

No limitations are imposed here on number of memories, either working or storage. In actual fact, the number used is not large.

Three particular lists have special locations in storage memory that can be referred to directly in IP's: (1) the theorem list, T, of all axioms and theorems that have previously been proved; (2) the active problem list, P; and (3) the inactive problem list, Q. Each list consists of the main elements of the appropriate expressions (theorems or problems, respectively) in arbitrary order. For the rest, the storage memory is entirely unspecialized.

Information Processes

A term that specifies an IP is called an instruction, by analogy with computer terminology. As Figure 1 shows, an instruction consists

OPERATION	REFERENCE PLACES LEFT CENTER RIGHT	BRANCH LOCATION

Fig. 1

of an operation part, three reference places (left, L, center, C, and right, R), and a branch location, B. The kinds of operations that can be performed by an IPS will depend, first, on what elementary IP's are postulated, and second, on what restrictions are placed on how they can be combined. For the moment, the exact nature of the elementary processes is unimportant; for concreteness, the reader may think of the following as typical: transferring information from memory x to memory y, or adding the number in memory x to the number in memory y.

The reference places refer to the working memories, so that the same operation may operate on different memories at different times and under different circumstances. The working memories will be designated by small integers, 1, 2, ..., and by the letters x, y, z.

No direct reference is made in an instruction to any storage memory, except T, P, and Q. Lists are located by the A stored within elements belonging to the lists; and elements within a list are located by their relation to known elements. An example will make this clear. A typical operation involving the storage memory is:

OPER	L	C	R	B
FR	x	y		

which reads: Find the element that is the right subelement of E(x)—i.e., of the element in working memory x—and put it in working memory y. The operation is executed thus: Working memory x contains the A(x) that is the location of the expression in which E(x) occurs. Memory x also contains the symbol P(x). Since we wish to put in y the right subelement of E(x), P(y) is by definition obtained by appending an R to P(x). Hence, we can determine P(y), and locate E(y) by going to storage memory A(x) and searching the list of its elements in order until we find the element with the correct P. We then transfer this element, which is the one we want, to working memory y.

Programs and Routines

The rule of combination of IP's is simple: any one IP may follow another. We shall consider time to be discrete, using it essentially as an index, and shall assume that only one process occurs at a time. We say that a particular IP has control when it is occurring. Thus, when a sequence of IP's occurs one after the other in consecutive time intervals, there occurs a series of transfers of control from each IP to the next in the sequence.

The operation of any IP includes a processing component and a control component. The processing component changes the memory content of the IPS; the control component transfers control to another IP. In some IP's, processing is the significant component. In these the transfer of control is independent of the memory contents at the time the IP occurs. In certain other IP's, control is the significant component. These do not alter memory contents, but transfer control to various IP's depending on the memory contents when they occur. In other IP's both processing and control components are significant.

Control. We allow only a binary branch in control at any one instruction. Normally, control passes in a linear sequence through a set of IP's. We write this sequence vertically. Each instruction is considered to have a location in the sequence. For branch instructions (those in which the control component transfers control to one of two IP's depending on memory content), control transfers either (1) to the next instruction in the sequence or (2) to the instruction named in the branch location, B. These locations are designated by letters A, B, C, ... In

Figure 2, Instruction #1 transfers controls to #2; #2 transfers control to #3 or branches to A (which is #4) depending on memory content; #3 transfers control to #4; #4 transfers control to #5 or branches back to B, which is #1.

Each control operation can be reversed in sense by putting a minus sign in front of the operation name. The effect of the minus sign is simply to reverse the condition of transfer. That is, if CC-A transfers to A when two specified numbers are equal, then -CC-A transfers to A when these numbers are unequal.

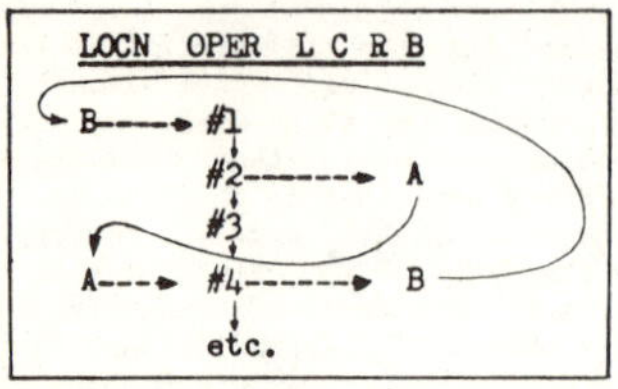

Fig. 2

Routines. We will call such a list of instructions with a control network a routine, again, in direct analogy to computer terminology. Notice that a routine satisfies our definition of a program (IPP): if all the memories referred to have specified initial contents, the routine determines their contents at all later times covered by its duration.

If we postulate a set of elementary information processes, each specified by an instruction, it might be supposed that each routine would define a new (non-elementary) information process. This is not the case, for in LL the format of an instruction (Figure 1) allows reference to not more than three working memories and to not more than one branch. Hence, only those routines may be regarded as definitions of IP's which satisfy the following conditions:

1. The routine contains branches to not more than two instructions outside the routine;

2. Not more than three working memories that are to be referred to subsequently are changed by the routine. This means that even though other working memories are changed, there is no way to refer to these memories in subsequent routines.

Within these restrictions we can define a set of new IP's in terms of the elementary IP's, then another set of IP's in terms of both the elementary and defined IP's, and so on; thus creating a whole hierarchy of IP's and their corresponding routines. The elementary IP's and the hierarchy of defined IP's for LT are given in Section III, and its structure as explained in some detail in Section II.

The restrictions imposed above on numbers of branches and working memories in IP's have the following two consequences for the structure of the routines that are used to define IP's:

1. A working memory can be used only within the routine in which it is introduced. That is, working memories introduced in a particular routine cannot be referred to when control is in any other routine, except as noted in rule 2. For this reason, no ambiguity arises from using the same names, 1, 2, . . ., for different memories in distinct routines.

2. Within the routine that defines a particular IP, reference may be made to the working memories that are designated in the reference places of that IP. Let I_1 be an instruction that appears in the routine defining I_2. The symbols L, C, R in I_1 refer, respectively, to the working memories in the left, center, and right reference places of instruction I_2, in whose definition I_1 occurs. (See, for example, the first instruction, FEF, in the routine given in full at the end of the section.) Some such arrangement is obviously required if the defining routine is to have any connection with the instruction it defines.

Elementary Processes

In LT there are forty four different elementary processes. These represent variations on eight types of operations. The remainder of this section will be devoted to a description of these types, and an enumeration of the elementary processes that belong to each type. Separate, explicit definitions for each elementary IP are given in Section III. The first letter in the name of an operation designates the type to which it belongs: A for assign, B for branch, C for compare, F for find, N for numerical, P for put, S for store, and T for test.

Find instructions obtain information from storage memory on the basis of stated relationships, and put it in specified working memories. An example, FR-x-y (Find the right subelement of E(x) and put it in y), has already been described. Two other Find instructions are very similar: FL (Find the left subelement) and FM (Find the main element).

Other Find instructions involve the ordering relation on the lists. An example is:

OPER	L	C	R	B
FEF	x	y		A

This reads: Find the first element in X(x)—the expression associated with E(x)--in the list A(x), and put this element in y. Then go to next instruction, but if no element is found, branch to instruction A. Here the order of elements is essential since there may be many elements in X(x). This kind of operation is used to start a search, and it is always combined with an instruction, FEN, for continuing and terminating the search:

OPER	L	C	R	B
FEN	x	y		A

This reads: Find the element in X(x) that is next in order after E(y) and put it in y. When such an element is found, branch to A; if none is found, transfer control to the next instruction in sequence. FEF and FEN together allow the familiar cycling or iteration that is a common feature of computing routines:

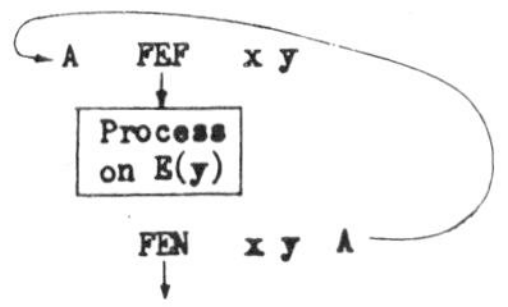

(after all elements of X(x) have been processed)

The complete list of elementary Find instructions is:

FEF FL FM
FEN FR

Store instructions transfer information from working memory back to storage memory. An example is:

OPER	L C R B
S	x

This simply reads: Store E(x) in the storage memory. If the element in x is one that was previously withdrawn from storage, it will be replaced in its original location within A(x); if it is a new element in List A, it will be placed at the end of the list.

Another elementary Store instruction is SEN, which puts E(x) into storage memory at the end of the list A(y). A third is *SX, which simply stores a copy of X(x) in memory location A(y).[8]

The complete list of elementary store instructions is:

S *SX *SXL *SXM
SEN *SXE *SXR

Instructions belonging to the remaining six types are concerned only with working memory (See Figure 3). No complex processing may take place in storage memory, and conversely, as we have seen, no information may be stored in working memory except on a temporary basis.

Put instructions transfer information and symbols around the working memory. A typical Put instruction is:

OPER	L C R B
PE	x y

This reads: Put E(x) in E(y). The operation leaves E(x) unchanged and duplicates it in E(y). The variations on this instruction correspond to the different symbols in an element that may need to be transferred. The list of Put instructions is:

PE PCv PU
PK PC→ PUB

[8]Certain of the Store instructions are marked with an asterisk. These are treated as elementary operations in the present section and in Part I of Section III, but in Part II of Section III they are defined in terms of simpler operations.

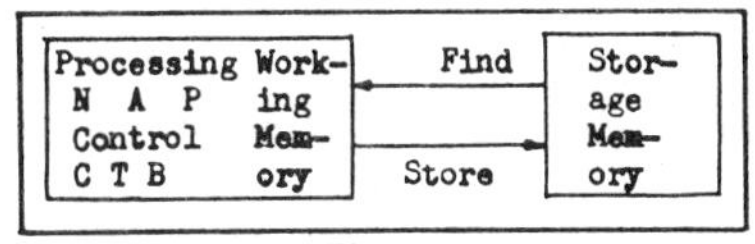

Fig. 3

Numerical instructions carry out the arithmetic operations. An example is:

OPER	L C R B
NAG	x

This reads: Add 1 to G(x). Operations are required to permit addition and subtraction for symbols G, H, J, K, and W. The list of Numerical instructions is:

NAG NAH NAJ NSG
NAGG NAK NAW NSGG

Assign instructions write in new names and locations in elements that are in working memory. One Assign instruction is:

OPER	L C R B
AN	x

This reads: Assign an unused name to E(x). The other Assign instruction, AA, assigns new list locations. There are, then only two Assign instructions:

AA AN

Compare instructions belong to a class of pure control instructions. They compare two symbols for equality (or, if appropriate, for the relation "greater"); then transfer to the branch location if the condition is satisfied or to the next instruction in sequence if the condition is not satisfied. The sense of the branch on these and all other branch instructions can be reversed by a minus sign preceding the operation. A typical example is:

OPER	L C R B
CC	x y A

This reads: If C(x) = C(y), branch control to location A; if not, go to the next instruction in sequence. That is, if the connective in x is identical with the connective of y, we branch to A. Notice that there is no change in memory content; only a transfer of control has occurred. The compare instructions are:

CC CGG CWG
CN CKG CPS

Test instructions are also control instructions. They test the properties of a single element, and transfer control accordingly. The variations of the type deal with different properties. An example is:

OPER	L C R B
TU	x A

66

This reads: If E(x) is a unit, transfer control to A; if not, go to the next instruction in sequence. TC→ transfers control if C(x) is "implies"; goes to the next instruction if C(x) is "or". The Test instructions are:

TV TB TU TF
TC→ TN TGG

<u>Branch</u> instructions are unconditional control instructions that cause the program to branch to the indicated address instead of going to the next instruction in sequence. The simplest example is:

OPER	L	C	R	P
B				b

When this instruction is reached, the program simply branches to instruction b in the same routine.

When the instructions BHB or BHN occur in a routine, they cause the program to branch to an address determined by the higher-level instruction that the routine defines. For example, suppose BHB appears as one of the defining instructions within the routine:

OPER	L	C	R	B
MSb	x			b

Then, the occurrence of BHB will cause control to branch to the address b of MSb.

Suppose, further, that MSb appears as one of the instructions in the routine Ex, and that the instruction MDt appears immediately after MSb in Ex. Then, if BHN is one of the instructions in the routine MSb, its occurrence will cause control to branch to the <u>next</u> instruction after MSb in the higher routine, Ex, i.e., to MDt. Thus BHB and BHN are the instructions that terminate control by a particular routine, and cause control to transfer, respectively, to the branch designated in the higher-level instruction defined by the routine, or to the higher-level instruction that follows the routine. Instruction BHB produces the former transfer, BHN, the latter. The three Branch operations are:

B BHB BHN

<u>Example</u>. It will clarify matters and provide some introduction to the complete program given in Section III if we set forth in detail one of the simpler defined routines, the routine NH. This routine consists of six instructions, all of them primitives included in the list we have already given:

A	OPER	L	C	R	B	
	NH	x				Count the number of variable places in X(x), and <u>record the result in H (x).</u>
	FEF	L	1		C	
A	-CPS	1	L		B	
	-TU	1			B	
	NAH	L				
B	FEN	L	1		A	
C	BHN					

(1) FEF finds the first element in X(x) and puts it in working memory 1. If there is no element, it branches to C. (2) -CPS (note the negative sense) determines whether E(1) is a subelement of E(x). If it is <u>not</u>, control transfers to B; if it is, control transfers to the next instruction in sequence. (Henceforth we will abbreviate these transfers as →B and →next, respectively.) (3) -TU determines whether E(1) is a unit (i.e., is to be viewed as a variable). If it is <u>not</u> (negative sense), →B, if it is, →next. (4) NAH increases by 1 the number H(x). (Because of the previous branches, NAH will occur only if the element in 1 is viewed as a variable and is a subelement of the element in x.) (5) FEN finds the next element in X(x), puts it in working memory 1, and returns control to instruction A, whereupon the cycle is repeated from step (2). If there are no more elements, →next. (6) BHN terminates the routine after all elements in X(x) have been examined, and transfers control to the instruction that follows NH at the next higher level of the hierarchy of routines.

<u>Conclusion</u>

We have now completed our description of the language LL. We have outlined the coding system, the memory structure, the structure of the information processes, the routines, and the types of elementary processes. Further detail can be found by consulting Section III. In Section II we shall construct in this language a program, LT, that will permit the information processing system to solve problems in symbolic logic.

II

The Logic Theory Machine

In the language we have constructed, we have <u>variables</u> (atomic sentences): p, q, r, A, B, C, ... and <u>connectives</u>: - (not), v (or), → (implies). The connectives are used to combine the variables into <u>expressions</u> (molecular sentences). We have already considered one example of an expression:

1.7 $-p \;.\!\rightarrow\!.\; q \vee -p$

The task set for LT will be to prove that certain expressions are <u>theorems</u>--that is, that they can be derived by application of specified rules of inference from a set of primitive sentences or <u>axioms</u>.

The two connectives, - and v, are taken as primitives. The third connective, →, is defined in terms of the other two, thus:

1.01 $p \rightarrow q =_{def} -p \vee q$

The five axioms that are postulated to be true are:

1.2 $p \vee p \;.\!\rightarrow\!.\; p$
1.3 $p \;.\!\rightarrow\!.\; q \vee p$
1.4 $p \vee q \;.\!\rightarrow\!.\; q \vee p$
1.5 $p \;.\!\vee\!.\; q \vee r \;:\!\rightarrow\!:\; q \;.\!\vee\!.\; p \vee r$
1.6 $p \rightarrow q \;.\!\rightarrow\!:\; r \vee p \;.\!\rightarrow\!.\; r \vee q$

Each of these axioms is stored as a list in the theorem memory, T, with all its variables marked free, F, in their respective elements.

From the axioms other true expressions can be derived as theorems. In the system of Principia Mathematica, there are two rules of inference by means of which new theorems can be derived from true expressions (theorems and axioms). These are:

Rule of Substitution: If A(p) is any true expression containing the variable p, and B any expression, then A(B) is also a true expression.

Rule of Detachment: If A is any true expression, and the expression A → B is also true, then B is a true expression.

To these two rules of inference is added the rule of replacement, which states that an expression may be replaced by its definition. In the present context, the only definition is 1.01, hence the rule of replacement permits any occurrence of (-pvq) in an expression to be replaced with (p→q), and any occurrence of (p→q) to be replaced with (-pvq).[9]

In this system, then, a proof is a sequence of expressions, the first of which are accepted as axioms or as theorems, and each of the remainder of which is obtained from one or two of the preceding by the operations of substitution, detachment, or replacement.

Example: prove 2.01, p → -p .→. -p:

(1) ! p v p .→. p (axiom 1.2)[10]
(2) ! -p v -p .→. -p (by subst. of -p for p)
(3) ! p → -p .→. -p (by replacement on left)

The problem now is to specify a program for LT such that, when a problem is proposed in the form of a theorem to be proved (like 2.01 above), a proof will be discovered and constructed. First, it should be observed that there is a systematic algorithm for constructing such a proof should one exist. Starting with the five axioms, we construct all the theorems that can be obtained from them by a single application of the rules of substitution, detachment, or replacement.[11] We thus obtain the set of all theorems that can be obtained from the axioms by proofs not more than one step in length. Repeating this process with the enlarged set of theorems, we obtain the set of all theorems that can be derived from the axioms by proofs not more than two steps in length. Continuing, we finally obtain the set of theorems that can be derived by proofs not more than n steps in length.

Now, if the theorem in which we are interested possesses a proof k steps in length, we can, in principle, discover it by constructing all valid proof chains of length not more than k, and selecting any one of these that terminates in the theorem in question. This "in principle" possibility is in fact computationally infeasible because of the very large number of valid chains of length k that can be constructed, even when k is a number of moderate size. Under these circumstances, the rules of inference do not give us sufficient guidance to permit us to construct the proof we are seeking; and we need additional help from some system of heuristic.

The problem will be solved if we can devise a program for constructing chains of theorems, not at random, but in response to cues that make discovery of a proof probable within a reasonable computing time. For example, suppose the rules of inference were such as to permit any given proof chain to be continued, on the average, in ten different ways. Then there would be ten thousand proofs chains four steps in length (10^4). The expected number of proof chains that would have to be examined to find any particular proof by random search is five thousand. Suppose, however, that LT responded to cues that permitted eight of the ten continuations at each step to be eliminated from consideration. Then the number of proof chains four steps in length that would have to be examined in full would be only sixteen (2^4), and the expected number would be only eight.

The Program of LT

We wish now to describe the program of LT, which is given in full in Section III; hence, in the text we shall refer frequently to Section III for detail. We shall refer to each routine by its name (e.g., LMc for the matching routing), but we shall need some additional notation to refer to the main segments of routines that do not themselves have names. The names of these segments are given in Section III in the column marked "Seg." In each segment there is generally one main operation to be performed; and this main operation, or sub-routine, is usually surrounded by a number of procedural and control operations that fit into the larger routine. In ordinary language, we would say that the "function" of the segment is to perform the main operation that is contained in it. For example, the main operation in the third segment of LMc is LSby, a substitution. The function of this segment in the matching program is to substitute one sub-expression for another in one of the expressions being matched. Hence, we will name the segment after the main operation: LMc(Sby). Similar designations will be used for the other segments of routines. This notation emphasizes the fact that each routine consists in a sequence (or branching tree) of main operations that are connected by procedural and test operations. Thus, an abbreviated description of the matching routine might be given as:

---

[9] As we shall see, 1.01 is not held in storage memory, but is represented, instead, by two routines for actually performing the replacements.

[10] The exclamation point in front of an expression indicates that the expression in question is asserted to be true. To designate an expression whose truth has not been demonstrated, we will use a question mark preceding the expression.

[11] A technical difficulty arises from the fact that there is an infinite number of valid substitutions. This difficulty can be removed rather easily, but the question is irrelevant for the purposes of this paper.

LMc
T Perform diagnostic tests
LMc Recursion of matching with next elements in logic expression
Sby Substitute the element y for the element x
Sbx Substitute the element x for the element y
CN Compare variables in x and y
Rp Replace connectives, if required and possible

The Substitution Method

Let us take as our first example the very simple expression, 2.01, for which we have already given a proof. We suppose that, when the problem is proposed, LT has in its theorem memory only the axioms, 1.2 to 1.6. We wish to construct a proof (the one given above, or any other valid proof) for 2.01.

As the simplest possibility, let us consider proofs that involve only the rules of substitution and replacement. We are now able to state the problem thus: how can we search for a proof of the expression by substitution without considering all the valid substitutions in the five axioms? We use two devices to focus the search. Both of these involve "working backward" from the expression we wish to prove--for by taking account of the characteristics of that expression, we can obtain cues as to the most promising lines to follow:

1. In attempting substitutions, we will limit ourselves to axioms (or other true theorems, if any have already been proved) that are in some sense "similar" in structure to the theorem to be proved. The routine that accomplishes this will be called the test similarity routine, CSm.

2. In selecting the particular substitutions to be made in a theorem that has been chosen for trial, we will attempt to match the variables in that theorem to the variables in the expression to be proved. Similarly, we will try to use the rule of replacement to match connectives. The routine in which these various operations occur is called the matching routine, LMc.

Using these devices, the proposed routine for proving theorems—the method of substitution, MSb—works as follows. MSb(Sm): search for an axiom or theorem that is similar to the expression to be proved. MSb(Mc): when one is found, try to match it with the expression to be proved; if a match is successful, the expression is proved; if the list of axioms and theorems is exhausted without producing a match, the method has failed. (Reference to Section III will show that there is another segment, MSb(NAW), that we have not mentioned. The function of this segment will be discussed later in connection with the executive routine.)

To see in detail how the method operates, we next examine the main operations, CSm and LMc, of the two segments of the substitution method. For concreteness, we will carry out these operations explicitly for the proof of the expression 2.01.

2.01 ? p→ -p .→. -p

Test for Similarity, CSm. We must state what we mean by similarity. We start from a common-sense viewpoint and regard two propositions as similar if they "look" similar to the eye of a logician. In Section I we have already defined three characteristics of an expression that can be used as criteria of similarity. These are: K, the number of levels in the expression; J, the number of distinct variables in the expression; and H, the number of variables in the expression.[12]

Applying these definitions to 2.01 (routines NK, NJ, and NH, respectively), we find that K = 3, J = 1, and H = 3. That is, 2.01 has three levels, one distinct variable (p), and three variable places. We may write this:

$$D(2.01) = (3,1,3)$$

In the same way, we can write descriptions for the various sub-expressions contained in 2.01--in particular, the sub-expressions to the left and to the right of the main connective, respectively. We have for these:

$$DL(2.01) = (2,1,2); \text{ and } DR(2.01) = (1,1,1)$$

Now, we say that two expressions, x and y, are similar if they have identical left and right descriptions; i.e., if DL(x) = DL(y) and DR(x) = DR(y). The routine for determining whether two theorems are similar, CSm, consists of two segments: (1) CSm(D), a description segment, and (2) CSm(CD), a comparison of descriptions. The description segment is made up of four description routines, D, one each to compute DL(x), DR(x), DL(y), and DR(y). The comparison segment is made up of two compare description routines, CD, one of which compares DL(x) with DL(y), the other DR(x) with DR(y).

A diagram of the hierarchy of principal subroutines in testing similarity will look like this:

[12]The assertion is that two expressions having the same description "look alike" in some undefined sense; and hence if we are seeking to prove one of them as a theorem, while the other is an axiom or theorem already proved, then the latter is likely construction material for the proof of the former. Empirically, it turns out that with the particular definition of similarity introduced here, in proving the theorems of Chapter 2 of Principia Mathematica about one theorem in five that is stored in the theorem memory turns out to be similar to the expression we are seeking to prove. It is easy to suggest a number of alternative, and quite different criteria that would be equally symptomatic of "similarity." Uniqueness is of no account here; all we are concerned with is that we have some criteria that "work"— that select theorems suitable for matching.

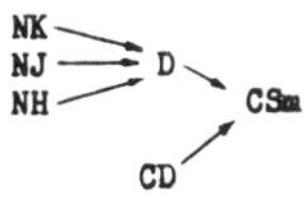

In the case of 2.01, the segment MSb(Sm) will search the list of axioms and theorems and will find that axiom 1.2 is similar to 2.01:

1.2 ! $p \vee p .\rightarrow. p$

for it, too, has the descriptions: DL(1.2) = (2,1,2); DR(1.2) = (1,1,1). Moreover, 1.2 is the only axiom that has this description.

<u>Matching Expressions</u>, <u>LMc</u>. Next we carry out a point-by-point comparison between 2.01, the expression to be proved, and 1.2, the axiom that is similar to it. We start with the main connectives, and work systematically down the tree of the logic expressions—always as far as possible to the left. In the present case the order in which we will match is: main connective (P = none), connective of left sub-expression (P=L), left variable of sub-expression, (P=LL), right variable of sub-expression (P=LR), and right sub-expression (P=R).

The matching routine is fairly complicated, consisting of six segments, but not all segments are employed each time two elements are matched. The first segment, LMc(T), and the initial operations of most of the other segments consist of tests that determine whether the two elements to be matched are already identical, whether they can be made identical by substitution (if one is a free variable) or by replacement (if both are connectives), or—finally—whether matching is impossible. The second segment, LMc(LMc), is a recursion of the matching routine with each of the next lower pair of elements in the tree of the expression. This recursion segment operates only if the elements to be matched in LMc are identical connectives (or have been made so).

The third and fourth segments, LMc(Sby) and LMc(Sbx), apply the rule of substitution when the tests have shown this to be appropriate. LMc(Sby), which is executed whenever E(x) is a free variable,[13] simply substitutes the expression X(y) for E(x). LMc(Sbx), which is executed whenever E(y) is a free variable, substitutes the expression X(x) for E(y). In both cases, of course, substitution must take place throughout the whole expression in which the free variable occurs. This is taken care of automatically by the process LSb. Also, since LMc matches X(x) to X(y), LMc(Sby) has priority over LMc(Sbx), as a careful examination of the test network will reveal.

The fifth segment, LMc(CN), reports the successful termination of the matching program if E(x) and E(y) are identical variables, its failure if they cannot be made identical by substitution.

The sixth segment, LMc(Rp), operates when E(x) and E(y) have different connectives. The segment replaces the connective in x by the connective in y whenever this replacement is legitimate, and then returns control to the recursion segment.

By virtue of the recursion segment, the matching routine will attempt to match each pair of elements; if successful, will proceed to the next pair; if unsuccessful, will report failure. Hence, the routine will continue until it makes the theorem that is being matched identical with the expression to be proved, or until the matching fails.

The hierarchy of principal routines looks like this:

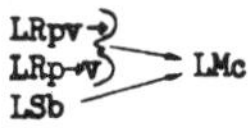

Returning to our specific example of the two similar expressions, 1.2 and 2.01, we carry out the matching routine as follows:

2.01 ? $p \rightarrow -p .\rightarrow. -p$
1.2 ! $A \vee A .\rightarrow. A$

(We use A instead of p in 1.2 to indicate that the variable is <u>free</u> (F).)

a. The main connectives agree: both are →.
b. Proceeding downward to the left, the connective is → in 2.01, but ∨ in 1.2. To change the ∨ to →, we must have (because of the definition, 1.01, a - before the left-hand A in 1.2. This we can obtain by making the substitution of -B for A in 1.2. Having carried out this substitution, and having then replaced (-B ∨ -B) with (B→ -B), we have the following situation:

2.01 ? $p \rightarrow -p .\rightarrow. -p$
1.2' ! $B \rightarrow -B .\rightarrow. -B$

c. Proceeding again to the left, we find B in 1.2', but p in 2.01. We therefore substitute p for B in 1.2', and now find (after recursion through the remaining two elements) that we have a complete match:

2.01 ? $p \rightarrow -p .\rightarrow. -p$
1.2'' ! $p \rightarrow -p .\rightarrow. -p$

Thus, we have discovered a proof of 2.01 (in fact, precisely the proof we gave before), which consists in substituting the variable -p for the variable in 1.2, and replacing the connective ∨ in 1.2 with →.

This completes our outline of the method of substitution as a routine for discovering proofs in symbolic logic. The method may be viewed as an information process that is composed of a considerable number of more elementary in-

[13]Essentially, a variable is <u>free</u> when no substitution has yet been made for it. After any substitution it is <u>bound</u> and no longer available for subsequent substitutions. As previously noted, all variables in expressions stored in the theorem memory are free.

formation processes arranged to operate in highly conditional sequences. Each of the main components—the test for similarity routine, and the matching routine—is made up, in turn, of subroutines. The test conditions that control the branchings of the sequences depend in a number of instances upon the outcomes of searches through the theorem memory. Hence, the method of substitution represents a complex information process in the sense in which we have defined the term. Combining the two diagrams depicted above, we can illustrate the hierarchy of the main operations that enter into the substitution method:

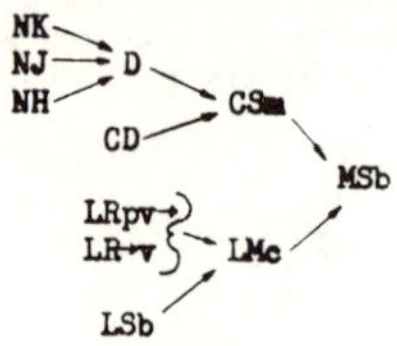

The method is a heuristic one, for it employs cues, based on the characteristics of the theorem to be proved, to limit the range of its search; it does not systematically enumerate all proofs. This use of cues represents a great saving in search, but carries the penalty that a proof may not in fact be found. The test of a heuristic is empirical: does it work?

Moreover, the cues that are used in the method are not without cost. For example, in order to limit matching attempts to "similar" theorems, theorems must be described and compared. The net saving in computing time, as compared with random search, is measured by the reduction in the number of theorems that have to be matched <u>less</u> the cost of carrying out the search and compare for similarity routines. Stated otherwise, cues are economical only if it is cheaper to obtain them than to obtain directly the information for which they serve as cues.

To be sure, we have found a proof for one proposition in <u>Principia</u>; but how general is the substitution method? On examination of the 67 propositions in Chapter 2 of <u>Principia</u>, it appears that some 21 can be proved by the method of substitution, including for example: 2.01, 2.02, 2.03, 2.04, 2.05, 2.10, 2.12, 2.21, 2.26, 2.27. The remaining propositions evidently require more powerful techniques of discovery and proof. It is evident, for instance, that we must employ the rule of detachment.

<u>The Method of Detachment</u>

We will describe next the <u>method of detachment</u>, <u>MDt</u>, which, as its name implies, incorporates the rule of detachment. The method, of course, is not synonymous with the rule, but includes also heuristic devices that select particular theorems to which the rule is applied.

Let us review the principle of logic that underlies the method. Suppose LT must prove that expression A is a theorem; and assume that there are in the theorem memory two theorems, B and B→A. Then, by application of the rule of detachment to B and B→A, A is derivable immediately.

We can generalize this procedure by combining matching (substitution and replacement) with detachment. Assume that the theorem memory contains B" and B'→A'; that <u>A</u> is obtainable from A' by matching; and that B' is obtainable from B" by matching. Then we can construct a proof of A as follows: (1) By matching with B", B' is a theorem. (2) Since B'→A' is also a theorem, it follows by detachment that A' is a theorem. (3) By matching with A', A is a theorem.

This settles the problem of constructing a <u>valid</u> proof by the method of detachment. From the standpoint of the <u>discovery</u> of a proof employing this method, the trick lies again in narrowing down the search for B'→A' and B", so that these do not have to be sought through a very large scale trial-and-error search and substitution program.

<u>Structure of the Detachment Method</u>. The basic structure of the detachment method is quite similar to that of the substitution method, for both methods utilize the same basic operations. The first two segments of the detachment method, MDt(SmV) and MDt(SmCt), carry out searches for similar expressions, in a way that will be indicated more precisely below. The next segment, MDt(Mc), carries out a matching of any expression so found with the theorem to be proved. If the matching is successful, a new problem is created by the segment MDt(F). This problem is then attacked, in the final segment, MDt(MSb), by the method of substitution.

Again, designate by A the expression to be proved. In MDt(SmV) we search the theorem memory for theorems whose <u>right sides</u> are similar (by the test, CSm, described previously) to the <u>whole</u> expression A. If we find such a theorem (call it T), we go to segment MDt(Mc), and apply the matching operation to the right side of T and to A. If we are successful in the matching, we find the left side of T, MDt(P); and seek to prove by the method of substitution that it is a theorem, MDt(MSb). For if the left side of T is a theorem and T is a theorem, then by detachment, the right side of T is a theorem. But A can be obtained from the right side of T by substitution, hence is a theorem. (Note that a check is made to see that T has → for a connective.)

<u>Contraction</u>. If the detachment method fails to find a proof in the manner just described, a new attempt is made by means of the second segment, MDt(SmCt), employing a different criterion of similarity from the one we have used thus far. If the theorem is similar, the method proceeds with the matching segment exactly as before.

To see what is involved in this generalized notion of similarity, let us consider two expressions, A and A', with different descriptions. If A has more levels and variable places than A', it is still possible that A is derivable from A' by substitution—specifically, by substituting appropriate <u>molecular</u> expressions for the variables of A. For example, take as A the expression:

2.06 ? p→q .→: q→r .→. p→r

for which we have DL(2.06) = (2,2,2), DR(2.06) = (3,3,4); and take as A' the expression:

A' ? a .→. b→c

for which we have DL(A') = (1,1,1), DR(A') = (2,2,2).

If in A' we substitute p→q for a, q→r for b, and p→r for c, we obtain 2.06. Operating in the reverse direction, if we <u>contract</u> 2.06 by making the inverse substitutions, we obtain A'. We can therefore refer to A' as "2.06 viewed as contracted."

Since the purpose in searching for similar theorems is to find appropriate materials to which to apply the matching routine, there is no reason why we should not use this more general notion of similarity if it proves effective in finding materials that are useful.

In general, what parts of an expression should be considered as units in the search for proofs is not a "given" for the problem solver. LT makes an explicit decision each time it looks for similar expressions as to what subexpressions will be taken as units. In contracting 2.06, a decision has been made that the elements p, q, and r are too small, and that more aggregative elements, e.g., (p→q) = a, should be perceived as units.

Examination of the routines for describing expressions (NH, NK, NJ) will reveal that these routines in fact count <u>units</u> rather than <u>variables</u>. Normally, the variables are the units used in description, for VV precedes CSm in every program except MDt. In the latter program, however, it is sometimes useful to view expressions as contracted, by means of VCt.

<u>Example of Proof by Detachment</u>. To illustrate the method of detachment, let us carry out explicitly the proof of 2.06:

2.06 ? p→q .→: q→r .→. p→r

The reader may verify that this theorem cannot be proved by substitution in the axioms and earlier theorems. Moreover the detachment method without contraction will also fail, for there is no theorem whose right side is similar to 2.06. However, we have already seen that when we contract 2.06, we obtain:

A' ? a .→. b → c

where p→q has been contracted to <u>a</u>, q→r to b, and p→r to c. We now have DL(A') = (1,1,1) and DR(A') = (2,2,2), descriptions that are identical with the descriptions of the sub-expressions of the right side of 2.04.

2.04 ! A →. B → C : → : B → . A → C
A' a → . b → c

Having selected 2.04 by use of the routine MDt(SmCt), we now proceed to match its right side with 2.06 in segment MDt(Mc):

2.04 ! A .→. B → C :→: B .→. A → C
2.06 ? p→q .→: q→r.→.p→r
2.04' ! q→r .→: p→q.→.p→r .:→:. p→q .→: q→r.→.p→r

We have now created a new problem to replace the original one: to prove that the left side of 2.04' (the part underscored) is a theorem. We apply the method of substitution, MDt(MSb). The search of the theorem memory discloses 2.05 to be similar to the left side of 2.04', and we proceed to match them:

2.04'L ? q→r .→: p→q .→. p→r
2.05 ! A→B .→: C→A .→. C→B

It is easy to see that with the substitution of q for A, r for B, and p for C, the matching will be successful. Hence we have B (2.05 with the indicated substitution), and B→A (2.04'), from which A (2.06) follows by the rule of detachment.

The diagram below summarizes the principal routines incorporated in the method of detachment. A comparison of this diagram with the one for the substitution method shows clearly that both methods rest on the same component processes, with minor modifications and new combinations and conditions. The sole new process involved in detachment is the viewing of theorems as contracted.

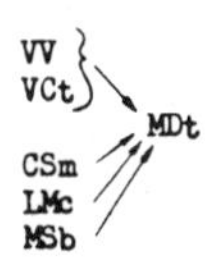

<u>The Chaining Method</u>

A number of expressions that do not yield to the method of substitution can be proved by the method of detachment. We shall add an additional method, however, to the repertoire available to LT. We shall call this method <u>chaining</u>, <u>MCh</u>. Like the methods previously described, chaining involves heuristic procedures which we shall consider first.

Theorem 2.06, which we have just proved, embodies one form of the principle of the syllogism (2.05 is another form of this principle). Now suppose T_1, (p→q) is a true theorem, and T_2, (q→r) is another true theorem. Theorem 2.06 is of the form:

$$T_1 \;.\!\to\!.\; T_2 \to E$$

where E is (p→r), an expression not known to be true. By detachment, from ! T_1 and ! T_1.→.T_2→E, we get ! T_2→E. By a second detachment, from ! T_2 and ! T_2→E, we get ! E. Hence, if we know p→q and q→r to be true, we can construct a proof of p→r by means of two detachments with the use of 2.06. Instead of carrying through this derivation explicitly in each instance, we simply construct a program that makes direct use of the transitivity of syllogism. This proof method is the basis for chaining.

Suppose that we wish to prove A→C. We search for a theorem, T (with → for a connective) whose left side is similar to A, using the segment MCh(SmF). We match the left side of T with A, MCh(McF), and if we are successful, we have then proved a theorem of the form A→B, for T, as modified by matching, is of this form. We check first, in segment MCh(McR) whether we can simply match B to C. If we succeed, we have proved the theorem. If we fail, we now construct, by segment MCh(S), the expression B→C, and attempt to prove this expression by substitution, MCh(MSb). If we are successful, we now have a chain: A→B, B→C. Then by syllogism, as indicated above, we obtain A→C, the expression we wished to prove.

The procedure just described is chaining forward. Alternatively, we may chain backward. That is, to prove A→C, we may search for a theorem of the form B→C; then try to prove A→B by substitution.

Proof by the chaining method is illustrated by:

2.08 ? p → p

A search for theorems that have left sides similar to 2.08 yields 1.3, 2.02, and 2.07. The latter is:

2.07 ! p .→. pvp

If we take 2.07 as the (A→B) of the schema given above, then B is (pvp). Two theorems have left sides similar to B: 1.2 and 2.01. An attempt to match the left side of 2.01 to the right side of 2.07 will be unsuccessful, but the matching is immediate with 1.2:

2.07 ! p .→. pvp
1.2 ! pvp .→. p

Hence we can take 1.2 as the (B→C) of the chaining method. We now form (A→C) by joining the left side of 2.07 to the right side of 1.2 by →. The result is 2.08:

2.08 ! p .→. p

The chaining method is summarized by the following diagram:

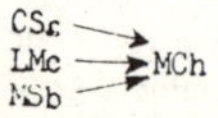

The Executive Routine

It remains to complete the specification of LT in two directions; first, to assemble the three methods that have been described into a coherent program; and second, to show how the information processes in terms of which LT has been described here can be specified precisely in terms of the elementary processes listed in Section I. The latter task is carried out in detail in Section III. We will turn our attention here to the former, which is embodied in the executive routine, Ex.

In its first segment, Ex(R), the executive routine reads a new expression that is presented to it for proof, and places it in a working memory.[14]

In the next three segments, Ex(MSb), Ex(MDt), and ExMCh), successive attempts are made to prove the expression by the methods of substitution, detachment, and chaining, respectively. If a proof is obtained by one of these methods, the executive routine writes the proof, Ex(WP); and stores the newly-proved theorem (changing all its variables to free variables) in the theorem memory, Ex(ST).

To explain what happens if the three methods are unsuccessful, we have to take up some details that were omitted above. These have to do with the creation of subsidiary problems and with stop rules.

Subsidiary problems. Both detachment and chaining are two-step methods. Suppose we wish to prove A. In detachment, we try to find a theorem, B→A, and if we are successful, we then try to prove B. The task of proving B we may call a subsidiary problem.

Suppose we wish to prove a→b. In chaining, we try to find a theorem, a→c, and if we are successful, we then try to prove c→b. The task of proving c→b is also a subsidiary problem.

Within both the detachment and chaining methods, only the method of substitution is applied to the subsidiary problem. If that method fails, failure is reported for the main problem. But before control is shifted back to the executive routine, the main element of the subsidiary problem is stored in the problem list, P, in the storage memory. (The operation that stores the problem in the problem list is the operation SEN that can be found in segment MDt(P) and segment MCh(P).)

When the three methods have failed for a given problem, the executive routine stores it in the inactive problem list, Q. It then selects from the problem list, P, an expression that is, in a certain sense, the simplest--specifically, an expression with the smallest possible number of levels, K, Ex(CK). It erases this new subsidiary problem from P; checks to make certain it does not duplicate one previously attempted, Ex(CX); and then tries to solve this subsidiary problem by the methods of detachment and chaining.[15] This sequence is repeated until some subsidiary problem is solved (in which case the main problem is also solved), or until no problems remain on the problem list, or until the other stop rule, to be described, comes into operation. In the latter two cases, the routine reports that it is unable to prove the theorem, Ex(WNP).

[14] Certain segments of Ex, in particular Ex(R), Ex(WP), Ex(ST) and Ex(WNP), are not written in Section III in terms of the primitives but are simply indicated by parentheses. It would be rather simple to formalize them, but this would further lengthen the description of the program.

[15] There is no need to attempt to prove the subsidiary problem by substitution, since an unsuccessful substitution attempt was made immediately before the expression was stored in the subsidiary problem list.

The check to prevent duplication of subsidiary problems, Ex(CX), is handled as follows: for each problem that is selected from list P by Ex(CK), a check is made, by Ex(CX), against all expressions in the inactive problem list, Q, and if the new problem duplicates any expression found there, it is dropped. The main operation of this segment, CX, applies the same basic tests of identity of elements that are applied in the matching program, but does not modify the expressions to make them match.

Stop Rules. Since all proof methods may fail, even if the expression given to LT is a genuine theorem, the executive routine needs a stop rule. One stop rule is provided by the exhaustion of list P, but there is no guarantee that the list will ever be exhausted. A second stop rule is provided by an operation that measures the total amount of "work" that has been done in attempting to prove a theorem, and that terminates the program with a "no proof" report when the total work exceeds a specified amount. The first operation in the substitution routine, NAW, tallies one for each time the routine is used. This tally is kept in a special location, W, in the storage memory. The executive routine, just before it seeks a new subsidiary problem, checks the cumulative tally in this register, Ex(CW), and if the tally exceeds a given limit, terminates the program. Since the substitution routine is used in each of the methods, the number of substitutions attempted seems to be one reasonable index of the amount of work that has been done.

This stop rule operates as a global constraint on the total work applied in trying to prove a single theorem. The rule does not govern the direction in which this effort is expended. The latter is determined by the priority rule previously described for selecting subsidiary problems from the problem memory and by the other elements of LT's program.

Learning Processes

The program we have described is primarily a performance program rather than a learning program. But, although the program of LT does not change as it accumulates experience in solving problems, learning does take place in one very important respect. The program stores the new theorems it proves, and these theorems are then available as building blocks for the proofs of subsequent theorems. Thus, in the theorems used as examples in this paper, 2.06 was proved with the aid of 2.05 and 2.04, and 2.08 was proved with the aid of 2.07. Without this form of learning it is doubtful whether the program would prove any but the first few theorems in Chapter 2 in a reasonable number of steps.

III

The Complete Program for the Logic Theorist

This Section is divided into two parts. The first part constitutes the program as described in the text, including the following routines: Ex; MCh, MDt, MSb; LMc, LSb, LRp→v, LRpv→, VV, VCt; CX; CSm, CD, D, NK, NH, NJ. These routines are preceded by a list of the most important primitive IP's—those that are used in several routines. Following each routine is a supplementary list of primitive IP's used in the definition of that routine.

The second part of this Section consists of routines for five IP's—those Store instructions that are marked with asterisks (*)—which up to this point have been treated as primitives.

Principal Primitive Instructions

A	OPER	L	C	R	B	
	B				b	Branch to b (→b).
	BHB					In higher instruction, →b.
	BHN					In higher instruction, →next.
	FEF	x	y		b	Find the first E in A(x) and put in y; if none, →b.
	FEN	x	y		b	Find the E in A(x) next after E(y), put in y; then →b. If none (end of list), →next.
	FL	x	y			Find EL(x) and put in y; if none, leave y blank.
	FR	x	y			Find ER(x) and put in y; if none, leave y blank.
	PE	x	y			Put E(x) in E(y);E(x) remains.
	S	x				Store E(x) back in A(x)(match on P); if not there,store E(x) at end of A(x).
	SEN	x	y			Store E(x) as next E in A(y); E(x) now last item in A(y).
	*SX	x	y			Store a copy of X(x) at (new) A(y). E(x) = M.
	TC	x			b	If C(x) = → (implies), →b.
	TV	x			b	If E(x) = V, →b.

A	OPER	L	C	R	B	Seg.	
	Ex						**Executive routine**
	(Read problem X)					R	
	(Put EM(X) in 1)						
	-MSb	1			C	MSb	
A	-MDt	1			G	MDt	
	-MCh	1			G	MCh	
	SEN	1	Q				X(1) is finished.
	CWG				H	CW	
B	FEF	P	1		H	CK	Find problem with lowest K.
	NK	1					
C	-FEN	P	2		D		
	NK	2					
	CKG	2	1		C		
	PE	2	1				
	PK	2	1				
	B				C		
D	E	1	P			CX	Remove duplicates of previous problems.
	FEF	Q	3		F		
E	CX	1	3		B		
	FEN	Q	3		E		
F	B				A		
G	(Write proof.)					WP	Succeeds in proving P.
	(X(1) a theorem)					ST	
	(Stop)						

```
H  (Write:no proof) WNP  Fails to find proof.
   (Stop)
```

Primitives

```
   CKG   x y   b    If K(x)>K(y), →b.
   CWG         b    If W (work done) > limit, →b.
   E     x y        Erase E(x) in A(y).
```

Note: There are six IP's in the executive routine that are not formally defined in LT. These are written in parentheses above: read problem, find problem and put in working memory 1, write proof, store expression as theorem, write "no proof", and stop.

```
A  OPER  L C R B    Seg.
                       Substitution method
                        If can't prove X(x) by
   MSb   x     b        substitution, →b.

   NAW              NAW  Count one unit of work.
   VV    L          Sm
   FEF   T 1   C
A  VV    1
   CSm   L 1   D
B  FEN   T 1   A         Find next T and repeat.
C  BHB

   SX    1 2        Mc
   LMc   2 L
   BHN
```

Primitives

```
   NAW                   Add one to W (work done).
```

```
A  OPER  L C R B    Seg.
                       Matching routine
                        Match X(x) to X(y); if
   LMc   x y   b        can't, →b.

   CGG   C L   A    T
   CGG   L C   C         Now G(x) = G(y).
   TV    L     E
   TV    C     D
  -CC    L C   F
   FL    L 1        LMc
   FL    C 2
   LMc   1 2   H         Mc left subexpression.
   FR    L 3
   FR    C 4
   LMc   3 4   H         Mc right subexpression.
   BHN

A  TV    L     H    Sby
  -TF    L     H
B  NSGG  L C
   FM    L 5             Assures Sb everywhere.
   LSb   C L 5
   BHN

C  TV    C     H    Sbx
D -TF    C     H
   NSGG  C L
   FM    C 5             Assures Sb everywhere.
   LSb   L C 5
   BHN
```

```
E  TF    L     B    CN
  -TV    C     H
  -CN    L C   D
   BHN

F -LRp→v L     G    Rp    LRp's are self-testing.
   LRpv→ L     H
G  LMc   L C   H
   BHN
H  BHB
```

Primitives

```
   CC    x y   b    If C(x) = C(y), →b.
   CGG   x y   b    If G(x) > G(y), →b.
   CN    x y   b    If N(x) = N(y), →b.
   FM    x y        Find EM(x) and put in y.
   NSGG  x y        Subtract G(x) from G(y).
   TF    x     b    If E(x) is free, →b.
```

```
A  OPER  L C R B    Seg.
                       Substitution routine
                        Substitute X(x) for
   LSb   x y z          E(y) (=V) in X(z) (=M).

   FEF   L 1   F    F
A  CPS   1 1   B         E(1) must belong to X(x).
   CN    1 C   G
B  FEN   L 1   A
C  FEF   R 2   F    Sb   Search through X(z).
D -CN    2 C   E
   PE    L 3
   NAGG  2 3             G's add in Sb.
   SXE   3 2
E  FEN   R 2   D         Find next E(z), repeat.
F  BHN

G  AN    4          LSb
   LSb   4 C R
   B           C
```

Primitives

```
   AN    x               Assign an unused name to E(r).
   CN    x     b         If N(x) = N(y) →b.
   CPS   x y   b         If E(x) subelement of E(y)→b
                          (P(x) ⊃ P(y)).
   NAGG  x y             Add G(x) to G(y); result in
                          G(y).
  *SXE   x y             Store X(x) in A(y) in place
                          of E(y) (=V).
```

```
A  OPER  L C R B    Seg.
                       Detachment method
                        If can't prove X(x) by
                        detachment, →b. Store
   MDt   x     b        new problems in P.

   FEF   T 1   C    T
A  TC→   1     B         T must have C = →.
   VV    1
   FR    1 2
   VV    L          SmV
   CSm   L 2   D
   VCt   L          SmCt Change view.
   CSm   L 2   D
B  FEN   T 1   A         Find next T and repeat.
C  BHB
```

```
D  SX     1 3             Copy, to work on T.
   FR     3 4
   LMc    4 L    B  Mc
   FL     3 5       P
   SXM    5 6             Create new X.
   S      6               Stored away fixed ME.
   SEN    6 P
   MSb    6      B  MSb
   BHN
```

Primitives

```
   *SXM   x y       Store X(x) at (new) A(y) as
                     main expression.
```

```
A  OPER   L C R B   Seg.
                          Chaining Method
                          If can't prove X(x) by
                          chaining, →b; Store new
   MCh    x     b         problems in P.

   -TC→   L     D   T     C(x) must be →.
   VV     L
   FL     L 1
   FR     L 2
   FEF    T 3   D
A  -TC→   3     C         T must have C = →.
   VV     3
   SX     3 4             Copy, to work on T.
   FL     4 5
   FR     4 6
   -CSm   1 5   B   SmF
   -LMc   5 1   E   McF
B  -CSm   2 6   C   SmB
   -LMc   6 2   F   McB
C  FEN    T 3   A         Find next T and repeat.
D  BHB
E  PE     2 5             Put E(2) and E(6) in
   PE     6 1              proper wkg. memory.
   -LMc   1 5   G   McR
F  AM     7         S     Create EM for new X.
   PC→    7               Fix connective.
   S      7               Store parts.
   SEN    7 P
   SXL    1 7
   SXR    5 7
   MSb    7     C   MSb
G  BHN
```

Primitives

```
   PC→    x         Put C(x) = → (implies).
   *SXL   x y       Store X(x) in A(y) as XL(y).
   *SXR   x y       Store X(x) in A(y) as XR(y).
```

```
A  OPER   L C R B   Seg.
                          Replacement of → with v.
                          If C(x) = →, replace
   LRp→v  x     b         with v; if not →b.

   TC→    L     A   T
   BHB
A  PCv    L         Pv    Fix E(x).
   S      L
   FL     L 1             Fix EL(x).
   NAG    1
   S      1
   BHN
```

Primitives

```
   NAG    x             Add one to G(x).
   PCv    x             Put C(x) = v.
```

```
A  OPER   L C R B   Seg.

   VV     x             View variables as units.

   FEF    L 1       T
A  PUB    1             Erase old unit.
   -TV    1     B
   PU     1         P
B  S      1
   FEN    L 1   A       Find next E and repeat.
   BHN
```

Primitives

```
   PU     x             Make E(x) a unit, (U).
   PUB    x             Make U(x) blank.
```

```
A  OPER   L C R B   Seg.
                        View as contracted
                        Make units of binary
                        expressions and
   VCt    x             isolated variables.

   TV     L     C   T
   FL     L 1       VCt
   FR     L 2
   TV     1     B
   VCt    1             Recursion
   TV     2     E
A  VCt    2             Recursion
   PUB    L
   S      L
   BHN

B  -TV    2     D
   PUB    1         Ct  Blank V's of Ct unit.
   S      1
   PUB    2
   S      2
   TN     L     C       Give X(x) a name if
   AN     L              one needed.
C  PU     L
   S      L
   BHN

D  PU     1         VV  Make left (isolated)
   S      1              variable a unit.
   B            A       XR(x) still to be done

E  PU     2
   S      2             Make right (isolated)
   BHN                   variable a unit.
```

Primitives

```
   AN     x         Assign E(x) an unused name.
 (See VV for PU and PUB)
   TN     x     b   If E(x) has a name →b.
```

```
A  OPER   L C R B   Seg.
                        Replacement of v with →.
                        If C(x)=v and G(EL(x))
                        >0, replace v with →;
```

```
   LRpv→ x      b          if not →b.

   -TCv  L      A   T
    FL   L 1
    TGG  1      C
   -TV   1      A
   -TSb  1      B
A   BHB

B   PE   1 2        Sb
    NAG  2
    FM   2 3
    LSb  2 1 3
    FL   L 1
C   PC→  L          P      Fix x.
    S    L
    NSG  1
    S    1
    BHN
```

Primitives

```
    FM   x y               Find EM(x) and put in y.
    NAG  x                 Add one to G(x).
    NSG  x                 Subtract one from G(x).
    PC→  x                 Put C(x) = →.
    TGG  x      b          If G(x) >0 →b.
```

```
A   OPER  L C R B  Seg.
                           Compare expressions
                           Compare X(x) with X(y); if
    CX    x y   b          they match, →b.

    CGG  L C    B   T
    CGG  C L    B          G(L) = G(R), otherwise →B.
    TV   L      A
    TV   C      B
   -CC   L C    B          C(L) = C(R)
    FL   L 1        CX     Recursion down tree of
    FL   C 2                expressions.
   -CX   1 2    B
    FR   L 3
    FR   C 4
   -CX   3 4    B
    BHB

A  -TV   C      B   CN     L and C both variables;
   -CN   L C    B           with identical names.
    BHB

B   BHN
```

Primitives

(For CC, CGG, and CN, see LMc)

```
A   OPER  L C R B  Seg.
                           Similar expressions test
                            If DL(x) = DL(y) and
    CSm   x y   b          DR(x) = DR(y), →b.

    FL   L 1        D
    FR   L 2
    D    1
    D    2
    FL   C 3
    FR   C 4
    D    3
    D    4
   -CD   1 3    A   CD
   -CD   2 4    A
    BHB

A   BHN
```

```
A   OPER  L C R B  Seg.
                           Compare descriptions
                            If K(x) = K(y), J(x) = J(y),
    CD    x y   b           and H(x) = H(y) →b.

   -CK   L C    A          Def: If K(x) = K(y) →b.
   -CJ   L C    A          Def: If J(x) = J(y) →b.
   -CH   L C    A          Def: If H(x) = H(y) →b.
    BHB

A   BHN
```

```
A   OPER  L C R B  Seg.

    D     x                Describe

    NK   x
    NJ   x
    NH   x
    BHN
```

```
A   OPER  L C R B  Seg.

    NH    x                Count variable places

    FEF  L 1    C
A  -CPS  1 L    B
   -TU   1      B
    NAH  L
B   FEN  L 1    A
C   BHN
```

Primitives

```
    CPS  x y    b          If E(x) subelement of E(y) →b.
                            (P(x) ⊃ P(y)).
    NAH  x                 Add one to H(x)
    TU   x      b          If E(x) is a unit, →b.
```

```
A   OPER  L C R B  Seg.

    NJ    x                Count distinct variables

    AA   1                 List for counted-V.
    FEF  L 2    E   F      Find first E of X(x).
A  -CPS  2 L    D
   -TU   2      D
    FEF  1 3    C          Find first V of list.
B   CN   2 3    D   CN
    FEN  1 3    B          Find next V of list.
C   SEN  2 1
    NAJ  L          A
    FEN  L 2    A          Find next E of X(x).
E   BHN
```

Primitives

```
    AA   x                 Assign an unused list of A(x).
    CN   x y    b          If N(x) = N(y), →b.
```

77

```
CPS    x y   b   If E(x) subelement of E(y), →b.
                  (P(x)⊃ P(y)).
NAJ    x         Add one to J(x).
TU     x     b   If E(x) is a unit, →b.
```

```
A  OPER   L C R B  Seg.

   NK     x               Count levels

   TU     L     A  T
   TB     L     B
   FL     L 1      NK
   NK     1
   FR     L 2
   NK     2
   CKG    2 1   C  CK
   PK     1 L      KL
A  NAK    L
B  BHN

C  PK     2 L      KR
   B            A
```

Primitives

```
CKG    x y   b   If K(x) > K(y), →b.
NAK    x         Add one to K(x).
PK     x y       Put K(x) in K(y).
TB     x     b   If E(x) is blank →b.
TU     x     b   If E(x) is a unit →b.
```

PART 2: Reduction of procedural processes [*S]

The Store instructions that rewrite expressions in various ways can be reduced to processes more like the rest of the primitive set. The new primitives required are (a) two (PA and CP) which belong to types of operations already considered, and (b) four of a new type to manipulate the P sequences. The latter operations insert and delete subsequences from the <u>front</u> end of a given sequence. Thus if P = LRRL and P' = LRRLRLR, then P'' = P' - P = RLR and P'' + P = LRRLRLR. Observe that subtraction can only be performed when the subtrahend is an initial segment of the minuend, and also that addition is not commutative All these routines involve bringing in the elements, one by one, modifying them and storing them in the new list.

Store a copy of X(x) at (new) A(y) (E(x) = M).

```
A  OPER   L C R B

   SX     x y

   AA     C
   FEF    L 1   B
A  PE     1 2
   PM     C 2
   S      2
   FEN    L 1   A
A  BHN
```

Store X(x) in A(y) in place of E(y) (E(y) =V) (take E(x) from w.m.)

```
A  OPER   L C R B

   SXE    x y

   FEF    L 1   D
A  CP     L 1   E
   CPS    1 L   C
   PE     1 2
B  PM     C 2
   HSPP   L 2
   HAPP   C 2
   S      2
C  FEN    L 1   A
D  BHN

E  PE     L 2
   B            B
```

Store X(x) at (new) A(y) as main expression

```
A  OPER   L C R B

   SXM    x y

   AA     C
   FEF    L 1   C
A  CPS    1 L   B
   PE     1 2
   PM     C 2
   HSPP   L 2
   S      2
B  FEN    L 1   A
C  BHN
```

Store X(x) in A(y) as XL(y).

```
A  OPER   L C R B

   SXL    x y

   FEF    L 1   C
A  CPS    1 L   B
   PE     1 2
   PM     C 2
   HSPP   L 2
   HAPL   2
   HAPP   C 2
   S      2
B  FEN    L 1   A
C  BHN
```

Store X(x) in A(y) as XR(y).

```
A  OPER   L C R B

   SXR    x y

   FEF    L 1   C
   CPS    1 L   B
   PE     1 2
   PM     C 2
   HSPP   L 2
   HAPR   2
   HAPP   C 2
   S      2
   FEN    L 1
   BHN
```

Primitives

```
AA     x           Assign an unused list to A(x).
CP     x y   b     If P(x) = P(y) →b locates
                   "same" element even though V,
                   G, etc. have been modified).
CPS    x y   b     If E(x) subelement of E(y),→b
                   (P(x)⊃ P(y)).
HAPL   x           Add a Left to front of P(x).
HAPR   x           Add a Right to front of P(x).
HAPP   x y         Add P(x) to front of P(y).
HSPP   x y         Subtract P(x) from front of
                    P(y).
PA     x y         Put A(x) in A(y).
```

Conclusion

In this paper we have specified in detail an information processing system that is able to discover, using heuristic methods, proofs for theorems in symbolic logic. We have confined ourselves to description, and have not attempted to generalize in abstract form about complex information processing. Because of the nature of the description, involving considerable rigor and detail, it may be useful to set out in conclusion the main features of LT, especially as these appear to reflect basic characteristics of complex systems.

First of all, LT can be specified at all only because its structure is basically hierarchical, and makes repeated use of both iteration and recursion. So true is this, that one of LT's main features, the use of a problem-subproblem hierarchy, is hardly visible in the program at all.

LT offers no guarantee of finding a proof; on the other hand, it brings to its task a number of different heuristic methods for achieving its goals. All of these methods are important in making LT sufficiently powerful to find proofs in most cases, and to find them with a reasonable amount of computation, but not all of them are essential. Without chaining, for instance, LT could still function. The methods MSb and MDt still provide it with ways to prove theorems—and even some theorems more easily provable by MCh would yield to the more directly "brute force" approach of the other two.

LT is still a very simple process compared, for instance, with the array of methods, techniques, and concepts used by a human logician. For example, the concepts of commutativity and associativity are nowhere to be found in LT. The analysis of LT and its variations is a subject for later papers. However, the following facts, based on hand simulation, may help put LT in perspective. LT will prove in sequence most of the 60 odd theorems in Chapter 2 of Principia Mathematica. With some extension in the variety of methods and cues employed, it will prove most of the theorems in Chapter 3, in which another connective, "and," is introduced.[16] We know nothing, as yet, about what will be required for an extension to the predicate calculus or to other types of problem solving.

LT uses similarity-testing and matching as a multi-stage search and selection process. The questions of efficiency involved in such processes have already been commented upon in Section II. Additional variation and complexity enters the program through the alternative modes, VV and VCt, for perceiving the logic expressions in the course of testing similarity and of matching.

In these and other ways, the logic theorist is an instructive instance of a complex information process. We expect to learn more about such processes when we have realized the logic theorist in a computer and studied its operations empirically; and when the logic theorist will have been joined by similar systems capable of performing other complex information processing tasks.

References

1. Bowden, B. V. (ed.), Faster Than Thought (London: Pitman, 1953), pp. 181-198.

2. Hilbert, D., and W. Ackermann, Principles of Mathematical Logic (New York: Chelsea, 1950), Chapter 1.

3. Whitehead, A. N., and Bertrand Russell, Principia Mathematica, vol. 1, 2nd ed. (Cambridge: Cambridge U. Press, 1925).

[16] A program to do this has been developed and hand simulated by Mr. Kalman Cohen.

Reprinted from *IEEE Trans. Inform. Theory,* **IT–11,** No. 3, 1965, pp. 353–362.

Threshold Training of Two-Mode Signal Detection

JACK SKLANSKY, SENIOR MEMBER, IEEE

17

***Abstract*—In certain systems of signal detection and pattern recognition, the process of training an observer to distinguish levels of sensory excitation or to recognize patterns, involves an adaptive threshold adjustment. These "threshold learning processes" (TLPs) can be modeled by finite-state Markov chains. When the output statistics of these TLPs move at random between two sets of parameters, we have a "two-mode" TLP.**

A probabilistic measure of the training and working performance of two-mode TLPs is proposed. A method of designing periodic train-work schedules for two-mode TLPs is described. For many two-mode TLPs the ratio of working time to retraining time yielding a desired performance level is maximized when the work-retrain period is made as small as possible. The final success probability in a working phase of any two-mode Markov chain cannot be less than one-half of the success probability at the beginning of that working phase. Train-work schedules can exploit the adaptive properties of trainable detectors to overcome not only the unpredictability of the mode, but also the designer's ignorance of the channel statistics.

I. Introduction

WE SHALL DISCUSS the learning dynamics of a trainable threshold detector [1] "looking" at a two-mode channel. One attraction of this model is that it provides a simple framework for the study of adaptation and learning. Another attraction of the model is that it appears in several applications: signal detection [2], pattern recognition [3], discrimination learning [4], and information retrieval [5].

The work reported here is part of a study of how the choice of training strategy (or feedback policy) affects the adaptive properties of certain trainable stochastic systems.

In our model of trainable signal detection, a binary signal is transmitted through a noisy channel. The observer (or receiver) guesses the value of the transmitted signal by comparing the observed signal to a "threshold." The observer "learns" by moving his threshold to a new value whenever he receives a reinforcement signal.[1] The reinforcement signal, in simple cases, consists merely of the information that the latest guess was right or wrong.

To present a challenge to the observer, we have given the channel a pseudo-nonstationary character. The channel moves at random between two modes, $\mathcal{A}$ and $\mathcal{B}$: in mode $\mathcal{A}$ the channel has one set of stationary statistics, in mode $\mathcal{B}$ another set of stationary statistics. (An example of such a channel appears in telephone communication [6].) When the observer is trained on this channel, he tends to learn implicitly the statistics of one of the modes—say mode $\mathcal{A}$. Then, at a selected instant, the observer's training phase ends, and the working phase begins. After some time in the working phase, the observer will see mode $\mathcal{B}$, while his threshold is better suited to mode $\mathcal{A}$. Consequently, periodic retraining is called for.

We shall describe how train-work schedules for two-mode channels may be synthesized, and we shall show how the observer's learning dynamics on a two-mode channel is related to the constituent one-mode channels.

II. Philosophy and Terminology

The philosophy underlying our study stems from classical feedback-control theory. We assume that every trainable system is describable as consisting of a "plant," a "critic," and a "controller" (Fig. 1). The plant refers to that part of the system which is to be trained; the critic, incorporated in the experimenter or system designer, is a mechanism that computes a performance index; the controller is that part of the system that adjusts the plant parameters in response to the input/output behavior of the plant. The controller may be viewed as a teacher that trains the plant during a "training phase"; during a "working phase" the plant operates without the controller.

In most control systems, the controller adjusts the plant in response to an "error" detector. In Fig. 1, we have embedded this error detector inside the controller. The error detector may be identical to the critic, but not necessarily so. In fact, the error detector may not be distinguishable as a physical entity.

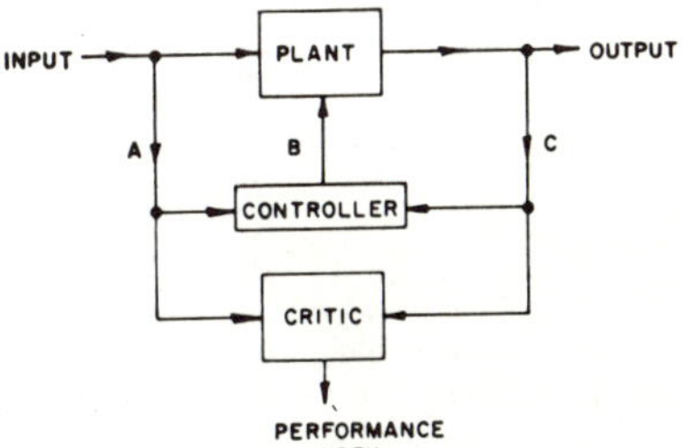

Fig. 1. Block diagram of a trainable system.

A system is viewed as *adaptive* if it exhibits one or both of the following *adaptation characteristics* [7]:

1) *Stability*: The performance index remains within prescribed bounds when the environment changes.
2) *Reliability*: The performance index remains within prescribed bounds when the plant's internal structure changes.

Manuscript received February 21, 1964; revised February 11, 1965. The research reported in this paper was sponsored by the Aerospace Medical Division, Air Force Systems Command, Wright-Patterson Air Force Base, Ohio, under Contract Number AF33 (657)-11336.

The author is with the National Cash Register Co., Dayton, Ohio. He was formerly with RCA Labs., Princeton, N. J.

[1] We use the anthropomorphic terms "he" and "his" for convenience, even though the observer is just a mathematical model. The model may represent either a human being or a machine.

Learning is viewed as a favorable time variation of the performance index in response to a step transition in the environment. Thus, we consider learning to be a particular facet of stability.

Feedback is often a means to enhance the adaptation characteristics of a plant. On the other hand adaptive behavior may be achieved without feedback—both "open-loop" and "closed-loop" adaptive systems are possible.

The work reported in this paper is part of an effort directed toward understanding the ways in which particular forms of feedback affect the adaptation characteristics of trainable stochastic systems. In this way we hope to contribute toward the development of a theory of adaptation [8].

This approach to the study of adaptation is to be distinguished from the many current studies of "optimal" control systems. The optimality criteria in those studies do not, as a rule, account for the fabrication and operating costs of the control policies, and as a result the optimal policies often require expensive machinery (such as digital computers) for their realization. In the present approach, simple feedback policies are assumed a priori.

III. One-Mode Threshold Learning Processes

In this section we review the analysis of a trainable threshold detector on a one-mode channel [9]. We refer to this model as a one-mode "threshold learning process."

A. Definition of Threshold Learning Processes

A threshold learning process (TLP) is a discrete trainable version of simple threshold detection [1]. It is illustrated in Fig. 2. It consists of a binary source, a channel, and an observer.

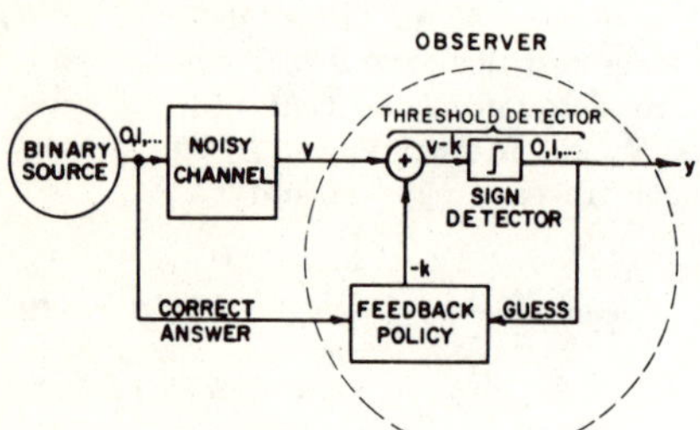

Fig. 2. The "threshold learning process."

The binary source emits a stationary, statistically independent sequence u, of 0's and 1's. The channel mixes u and a noise sequence to form a sequence of received signals v. The channel is described by two *constituent densities*: $f_0(v) \triangleq \rho p(v \mid u = 0), f_1(v) \triangleq (1 - \rho)\, p(v \mid u = 1)$, where ρ is the frequency of 0's; $p(v \mid u = 0)$ is the conditional probability density of v, given that $u = 0$.

The observer compares v with a threshold k. If $v - k$ is nonnegative, then the observer's guess is $y = 1$, which represents the guess that the source emitted a 1. If $v - k$ is negative, then $y = 0$, which represents the guess that the source emitted a 0.

During a training phase the observer checks the guesses against a set of stored answers. When his guess and the stored answer disagree, the observer moves his threshold to a new value in accordance with an algorithm. We call this algorithm the "feedback policy". After the training phase, the observer enters a "working phase", during which he has no access to correct answers.

In this paper, as in our earlier work, we consider the following "simple incremental" feedback policy: A threshold having K possible values is moved up or down to an adjacent available value in response to a false alarm or false rest, respectively. The threshold remains fixed if no error is incurred or if a boundary threshold prevents a desired adjustment.

B. Analysis of One-Mode TLPs

With simple incremental feedback, the probabilistic behavior of the thresholds is given by a random walk of the form shown in Fig. 3. In this random walk, each node is associated with a "state", and each state is associated with a threshold. In the specific random walk in the figure, the number of thresholds, K, is three. In terms of the random walk, the probability of a correct guess at time n, i.e., the success probability at time n, is[2]

$$z(n) = \mathbf{r}(0)\mathbf{P}^n\mathbf{q} \tag{1}$$

where

$\mathbf{r}(0) \triangleq$ row vector each of whose elements $r_i(0)$ is the probability that the state at time 0 is i.

$\mathbf{P} \triangleq$ stochastic matrix each of whose elements p_{ij} is the conditional probability that the next state[3] is j, given that the present state is i.

$\mathbf{q} \triangleq$ column vector each of whose elements q_j is the conditional probability of a correct guess, given that the present state is j.

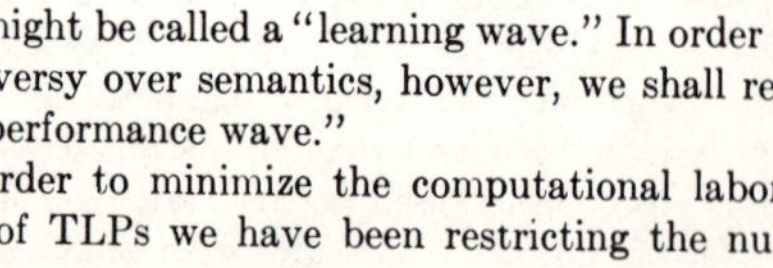

Fig. 3. State transition graph of the Markov chain of a three-threshold *TLP*.

When $z(n)$ is plotted as a function of time we have what might be called a "learning wave." In order to avoid controversy over semantics, however, we shall refer to it as a "performance wave."

In order to minimize the computational labor in our study of TLPs we have been restricting the number of

[2] In the earlier paper we used a slightly different time origin for $z(n)$. By the definition for $z(n)$ in that paper, the variable n in the left member of (1) would be replaced by $n + 1$. The change in time origin is just a matter of convenience.

[3] In the model under discussion, "state" and "threshold" are equivalent. Later in this paper we shall see that this is not so in the case of two-mode TLPs.

thresholds to three; and we have been assuming that the constituent densities, $f_u(v)$, are piecewise constant, with each of the discontinuities occurring at one of the available thresholds. The resulting model—the "quantal" TLP—is a very simple yet nontrivial example of a discrete adaptive stochastic process. Empirical data indicate that certain qualitative characteristics of the transient and steady-state behavior of three-threshold quantal TLPs hold true for TLPs having more than three thresholds and having continuous constituent densities.

An example of a quantal TLP—"Model I"—is illustrated in Fig. 4. In this figure the constituent densities are characterized by three parameters:

$\rho \triangleq$ frequency of occurrence of zeros in the sequence u
$\alpha \triangleq$ amplitude of the central part of $\rho^{-1}f_0(v)$
$\beta \triangleq$ amplitude of the central part of $(1 - \rho)^{-1} f_1(v)$.

The crosses in Fig. 4 mark the available threshold values $\{k\}$. If $\alpha = \beta$, the Markov chain of this model has the following stochastic matrix:

$$\mathbf{P} = \begin{array}{c|c|c|c|} & 1 & 2 & 3 \\ \hline 1 & 1 - \frac{\rho}{2}(1+\alpha) & \frac{\rho}{2}(1+\alpha) & 0 \\ \hline 2 & \frac{1-\rho}{2}(1-\alpha) & \frac{1}{2}(1+\alpha) & \frac{\rho}{2}(1-\alpha) \\ \hline 3 & 0 & \frac{1-\rho}{2}(1+\alpha) & 1 - \frac{1-\rho}{2}(1+\alpha) \\ \hline \end{array} \quad (2)$$

Two other models, Models II and III, in which the constituent densities overlap by lesser amounts than in Model I, have also been studied [9].

The TLP and the Markov chain model constitute the basis for our work toward a theory of adaptation [8]. Another Markov chain approach has been taken by Tsetlin and other workers in the Soviet Union [10]–[12]. Tsetlin's approach, however, differs from ours in certain important respects. One distinguishing feature is the fact that even in the very simple learning modeled by the TLP there are two types of punishments—one type in response to a false rest, and the other in response to a false alarm. Tsetlin's models, on the other hand, have just one type of punishment and one type of reward. Another distinguishing feature is the fact that the probability of a threshold transition in a TLP depends on the latest state of the Markov chain, while the values of Tsetlin's transition probabilities are independent of the states, so long as the states remain in one of the arms of his star-shaped model.

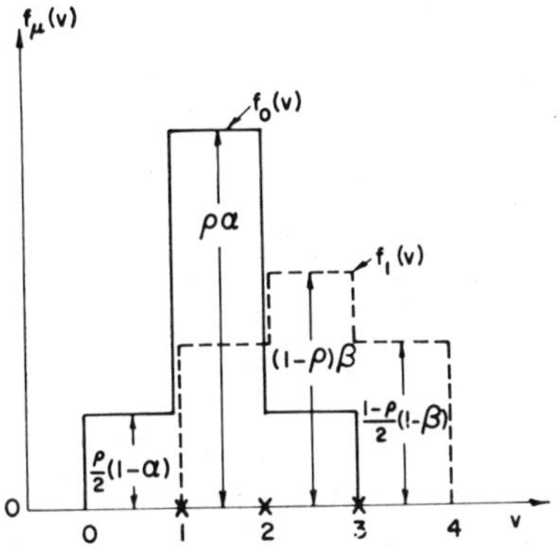

Fig. 4. Constituent probability densities for Model I.

IV. Two-Mode Threshold Learning Processes

In some stochastic processes it is convenient to assume that the statistical parameters of the process are themselves subject to statistical fluctuation. Here we have one stochastic model superimposed on another stochastic model. Tsetlin [10] refers to such a process as a "composite medium;" we call it a "two-mode process." The two-mode TLP, described, is the particular form of two-mode process analyzed in this paper.

Consider a communication link in which a binary signal is transmitted through a two-mode channel. If the channel is fixed in mode $\mathcal{A}$, it acts as a zero-memory channel with relatively good transmission statistics. If the channel is fixed in mode $\mathcal{B}$, it acts as a different zero-memory channel with relatively bad transmission statistics. In a one-mode operation, the channel is fixed at either mode $\mathcal{A}$ or mode $\mathcal{B}$. In the two-mode operation, the channel is only temporarily fixed at either $\mathcal{A}$ or $\mathcal{B}$, and the transmission statistics follow a random square wave as a function of time, such as the uppermost wave in Fig. 5. In the model to be discussed, the transitions between $\mathcal{A}$ and $\mathcal{B}$ are described by a two-state Markov chain.

Suppose the observer in this communication link is trained by a three-threshold simple incremental feedback policy. As a result of this feedback each mode is describable by a three-state random walk (Fig. 3). The two-mode process is a special case of the situation where each transition probability of a Markov chain shifts at random from one value to another. We shall show that this apparently complicated model is equivalent to a Markov chain with constant transition probabilities.

The following question arises: how may the two-mode process be described in terms of the individual mode matrices **A**, **B**, and the mode-to-mode transition matrix **Γ**, where

$$\mathbf{A} \triangleq \{a_{ij}\}, \mathbf{B} \triangleq \{b_{ij}\},$$
$$\mathbf{\Gamma} \triangleq \begin{bmatrix} 1-\delta & \delta \\ \epsilon & 1-\epsilon \end{bmatrix}. \qquad (3)$$

(The quantities δ and ϵ are the mode-to-mode transition probabilities.)

The specific answer to this question depends on the way in which the states of the two-mode Markov chain are defined. We define these states as follows. Let A1, A2, A3, B1, B2, B3 denote the six states of a two-mode Markov chain in which the constituent modes each have three thresholds. (The extension to modes of more than three thresholds is obvious.)

Consider the sequence of events illustrated in Fig. 5. These events refer to the guesses and the error signals generated in a TLP. Just before the "observer" in Fig. 2 generates a guess, he receives a sampling pulse which tells him: during this sampling interval guess whether the observed signal v was caused by a 0 or a 1 at the information source. During the sampling interval the channel will be either in mode $\mathcal{A}$ or mode $\mathcal{B}$. If it is in $\mathcal{A}$, then the two-mode process is said to be in the state Ak from the time that the threshold takes on the value k chosen by the feedback policy until the next time a threshold value is established. (The next established threshold value may or may not be different from the "present" value.) Similarly, if the channel is in mode $\mathcal{B}$ during the sampling pulse then the next state of the two-mode process will be Bk, where the sign of the increment in k depends on the sign of the error. Note that by this definition of Ak and Bk, the model of the process may occupy state Ak even though the process itself may have shifted to $\mathcal{B}$. Similarly

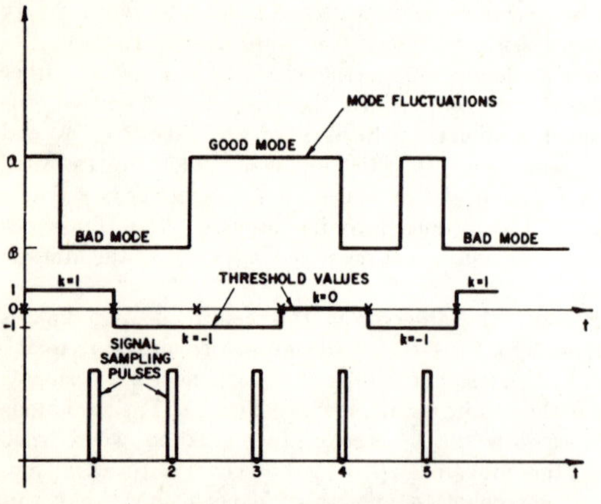

Fig. 5. Timing relations between mode-to-mode transitions, threshold shifts, and sampling pulses.

the model may be in state Bk even though the channel is in $\mathcal{A}$. The reason for the proposed definition is the nonambiguity and simplicity of the resulting mathematical analysis. (A definition by which the model is in state Ak if and only if the channel is in $\mathcal{A}$ at the time of threshold adjustment results in an ambiguous mathematical formulation [13].)

By the foregoing definition, a transition from state Ai to Bj occurs with probability δb_{ij}, Bi to Bj occurs with probability $(1-\epsilon)b_{ij}$, Ai to Aj occurs with probability $(1-\delta)a_{ij}$, and Bi to Aj occurs with probability $\epsilon\, a_{ij}$. Consequently the process may be described by the signal flow graph ([14], [15]) of Fig. 6(b). Figure 6(a) is a signal flow graph displaying only the mode-to-mode transitions. (The quantity x in these graphs represents a unit-delay operator. For example, $\delta b_{11}x$ is the "x transform" of an impulse of area δb_{11} occurring at time 1 at node $B1$ in response to an impulse of area 1 occurring at time 0 at node $A1$. An impulse is a spike-shaped signal of zero width but finite area.) To help us in our analysis, the graph of Fig. 6(b) may be represented by a "vector flow graph" each of whose nodes represents a vector having state probabilities as elements, and each of whose branches represents a matrix operating on the node vector at the tail of the branch. A convenient partition of the state probabilities into vectors is $\mathbf{r}_A(n)$ and $\mathbf{r}_B(n)$, where the elements of $\mathbf{r}_A(n)$, $\mathbf{r}_B(n)$ are the probabilities of states Ak, Bk, respectively, for $k = 1, 2, 3$. The resulting vector flow graph is shown in Fig. 7. The stimulus-response matrix equation is obtainable directly from this graph. This equation is:

$$r(x) = s(x) + r(x)\mathbf{\Gamma P}x \qquad (4)$$

where

$$r(x) \triangleq [r_A(x),\ r_B(x)] \qquad (5)$$

$$s(x) \triangleq [\mathbf{s}_A(x),\ s_B(x)] \qquad (6)$$

$$\mathbf{P} \triangleq \begin{bmatrix} \mathbf{A} & \mathbf{0} \\ \mathbf{0} & \mathbf{B} \end{bmatrix}. \qquad (7)$$

The vectors $r(x)$, $s(x)$, etc., are x transforms. For example,

$$r(x) \triangleq \sum_{n=0}^{\infty} \mathbf{r}(n)x^n.$$

Solving (4) for $r(x)$, we have

$$r(x) = s(x)[\mathbf{I} - \mathbf{\Gamma P}x]^{-1}. \qquad (8)$$

If $s(x)$ is the x transform of an impulse vector, i.e., a vector each of whose elements is an impulse, then

$$\mathbf{r}(n) = \mathbf{r}(0)(\mathbf{\Gamma P})^n. \qquad (9)$$

Note that $(\mathbf{\Gamma P})^n \neq \mathbf{\Gamma}^n\mathbf{P}^n$, because $\mathbf{\Gamma P} \neq \mathbf{P\Gamma}$, except in trivially degenerate cases.

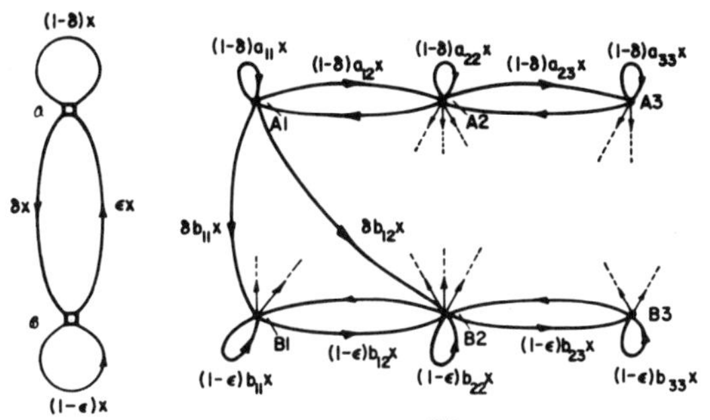

(a) (b)

Fig. 6. Markov chain model of a two-mode process.

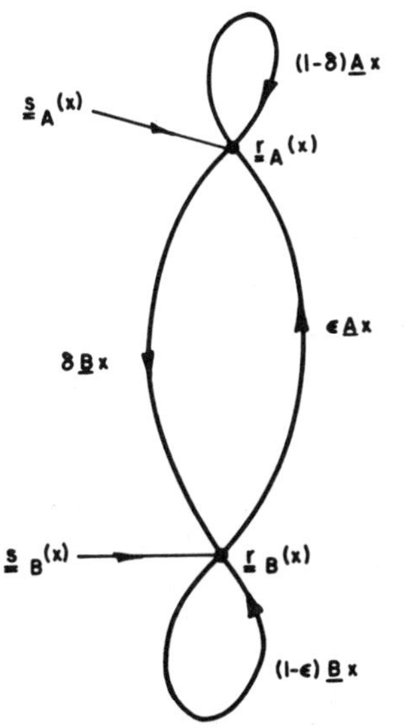

Fig. 7. The vector flow graph of a two-mode Markov chain.

V. The Training Phase

During the training phase of a TLP, the observer guesses the "cause" u of the "effect" v. After his guess, the observer is told the correct answer. During the working phase, the observer is not informed of the correct answers to his guesses.

In this section we shall derive an expression for the success probability $z(n)$ in response to an impulse vector. (An impulse vector represents the situation where the initial probability distribution over the available threshold values is known.) The function $z(n)$ is then a measure of success as a function of the length of training.

Equation (4) can be solved for $r_A(x)$ by treating it as two simultaneous matrix equations, and replacing $r_B(x)$ by an expression involving $r_A(x)$ and *not* involving $r_B(x)$. This yields

$$r_A(x) = \{s_A(x) + s_B(x)[\mathbf{I} - (1-\epsilon)\mathbf{B}x]^{-1}\epsilon\mathbf{A}x\}\, M(x) \qquad (10)$$

where

$$M(x) \triangleq \{[\mathbf{I} - (1-\epsilon)\mathbf{B}x][\mathbf{I} - (1-\delta)\mathbf{A}x] - \delta\epsilon\mathbf{B}\mathbf{A}x^2\}^{-1}[\mathbf{I} - (1-\epsilon)\mathbf{B}x]. \qquad (11)$$

A similar expression is obtained for $r_B(x)$.

Generally, the training process will start with an initial probability distribution spread over the range of available threshold values, rather than one specific value. For the case of a spread distribution, assuming the mode-to-mode transitions have reached steady-state statistics, we have

$$s_A(x) = \mathbf{r}_A(0) = \gamma\mathbf{r}(0), \quad \text{and} \quad s_B(x) = \mathbf{r}_B(0) = (1-\gamma)\mathbf{r}(0), \qquad (12)$$

where

$$\gamma \triangleq \frac{\epsilon}{\delta + \epsilon}, \qquad (13)$$

and where $\mathbf{r}(0)$ is a probability vector—i.e., a vector having non-negative real elements summing to unity.

The success probability $z(n)$ may be found from the following formula:

$$z(n) = \mathbf{r}_A(n)\mathbf{q}_A + \mathbf{r}_B(n)\mathbf{q}_B \qquad (14)$$

where

$\mathbf{q}_A \triangleq$ a column vector of conditional success probabilities for states in mode $\mathcal{A}$

$\mathbf{q}_B \triangleq$ a column vector of conditional success probabilities for states in mode $\mathcal{B}$.

The vectors $\mathbf{q}_A$ and $\mathbf{q}_B$ are obtainable from an inspection of the state transition graph and from a knowledge of the conditional success probabilities.

We may think of the two modes as "weakly coupled" or "strongly coupled," depending on the size of δ and ϵ. Weak coupling corresponds to $\delta \ll 1$ and $\epsilon \ll 1$, i.e., infrequent transitions. Strong coupling corresponds to $1 - \delta \ll 1$ and $1 - \epsilon \ll 1$, i.e., frequent transitions.

The preceding development leads to the following weak-coupling approximation for the two-mode training performance wave:

$$z(n) \cong \gamma z_{A_o}(n) + (1-\gamma)z_{B_o}(n). \qquad (15)$$

(The subscripts Ao and Bo stand for "$\mathcal{A}$ only" and "$\mathcal{B}$ only." Thus $z_{A_o}(n)$ is the performance wave of the one-mode TLP characterized by matrix $\mathbf{A}$.)

VI. The Working Phase

When the success probability $z(n)$ is brought to a specified "acceptable" value, or higher, by the training, the training may be stopped. The process then begins its working phase (i.e., open-loop operation). If the process is a one-mode TLP, $z(n)$ will remain, throughout the working phase, at the value it attained at the end of the training phase. But suppose the process is a two-mode TLP. There exists a nonzero probability of a mismatch between the threshold and the mode—i.e., there is a nonzero probability that the threshold of the process is not optimum for the particular mode the channel happens to occupy. In a two-mode process this mismatch probability is relatively small at the end of the training phase, and becomes greater and greater as the process moves further along in the working phase. (In a one-mode process the mismatch probability remains constant throughout the working phase.) Hence, one expects the success probability during the working phase of a two-mode process to diminish monotonically from a peak at the beginning of the working phase, finally leveling off at an asymptotic value ζ_F. (The subscript F stands for "fixed threshold".) The Markov chain model permits an exact analysis of the dynamics of the working-phase success probability. It also permits a determination of ζ_F.

Suppose we want the success probability to remain above a prescribed lower bound ζ_L throughout the working phase. If $\zeta_L > \zeta_F$, then the working phase will have to be interleaved with "retraining" phases. The Markov chain permits us to find an optimum train-work schedule for any specific ζ_L.

The formula for the working phase performance wave is

$$z_F(n) = \zeta_F + [z_F(0) - \zeta_F](1 - \delta - \epsilon)^n \tag{16}$$

where:

the time origin is the beginning of the working phase,
ζ_F is the final value of $z_F(n)$
$z_F(0)$ is the initial value of $z_F(n)$.

This formula is exact for all δ and ϵ; no approximation is involved. The quantities ζ_F and $z_F(0)$ are given by:

$$\zeta_F = \gamma^2\psi_A + (1 - \gamma)^2\psi_B + \gamma(1 - \gamma)(\psi_{AB} + \psi_{BA}) \tag{17}$$

$$z_F(0) = \gamma\psi_A + (1 - \gamma)\psi_B \tag{18}$$

where

$$\psi_A \triangleq \frac{1}{\gamma}\mathbf{r}_A(0)\mathbf{q}_A \tag{19}$$

$$\psi_B \triangleq \frac{1}{1-\gamma}\mathbf{r}_B(0)\mathbf{q}_B \tag{20}$$

$$\psi_{AB} \triangleq \frac{1}{\gamma}\mathbf{r}_A(0)\mathbf{q}_B \tag{21}$$

$$\psi_{BA} \triangleq \frac{1}{1-\gamma}\mathbf{r}_B(0)\mathbf{q}_A. \tag{22}$$

These equations lead to the following interesting observation: *the final success probability in a working phase of any two-mode Markov chain cannot be less than one-half of the success probability at the beginning of that working phase* [13].

Equation (16) displays the degradation in performance associated with the working phase. That this degradation is brought about by the mode-to-mode fluctuations is displayed by the fact that the exponentially decaying portion of (16) decays at a rate determined only by δ and ϵ. Another factor involved in determining the extent of the working phase degradation is the degree of mismatch that occurs when a threshold optimized for one mode coexists whth the other mode. This is seen when we compare (17) and (18), and take note of the definitions in (19)–(22). If modes $\mathcal{A}$ and $\mathcal{B}$ were identical, then ζ_F would equal $z_F(0)$. The degree to which ζ_F and $z_F(0)$ differ depends on the sizes of ψ_{AB} and ψ_{BA}.

Note also that $z_F(n)$ is not sensitive to changes in the initial threshold probability vector $\mathbf{r}(0)$ provided $z_F(0)$ and ζ_F are fixed. Thus $z_F(0)$ and ζ_F completely determine the working phase performance—no knowledge of the individual initial threshold probabilities is required.

VII. Train-Work Cycles

We have seen that the mode-to-mode fluctuations of a two-mode process effect a degradation of performance during a working phase. Hence a schedule of train, work, retrain, work, retrain, etc., will be necessary if the lowest acceptable success probability ζ_L, is greater than ζ_F. This is to be contrasted to one-mode processes, where a single training phase can bring the success probability permanently to a desired value.

We shall describe how train-work schedules may be constructed from a knowledge of the $\mathcal{A}$-only and $\mathcal{B}$-only threshold dynamics.

An exaggerated example of a train-work cycle is illustrated in (Fig. 8.) During the training phase, the threshold probability vector is

$$\mathbf{r}(n) = \mathbf{r}(0)\,(\mathbf{\Gamma P})^n. \tag{23}$$

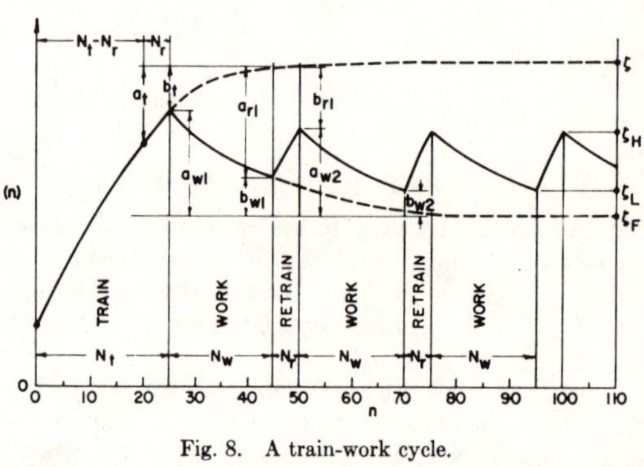

Fig. 8. A train-work cycle.

Suppose the available thresholds range over the values $k = 1, 2, \cdots, K$. At the end of the training phase, the $2K$ elements of the threshold probability vector $\mathbf{r}(N_t)$ are grouped into pairs—each pair consisting of the two joint probabilities associated with the same threshold k. These pairs are then used in the following equation to find the corresponding pairs throughout the working phase:

$$\mathbf{r}_k(N_t + m) = [r_{\mathcal{A}k}(N_t), r_{\mathcal{B}k}(N_t)]\begin{bmatrix} 1-\delta & \delta \\ \epsilon & 1-\epsilon \end{bmatrix}^m \tag{24}$$

for $m = 1, 2, \cdots, N_w$. The quantity $r_{\mathcal{A}k}(N_t)$ is defined as the joint probability of mode $\mathcal{A}$ and threshold k at time N_t. At the end of the working phase the pairs are regrouped into a $2K$-dimensional vector $\mathbf{r}(N_t + N_w)$. This new vector is used as the "initial condition" for the retraining phase, and used in (23), with a proper shift of time origin, to find the threshold probability throughout the retraining phase.

A significant computational difficulty in the exact analysis of the two-mode process is the task of regrouping $\mathbf{r}(n)$ at the transition between training and working phases. The "RC-circuit" approximation is an analysis technique in which these transition regroupings are ignored. This approximation is based on the assumption that when the training performance wave $z(n)$ is near its asymptote, $z(n)$ may be approximated by the sum of a constant term and only one exponentially decaying term—i.e., only one nonconstant eigenfunction. (Actually, the $z(n)$ of a two-mode three-threshold TLP contains five nonconstant eigenfunctions.) This assumption automatically implies that the transition regroupings may be ignored, since a change in the transition regroupings only affects the relative contribution of each eigenfunction to $z(n)$. The value of ζ is unaffected by the transition regroupings, because the associated stochastic matrix is ergodic.

The form of the train-work cycle that we shall analyze is illustrated in Fig. 8. This cycle consists of three types of "phases": a training phase, a working phase, and a retraining phase, with phase lengths of N_t, N_w, and N_r, respectively.

Under the foregoing assumptions the train-work cycle of a two-mode TLP is analogous to the charge-discharge cycle of a resistor-capacitor (RC) circuit, such as that illustrated in Fig. 9.

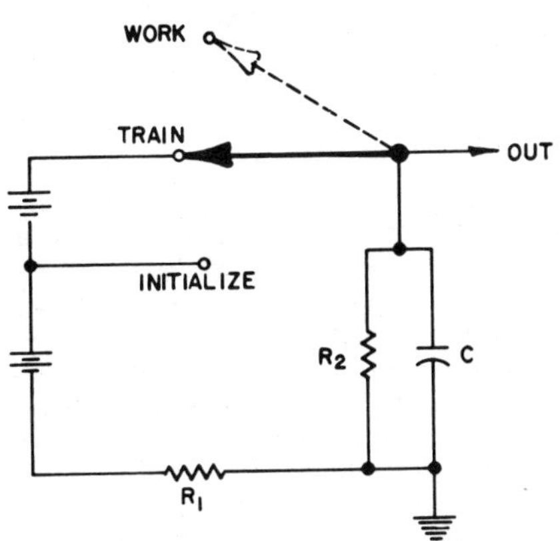

Fig. 9. An approximate electrical analog of the train-work cycle.

We found that in train-work cycles where the RC-circuit approximation is valid, the ratio of working time to retraining time is maximized when the work-retrain period is made as small as possible [13]. We shall observe this property in the numerical example.

VIII. Numerical Example

Consider the two-mode TLP having the constituent densities shown in Fig. 10. (This is a version of Gilbert's "burst-noise" channel [6].)

In this example, the constituent densities have the following properties: 1) the frequencies of occurrence of the transmitted signals in mode $\mathcal{A}$ are equal to the corresponding frequencies in mode $\mathcal{B}$; and 2) the constituent densities in mode $\mathcal{A}$ do not overlap. Expressed symbolically, these properties are a) $\rho_A \equiv \rho_B$; and b) $\alpha_A \equiv 1$. Thus the four constituent densities can be specified by only two parameters: ρ_A (or ρ_B) and α_B. Let

$$\rho \triangleq \rho_A \equiv \rho_B \tag{25}$$

and

$$\alpha \triangleq \alpha_B. \tag{26}$$

If we assume $\delta \ll 1$, $\epsilon \ll 1$, the approximate TLP dynamics are completely specified by ρ, α, and γ, as defined in (25), (26), and (13).

For the specific densities shown in Fig. 10, the best performance for mode $\mathcal{A}$ is obtained when the threshold is fixed at $k = 2$, and the best threshold for mode $\mathcal{B}$ is obtained when the threshold is fixed at $k = 3$. One will suspect, therefore, that for certain values of α and ρ, no fixed threshold will yield near-optimal performance in the two-mode process, and that continual retraining of the threshold is necessary in order to obtain near-optimal performance. This conjecture turns out to be correct over a wide range of ρ, α, and γ [13].

To illustrate the techniques for synthesizing train-work cycles, we consider the case $\alpha = 0.6$, $\rho = 0.9$, $\delta = \epsilon = 0.01$ for the process of Fig. 10. (Equations (25) and (26) still apply.) The point (α, ρ) was chosen well within a region of the $\alpha\rho$ plane where we expect the working phase asymptote ζ_F to be significantly different from the training phase asymptote ζ [13]. We shall assume that the initial threshold is at $k = 1$.

The mode matrices for our example are

$$\mathbf{A} = \begin{bmatrix} 0.1 & 0.9 & 0 \\ 0 & 1 & 0 \\ 0 & 0.1 & 0.9 \end{bmatrix}$$

$$\mathbf{B} = \begin{bmatrix} 0.280 & 0.720 & 0 \\ 0.020 & 0.800 & 0.180 \\ 0 & 0.080 & 0.920 \end{bmatrix}.$$

[The elements of $\mathbf{A}$ and $\mathbf{B}$ were computed in accordance with the right member of (2).]

Applying the weak-coupling approximation (15), we obtained the approximate performance wave $\tilde{z}(n)$ of the training phase. This wave is shown in Fig. 11.

We found the exact training performance wave $z(n)$ by the method of Section V, using a digital computer. The resulting function $z(n)$ is so close to $\tilde{z}(n)$ that no difference between the two would be visible in Fig. 11. In order to make this difference visible, the difference $\Delta(n) \triangleq \tilde{z}(n) - z(n)$ is plotted in Fig. 11 on a magnified scale. Note that $\Delta(n)$ approaches its maximum as $n \to \infty$, and that $\Delta(\infty)$ is quite small—approximately 0.004.

To synthesize train-work cycles by the RC-circuit approximation, we computed ψ_A, ψ_B, ψ_{AB}, and ψ_{BA} for $n = \infty$ (infinite training). These quantities are defined in (19) to (22), where the argument 0 refers to a new time origin at the beginning of the working phase. Using the ψ's, we found ζ and ζ_F via (17) and (18). The following values were obtained:

$$\zeta = z_F(0) = 0.9343$$

$$\zeta_F = 0.9004.$$

At first sight it may seem surprising that ζ and ζ_F differ by only about four percent even though $(\alpha, \rho) = (0.6, 0.9)$ falls well within the region of the $\alpha\rho$ plane where we expect a significant difference between ζ and ζ_F. The question arises: Under what circumstances will ζ_F differ substantially from ζ? We suggest that this will occur when the number of available thresholds, K, is larger than three. Intuition tells us that when K is large it will be possible to reduce the "cross-correlations" ψ_{AB} and ψ_{BA}.

Using the above values of ζ and ζ_F, and setting ourselves a design goal of

$$\zeta_L \cong 0.9250$$

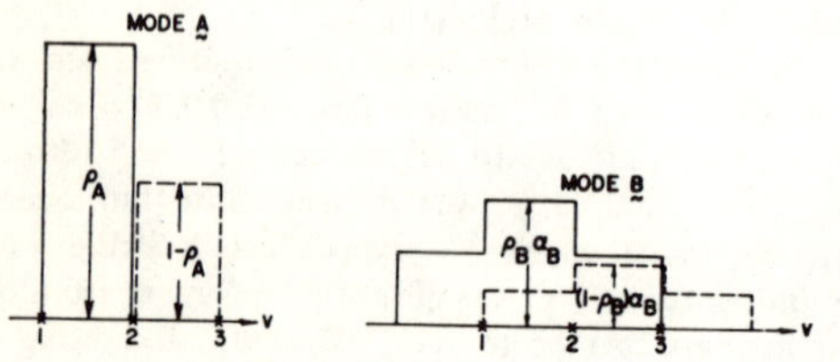

Fig. 10. The constituent probability densities in the illustrative example.

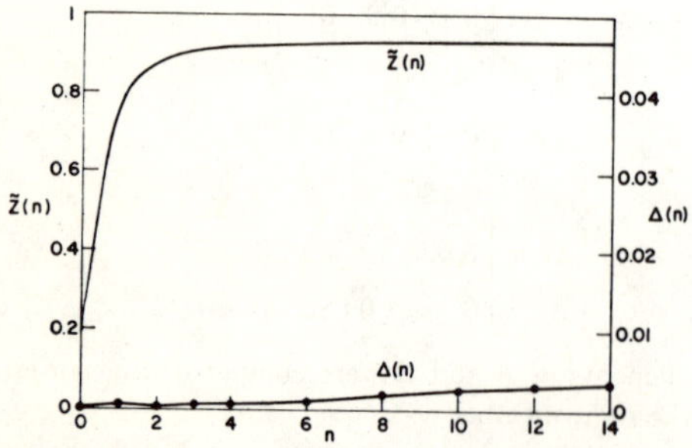

Fig. 11. Training performance wave of numerical example.

we computed a number of train-work schedules, using the RC-circuit approximation. [A train-work schedule is identified by (N_t, N_w, N_r).] The choice of the goal $\zeta_L \cong 0.9250$ was based on the intuitive idea that a reasonable value of achievable ζ_L lies roughly midway between ζ and ζ_F. The results are displayed in Table I.

TABLE I
SEVERAL SCHEDULES ACHIEVED BY SYNTHESES IN WHICH THE DESIRED ζ_L IS 0.9250

Train-work schedule			Work ratio	The achieved ζ_L
N_t	N_w	N_r	N_w/N_r	
	0	0	7.10	
6	6	1	6	0.9201
7	10	2	5	0.9202
9	15	4	3.75	0.9206
12	18	7	2.57	0.9215
15	19	10	1.90	0.9221
25	20	20	1	
∞	20	∞	0	

The fourth column in this table gives the "work ratio" N_w/N_r for each schedule. As predicted, the work ratio decreases monotonically as the work-retrain period increases.

Using the same approximation techniques, we found that if the work ratio is to exceed unity and if $\delta = \epsilon$, then δ must lie in the interval $0 \le \delta < 0.077$ in order to achieve $\zeta_L = 0.9250$. We found that for this range of δ the maximum error of the weak-coupling approximation is less than 2.5 percent. These results suggest that the weak-coupling approximation will be valid whenever the coupling is weak enough to permit "reasonable" values of ζ_L to be achieved by work ratios greater than unity.

We tested the RC-circuit approximation by computing ζ_L for $N_t = 3, 6, 7$, and 16, keeping N_w and N_r fixed at $N_w = 6$ and $N_r = 1$. We found that the effect of this range of values of N_t on the computed values of ζ_L is less than 0.1 percent. This lends support to the RC-circuit approximation as a design tool.

IX. Trainable vs. Fixed Detectors

One reason for using a trainable rather than fixed detector is the unpredictability of the channel modes. The designer may know the statistics of both modes completely—i.e., he may know the constituent densities of modes $\mathcal{A}$ and $\mathcal{B}$—and he may know the mode-to-mode transition probabilities exactly. Yet in many cases he will find that a trainable detector on a train-work cycle will give better performance than *any* fixed detector. For some cases, however, a fixed detector can be better than any periodically trained detector, provided the threshold is properly chosen.

Figure 12 illustrates this situation for the two-mode channel of Fig. 10 under the constraint of (25) and (26) and under the assumption $\gamma = \frac{1}{2}$. The unbroken curves

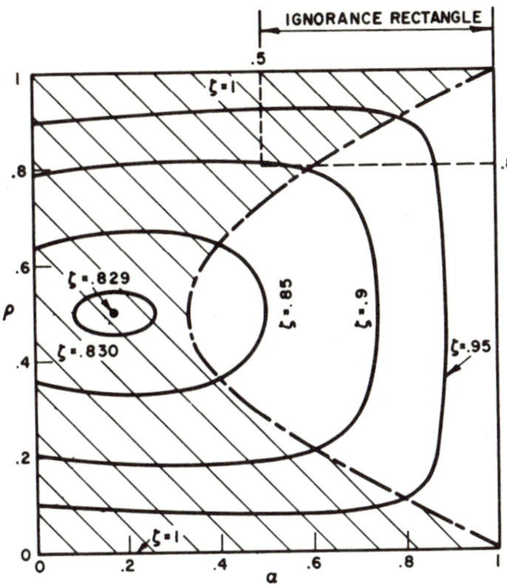

Fig. 12. ζ contours for the two-mode *TLP*, $\gamma = \frac{1}{2}$.

are the contours of constant asymptotic success probability, $\zeta \triangleq z(\infty)$, plotted on the $\alpha\rho$ plane. The quantity ζ is the probability of a correct guess after infinite training on the two-mode channel. In the shaded region of Fig. 12, ζ is larger than the success probability of any fixed-threshold detector. In the unshaded region, however, a threshold of $k = 2$ will yield success probabilities larger than that of an infinitely trained TLP. (A derivation of these properties has been given elsewhere [13].)

Recall that $(\alpha, \rho) = (0.6, 0.9)$ in the numerical example. Since this point falls in the shaded region of Fig. 12, a trainable detector for this (α, ρ) will have an asymptotic performance superior to that of any fixed detector.

The unshaded region in Fig. 12 occupies a substantial fraction, about one-third, of the $\alpha\rho$ square. (We define the $\alpha\rho$ square as the region of the $\alpha\rho$ plane satisfying $0 \leq \alpha \leq 1, 0 \leq \rho \leq 1$.) This fraction, we believe, will be smaller in cases where the distance between the constituent modes' optimum thresholds is greater than the example of Fig. 10. In other words, if the optimum thresholds of the two modes are substantially different, and if the a priori probabilities of (α, ρ) are distributed uniformly over the $\alpha\rho$ square, then the chance is strong that the best trained detector is better than the best fixed detector.

X. Synthesis in the Face of Ignorance

In Section IX we pointed out that important applications of trainable detectors occur in situations where the channel moves unpredictably among two or more modes. In the numerical example a trainable detector was shown to be better than any fixed detector, even though all the channel statistics were known.

Another application of trainable detectors occurs in situations where the channel statistics are unknown. The designer's ignorance can take a variety of forms. He may be ignorant of the constituent modes' statistics, he may be ignorant of the statistics of the mode-to-mode fluctuations, or he may be ignorant of the number of modes in the channel. In all of these cases, a trainable detector is usually better than a fixed detector.

Consider, for example, the channel of Fig. 10 under the constraints of (25) and (26). Assume that the exact values of $\alpha, \beta, \delta, \epsilon$ are not known. More specifically, assume that $0.5 \leq \alpha \leq 1$, $0.8 \leq \rho \leq 0.1$, $\delta = \epsilon$. An important consideration in the synthesis of a train-work schedule is the asymptotic success probability ζ. Since δ and ϵ are small, the weak-coupling approximation equation (15) is applicable, and ζ may be calculated from the ζ's of the constituent modes. That is,

$$\zeta = \tfrac{1}{2}(\zeta_{A_0} + \zeta_{B_0}) \tag{27}$$

where ζ_{A_0} is the success probability of the threshold detector after infinite training in mode $\mathcal{A}$. (When using (15), recall that $\gamma = \epsilon/(\delta + \epsilon) = \frac{1}{2}$.) In our earlier paper [9] we presented contours of ζ on the $\alpha\rho$ square for single-mode TLPs of the same type as the constituent modes in Fig. 10. These contours may be combined by (27) to yield composite contours for the two-mode case. The resulting contours are given in Fig. 12.

Another important consideration in the synthesis of train-work schedules is learning time or some measure of the slowness of learning. One such measure is the number of samples consumed by the slowest eigenfunction in $z(n)$ to decay to one-tenth of its initial value. This quantity, which we call ν, is reasonably easy to compute [9]. In our earlier paper are presented contours of ν on the $\alpha\rho$ plane for single-mode TLPs of the same type as the constituent modes in Fig. 10. These contours are reproduced here in Fig. 13. By (15), we see that, at least for small δ and ϵ, the two-mode learning time is approximately the larger of the learning times of the constituent modes. By Fig. 10 and 13, we see that this learning time must lie on the line $\alpha = 1$, $0.8 \leq \rho \leq 1$.

Recall that (α, ρ) lies somewhere in the "ignorance rectangle" $0.5 \leq \alpha \leq 1$, $0.8 \leq \rho \leq 1$. In Fig. 12, we see that the smallest ζ in this rectangle occurs at $(\alpha, \rho) = (0.5, 0.8)$. Furthermore, since the shaded portion of the rectangle covers more area than the unshaded portion, a trainable detector with an appropriate train-work cycle is likely to be better than any fixed detector.

In Fig. 13, we see that the longest learning time—namely, infinity—occurs at $(\alpha, \epsilon) = (1, 1)$. However, we need not consider this possibility, because $z(0) = \rho$ when $\alpha = 1$. Hence we need only consider the ν's lying on the line segment $\alpha = 1$, $0.8 \leq \rho \leq \zeta_L$, where the value of ζ_L may be chosen somewhere between the smallest ζ in the ignorance rectangle and the ζ_F computed from (17). Then the longest learning time we need consider occurs at $(\alpha, \rho) = (1, \zeta_L)$.

To design the train-work cycle we suggest a worst-case approach. Synthesize two train-work schedules by the method illustrated in Section VIII: one schedule for

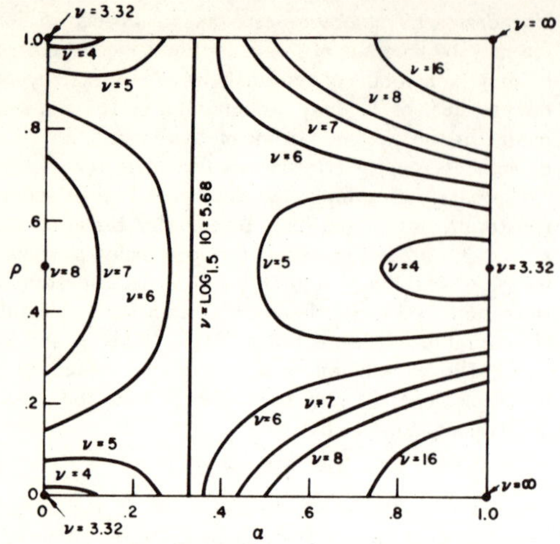

Fig. 13. ν-contours for the constituent modes.

$(\alpha, \rho) = (0.5, 0.8)$ and the other schedule for $(\alpha, \rho) = (1, \zeta_L)$. In both cases, assume $\delta = \epsilon = 0.1$. Denote the two schedules by $(N_{t_1}, N_{w_1}, N_{r_1})$ and $(N_{t_2}, N_{w_2}, N_{r_2})$. For the final schedule, (N_t, N_w, N_r), use

$$N_t = \text{Max}(N_{t_1}, N_{t_2})$$

$$N_w = \text{Min}(N_{w_1}, N_{w_2})$$

$$N_r = \text{Max}(N_{r_1}, N_{r_2}).$$

This schedule will accommodate fluctuations between any two modes of the type described by Fig. 10 and (25) and (26) for any α, ρ in the ignorance rectangle and for any δ, ϵ satisfying $0 \leq \delta = \epsilon \leq 0.1$.

In our earlier paper we showed how trainable TLPs maintain acceptable ζ's over a larger part of the $\alpha\rho$ square than fixed-threshold detectors [9]. Consequently a worst-case approach to the synthesis of single-mode TLPs will usually yield better performance over a given ignorance rectangle than a fixed detector. The same situation holds in the case of trainable vs. fixed detectors on a two-mode channel.

XI. Conclusions

We have shown how the performance wave (or learning wave) of a two-mode TLP may be represented by a Markov chain, and how the performance wave of the two-mode TLP is related to the constituent one-mode TLPs. We have seen that under the weak-coupling condition the performance wave of a two-mode TLP is a linear sum of the performance waves of the constituent one-mode TLPs.

A method of analyzing the train-work dynamics of two-mode TLPs was described. We found that the final success probability in a working phase of any two-mode Markov chain (of which the two-mode TLP is a special case) cannot be less than one-half of the success probability at the beginning of that phase.

A simplified method of designing train-work schedules is possible in cases where the "*RC*-circuit approximation" is applicable. In these cases, the ratio of working time to retraining time yielding a desired performance level is maximized when the work-retrain period is made as small as possible.

The numerical example suggests that the *RC*-circuit approximation, together with the weak-coupling approximation, provide a convenient technique for synthesizing train-work schedules for two-mode TLPs whenever the work ratio N_w/N_r exceeds unity.

We showed how trainable detectors can be superior to fixed detectors even when the channel statistics are known exactly, provided the channel moves randomly among two or more modes.

We indicated how a worst-case approach to the synthesis of train-work schedules can exploit the adaptive properties of trainable detectors to overcome not only the unpredictability of the mode, but also the designer's ignorance of the channel statistics.

Acknowledgment

The author is indebted to his colleagues at RCA Labs.: particularly to H. J. Kishi for pointing out the burst-noise problem, and to K. R. Kaplan and J. Wilder for several general discussions.

References

[1] Lawson, J. L., and G. E. Uhlenbeck, *Threshold Signals.* New York: McGraw-Hill, 1950, ch. 7.
[2] Peterson, W. W., J. G. Birdsall, and W. C. Fox, The theory of signal detectability, *IRE Trans. on Information Theory,* vol IT-4, Sep 1954, pp 171–212.
[3] Chow, C. K., An optimum character recognition system using decision functions, *IRE Trans. on Electronic Computers,* vol EC-6, Dec 1957, pp 247–254.
[4] Norman, D. A., Stochastic learning and a quantal model of signal detection, in *Discrete Adaptive Processes—Symposium and Panel Discussion,* J. Sklansky Ed. New York: AIEE, 1962.
[5] Swets, J. A., Information retrieval systems, *Science,* vol 141, no 3577, Jul 1963, pp 245–250.
[6] Gilbert, E. N., Capacity of a burst-noise channel, *Bell Sys. Tech. J.,* vol 39, Sep 1960, pp 1253–1266.
[7] Sklansky, J., Adaptation, learning, self-repair, and feedback, *IEEE Spectrum,* May 1964, pp 172–174.
[8] ——, Adaptation theory—A tutorial introduction to current research, *RCA Engineer,* Apr–May 1965, pp 24–30.
[9] ——, A Markov chain model of adaptive signal detection, Pre-prints 1963 Bionics Symp., Air Force Systems Command, Wright-Patterson Air Force Base, Ohio.
[10] Tsetlin, M. L., On the behavior of finite automata in random media, *Automatika i Telemekhanika,* vol 22, no 10, Oct 1961, pp 1345–1354. (English translation in *Automation and Remote Control,* pp 1210–1219.)
[11] Varshavskii, V. I., and I. P. Vorontsova, On the behavior of stochastic automata with a variable structure, *Automatika i Telemekhanika,* vol 24, no 3, Mar 1963, pp 353–360. (English translation in *Automation and Remote Control,* pp 327–333.)
[12] Krylov, V. Y., On one automaton that is asymptotically optimal in a random medium, *Automatika i Telemakhanika,* vol 24, no 9, Sep 1963, pp 1226–1228. (English translation in *Automation and Remote Control,* pp 1114–1116.)
[13] Sklansky, J., Two-mode threshold learning, Tech. Documentary Rept. No. AMRL-TDR-64-39, Aerospace Medical Research Labs., Wright-Patterson Air Force Base, Ohio, May 1964.
[14] Huggins, W. H., Signal flow graphs and random signals, *Proc. IRE,* vol 45, Jan 1957, pp 74–86.
[15] Kaplan, K. R., and J. Sklansky, Analysis of Markov chain models of adaptive processes, Tech. Documentary Rept. No. AMRL-TDR-65-00, Aerospace Medical Research Labs., Wright-Patterson Air Force Base, Ohio, 1965.

Image Processing

V

Editor's Comments on Papers 18 Through 23

One of the most important types of patterns in recognition technology is the pictorial pattern. In fact, other types of patterns (e.g., sound patterns) are often transformed into two-dimensional pictorial patterns to facilitate analysis by humans. Hence an important branch of recognition technology is that of transforming pictures into forms that are readily analyzed by machines and/or humans. We refer to this branch as "image processing." Much of image processing has been concerned with (1) enhancement of pictures for improved human viewing, (2) compression of pictures for efficient communication of pictorial data, (3) transformation of continuous-tone pictures into line drawings, and (4) analysis of two-valued pictures by computer.

So far, the great majority of the important contributions to automatic image processing have been primarily or exclusively concerned with two-valued pictures (i.e., pictures represented by symbols from a two-valued alphabet—typically 0's and 1's). Dineen's paper [Din], the first paper in this part, contains one of the earliest descriptions of parallel algorithms for analyzing pictures by computer.

The next two papers, by Freeman [Fre] and by Sklansky, Chazen, and Hansen [Skl-1], describe schemes for representing on a computer line drawings and the edges of silhouettes. Freeman's representation, a sequence of unit vectors called the "chain code," is particularly efficient when the represented curves are complex and involuted. Sklansky et al.'s representation, the "minimum-perimeter polygon," is particularly efficient when the curves are smooth and relatively simple; it has the special advantage of taking account of digitization in its description of closed curves [Skl-1, Skl-4].

One of the important ways of summarizing a two-valued picture is to replace all the thick lines by thin lines. Another approach is to imagine that each object in the picture is composed of a "skeleton" and "flesh," and to use the skeleton as a summary of the object. This approach has been formalized in the notion of the "distance skeleton" and in various "thinning algorithms." The next two selections discuss these techniques.

The first of these two papers, by Rosenfeld and Pfaltz [Rose], defines the distance skeleton in precise terms and presents an algorithm for finding distance skeletons for arbitrary two-valued pictures. Their definition of distance skeleton has the special advantage that the flesh can be fully determined from the skeleton. Their algorithm for finding the skeleton has the advantage of being a parallel computation. Parallelism in a computation contributes to the simplicity of the implementation of the algorithm on present-day digital computers and, of course, provides support for the future development of parallel-structured picture-processing computers (discussed further in Part VI).

The next selection by Hilditch [Hil], presents an algorithm for thinning arbitrarily shaped digitized silhouettes. This algorithm has two special advantages: (1) it produces a line figure whose connectivity is the same as the original silhouette, and (2) it can operate effectively on images whose range of gray levels is greater than two.

An optical technique for character recognition by spatial filtering was introduced by Vander Lugt in the last paper of this part [Van]. Since the appearance of this paper in 1964, spatial filtering and its modern descendent, holography, have been used for several forms of enhancement and recognition of pictures.

Reprinted from *Proc. Western Joint Comput. Conf.*, Los Angeles, 1955, pp. 94–100

18

Programming Pattern Recognition*

G. P. DINNEEN†

EVERYONE LIKES to speculate, and recently there has been a lot of talk about reading machines and hearing machines. We know it is possible to simulate speech. This raises lots of interesting questions such as: If the machines can speak, will they squawk when you ask them to divide by zero? And can two machines carry on an intelligent conversation, say in Gaelic? And, of course, there is the expression "electronic brain" and the question, Do machines think? These questions are more philosophical than technical and I am going to duck them.

Over the past months in a series of after-hour and luncheon meetings, a group of us at the laboratory have speculated on problems in this area. Our feeling, pretty much unanimously, was that there is a real *need* to get practical, to pick a real live problem and go after it. As the title of this session suggests, we picked pattern recognition. Selfridge has already explored some of the implications of this problem and indicated at least three levels of complexity.

Selfridge and I have begun an investigation of one aspect of pattern recognition, that is, the recognition of simple visual patterns. Consider, for example, how many different representations of the block capital A we recognize as A. A great number of variations in such things as orientation, thickness, and size can occur without loss of identity. Our real live problem then is to design a machine which will recognize patterns. We shall call any possible visual image, no matter how cluttered or indistinct, a configuration. A pattern is an equivalence class consisting of all those configurations which cause the same output in the machine. For example, if the machine had just two outputs, yes and no, then one pattern would be all those inputs which caused the machine to say no.

The visual patterns we have used in our experiments have been mostly block capital A's and O's, and some squares and triangles. Why did we choose letters? Probably because of the interest in reading machines. Why A and O? Perhaps because O upside down is still O, like radar spelled backwards. Capital letters and geometric figures seem like a good start. Straight lines are too simple and most other things, such as faces, are too complicated. Let me emphasize again that we are not trying to build an efficient reading machine, but rather to study how such a machine might work.

* The research in this document was supported jointly by the Army, Navy, and Air Force under contract with the Massachusetts Institute of Technology.

† Lincoln Laboratory, Massachusetts Institute of Technology, Lexington, Mass.

Our theory of pattern recognition is that it is possible to reduce by means of a sequence of simple operations a configuration to a single number, or by means of a set of such sequences to a set of numbers. We believe that for the proper sequences, almost all of the configurations belonging to a given pattern reduce to the same number or set of numbers. At least one of the operations of this machine must be a counting operation.

A machine for pattern recognition should place a configuration, such as one representation of the block capital A, into its proper equivalence class. The decision as to what things belong to an equivalence class or pattern is made at this stage by the designer. The machine must extract the essential characteristics of the configuration in order to recognize the pattern to which it belongs.

One of the first steps is the design of basic operations which the machine uses to reduce the input image. Although this is a preliminary and experimental phase of the study, the results obtained have been very interesting and extremely valuable in formulating future studies. For this reason, it seems worthwhile to discuss these results now.

The problem we have stated is not basically arithmetic, and it is not even clear that a machine for pattern recognition should be completely digital. However, one of the very important applications of a high-speed digital computer is the *simulation* of just such problems. We have used MTC—the Memory Test Computer—at Lincoln Laboratory for our investigation.

The Image

From now on, we are considering the simulation of this problem on MTC. The first problem is "how does MTC see the image?" The field of view is a 90×90 array (Fig. 1). A picture is constructed by making each of the 8,100 cells black or white, similar to a newspaper photograph, except that there are only two gradations in intensity, zero to one. If black is interpreted as one and white as zero, and storage registers are assigned to the 90×90 array, six to a row, as in Fig. 2, a simple image may be described by giving the contents of the 540 register as octal numbers. A flexowriter tape giving the contents of 540 registers is read into the machine and the visual image is thus stored by the computer. We chose a 90×90 array because we wanted the image to be as large as was practical in terms of computer storage. The larger the image, of course, the greater the resolution and the variety of inputs.

For purposes of pattern recognition, certain basic

operations will be performed on the input image. Each operation performs a mapping of the input image, or working image. The result of this mapping is also stored in the machine. Thus another bank of 540 registers is required for storage of this new image. If a sequence of operations is to be performed, then the transformed image is transferred back to the input storage or working image after each operation. If it is desired to retain the original image, then three banks are required, as shown in Fig. 3.

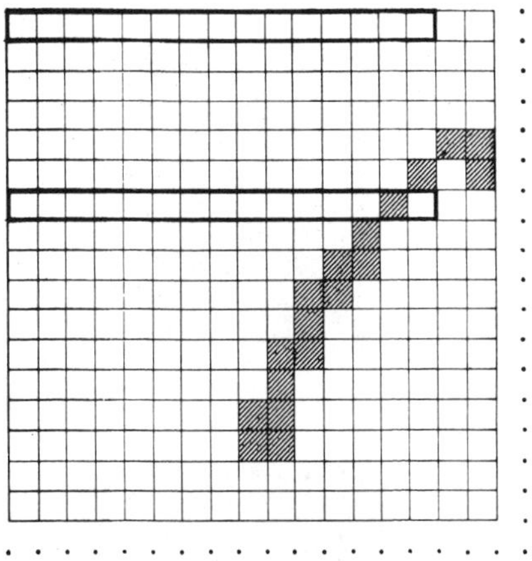

Fig. 1—90×90 input array.

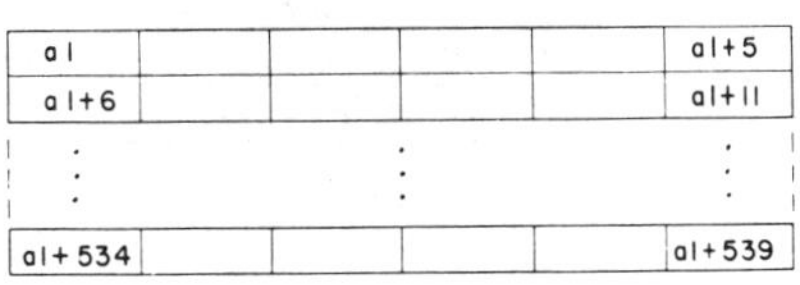

Fig. 2—The input image.

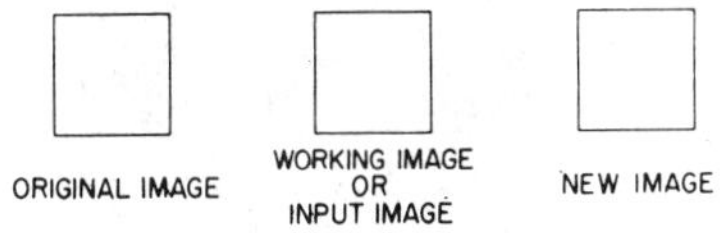

Fig. 3

Averaging Operation

The first of the basic operations is an averaging operation which was designed to eliminate spurious noise and to smooth irregularities in the image. The point of this operation is that those elements or cells which agree with their neighbors are unchanged, but those which do not are changed. The notion is that the resulting image is more homogeneous. The averaging operation is performed by observing the contents of all the elements in some $n \times n$ square surrounding an element. In Fig. 4 we are considering element a_{ij}, thus we look at the elements in the 5×5 square surrounding it. Let us agree to call this square a "window." To complete the operation we count the number of ones in this window and compare the total with some threshold. If the count is greater than or equal to the threshold then the corresponding element in the new image, a_{ij}' is "one," otherwise $a_{ij}'=0$. For example, a zero surrounded by all zeros remains zero, but a zero surrounded by some ones may become zero or one, depending on the threshold.

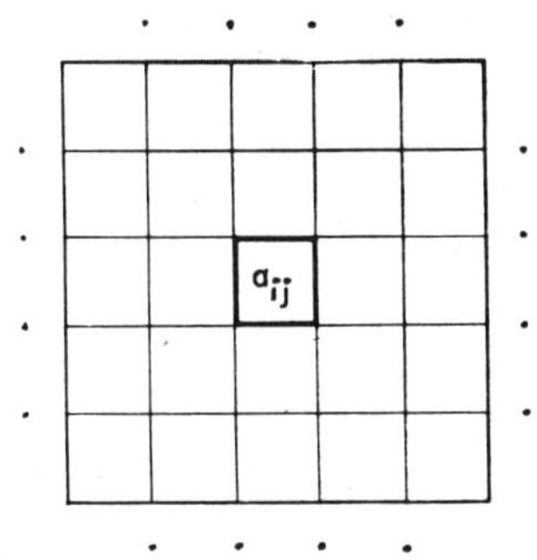

Fig. 4—Averaging operation.

The first averaging operation uses a 5×5 square. A count of the number of ones inside this square is made (Fig. 4).

$$N = \sum_{m=-2}^{+2} \sum_{n=-2}^{+2} a_{i+m,j+n}.$$

The N is compared with the threshold T and

$$N \geqq T \qquad a_{ij}' = 1$$

$$N < T \qquad a_{ij}' = 0.$$

The threshold T is held constant over the entire working image.

Results of the Averaging Operation

A large number of experimental runs were made using the computer to test the operation. As predicted, averaging with a 5×5 window and a threshold of 5 eliminated scattered "ones" and filled in holes. Fig. 5 is an input image, and Fig. 6 is the same image after this averaging operation. These are photographs of one of the MTC scopes.

Fig. 5—A3, input image.

Fig. 6—A3, after averaging with threshold 5.

For a low threshold, such as 5 for a 5×5 window, the image will be thickened. As the threshold is raised a thinning takes place. This is evident in Figs. 7 through 11. It is particularly significant that for a threshold of 15, the corner point and two junction points are isolated. The same phenomenon is shown in Figs. 12 through 17. The thick A of Fig. 18 has a blank strip and one small hole. For the low thresholds these irregularities are removed and for the high thresholds they are emphasized, as shown in Figs. 18 through 25.

Fig. 7—A4, input image.

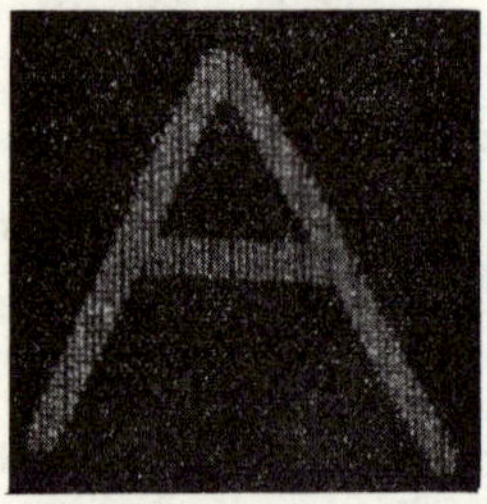

Fig. 8—A4, after averaging with threshold 5.

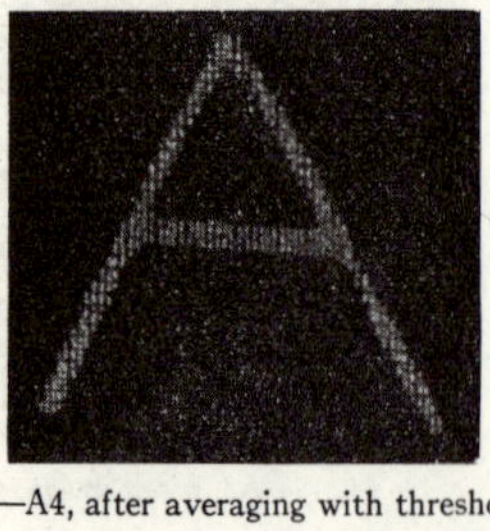

Fig. 9—A4, after averaging with threshold 10.

Fig. 10—A4, after averaging with threshold 13.

Fig. 11—A4, after averaging with threshold 15.

Fig. 12—A5, input image.

Fig. 13—A5, after averaging with threshold 5.

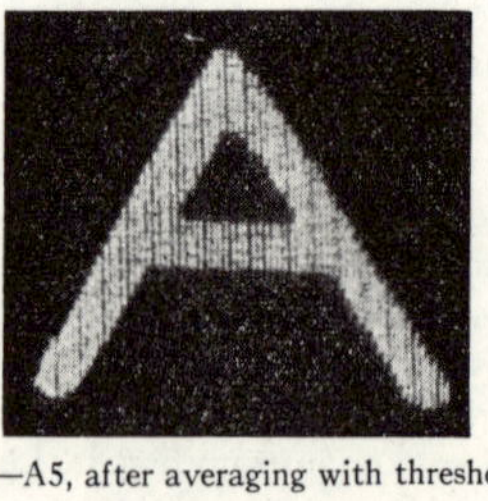

Fig. 14—A5, after averaging with threshold 10.

Fig. 15—A5, after averaging with threshold 15

Fig. 16—A5, after averaging with threshold 20.

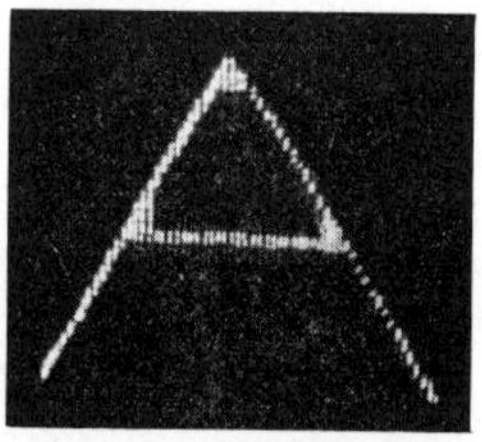

Fig. 17—A5, after averaging with threshold 25.

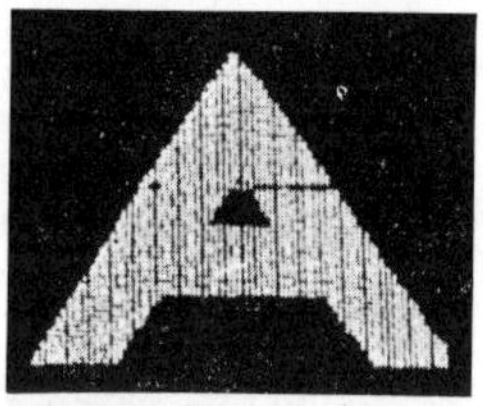

Fig. 18—A6, input image.

Fig. 19—A6, after averaging with threshold 3.

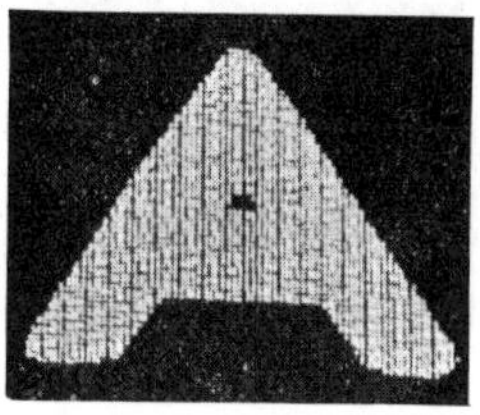

Fig. 20—A6, after averaging with threshold 5.

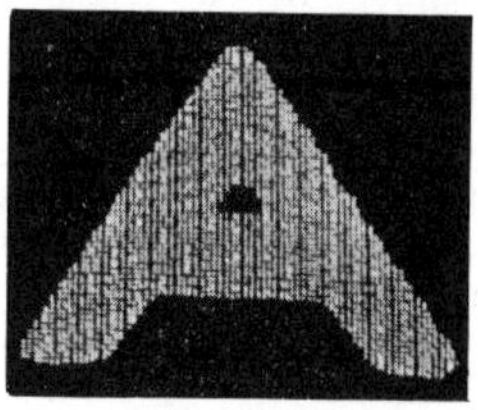

Fig. 21—A6, after averaging with threshold 10.

Fig. 22—A6, after averaging with threshold 15.

Fig. 23—A6, after averaging with threshold 20.

Fig. 24—A6, after averaging with threshold 22.

Fig. 25—A6, after averaging with threshold 25.

We see that for rough smoothing we like a low threshold, and for thinning we like a high threshold. Our notion of sequence of operations is now brought to mind. For if a letter such as the last one were first averaged with a low threshold the gaps would be filled. Then successive averaging with a higher threshold would thin the letter. The problems one encounters in this next phase are apparent. How often should these operations be repeated? What thresholds should be used?

You will have noticed that although the transformation is not sensitive to small changes in the threshold, large changes have a major effect. To attack the problem of setting the threshold, we have considered another averaging operation where the threshold for the small 5×5 window is determined by the degree of homogenity inside a larger window, say 15×15. In particular, for each cell we count the number of ones inside a 15×15 window surrounding it and use this number to set the threshold for the 5×5 window. This is like an automatic gain control. When the 15×15 window is very dense, we use a high threshold, and conversely. This operation has been tried and the results look favorable, but unfortunately we have no photographs yet.

An Edging Operation

The edging operation, quite unlike the averaging operation, preserves elements which are centers of asymmetry, that is, those which are located in the regions of discontinuity of the image. The operation sharpens differences. It picks out the edges of letters and for certain choices of thresholds locates the corners, junctions, and end points of letters. This operation is performed by observing the contents of all the elements in some $n \times n$ square surrounding an element which is one; zeros remain zero. In Fig. 26 we are considering element a_{ij}.

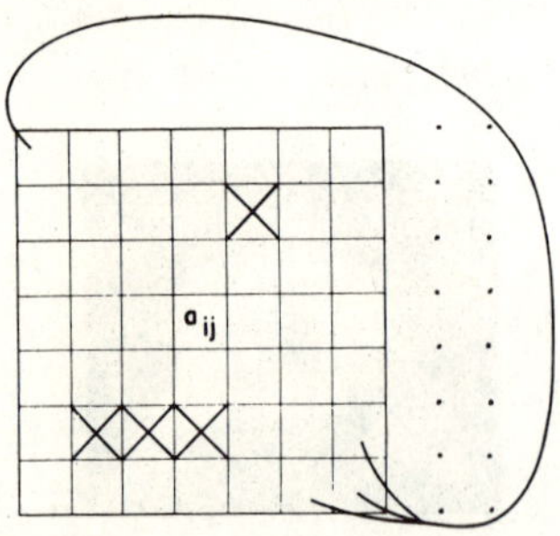

Fig. 26—The edging operation.

The edging operation is like a two-dimensional derivative, since we count changes about the center element. In particular, we scan the elements in the 7×7 window starting at $a_{i-3,j-3}$. When we reach a "one" we observe the three diagonally opposite elements in the same ring. If these are all zero we count one, otherwise we count zero. We consider the three diagonally opposite bins so that lines with small curvature give a zero count of differences. After the entire window has been scanned, with the exception of element a_{ij}, the total count of differences is compared with a threshold T. If the count is greater than the threshold, we enter a one in the element a_{ij}' of the new image. If the count is less than or equal to the threshold, we enter a "zero" in the element a_{ij}' of the new image. To fix the threshold, we first count the total number of ones in the window and take some proportion of this as the threshold. A further modification of this operation is the weighting of the count of differences depending on the ring, that is, we put weight W_1 on the elements in the first ring around the element a_{ij}, W_2 for the second ring, and so on. To identify this operation, we must specify the size of the window, the weighting, and the threshold.

We first tried an edging operation which used a 7×7 window with a weight of two on all differences which occur in the first and second ring, and a weight of one on all differences in the outer ring. The total number of ones in the 7×7 window, exclusive of the center element, will be denoted by N. The threshold T of the operation was taken to be $(j/8) \cdot N$ for $j = 0, 1, 2, \cdots, 8$.

Results of the Edging Operation

In testing the edging operation we were interested in its ability to pick out singular points, that is, junction points, end points, corners in the case of letters, and in its ability to transform the input image into a new image where only the outline remains.

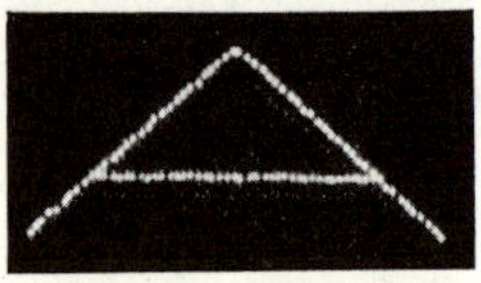

Fig. 27—Thin A.

For an input image, Fig. 27, edging with thresholds 2/8, 4/8, and 6/8 of the ring total isolates the singular points as shown in Figs. 28, 29, and 30. Edging with a threshold of 0/8 of the ring total is equivalent to removing only those points which are centers of symmetry. This effect is shown in Fig. 31 for the input image of Fig. 12. The outline of the letter is shown in Fig. 32, the result of edging with a threshold of 2/8 times the ring

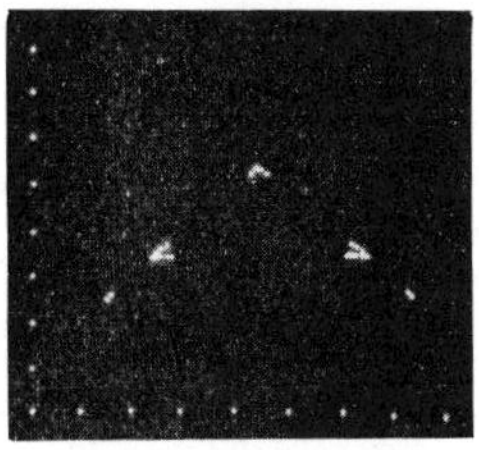

Fig. 28—Edging with threshold 2/8.

Fig. 29—Edging with threshold 4/8.

Fig. 30—Edging with threshold 6/8.

Fig. 31—Edging with threshold 0/8.

Fig. 32—Edging with threshold 2/8.

total. For a thick *A* (see Fig. 18) the results are shown in Figs. 33 through 35. It is significant that the irregularities are emphasized for low thresholds and suppressed for the high thresholds. Figs. 36 through 39 demonstrate the way corners are isolated in a square and the edging effect for a 0 is shown in Figs. 39 and 40.

Fig. 33—Edging with threshold 0/8.

Fig. 34—Edging with threshold 4/8.

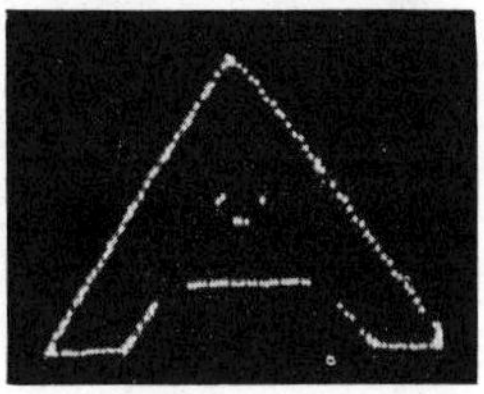

Fig. 35—Edging with threshold 6/8.

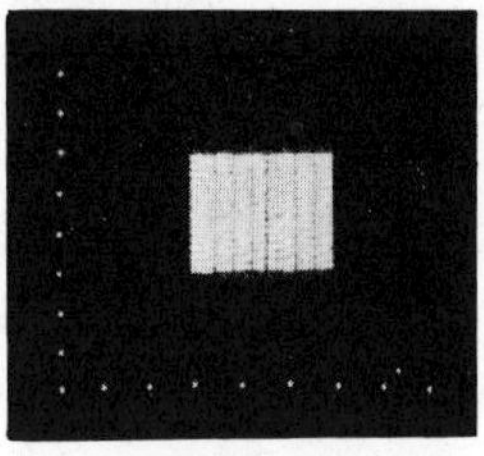

Fig. 36—Square.

Fig. 37—Edging with threshold 4/8.

Fig. 38—Edging with threshold 8/8.

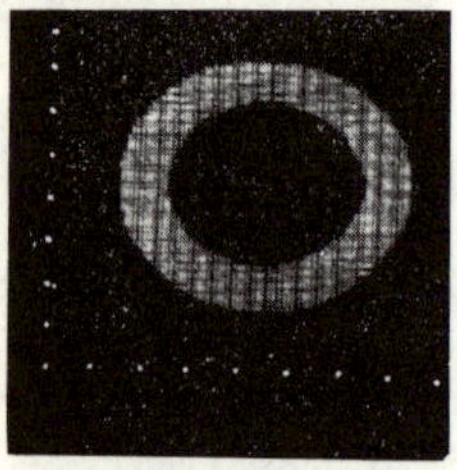

Fig. 39—Thick 0.

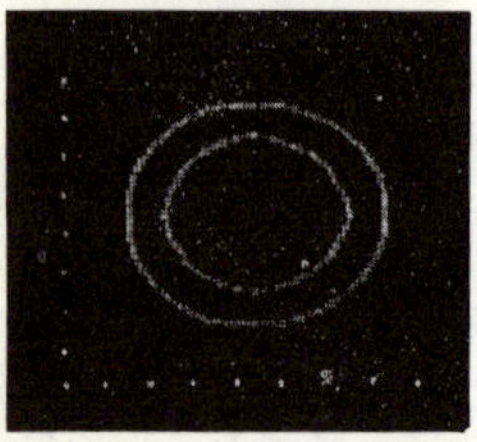

Fig. 40—Edging with threshold 2/8.

Other Operations

Before I say anything about new operations, a word about our reasons for these first two operations is in order. We tried to pick operations which were simple in structure and unrelated to particular patterns. In other words, we avoided special operations which might work very well for A's and O's, but not very well for other shapes. There is evidence in neurophysiology, moreover, that both averaging and edging of visual images are performed by the nervous system of many animals.

Many other operations have been proposed but I would like to discuss just one of these. Selfridge talked about identifying a letter by counting blobs. By blob we mean a region of ones with no separation of more than one cell. For example, there were five blobs in Fig. 29. A blob counter is then simply an operation which counts these blobs. We propose to do this by scanning the image until a one is reached. Then a rectangle with a perimeter two cells wide will be constructed and gradually enlarged until the entire perimeter is empty. Thus the blob is isolated and counted.

Certainly some operation to measure curvature will be needed, as well as some way to describe relative positions of blobs.

Although the first two operations are very simple, the coding of the program is quite complicated. This is due to a large extent to the necessity of using the individual bits of the storage registers as independent storage bins. We need a lot of shifting and cycling; the simple averaging operation takes about 300 instructions and requires about 20 seconds a letter. The two window averaging takes about 400 instructions and requires about 4 minutes. The edging requires 700 registers of instructions and takes 2 minutes.

Conclusion

In his paper, Selfridge has given our model for pattern recognition. I think we have shown that even with just two simple operations, a sequence can be found such that some A's can be reduced to five blobs. One of our next tasks will be to choose such a sequence, try it on many A's, and plot the distribution of the number of blobs. In this way we shall determine the useful sequences. This leads naturally to the next phase of the study, which is the study of the model for pattern recognition.

Acknowledgment

For their advice and encouragement, I wish to thank J. V. Harrington, I. S. Reed, O. G. Selfridge, H. Sherman, and G. E. Valley, who participated in the seminar which launched this study. It would have been impossible to obtain the experimental results without the excellent assistance of Miss B. Jensen and Mrs. M. Kannel in programming, coding, and operating the Memory Test Computer. I wish to acknowledge the excellent co-operation of those responsible for the operation of the Memory Test Computer.

Reprinted from *IRE Trans. Electron. Comput.*, **EC–10,** No. 2, 1961, pp. 260–268

On the Encoding of Arbitrary Geometric Configurations* 19

HERBERT FREEMAN†, SENIOR MEMBER, IRE

Summary—**A method is described which permits the encoding of arbitrary geometric configurations so as to facilitate their analysis and manipulation by means of a digital computer. It is shown that one can determine through the use of relatively simple numerical techniques whether a given arbitrary plane curve is open or closed, whether it is singly or multiply connected, and what area it encloses. Further, one can cause a given figure to be expanded, contracted, elongated, or rotated by an arbitrary amount. It is shown that there are a number of ways of encoding arbitrary geometric curves to facilitate such manipulations, each having its own particular advantages and disadvantages. One method, the so-called rectangular-array type of encoding, is discussed in detail. In this method the slope function is quantized into a set of eight standard slopes. This particular representation is one of the simplest and one that is most readily utilized with present-day computing and display equipment.**

Introduction

CONCOMITANT with present-day advances in the fields of control and communications, a growing need is being felt for precise means of describing arbitrary geometric configurations. This need arises in two ways: 1) from the desire to communicate geometric information, and 2) from the requirement for analysis and synthesis of geometric configurations.

If one wishes to transmit the outline of a lake, the information relating to the contour must first be identified (a description process) and then encoded in a manner which permits efficient transmission. Decoding and reconstruction of the contour in terms of a pictorial representation is required at the receiving end of the transmission. The twin objectives of communication are efficient transmission and faithful reproduction. Any scheme for communicating geometric information must be able to withstand critical examination on these objectives.

The analysis and synthesis of arbitrary geometric configurations have, until recently, received only scant attention; the tedium of lengthy hand computation was too discouraging. With the availability of modern high-speed digital computers, however, labor of computation is no longer a deterrent. Thus it is now entirely feasible to use a computer to determine the surface area of a lake from its contour, or, given a set of past weather maps, to compute a most probable future weather map. One need merely develop the necessary algorithms for the computer and devise methods for encoding the geometric information in a way which will facilitate such analysis.

* Received by the PGEC, August 8, 1960; revised manuscript received, January 27, 1961.

† Dept. of Elec. Engrg., New York University, New York, N. Y.

An arbitrary geometric curve is a curve which is pictorially defined (*e.g.*, the outline of a knife), but for which no analytic description exists. It thus differs from a mathematical (or nonarbitrary) curve, such as a triangle, sine wave, or hypocycloid, which can be precisely formulated in mathematical terms. A circle is a mathematical curve perfectly described by a simple equation. In contrast, a wheel is an arbitrary geometric curve which, to a certain limited degree of precision, can be approximated (described) by a circle. If one desires descriptions which will take into account more and more of the wheel's minute irregularities, the descriptions must become progressively more complex and unwieldy.

Description Processes

Consider the problem of describing arbitrary geometric curves to permit their transmission over a telegraph communication link or their manipulation by a digital computer. The curves are assumed to be continuous plane curves, open or closed, and either singly or multiply connected. One approach to this problem is to cut the curve into arbitrarily fine segments and then to approximate each segment with a standardized mathematical curve.

The segmentation of curves raises some important questions. Should the segments be large and few in number, or should they be small and much greater in number? If the former, the mathematical representation of the segments will be relatively complex (*e.g.*, high-order polynomials may be required), while, if the latter, a straight-line approximation will suffice. Further, should the segments all be equal or should segmentation be dependent on the curve itself? Uniform segmentation has the advantage of simplicity; however, segmentation which is based on the properties of a particular curve may lead to more efficient encoding.

An encoding scheme for arbitrary geometric curves should be simple, highly standardized, and universally applicable to all continuous curves. Further, the encoding scheme should be such that it facilitates digital computer analysis of curve properties. For these reasons subsequent discussion will be limited to straight-line segmentation using either a single length or a small number of standard lengths. It is not intended to imply that other approaches are without merit; their consideration will, however, be outside the scope of this paper.

A question that arises at once concerns the fineness to which a curve is to be segmented. Consider the curve of Fig. 1, drawn in the x-y plane. One may introduce a parameter t which will be a measure of distance along the curve as the curve is traversed in the direction indicated, beginning at the starting point x_0y_0. This makes it possible to represent the original curve by two parametric curves, $x(t)$ and $y(t)$, as shown in Fig. 2.

Approximating a plane curve with straight-line segments is a sampling-type operation, and its validity can be tested by means of the sampling theorem. This can be done by obtaining the Fourier transforms of the two parametric curves and examining their frequency spectra. Generally, the frequency spectra will be infinite, with progressively increasing attenuation of the higher-frequency components. A qualitative interpretation of the sampling theorem states that the sampling interval T must be less than one half the reciprocal of the highest significant frequency component. If the precision of representation is to be such that over a square-meter x-y plane any errors in location of points on the curve will not exceed one millimeter, one may refer to the representation as having a precision of 60 db. In a loose sense this can be carried over into the frequency spectrum, where components which are attenuated 60 db or more may then be considered insignificant.

Once the desired segment-length T has been determined, one may replace the original arbitrary curve with a curve consisting of a chain of straight-line segments of length T. The curve can then be described simply by a sequence of angles and a standard distance. When reconstructing the curve from the given data, the scale can be arbitrarily selected by choosing the appropriate standard length. A coded representation of

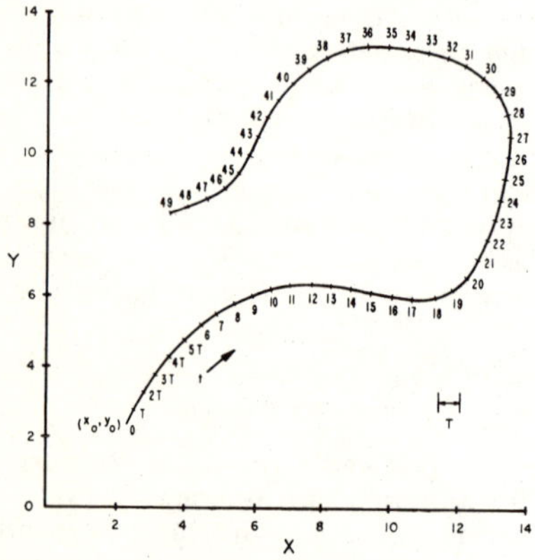

Fig. 1—Arbitrary plane curve.

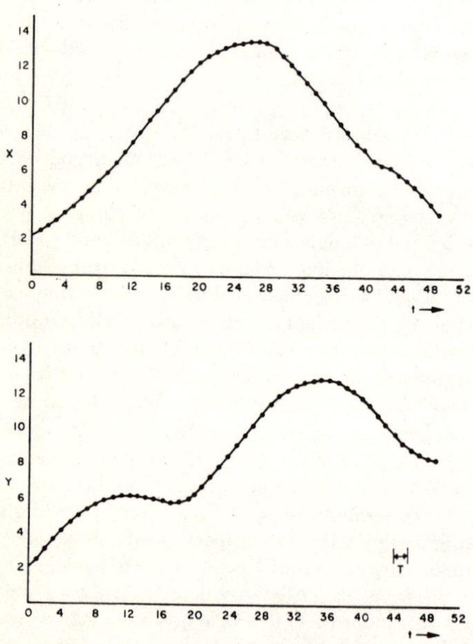

Fig. 2—Parametric curves.

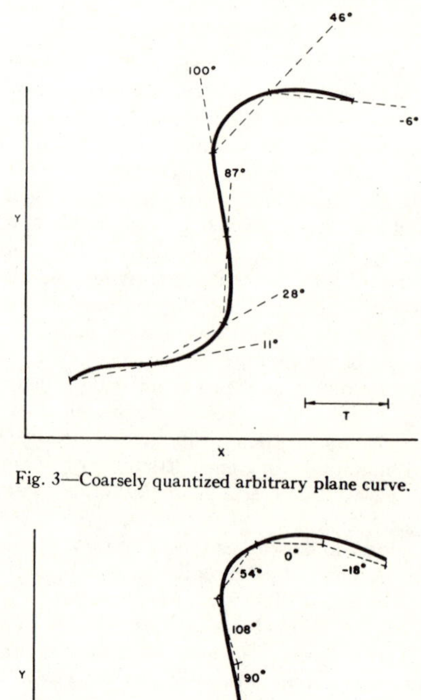

Fig. 3—Coarsely quantized arbitrary plane curve.

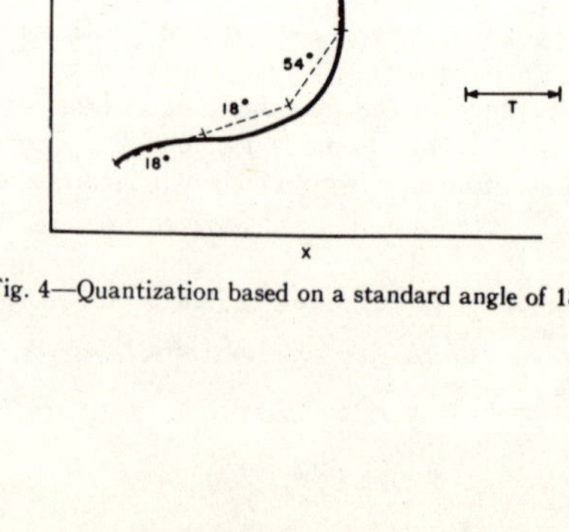

Fig. 4—Quantization based on a standard angle of 18°.

the curve shown in Fig. 3 would appear as follows:

$$11°, 28°, 87°, 100°, 46°, -6°.$$

The actual encoding procedure can be simplified by severely limiting the number of permissible angles. Thus if one were to limit the encoding to 20 standard angles (18° increments) and to number these consecutively from 0 to 19, the curve of Fig. 4 could be represented by the following number series (read from left to right):

$$1, 1, 3, 5, 6, 3, 0, 19.$$

It is evident that any desired precision (fineness of resolution) can be obtained with a relatively coarse angle quantization by making the standard distance arbitrarily small.

This method of describing an arbitrary geometric curve may be termed the unit-vector method. In essence, a curve is represented by a sequence of small vectors of unit length and a limited set of possible directions. For reasons of data handling, it is sometimes preferable to use a grid or array type of description. Thus, one may lay a rectangular grid over the curve and describe the curve by identifying the grid points which lie closest to it. Such a grid system has the advantage over the unit vector scheme of being much less susceptible to error build-up during encoding.

Rectangular-grid representations of arbitrary geometric curves are frequently encountered in connection with digital-computer output displays. Thus, a common type of display consists of a cathode-ray tube on the face of which the beam spot can be positioned to, say, one part in 1024 in both the x and the y direction. Two ten-place binary numbers (20 bits) are required to locate a particular point on the face of the tube. Although a typical curve display may require a very large number of points, the full 20-bit coordinates of each point are usually given. This is unnecessarily wasteful.

The rectangular grid method is somewhat similar to a unit-vector method based on eight angles. The significant difference lies in the use of two standard distances which are in the ratio of $\sqrt{2}$ to each other; *i.e.*, one is the side and the other is the diagonal of a small square in the grid.

The unit-vector representation for six angles has properties that merit special consideration; it can also be regarded as being a representation based on a hexagonal grid. This is the only grid utilizing a single standard distance. The use of a hexagonal grid for computer output display can be achieved with a cathode-ray tube having its pairs of deflection plates mounted at 60° to each other instead of the conventional 90°.

Coding Processes

The process of adopting a symbolism convention and then quantitatively identifying the describing properties in terms of the convention is called encoding. It is desired here to develop means for encoding arbitrary geometric curves so as to facilitate their handling in communications systems and digital computers. A general objective of all encoding is that the process be efficient, *i.e.*, that it use a minimum of bits to represent some given information.

Consider the rectangular-grid representation mentioned previously. The conventional manner of representing a curve consists of giving the full twenty-bit coordinates of each point of a curve (for a 1024×1024 array). Such coding would be necessary if all points were fully independent of each other. If the points describe a continuous curve, they are, of course, far from independent. An important restriction which holds for continuous curves (and which may be considered a definition of a continuous curve) is that successive points are adjacent to each other. Once one point on a continuous curve is given, the next point's location is very much restricted. This knowledge can be utilized to locate successive points with far fewer bits than the number required if each point were to be independently located.

For the rectangular grid it is clear that if a point on a continuous curve is known, the next point can assume only one of eight possible adjacent positions, as shown in Fig. 5(a). If one assigns the decimal digits zero through seven to these eight positions, starting with the one which is horizontally to the right and progressing in a counter-clockwise direction, the code of Fig. 5(b) is obtained. One notes that in this manner each point on a curve is located relative to the previous one, and only the first need be located in an absolute sense. To shift a curve vertically or horizontally, only the coordinates of the first point require changing. As an illustration, consider the curve of Fig. 6 which can be represented by the code sequence (read from left to right).

$$107643,$$

or in binary form,

$$001 \quad 000 \quad 111 \quad 110 \quad 100 \quad 011.$$

One notes that only three bits are required to specify one point on the curve. The required memory capacity for a continuous curve encoded in this way is then only 15 per cent of that required for a curve which has all its points independently specified in a 1024×1024 point array.

One property of the rectangular-array code is at once apparent. Adding "2" (modulo 8) to each of the digits in the decimal representation of a curve causes the curve to be rotated 90° in a counter-clockwise direction. A subtraction will result in clockwise rotation. The addition (or subtraction) of any even number n will cause a rotation equal to $n/2$ times 90°. If "1" is added to each digit, a rotation of 45° is achieved; however, this rotation is nearly always accompanied by distortion or at least a change of scale. This is true for the addition (or subtraction) of any odd number.

The encoding method discussed thus far is by no means unique. Nor is it necessarily the one which is most

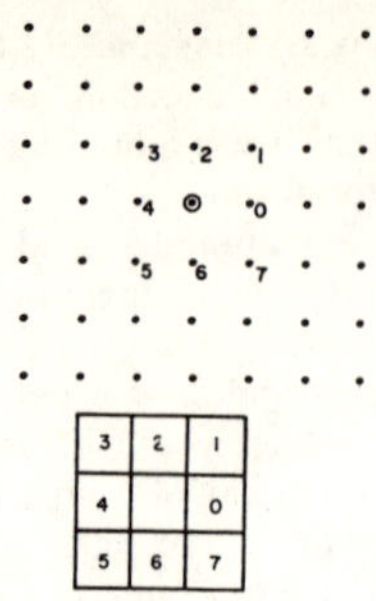

(a)

(b)

Fig. 5—Rectangular array.

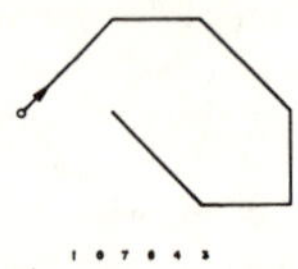

Fig. 6—Illustration of rectangular-array representation.

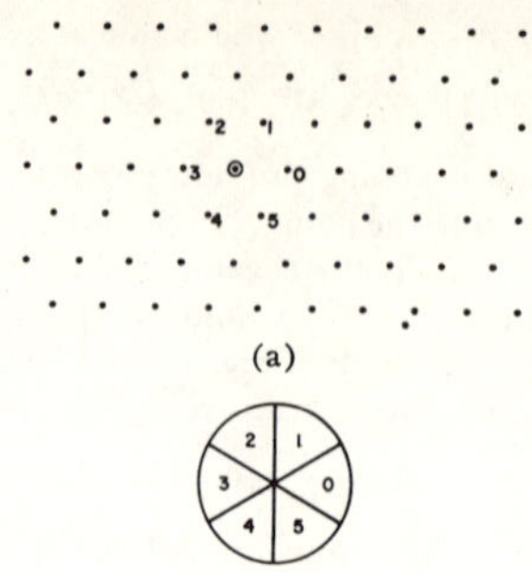

(a)

(b)

Fig. 7—Hexagonal array.

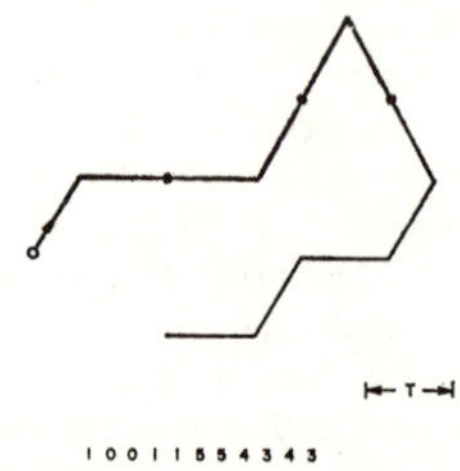

Fig. 8—Illustration of hexagonal-array representation.

economical in its use of memory capacity. In developing the method it was supposed that, given one point, the next point could assume one of eight neighboring positions with equal likelihood. If certain conditions are imposed on an arbitrary curve (in addition to continuity), a two-bit or even a one-bit code can be utilized. For example, if it is known that the slope of the arbitrary curve changes very slowly, *i.e.*, if the values of dx/dt and dy/dt at $t=n$ differ only slightly from those at $t=n+1$, then a one-bit code may suffice. Such a code would be associated with the second difference, and would be used as follows. Given the slope between the previous two points, the slope to the next point would be formed by increasing the last slope by 45° if the digit is "1," or decreasing the slope by 45° if the digit is "0." A straight line would be represented by a sequence of alternating ones and zeros.

The rectangular-array code of Fig. 5 has the disadvantage, as has been noted, that the addition of an odd number to each digit results in distorted rotation. This drawback can be avoided by using instead the hexagonal array shown in Fig. 7(a). For each given point, there are six possible locations for the next point, all of which are equidistant from the given point. The six next-point locations can be numbered from zero to five in a counter-clockwise direction, starting with the location horizontally to the right. Three bits per digit are required to represent the six next-point locations. The code is unsaturated since there are two unused combinations, and special techniques must be used to obtain modulo-six additions. An example of a hexagonal-array display is given in Fig. 8. The curve is represented by the sequence (read from left to right):

10011554343.

The hexagonal-array representation has the property that addition (modulo six) of unity to each digit causes a 60° distortion-free rotation of the curve. The method suffers from the disadvantage of being based on an uncommon, nonorthogonal coordinate system, of having its angular resolution limited to 60° (in contrast to 45° for the rectangular array), and of resulting in an unsaturated binary code representation.

The simplicity of the rectangular array, as well as the ease with which it can be adapted to standard display techniques, suggests that this array be given special attention. Accordingly, the remaining sections of this paper are devoted entirely to this encoding method. It is usually not difficult to see, however, that most techniques applicable to the rectangular array can be extended to the hexagonal and the unit-vector arrays.

Rectangular-Array Encoding

In the rectangular-array method, based on the code of Fig. 5(b), a number sequence utilizing only one kind of digit represents a straight line; *e.g.*, the sequence 22222222 · · · 2 describes a vertical straight line. A total of eight such straight lines can be represented in this manner with the digits "0" through "7." Each of these lines makes an angle with the horizontal which is equal to the digit multiplied by 45°. Straight lines making angles with the horizontal of other than multiples of 45° can be formed with digit pairs, triplets, or higher-order digit groups. Thus the sequence 121212121212 · · · 12 represents a "straight" line making an angle of +63.43°. The total number of straight lines which can be represented with digit pairs is 16. For triplets this increases to 32. One notes that these digit groups can contain only two kinds of digits, and that these cannot differ by more than unity, *e.g.*, 0 and 1, 1 and 2, etc.

Examples of a variety of straight-line representations are given in Fig. 9.

All first-quadrant straight-line digit groups up to five digits in length are listed in Table I. Angles in other quadrants can be obtained by adding either 2, 4 or 6 to each of the digits in a group.

The digit groups given in Table I are not necessarily unique. Thus, the digit groups 01010 and 00011 are equivalent; *i.e.*, they describe the same straight-line slope. However, the first digit group is to be preferred because of its greater smoothness. To assure minimum deviation from the true straight-line path, the two kinds of digits making up a digit group should alternate to the maximum extent.

The representation of an arbitrary curve of any significance will usually consist of a sequence of many hundreds of digits. The more precisely an arbitrary curve is to be represented, the more finely it must be quantized, and, therefore, the greater the number of digits required in its representation. If a curve is completely arbitrary (except for continuity), no condensation or abbreviated representation is possible. However, if there is some regularity in the curve, this *pattern* can be exploited to simplify the representation.

Consider, for example, the straight line which makes an angle of $+26.57°$ with the horizontal. It is represented by the sequence

$$0101010101010101 \cdots 01.$$

One may regard this number sequence as a function of a parameter n where $n=0, 1, 2, \cdots, N$. A more compact representation is then possible through the introduction of the concept of the generating function.[1]

Given a function $f(n)$, one defines another function $u(x)$ as follows:

$$u(x) = \sum_{n=0}^{N} f(n)x^n,$$

where $u(x)$ is the generating function of $f(n)$. For the straight line just mentioned, the generating function is given by the following:

$$(0) + (1)x + (0)x^2 + (1)x^3 + (0)x^4 + (1)x^5 + \cdots$$

This infinite sequence has the closed form

$$\frac{x}{1-x^2}.$$

In obtaining $f(n)$ from the corresponding generating function, one must recognize that a zero is a meaningful digit which represents a finite segment of the curve being described. Generating functions corresponding to the first eight entries of Table I are given in Table II.

[1] C. Jordan, "Calculus of Finite Differences," Chelsea Publishing Co., New York, N. Y., p. 20; 1950.

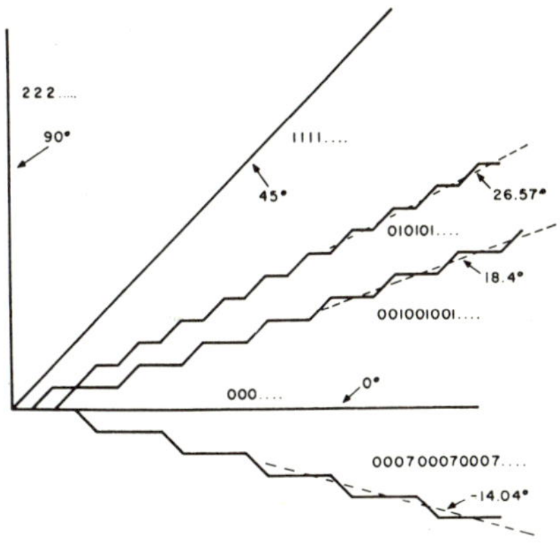

Fig. 9—Straight-line representations.

TABLE I

FIRST-QUADRANT, STRAIGHT-LINE DIGIT GROUPS

Digit Group	Tangent	Angle (Degrees)
0	0	0
00001	0.2	11.32
0001	0.25	14.04
001	0.33	18.4
01010	0.4	21.8
01	0.5	26.57
10101	0.6	30.09
110	0.67	33.7
1110	0.75	36.85
11110	0.8	38.65
1	1.0	45
11112	1.25	51.3
1112	1.33	53.1
112	1.5	56.3
12121	1.67	59.01
21	2	63.4
21212	2.5	68.2
221	3	71.6
2221	4	75.97
22221	5	78.7
2	∞	90

TABLE II

	Digit Group	$u(X)$
1	0	$\frac{0}{1-X}$
2	00001	$\frac{X^4}{1-X^5}$
3	0001	$\frac{X^3}{1-X^4}$
4	001	$\frac{X^2}{1-X^3}$
5	01010	$\frac{X+X^3}{1-X^5}$
6	01	$\frac{X}{1-X^2}$
7	10101	$\frac{1+X^2+X^4}{1-X^5}$
8	110	$\frac{1+X}{1-X^3}$

The concept of generating function representation is not limited to straight lines. Consider the sequence 01234567. This sequence will be called the minimal circle and is shown in Fig. 10. It is the smallest figure which possesses the circle property of permitting arbitrary rotation without any visible effect. It is minimal in that there is no smaller figure for which this property holds.

The minimal circle is a closed curve and is represented by a short sequence of digits. Even when dealing with short sequences, it is sometimes desirable to employ the generating function representation. For the minimal circle the generating function is given by

$$\frac{x}{(1-x)^2},$$

as is easily verified by performing the indicated long division. This generating function leads to an infinite series; however, since the numbers are all modulo eight, the series is periodic and simply causes the same path to be traversed over and over again.

Various minimal waveforms, such as square waves or triangular waves, can be represented in a straightforward manner. Minimal waveforms are waveforms which cannot be reduced without destroying the characteristics of the waveform. A set of common minimal waveforms, together with their digit groups and generating functions, is shown in Fig. 11. The numerators of the generating functions bear a one-to-one correspondence to the digits of the respective digit groups, *i.e.*, to the digits in one period of the sequences. The denominators are determined by the period lengths of the sequences. Thus, if a sequence has a period of three digits, the denominator of the corresponding generating function becomes $1-x^3$.

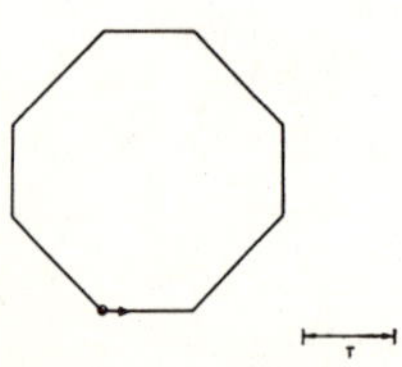

Fig. 10—Minimal circle 01234567.

NAME	WAVEFORM	DIGIT GROUP	GENERATING FUNCTION
SQUARE	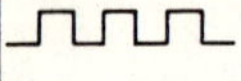	0206	$\frac{2x+6x^3}{1-x^4}$
SAWTOOTH	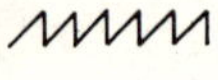	16	$\frac{1+6x}{1-x^2}$
TRIANGULAR	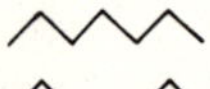	17	$\frac{1+7x}{1-x^2}$
SINE	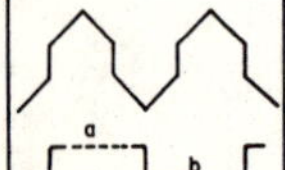	121767	$\frac{1+2x+x^2+7x^3+6x^4+7x^5}{1-x^6}$
RECTANGULAR	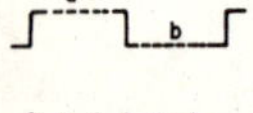	$2\underbrace{0\ldots0}_{a}6\underbrace{0\ldots0}_{b}$	$\frac{2+6x^{a+1}}{1-x^{a+b+2}}$
BACKWARD SAWTOOTH	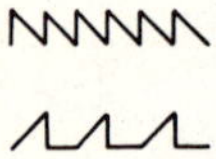	27	$\frac{2+7x}{1-x^2}$
SPACED SAWTOOTH	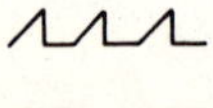	160	$\frac{1+6x}{1-x^3}$

Fig. 11. Minimal waveforms.

Elementary Manipulations

One of the objectives of encoding an arbitrary geometric curve is to translate the significant information contained in the curve into a representation which will facilitate manipulation of the curve by a digital computer. The problem may be one of analysis, *i.e.*, to discern certain properties of a curve such as its area or axes of symmetry, or it may be one of synthesis, where a curve is to be constructed having specified properties. The following section will describe some of the simpler techniques for manipulating curves encoded in accordance with the three-bit rectangular array.

Expansion

Consider a curve stored in the memory of a digital computer. If displayed by the computer's graphical output unit (CRT or similar device), the curve will have an over-all size determined jointly by the coded representation of the curve and the scale factor of the display device. If it is desired to expand a portion of a curve relative to the rest of the curve, an operation must be performed on the coded representation of the curve. Changing the scale factor of the display device would have a uniform effect and could not be utilized for selective expansion.

The process of expansion is performed as illustrated by the following example. Given a curve represented by 012075, a curve exactly twice this size, but otherwise indistinguishable, is given by 001122007755. To expand a curve by a ratio n, each of the digits of the curve must be replaced by a set of n identical digits. One notes that n must be an integer.

If a curve is represented by a generating function, expansion can be performed analytically by replacing x by x^n and then multiplying by $(1-x^n)/(1-x)$. Thus the minimal circle 01234567 can be tripled in size by performing the appropriate operation on its generating function:

minimal form:

$$\frac{x}{(1-x)^2},$$

expansion to triple size:

$$\frac{x^3}{(1-x^3)^2}\,\frac{1-x^3}{1-x}=\frac{x^3}{1-x-x^3+x^4}.$$

Contraction

Over-all contraction is readily accomplished by an appropriate change of scale; however, selective contraction requires a special procedure and is almost always accompanied by distortion. This distortion is introduced because contraction implies (except for trivial cases) a reverting to a more primitive representation, and, consequently, a loss of information. Consider the contraction to one-half size of the curve 22101076. If the digits could be grouped into pairs of identical digits, the contracted curve would be given merely by selecting one digit from each pair. The first two digits are identical and meet this requirement. All the remaining digits, however, do not occur in pairs. One notices that the next four digits can be arranged to give two pairs, "11" and "00." The last two digits differ by unity and their mean does not favor any integer. In such a case, the previous digit is also considered and a mean of these three digits is obtained. The mean for 0 (*i.e.*, 8), 7, and 6 is the digit 7. The contraction is thus as follows:

22101076
22110076
22110077
2107.

Rotation

Rotation has already been discussed. Where the rotation is in multiples of 90°, one need merely add the appropriate even digit to each digit of the curve. Rotations of odd multiples of 45° are obtained by adding the appropriate odd digit. Such rotations are almost always accompanied by distortion. Rotations of arbitrary amounts involve digit-group substitutions and are beyond the scope of the present discussion.[2]

Curve Length

The length of a curve is given by the number of even digits plus the square root of two times the number of odd digits.

Inverse Digits

Inspection of the array of Fig. 5(b) shows that digits which are diametrically opposite in the array have a canceling effect on each other. Accordingly, such digits are referred to as inverses of each other. Thus the inverse of "1" is "5," etc. Numerically, the inverse of a digit is obtained simply by adding either plus or minus "4" to the digit—whichever gives a positive sum less than "8" (hence, adding "4" modulo 8).

Path Reversal

A curve is defined by selecting a starting point and giving a sequence of slope segments which trace out the path of the curve from this point. Path reversal is the process of tracing out a curve in reverse direction. It is achieved by replacing each digit of a curve sequence by its inverse and reversing the sequence end for end. As an example, path reversal changes the curve sequence 1232076 to 2346765.

[2] For example, one notes from Table I that rotating the straight line which makes an angle of 26.57° with the horizontal so that its angle will be 30.09°, requires replacement of the digit group 01 by the digit group 10101.

Path Reduction

Path reduction is defined as the process of obtaining the shortest distance between the end points of an open curve and is found by reducing the given curve in the following manner. If a curve contains two digits which are inverses of each other, they may both be deleted without affecting the location of the end points. Further, there are many digit pairs which can be replaced by a single equivalent digit. Thus, the digit pair "42" can be replaced by the single digit "3." The two digits need not be adjacent for either a cancellation or a replacement to be possible. Table III lists all possible sum-replacement and inverse-digit pairs. There are some digit combinations which, although not permitting reduction, can be replaced by a pair of identical digits. Such digit combinations are presented by the double-digit entries in Table III.

TABLE III

	0	1	2	3	4	5	6	7
0			1	2	x	6	7	
1				22	2	x	0	00
2	1				3	4	x	0
3	2	22				44	4	x
4	x	2	3				5	6
5	6	x	4	44				66
6	7	0	x	4	5			
7		00	0	x	6	66		

x = Inverse

As an illustration, let it be desired to find the shortest curve connecting the end points of the curve 7107542. The length of this curve is $3+4\sqrt{2}$. The curve has two cancellation pairs, "15" and "04," which gives a partially reduced curve 772. Sum-replacement reduces this further to the two-digit curve 70. The minimum distance between the curve's end points is thus equal to $1+\sqrt{2}$.

Closure

To determine whether a given curve is open or closed, one performs a path reduction. If the curve vanishes, it is closed. If it does not vanish, it is open, and the residue (referred to as the closure) is the minimum distance between the end points.

As a corollary to the above, one notes that the digits of a given curve may be arbitrarily rearranged without changing the length of the curve or the minimum distance between its end points.

Multiple-Loop Curves

To determine whether a given curve consists of multiple loops, one must examine the curve for subsets of adjacent digits for which the closure vanishes. Thus the curve 7012345667012345 has a total of seven subsets (including one for the curve itself), for which the closure vanishes, indicating the existence of seven possible ways of tracing out a closed path within the curve; however, only three of these loops are independent.

If a curve has more than one subset for which the closure vanishes, and if the subsets are nonoverlapping and separated by an ordered set of cancellation pairs, the curve is multiply connected except that the customary connecting branch has been provided (represented by the ordered set of cancellation pairs). The curve 0112334556772321076546 is an example of a multiply connected curve. Both this and the previous curve are illustrated in Fig. 12.

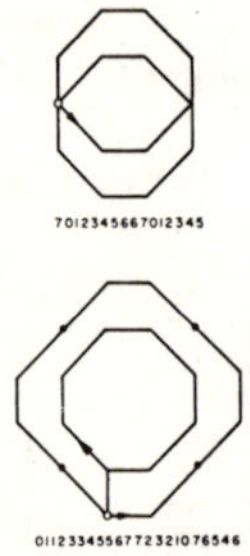

Fig. 12—Multiple-loop curves.

Intersection

To find the point of intersection of two curves, one must first specify a connecting branch which will place the two starting points into relative position. The connecting branch may be any simple curve tracing out a path from the starting point of one curve to the starting point of the other. It may not, however, touch the two curves except at their starting points. Tracing out first one curve and then the other (from the starting point of the connecting branch), a progressive path reduction is performed by considering one additional digit at a time. Each reduced curve is rearranged to place its digits in numerically ascending order. The corresponding lengths of the reduced curves are also computed. The two sets of path reductions are then compared. For each path-reduction sequence which is *common to both curves*, a nodal intersection exists (*i.e.*, the curves intersect at a grid point). If a comparison of the path-reduction sequences of the two curves shows them to differ by only one digit (either by a difference in value of one or the absence of one digit) twice in succession, and if simultaneously the corresponding lengths of the sequences interchange their roles as to which is the longer, a non-nodal intersection exists (*i.e.*, an intersection between grid points).

As an example, consider the two curves $A=01066112$ and $B=020117$, connected by a branch 66 from A to B. The successive path-reduction sequences and lengths are as follows:

		Sequence	*Length*
For A:	1)	0	1
	2)	01	$1+\sqrt{2}$
	3)	010=001	$2+\sqrt{2}$
	4)	0016=000	3
	5)	0006=007	$2+\sqrt{2}$
	6)	0071=0000	4
	7)	00001	$4+\sqrt{2}$
	8)	000012=00011	$3+2\sqrt{2}$
For B:	1)	6	1
	2)	66	2
	3)	660=67	$1+\sqrt{2}$
	4)	672=7	$\sqrt{2}$
	5)	70=07	$1+\sqrt{2}$
	6)	071=000	3
	7)	0001	$3+\sqrt{2}$
	8)	00017=00000	5

Inspection of the two sets of path reductions shows that $A(4)$ matches $B(6)$, indicating the presence there of a nodal intersection. Further, $A(6)$ and $B(7)$ differ by only one digit and the same is true for $A(7)$ and $B(8)$. Simultaneously, the length of A increases from 4 to 5.414 and that of B increases from 4.414 to 5, making A now longer than B. Hence the curves intersect non-nodally within the grid square defined by the end points of the four sequences $A(6)$, $A(7)$, $B(7)$, and $B(8)$.

Determination of Area

A fairly simple procedure exists for determining the area enclosed by an arbitrary curve. Consider the curve 10127 shown in Fig. 13(a). The area under this curve, *i.e.*, its integral with respect to x, can be obtained by adding the area covered by four vertical columns of unit width along the x axis:

$$2\tfrac{1}{2} + 3 + 3\tfrac{1}{2} + 4\tfrac{1}{2} = 13\tfrac{1}{2} \text{ square units.}$$

This suggests the following procedure for determining area. Define a modifier B to represent the instantaneous distance of the curve from the x axis. Thus in Fig. 13(a), the area A is initially zero and the modifier B is equal to "2." The initial slope of "1" (*i.e.*, 45°) causes the area to increase by the amount of the first vertical column to $2\frac{1}{2}$ and the modifier to change to 3. The next slope, "0," causes no change in the modifier since the curve is running parallel to the x axis, but the area is increased by the amount of the modifier, *i.e.*, to $5\frac{1}{2}$. It should be noted that the modifier gives the value of the leading edge of the particular vertical column. In the next step, the slope "1" increases the area by the modifier plus $\frac{1}{2}$ (to 9), and then increases the modifier to 4.

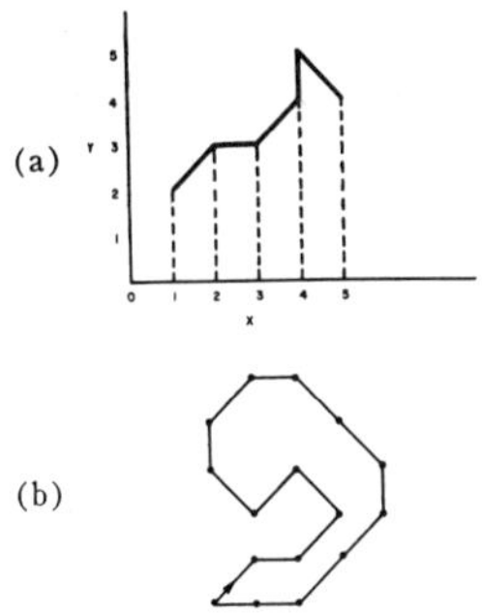

Fig. 13—Arbitrary curves to illustrate integration.

The slope "2" gives no change in area but increases the modifier to 5. The next slope, "7," increases the area by the modifier minus ½ (to 13½) and decreases the modifier to 4.

The foregoing procedure can be generalized to develop a set of rules for all eight slopes, as shown in Table IV. The table gives the slope (N), the change in area resulting from this slope (*i.e.*, the area in the vertical column), and the change to be made in the modifier. If the starting point coincides with the origin, the modifier is initially zero, if it does not, one must use the appropriate initial-condition value.

TABLE IV

Slope	Change in Area	Change in Modifier
0	$+B$	+0
1	$+B+\frac{1}{2}$	+1
2	+0	+1
3	$-B-\frac{1}{2}$	+1
4	$-B$	+0
5	$-B+\frac{1}{2}$	−1
6	+0	−1
7	$+B-\frac{1}{2}$	−1

As an example consider the curve 1013532107765544, shown in Fig. 13(b). This curve is traversed in a positive (clockwise) sense and has an area of 11 square units. The initial value of B is taken as zero.

N	A	B
1	½	1
0	1½	1
1	3	2
3	½	3
5	−2	2
3	−4½	3
2	−4½	4
1	0	5
0	5	5
7	9½	4
7	13	3
6	13	2
5	11½	1
5	11	0
4	11	0
4	11	0

Table IV can be expressed in the form of an algorithm and programmed for a digital computer. It is then a simple matter to determine the area enclosed by an arbitrary curve encoded according to the three-bit rectangular array. For open curves, single-valued in x, one can readily obtain their integral with respect to x. Integration with respect to y can be accomplished by first rotating the curve 90°.

Conclusion

A procedure has been developed for the description and encoding of arbitrary geometric curves which will facilitate the computer manipulation of such curves. Various approaches to the twin problems of describing and encoding have been discussed. Particular attention has been given to the rectangular-array type of representation which is one of the simplest and most natural, and one which lends itself easily to manipulation. Elementary manipulative techniques for the rectangular array have been described. Although consideration has been limited to plane (two-dimensional) curves, extension to three or more dimensions is readily visualized.

Reprinted from *IEEE Trans. Comput.*, **C–21,** No. 3, 1972, pp. 260–268

Minimum-Perimeter Polygons of Digitized Silhouettes

20

JACK SKLANSKY, SENIOR MEMBER, IEEE, ROBERT L. CHAZIN, AND BRUCE J. HANSEN, ASSOCIATE MEMBER, IEEE

Abstract—The minimum-perimeter polygon of a silhouette has been shown to be a means for recognizing convex silhouettes and for smoothing the effects of digitization in silhouettes.

We describe a new method of computing the minimum-perimeter polygon (MPP) of any digitized silhouette satisfying certain constraints of connectedness and smoothness, and establish the underlying theory. Such a digitized silhouette is called a "regular complex," in accordance with the usage in piecewise linear topology. The method makes use of the concept of a stretched string constrained to lie in the cellular boundary of the digitized silhouette.

We show that, by properly marking the virtual as well as the real vertices of an MPP, the MPP can serve as a precise representation of any regular complex, and that this representation is often an economical one.

Index Terms—Artificial retina, cellular convexity, digitization of pictures, image processing by computer, minimum-perimeter polygon, pattern recognition, smoothing of silhouettes.

I. Introduction

When a computer is programmed to analyze a two-dimensional geometric object, the object is usually represented as a rectangular array of ones and zeros in the computer's memory. This digitization of the object affects the computer's ability to analyze the shape of the object. We call such digitizations "cellular images" or, using a more precise terminology, "cellular complexes."

A theory of the relations between silhouettes and their cellular images is gradually emerging. In this paper, we describe the basic elements of this theory, including a number of new results. A principal result is Theorem 9, which describes the conditions under which a cellular complex can be represented perfectly by a minimum-perimeter polygon (MPP). (An MPP of a cellular complex is a polygon of shortest perimeter among the polygons whose images coincide with the given cellular complex.)

Earlier papers have shown how the MPP of a cellular binary-valued image can be instrumental in automating the recognition of convexity on a rectangular mosaic [1], [2]. Another paper has shown how the MPP provides a means of smoothing the edge of a digitized silhouette [3]. In order to guarantee the existence and uniqueness of the MPP (although uniqueness does not seem essential to the utility of the MPP), the cellular image must satisfy certain constraints of connectedness, and the boundary of the cellular image must satisfy certain constraints of smoothness. The so-called "regular cellular complexes" satisfy these requirements. In this paper, we describe and establish the validity of an algorithm that finds the MPP of any regular cellular complex. An earlier algorithm for finding the MPP makes use of nonlinear programming techniques [3]. Our algorithm is simpler, and is based on the intuitively appealing concept of a stretched thread constrained to lie in the cellular boundary of the digitized silhouette.

The present algorithm is an outgrowth of an earlier computer program for recognizing convex cellular complexes [10]. That program, in turn, was based on a previously developed theory of convex cellular "blobs" [1].

We show that the class of convex cellular complexes recognized by MPPs is somewhat larger than the class of convex images suggested indirectly by Minsky and Papert [4].

II. Basic Theory

In this section, we present the elements of the theory of cellular convexity and MPPs, including a summary of earlier work [1], [2]. In summarizing the earlier results, we have revised some of the terminology and notation to achieve closer agreement with the usage in piecewise linear topology [5].

Let $I=[0, 1]$ denote the closed unit interval. A *curve* in the plane is then a continuous mapping $f\colon I\rightarrow R^2$, where R^2 is the Euclidean plane. If $f(0)=f(1)$, f is said to be a closed curve. In this paper, all curves are differentiable of class C^1, i.e., f has a continuous derivative. To any curve f in the plane we may associate its *image* $\{f(x)|\,x\in I\}$. Thus, a curve is a function, while its image is a set of points in the plane. A curve will be called *simple* if it is 1-1. This means that its image will have no self-intersections.

A *domain* is a set of points in the plane that consists of the image of a piecewise C^1 simple closed curve, together with all points interior to it. A domain is thus a compact subset of the plane and is topologically homeomorphic to a disk.[1] Let ∂D denote the *boundary* (or the topological frontier [14]) of the domain D.

A *cellular mosaic* is a set of convex domains in the plane, called *cells*, that overlap only at their boundaries, that cover the entire plane, and exist such that any arbitrary domain in the plane meets only a finite number of cells. A *polygon* is a domain whose boundary consists of a finite number of line segments. Each of these line segments (which we take to be closed unless otherwise specified) will be called an *edge* of the polygon. Note that the cells of a cellular mosaic must be polygons. A *rectangular mosaic* is a cellular mosaic each of

Manuscript received December 1, 1969; revised July 2, 1971. This research was supported by the National Science Foundation under Grant GK-4226.

J. Sklansky is with the School of Engineering, University of California, Irvine, Calif. 92664.

R. L. Chazin is with the Department of Mathematics, University of California, Irvine, Calif. 92664.

B. J. Hansen is with Raytheon Data Systems, Norwood, Mass. 02067.

[1] The standard disk D^2 in the plane consists of the unit circle and all points interior to it. By a *homeomorphism* we mean a 1-1 map of one space onto another, with a continuous inverse [14].

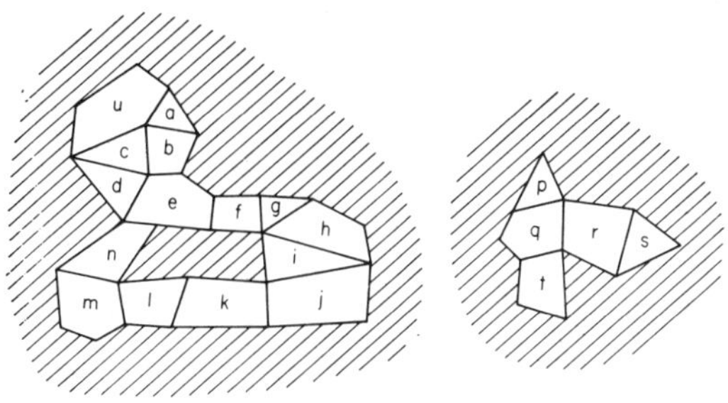

(a) (b)

Fig. 1. Examples of cellular complexes.

whose cells is a rectangle sharing each of its edges with precisely one adjacent cell.

A proper subset of a cellular mosaic will be called a *cellular complex*.[2] We will usually omit the word "cellular" when it is clear from the context. A cell belonging to a given complex will be called an *element* of the complex. Examples of cellular complexes are shown in Fig. 1. The *space* of a complex J, denoted by $|J|$, is the union of all points belonging to elements of J. It is thus a subset of the plane. J is a *cellular image*, or briefly, *image*,[3] of a set of points p, if: 1) $p \subseteq |J|$; and 2) every element of J containing an exterior point of p also contains a boundary point of p, or, if p is the limit, in the sense defined below, of a sequence of domains each of which satisfies 1) and 2).[4] Note that a set of points p may have more than one image.

We now define "limit[5] of a sequence of domains." First consider the spaces of curves, i.e., mappings

$$f: I \rightarrow R^2$$

as a metric space in the sup-norm topology. Let $\rho(f, g)$ denote the distance between f and g in the sup-norm topology, and let $d(P, Q)$ denote the Euclidean distance between points P and Q in R^2. We define $\rho(P, Q)$ as follows:

$$\rho(P, Q) = \sup_{x \in I} d[P(x), Q(x)].$$

Convergence of a sequence in this space is the same as uniform convergence on the real line. Recall that, by our definition of "domain," the boundary of a domain always has a given parametrization. Let p be a domain and f the associated parametrization. Let p_n be a sequence of domains, and f_n the associated parametrizations of the boundaries. Then we will say that $\lim p_n = p$ if $\lim f_n = f$ in the usual pointwise sense and if, also, $\lim f_n'$ exists in the above metric. A standard theorem of real analysis [15] guarantees that f exists, is piecewise C^1, and that f_n' converges to f' in the above metric, where f_n' denotes the derivative of f_n with respect to x, $x \in I$.

[2] This definition of cellular complex is very similar to that of "convex linear cell complex" as used in piecewise linear [5] or algebraic topology. The difference is that we allow T-shaped junctions of cellular boundaries, whereas in the definition of piecewise linear topology, the intersection of two cells is either empty or else is a common edge of each.

[3] This definition of "image" is distinct from, and we hope, will not be confused with, the definition of the "image of a curve."

[4] By "$\subseteq$" we mean "is a subset of," and "$\subset$" denotes "is a proper subset of."

[5] Our definition of limit is partially based on our desire to have a domain have a piecewise C^1 boundary. This modest degree of smoothness insures, for instance, that the boundary of a domain is parametrized by a rectifiable curve, i.e., one with a finite arclength. The conditions could be relaxed; more delicate (and less intuitive) conditions would then be required.

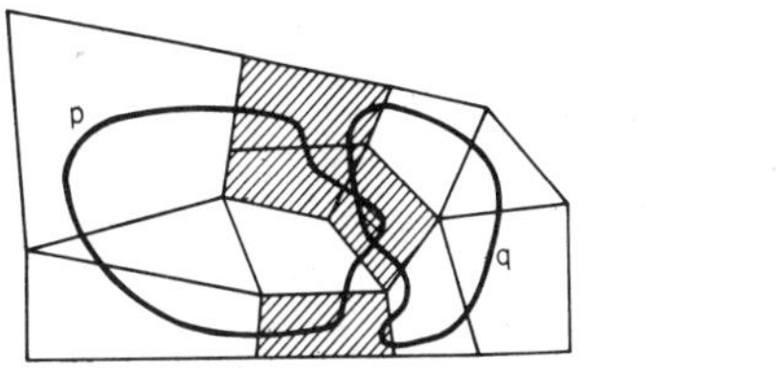

Fig. 2. Illustration of the image of $p \cap q$ properly contained in $I \cap J$.

By the following theorem, the image of a finite union of cells is the union of their images.

Theorem 1: Let p and q be domains on some cellular mosaic, let I be a cellular image of p, and J be a cellular image of q. Then $I \cup J$ is a cellular image of $p \cup q$.

Proof: Let c be a cell of the mosaic. Then

$$\begin{aligned} c \in I \cup J &\text{ if and only if } c \in I \text{ or } c \in J \\ &\text{ if and only if } c \cap p \neq \emptyset \text{ or } c \cap q \neq \emptyset \\ &\text{ if and only if } c \cap (p \cup q) \neq \emptyset \\ &\text{ if and only if } c \text{ is a cellular image of } p \cup q. \end{aligned}$$

Theorem 2: Under the same notation as in Theorem 1, any cellular image of $p \cap q$ is contained in $I \cap J$.

Proof: Let K be an image of $p \cap q$. If $c \in K$, then $p \cap q \cap c \neq p$. Hence $p \cap c \neq \emptyset$ and $q \cap c \neq \emptyset$. Hence $c \in I$ and $c \in J$, which implies $c \in I \cap J$.

On the other hand $I \cap J$ is not necessarily contained in an image of $p \cap q$, as illustrated in Fig. 2. In this figure $I \cap J$ is shown shaded, $p \cap q$ is cross-hatched, and the image of $p \cap q$ is indicated by a heavy boundary.

We adopt the convention "c is black," meaning that c is an element of a given cellular complex, and "c is white" meaning that c is *not* an element of a given complex.

Two cells are *neighbors* if they intersect in a (finite) line segment of nonzero length. A chain is any finite sequence of cells, each of which, except for the first, is a neighbor of its predecessor. If α and β are chains, we denote by $\alpha\beta$ the chain obtained by following the last cell of α by the first cell of β. A chain containing no cells is a *null chain.* We will call α a *subchain* of β if α and β are chains, and if there are chains γ and δ such that $\gamma\alpha\delta = \beta$. Note that γ and δ may be null. A chain is *regular* [2] if the predecessor and successor of every element of the chain are distinct. Otherwise a chain is said to be irregular. Thus, in Fig. 1, *abcdefghijklmn* is a regular chain, and *pqrsrqt* is an irregular chain.

A chain is said to be *closed* if the first and last elements are neighbors. A chain is *nonrepeating* if all elements of the chain are distinct. In Fig. 1, if we put $\gamma = efghijklmn$, then γ

is a closed nonrepeating chain, and $\gamma\gamma$ is a closed repeating chain.

A complex J is *chained* if $J \neq \varnothing$ and if every pair of elements of J lies on a chain belonging entirely to J. J will be said to be *simply chained* if $\partial|J|$ is a simple closed curve, where $\partial|J|$ is the boundary of $|J|$. The terms "chained" and "simply chained" are analogous, but not equivalent, to "connected" and "simply connected." On a rectangular mosaic a chain is equivalent to a "4-path," and a chained complex is equivalent to a "4-connected" set of points [6].[6] Parts (a) and (b) of Fig. 1 are both chained, but only part (b) is simply chained.

The *cellular boundary* $\mathcal{B}J$ of a complex J is the set of cells of J that meet $\partial|J|$ (i.e., that have a nonempty intersection with $\partial|J|$). It is clear that the cellular boundary of a complex is unique. A *boundary chain* of J, denoted by $\beta(J)$, is any closed chain of cells in $\mathcal{B}J$ such that every cell of $\mathcal{B}J$ is an element of the chain. A boundary chain may be repeating; and a complex may have more than one boundary chain. For example, if J is the complex of Fig. 1, *pqrsrqt* is not a boundary chain of J, but *pqrsrqtq* is a boundary chain of J. Note that a complex has a boundary chain only if $\partial|J|$ is connected.

A *transverse edge* of any chain γ is the edge shared by some two-element subchain of γ.

We say that a chain *encloses* a point P if P lies inside or on every simple closed curve passing through all the elements of γ successively without meeting the nontransverse edges of γ. Then we have the following theorem.

Theorem 3: A closed regular chain encloses at least one point.

Proof: Since γ is closed and regular, there exists a nonempty set κ of simple closed curves, each of which passes successively through all the elements of γ without meeting the nontransverse edges of γ. Let K denote an arbitrarily chosen member of κ.

Since K does not meet the nontransverse edges of γ, K must meet every transverse edge of γ. Hence one of the endpoints of any transverse edge of γ lies inside or on K. Let P denote such an endpoint. Since K was chosen arbitrarily, γ encloses P, thereby proving the theorem.

A *core boundary* of J, denoted by ∂cJ, is the set of points in the boundaries of the cells of $\mathcal{B}J$ that are neither in $\partial|J|$ nor in the interiors of the transverse edges of $\beta(J)$. The *core* of J, denoted by cJ, is the union of the core boundary and all points interior to it. J is said to be *cored* if it has a nonempty core.

The class of cored complexes is partially described by the following theorem.

Theorem 4: If a simply chained cellular complex J has a boundary chain $\beta(J)$ enclosing at least one point, then J is cored.

Proof: Suppose J is a simply chained complex, and suppose $\beta(J)$ encloses a point P. Then $\partial|J|$ is a simple closed curve enclosing P. P cannot lie on $\partial|J|$, since $\beta(J)$ encloses P. Hence $P \in cJ$. Thus $cJ \neq \varnothing$, and J is cored. This completes the proof.

We say that J is *simply cored* if J is cored and there exists a nonrepeating boundary chain $\beta(J)$. (A simply cored cellular complex has been referred to in an earlier paper [1] as a "cellular blob." We refrain from using this terminology here in order to free "cellular blob" for a less restricted use.)

From these definitions, it follows that every simply cored complex is simply chained, but not conversely.

Theorem 5: Every simply cored complex is simply chained.

Proof: Let J be simply cored. By the definition of core boundary, ∂cJ does not contain any points of $\partial|J|$. If the interior of ∂cJ contains a point of $\partial|J|$, then $\partial|J|$ is not connected, in which case J has no boundary chain, contradicting the assumption that J is simply cored. Hence cJ contains no points of $\partial|J|$. Hence $\partial|J|$ is a simple closed curve, and J is simply chained.

The converse to Theorem 5 is false. An example of a simply chained complex which is cored but not simply cored is shown in Fig. 3.

A cellular complex J is *regular* if it is simply chained, and if there exists a regular boundary chain $\beta(J)$. By Theorems 3 and 4, every regular complex is cored. Note that every nonrepeating chain is regular, but not every regular chain is nonrepeating. Hence, every simply cored complex is a regular complex, but not conversely. An example of a regular but not simply cored complex is shown in Fig. 4. Since every regular complex is simply chained, it follows from Theorem 3 that if the boundary chain of a regular complex is nonrepeating, then the complex is simply cored.

A cellular complex J is *cellularly convex* if there exists at least one convex domain of which J is an image. According to this definition, the space of a complex may be concave,[7] even though the complex is cellularly convex.

Two other definitions of cellular convexity have been proposed. Feder [7] proposed that a cellular complex be convex if the chain code [8] of its cellular boundary forms a convex polygon. By this definition, a cored cellular image of any triangle on a rectangular mosaic is concave. Since all triangles are convex, this result contradicts our intuitive requirements for cellular convexity. Minsky and Papert [4] proposed a definition of convexity that can be extended to cellular complexes on a rectangular mosaic as follows. A triplet of cells is *collinear* if their centroids (barycenters) can be joined by a straight line. A complex J is then convex if there is no collinear triplet of cells (a, b, c) such that $a \in J$, $b \notin J$, and $c \in J$. We refer to this definition as the "extended Minsky–Papert definition" of convexity. Fig. 5 shows a complex which, as a result of cells (a, b, c), is not convex by the extended Minsky–Papert definition. However, this complex is cellularly convex by our definition of cellular convexity because the complex is a cellular image of the heavily outlined rectangle. Thus the classes of "convex" complexes determined by the Feder definition and the classes deter-

[6] This terminology is *not* the same as that used in algebraic topology, which deals with maps of the n sphere into a space.

[7] By "concave" we mean "not convex."

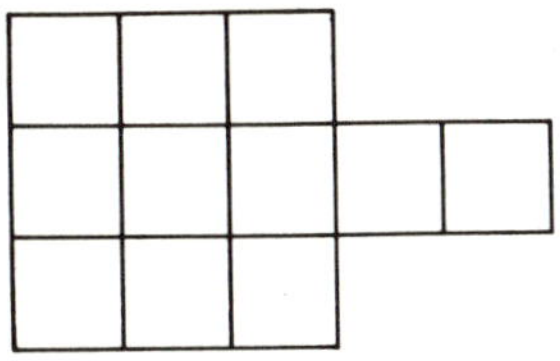

Fig. 3. This simply chained complex is cored but not simply cored.

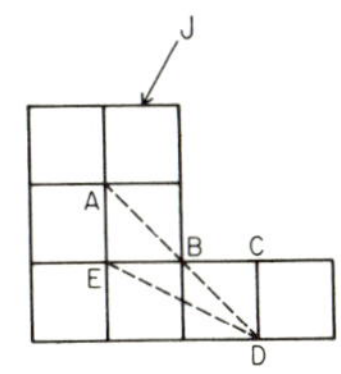

Fig. 6. This irregular convex complex has a concave MPP.

Fig. 4. This regular complex is not simply cored.

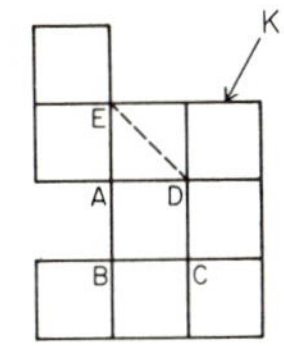

Fig. 7. This irregular convex complex has a convex MPP.

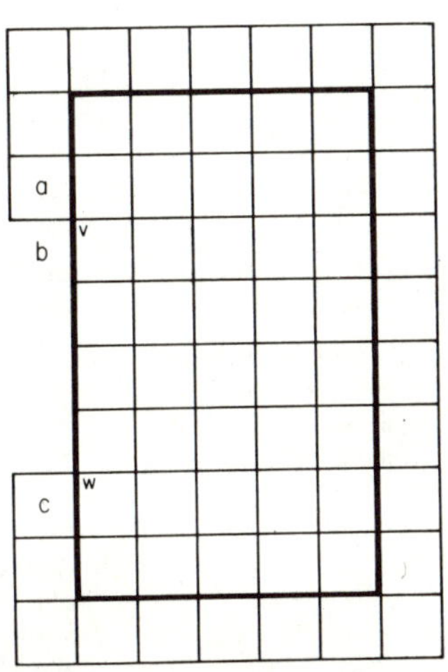

Fig. 5. A cellularly convex complex.

mined by the extended Minsky–Papert definition are proper subsets of the set of cellularly convex complexes determined by our definition.

A *minimum-perimeter polygon* (MPP) of a complex J is any polygon p having J as an image, and such that there is no polygon of shorter perimeter also having J as an image.

In an earlier paper we showed that: 1) a simply cored complex on a rectangular mosaic has a unique MPP, and 2) a simply cored complex J on a rectangular mosaic is convex if and only if the MPP of J is convex [1]. Recently, Montanari has shown that these results remain correct when "simply cored" is replaced by "regular" [2]. Thus we have the following two theorems. (The proofs of these theorems make use of our definitions of "cellular image" and "limit of a sequence of domains.")

Theorem 6: A regular cellular complex on a rectangular mosaic has a unique MPP.

Theorem 7: A regular cellular complex J on a rectangular mosaic is cellularly convex if and only if the MPP of J is convex.

These theorems provide a convenient convexity–concavity test for all regular complexes. The convexity or concavity of the MPP of a regular complex implies the convexity or concavity of the complex.

If a convex simply chained complex is *not* regular, then it may have either a concave or convex MPP. A case in which a convex irregular complex J has a concave MPP is shown in Fig. 6. In this figure, the concave polygon $ABCBEA$ is the MPP of the complex, while the complex is a cellular image of the convex polygon $ABDEA$. A case in which a convex irregular complex K has a convex MPP is shown in Fig. 7. In this figure the MPP of K is $ABCDEA$.

In the proof of [1, Theorem 2], it was shown that every convex vertex of an MPP must lie on ∂cJ. Further, by [1, Theorem 3], the MPP of any regular complex must contain cJ. (Note: By the definitions in [1], Theorem 3 is applicable to simply cored complexes. However, using the same proof, one can show that the applicability of Theorem 3 may be extended to any cored complex.) Hence, every convex vertex of the MPP of any regular complex J—for example, the vertex found by Algorithm 1 in Section III of this paper—is a convex vertex of the core of J. (Note: if cJ contains isolated points, isolated line segments, or protruding line segments, we interpret the isolated points, the endpoints of the isolated line segments, and the tips of the protruding line segments as convex vertices of cJ.) Similarly, every concave

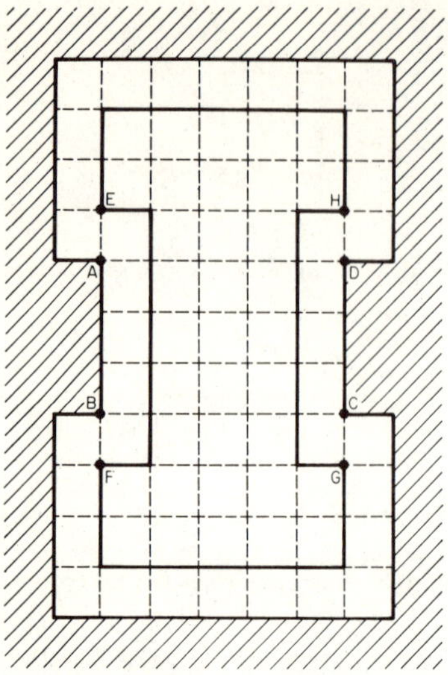

Fig. 8. Examples of virtual vertices.

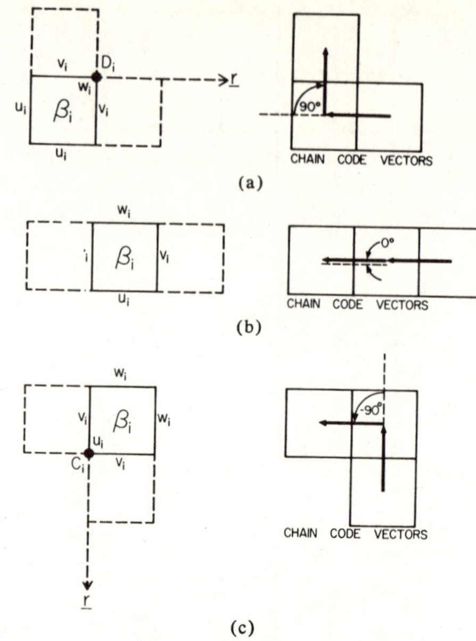

Fig. 9. Relations between boundary chain segments and chain code vectors.

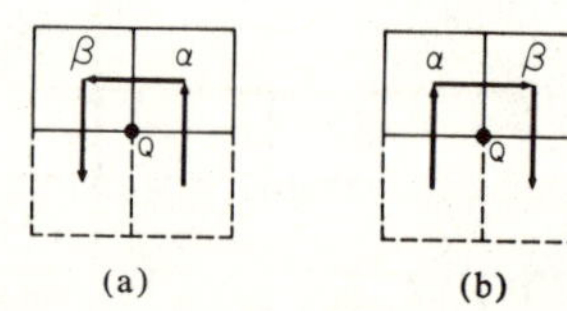

Fig. 10. Examples of 180° turns in boundary chain segments.

vertex of the MPP of J is a concave vertex of $|J|$. Thus we have the following theorem.

Theorem 8: a) Every concave vertex of the MPP of a regular complex J coincides with a concave vertex of $|J|$; b) every convex vertex of the MPP of J coincides with a convex vertex of cJ.

Let p denote the MPP of a cellular complex J. Suppose ∂p lies on a vertex of a cell of $\mathcal{B}J$ at a point Q, and suppose that p has no vertex at Q. Then depending on whether Q lies on $\partial|J|$ or ∂cJ, we identify Q as a *concave virtual vertex* or a *convex virtual vertex*, respectively. Thus a virtual vertex has an interior angle of 180°. (Examples of concave virtual vertices are A, B, C, and D in Fig. 8. Examples of convex virtual vertices are E, F, G, and H in that figure.) When we have identified every concave and convex virtual vertex of an MPP, we call it a *marked virtual-vertex MPP*.

Theorem 9: The marked virtual-vertex MPP p of a regular complex J on a rectangular mosaic uniquely determines the boundary chain of J, and the converse is true.

In this case we denote the boundary chain of J by $\beta(J)$.

Proof: We first prove that the marked virtual-vertex MPP of J uniquely determines $\beta(J)$.

We introduce the following terminology. Let γ be a chain on J, with $\gamma = c_1, c_2, \cdots, c_n$. To every pair of adjacent cells of γ we associate a line segment s_{ij}, joining the barycenters of c_i and c_j. s_{ij} will be called the *spine* of the pair (c_i, c_j) and this notion obviously extends to any finite sequence of cells, and so to γ itself. The spine $s(\gamma)$ of a chain may be directed, if we wish, and in that case we may think of the spine as a sequence or a vector. Thus the spine is a polygonal path lying in γ. Now let c_{j-1}, c_j, c_{j+1} be a sequence of three cells in γ, with associated spines $s_{j-1,j}$, $s_{j,j+1}$. On the rectangular mosaic, the angle between $s_{j-1,j}$ and $s_{j,j+1}$ is either 0° or 90°, $\pm 180°$. In the case where the angle is $90° \pm 180°$, we call the triple (c_{j-1}, c_j, c_{j+1}) a *right angle sequence* of cells, and refer to c_j as a *corner* cell.

Let p denote, as before, the MPP of J. In the derivation of Theorem 8, we showed that if J is regular, then the concave vertices of p lie on $\partial|J|$ and the convex vertices of p lie on ∂cJ. Using essentially the same argument, it can be shown that this property of the vertices of p also holds when the virtual as well as the real vertices of p are included.

We now determine a boundary chain β as follows. A cell is included in β if it is determined by a point Q of ∂p. A point of ∂p that is not a real or virtual vertex determines two successive cells of β or one cell, depending on whether or not Q lies on a transverse edge of a pair of adjacent cells. If Q lies on a real or virtual vertex of p, Q determines a corner cell of β as in (a) and (c) of Fig. 9. In Fig. 9, Q is located at C_i and D_i, and determines cell β_i. Q can also determine *two* corner cells of a pair of right-angle sequences of β, as in Fig. 10. These are the only possible cases; and the chain β is obviously the only one determined by p.

The converse follows immediately by Theorem 6. This completes the proof of Theorem 9.

III. The Stretched Thread

In the remainder of this paper, all the mosaics are assumed to be rectangular.

Theorems 6 and 7 show that the convexity or concavity of a regular complex on a rectangular mosaic is determined by the convexity or concavity of the complex's MPP. Since the application of the theorems is restricted to regular complexes, it would be useful to transform irregular 8-connected complexes to regular complexes with little change in shape. (An "8-connected" complex is, following Rosenfeld [6], a complex whose space is connected.) Such a transformation is described in a subsequent paper [9].

To find the MPP of a regular complex J on the rectangular mosaic, we imagine a "spider" that spins a taut elastic thread through the transverse edges of $\beta(J)$, with the thread constrained to lie in $|\mathcal{B}J|$. As the spider moves along, the thread provides an estimate of a portion of the minimum-perimeter path through $\beta(J)$. If, during the spinning process, the spider is forced to generate a concave vertex on $\partial|J|$ in the stretched thread, J is proved concave, provided the initial point of the thread lies on ∂cJ. If, after one or more revolutions around the boundary, the path of the string is stabilized, then this path is the MPP of J.

Note that since the initial point of the stretched thread is chosen arbitrarily in $|\mathcal{B}J|$, the initial point does not necessarily lie on the MPP, so that more than one revolution of the spider around the core may be needed before a stable path is found. Hence, in implementing the concept of the stretched thread, we encounter the problem of ensuring a stable path, preferably in a single revolution. A solution to this problem is given by Theorem 10 and Algorithm 1. A line L is a *supporting line* of a domain if it passes through at least one boundary point of p and if the entire domain lies on one side of L [13]. Note that every domain has two horizontal and two vertical supporting lines. If the domain is a polygon, each of these supporting lines contains at least one convex vertex of the polygon.

Let p denote the MPP of a regular complex J. (Recall that the mosaic is assumed to be rectangular.) Let L denote the upper horizontal supporting line of p. Line L touches p at at least one convex vertex. In particular the leftmost point Q in $L\cap p$ is a convex vertex of p. Point Q must lie in the lower right corner of the leftmost cell c in the top row of J, since if Q were anywhere else in c, the existence of a polygon q such that $I(q)=J$ and ∂q is shorter than ∂p could be demonstrated. The demonstration depends on the fact that c has precisely two neighbors in J—one to the right of c and one below c—and that both neighbors lie in $\mathcal{B}J$. This leads to the following theorem.

Theorem 10: If p is the MPP of a regular complex J on a rectangular mosaic, the lower right corner of the leftmost cell in the top row of J lies on a convex vertex of p.

This theorem leads to Algorithm 1, for finding a convex vertex of p. In this algorithm, as well as in subsequent ones, we need the concept of a "cellular picture."

A *cellular picture*, or briefly, *picture*, is a simply chained complex containing the complex of interest in a given mosaic. Usually every element of the picture, together with a tag labeling the membership or nonmembership of the element in a given complex, is stored in a memory of a computer for use in various "picture-processing" algorithms.

Algorithm 1—Convex Vertex Finder: Scan the picture horizontally from left to right, and let successive horizontal scans progress downward one row at a time. By Theorem 9, if the lower right vertex of the first encountered black cell belongs to a regular complex J, that vertex lies at the leftmost of the top convex vertices of the MPP of J.

Algorithm 1 and Theorem 10 ensure that the path of the thread is completed in a single revolution around $\beta(J)$.

A basic property of the stretched thread is that its convex vertices lie on convex vertices of cJ and its concave vertices lie on concave vertices of $|J|$, as indicated in Theorem 8.

IV. Finding the Minimum-Perimeter Polygon

In this section we formally describe our algorithm for finding the MPP of any regular complex, and we prove the validity of the algorithm. The algorithm is based on the concept of the stretched thread. We refer to this algorithm as *Algorithm 2* or the *MPP Finder.*

Definitions: The principal geometric concepts in Algorithm 2 are illustrated in Fig. 11. The unshaded portion of this figure shows a position of the cellular boundary of a regular complex J. Point O_n in this figure represents the nth vertex of the MPP of J. We refer to O_n as the nth *source*. The first source is obtained by Algorithm 1. Subsequent sources are obtained sequentially by Algorithm 2.

Let β_i denote the ith cell of $\beta(J)$, beginning with β_0 defined as the leftmost cell of the top row of J. This numbering is illustrated in Fig. 12. In this figure each cell of $\mathcal{B}J$ contains the subscripts of the elements of $\beta(J)$ that coincide with that cell of $\mathcal{B}J$. Any cell that appears twice in $\beta(J)$ contains two numbers, namely, the subscripts of the two elements of $\beta(J)$ associated with that cell.

For any i, divide the boundary of β_i into three parts: u_i, v_i, w_i. w_i is defined recursively as follows: $w_0=\beta_0\cap\partial|J|$; w_i= set of all points on $\beta_i\cap\partial|J|$ that are connected to w_{i-1}, i.e., the set of points in $\beta_i\cap\partial|J|$ such that for every point in w_i there exists a path from that point in w_{i-1} lying entirely in $\beta_i\cap\partial|J|$.

v_i is defined as the set of points consisting of the two transverse edges of β_i. Let $u_i=\partial\beta_i-w_i-\mathring{v}_i$, where $\mathring{v}_i$ is the interior of v_i. u_i, v_i, and w_i are illustrated in Fig. 9. Thus, in cell β_6 of Fig. 12, u_6 is the upper horizontal edge of β_6, v_6 is the pair of vertical edges of β_6, and w_6 is the lower horizontal edge of β_6.

Proposition 1: If a complex J is simply cored, then u_i must lie on ∂cJ for every i.

Proof: By the definition of core boundary

$$\partial cJ = \bigcup_i u_i.$$

Hence $u_i\subseteq\partial cJ$ for every i, which completes the proof.

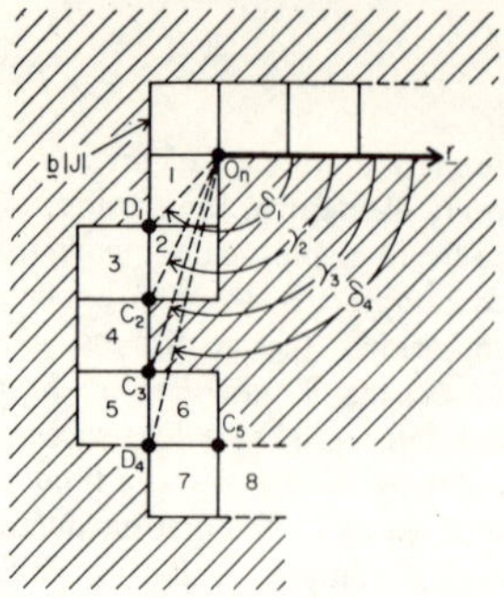

Fig. 11. Notation for Algorithm 2.

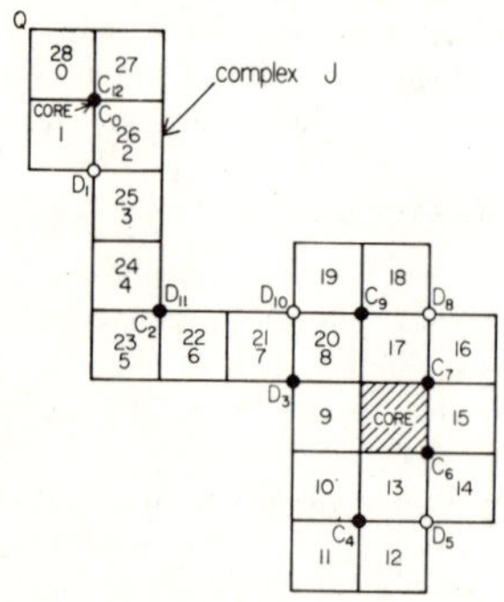

Fig. 12. Notation for numbering of cells and corners in a regular complex that is not simply cored.

Note that if J is simply cored, then $u_i \neq \varnothing$ for every i, by the above proposition.

It also follows from Proposition 1 that if J is simply cored, then $w_i \cap \partial|J|$ for every i. For, suppose $w_i \subset (\beta_i \cap \partial|J|)$. Then u_i would contain points of $\partial|J|$. This contradicts the proposition, since in a simply cored complex, $\partial|J|$ and ∂cJ are disjoint.

There are only three distinct arrangements of (β_{i-1}, β_i, β_{i+1}), allowing for possible 90° rotations. These arrangements are shown in Fig. 9. In this figure the boundaries of β_{i-1} and β_{i+1} are indicated by dashed lines.

We now define two sequences of points, $\mathcal{C}$ and $\mathcal{D}$. The elements of $\mathcal{C}$ and $\mathcal{D}$ are determined by the following two rules.

Rule 1: If w_i consists of just one point, then $w_i \in \mathcal{D}$, as in part (a) of Fig. 9.

Rule 2: If w_i consists of two adjacent edges of β_i, then u_i consists of single point, and $u_i \in \mathcal{C}$, as in part (c) of Fig. 9.

Rule 3: The only points in $\mathcal{C}$ and $\mathcal{D}$ are those determined by Rules 1 and 2.

Clearly, any cell β_k can satisfy at most one of Rules 1 and 2. Hence the application of the above rules of β_k determines, at most, one element of $\mathcal{C} \cup \mathcal{D}$. Note that it is possible that β_k contains no element of $\mathcal{C} \cup \mathcal{D}$, as in Fig. 9(b).

The members of $\mathcal{C} \cup \mathcal{D}$ are numbered consecutively in the order in which they are generated by Rules 1, 2, and 3. A typical sequence is C_0, D_1, C_2, D_3, C_4, D_5, C_6, C_7, D_8, C_9, D_{10}, D_{11}, $C_{12}(=C_0)$, as in Fig. 12. In this case

$$\mathcal{C} = \{C_0, C_2, C_4, C_6, C_7, C_9, C_{12}\}$$

$$\mathcal{D} = \{D_1, D_3, D_5, D_8, D_{10}, D_{11}\}.$$

Each node marked by a dot (•) or a small circle (o) in this figure is an element of $\mathcal{C} \cup \mathcal{D}$, with the dots identifying the vertices of the MPP.

Let $I(k)$ denote the index of the element, if it exists, of $\mathcal{C} \cup \mathcal{D}$ determined by β_k. We denote the $I(k)$th member of $\mathcal{C} \cup \mathcal{D}$ in β_k by $C_{I(k)}$ if it belongs to $\mathcal{C}$, $D_{I(k)}$ if it belongs to $\mathcal{D}$. Thus, if $k=5$ and β_k contains the third element of $\mathcal{C} \cup \mathcal{D}$, then $I(5)=3$.

From Fig. 9(c) it is clear that when u_i is a single point lying on ∂cJ, then u_i is a convex vertex of cJ. Thus, by Proposition 1, $\mathcal{C}$ is the set of convex vertices of the core of any simply cored complex. Furthermore, if V is any convex vertex of cJ, then there is a cell β_i in $\beta(J)$ for which $u_i = V$, as in Fig. 9(c). We also see that every element of $\mathcal{D}$ is a concave vertex of $|J|$.

Fig. 12 illustrates the C_i and D_i for a case in which J is regular but not simply cored. Here we see how some cells are numbered more than once, and how some vertices of $|J|$ are D_i while other vertices of $|J|$ are members of both $\mathcal{C}$ and $\mathcal{D}$. In particular, a vertex of cell β_5 is both C_1 and D_6. We also see that the C_k of cells $\{\beta_i | i=8, 11, 14, 16, 18, 27\}$ are convex vertices of cJ.

Construct vectors $\underline{c}_i$, $\underline{d}_i$ drawn from O_n to C_i, D_i, respectively, as illustrated in Fig. 11. Construct a reference vector $\underline{r}$ through O pointing clockwise along $\partial|J|$ or ∂cJ, depending on whether O_n lies on $|J|$ or cJ, respectively. Possible directions of $\underline{r}$ are illustrated in Fig. 9(a) and (c) for cases where O_n coincides with D_i (and hence lies on $|J|$) and where O_n coincides with C_i (and hence lies on cJ).

Let P denote any point in the plane. We define the "angle of P" as the absolute value of the angle swept out by a vector through O_n starting from $\underline{r}$ and rotating counterclockwise to P. In particular γ_i is the angle of C_i, and δ_j is the angle of D_j. Thus, in Fig. 11, δ_1 is the angle of D_1, γ_2 is the angle of C_2, γ_3 is the angle of C_3, etc.

Let η_k denote the largest of the angles of the points of u_k, and let θ_k denote the smallest of the angles of the points of w_k. Note that η_k and θ_k may be computed from the angles of at most three points of u_k (the endpoints and the midpoint) and three points of w_k. Let H_k, Θ_k be defined recursively as follows. $K(n)=$ value of k such that: 1) O_n lies in the upper right-hand corner of $\beta_{K(n)}$ when r_n points to the right, and 2) $K(1)=1$.

$$H_k = \operatorname*{Max}_{K(n) \leq i \leq k} (\eta_i)$$

$$\Theta_k = \operatorname*{Min}_{K(n) \leq i \leq k} (\theta_i).$$

We define P_k as the last member of $\mathcal{C} \cup \mathcal{D}$ encountered in moving along $\beta(J)$ from $\beta_{K(n)}$ to β_k. Thus

$$P_k = \begin{cases} C_{I(k)} & \text{if } \beta(J) \text{ contains an element of } \mathcal{C} \\ D_{I(k)} & \text{if } \beta_k \text{ contains an element of } \mathfrak{D} \\ P_{k-1} & \text{if } \beta_k \text{ contains no element of } \mathcal{C} \cup \mathfrak{D}. \end{cases}$$

Algorithm 2—MPP Finder:

Step 1: Choose the first source O_1 by Algorithm 1.

Step 2: Let O_n denote the current source. Number the cells of $\beta(J)$ counterclockwise from O_n, as shown in Fig. 11. Starting at cell 1, move along $\beta(J)$ counterclockwise. For each β_k compute H_k and Θ_k.

Step 3: Compute P_k.

Step 4: If $H_k < \Theta_k$, go to Step 2. If $H_k > \Theta_k$, then P_k becomes the $(n+1)$th source O_{n+1}.

Step 5: Replace n by $n+1$, i.e., add 1 to the numerical value of the contents of the register labeled "n." (Thus O_{n+1} becomes O_n.) If $O_n = O_1$, stop. Otherwise, go to Step 2.

End of algorithm.

We now show that the above algorithm yields the MPP of any regular complex J.

Theorem 11: When Algorithm 2 is applied to any regular complex J, the sequence of sources $\{O_n\}$ found by the algorithm is a counterclockwise sequence of successive vertices of the MPP of J.

Proof by Induction: Let p denote the MPP of J. The first source, O_1, is a convex vertex of p, by Theorem 10.

Let O_n denote any vertex of p. We shall show that if O_n is a source in Algorithm 2, then the source O_{n+1} found by Algorithm 2 is the next vertex of p, moving counterclockwise around p. Let V denote this next vertex of p.

Since J is regular, all possible geometric configurations of subsequences of length 3 in $\beta(J)$ are accounted for in Fig. 9. Furthermore, since J is regular, every concave vertex of p coincides with a concave vertex of $|J|$, and every convex vertex of p coincides with a convex vertex of cJ, by Theorem 8. Recall in our discussion of Rules 1, 2, and 3 that every convex vertex of cJ is an element of $\mathcal{C}$, and every concave vertex of $|J|$ is an element of $\mathfrak{D}$. It follows that every convex vertex of p belongs to $\mathcal{C}$, and that every concave vertex of p belongs to $\mathfrak{D}$. Hence the vertices of p are a subset of $\mathcal{C} \cup \mathfrak{D}$.

Let s_k denote the interior of a segment of ∂p joining O_n counterclockwise to any point in cell β_k, $k > j \geq K(n)$, where β_j contains a member of $\mathcal{C} \cup \mathfrak{D}$.

Suppose $H_k > \Theta_k$ for the first time since establishing the current source O_n. Then s_k contains at least one vertex of p. Suppose s_k has no vertex of p. Then s_k must be straight and must lie in $|\mathcal{B}J|$. It follows that $H_k \leq \Theta_k$, a contradiction of $H_k > \Theta_k$. Hence s_k contains at least one vertex of p.

Since every element of $\beta(J)$ contains at most one member of $\mathcal{C} \cup \mathfrak{D}$, and since $\mathcal{C} \cup \mathfrak{D}$ contains all the vertices of p, it follows that s_k contains precisely one vertex of p, and that this vertex is the last member of $\mathcal{C} \cup \mathfrak{D}$ encountered in moving along $\beta(J)$ from O_n, namely, P_k. This completes the proof.

Since O_1 lies on p, we have the following corollary.

Corollary: Algorithm 2 computes the MPP of any regular complex J in a single revolution around $\beta(J)$.

The Spine Code: To facilitate the implementation of an MPP Finder on a computer, we devised the "spine code" for representing $\beta(J)$. The spine code, a compressed version of the chain code [8], [16], provides a convenient means for computing the elements of $\mathcal{C} \cup \mathfrak{D}$. A description of the spine code is given in Appendix I.

V. Summary and Conclusions

We have shown how the MPP of any regular complex may be found by a relatively simple algorithm (Algorithm 2) based on the concept of the stretched thread. We also proved the validity of the algorithm.

Since Algorithm 2 finds the vertices of the MPP sequentially around $\beta(J)$, this algorithm may be made to terminate at the first encountered concave vertex of the MPP if one merely wishes to detect cellular convexity. This change in Algorithm 2 will shorten significantly the average computation time for recognizing cellularly concave complexes.

In Theorem 9 we showed how the marked virtual-vertex MPP is a complete representation of any regular complex. It follows that the marked virtual-vertex MPP provides an alternative to the distance skeleton for representing a digitized silhouette economically [11], [17].

We have constructed an MPP Finder in the form of a computer program based on Theorems 6 and 7, and have tested it successfully [10]. Our computer program not only detects convexity, but also lists the coordinates of the vertices of the MPP, and indicates whether each of these vertices is convex or concave.

Appendix

The Spine Code

The *spine code* facilitates the determination of the corners of the cells of $\beta(J)$ and the angles of these corners with respect to the current source. These corners and anglés form the data for the MPP Finder.

The *spine sequence* of a chain γ is a sequence of signed digits representing the sequence of directed edges of the *spinal path* formed by the spines of γ. ("Spine" is defined in the proof of Theorem 9.) A spine sequence and the associated spinal path are illustrated in Fig. 13. The magnitude of the ith digit of a spine sequence is the length of the ith edge of the spinal path, with the unit of length equal to the width of a cell. The sign of the ith digit is the sign of the change of slope at the first endpoint of the ith edge of the spinal path.

Special treatment is given to a 180° change of direction, such as point A in Fig. 13. In the spine code, this is represented by a 90° rotation to a vector of length 0, followed by a 90° rotation in the same direction to a vector whose length is the distance to the next vertex of the spinal path. The sign of the change of direction is indicated by the sign of the digit following O. Thus, in Fig. 13, the chain γ is represented by the following spine sequence: $2, -1, 3, 4, 0, 2, -1 \cdots,$

By restricting the alphabet of Freeman's "chain code" to four mutually perpendicular unit vectors, Freeman's "difference sequence" [12] become similar to our spine sequence. To obtain Freeman's difference sequence from our spine sequence, replace $+k$ by 1 followed by a sequence of $k-1$ 0's, and replace $-k$ by -1 followed by $k-1$ 0's. An ex-

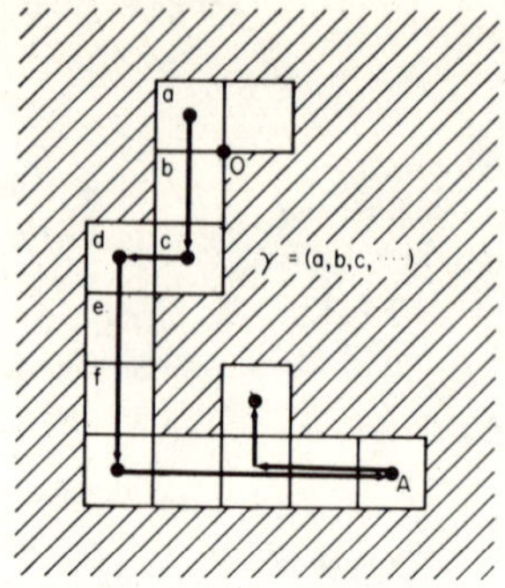

Fig. 13. This complex has the spine sequence $\{2, -1, 3, 4, 0, 2, -1\}$.

ception to this rule occurs at each 0 in the spine sequence. In this case replace the pair $(0, k)$ by 2 and $k-1$ 0's, and replace $(0, -k)$ by -2 and $(k-1)$ 0's.

Clearly the spine sequence of $\beta(J)$ is independent of integer multiples of 90° rotations in $\beta(J)$'s orientation, a property that the spine sequence shares with Freeman's difference sequence.

References

[1] J. Sklansky, "Recognition of convex blobs," *Pattern Recognition*, vol. 2, pp. 3–10, Jan. 1970.
[2] U. Montanari, "On limit properties of digitization schemes," *J. Ass. Comput. Mach.*, vol. 17, pp. 348–360, Apr. 1970.
[3] ——, "A note on minimal length polygonal approximation to a digitized contour," *Commun. Ass. Comput. Mach.*, vol. 13, pp. 41–47, Jan. 1970.
[4] M. Minsky and S. Papert, *Perceptrons.* Cambridge, Mass.: M.I.T. Press, 1969.
[5] J. F. P. Hudson, *Piecewise Linear Topology.* New York: Benjamin, 1969.
[6] A. Rosenfeld, "Connectivity in digital pictures," *J. Ass. Comput. Mach.*, vol. 17, pp. 146–160, Jan. 1970.
[7] J. Feder, "Languages of encoded line patterns," *Inform. Contr.*, vol. 13, pp. 230–244, Sept. 1968.
[8] H. Freeman, "On the encoding of arbitrary geometric configurations," *IRE Trans. Electron. Comput.*, vol. EC-10, pp. 260–268, June 1961.
[9] J. Sklansky, "Measuring concavity on a rectangular mosaic," School Eng., Univ. Calif., Irvine, Tech. Rep. TP-71-4, Sept. 1971.
[10] B. J. Hansen, "Recognizing convex blobs by computer," M.S. thesis, School Eng., Univ. Calif., Irvine, 1969.
[11] J. L. Pfaltz and A. Rosenfeld, "Computer representation of planar regions by their skeletons," *Commun. Ass. Comput. Mach.*, vol. 10, pp. 119–125, 1967.
[12] H. Freeman, "On the digital computer classification of geometric line patterns," in *Proc. Nat. Electron. Conf.*, vol. 18, pp. 312–324, Oct. 1962.
[13] I. M. Yaglom and V. G. Boltyanskii, *Convex Figures.* New York: Holt, Rinehart and Winston, 1961.
[14] J. K. Kelley, *General Topology.* Princeton, N. J.: Van Nostrand, 1955.
[15] W. R. Rudin, *Principles of Mathematical Analysis*, 2nd ed. New York: McGraw-Hill, 1964.
[16] H. Freeman, "Boundary encoding and processing," in *Picture Processing and Psychopictorics.* New York: Academic, 1970.
[17] A. Rosenfeld, *Picture Processing by Computer.* New York: Academic, 1969.

Reprinted with permission from *J. Assn. Comput. Machinery*, **13**, No. 4, 1966, p. 471–494

Sequential Operations in Digital Picture Processing

AZRIEL ROSENFELD AND JOHN L. PFALTZ

University of Maryland, College Park, Maryland*

21

Abstract. The relative merits of performing local operations on a digitized picture in parallel or sequentially are discussed. Sequential local operations are described which label the connected components of a given subset of the picture and compute a "distance" from every picture element to the subset. In terms of the "distance" function, a "skeleton" subset is defined which, in a certain sense, minimally determines the original subset. Some applications of the connected component and distance functions are also presented.

1. *Introduction*

Computer programs for processing digitized pictorial information have received increasing attention in recent years. Much of the work done in this field has involved performing "local" operations on picture "neighborhoods." As several investigators have shown, a wide variety of picture processing transformations can be accomplished by applying such operations independently, or "in parallel," to each element of the given picture.

In this paper it is suggested that local operations performed on picture elements *taken in a definite sequence*, using at each step the results obtained by operating on the preceding elements in the sequence, may be preferable to the parallel approach in some cases. It is shown that the parallel and sequential approaches are mathematically equivalent, and that the latter should be competitive in processing time required if a sequential computer is used.

"Sequential" local operations for performing two basic picture transformations are next described. The first of these labels the connected components of any given picture subset, while the second determines the "distance" (in a certain sense) from every picture element to the nearest element of a given subset. In connection with the latter transformation, a "skeleton" subset is defined which can be used in place of the given subset to generate the same transformed picture by applying the "reverse" local operations sequentially. Examples of the outputs of sequential computer programs which perform these transformations are given.

In the concluding sections of this paper, various applications of these basic picture transformations to the analysis of picture subsets are indicated. Programs are described which construct the graphs corresponding to dissections of a picture into regions and which determine the orders of connectivity of the multiply connected regions. Two approaches to the discrimination of elongated from non-elongated regions or parts of regions using the distance transformation are presented, one of them involving components of the skeleton subset.

2. *Sequential and Parallel Neighborhood Operations*

2.1. *Operations on digitized pictures*

A digitized picture, for the purposes of this discussion, is a finite rectangular array of "points" or "elements," each of which has associated with it one of a dis-

* Computer Science Center. The research described in this paper was supported in part by NASA Grant NsG-398 to the University of Maryland, and in part under NASA Contract NAS5-3461 with the Budd Company, McLean, Virginia.

crete finite set of "values." If the array has m rows and n columns, any "point" in it is specified by a pair of numbers i, j $(1 \leqq i \leqq m, \quad 1 \leqq j \leqq n)$ denoting its row and column. The picture can thus be represented as an m by n matrix in which each entry a_{ij} has one of the "values," say $v_1, \cdots, v_k$. In practice, m and n are usually not greater than 2^{10}, and k is rarely greater than 2^6. We assume in what follows that the values are nonnegative integers.

By an *operation* on a digitized picture is meant a function which transforms a given picture matrix into another one. A general function of this type has mn numerical arguments (one for each position in the matrix), and is correspondingly difficult to handle computationally. For practical purposes, it is desirable to work with operations on digitized pictures which can be defined in terms of functions having considerably fewer arguments.

By a *local operation* or *neighborhood operation* on a picture is meant a function which defines a value for each element in the transformed picture in terms of the values of the corresponding element and a small set of its neighbors in the given picture. For example, such operations can be defined using a neighborhood which consists of the given element and its eight immediate neighbors; an operation of this type has only nine arguments and is of the form

$$a^*_{i,j} = f(a_{i-1,j-1}, a_{i-1,j}, a_{i-1,j+1}, a_{i,j-1}, a_{i,j}, a_{i,j+1}, a_{i+1,j-1}, a_{i+1,j}, a_{i+1,j+1}).$$

In what follows only operations of this type are considered.[1]

Local operations can also be used to define *local properties* of a picture. If $f: a_{i,j} \to a^*_{i,j}$ is a local operation, one can speak of *the property that* $a^*_{i,j} = v$, where v is a picture element value.

It is sometimes convenient to consider operations which involve more than one picture at a time. Strictly speaking, however, this is no more general than operating on a single picture. In fact, we have:

LEMMA. *Let (a_{ij}), (b_{ij}) be m by n pictures; then there exist an m by n picture (c_{ij}) and two functions g, h such that $g(c_{ij}) = a_{ij}$, $h(c_{ij}) = b_{ij}$ for all i, j.*

PROOF. Let $c_{ij} = 2^{a_{ij}}3^{b_{ij}}$, so that c_{ij} is a positive integer; let $g = \phi_2$, $h = \phi_3$, where ϕ_2, ϕ_3 are defined for positive integer x by

$$\phi_2(x) = \max \{k \mid k \text{ nonnegative integer; } 2^k \text{ divides } x\},$$

$$\phi_3(x) = \max \{k \mid k \text{ nonnegative integer; } 3^k \text{ divides } x\}.$$

COROLLARY. *Let f be any function which takes a* pair *of m by n pictures into an m by n picture, say $f((a_{ij}), (b_{ij})) = (d_{ij})$. Then there exist a picture (c_{ij}) and a function f^* such that $f^*(c_{ij}) = (d_{ij})$.*

PROOF. Take (c_{ij}), g, h, as in the proof of the Lemma and define $f^*(c_{ij}) = f(g(c_{ij}), h(c_{ij}))$.

Evidently this argument generalizes immediately to operations on any number of pictures. Note also that if f is local—in other words, if d_{ij} depends only on $a_{i-1,j-1}$,

[1] The function f is not defined for "border" picture elements which do not have all eight neighbors. To avoid such exceptions, one can "augment" the picture matrix by adding a zeroth row and column, an $(m+1)$-st row and an $(n+1)$-st column, giving these fictitious elements a value which does not occur in the "real" picture array, and defining the function appropriately when some of its arguments have this value. In many of the cases considered in what follows, one can avoid this complication by simply adding to the definition of f the phrase "for whichever of these elements is defined."

$\cdots, a_{i+1,j+1}$ and on $b_{i-1,j-1}, \cdots, b_{i+1,j+1}$—then f^* is also local, since c_{ij} depends only on a_{ij} and b_{ij}.

When processing a picture using local operations, it is often convenient to store the results of intermediate processing steps as auxiliary pictures. By the Lemma and the last remark, local operations involving such auxiliary pictures can be regarded as operations on a single picture. In Section 3 and in the Appendix repeated advantage is taken of this convenience.

2.2 *Parallel operations*

Many useful transformations of a given picture can be achieved by performing a single local operation, or at most a few of them in succession, on each point of the picture. For example, a "noisy" picture can often be effectively "smoothed," or an "unsharp" picture "enhanced," by a single neighborhood operation which takes a local average or computes a finite-difference Laplacian. Similarly, a picture which contains thick "roads" (lines or curves of points having given values) can be "thinned" by iterating a "border element deletion" operation, perhaps alternated with a smoothing operation, where the number of iterations required is relatively small since the roads are narrow compared to the picture size. Transformations of these types have been demonstrated by Dinneen [1], Kirsch [2], Unger [3], Narasimhan [4] and others. These operations can also be used to define picture subsets consisting of points which have smooth or broken neighborhoods, lie on edges or roads, and so on.

Each of the local operations used in the examples just given is performed independently on every point of the picture. The arguments $(a_{i-1,j-1}, \cdots, a_{i+1,j+1})$ are always the original picture matrix values; the new values $a^*_{ij} = f(a_{i-1,j-1}, \cdots, a_{i+1,j+1})$ are stored, but are not used until the operation has been performed for every (i, j), when they then become arguments for the next operation (if any). Since the sequence in which the points are processed is thus entirely irrelevant, the operation can be thought of as being performed "in parallel," simultaneously for every picture point. Extensive consideration has in fact been given to the design of computers which actually do perform identical operations simultaneously on each of a large number of stored quantities. Even when processing digitized pictures on conventional sequential computers, many investigators have used programs which simulate the operation of such "parallel" machines.

The wide variety of picture transformations which can be performed using local operations applied in parallel has given rise to the widespread belief that this approach is optimum for local picture processing in general. In this paper the counter-suggestion is made that an alternative type of processing, in which *sequential* application of local operations plays a crucial role, is equally general in scope, and may even have significant advantages, particularly when processing is being done on a sequential computer.

The concept of a sequentially applied neighborhood operation will be defined in what follows, and the relative merits of the parallel and sequential approaches considered.

2.3 *Sequential operations*

Suppose that a local operation is applied to the points of a digitized picture in some definite sequence. For simplicity, suppose that the points are processed row by row beginning at the upper left—that is, in the sequence $a_{11}, a_{12}, \cdots, a_{1n}$,

$a_{21}, \cdots, a_{2n}, \cdots, a_{m1}, \cdots, a_{mn}$. Unlike the cases described in Section 2.2, however, suppose that as soon as a point is processed, its *new* value rather than the original value is used in processing any succeeding points which have it as neighbor. If this is done, the general form of the operation becomes

$$a_{i,j}^* = f(a_{i-1,j-1}^*, a_{i-1,j}^*, a_{i-1,j+1}^*, a_{i,j-1}^*, a_{i,j}, a_{i,j+1}, a_{i+1,j-1}, a_{i+1,j}, a_{i+1,j+1}),$$

since points $(i-1, j-1)$, $(i-1, j)$, $(i-1, j+1)$ and $(i, j-1)$ have already been processed, while the remaining points have not yet been processed. Such an operation will be called *sequential.*

The particular processing sequence just described will be called the (forward) *raster* sequence. There will be occasion in the next two sections to use other sequences as well.

At first glance, this type of operation seems more complex, and hence presumably less basic, than the "parallel" type, which uniformly uses "old" values until the entire picture has been processed. However, it is easily shown that the two types of operation are entirely equivalent in the sense of the following.

THEOREM. *Any picture transformation that can be accomplished by a series of parallel local operations can also be accomplished by a series of sequential local operations, and conversely.*

A proof of this Theorem is given in Appendix A.

In the proof, it is shown that any parallel local operation is equivalent to just two sequential local operations; but to guarantee that a sequential local operation is matched by parallel local operations, a long sequence of the latter may be required. In practice, one can often obtain the result of a sequential operation using relatively few parallel operations which produce the result without following the stepwise progress of the sequential operation. However, it at least appears plausible that there exist picture transformations which are more efficiently performed using sequentially applied operations, particularly if a sequential computer must be used.

As an illustration, consider the distance transformation defined in Section 4. It can be performed by two sequentially applied local operations, involving a total of $2mn$ individual local operations. On the other hand, it is easily verified that this transformation can also be accomplished by applying the local operation

$$f(a_{i,j}) = \min(a_{i-1,j}, a_{i+1,j}, a_{i,j-1}, a_{i,j+1}) + 1 \quad \text{if} \quad a_{i,j} \neq 0, \quad f(0) = 0,$$

$m+n$ times in parallel to every picture element. If this is done on a sequential computer, it involves $mn(m+n)$ individual local operations—that is, $(m+n)/2$ times as many as required by the method of Section 4. Note, however, that if a parallel computer is available, it need perform only $m+n$ local operations on the picture in parallel, a saving by a factor of $2mn/(m+n)$ over the method of Section 4. Thus if $m = n$, parallel processing on a parallel computer is n times faster than sequential processing on a sequential computer; but this in turn is n times faster than parallel processing on a sequential computer even when this efficient parallel method of performing the transformation is used.

3. *Sequential Operations for Connected Component Discrimination*

A set of sequentially applied local operations which "labels" the connected components of any given picture subset is described in this section. For simplicity, it is

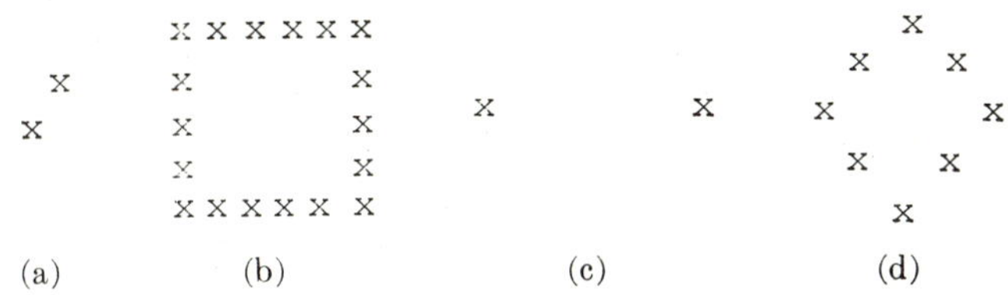

FIG. 1. Examples of connected and nonconnected sets

assumed that the given subset consists of picture elements which have value 0, while every other element has value 1. The results can be immediately extended to subsets consisting of elements which have any given property; it suffices to first transform the picture using the characteristic function of the complementary property.

3.1 *Connectivity*

A subset of a digitized picture is called *connected* if for any two points P and Q of the subset there exists a sequence of points $P = P_0, P_1, P_2, \cdots, P_{n-1}, P_n = Q$ of the subset such that P_i is a neighbor of P_{i-1}, $1 \leqq i \leqq n$. In Figure 1(a), the set of x's and the set of blank points are both connected; in Figure 1(b), the x's are connected but the blanks are not; in Figure 1(c), the blanks are connected but the x's are not. For these examples, the definition agrees with the intuitive concept of connectivity. On the other hand, both the x's and blanks in Figure 1(d) are connected, which runs counter to intuition. This results from the fact that a point is connected to any of its eight neighbors, including the diagonal ones. If connectivity were redefined to require that P_i be one of the four horizontal and vertical neighbors of P_{i-1}, both the x's and blanks in Figure 1d would become disconnected, which is still not consistent with intuition. The "paradox" of Figure 1d can be rephrased as follows: If the "curve" of shaded points is connected ("gapless"), it does not disconnect its interior from its exterior; if it is totally disconnected, it *does* disconnect them. This is of course not a mathematical paradox, but it is unsatisfying intuitively; nevertheless, connectivity is still a useful concept. It should be noted that if a digitized picture is defined as an array of hexagonal, rather than square, elements, the paradox disappears; this is because in the hexagonal case an element has an edge in common with every one of its six neighbors.

In general, a subset of a picture (say the subset of "0" points) consists of a number of connected parts or *components*.[2] The problem of distinguishing among these components is now to be considered. Specifically, it is desired to construct a transformed picture in which the 0 points have new values $v_1, \cdots, v_k$ (positive integers each greater than 1), two points having the same value if and only if they belong to the same connected component of 0 points on the original picture.

Neighborhood operations lend themselves naturally to the study of connectivity, since it is defined in terms of neighbors. If the operations are applied in parallel, it is not easy to distinguish among connected components, since the parallel operations treat every point of the given set identically. Using sequentially applied operations, however, one can "track" each connected region, assigning a value to each point of it as the tracking proceeds. If two of the tracked regions merge, a

[2] Formally, these components are the *equivalence classes* of picture points defined by the relation "is connected to" (that is: "is a neighbor of a neighbor . . . of a neighbor of"), which is evidently an equivalence relation.

special value is assigned. Further processing is then applied to these special values so as to eliminate redundant values from the picture.

In Section 3.2 a set of sequential local operations is defined which assigns to every point of each connected region on the picture a value which labels the region. In Section 3.3 a computer program is described which generally follows this sequence of operations but which does not adhere strictly to the requirement that only local operations are permitted, and which in consequence is considerably more efficient.

3.2 *Sequential operations for determining connected components of a picture*

Let f be the local operation which takes $a_{i,j}$ into $a'_{i,j}$ defined by:

(a) If $a_{i,j} = 1$, then $a'_{i,j} = 1$.

(b) If $a_{i,j} = 0$, and $a'_{i-1,j-1} = a'_{i-1,j} = a'_{i-1,j+1} = a'_{i,j-1} = 1$, then $a'_{i,j} = v_k$, where v_k is one of a set of as yet unused labels. (This indicates that $a_{i,j}$ is possibly the start of a new connected component of 0's. If it is not desired to allow an operation which can draw on a set of labels in this way, one can simply use 2^i3^j as the label; these labels are automatically distinct for all i, j.)

(c) If $a_{i,j} = 0$ and each of $a'_{i-1,j-1}$, $a'_{i-1,j}$, $a'_{i-1,j+1}$ and $a'_{i,j-1}$ is either 1 or some v_k (but not all of them are 1), then $a'_{i,j}$ is the smallest of the v_k's. (If there is only one v_k, this indicates that $a'_{i,j}$ belongs to that same component. If there is more than one, it indicates that two or more components were actually parts of the same component.)

Furthermore, let f also create an auxiliary picture (b_{ij}) in which $b_{i,j} = 1$ when more than one v_k is involved in case (c), and $b_{i,j} = 0$ otherwise. (These 1's thus label points at which two or more components have "merged." It is clear that (b_{ij}) could be combined with (a'_{ij}), if desired, by the method of the Lemma in Section 2.1.) When f is applied to a binary picture sequentially, e.g., in forward raster sequence, it labels the 0's in such a way that 0's which get the same label must belong to the same connected component; note, however, that the 0's in a given component may have several labels.

To complete the task of labeling the connected components, it remains only to eliminate all labels which have merged with other ones. For example, if v_r has "met" v_s, where $v_r < v_s$, one should replace all the v_s's prior to the meeting point with v_r's.

If one were not restricted to performing only local operations on the picture, it would be fairly easy to eliminate the redundant labels by processing a list of the redundant pairs. A method for doing this is described in Section 4. In the remainder of this section, elimination of redundancies using local operations only is described.

After f has been performed, the redundancies are identified by 1's in (b_{ij}) at the points where they were detected. To eliminate a redundancy, say of v_s with v_r, *using only local operations*, it is necessary to convey the information that v_s "equals" v_r to the neighborhood of every point (i, j) of the picture, so that if $a'_{i,j}$ has value v_s, it can be replaced by v_r. This is done for one redundancy at a time by proceeding as follows.

(1) *Pick the first redundancy not yet processed.* This can be done by applying a local operation to (b_{ij}) in *zigzag* sequence $(1, 1), \cdots, (1, n), (2, n), \cdots, (2, 1), (3, 1), \cdots, (3, n), \cdots, (m, 1), \cdots, (m, n)$ if m is odd; $\cdots, (m, n), \cdots, (m, 1)$ if m is even. This operation g takes (b_{ij}) into (b'_{ij}), and also generates an auxiliary pic-

ture (c_{ij}), such that $b'_{1,1} = c_{1,1} = 0$ and the succeeding elements are defined as follows:

For $(i, j) \neq (1, 1)$, let (i', j') denote the predecessor of (i, j) in the zigzag sequence.

If $c_{i',j'} = b_{i,j} = 0$, then $b'_{i,j} = c_{i,j} = 0$.

If $c_{i',j'} = 0$ and $b_{i,j} = 1$, then $b'_{i,j} = 0$ and $c'_{i,j} = 1$.

If $c_{i',j'} = 1$ or 2, then $b'_{i,j} = b_{i,j}$ and $c_{i,j} = 2$.

Thus g "erases" the first 1 in (b_{ij}) ("first" in the sense of the zigzag sequence) and stores a 1 in the corresponding position in (c_{ij}). (Note that the first 1 in (b_{ij}) cannot be in the first row, since components cannot yet have merged; hence setting $b'_{1,1} = c_{1,1} = 0$ is safe.) As soon as it has done this, it stores 2's in (c_{ij}) thereafter; this keeps it from mistaking subsequent 1's in (b_{ij}) for "first." The reason for using the zigzag sequence is to ensure that (i', j') is always a neighbor of (i, j), so that g is local.

(2) *"Transmit" the information about this redundancy to every point.* Let $c_{x,y} = 1$, and let $v_p < v_q \leqq v_r \leqq v_s$ be labels of $a'_{x-1,y-1}$, $a'_{x-1,y}$, $a'_{x-1,y+1}$ or $a'_{x,y-1}$. It is desired to express the fact that the labels v_q, v_r, v_s are to be replaced by v_p. This can be done by using the integer $v = 2^{v_p}3^{v_q}5^{v_r}7^{v_s}$ as a label, since this integer carries the values v_p, v_q, v_r, v_s in retrievable form, as well as indicating which of them is to replace the others. To get this information to every point, one constructs an auxiliary picture every element of which has value v. Specifically, one defines the local operation h_1, taking (c_{ij}) into (d_{ij}) such that $d_{1,1} = 0$ and:

If $d_{i',j'} = 0$ and $c_{i,j} \neq 1$, then $d_{i,j} = 0$.

If $d_{i',j'} = 0$ and $c_{i,j} = 1$, then $d_{i,j} = v$, where v is defined in terms of the elements $a_{i-1,j-1}$, $a_{i-1,j}$, $a_{i-1,j+1}$ and $a_{i,j-1}$ as described just above.

If $d_{i',j'} = v$, then $d_{i,j} = v$.

Thus h_1, applied in zigzag sequence, constructs a picture (d_{ij}) in which every element after the 1 in (c_{ij}) is v. (In particular, $d_{m,n} = v$.) To make the remaining elements v's, one need only apply a simple local operation h_2, in *reverse* zigzag sequence. Let (i'', j'') denote the predecessor of (i, j) in this sequence, and let h_2 take (d_{ij}) into (d^*_{ij}) such that $d^*_{m,n} = d_{m,n} = v$, and $d^*_{i,j} = v$ whenever $d_{i'',j''} = v$.

(3) *Use this information to correct the redundancy.* It remains only to define the function h by

$$h(a'_{i,j}) = v_p \quad \text{if} \quad a'_{i,j} = v_q,\ v_r \text{ or } v_s,$$

$$h(a'_{i,j}) = a'_{i,j} \qquad \text{otherwise.}$$

This is a local operation—indeed, it operates only on a single (i, j) at a time—since $(d^*_{i,j})$ has brought these v's to every (i, j); it can be applied in any sequence. The resulting transform of (a'_{ij}) has all its v_q's, v_r's and v_s's replaced by v_p's, and is otherwise the same as a'_{ij}.

We now *repeat the process* described in (1)–(3), but starting with the new (a'_{ij}) and with (b'_{ij}). Application of g in zigzag sequence now erases the first 1 in (b'_{ij}), say $b_{z,w}$ (which was the second 1 in (b_{ij})), and leaves the rest of it unchanged; it also constructs a new (c_{ij}) with a 1 in the (z, w) position. Application of h_1 and h_2 then yields a new (d^*_{ij}) with appropriate label v (not the same as the previous v). It is quite possible that the redundancy at (z, w) involved only v_p, v_q, v_r or v_s, and is now eliminated; in this case the new v reduces to 2^{v_p}, and application of h does nothing to (a'_{ij}). In any event, this second cycle of (1)–(3) yields an (a'_{ij}) in which further possible redundancies have been eliminated.

Let this entire process be repeated as many times as necessary. (One can, of course, stop when there are no more 1's in (b_{ij}), but if only local operations are involved, this can only be detected by performing a counting operation on (b_{ij}) after each iteration. Certainly mn repetitions—in fact, considerably fewer—will suffice to clear up all the redundancies in (a'_{ij}).)

In summary: Given (a_{ij}) in which every element is 0 or 1, one can construct (a'_{ij}) in which every connected component of 0's has a unique label by proceeding as follows:

(a) Apply f to (a_{ij}) in (e.g.) raster sequence (zigzag would do just as well).

(b) Iterate the following sequence mn times: (g in zigzag sequence; h_1 in zigzag sequence; h_2 in reverse zigzag sequence; h in any sequence).

3.3 *Programming considerations*

A practical computer program for determining connected components along the lines described above need not be as elaborate, since it need not restrict itself to local operations alone. Some immediate shortcuts, once other types of operations are permitted, include the following:

(a) The "redundancies" can be stored as a *table* "outside" the picture; this greatly reduces storage requirements.[3]

(b) Elimination of redundancies can be performed by processing this table. When this has been done, the redundant picture element labels can be "translated" into irredundant ones as the very last step, by making one scan of the picture, "looking up" each value in the processed table and substituting the equivalent irredundant value if different from the given value.

(c) The table can be processed in many fewer steps than are required to process redundancies within the picture, since (1) the table is in general much smaller; (2) when a redundancy is being "reduced," it need not be "carried" through the table, since processing is not constrained to neighborhoods within the table; (3) it is easy to stop the processing when the table is exhausted, rather than blindly repeating it mn times.

In the light of these simplifications, a program for labeling connected components can proceed as follows:

(1) Apply f as described in Section 3.2; but rather than generating an auxiliary picture (b_{ij}), simply store the redundant labels in the first unused place in a table T. The ith entry in this table thus has the form $(v_{pi}, v_{qi}, v_{ri}, v_{si})$, where $v_{pi} < v_{qi} \leqq v_{ri} \leqq v_{si}$.

(2) To process the table:

(a) Order the entries lexicographically (in order of increasing first value; for each of these, in order of increasing second value; and so on).

(b) Store $(v_{p1}, v_{q1}, v_{r1}, v_{s1})$ in a second table T'. In the remaining entries, replace every v_{q1}, v_{r1} and v_{s1} by v_{p1}. Reorder each entry (if necessary) to re-establish $v_{pi} < v_{qi} \leqq v_{ri} \leqq v_{si}$; if all terms are equal, erase the entry.

---

[3] Since auxiliary tables which contain stored information about the picture are used in this and the following steps, the operations performed are no longer local; the table makes available information about picture elements which are not neighbors of the element being processed.

Repeat steps (a) and (b) until every entry has been erased or stored in T'. When this is finished, T' consists of a set of entries in lexicographic order. The first term of each entry is the smallest representative of an equivalence class of redundant values; the remaining terms of the entries which have first term v are the remaining elements of its equivalence class.

(3) Scan the picture in any sequence, comparing the value of each element with the entries in T'. Whenever a value is found to be in T', but not as a first term, replace it by the corresponding first term. (If desired, gaps in the sequence of labels can be "closed up" before output.)

Note that this program consists basically of a single sequentially applied local operation (step (1), except that the redundancies are stored outside the picture to simplify the remaining steps), followed by sequential processing of the table and sequential relabeling of the picture. The approach is still essentially sequential, even though for simplicity the restriction to "pure" neighborhood operations has been relaxed.

An IBM 7090/94 program along these lines has been written and tested. The program, originally written in the FAP symbolic assembly language, has been adapted so that it can be called as a FORTRAN subroutine. It accepts as input a digital picture on magnetic tape. Each record on the tape contains information about one row of the picture. A picture element can have any value from 0 to 2^6-1, and each row can consist of up to 2,000 elements. The number of rows is limited only by the capacity of the tape.

The program selects any prespecified rectangular subpicture (rows r through $r+u$, columns s through $s+v$, for example). It slices the picture element values between any two prespecified levels t_1, t_2 ($0 \leqq t_1 \leqq t_2 < 2^6-1$), treating all values between t_1 and t_2 as 0 and all values outside the range as 1. The program then proceeds to label the connected components of the set of 0's essentially as described above. The labels used for processing are simply the integers. For printout purposes, only the 46 distinct labels

ABCDEFGHIJKLMNOPQRSTUVWXYZ123456789+−/=|.) $*,(

are used, in that order. If there are more than 46 connected components, these symbols are used over and over again, as many times as necessary. The output is a matrix of alphanumerics in which the symbol printed at each 0 point is the label of the connected component which contains the point; 1 points are left blank. A labeled version of the picture is also written on tape for input to succeeding processing routines.

An example of a simple picture input to the program is shown as Figure 2 (1 ≡ black, 0 ≡ white). The corresponding output for this picture is shown as Figure 3. In this picture, the component labeled I, for example, had three labels in the original processing, since it was detected as a possible "new" component at each of the three elements which are circled in the figure. Component D obviously had many labels originally, while components A and C had unique labels throughout the processing.

4. *Sequential Operations for Distance Determination*

Several investigators over the past decade have considered picture transformations in which a given subset is "propagated" over the picture, or dually in which the

FIG. 2. Picture input to processing programs

FIG. 3. Connected component transform of Figure 2

subset is examined by an expanding array of sensors. (For the latter approach see Harmon [5] and Singer [6–8]; compare also Stevens [9].) In early work on digital picture processing (Kirsch [2]), a transformation of this type was performed by a sequence of local operations performed in parallel; this approach requires two operations for each incremental propagation step. More recent discussions of this type of transformation and its implications for shape description may be found in several papers by Blum [10–12] (see also Kotelly [13]), who also considers the possible role of such transformations in visual form perception.

"Propagating" a subset over a picture is tantamount to finding the "*distance*," in the sense of the propagation process, between the subset and each point of the picture. In this section a simple "distance" concept, appropriate to digitized pictures, is introduced, and a transformation is defined which determines the distance from every picture element to a given subset.

4.1 *Distance*

Let P and Q be any two distinct points in a digitized picture, and let $d^*(P, Q)$ be the smallest positive integer such that there exists a sequence of distinct points $P = P_0, P_1, \cdots, P_n = Q$ with P_i a neighbor of P_{i-1}, $1 \leqq i \leqq n$. This d^* is called the *distance* from P to Q; if $P = Q$, the distance between them is defined as zero. The distance from P to a given subset S of the picture is defined as the smallest of the distances from P to the points in S.

Like connectivity, the distance concept is defined by iterating the property of being a neighbor. Here, however, the minimum number of iterations required to "reach" Q from P is of interest, whereas in the case of connectivity, the question considered was whether Q could be reached at all from P using only points in a given subset as intermediate points. As was pointed out for connectivity in Section 3.1, a distance can also be defined using only horizontal and vertical neighbors as "steps." If $d(P, Q)$ is the distance from P to Q using this more restricted definition, it is clear that $d \geqq d^*$. For simplicity, the restricted definition is used in the remainder of this paper.

Evidently, $d(P, Q)$ (and similarly for d^*) has all the properties of a *metric*.[4] It should be emphasized, however, that d is not even approximately the Euclidean distance. In fact, the locus of points at a given distance $d > 0$ from a given point P is a diagonally oriented square of side $d+1$ centered at P, rather than a circle.[5]

4.2 *Distance transformation*

Given a digitized picture whose elements have only the values 0 and 1, it is desired to construct a distance transform of the picture in which each element has an integer value equal to its distance from the set of 0's. (It is assumed that the set of 0's is nonempty.) Thus in particular, the 0's remain unchanged, since they are at zero distance from themselves; the 1's which are horizontal or vertical neighbors of 0's also remain unchanged; the 1's which are horizontal or vertical neighbors of such 1's become 2's; and so on.

This transform can be performed using just two sequentially applied local operations as follows. Let

$$\begin{aligned} f_1(a_{i,j}) &= 0 && \text{if } a_{i,j} = 0, \\ &= \min(a_{i-1,j} + 1, a_{i,j-1} + 1) && \text{if } (i,j) \neq (1,1) \text{ and } a_{i,j} = 1, \\ &= m + n && \text{if } (i,j) = (1,1) \text{ and } a_{1,1} = 1, \\ f_2(a_{i,j}) &= \min(a_{i,j}, a_{i+1,j} + 1, a_{i,j+1} + 1). \end{aligned}$$

Since no two points of the picture can be distance $m+n$ apart, we know that $a_{1,1}$ is at a distance less than $m+n$ from the set of 0's, if this set is nonempty; thus the

[4] It is positive definite by definition, and is clearly symmetric (the reversal of a sequence from P to Q is a sequence from Q to P and vice versa). Moreover, since any two sequences from P to Q and Q to R, respectively, can be put end to end to give a sequence from P to R, it evidently satisfies the triangle inequality.

[5] For the metric d^*, the corresponding locus is an upright square of side $2\,d+1$ centered at P.

final value of $a_{1,1}$ (or of any other element labeled $m+n$ by f_1) will be the value assigned to it by f_2.

THEOREM. *Let $C = (c_{i,j})$ be the picture which results when f_1 is applied to the picture $A = (a_{i,j})$ in forward raster sequence, followed by f_2 in* reverse *raster sequence. Then C is the distance transform of A.*

PROOF. Note first that if $a_{i,j} = 1$ and a horizontal or vertical neighbor of $a_{i,j}$ is zero, evidently $c_{i,j} = 1$, and conversely. Suppose now that $c_{i,j}$ is equal to the distance from the (i, j) element to the closest zero element in A for all (i, j) such that this distance is less than k. Let $B = (b_{i,j})$ be the picture which results from applying f_1 in forward raster sequence to A. If $c_{i,j} = k$, by the induction hypothesis the distance from the (i, j) element to the nearest zero must be at least k. If it is greater than k, by definition of distance it must be at least k for each of the (i, j) element's horizontal and vertical neighbors. In particular, $c_{i+1,j}$ and $c_{i,j+1}$ each are greater than or equal to k, so that $c_{i,j} = k$ implies $b_{i,j} = k$ by definition of f_2. But then $b_{i-1,j}$ or $b_{i,j-1}$, say the former, must be $k-1$ by definition of f_1, so that $c_{i-1,j} \leqq k - 1$; contradiction.

The distance transforms for a circle, two rectangles[6] and regions F, J and K of Figure 3 are shown as Figure 4. These transforms illustrate the output of an IBM 7090/94 program, written in FORTRAN, which accepts input digital picture data as described in Section 3.3. For simplicity, only the odd distance values are printed out modulo 10, while the even values are left blank; the points with value zero are printed as X's.

4.3 *Distance skeleton*

Blum has suggested [12] that the locus of points at which the propagation wave front "intersects itself" may be perceptually important. This locus defines a sort of "skeleton" (Blum: "medial axis") for the original picture. In this subsection, a skeleton subset is defined for the distance transform introduced above,[7] and it is shown that this skeleton is the smallest subset of the transform picture from which the entire transform picture can be reconstructed by "reversing" the distance-measuring process.

Define the local operations g_1 and g_2 by

$$g_1(a_{i,j}) = \max(a_{i,j}, a_{i,j-1} - 1, a_{i-1,j} - 1),$$

$$g_2(a_{i,j}) = \max(a_{i,j}, a_{i,j+1} - 1, a_{i+1,j} - 1).$$

Let $G_1(P)$ be the picture which results when g_1 is applied to P in forward raster sequence; $G_2(P)$, the result of applying g_2 to P in backward raster sequence; and $G(P) = G_2(G_1(P))$.

LEMMA 1. *If A is any picture and $G(A) = (c_{ij})$, then all of $|c_{i,j} - c_{i+1,j}|$, $|c_{i,j} - c_{i,j+1}|$, $|c_{i,j} - c_{i-1,j}|$ and $|c_{i,j} - c_{i,j-1}|$ which are defined are less than or equal to* 1.

PROOF. Let $A = (a_{ij})$, $G_1(A) = (b_{ij})$. By definition of g_1,

$$b_{i,j} \geqq b_{i,j-1} - 1 \quad \text{and} \quad b_{i,j} \geqq b_{i-1,j} - 1, \qquad \text{for all } i, j,$$

[6] The two rectangles actually have the same proportions; the difference between their shapes in the figure results from the unequal horizontal and vertical size of a character space. The circle appears distorted for the same reason.

[7] It should be emphasized that since the distance considered here is non-Euclidean, as already pointed out, the resulting skeleton is not likely to have any special significance for visual form perception; however, it is still a useful picture processing tool.

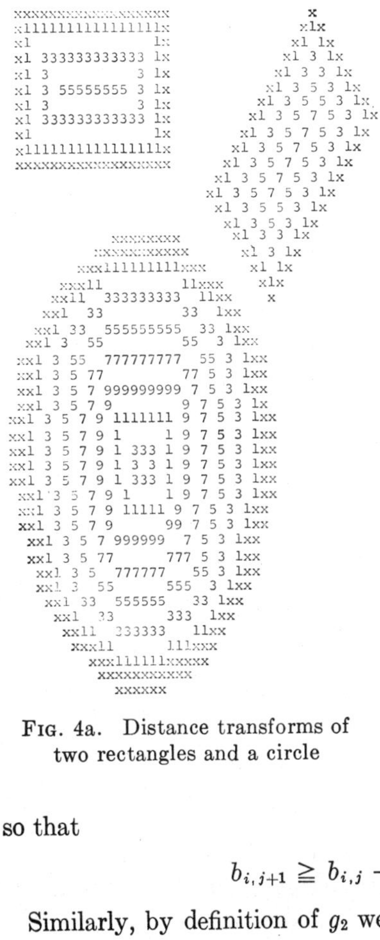

FIG. 4a. Distance transforms of two rectangles and a circle

FIG. 4b. Distance transforms of components F, J, K of Figure 3

so that

$$b_{i,j+1} \geqq b_{i,j} - 1 \quad \text{and} \quad b_{i+1,j} \geqq b_{i,j} - 1, \qquad \text{for all } i, j.$$

Similarly, by definition of g_2 we have for any $B = (b_{ij})$ and for all i, j,

$$c_{i,j} \geqq c_{i,j+1} - 1, \qquad c_{i,j} \geqq c_{i+1,j} - 1,$$

$$c_{i,j-1} \geqq c_{i,j} - 1, \qquad c_{i-1,j} \geqq c_{i,j} - 1,$$

where $G_2(B) = (c_{ij})$.

If it can be shown that the above relations on the b's remain true when the b's are replaced by c's (that is, when g_2 is applied), the assertion made in Lemma 1 will follow immediately, since (e.g.) $c_{i,j-1} \geqq c_{i,j} - 1$ and $c_{i,j} \geqq c_{i,j-1} - 1$ are equivalent to $|c_{i,j} - c_{i,j-1}| \leqq 1$.

Suppose that these relations hold for all the c's through the (i, j)-th in the sense of the backward raster sequence. Since g_2 can never decrease the value of a picture element, we have $b_{i,j-1} \leqq b_{i,j} + 1 \leqq c_{i,j} + 1$. By the induction hypothesis, $c_{i+1,j-1} - 1 \leqq c_{i+1,j}$, and by the relations on the c's, this is less than or equal to $c_{i,j} + 1$. Hence

$$c_{i,j-1} = \max (b_{i,j-1}, c_{i,j} - 1, c_{i+1,j-1} - 1) \leqq c_{i,j} + 1,$$

proving the induction step. Finally,

$$c_{m,n-1} = \max (b_{m,n-1}, c_{m,n} - 1) \leqq \max (b_{m,n} + 1, c_{m,n} + 1) = c_{m,n} + 1,$$

and similarly $c_{m-1,n} \leqq c_{m,n} + 1$. This completes the proof.

LEMMA 2. *Let A be a picture such that $a_{i,j} \geqq a_{i,j-1} - 1$ and $a_{i,j} \geqq a_{i-1,j} - 1$ for all i, j; then $G_1(A) = A$. Similarly, if A is such that $a_{i,j} \geqq a_{i,j+1} - 1$ and $a_{i,j} \geqq a_{i+1,j} - 1$ for all i, j, then $G_2(A) = A$.*

PROOF. Clearly $g_1(a_{11}) = a_{11}$. If $G_1(A) = A$ for all elements up to the i, jth (in the sense of the forward raster sequence), then

$$\begin{aligned} g_1(a_{i,j}) &= \max (a_{i,j}, g_1(a_{i,j-1}) - 1, g_1(a_{i-1,j}) - 1) \\ &= \max (a_{i,j}, a_{i,j-1} - 1, a_{i-1,j} - 1) \end{aligned}$$

by induction hypothesis, and this equals $a_{i,j}$ by the original assumption about A. The proof of the second part is exactly analogous.

COROLLARY. $G_1(G_1(A)) = G_1(A)$, $G_2(G_2(A)) = G_2(A)$ *and* $G(G(A)) = G(A)$ *for all* A.

PROOF. By the proof of Lemma 1, $G_1(A)$ has the properties of the first part of Lemma 2, so that $G_1(G_1(A)) = G_1(A)$; similarly for $G_2(A)$. By Lemma 1, $G(A)$ has the properties of both parts of Lemma 2; hence by Lemma 2 $G(G(A)) = G_2(G_1(G(A))) = G_2(G(A)) = G(A)$.

LEMMA 3. *The distance transform of any picture has the property of Lemma* 1.

PROOF. By the Theorem of Section 4.2, in such a picture each element value is equal to the distance from the element to a zero-valued element, and clearly these distances for an element and any of its neighbors can differ by at most 1.

COROLLARY. *If T is any distance transform picture, $G(T) = T$.*

Proof. The proof is as for the Corollary to Lemma 2.

LEMMA 4. *Let $A = (a_{ij})$, $B = (b_{ij})$ be pictures such that $a_{i,j} \leqq b_{i,j}$ for all i, j. Let $G(A) = (c_{ij})$, $G(B) = (d_{ij})$, and let $a_{h,k} = b_{h,k} = d_{h,k}$ for some h, k. Then $a_{h,k} = c_{h,k}$.*

PROOF. Evidently we must have $c_{i,j} \leqq d_{i,j}$ for all i, j, so that $c_{h,k} \leqq d_{h,k} = a_{h,k}$. But G never decreases the value of a picture element; hence $a_{h,k} \leqq c_{h,k}$.

If $P = (p_{ij})$ is any picture, $P' = (p'_{ij})$ will be called a *partial picture* of P if $p'_{i,j} = p_{i,j}$ or 0 for all i, j.

COROLLARY. *Let T be any distance transform picture, T' any partial picture of T. Then all the elements of T' which are equal to the corresponding elements of T are invariant under G.*

PROOF. Take $A = T'$, $B = T$ in Lemma 4. By Lemma 3, $b_{i,j} = d_{i,j}$ for all i, j; hence for all $a_{h,k}$ such that $a_{h,k} = b_{h,k}$ we have $a_{h,k} = c_{h,k}$ as required.

LEMMA 5. *Let $A = (a_{ij})$ be a picture, $G(A) = (c_{ij})$, and let $a_{h,k} < V$; let $c_{h-1,k}$, $c_{h,k-1}$, $c_{h+1,k}$, $c_{h,k+1}$ all be less than or equal to V. Then $c_{h,k} < V$.*

PROOF. Let $G_1(A) = (b_{ij})$. Since G_2 never decreases the value of an element, we have $b_{h-1,k} \leqq c_{h-1,k} \leqq V$, $b_{h,k-1} \leqq c_{h,k-1} \leqq V$, so that

$$b_{h,k} = \max (a_{h,k}, b_{h-1,k} - 1, b_{h,k-1} - 1) < V,$$

and

$$c_{h,k} = \max (b_{h,k}, b_{h+1,k} - 1, b_{h,k+1} - 1) < V.$$

If $T = (t_{ij})$ is a distance transform picture, the partial picture $T^* = (t^*_{ij})$ defined by $t^*_{i,j} = t_{i,j}$, if none of $t_{i-1,j}$, $t_{i+1,j}$, $t_{i,j-1}$, $t_{i,j+1}$ is $t_{i,j} + 1$; 0, otherwise, will be called the *skeleton* of T. In order words, T^* is the set of *local maxima* of the distance transform. We assume that T is not the trivial picture every element of which has value $m+n$.

THEOREM. *$G(T^*) = T$, and if T' is any partial picture of T such that $G(T') = T$, then T^* is a partial picture of T'.* In other words, T^* is the partial picture of T with fewest nonzero elements such that $G(T^*) = T$.

PROOF. If P is any picture with integer-valued elements, let P_k be the set of elements of P which have value k. Let N be the highest value of any element of T; then by definition, $(T^*)_N = T_N$, so that by the Corollary to Lemma 4, $G(T^*)_N = T_N$. Suppose that $G(T^*)_{M+1} = T_{M+1}$. By definition, T^* contains every element of value M which has no element of value $M+1$ as a neighbor in T (or equivalently, in $G(T^*)$), and by the Corollary to Lemma 4, $G(T^*)$ still contains these elements. On the other hand, if $t_{h,k} = M$ and has a neighbor in $G(T^*)$ with value $M+1$, then by definition of G, the (h, k) element in $G(G(T^*))$ has value at least M. But $G(G(T^*)) = G(T^*)$ (Corollary to Lemma 2), and by the proof of Lemma 4, the (h, k) element in $G(T^*)$ can have value at most that of the (h, k) element in $G(T) = T$ (Corollary to Lemma 3); hence every such element has value M in $G(T^*)$, proving that $G(T^*)_M = T_M$. This induction argument proves $G(T^*)_k = T_k$ for all $k(= N, N - 1, \cdots, 1, 0)$, so that $G(T^*) = T$. Conversely, let T' be any partial picture of T such that $G(T') = T$, and let $t_{h,k}$ be an element of T of value $M > 0$ which has no neighbor in T of value $M+1$ and which fails to be in T'. Then the values of its neighbors in $G(T') = T$ are less than or equal to M (Lemma 1), while its value in T' is $0 < M$, so that by Lemma 5 its value in $G(T')$ is still less than M, contradicting $G(T') = T$. Thus T' must contain every element of T^* of value greater than 0; this completes the proof.

Skeletons for the pictures of Figure 4 are shown as Figure 5. In this figure, the nonzero skeleton point values are printed out modulo 10. As the two rectangles in Figure 5 show, the skeleton is not invariant under rotation. Note also that the Euclidean skeleton for a circle would evidently be just the point at its center, unlike the skeleton shown for the circle in Figure 5.

5. *Applications: Connectivity and Proximity*

The connectivity transformation described in Section 3 has several immediate applications. Once a label has been assigned to each connected component of a picture, it is trivial to count the number of such components by simply counting the number of labels which were used. (A special-purpose version of the connected component program can be written which only counts the components but does not label each element of each component; see Nuttall [14] and Sabbagh [15, pp. 43–48].

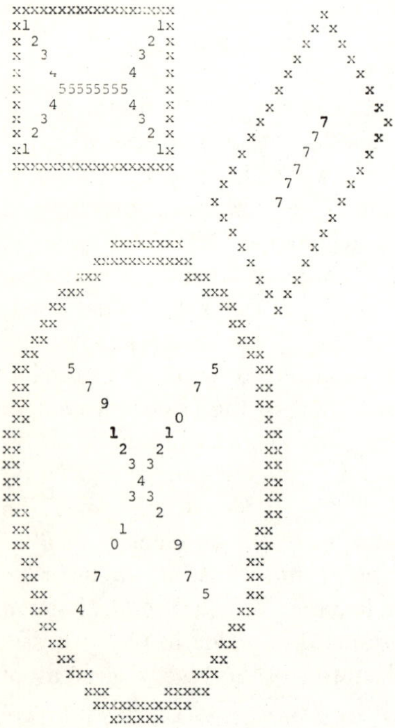

FIG. 5a. Skeletons for Figure 4a

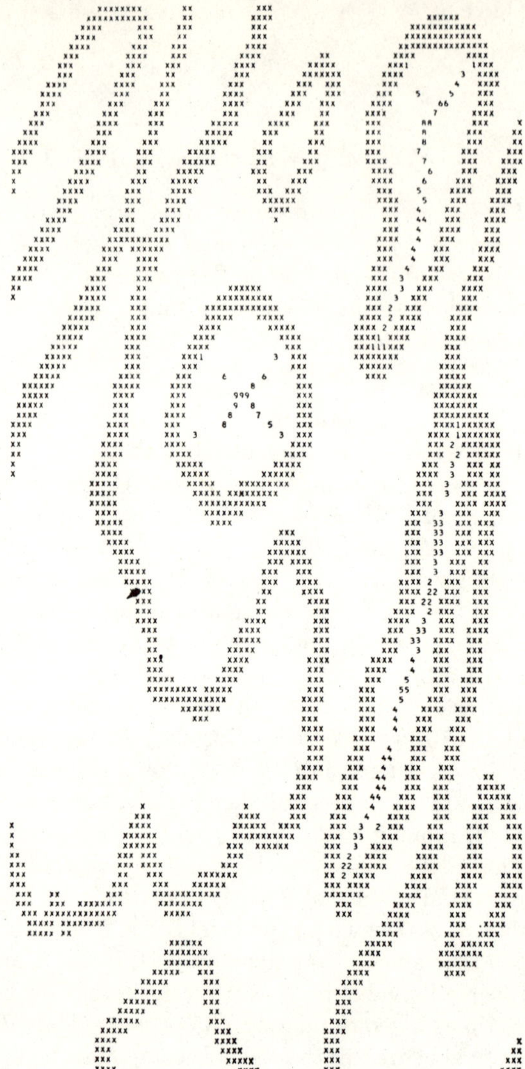

FIG. 5b. Skeletons for Figure 4b

It is also possible to perform this blob-counting operation by a process of successively deleting from each component border elements which do not disconnect the component until only one element per component remains[8]; for this approach, which is easily implemented using parallel local operations, see Kirsch [2], Minot [16] and Izzo [17, 18]. A closely related approach, using accretion rather than deletion, has been implemented by von Foerster and his colleagues [19–21].) One can also measure the area of any given component by counting the number of times its label occurs.

5.1 *Adjacency and order of connectivity*

Two somewhat less trivial problems which can be solved with the aid of the basic

[8] Provided that the components are simply connected; if they have "holes" in them, a more complicated procedure is necessary.

connectivity transformation are: (a) constructing the *graph* corresponding to a given dissection of a picture into connected components, and (b) determining the *order of connectivity* of a given connected component.

In the graph of any dissection of the picture, each connected component is represented by a single node or vertex; for simplicity, these may be taken to be the vertices of a regular polygon. Two nodes are joined by an arc (a side or diagonal of the polygon) if and only if the corresponding components are adjacent. For many purposes it is convenient to represent the exterior of the picture by a single additional node, which is considered to be adjacent to every component having elements on the boundary of the picture. A graph with k nodes is completely specified by its *incidence matrix*; this is a $k-1$ by $k-1$ triangular matrix (a_{ij}), $i < j$, in which $a_{ij} = 1$ if the ith and jth nodes are joined by an arc; $a_{ij} = 0$ otherwise.

In Figure 3, the connected components labeled A, ···, M, together with the connected components of the set of blank points, constitute a dissection of the picture. Since the border of Figure 2 was black, the additional exterior component is connected to all of these blank points except those in the belts immediately surrounding regions F, G and J. The set of blank points thus has four components, namely the one of which the picture border is a part and the ones surrounding F, G, J. The nonzero entries in the incidence matrix of the graph of Figure 3 are shown in Table I.

A computer program for constructing the graph of a given dissection is easily written, once the connected components of the dissection have been labeled. It suffices, for example, to examine every 2 by 2 subpicture and to enter 1's in the

TABLE I

Region	*Border of* F	*Border of* G	*Border of* J	A	B	C	D	E	F	G	H	I	J	K	L	M
Picture border	0	0	0	1	1	1	1	1	0	0	1	1	0	1	1	1
Border of F		0	0	0	0	0	1	0	1	0	0	0	0	0	0	0
Border of G			0	0	0	0	1	0	0	1	0	0	0	0	0	0
Border of J				0	0	0	1	0	0	0	0	0	1	0	0	0

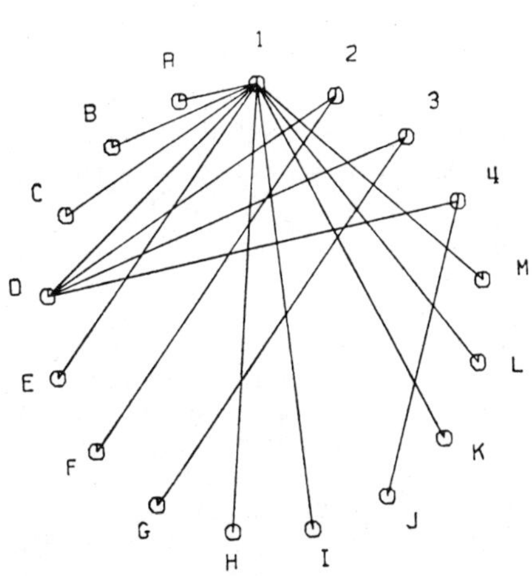

FIG. 6. Graph for Figure 3

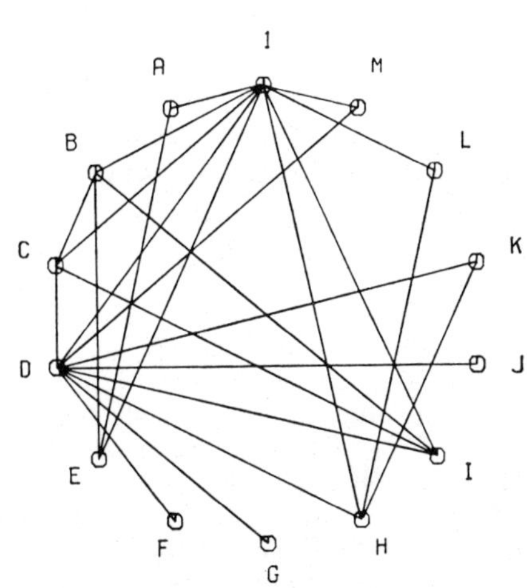

FIG. 7. Proximity graph for Figure 3

TABLE II

Region		Order of Connectivity
1	Boundary of picture	10
2	Boundary of region F	2
3	Boundary of region G	2
4	Boundary of region J	2
D		4

appropriate positions in an incidence matrix whenever such a subpicture contains points which have two or more different labels. The graph of Figure 3, constructed in this way by a FORTRAN program and output by a tape-controlled plotter, is shown in Figure 6.

Once the graph has been constructed, it is easy to solve the second problem posed earlier. It is easily seen that the order of connectivity of a connected component is equal to the number of nonadjacent "pieces" into which the picture is divided if the given component is deleted. Evidently, this is just the number of connected components into which the *graph* is divided if the corresponding *node* and the arcs emanating from it are deleted. This number can be determined by examining the incidence matrix of the graph after deleting the corresponding row and column.[9] A FORTRAN program which performs this analysis has been written; its output for Figure 3 is shown in Table II.

5.2 *Proximity*

Closely related to the two problems just discussed is the question of defining a "graph" for a picture such as Figure 3 ignoring the unlabeled "borders," and considering two of the labeled regions as being "adjacent" if they are separated only by a border. Intuitively, region I on Figure 3 is adjacent in this sense to regions B, C and D, but region B is not adjacent to region D. The graph for the labeled regions and "exterior region" of Figure 3 corresponding to this notion of adjacency is shown as Figure 7.

The concept of adjacency in the intuitive definition just given requires careful consideration. If the borders between regions in a picture all have approximately the same thickness, the adjacency of two regions in this sense essentially reflects their degree of *proximity*; regions are adjacent provided they approach one another within a distance just greater than the border thickness.[10] As in the case of true adjacency, this can be determined by examining all possible subpictures of the appropriate size and entering 1's in the incidence matrix whenever points with two or more labels are contained within such a subpicture. The graph in Figure 7 was drawn by a FORTRAN program which analyzed 4 by 4 subpictures of Figure 3 in this manner.

[9] This number could be determined directly from the picture as follows: Temporarily label the points of the given component 1, the points of its complement 0, whether these points were 1 or 0 in the original picture. Apply the connected component labeling program to this new set of 0's and simply count the number of its components. However, it is much simpler and faster to determine the orders of connectivity from the graph, once this has been constructed.

[10] One should certainly *not* define two regions as being adjacent if it is merely possible to go from one to the other by moving through border elements only; by this criterion, regions A and B, B and D of Figure 3 would be adjacent, and K would be adjacent to the picture exterior.

A more difficult problem is presented if the borders between regions are of varying thickness. Even in this case, however, one might proceed by determining the degree and direction of the *elongation* of any segment of border (see Section 6.2). Adjacent could then be defined as "separated by a segment of border which is tangentially elongated." This definition would be consistent with the intuitive concept of adjacency for the labeled regions of Figure 3.

It should be pointed out that the intuitive definitions of adjacency suggested in the last three paragraphs are of more limited usefulness than the mathematical definition. For example, one cannot in general determine the order of connectivity of a region from a graph based on such a definition. Examination of the graph in Figure 7 does indeed show, in agreement with intuition, that all the regions except D are simply connected, while D has order of connectivity 4. However, suppose that in Figure 3 the six D's to the right of the top row of F's are replaced by blanks, making a "cut" in region D. This does not change the graph of the figure (region D is still connected, and region F still not adjacent, in the intuitive sense, to the picture exterior); but region D now has order of connectivity only 3.[11]

6. *Applications: Shape (Elongation)*

The distance transform can be used to obtain a variety of information about the shapes of regions on a picture. In this section, two applications of this transform to the definition of *elongation* are discussed. The elongation considered here is an *intrinsic* shape property; a snake is considered to be elongated even when it is coiled. It is difficult to define this property in conventional geometrical terms, in spite of its evident intuitive significance.

Since the connected component transformation provides the ability to single out any component of a picture for analysis of its shape, it will be assumed in what follows that the given picture contains only a single connected region ("figure") consisting of 1's, and that the remainder of the picture consists of 0's.

6.1 *Elongation as the proportion of a figure which lies close to its boundary*

In his original papers [10–11] on the propagation concept, Blum suggested that the successive wavefronts—that is, the sets of points which are at a given distance from the original figure boundary—could provide useful information about the shape of the figure. For example, if the figure is a square, the wavefronts are concentric squares, and the numbers of points in them decrease linearly to zero. (See the solid curve in Figure 8(a)). On the other hand, if the figure is a very elongated rectangle (Figure 8(b)), the number of points in a wavefront decreases linearly until the center line of the rectangle is reached, when it drops abruptly to zero. Analogous plots of number of points vs. number of steps for three irregular figures of approximately equal area (regions F, J and K of Figure 3) are shown in Figures 8(c)–(e).

As the solid curves in Figure 8, especially parts (a) and (b), indicate, the manner in which wavefront perimeter decreases provides a measure of the elongation of a given figure. This measure represents the degree to which the interior of the figure lies close to its boundary, which is intuitively related to the intrinsic elongation of the figure.

[11] Note that making this cut *does* change the graph in Figure 6, since it combines the "border of F" region with the "picture border" region. The modified graph does in fact reflect the orders of connectivity which result from making the cut.

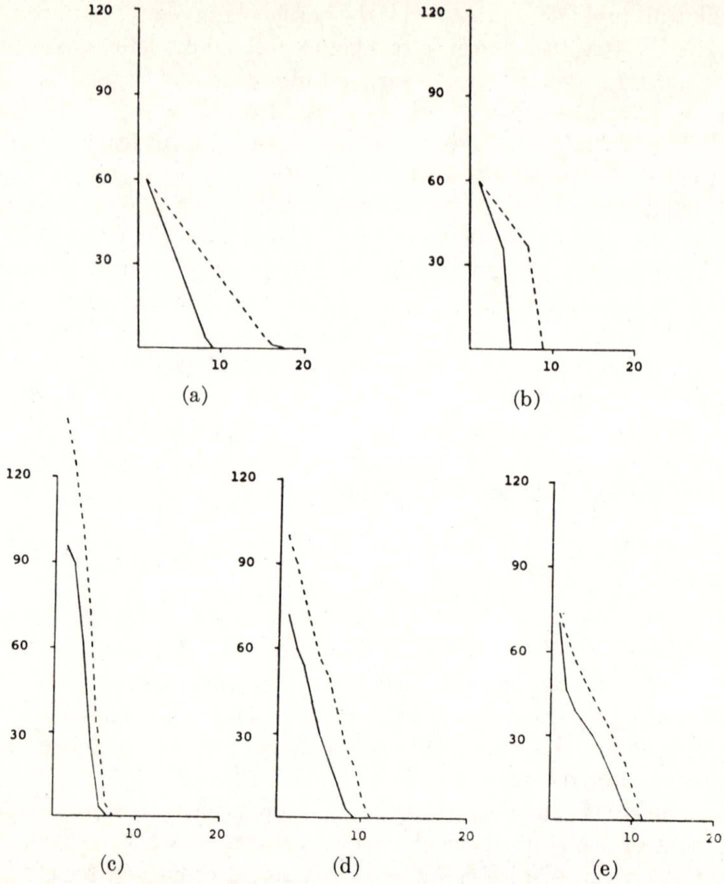

FIG. 8. Wavefront perimeter and boundary-touching square plots for (a) a square; (b) an elongated rectangle; (c) component K of Figure 3 (elongated); (d) component F of Figure 3 (partly elongated); (e) component J of Figure 3 (roughly circular)

A shape descriptor closely allied to wavefront perimeter is the number of different squares of a given size which are contained within a given figure and touch its boundary. For simplicity, only squares whose sides are parallel to the sides of the picture will be considered. These numbers can be computed by systematically erecting all possible squares on the cross-sections of the figure by the rows of the picture. An IBM 7090/94 program for doing this has been written in FAP. In Figure 8, the numbers of boundary-touching squares are plotted as dashed curves for comparison with the wavefront perimeters.[12]

The measure of elongation provided by these shape descriptors is relatively crude, since they are computed over the entire figure. A much more sensitive measure of elongation is defined in Section 6.2, using the distance skeleton concept introduced in Section 4.3.

[12] The wavefront and enclosed squares descriptors are conceptually related, but not equivalent, to the "Buffon needle" shape descriptor proposed by Tenery [22–23], which involves the probability that a line segment of given length randomly dropped on a figure with one end inside the figure also has the other end inside.

FIG. 9a. Lake, river and streams

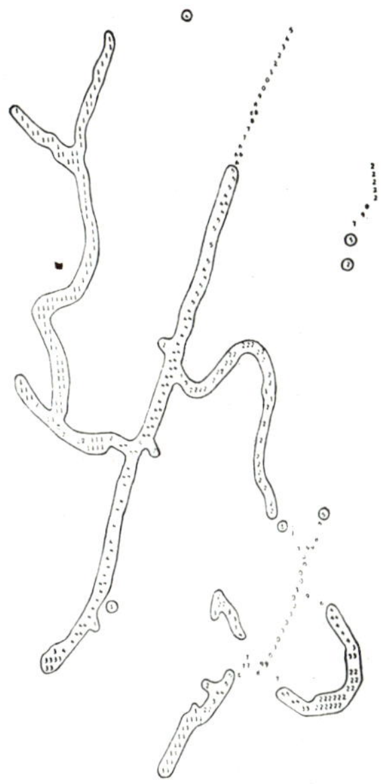

FIG. 9b. Skeleton of Figure 9a

FIG. 9c. "Elongated" parts of Figure 9a

6.2 *Elongated parts of a figure*

The skeleton subset introduced in Section 4.3 can be used to define a variety of useful shape properties. In this section it is applied, in combination with proximity analysis (see Section 5.2), to the problem of determining elongated parts of a given figure. The approach described in what follows is based on the intuitively appealing idea that any elongated figure part should give rise to a skeleton subset similar to that of an elongated rectangle. Such a skeleton should contain a large number of adjacent or proximate points located a relatively short distance away from the figure border. If the "reverse" distance transformation (Section 4.3) is applied to this set of points, the elongated part of the original figure should be regenerated.

Consider as an example the fictitious "hydrography" of Figure 9(a), in which the X's are water and the blanks land. Intuitively, the river, tributaries and creeks are elongated, but the lake and bay are not. Figure 9(b) shows the corresponding skeleton locus modulo 10, where the land points have been treated as 0's, the water points as 1's. In this figure the components of the points with values 5 or less, defined by a proximity criterion using a 3 by 3 subpicture, have been circled.[13] The *large* components (25 elements or more) evidently correspond to elongated portions of the hydrography, the one at the lower right to the elongated loop of lake around the island. In Figure 9(c) these elongated pieces have been regenerated by applying the reverse distance transform starting with these large components only. The regenerated parts are represented by E's, the remaining original water points by dots.

[13] The number 5 is an arbitrary threshold, not necessarily optimum. Skeleton points contained in the same 3 by 3 subpicture were considered to belong to the same component only if their values differed by two or less.

This example suggests the following general procedure for determining elongated parts of a figure:

1. Apply the distance transform to the figure and determine the skeleton locus.
2. For each $k = 2, 3, \cdots$, up to half the picture diameter if necessary, consider the set S_k of skeleton points which have values less than or equal to k.
3. Determine "proximity components" of each S_k, and count the number of points in each component.
4. Select those components, if any, which have more than t_k points. A reasonable value for t_k is in the range $5k$–$10k$,[14] corresponding to a set of proximate skeleton points whose "length" is at least $2\frac{1}{2}$ times the "width" of the piece of figure which gave rise to it.
5. Apply the reverse distance transform to these components to reconstruct the elongated parts of the original figure.

Appendix. Proof of the Equivalence of Parallel and Sequential Local Operations

It must be shown that any local operation applied in parallel is equivalent to a series of local operations applied sequentially, and vice versa.

Note first that if the local operation f is applied to each element of the picture A, and the results are stored in another picture B, rather than modifying A, then it makes no difference whether f is applied to A in parallel or sequentially, since the arguments of f are always the original elements of A. Hence if f applied in parallel takes A into A^*, then f applied in any sequence, *using B for storage of the results*, yields $B = A^*$. By the Lemma of Section 2.1, it is known that if necessary, this procedure can be re-expressed in terms of A alone (for example, one could transform A in such a way as to "keep" the original element values as exponents of 2, while storing the transformed values as exponents of 3). It has thus been shown that the result of any parallel local operation can be obtained by applying a local operation sequentially. (Strictly speaking, an additional operation of "erasing" A and "replacing" it by $B = A^*$ should also be performed; this operation does not even involve neighbors, and can be performed either sequentially or in parallel. In the example using exponents given just above, this operation is simply ϕ_3 (see Section 2.1).)

Conversely, let f be a local operation which takes A into A^* when applied sequentially. Let $A = (a_{ij})$, $A^* = (a^*_{ij})$, $1 \leqq i \leqq m$, $1 \leqq j \leqq n$, and define $a_{0,j} = a_{m+1,j} = a_{i,0} = a_{i,n+1} = v$, $1 \leqq i \leqq m$, $1 \leqq j \leqq n$, where v is different from every $a_{i,j}$ and $a^*_{i,j}$, $1 \leqq i \leqq m$, $1 \leqq j \leqq n$. Now define:

$$\text{(1)}\quad f_1(a_{i,j}) = f(a_{i-1,j-1}, \cdots, a_{i+1,j+1}), \quad \text{if} \quad a_{i-1,j} = a_{i,j-1} = v;$$
$$= a_{i,j} \text{ otherwise}; \qquad 1 \leqq i \leqq m, \quad 1 \leqq j \leqq n.$$

(Since $a_{i-1,j} = a_{i,j-1} = v$ is equivalent to $(i, j) = (1, 1)$, applying this f_1 in parallel to all of A is equivalent to applying f to $a_{1,1}$ only.) At the same time, let f_1 generate an auxiliary picture (b_{ij}) such that

$$\left.\begin{aligned} b_{i,j} &= w \quad \text{if } a_{i-1,j} = a_{i,j-1} = v \\ &\qquad\quad (\text{i.e., if } (i, j) = (1, 1)) \\ &= a_{i,j} \quad \text{otherwise} \end{aligned}\right\}, \quad 1 \leqq i \leqq m, \quad 1 \leqq j \leqq n,$$

[14] This uncertainty can be reduced if the skeleton locus is "thinned" before this step is performed.

where w is different from every $a_{i,j}$ and $a^*_{i,j}$ as well as from v.

$$(2)\quad \left.\begin{aligned} f_2(a_{i,j}) &= f(a_{i-1,j-1}, \cdots, a_{i+1,j+1}) \\ &\qquad \text{if } a_{i-1,j} = v \text{ and } b_{i,j-1} = w \\ &= a_{i,j} \text{ otherwise} \\ f_2(b_{i,j}) &= w \text{ if } a_{i-1,j} = v \text{ and } b_{i,j-1} = w \\ &= b_{i,j} \text{ otherwise} \end{aligned}\right\}, \quad 1 \leqq i \leqq m, \quad 1 \leqq j \leqq n.$$

(If f_1 has been applied to A, the unique (i, j) satisfying $a_{i-1,j} = v$ and $b_{i,j-1} = w$ is $(1, 2)$. Thus applying f_2 in parallel to $f_1(A)$ is equivalent to applying f to $a_{1,2}$. Application of f_2 also puts a w in the $(1, 2)$ position; hence if it is applied *again*, the unique (i, j) satisfying the conditions is now $(1, 3)$. Hence repetition of f_2 $n-1$ *times* is equivalent to applying f sequentially to $a_{1,2}, \cdots, a_{1,n}$.)

$$(3)\quad \left.\begin{aligned} f_3(a_{i,j}) &= f(a_{i-1,j-1}, \cdots, a_{i+1,j+1}) \\ &\qquad \text{if } a_{i-1,j} = w \text{ and } a_{i,j-1} = v \\ &= a_{i,j} \text{ otherwise} \\ f_3(b_{i,j}) &= w \text{ if } b_{i-1,j} = w \text{ and } a_{i,j-1} = v \\ &= b_{i,j} \text{ otherwise} \end{aligned}\right\}, \quad 1 \leqq i \leqq m, \quad 1 \leqq j \leqq n.$$

(If f_1 has been applied, these conditions are satisfied by $(i, j) = (2, 1)$ only. Hence applying f_3 after f_1 and $n-1$ f_2's have been applied has the same effect as applying f to $a_{2,1}$ after having applied it to $a_{1,1}, \cdots, a_{1,n}$.)

$$(4)\quad \left.\begin{aligned} f_4(a_{i,j}) &= f(a_{i-1,j-1}, \cdots, a_{i+1,j+1}) \\ &\qquad \text{if } b_{i-1,j} = b_{i,j-1} = w \\ &= a_{i,j} \text{ otherwise} \\ f_4(b_{i,j}) &= w \text{ if } b_{i-1,j} = b_{i,j-1} = w \\ &= b_{i,j} \text{ otherwise} \end{aligned}\right\}, \quad 1 \leqq i \leqq m, \quad 1 \leqq j \leqq n.$$

(Readily, after f_1, $n-1$ f_2's and f_3 have been applied, this f_4 singles out the $(2, 2)$ element; and repeating it a total of $n-1$ times singles out the $(2, 3), \cdots, (2, n)$ elements, successively. Moreover, after this has been done, application of f_3 again will single out the $(3, 1)$ element; successive applications of f_4 after this will pick the $(3, 2), \cdots, (3, n)$ elements; and so on.)

In summary: Applying f to A sequentially is equivalent to applying the following series of parallel local operations to A:

$$f_1\,; f_2, \cdots, f_2, \quad (n-1 \text{ times}); \qquad [f_3\,; f_4, \cdots, f_4, \quad (n-1 \text{ times})],$$

with the bracketed series of operations repeated a total of $m-1$ times, giving a total of mn parallel operations.

Acknowledgments. The assistance of Mr. David Wilson, who made several significant contributions to the development of the distance transformation program, is gratefully acknowledged. Early versions of both this and the connected component program were developed by the senior author and his colleagues at the Budd Information Sciences Center, McLean, Virginia. This initial work was accomplished through the efforts of Mr. James N. Orton of Budd, with the assistance of Messrs. Ernest W. Smith and Bernard Altschuler.

RECEIVED JANUARY, 1966; REVISED APRIL, 1966

REFERENCES

1. DINNEEN, G. P. Programming pattern recognition. Proc. Western Joint Comput. Conf., Vol. 7, 1955, pp. 94–100.
2. KIRSCH, R. A., ET AL. Experiments in processing pictorial information with a digital computer. Proc. Eastern Joint Comput. Conf., Vol. 12, 1957, pp. 221–229.
3. UNGER, S. H. A computer oriented toward spatial problems. *Proc. IRE 46* (1958), 1744–1750.
4. NARASIMHAN, R. Labeling schemata and syntactic descriptions of pictures. *Inform. Control 7* (1964), 151–179.
5. HARMON, L. D. Line drawing pattern recognizer, *Electronics 33* (Sept. 2, 1960), 39–43; Proc. Western Joint Comput. Conf., Vol. 17, 1960, pp. 351–364.
6. SINGER, J. R. Model for a size invariant pattern recognition system. Bionics Symposium, WADD Tech. Rep. 60–600, Dec. 1960, pp. 239–245.
7. ——. Electronic analog of the human recognition system. *J. Opt. Soc. Amer. 51* (1961), 61–69.
8. ——. A self organizing recognition system. Proc. Western Joint Comput. Conf., Vol. 19, 1961, pp. 545–554.
9. STEVENS, M. E. Abstract shape recognition by machine. Proc. Eastern Joint Comput. Conf., Vol. 20, 1961, pp. 332–351.
10. BLUM, H. An associative machine for dealing with the visual field and some of its biological implications. In Bernard, Eugene E., and Kare, Morley R., Eds., *Biological Prototypes and Synthetic Systems, Vol. 1.* (Proc. Second Annual Bionics Symp., Cornell U., 1961). Plenum Press, New York, 1962, pp. 244–260.
11. ——. A machine for performing visual recognition by use of antenna-propagation concepts. *Proc. IRE Wescon*, Pt. IV, 1962.
12. ——. A transformation for extracting new descriptors of shape. Symp. on Models for the Perception of Speech and Visual Form (Boston, Nov. 1964); in press, M.I.T. Press, Cambridge, Mass.
13. KOTELLY, J. A Mathematical Model of Blum's Theory of Pattern Recognition. AFCRL Res. Rep. 63–164, April, 1963.
14. NUTTALL, T. C. Apparatus for Counting Objects. U. S. Patent 2803406, Aug. 20, 1957.
15. SABBAGH, E. N. Aerial reconnaissance electronic reader. RADC Tech. Rep. 60–132, June, 1960.
16. MINOT, O. N. Counting and outlining of "two-dimensional" patterns by digital computer. U. S. Naval Elect. Lab. TM-414, Aug. 1960.
17. IZZO, N. F., AND COLES, W. Blood-cell scanner identifies rare cells. *Electronics 35* (April 27, 1962), 52–57.
18. IZZO, N. F. Electro-optical enhancement of microscopic images. Proceedings S.P.I.E. Image Enhancement Seminar, March, 1963, Society of Photographic Instrumentation Engineers, Redondo Beach, Calif., pp. 1–13.
19. VON FOERSTER, H. Circuitry of clues to Platonic ideation. In Muses, C. A., Ed., *Aspects of the Theory of Artificial Intelligence* (Proc. First Int. Symp. on Biosimulation, Locarno, Switz., 1960). Plenum Press, New York, 1962, pp. 43–81.
20. BABCOCK, M. L. Some physiology of automata. Proc. Western Joint Comput. Conf., Vol. 19, 1961, pp. 291–298.
21. WESTON, P. Photocell field counts random objects. *Electronics 34* (Sept. 22, 1961), 46–47.
22. TENERY, G. A pattern recognition function of integral geometry. *IEEE Trans. MIL-7* (1963), 196–199.
23. ——. Information flow in a bionics image recognition system. Symp. on Models for the Perception of Speech and Visual Form. (Boston, Nov. 1964); in press, M.I.T. Press, Cambridge, Mass.

Reprinted from *Machine Intelligence IV*, B. Melzer and D. Hichie (eds.), 1969, pp. 403–420

22

22

Linear Skeletons from Square Cupboards

C. Judith Hilditch
Medical Research Council,
Clinical and Population Cytogenetics
Research Unit

INTRODUCTION

The problem of reducing the line-like elements of a digitized picture to idealized thin lines is of general interest in pattern recognition. As early as 1957 the idea of obtaining a thin-line representation of certain patterns was suggested (Kirsch *et al.* 1957); recently McCormick (1963) and Narasimhan (1964) have described computer programs for doing this (for use in particular on bubble chamber photographs), and similar work has been done in character recognition, for example by Deutsch (1967). Blum (1964) has put forward an approach for dealing with more general shapes. In this the boundary of a shape is considered as being the source of a wavefront. The points at which wavefronts originating at different parts of the boundary first meet form a 'skeleton' which, with a function giving the time taken for the wavefront to reach each point of the skeleton, completely defines the original shape. Programs for generating this skeleton for digitized pictures have been described by Rosenfeld and Pfaltz (1966), and also by Philbrick (1966). A technique which we at the MRC have implemented for reducing line-like shapes to idealized thin lines is similar to the last of these, in that it involves working inwards from the boundary of the shape under consideration, removing all points except those which are considered part of the skeleton. It is also similar to a stripping routine described by Izzo and Coles (1962) and Preston (1961) in a rather different context.

AIMS

The problem with which we have been primarily concerned is the automatic analysis of chromosome spreads, a typical example of which is shown in figure 1.

The aim of the algorithm described in this paper is to reduce such a picture to a 'skeleton' of idealized thin lines which satisfy not only the obvious requirement that they should lie approximately along the centre of each line-like part of the picture but also satisfy, as nearly as is possible in a discrete space, the definition of a line as 'that which has length without breadth' while still retaining the connectivity of the original.

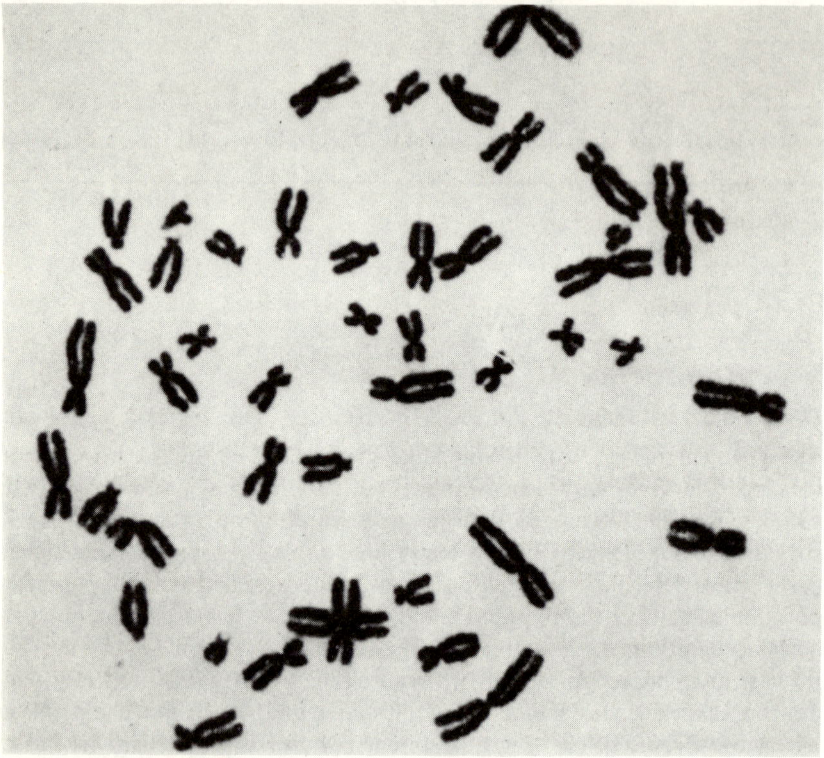

Figure 1. A typical human chromosome spread

THE PICTURE

Before describing how this has been done it is necessary to describe more fully the form which the picture takes. Let J be the set of all pairs of integers. Then a picture is defined as a function f on a subset P of J. In particular P is usually rectangular, i.e., $P=\{(i,j) \mid 1 \leqslant i<m, 1 \leqslant j<n\}$, and the elements of P can be regarded as the elements of a matrix, or as points with integer co-ordinates in the Euclidean plane. Usually the function f will initially take values such that each element or point represents in some way the darkness of that part of the picture. Subsequent transformations of the picture will, however, alter the values of the points and hence of course their significance.

The work described here is concerned not with whole pictures, which in our case consist of about a quarter of a million points, but with sub-pictures, that is restrictions of f to a subset Q of P; formally we denote this by $f \mid Q$. Q may for example be the set of all points of P with value greater than some threshold or a connected component of such points. The problem which we are considering here is that of producing a skeleton for such a sub-picture which satisfies all the requirements for a skeleton listed above.

CONNECTIVITY

At this stage it is necessary to define what we mean by connectivity in the case of a digitized picture. Each point of a picture is considered to have eight neighbours, these being the eight points which differ from it by one in either or both co-ordinates. For convenience these neighbours are numbered n_1, $n_2, \ldots, n_8$ as shown in figure 2. The numbers are taken modulo eight so that, for example, neighbour nine is the same point as neighbour one.

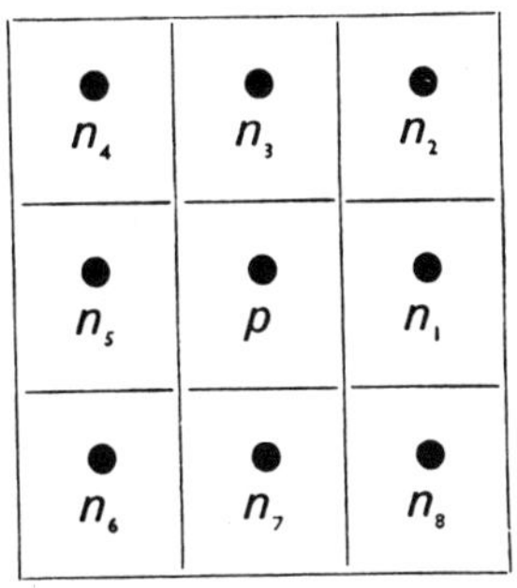

Figure 2. The eight neighbours n_1 to n_8 of a point p

Following Rosenfeld and Pfaltz (1966) we say that a subset of a digitized picture is *connected* if for any two points p and q of the subset there exists a sequence of points

$$p=p_0, p_1, p_2, p_3, \ldots, p_{n-1}, p_n=q,$$

such that p_i is a neighbour of p_{i-1}, $1 \leqslant i \leqslant n$. This corresponds with the usual concept of connectivity in the Euclidean plane, if one considers the area defined by taking each point of the subset as the centre of a closed unit square.

However, as pointed out by Rosenfeld and Pfaltz (1966), if one then considers whether the complementary subset of the picture is connected, paradoxical situations can arise. For example, both the set of black points and the set of white points in figure 3a are connected, as is illustrated in figure 3b. This paradox is not resolved by considering a point as having only four neighbours, namely n_1,n_3,n_5 and n_7. In this case we simply have the reverse situation that neither the set of black points nor the set of white points is connected.

The paradox arises because the connectivity of a subset of the picture and the connectivity of its complementary subset are both being considered at the same time. In practice one is usually interested only in the connectivity of a given subset, say the black points in figure 3a. In this case confusion can be avoided by considering the connectivity of the area defined by this subset in the Euclidean plane and the connectivity of the complementary area, rather than the area defined by the complementary subset.

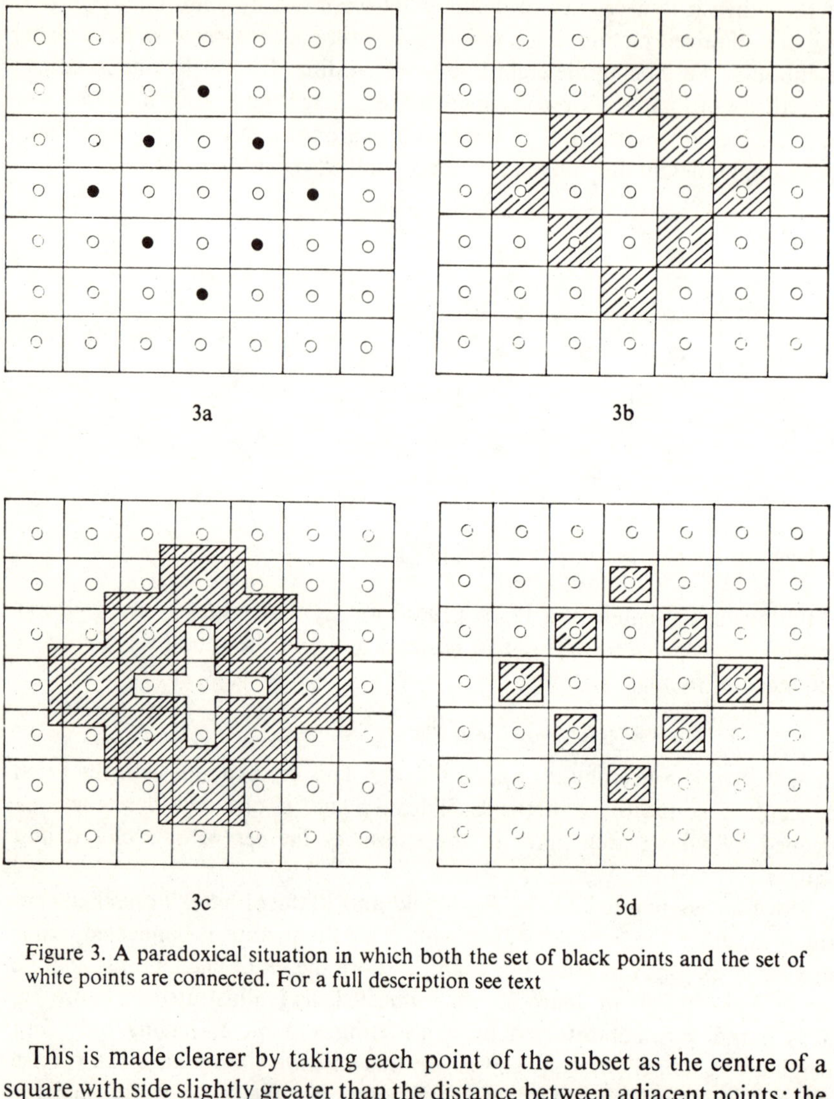

3a 3b 3c 3d

Figure 3. A paradoxical situation in which both the set of black points and the set of white points are connected. For a full description see text

This is made clearer by taking each point of the subset as the centre of a square with side slightly greater than the distance between adjacent points; the area defined by the set of black points is then given by the shaded part of figure 3c and clearly is connected, whereas its complement clearly is not. On the other hand the area defined by the set of white points (given by the unshaded part of figure 3d) is also connected and its complement is not. We choose to consider each point of a given subset of the points of a picture as representing a square of slightly greater than unit area, in this way, and define the subset as connected if the area which it represents is connected in the usual sense in the Euclidean plane.

This is equivalent to defining connectivity on the neighbourhood basis with the points of the given subset each having eight neighbours n_1 to n_8, but allowing the points of the complementary subset to have only four neighbours n_1,n_3,n_5 and n_7.

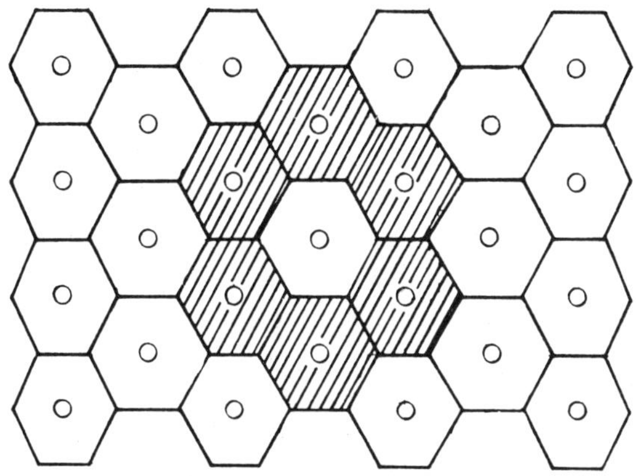

Figure 4. In the hexagonal case each point has six neighbours, and the paradoxical situations cannot arise

It may be interesting to note an alternative approach which avoids this difficulty altogether. This requires alternate lines of the picture to be displaced by half a unit, and each point taken to have six neighbours, as shown in figure 4. This is equivalent to considering each point as the centre of a hexagon, and in this case it is clear that the paradoxical situations do not arise.

REQUIREMENTS TO BE MET BY THE SKELETON

We are now in a position to consider in greater detail the requirements to be met by the skeleton and how these are satisfied. The requirements are:

1. Thinness

First, the skeleton is required to consist of thin lines. This is achieved simply by eroding away the subset by successively removing points which lie on its edge until all that remains is lines which are one point wide. The algorithm is intended for use on a general purpose digital computer in which the points must be treated sequentially and not in parallel. However, if the points are removed sequentially – a point being removed from the subset as soon as it has been found to lie on the edge of the subset – then subsequent nearby points will appear to lie on the edge and will be deleted in their turn. The result is that the skeleton will tend to be biased towards one side or the other of the original subset, depending on the order in which the points are taken.

2. Position

The second condition is that the idealized thin lines should lie along the centres of the line-like parts of the subset. To achieve this the process of removing points on the edge of the subset is made essentially parallel. A point is removed only if it lies on the edge of the initial subset, regardless of which other points have been removed. This means that several passes through the points of the subset are required. At each pass the outer layer of points is removed to give a 'thinner' subset for the next pass.

However, once this thinning process has reached a stage where some or all of the subset has been reduced to thin lines of points, these lines must not be thinned away to nothing. This is ensured by the next two conditions.

3. Connectivity

The third requirement is that the process should not alter the connectivity of the subset. This is achieved by testing each point that is to be removed to find whether its removal will alter connectivity. If it does, then the point is retained even though it lies on the edge.

However, if this is performed in parallel, a difficulty arises in the case where the subset has been reduced to a line that is two points wide, such as is shown in figure 5.

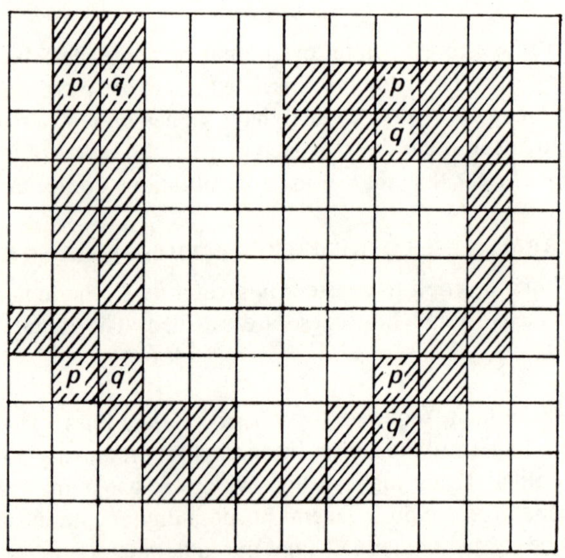

Figure 5. In each of the cases shown above neither the deletion of point p nor the deletion of point q will disconnect the area of shaded points; however, in each case the deletion of both p and q will.

In this case the removal of point p would not alter the connectivity of the subset, neither would the removal of point q. Unfortunately, the removal of both together most certainly will. This difficulty is overcome by taking advantage of the fact that the points are really being dealt with sequentially. Suppose, for example, that point p in figure 5 is tested before point q. Since the removal of p does not alter the connectivity of the subset, this point is removed. Subsequently, when point q is tested, the fact that p has been removed can be taken into consideration and the point q retained. This means that for a point to be removed, not only must its removal alone not alter connectivity, but if any one of its neighbours has been removed, then the removal of the two points together must not alter connectivity either.

4. Stability

Finally, it is necessary that as soon as a satisfactory skeleton, or part of a skeleton, is obtained, this should be stable and not be eroded away by subsequent passes. For most points of the skeleton this is ensured by the connectivity condition. However, a point which lies at the tip of a thin line can be removed without altering connectivity. An additional condition is therefore required to the effect that such a point may not be removed, otherwise the lines of the skeleton will gradually become shorter and shorter. Also, in order that an approximately circular subset should not disappear entirely, we need a condition which ensures that the last remaining point of such a subset is not removed.

THE ALGORITHMS

To meet these requirements the various algorithms that we have implemented each require several passes. At the start of a pass a subset Q of some subpicture $f_0 \mid P$ is given[1]; at the end of the pass a subset Q' of Q, which is one layer 'thinner', has been defined. Initially, Q is the subset to be reduced to idealized thin lines; the resulting Q' then becomes Q for the second pass, and so on; eventually a Q' is obtained which is a skeleton of the required form. Thereafter, no further points can be removed, and this fact is used to recognize when no more passes are required.

We have found it convenient to assume that the subset Q is defined as those points of P for which f_0 takes one of a given set of values, I, say, and that all other points of P take one of a set of values N. In particular, the picture usually takes the form of either a characteristic function with points in Q having value one and all other points zero, or f_0 takes values on the non-negative integers, points in Q having values greater than some threshold and other points less. However, this assumption causes no loss in generality since it can be extended to a subset Q consisting of points having *any* given property simply by making f_0 the characteristic function for these points.

[1] Since the algorithm requires the values of the neighbours of all points of Q to be defined, P should contain at least all neighbours of points of Q.

Throughout a pass through the points of the picture a record of the initial subset Q must be maintained. However, it has been found convenient, rather than retaining the original picture $f_0 \mid P$ as well as constructing point by point a new picture $f_1 \mid P$ which will define Q', to reserve a third set of values R for points which have been removed ($R \cap I = \phi$ and $R \cap N = \phi$). Only one picture is then required, and as each point $q \in P$ is tested the picture is changed by setting that point to a new value $f_1(q)$, where $f_1(q) \in R$ if the point is removed, or, if it is not, $f_1(q) \in I$ or $f_1(q) \in N$, depending whether the point was in Q in the first place or not.

At the stage when point p of the picture has just been set the value of any other point q is denoted by $f^{(p)}(q)$ (or $f(q)$ for short), where $f^{(p)}(q) = f_0(q)$, if q follows p, and $f^{(p)}(q) = f_1(q)$, if q precedes or is p. At this stage we have a *partially thinned picture* $f^{(p)} \mid P$; the initial subset Q is given by

$$Q = \{q \in P \mid f^{(p)}(q) \in I \cup R\}$$

and the *partially thinned subset* $Q^{(p)}$ is defined by

$$Q^{(p)} = \{q \in P \mid f^{(p)}(q) \in I\}$$

When all points of the picture have been tested

$$f^{(p)} = f_1 \text{ and } Q^{(p)} = Q' = \{q \in P \mid f_1(q) \in I\}$$

The picture is then ready for the next pass to begin, except that all points with values in R must first be reset to have values in N, or R and N must be redefined to the same effect.

It is sometimes useful, also, to reserve a subset U of I for the values of points which for some reason may not be removed at the current pass.

The crucial part of the algorithm is the determination of whether or not a point should be removed. This is independent of the choice of sets I, N, R and U and is described in full below.

CONDITIONS FOR THE REMOVAL OF A POINT

A point p will be removed, that is, it will be set to a new value $f_1(p)$ in R, if and only if it satisfies all the following conditions:

1. It belongs to Q and its removal is allowed, i.e.,

   $$f(p) \in I - U;$$

2. It lies on the edge of Q, that is, at least one of its axially adjacent neighbours n_1, n_3, n_5 and n_7 does not belong to Q; i.e., if

   $$\mu(p) = a_1 + a_3 + a_5 + a_7 \text{ (where } a_i = 1 \text{ if } f(n_i) \in N,\ a_i = 0 \text{ otherwise)}$$

   then we have the edge condition

   $$\mu(p) \geq 1;$$

3. It is not the tip of a thin line, that is, it has more than one neighbour which belongs to Q, i.e., if

$$v(p)=\sum_{i=1}^{8}(1-a_i) \qquad (a_i \text{ defined as above})$$

then we have the 'not tip' condition

$$v(p)\geqslant 2$$

4. It is not the last remaining point of small 'circular' subset, that is, it has at least one neighbour in Q which has not been removed; i.e., if

$$w(p)=\sum_{i=1}^{8}c_i \qquad (\text{where } c_i=1 \text{ if } f(n_i)\in I,\ c_i=0 \text{ otherwise})$$

then we have the condition

$$w(p)\geqslant 1$$

5. Its removal does not alter connectivity, that is, the area of the Euclidean plane defined by the subset Q can be continuously deformed to give the area defined by the subset $Q-\{p\}$. This will be so if and only if the set comprising those neighbours of p which are in Q consists of one connected component. (The case where the removal of p would produce a 'hole' is prevented by condition 2 above).

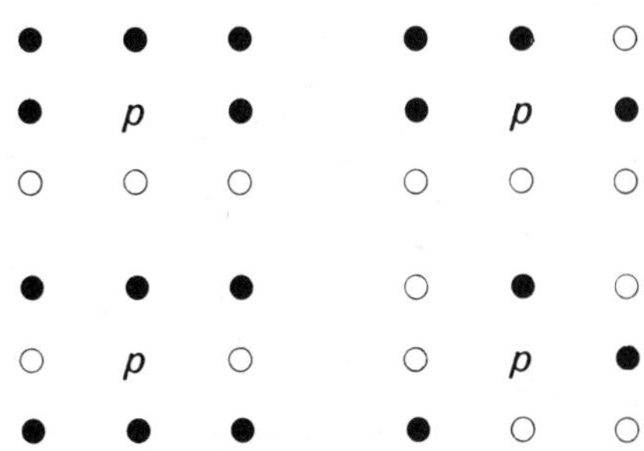

Figure 6. Crossing number. The crossing number at point p with respect to the set of black points is one in the two upper cases and two in the two lower cases. Note in the two right-hand cases that neighbour one is connected to neighbour three, so the fact that neighbour two is white does not cause an increase in crossing number.

The number of components is calculated by considering the number of times a 'bug' taking a walk around p by way of its neighbours would have to cross from outside to inside the subset. This number is called the *crossing number* of p with respect to the subset, and is generally equal to the number of components, but would be zero in the case where the 'bug' did not need to leave the subset at all. Note that to conform with our definition of connectivity the 'bug' must go from one axially adjacent neighbour of p to the next axially adjacent one, bypassing the diagonal if by so doing it avoids leaving the subset. Some examples are given in figure 6.

This crossing number $X(p)$ is calculated as follows:

$$X(p)=\sum_{i=1}^{4} b_i \text{ (where } b_i=1 \text{ if } f(n_{2i-1})\in N \text{ and either}$$
$$f(n_{2i})\in I\cup R \text{ or } f(n_{2i+1})\in I\cup R$$
$$\text{and } b_i=0 \text{ otherwise).}$$

The connectivity condition is then given by

$$X(p)=1$$

6. Its removal in conjunction with any one of its neighbours that has been removed does not alter the connectivity of Q; that is, if neighbour n_i of p has been removed, i.e., $f(n_i)\in R$, then if the value of this neighbour is temporarily altered so that $f(n_i)\in N$ and it thus appears that n_i is not in Q, then the new crossing number at p, $X_i(p)$, say, is still one. This gives us the additional 'two thick line' condition

$$f(n_i)\notin R \text{ or } X_i(p)=1 \quad (i=1,\ldots,8)$$

In general, the sequence in which the points are being tested is known, and it is therefore only necessary to test this last condition for those neighbours which precede p, since f can only take a value in R for a point *after* it has been tested. For example, if we start at the top of the picture and work from left to right along each line, it is only necessary to test the condition for $i=2,3,4$ and 5. In addition, if i is even and p satisfies all the preceding conditions, then the condition that either $f(n_i)\notin R$ or $X_i(p)=1$ is automatically satisfied and need not be tested. For, if $f(n_i)\in R$, then, since p has crossing number equal to one and has more than one neighbour in Q, and n_i belongs to Q, it follows that either n_{i-1} belongs to Q, or n_{i+1} belongs to Q, or both. If both belong to Q then deleting neighbour i does not alter the crossing number at p since the 'bug' can in this case 'cut the corner'. If on the other hand only one of these is in Q then deleting neighbour i cannot possibly alter the crossing number, so in each case we have $X_i(p)=1$. It is thus only necessary to test this last condition for $i=3$ and $i=5$, i.e.,

$$f(n_i)\notin R \text{ or } X_i(p)=1, \text{ for } i=3 \text{ and } i=5$$

APPLICATION TO BINARY PICTURES

The algorithm was initially implemented for use on pictures taking the form of a characteristic function. In this case points belonging to the subset Q have value one, all other points have value zero, and when a point is removed its value is set to minus one, i.e., the algorithm is applied with

$$I=\{1\}$$
$$N=\{0\}$$
$$\text{and } R=\{-1\}$$

Between each pass it is necessary to set those points which have been removed and so have value -1 to zero ready for the next pass.

This can be made more efficient in the following way. Consider a point p of the picture and suppose that at one pass neither this point nor any of its neighbours is removed. Then this point cannot possibly be removed at the next pass since its situation with regard to the conditions for removal has in no way changed. If all such points are set to two, therefore, and we define

$$U=\{2\}$$

this will avoid the unnecessary testing of the neighbours, crossing number, etc., of these points at the next pass. This is achieved by setting the value of *all* points of Q which are not removed to two; then at the end of the pass, when all points which have been removed are reset from -1 to zero, their neighbours with value two are reset to one.

Figure 7 shows the results obtained by applying this algorithm to several pictures.

An alternative method of improving the efficiency of the algorithm is by avoiding the need to reset the values of all points which have been removed, between passes, by re-defining the sets N and R instead. This is done by setting the value of those points which are removed at the mth pass to $-m$ instead of -1 and defining I, N and R as follows:

$$I=\{1\}$$
$$N=\{f \mid 0 \geqslant f > -m\}$$
$$R=\{-m\}$$

Thus, after each pass, N and R are re-defined by incrementing m, and the next pass can take place immediately.

SHORTCOMINGS OF THESE IMPLEMENTATIONS

With chromosome images we found that the type of approach described above had two disadvantages. First, the outlines of chromosomes tend to be rather noisy, with the adjacent arms of a chromosome not completely separate but touching in several places, and this results in a skeleton with many spurious branches, as illustrated in figure 8b. This can usually be overcome without much difficulty by a simple smoothing of the boundary and by expanding any 'holes' produced by touching arms until they are connected with the exterior of the object. Application of the algorithm then usually produces a skeleton with few or no spurious branches, as in figure 8c.

A second more serious shortcoming is that the resulting skeleton is completely defined by the original outline of the object. If the picture is essentially black and white and its outline well defined – as it frequently is in character recognition – this is exactly what is required. However, with chromosomes the density drops off gradually from the central ridge of each arm outwards, and the choice of boundary is somewhat arbitrary. In this case what is

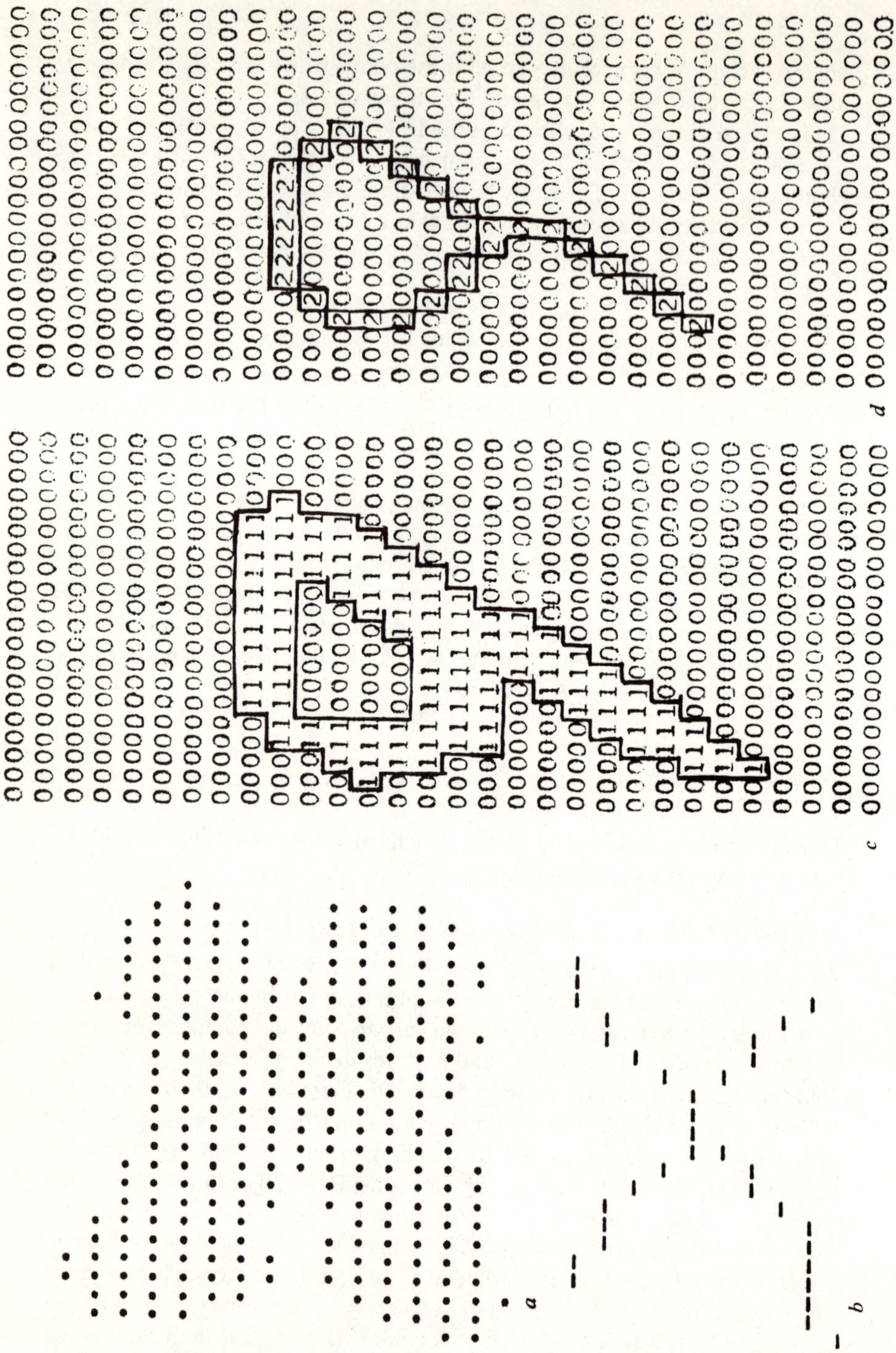

Figure 7. Binary pictures of a chromosome and of a hand-written digit, and the skeletons obtained from them.

required is that the skeleton should lie along the higher density ridges of the picture rather than in a central position determined by outline alone. An example illustrating this is shown in figure 9.

The way in which the algorithm can be varied in order to achieve this, for pictures in which f takes values that are positive integers representing the densities of the points, is given below.

IMPLEMENTATION FOR PICTURES WITH A RANGE OF DENSITY VALUES

It is possible to obtain a skeleton which tends to lie along ridges of higher density in a picture by removing only points at low density in the first few passes and allowing points with higher density to be removed later. This is done by restricting removal in any one pass to points with a given value. Thus, if d is the value of points which may be removed in the current pass, the algorithm is applied with I,N,R and U defined as follows:

$$I=\{\text{positive integers}\}$$
$$N=\{0\}$$
$$U=\{\text{all positive integers except } d\}$$
$$R=\{-1\}$$

Initially d is set to one. After each pass those points which have been removed are set to zero and the algorithm is re-applied until a pass is made in which no points are removed. At this stage any troughs of points with value one, which are not completely surrounded by points with a higher value, will have been deleted. d is now increased to two and the process repeated. In this way points with a low value lying between ridges of higher value points are deleted first, thus, for example, separating touching arms. When no further points with value two can be removed the program starts on value three, and so on. However, whenever the deletion of a point with value d uncovers a point with a lower value (i.e., a neighbour of a deleted point has value $g, 0<g<d$) d is reset to g at the next pass. Nevertheless, it may be desirable to consider that whenever there is an area of points with value d_1 completely surrounded by points with a higher value, d_2 say, then this represents a closed curve surrounding the d_1 points. To achieve a skeleton which reflects this, all that is necessary is that when all points with value less than or equal to d_2 which can be removed, have been, then any remaining points at level d_1 are deleted thus producing 'holes'. Thinning then continues at level d_1+1.

Unfortunately, application of the algorithm is very time-expensive since it requires a complete pass to be made through *all* the points of the picture even though there may be only very few points remaining with the current value d (and in general the greater the number of values the less the efficiency). This has been overcome by initially making a list of all points of the picture with each value. Therefore, when removing points with a given value, it is necessary to consider only the points given in the list for that value.

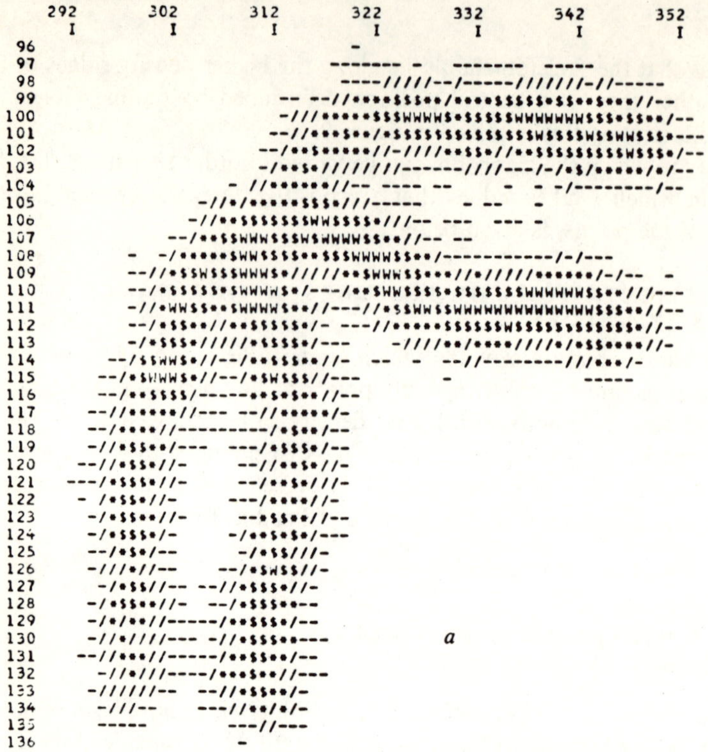

a

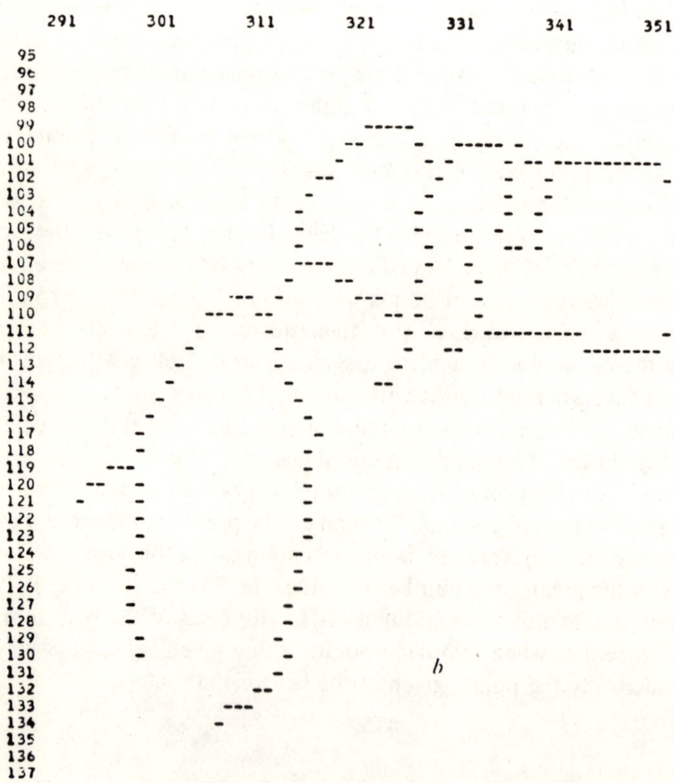

b

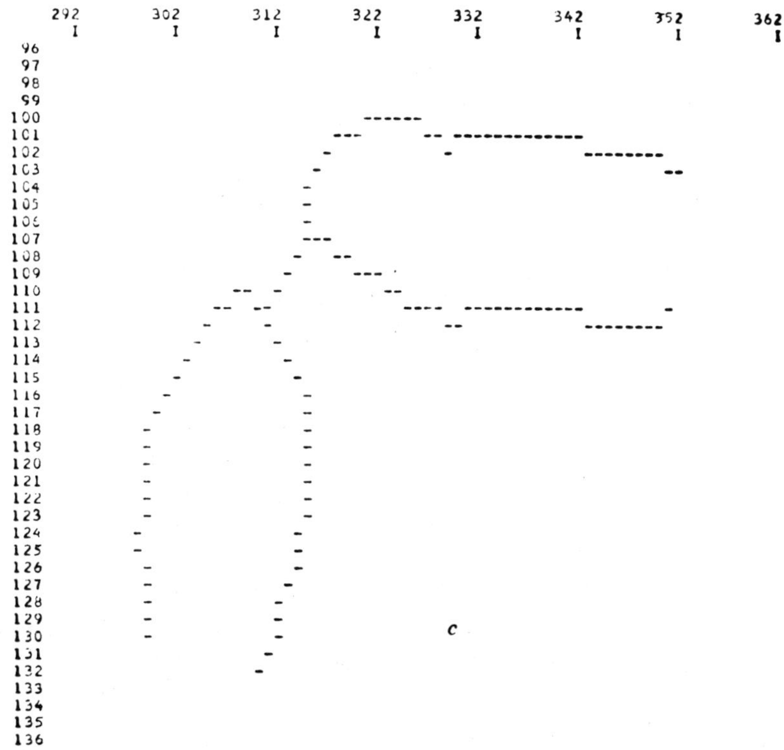

Figure 8. (*a*) A digitization of a chromosome. The chromosome is digitized on a seven-level density scale, and in the line printer representation shown here the characters are chosen so that the density at each point corresponds approximately to the overall darkness of the printed character.
(*b*) The skeleton obtained from this chromosome by using the binary application of the algorithm on its characteristic function.
(*c*) The skeleton obtained by pre-processing the picture before taking the characteristic function.

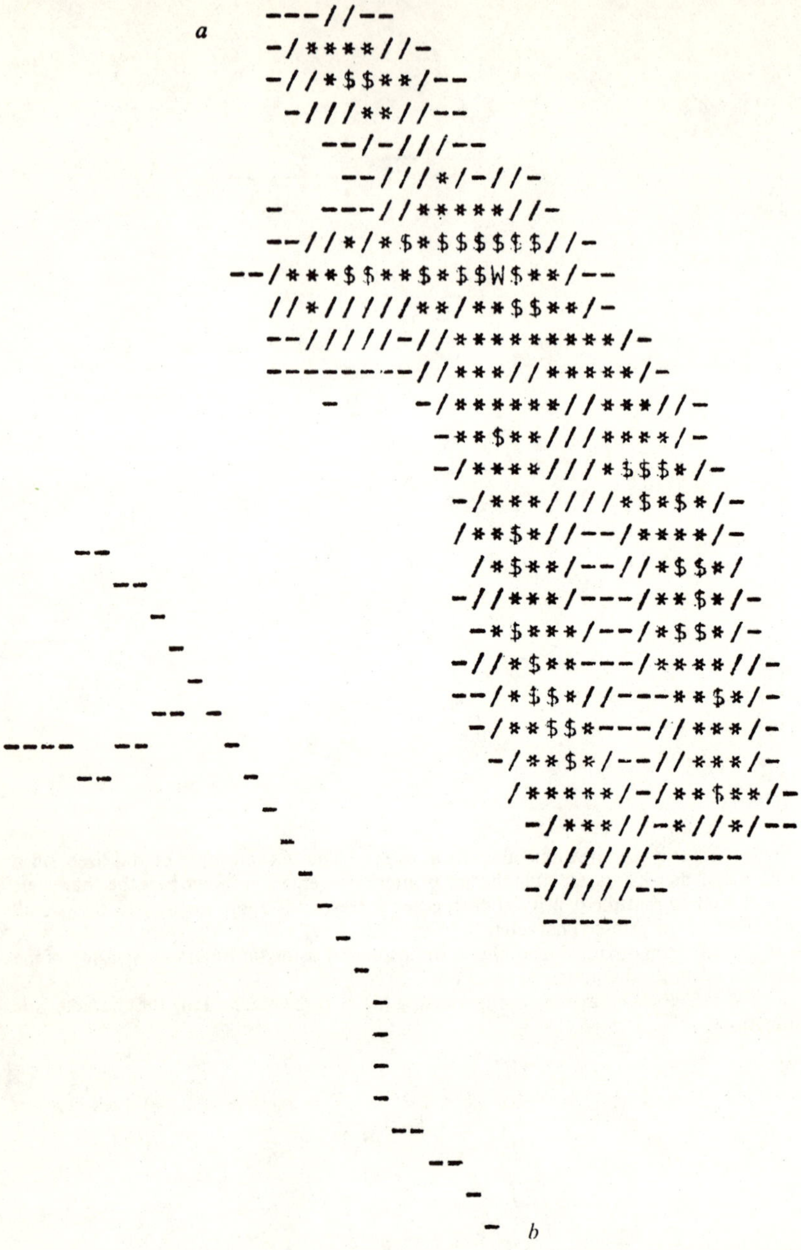

Figure 9. An example of a chromosome and its skeleton obtained by using the binary application of the algorithm. In this case it would be better if the skeleton were to lie along the high density ridges of the picture, rather than in a central position with respect to area alone.

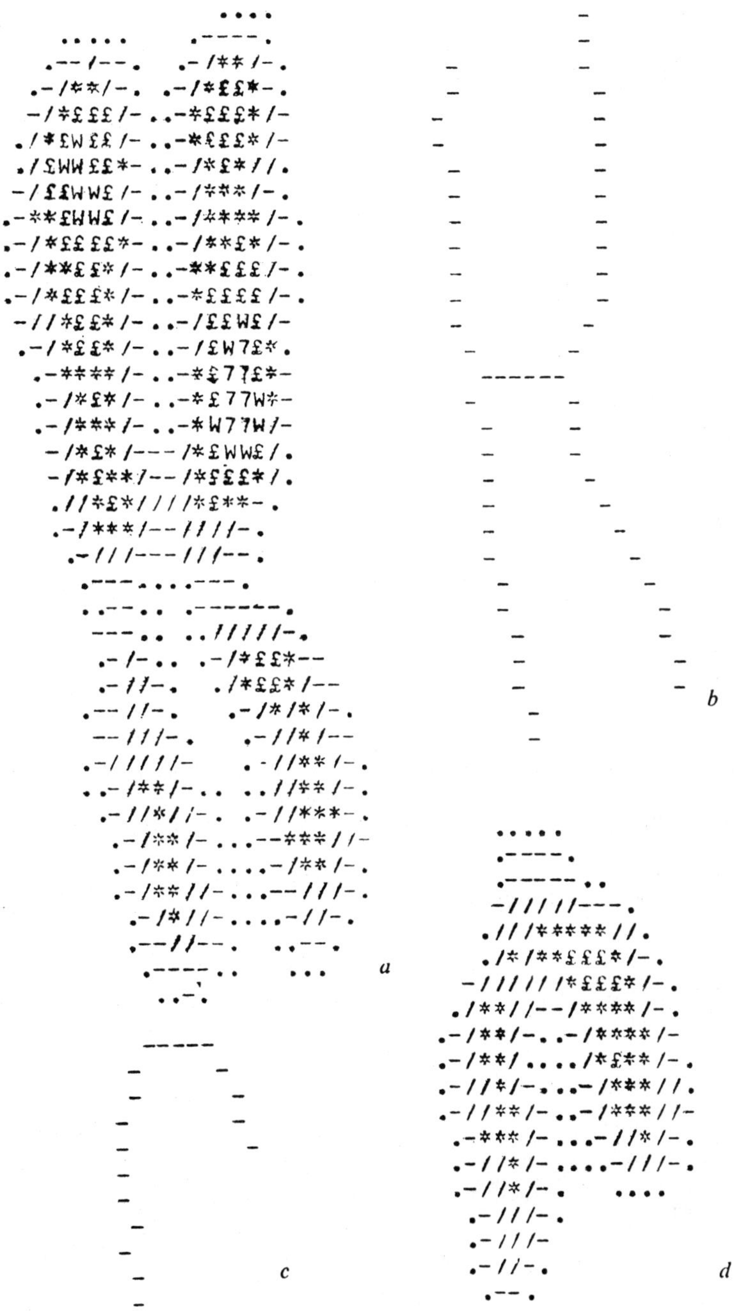

Figure 10. Some chromosome pictures and skeletons obtained using the version of the algorithm intended for pictures covering a range of density values.

The success of this algorithm is illustrated in figure 10. As well as being less sensitive to the choice of boundary for the picture it is also found to be much less sensitive to noise – the only pre-processing required to obtain satisfactory skeletons being a simple smoothing, by setting each point to a weighted average of itself and its neighbours.

Acknowledgements

Thanks are due to all members of the Clinical and Population Cytogenetics Research Unit, Pattern Recognition and Automation Section under the direction of Dr Denis Rutovitz.

The computing was done using the IBM 7090 computer at Imperial College in conjunction with a Fidac Scanner.

REFERENCES

Blum, H. (1964) *A Transformation for Extracting New Descriptors of Shape*. Boston: Air Force Cambridge Research Laboratories.

Deutsch, E.S. (1967) Computer simulation of a character recognition machine. *The Post Office Electrical Engineering Journal*, **60,** 39–44 and 104–9.

Izzo, N. & Coles, W. (1962) Blood-cell scanner identifies rare cells. *Electronics* **52.**

Kirsch, R.A., Cahn, L., Ray, C. & Urban, G.J. (1957) Experiments in processing pictorial information with a digital computer. *Proc. Eastern Computer Conference*, 221–9.

McCormick, B.H. (1963) The Illinois pattern recognition computer—Illiac III. *IRE Trans. Electronic Comp.* EC–12, **5.**

Narasimhan, R. (1964) Labelling schemata and syntactic descriptions of pictures. *Information and Control*, **7,** 151.

Philbrick, O. (1966) *A Study of Shape Recognition Using the Medial Axis Transform*. Boston: Air Force Cambridge Research Laboratories.

Preston, K. (1961) The Cell Scan system—a leukocyte pattern analyser. *Proc. Western Computer Conference*, 173.

Rosenfeld, A. & Pfaltz, J.L. (1966) Sequential operations in digital picture processing. *Journal of the ACM*, **13,** 471–94.

Reprinted from *IEEE Trans. Inform. Theory*, **IT–10**, No. 2, 1964, pp. 139–145

Signal Detection By Complex Spatial Filtering

A. VANDER LUGT

Summary—**In the past, spatial filtering in coherent optical systems has been limited by the inability to realize practically a general complex filter. This paper describes a technique for realizing such a filter, and gives an application of spatial filtering to the problem of detecting isolated signals in a variety of noise backgrounds. The experimental results obtained to date indicate that this technique provides an excellent two-dimensional filtering capability that will play a key role in such problems as shape recognition and signal detection.**

Introduction

The fundamental theory of optical spatial filtering has been formulated by several writers.[1,2] The close analogy of spatial filtering in coherent optical systems to optimum linear filtering in communication theory promised to open up new techniques for realizing those frequency domain filters which could not be synthesized in the time domain because of the realizability constraint; but spatial filtering has not advanced as far as one might have expected. Perhaps the main reason is that, though the formulation of the theory tacitly assumed that complex filters could be realized, the practical realization has presented a difficult problem. A major part of this problem is that photographic film, the most prominent candidate for use in the realization of spatial filters, can record only non-negative functions, so that auxiliary phase filters must be used to realize the complex filters.

The modulus of the transfer function for spatial filters is restricted to values between zero and one.[3] To demonstrate the theory, early experiments in spatial filtering used occluding filters with transfer functions having the values (0, 1) as band-pass filters.[2,3] Later, continuous amplitude control (*e.g.*, Gaussian weighting) was used to show how equalization could be accomplished in a coherent optical system. The next step was to add binary phase control to extend the range of filter values to the real axis between plus and minus one.[4,5] The binary phase functions were constructed by using ruled phase plates, evaporative techniques, or film reliefing techniques. These techniques are rather awkward to apply. Clearly, if more general filtering operations are to be performed, a fairly easy method for constructing a general complex filter must be found. This paper describes such a technique and gives some experimental results of major importance. This technique is especially attractive because it realizes the complex filter by a special process for recording on film without the use of an auxiliary phase filter.

Mathematical Nature of the Problem

The mathematical model shown in Fig. 1 describes the problem of sensing, recording and processing imagery. The scene will be denoted by $g(x, y)$, an intensity function of two space coordinates. The primary sensor makes a two-dimensional transformation of $g(x, y)$, and the recording process causes a further transformation. Because the recording medium is usually film, this transformation introduces film grain as a secondary source of noise. It has become common practice to refer to $f(x, y) = T_2\{T_1[g(x, y)]\}$ as the "scene." Though this is not strictly correct, transformation T_2 is usually a nonlinear process (and a poorly controlled one at that). Therefore, it becomes necessary to operate on the available data $f(x, y)$ rather than to attempt to recover $g(x, y)$ before the processing operation.

Processing of the imagery could involve several distinctly different operations, depending on the type of information desired. One such operation might be to differentiate the signal to emphasize large gradients in the image. In other cases, band-pass filtering will improve the imagery. The particular problem treated in this paper is that of maximizing the ratio of peak signal energy to mean square noise energy in the output of the processing system. The signal is any object of interest in the scene, and the noise is the rest of the imagery. This problem is familiar in signal detection theory, and the mathematical solution is well known. Suppose $n(x, y)$ is a homogeneous, isotropic random process with spectral density $N(p, q)$, and $s(x, y)$ is a known Fourier transformable function of space coordinates. If $h(x, y)$ denotes the impulse response of a linear space invariant filter with frequency response $H(p, q)$, we wish to find the optimum linear filter which operates on $f(x, y) = s(x, y) + n(x, y)$ to maximize the ratio of peak signal to rms noise.

Several writers have given the solution to this problem, but usually for the case where $N(p, q)$ is uniform. The general solution[6] is that the required filter response is

Manuscript received May 31, 1963. This work was jointly supported by Project MICHIGAN, under U. S. Army Electronics Command, Contract DA-36-039 SC-78801, and by Aeronautical Systems Division, Air Force Contract AF 33(616)-8433. A more detailed discussion of this subject is given in Report 2900-394-T/4594-22-T.

The author is with the Institute of Science and Technology, The University of Michigan, Ann Arbor, Mich.

[1] T. P. Cheatham, Jr. and A. Kohlenberg, "Optical filters: their equivalence to and differences from electrical networks, 1954 IRE Convention Record, pt. 4, pp. 6–12.

[2] E. O'Neill, "Spatial filtering in optics," IRE Trans. on Information Theory, vol. IT-2, pp. 56–65; June, 1956.

[3] L. J. Cutrona *et al.*, "Optical data processing and filtering systems," IRE Trans. on Information Theory, vol. IT-6, pp. 386–400; June, 1960.

[4] A. Marechal, "Filtering of optical images," in "*Communication and Information Theory Aspects of Modern Optics*," General Electric Co., Electronics Laboratory, Syracuse. N. Y.; August, 1962.

[5] J. Tsujiuchi, "Correction of optical images by compensation of aberrations and by spatial frequency filtering," in "Progress in Optics," E. Wolf, Ed., North-Holland Publishing Co., Amsterdam, The Netherlands, vol. 2, pp. 133–180; 1963.

[6] W. M. Brown, "Analysis of Linear Time-Invariant Systems," McGraw-Hill Book Co., Inc., New York, N. Y.; 1963.

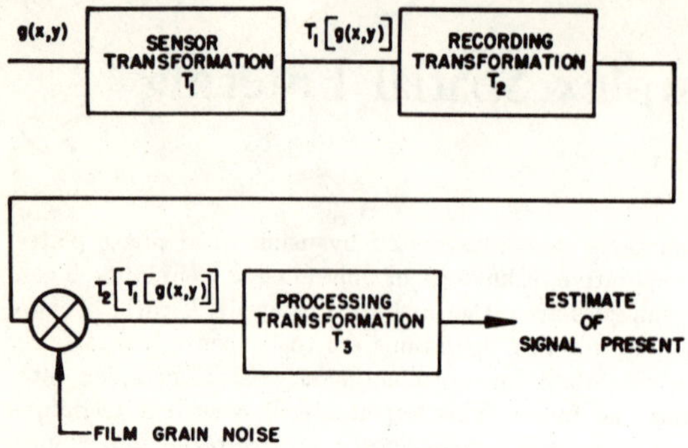

Fig. 1—Mathematical model of image processing.

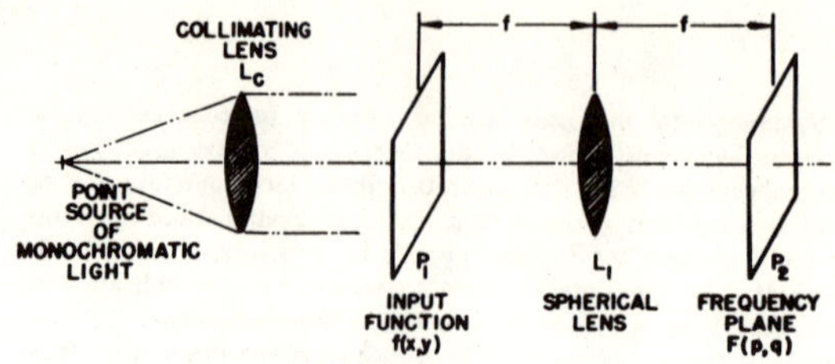

Fig. 2—Coherent Fourier analyzer.

$$H(p, q) = \frac{kS^*(p, q)}{N(p, q)} \tag{1}$$

where

$S^*(p, q)$ is the complex conjugate of the signal spectrum,
$N(p, q)$ is the spectral density of the background noise and
k is a constant chosen to make $|H(p, q)| < 1$ for passive spatial filters.

Eq. (1) reduces to the so-called matched filter case when $N(p, q)$ is uniform for all (p, q), as is usual in treatments of this problem for electronic systems. Almost always, the spectral density of the noise background in photographs is far from uniform. This fact might impose a limitation on the realizability of electronic filters, but, as we shall see later, it poses no problem in the realization of the optimum filter in coherent optical systems.

The output from the linear filter represented by (1), given here for future reference, is

$$r(x, y) = \frac{1}{4\pi^2} \iint_{-\infty}^{\infty} F(p, q)H(p, q)e^{j(px+qy)}\, dp\, dq. \tag{2}$$

Coherent Optical Processing Systems

Rhodes has shown that the optical system sketched in Fig. 2 functions as a two-dimensional Fourier analyzer.[7] If $f(x, y)$ denotes the specular amplitude transmission of the transparency in plane P_1, and $F(p, q)$ denotes the complex distribution of light in plane P_2, then

$$F(p, q) = \iint_{-\infty}^{\infty} f(x, y) \exp\,[j(px + qy)]\, dx\, dy. \tag{3}$$

In (3), p and q represent spatial frequency variables having the dimensions of radians/unit distance. The variables in plane P_2, which are in units of distance, are related to the frequency variables by

$$\xi = \frac{\lambda f}{2\pi} p \tag{4a}$$

$$\eta = \frac{\lambda f}{2\pi} q \tag{4b}$$

where

ξ is the direction parallel to x,
η is the direction parallel to y,
λ is the wavelength of the illumination and
f is the focal length of the spherical lens.

When a distribution of light is a function of frequency, the variables (p, q) will be used to emphasize that fact, as well as to simplify the notation associated with Fourier transform theory.

Since a spherical lens can take the Fourier transform of a complex distribution of light, one can construct an optical system by arranging a sequence of lenses which forms a succession of Fourier transform planes. An image of the input plane can be effected by placing a lens behind plane P_2 (see Fig. 3) which takes the transform of $F(p, q)$. A positive spherical lens always introduces a positive kernel in the transform relationship, hence the distribution in plane P_3 is

$$r(x, y) = \frac{1}{4\pi^2} \iint_{-\infty}^{\infty} F(p, q)e^{j(px+qy)}\, dp\, dq$$

$$= f(-x, -y). \tag{5}$$

We have assumed that the system has unity magnification and sufficient bandwidth to pass the highest spatial frequency of the input function. Note that the output is an inverted image of the input function, which is what one expects from an imaging system operating under any type of illumination.

It is convenient to realize separately the numerator and denominator of the optimum filter. If two transparencies are placed in contact, their complex transmissions

[7] J. E. Rhodes, Jr., "Analysis and synthesis of optical images," *Am. J. of Phys.*, vol. 21, pp. 337–343; May, 1953.

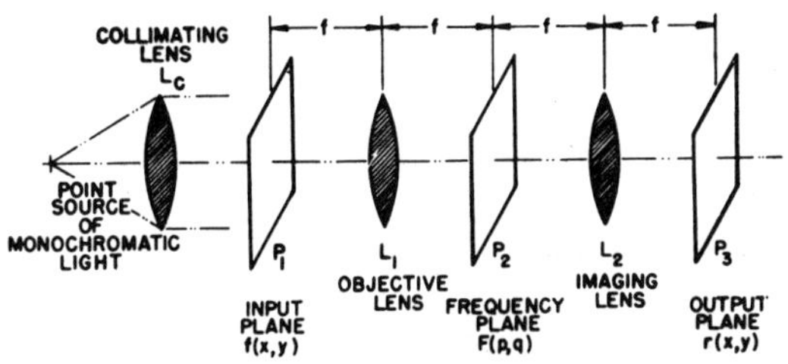

Fig. 3—Coherent optical processing system.

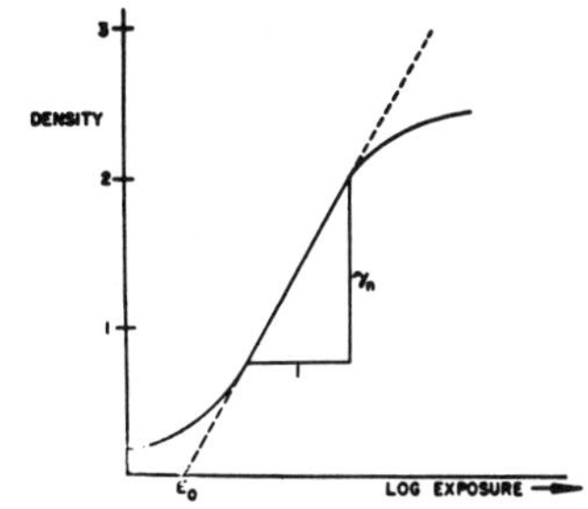

Fig. 4—Typical transfer curve for photographic film.

are multiplicative.[8] Consequently, to realize the filter described by (1), we need to insert in plane P_2 a transparency whose transmission is $1/N(p, q)$, as well as a transparency representing $S^*(p, q)$. When this filter is used, the output of the system essentially represents the probability that a signal has occurred. A bright spot in the output indicates a high probability, and low-light levels indicate a low one. (The output may not resemble the signal to any extent because the phase content of $S(p, q)$ is modified.) This process simultaneously detects signals with similar orientations regardless of their position in the input, as a result of the fact that the spectrum of a translated signal is modified by a linear phase factor. The phase factor contains precisely the information required to image the signal at the proper position in the output. In contrast, the system is sensitive to the orientation of the signals, but a rotation of the filter relative to the input provides a sequential search through all possible orientations.

Realization of the Optimum Filter

Having determined that the optimum filter which maximizes the ratio of peak signal energy to mean square energy is given by (1), we must find some method to realize $H(p, q)$. The denominator of $H(p, q)$ is always a non-negative function which can be realized on photographic film. The first step in this realization is a brief review of the transfer characteristics of films. Fig. 4 shows a typical curve of density vs log exposure, characterized in its linear region by

$$D_n = \gamma_n[\log E_n - \log E_0] \tag{6}$$

where

γ_n is the slope of the straight line,
E_n is the exposure,
E_0 is the intercept of the straight line,
D_n is the density and
n means that a negative transparency is used.

The coherent system operates on the specular amplitude transmission of the film, but using the relationship that $T = \exp[-D/2]$ and substituting (6), we have

$$T = CE_n^{-\gamma_n/2}. \tag{7}$$

If we make E_n proportional to $N(p, q)$ and require that $\gamma_n = 2$, we have realized the denominator of $H(p, q)$.

Since the numerator of (1) may represent a complex quantity, a different technique must be used to realize $S^*(p, q)$. One problem in realizing the numerator of the optimum filter is to determine both the amplitude and the phase of

$$S(p, q) = \iint_{-\infty}^{\infty} s(x, y) \exp[j(px + qy)]\, dx\, dy. \tag{8}$$

One cannot merely use a spherical lens, as previously described, to take the Fourier transform of $s(x, y)$, because any physical detector measures only the intensity of $S(p, q)$, not its phase. A Mach-Zehnder interferometer, however, can be used to determine the phase in a distribution of light by combining that distribution with a reference wave whose amplitude and phase distributions are known. This interferometer is modified for our purposes as shown in Fig. 5.

The signal $s(x, y)$ whose Fourier transform is to be found, and a spherical lens, are inserted in one beam of the interferometer. The lens displays the Fourier transform of $s(x, y)$ at its back focal plane outside the interferometer. If we neglect aberrations in the interferometer, the observed output in the back focal plane of the lens is

$$G(p, q) = |R(p, q) + S(p, q)|^2 = |R(p, q)|^2 + |S(p, q)|^2 + R^*(p, q)S(p, q) + R(p, q)S^*(p, q) \tag{9}$$

where $R(p, q) = |R(p, q)| \exp[j\phi(p, q)]$ represents the light coming from the reference beam, and $S(p, q) = |S(p, q)| \exp[j\theta(p, q)]$ is the signal spectrum. We can rewrite (9) as

$$G(p, q) = |R(p, q)|^2 + |S(p, q)|^2 + 2Re[R(p, q)S^*(p, q)] = |R(p, q)|^2 + |S(p, q)|^2 + 2|R(p, q)|\,|S(p, q)| \cos[\phi(p, q) - \theta(p, q)]. \tag{10}$$

[8] Unless otherwise noted, "transmission" will herein signify the specular amplitude transmission of the transparency.

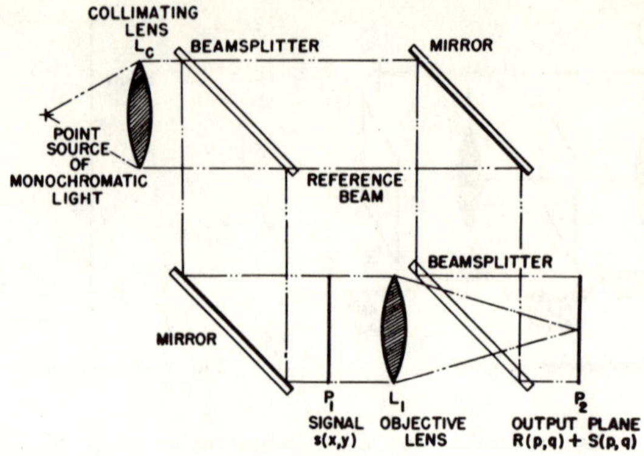

Fig. 5—Modified mach-zehnder interferometer.

Both the amplitude and phase of $R(p, q)$ could be adjusted to determine $\theta(p, q)$, but since the phase information of $S^*(p, q)$ is contained in $G(p, q)$, a non-negative function, $G(p, q)$ can be recorded on film to realize the optimum filter.

The film is exposed so that its transmission is proportional to $G(p, q)$. If we combine this film with the film on which $1/N(p, q)$ is realized, the transmission of the combination is

$$\frac{G(p, q)}{N(p, q)} = \frac{|R(p, q)|^2 + |S(p, q)|^2}{N(p, q)} + \frac{R^*(p, q)S(p, q)}{N(p, q)} + \frac{R(p, q)S^*(p, q)}{N(p, q)}. \tag{11}$$

Suppose we require $|R(p, q)|$ to be a constant, k, and $\phi(p, q)$ to be linear in (p, q), *i.e.*, $\phi(p, q) = bp + cq$. Then

$$\frac{G(p, q)}{N(p, q)} = A(p, q) + H^*(p, q)e^{-j(bp+cq)} + H(p, q)e^{j(bp+cq)} \tag{12}$$

where

$$A(p, q) = \frac{|R(p, q)|^2 + |S(p, q)|^2}{N(p, q)}$$

$$H(p, q) = \frac{kS^*(p, q)}{N(p, q)},$$

b, c are constants.

Thus, the third term of (12) represents the desired filter function, multiplied by a linear phase factor. The problem is to separate this term from the other two terms of (12). This can be accomplished by inserting the filter represented by (12) into the optical system (Fig. 3) at plane P_2. Lens L_2 separates the three terms in the output by taking the inverse transform of the light distribution in P_2; *i.e.*,

$$\text{output} = \frac{1}{4\pi^2} \iint_{-\infty}^{\infty} F(p, q) \frac{G(p, q)}{N(p, q)} e^{j(px+qy)} \, dp \, dq. \tag{13}$$

Substituting (12) in (13), we have

$$\text{output} = \frac{1}{4\pi^2} \iint_{-\infty}^{\infty} F(p, q)A(p, q)e^{j(px+qy)} \, dp \, dq$$
$$+ \frac{1}{4\pi^2} \iint_{-\infty}^{\infty} F(p, q)H^*(p, q)e^{j[(x-b)p+(y-c)q]} \, dp \, dq$$
$$+ \frac{1}{4\pi^2} \iint_{-\infty}^{\infty} F(p, q)H(p, q)e^{j[(x+b)p+(y+c)q]} \, dp \, dq. \tag{14}$$

The first term of (14), which appears on the optical axis, is of no particular interest in this discussion. Nor is the second term, which appears at $x = b$, $y = c$. The third term, $r(x + b, y + c)$, where $r(x, y)$ is defined by (2), is exactly the output expected from an optimum filter. This term appears with its center off the optical axis by an amount $x = -b$, $y = -c$. At this point it will be convenient to set $c = 0$ since it is arbitrary. To prevent overlap of the three outputs, the value of b must be such that $b \geq B$, where B is the length of the signal in the x direction. The fact that this output occurs off axis by a distance $x = -b$ is not important, since the output sensor can be located properly to detect it.[9]

In passing, a comment will be made on the significance of the second term of (14). If $N(p, q) = N$ for all (p, q),

[9] This method is the equivalent of recording a complex valued function as a real valued function on a carrier frequency.[6]

we can write the third term of (14) as a cross-correlation integral (for $c = 0$);

$$r(x + b, y) = \iint_{-\infty}^{\infty} f(u, v)s^*(x + b + u, y + v)\, du\, dv. \quad (15)$$

The second term of (14) can then be written as a convolution integral;

$$r(x - b, y) = \iint_{-\infty}^{\infty} f(u, v)s(x - b - u, y - v)\, du\, dv. \quad (16)$$

Thus, when $N(p, q)$ is uniform, the cross correlation and convolution of the signal with the input function are both displayed in the output plane.

Experimental Results

A few experimental results will serve to illustrate the theory and indicate the potential of spatial filtering when complex filters can be realized.

Detection of Simple Geometrical Shapes

The first example presented is the detection of one of the elementary geometrical shapes shown in Fig. 6(a). Any one of the shapes could be selected; we chose the small rectangle. We realized the filter for this signal (which is real because of symmetry), by the method described. The output of interest is shown in Fig. 6(b). Note the simultaneous detection of all signals with the proper shape and orientation.

The second signal selected was the "L" shape, which has a complex spectrum. The Fourier transform of the complex filter, shown in Fig. 7, illustrates the fidelity with which the filter was realized. The light distribution in the center of the output is the transform of the first two terms of (9). The "L" on the left is the transform of the third term of (9). The other "L" is the transform of the last term. These two images are inverted and reversed relative to each other, which graphically demonstrates that $\mathfrak{F}[S(p, q)] = s(x, y)$ and $\mathfrak{F}[S^*(p, q)] = s^*(-x, -y)$. Of course, since $s(x, y)$ is real, $s^*(-x, -y) = s(-x, -y)$.

Fig. 8(a) shows the output, which is the cross correlation of the "L" with the input function. Note the symmetry in the output which is a necessary feature of cross correlation. (The other "L" 's in the input, having different orientations, do not give as large an output, but a rotation of the filter relative to the input would sequentially detect them.) Fig. 8(b) shows the output which is the convolution of the signal with the input function. It is asymmetrical, as a consequence of convolution.

Detection of Alphanumerics

The second example is the detection of alphanumerics. An interesting variation of the first example is to record the alphabet shown in Fig. 9(a) via its complex spectrum as the filter function. It is a simple matter to select any one of the alphanumerics as the signal to be detected and use it as the input signal. The output, when the letter "g" is the input, is shown in Fig. 9(b). Since the filter (which is the normal input function in disguise) does not have to be changed while the search is being carried out, this technique suggests a method for scanning a printed page for the presence of any particular alphanumeric.

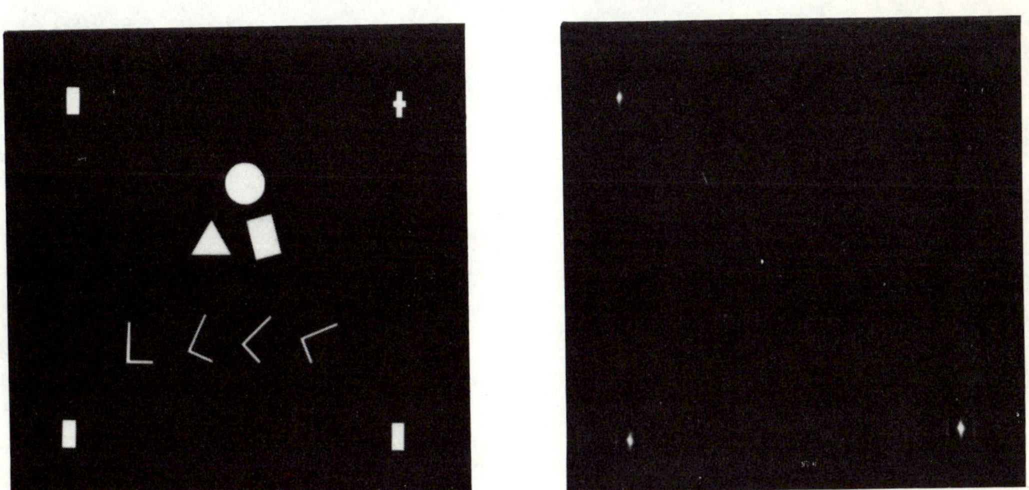

(a) (b)

Fig. 6—Detection of geometric shapes. (a) Geometric shapes. (b) Detection of rectangles.

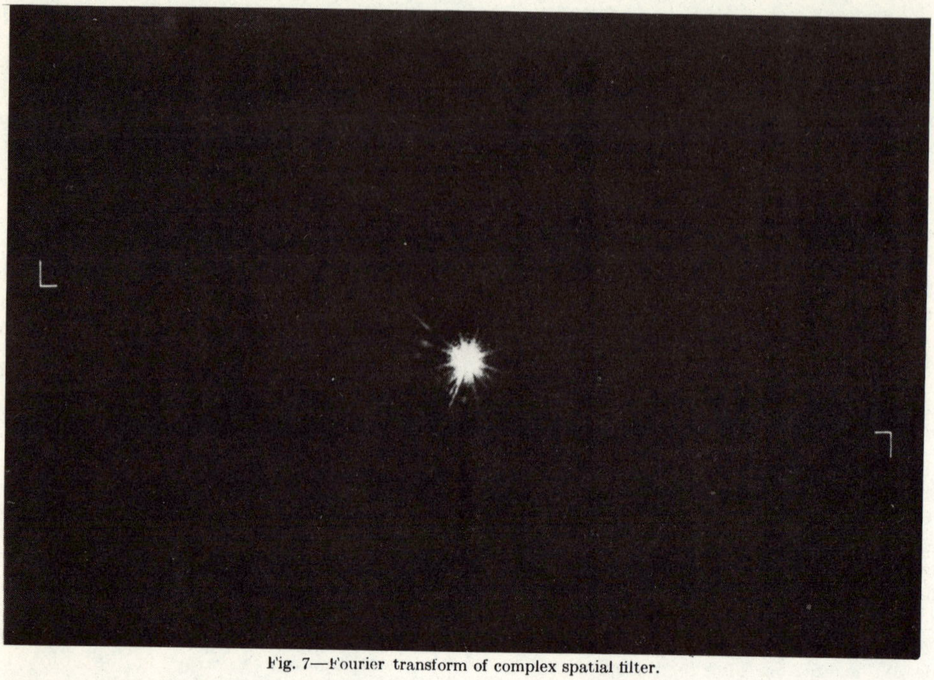

Fig. 7—Fourier transform of complex spatial filter.

(a)

(b)

Fig. 8—Detection of signal having complex spectrum. (a) Cross-correlation of "L" with geometric shapes. (b) Convolution of "L" with geometric shapes.

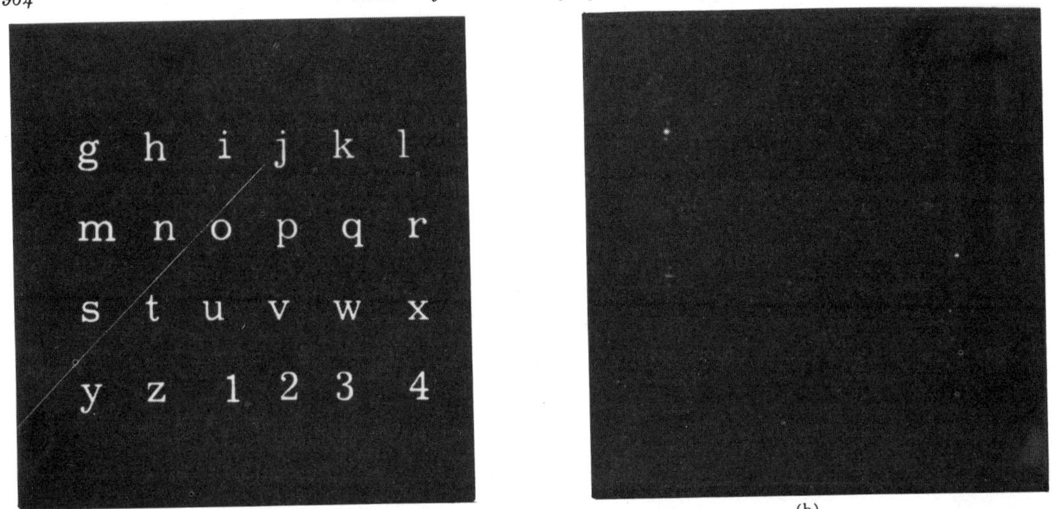

(a) (b)

Fig. 9—Detection of letter. (a) Alphanumerics. (b) Detection of the letter "*g*".

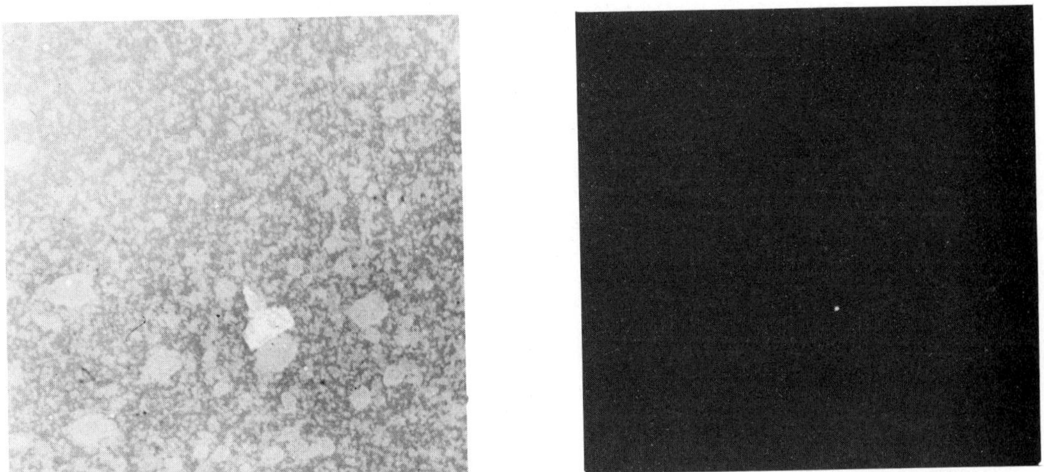

(a) (b)

Fig. 10—Detection of isolated signal in random noise. (a) Input scene. (b) Detection of signal.

Detection of Isolated Signal in Random Noise

In the preceding two examples the "noise" spectral density was uniform enough to be considered white. This final example shows the detection of a signal which is immersed in a noise background with nonuniform spectral density and demonstrates the power of using a coherent system for signal detection. Fig. 10(a) shows a signal in background noise. Since the noise spectral density is nonuniform, the denominator of the filter must be realized. Fig. 10(b) shows that the background noise has been completely suppressed and the signal has been detected.

ACKNOWLEDGMENT

The author wishes to thank A. Klooster, Jr., who carried out most of the experimental work. Helpful conversations with staff members, particularly E. N. Leith, are also acknowledged.

Picture Machines

VI

Editor's Comments on Papers 24, 25, and 26

24 Unger: *Pattern Detection and Recognition*

25 McCormick: *The Illinois Pattern Recognition Computer ILLIAC III*

26 Hawkins and Munsey: *A Parallel Computer Organization and Mechanization*

The use of computers for pattern recognition encounters special problems when the patterns are pictures. Consider an ordinary television picture satisfying the specifications for television broadcasting in the United States. Such a picture has about 500 × 500 picture elements or *pixels,* and each pixel is at one of at least 8 resolvable gray levels (i.e., the picture has a densitometric resolution of at least 3 bits). Thus at least 750,000 bits are required to represent this television picture in its full fidelity. In processing pictures by computer, a picture takes the same role that a number does in ordinary number processing. But in most number processing, each number is no longer than 40 bits. Thus the size of the high-speed memory in modern computers is a major limitation in the use of these machines for picture recognition.

Among the types of operations typically used in processing pictures, the following seem to be basic: (1) *threshold* (i.e., replace every pixel by 1 if the pixel exceeds a prescribed threshold, otherwise replace it by 0); (2) *add* (i.e., add the members of every pair of identically located pixels in two pictures of the same size to form the corresponding pixel of a sum picture); (3) *multiply* two pictures to form a product picture; (4) *shift* (i.e., shift every pixel of a given picture by a unit vector displacement); and (5) *count* or *accumulate* (i.e., add all pixels of a given picture). Among these five operations the first four are parallel in the sense that the operations may be executed as a set of simultaneous elementary operations, each elementary operation accepting as data only the pixel and its immediate neighbors at a specific location of the picture.

These considerations lead naturally to the invention of machines that are structurally highly redundant. Thus several proposals have appeared for the construction of parallel machines especially suited to the processing of pictures. None of them have yet resulted in a commercially viable machine—most likely because the technology of digital electronics has not yet reached the necessary low level of unit cost.

In the first selection of this part Unger [Ung] proposes a spatial computer consisting of an array of small computers, each computer operating on one pixel and its immediate neighbors. Unger's spatial computer was never built; but it was successfully simulated on an ordinary digital computer.

Later, Bruce McCormick proposed a much more detailed design of a parallel-structured picture analyzer—the ILLIAC III. This is described in the next paper. One of the significant features of this design is the use of "stalactites" for generalized parallel local operations.

The third paper, by Hawkins and Munsey [Haw], is notable for its constructive concern for the economics of parallel machines. Here digital computer technology is combined with optics, light amplifiers, and film to achieve relatively inexpensive implementations of picture-processing algorithms.

Reprinted from *Proc. IRE,* Oct. 1959, pp. 1737–1752

24

Pattern Detection and Recognition*

S. H. UNGER†, MEMBER, IRE

Summary—**Two types of pattern-processing problems are discussed in this paper. The first, termed "pattern detection," consists of examining an arbitrary set of figures and selecting those having some specified form. The second problem, "pattern recognition," consists of identifying a given figure which is known to belong to one of a finite set of classes. This is the problem encountered when reading alphanumeric characters.**

Both recognition and detection have been successfully carried out on an IBM 704 computer which was programmed to simulate a spatial computer[1] (a stored-program machine comprised of a master control unit directing a network of logical modules). One of the programs tested consisted of a recognition process for reading hand-lettered sans-serif alphanumeric characters. This process permits large variations in the size, shape, and proportions of the input figures and can tolerate random noise when it is well scattered in small specks.

Programs for detecting L-shaped (or A-shaped) figures in the presence of other randomly drawn patterns have also been successfully tested.

I. Introduction

A PRINCIPAL goal of the research upon which this report is based is to determine how machines can be made to duplicate some of the remarkable feats that humans perform daily when dealing with visual images. For example:

1) Presented with a new coloring book, a five-year-old child quickly points out all outlines of dogs.
2) A post-office clerk deciphers the name of a city in a carelessly written address.
3) A hold-up victim selects a photograph of his assailant from among the collection in police files.
4) A frequent visitor to an art museum identifies the creator of a newly acquired painting merely from its general appearance and style, and the knowledge that it was done by one of the better known nineteenth-century artists.

Examples 1 and 3 illustrate what we shall term *pattern detection*. This is the process of examining a set of figures and selecting those that fall into some particular class of patterns, defined as the *target set*. Examples 2 and 4 involve a different kind of operation, which we shall define as *pattern recognition*. Here a single input pattern known to belong to one of several known classes is to be identified. In other words, the problem is to specify which of a finite number of labels should be attached to the input. Thus, in example 2, the postal clerk knew that the scrawled word that he was trying to decipher was the name of one of the cities in the state of New Jersey, and his object was to decide *which* one. Compare this with the detection problem of example 1. Here, the child was required to search through an assortment of patterns selected from an unlimited ensemble and to indicate which, if any, were pictures of dogs. Note that detection subsumes recognition in that any recognition problem can be treated as a finite number of detection problems. The converse is not true.

Both detection and recognition will be discussed here in some detail with alphanumeric characters being used as the patterns of interest. Systems have been devised and successfully tested for accomplishing the following:

1) Recognizing any given hand-printed alphanumeric character.
2) Examining an input field consisting of a set of randomly drawn patterns and detecting all L-shaped figures that are present. (A-shaped figures have also been detected.)

The above-mentioned systems consist of programs written for the spatial computer.[1] A brief description of this machine (abbreviated SPAC) follows, and a somewhat more detailed description including the order structure, is included in an appendix.

SPAC consists of a rectangular network of logical modules directed by a master control unit. Each module has direct contact with its four immediate neighbors (Fig. 1) and receives orders from the master control, which issues identical commands to all modules in the network.

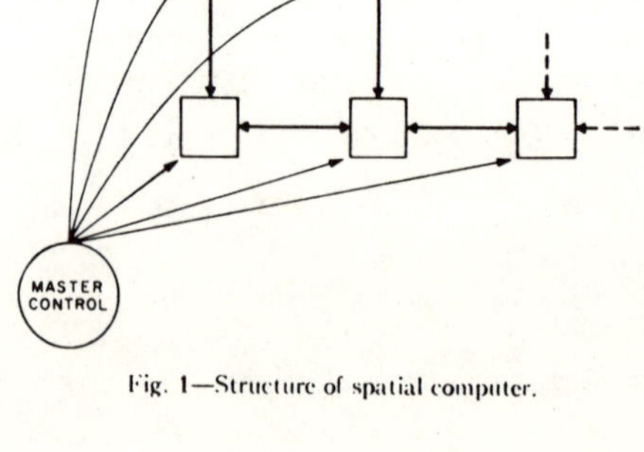

Fig. 1—Structure of spatial computer.

* Original manuscript received by the IRE, April 30, 1959; revised manuscript received, May 9, 1959.

† Bell Telephone Laboratories, Inc., Whippany, N. J.

[1] S. H. Unger, "A computer oriented toward spatial problems," Proc. IRE, vol. 46, pp. 1744–1750; October, 1958.

A module consists of some logical circuitry, a one-bit principal register (PR), and a set of one-bit memory registers (MR's) individually addressable as MR1, MR2, etc. (In the original description of SPAC,[1] the PR's are called accumulators.) A pattern can be stored in the PR's or in any of the MR arrays.

The master control includes a random-access memory for storing instructions, an instruction counter, and decoding circuitry. It operates like the control unit of a conventional digital computer, reading instructions out of memory in sequence, decoding them and sending appropriate control signals out on a set of buses feeding the modules.

The SPAC programs that will be discussed here were tested by means of a simulation program on an IBM 704 Computer. The simulated SPAC has a 36×36 array of modules, and there are nine MR's per module.

Important work in the pattern processing area has been done by Selfridge[2,3] and Dinneen[4] who performed a number of interesting experiments on a digital computer which indicated that much could be accomplished through the use of a small number of very elementary operations, such as local averaging, spatial differentiation, and blob counting. Their primary goal was to investigate the learning process and they were not concerned with finding efficient recognition or detection procedures.

Kirsch[5] and some of his colleagues at the Bureau of Standards have made use of the SEAC computer to study various pattern processing operations. Their objective was to develop a library of computer subroutines that might be useful in pattern processing. In addition to operations similar to those used by Selfridge and Dinneen, the Bureau of Standards group has demonstrated some interesting properties of an operation in which patterns are alternately complemented and spatially differentiated. No effort was made to develop specific recognition or detection systems.

A report by Greanias *et al.*[6] describes a system for recognizing members of a sixteen character alphabet (numerals and some miscellaneous printer symbols). The system has been tested via a computer program and has successfully identified samples of printed characters in the presence of background noise. As described in the paper, this method does not permit variations in the size and proportions of the input characters.

[2] O. G. Selfridge, "Pattern recognition and learning," Symp. on Information Theory, London, Eng.; 1955.

[3] O. G. Selfridge, "Pattern recognition and modern computers," *1955 Proc. WJCC*, pp. 91–93.

[4] G. T. Dinneen, "Programing pattern recognition," *1955 Proc. WJCC*, pp. 94–100.

[5] R. A. Kirsch, L. C. Ray, L. Cahn and G. H. Urban, "Experiments in processing pictorial information with a digital computer," *1957 Proc. EJCC*, pp. 221–230.

[6] E. C. Greanias, *et al.*, "Design of logic for recognition of printed characters by simulation," *IBM J.*, vol. 1, pp. 8–18; January, 1957.

T. L. Dimond[7] has developed a process for reading hand-printed numerals, provided that they are drawn in accordance with certain constraints that restrict size, proportion, and location.

The Solartron electronic reading automaton,[8] produced commercially in England, can read 120 printed numerals per second. Only small variations in size and style are permissible.

The amount of work being done on pattern processing problems is increasing too rapidly to permit a complete review of the field, but the preceding summary represents a reasonable cross section.

II. The Effects of Quantizing Patterns on a Grid

We shall not consider multi-color patterns or those represented in half-tones. The original inputs will be assumed to be representable in black and white.

As a first step in processing patterns, it is desirable to reduce the input field to a discrete form. This can be done by superimposing a grid or matrix of squares over the figure (assumed to be black on white) and placing a one in each square if the black area within that square exceeds a certain threshold. Zeros are filled in elsewhere (although zero-cells will usually be left blank in the diagrams). All of our input fields will be of this form.

Such a quantizing process (which can be physically realized by devices such as flying spot scanners) results in a loss of information concerning the original pattern, but this loss can always be reduced by decreasing the mesh of the grid (that is, by increasing the number of squares per unit area). If the grid is too coarse, certain details of the pattern will be lost. This effect can sometimes be made to serve a useful function in filtering out insignificant irregularities that might cause confusion. For example, if a character printed by a typewriter is magnified by a factor of several thousand diameters and projected on a screen it is generally somewhat difficult to identify because of the apparently random distribution of tiny blobs of ink on the paper. Thus, for a given input field, there is a limit on the amount of useful grid resolution.

Regardless of how fine a grid is used, there are still important transformations which occur when a continuous line is mapped onto a discrete grid. Assume that the threshold is set so that a one is placed in every cell touched by any portion of a black area. A straight vertical line will be mapped as a set of one-cells (squares with ones in them) one above the other, as shown in Fig. 2(a). Except for the change in thickness, if the one cells are blacked in the resulting picture will be the same as the original line.

[7] T. L. Dimond, "Devices for reading handwritten characters," *1957 Proc. EJCC*, pp. 232–237.

[8] "Typed figures translated into computer code," *Engineering*, vol. 183, pp. 348–349; March 15, 1957.

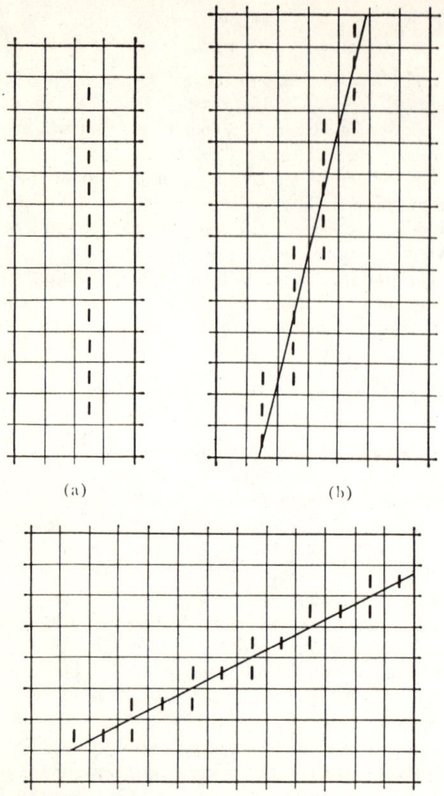

(a) (b) (c)

Fig. 2—Mappings of straight lines on a grid.

Consider now the mapping of a straight line whose slope exceeds unity, but is not infinite [Fig. 2(b)]. Such a map must have slope discontinuities, since the edges of the array of squares in the map must be either vertical or horizontal at all points. Thus, a map of a line with a slope anywhere between $+1$ and ∞ consists of a chain of vertical strips, with the top cell of each strip to the left of the bottom cell of the strip above. The numbers of cells in the strips corresponding to a particular straight line differ from one another by at most one (except for the uppermost and lowermost strips which may have fewer cells), and are approximately equal to the slope. Lines with absolute slopes less than one (lines closer to being horizontal) are similarly mapped into chains of overlapping horizontal strips, as shown in Fig. 2(c). In such cases, the number of one-cells per strip approximates the inverse slope of the line.

If a line is not quite straight, its map will still be qualitatively as above. The difference will show up in the form of variations in the lengths of some of the strips.

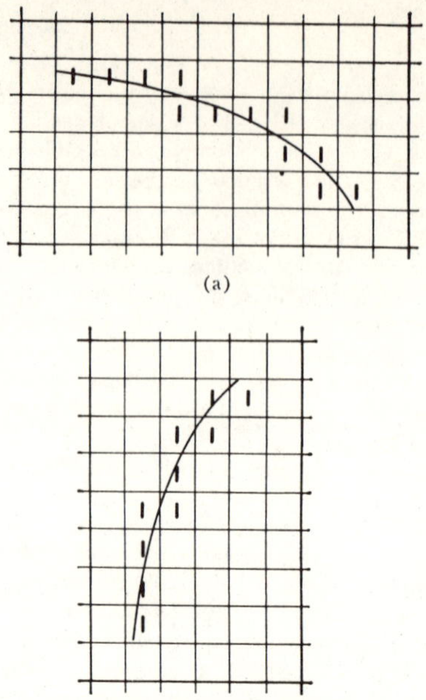

(a) (b)

Fig. 3—Mappings of curved lines on a grid.

The mapping of a curved line onto a discrete matrix can be thought of as the union of a set of maps derived from a series of nearly straight line segments approximating the curve. A more precise approach is suggested by an examination of Fig. 3(a), a mapping of a section of a curve that is convex upward. Note that the lengths of the horizontal strips that constitute the mapping decrease monotonically from the top down. In other words, the map consists of a staircase in which every step is as long as, or longer than, the step below.

Fig. 3(b) is a map of a curve convex to the left, with slope between $+\infty$ and $+1$. Here the lengths of the vertical strips decrease monotonically to the right. This monotonicity property can be used to characterize the curvatures of given lines.

III. Smoothing

It is important that any system for pattern detection or recognition be relatively insensitive to minor irregularities in the input fields. Interchanging zeros for ones in a few isolated cells should not cause significant changes in the output of a pattern processing system. As was pointed out previously, some smoothing is achieved merely by quantizing the input. This however is not adequate, and in some cases the quantization itself introduces irregularities.

There are at least two basic approaches to this problem. One is to carry out a preliminary smoothing operation on the input fields prior to the main task. Another approach is to incorporate the smoothing into the basic recognition or detection operations by making them insensitive to variations confined to any small area. Both of these techniques are used in the programs that will be described here.

The explicit smoothing process,

1) Fills in isolated holes in otherwise black areas,
2) Fills in small notches in straight edge segments,
3) Eliminates isolated ones,
4) Eliminates small bumps along straight edge segments,
5) Replaces missing corner points (under certain conditions).

Fig. 4 shows a cell x, and the eight cells around it. Treat each cell as a binary variable. That is, $b=1$ if cell b contains a one and $b=0$ if cell b contains a zero.

a	b	c
d	x	e
f	g	h

Fig. 4—Points involved in smoothing operations.

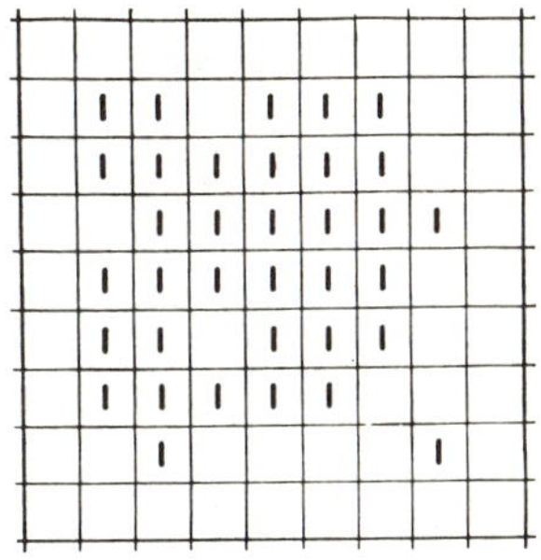

(a)

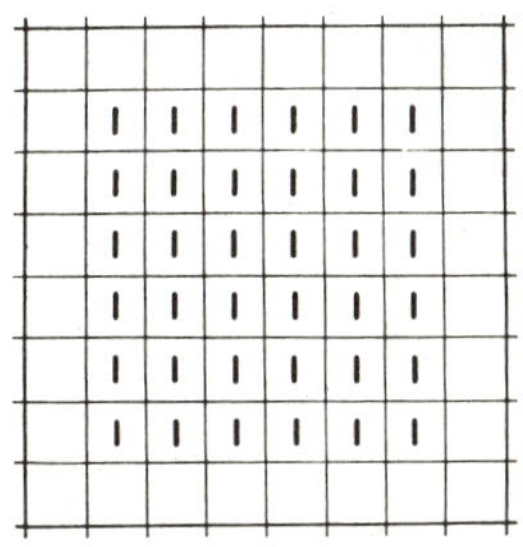

(b)

Fig. 5—Effects of smoothing.

The first step in the smoothing operation places a one in x if the Boolean function $f_1=x+bg(d+e)+de(b+g)$ is unity. (That is, x is changed from zero to one if three of the four variables b, d, e, and f are ones.) If this process is carried out simultaneously for every cell in the matrix, then steps 1 and 2 will be accomplished. (In the preceding sentence, "simultaneously" means that the next state of each cell is determined before any of the other cells have been changed.)

Steps 3 and 4 can be accomplished by replacing the contents of each cell x with $f_2=x[(a+b+d)(e+g+h)+(b+c+e)(d+f+g)]$. A series of four more operations of a similar nature serve to carry out step 5. The smoothing will transform Fig. 5(a) into Fig. 5(b).

About one hundred SPAC orders (each executed once) are required to accomplish the preceding operations.

A simple 25-step subroutine which closes breaks in lines, if the gaps are no wider than one unit, can be inserted ahead of the above described smoothing routine.

These programs will clean up only small noise "specks" affecting isolated cells or in some cases pairs of cells. However, smoothing operations for eliminating larger irregularities might be devised by considering larger regions around each cell and exploiting continuity properties.

Note that the smoothing operations discussed thus far are size dependent in an absolute sense. That is, the irregularities are smoothed out on the basis of absolute size, not on the basis of size relative to that of the over-all figure.

This situation is satisfactory only if the figures being processed do not vary in size by more than a factor of two or three in magnitude. If wider variations are to be permitted in the sizes of the input figures, then it would be necessary to insert parameters in the smoothing programs which would be functions of some dimension of the input figure, such as the over-all height. A preliminary part of the program would then measure this dimension and insert appropriate parameters in the smoothing program. These parameters would control the sizes of the irregularities to be smoothed out. All of this is doubteless possible, but it would add considerable complexity to the program. Possibly, the way to avoid the necessity for such an approach would be to use some sort of analog controlled lens system that would keep the sizes of input figures within a range of two or three to one.

IV. Edge Sequences

In order to be able to detect patterns in the sense defined in the introduction, it is necessary to be able to state precisely, for any target set, just what characteristics distinguish this set from all others. For most interesting target sets these characteristics must be independent of size, location, and, to a considerable extent, of the proportions of component parts.

An important property which goes far toward satisfying these requirements will now be introduced.

Consider the letter "L" in Fig. 6(a) (regarding it as a figure covering a non-zero area, not as a pair of intersecting line segments). Beginning at the starred corner and proceeding in a counter-clockwise direction along the edges (boundaries) of the figure, the following succession of edges is found: top, left, bottom, right, top, right. This sequence, abbreviated at TLBRTR (T for top, L for left, etc.), is cyclic, and if another starting point is used, then an equivalent form such as BRTRTL will be found. Such a sequence, which will be referred to as an *edge sequence,* is not affected by changes in size, proportion, or location.

The edge sequence of Fig. 6(b) is LBR (BL) B (TR), where (BL) and (TR) represent diagonal edges facing "bottom-leftward" and "top-rightward" respectively. Similar notation can be devised for curved edges.

In the case of a figure with a hole, such as is shown in Fig. 6(c), two edge sequences are required for a description; one for the outside, and one for the inside. For this case they are LBRT and R (TL) B, respectively.

Edge sequences constitute a powerful tool for pattern detection. As will be shown in a later section, the ideas concerning edges that were introduced earlier can be utilized by a machine to find the figures in a given input field that have edge sequences corresponding to the target set.

Edge sequences alone are not in general sufficient to completely characterize many interesting target sets. A particular edge sequence may, for example, be a necessary condition for membership in some target set, but there may be other requirements as well. Consider for example Fig. 7(a). This figure has the same edge sequence as a certain alphabetic character drawn in block capital form without serifs. But few readers would classify this figure as an H, although both (a) and (b) of Fig. 7 share the same edge sequence. An additional constraint that must be satisfied before a figure can be classified with 7(b) as an "H" is that the edge labelled p in Fig. 7(b) be directly above the edge labelled q. This condition is not satisfied by the corresponding edges in Fig. 7(a). Such "relative-edge-position" tests are frequently necessary after the edge sequence requirement has been met.

Questions of proportion may also arise. For example, it would be reasonable to exclude Fig. 8(a) from the H-set, while admitting Fig. 8(b). Both have the appropriate edge sequences and their edges are in the proper relation to one another. It is difficult to specify precisely which figures intermediate between the pair in Fig. 8 should be considered as acceptable H's. However, an arbitrary set of standards may be chosen for each target set, such as the requirement (as applied to the present example): "the width of the wider leg must not exceed twice the width of the narrower leg." The research reported on here has not yielded any more specific results concerning this aspect of the problem.

Still another question is posed by Fig. 9(a). Is this a respectable member of the H-set previously discussed? At first, the results of a lifetime of conditioning would lead one to immediately answer "yes." But, on second thought, it becomes obvious that the form of Fig. 9(a) is certainly significantly different from that of a block capital H without serifs, which is the target set under discussion [see Fig. 7(b)]. Only long established custom decrees that this is also an "H," and it would be perfectly possible to devise an alphabet in which the two forms represented different letters. The difference between Fig. 9(b) and Fig. 9(c) is of the same nature, and is smaller in magnitude than the difference between the two H's, and yet one is called a "C," and the other a "G."

Thus, it may be convenient to think of certain target sets as being ***compound;*** that is to say, of being composed of the union of two or more simpler sets. Just as it would not be wise to expect a single description to suffice for both a small "h" and a capital "H," it is similarly unreasonable to expect the same description to cover different styles of capital "H"'s.

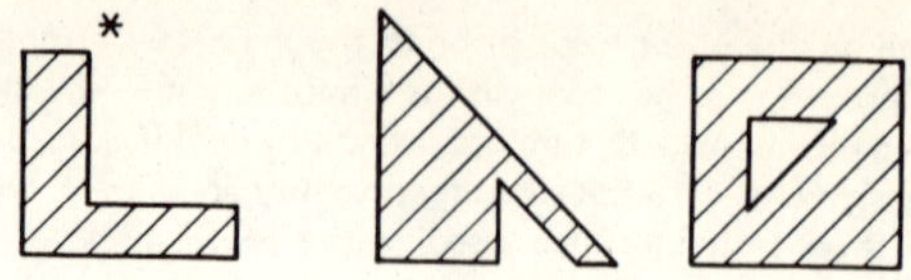
(a) (b) (c)

Fig. 6—Illustrating the use of edge sequences.

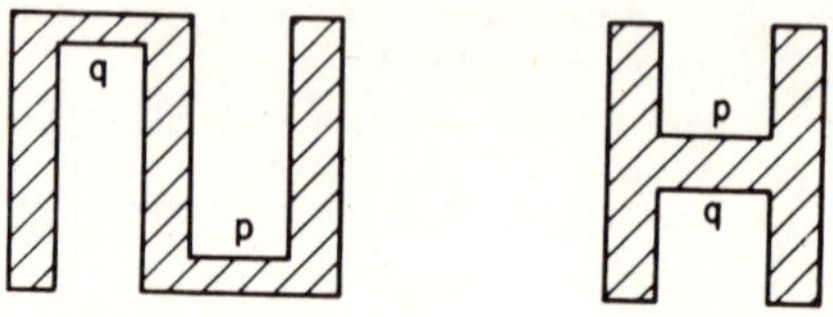

(a) (b)

Fig. 7—Limitations of edge sequence description.

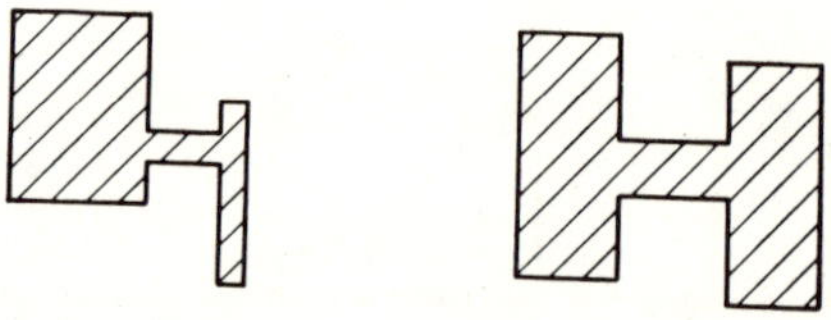
(a) (b)

Fig. 8—Variations in proportion.

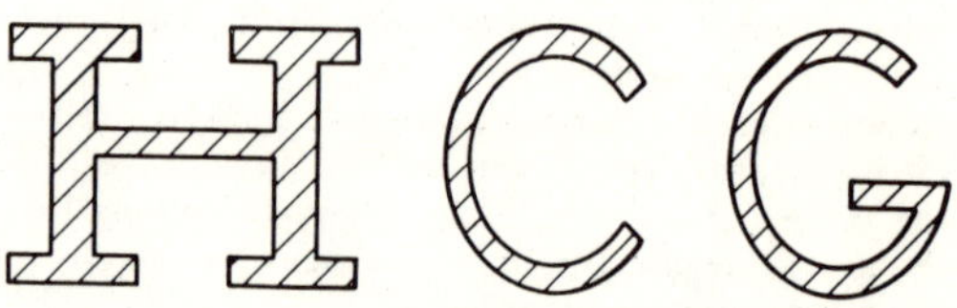
(a) (b) (c)

Fig. 9—Serifs.

Note that this argument holds only for the detection problem. Where pattern recognition is involved, it may well be feasible to devise (for example) a single scheme which can indicate that both forms of the capital "H" are sufficiently different from all other members of the alphabet as to be definitely classed as "H"'s.

V. Pattern Detection

In this section it will be shown how the ideas previously introduced can be utilized for the purposes of pattern detection. A SPAC program for detecting L-shaped figures will be presented and discussed in order to illustrate the principles involved. (The Appendix and an article mentioned previously[1] describe SPAC.)

The L-detection program has been executed successfully on an IBM 704 computer programmed to simulate SPAC. In order to make perfectly clear what the L-

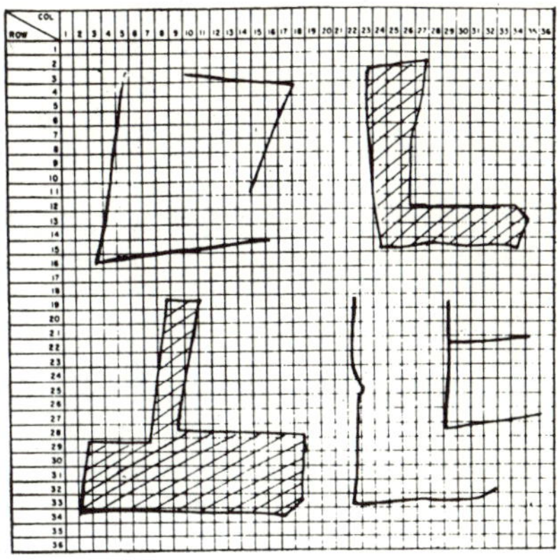

Fig. 10—Original drawing.

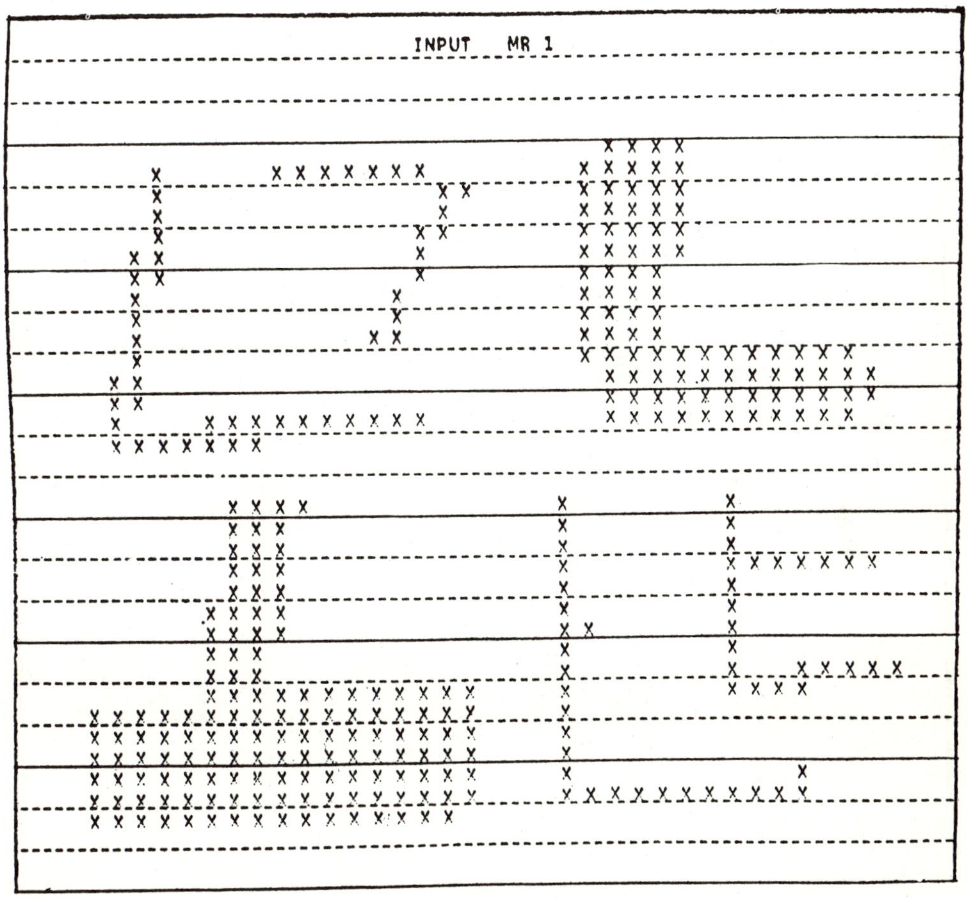

Fig. 11—Input to SPAC L-detection program.

detection program does, the results of one of the experimental 704 runs will be presented now.

The input to the system is a set of figures drawn freehand on a sheet of coordinate paper (Fig. 10). Since a suitable automatic scanning device was not yet available, its action was simulated by a key-punch operator, who was instructed to punch a set of IBM cards to represent the pattern; one column corresponding to each cell of the coordinate paper. A one was punched where the corresponding cell was black and a blank was punched where the corresponding cell was blank. The resulting deck of cards served as the input to the machine. (As can be seen in Fig. 10, a 36×36 array was used.) A print-out of this quantized input is shown in Fig. 11, with x's replacing ones in order to make the form of the figures more conspicuous.

The first step by SPAC was to smooth the input field using a routine carrying out the steps described in the section on smoothing. Details of the smoothing routine will not be presented here.

SPAC then executed the L-detection program, which will be discussed next, and then printed out the result shown in Fig. 12, in which only L-shaped figures (after smoothing) remain.

The program first selects those figures whose edge sequences include LBRTRT, where the first R-edge and the second T-edge can be arbitrarily small, while the other four edges must each be at least four units long. (This permits the detection of "thin" as well as "thick" L's.) From this set, the program eliminates all figures with any edges not in the LBRTRT sequence, leaving figures such as those shown in Fig. 6(b) and Fig. 13(a).

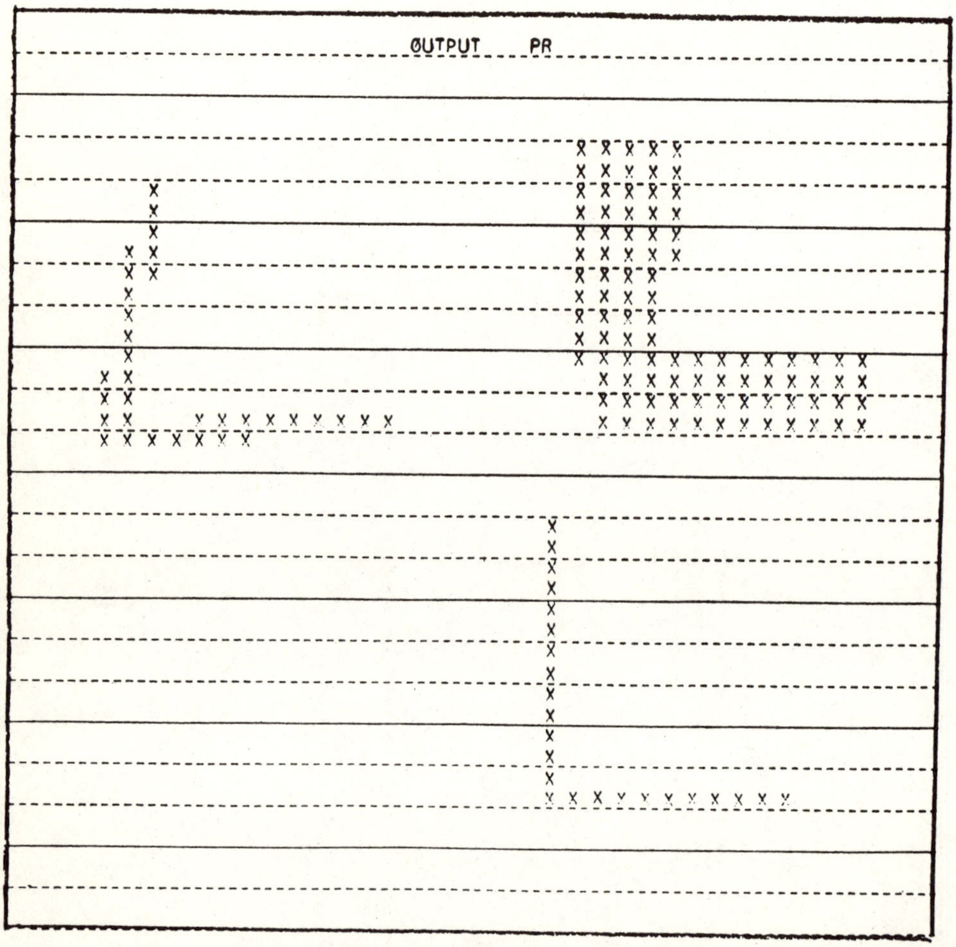

Fig. 12—SPAC output.

The following explanatory notes correspond to the parenthetically numbered points in the program shown in Table I, and the references to lettered edges in these notes pertain to Fig. 13(a).

(1) Left edge points (one-points with zeros to the left) which are in vertical strips of length at least equal to 4 (a-edges).
(2) Adds b-edges (vertical strips of left edge points diagonally below a-edges) to the a-edges found in (1).
(3) Corner points such as the one common to b and c.
(4) MR5 now includes edges a, b, c, and d.
(5) Adds edge e to MR5.
(6) Adds edge f to the edges already in MR5. Note that whereas the left edge of the L, consisting of m, a, and b-edges, must include an a-edge which is at least 4 units long, the portion of the L corresponding to f can be as small as one unit.
(7) Adds g-edge to MR5.
(8) Adds edge h to MR5.
(9) Edge i is added to MR5. The inside corner was "turned" 10 instructions prior to this order by the SHF L and SHF U instructions.
(10)–(13) Edges j, k, and l, are added to MR5.
(14) The PR now contains edge m (which is now also in MR3).
(15) MR2 now contains all edges which are in LBRTR sequences (or subsequences) and *only* such edges.
(16) MR3 now contains the edges found in (15) and the regions enclosed by these edges. In the case of Fig. 13(a), MR3 contains the entire figure. Since only the darkened edges of Fig. 13(b) comprise LBRTRT sequences, MR3 will contain only that part of this figure which is in MR2 (the darkened edges—which enclose no area). MR3 will contain Fig. 13(c) with the hole filled in. Thus, only in the case of true L's such as Fig. 13(a) will MR3 include the whole figure without additions. The remainder of the program consists of eliminating figures which are only partially contained in MR3 [Fig. 13(b)] and figures such as Fig. 13(c) which do not completely cover their counterparts in MR3.
(17) Figures such as 13(c) which have holes.
(18) PR now contains figures such as 12(b) with outer edge sequences including edges other than those in MR2.
(19) Figures found in (17) and (18) are eliminated, leaving only the desired L-shaped figures.

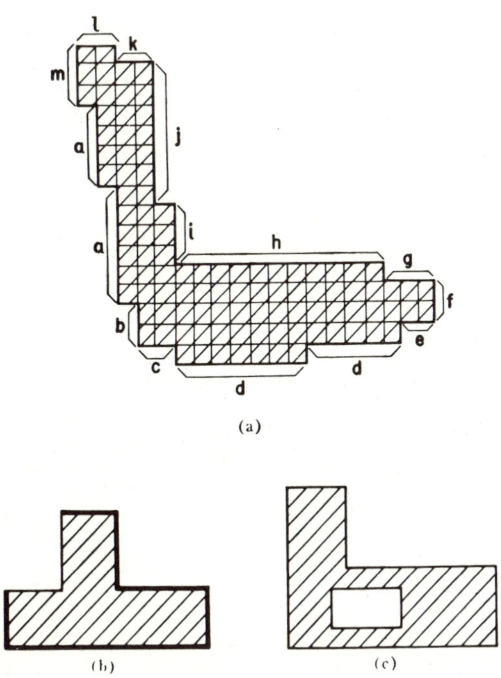

Fig. 13—Illustrating L-detection program.

TABLE I

L-Detection Program

SMOOTH	WRT 3	STR 3
WRT 1	SHF U	WRT 1
SHF R	ADD L, R	SHF D
INV	MPY 4	INV
MPY 1	EXP V, P, N	MPY 1
STR 2	ADD 3	STR 2
LNK	ADM 5 (6)	LNK
MPY U	SHF U	WRT 1
MPY U	ADD L, R	SHF L
MPY U	ADM 3	SHF D
ADD D	WRT 2	INV
ADD D	LNK	MPY 2, 3
ADD D	MPY 3	EXP H
STR 5 (1)	EXP V	STR 3
SHF D	ADM 5	WRT 2
ADD L, R	STR 3	MPY R
MPY 2	WRT 1	MPY R
EXP V	SHF D	MPY R
STR 3	INV	ADD L
ADM 5 (2)	MPY 1	ADD L
WRT 1	STR 2	ADD L
SHF U	LNK	LNK
INV	WRT 1	STR 4
MPY 1	SHF L	WRT 3
STR 2	SHF D	SHF L
LNK	INV	ADD U, D
MPM 3	MPY 2, 3	MPY 4
WRT 1	EXP H	EXP H, P, N
SHF R	ADM 5 (7)	ADD 3
SHF U	SHF L	ADM 5 (12)
INV	ADD U, D	SHF L
MPY 3 (3)	STR 3	ADD U, D
EXP H	WRT 2	ADM 3
ADM 5	MPY L	WRT 2
SHF R	MPY L	LNK
ADD U, D	MPY L	MPY 3
STR 3	ADD R	EXP H
WRT 2	ADD R	ADM 5 (13)
MPY R	ADD R	STR 3
MPY R	LNK	WRT 1
MPY R	MPY 3	SHF R
ADD L	EXP H, P, N	INV
ADD L	ADM 5 (8)	MPY 1
ADD L	SHF L	LNK
LNK	ADD U, D	STR 2
MPY 3	STR 3	WRT 1
EXP HPN	WRT 2	SHF R
ADM 5 (4)	LNK	SHF D
SHF R	MPY 3	INV
ADD U, D	EXP H	MPY 2, 3
STR 3	ADM 5	EXP V
WRT 2	SHF L	STR 3 (14)
LNK	SHF U	ADD 5
MPY 3	STR 3	LNK
EXP H	WRT 1	WRT 3
STR 3	SHF L	EXP H, V, P, N
ADM 5 (5)	INV	STR 2 (15)
WRT 1	MPY 1	INV
SHF L	STR 2	LNK
INV	LNK	MPY 2
MPY 1	MPY 3	ADR
STR 2	EXP V	EXP H, V
LNK	ADM 5 (9)	INV
WRT 1	SHF U	STR 3 (16)
SHF L	ADD L, R	LNK
SHF U	STR 3	WRT 1
INV	WRT 4	INV
MPY 2, 3	LNK	MPY 3
EXP V	MPY 3	EXP H, V, P, N
STR 3	EXP V, P, N	STR 4 (17)
WRT 2	ADM 5 (10)	WRT 1
MPY D	SHF U	LNK
MPY D	ADD L, R	WRT 3
MPY D	STR 3	INV
ADD U	WRT 2	MPY 1 (18)
ADD U	LNK	ADD 4
ADD U	MPY 3	EXP H, V, P, N
LNK	EXP V	INV
STR 4	ADM 5 (11)	MPY 1 (19)

Note that there are no loops in the program, so that each of the 237 SPAC instructions is executed exactly once.

Programs for detecting figures with holes are somewhat more complex. Both inner and outer edge sequences are traced, and, in place of the contents of MR3 described in (16) it is necessary to find the area enclosed between the outer and inner borders. This area is then used in the same manner as the MR3 contents were used in the L-program. However, it is then necessary to eliminate figures with the wrong *number* of holes, or with improperly located holes. This can be done in a variety of ways. One method is to eliminate points between one outer edge of the figure and the hole(s) and then check the edge sequence of the resulting figure, which no longer has any holes.

Figs. 14, 15 and 16 show the results of a test of an A-

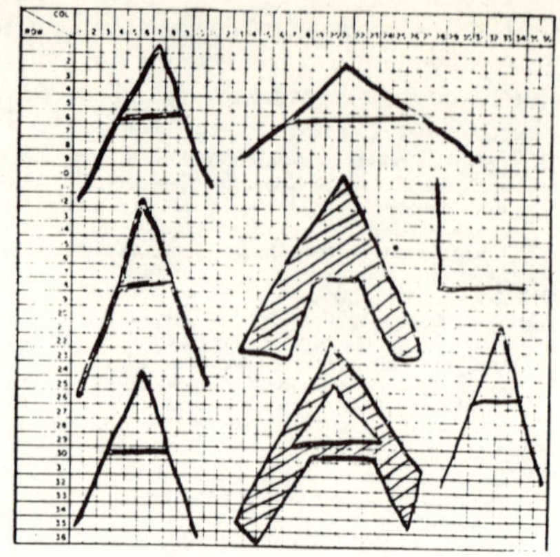

Fig. 14—Original drawing.

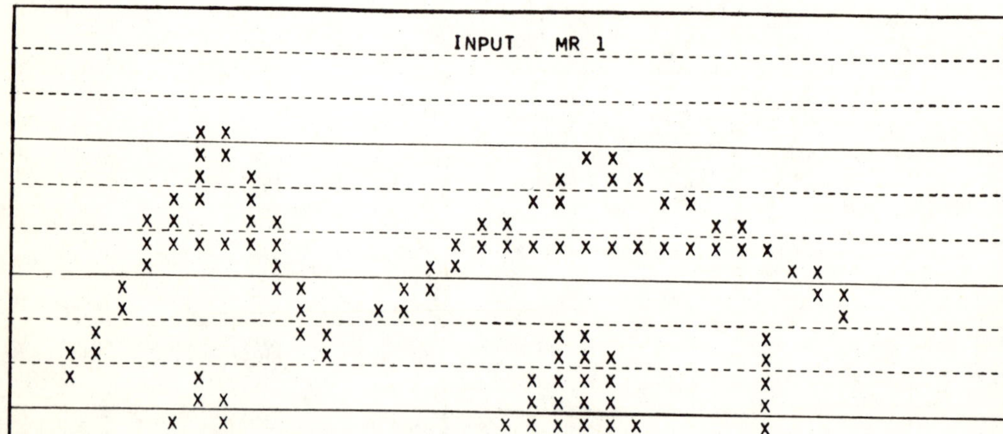

Fig. 15—Input to SPAC L-detection program.

detection program consisting of about 500 orders (including smoothing).

VI. Pattern Recognition

The pattern recognition problem defined earlier in this paper consists of identifying an input figure, given that it belongs to some member of a finite set of categories. For example, the set of categories (henceforth to be referred to as the *alphabet*) might consist of the digits from zero through nine inclusive.

For any alphabet there must exist at least one finite set of characteristics that can be used to distinguish amongst the members. That is, there must exist a set of yes or no questions, such that if these questions are answered with respect to any given figure, then there will be only one member of the alphabet to which this figure can belong. The questions might, for example, concern the presence or absence of such features as holes, straight left edges, or concavities open to the right.

It is not necessary to ask all of the questions in every case. A sequential process can be carried out in which the answer to the first question determines a subset of the alphabet to which the input figure may belong. Depending upon the subset, a second question is asked, the answer to which further narrows the field of possible categories. This process is repeated until a single candidate remains. If the questions can be so chosen that each one halves the number of remaining candidates, then the number of questions necessary to identify any given figure is about $\log_2 n$, where n is the number of members of the alphabet. This is the minimum average

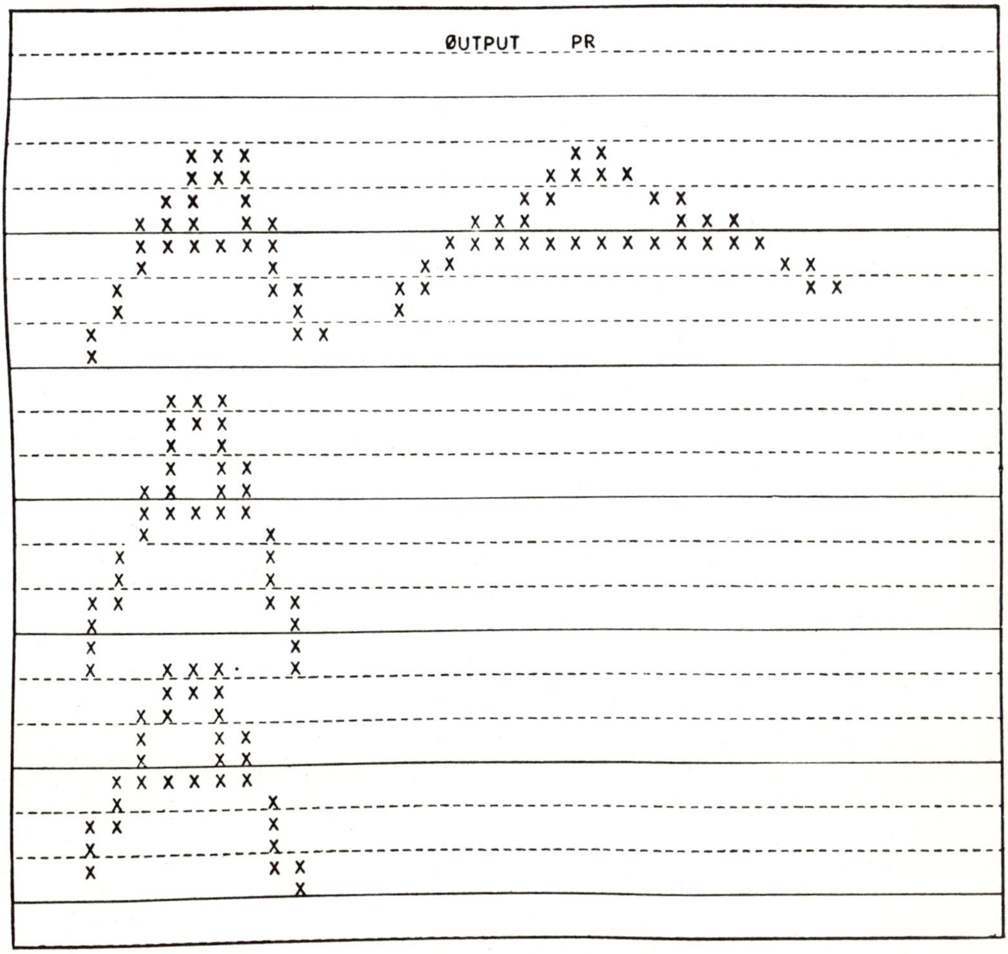

Fig. 16—SPAC output.

number of questions, assuming that the input figure is equally likely to belong to any of the n categories.

A good set of questions should have the following characteristics (insofar as they are mutually compatible):

1) They should be sufficient to distinguish any pair of allowable input patterns that belong to different members of the alphabet.
2) The necessary number of tests that must be performed for each identification should be minimal.
3) The number of orders necessary to perform each test should be minimal.
4) The total number of tests should be minimal.

An ideal property is thus easy to test for, possessed by half of the members of the alphabet (each test must produce a *different* dichotomy), and invariant with respect to all distortions that leave a pattern in the same category within the alphabet. Needless to say, it is not generally possible to attain such an ideal.

A pattern recognition scheme for alphanumeric characters will now be described. It is intended to recognize hand drawn sans-serif capital letters and numerals with very broad limits on the permissible over-all sizes and thicknesses of the input figures. A preliminary smoothing routine as described in Section III serves to cancel out the effects of noise, provided that the noise is not concentrated in any one locale.

The 34 properties described in Table II are used to distinguish among the 34 members of the alphabet (ones do not differ from I's, and zeroes do not differ from O's). Fig. 17 is a flow chart indicating how the tests are used. Starting with property 2 at the top, movement is downward. At each branch point the left branch is taken if the answer to the question referred to by the number is no. The right branch is taken for a yes answer. The following two definitions pertain to Table II:

1) A figure is *vertically concave* if there exist points not on the figure whose vertical projections *both* upward and downward touch the figure. Such points constitute *vertical cavities*. Similar definitions apply to horizontally concave figures, and to +45° and −45° concave figures. Parts (a), (b), (c), and (d) of Fig. 18 illustrate vertical, horizontal, −45° and +45° concave figures respectively, the dotted regions indicating the respective cavities. (This definition will be further qualified later on in the text.)
2) A cavity is *open to the right* if a directed path can be found starting at a point in the cavity, passing through points not on the figure, with no component in a leftward direction, and terminating at a point on the margin of the matrix. Cavities open to the left, or in other specified directions, are similarly defined.

TABLE II

FEATURES USED IN CHARACTER RECOGNITION PROGRAM

1) Horizontal cavity open above, (begj).
2) Vertical cavity open to the right, (aghk).
3) Vertical cavity open to the left, (efghl).
4) Horizontal cavity open below, (fhk).
5) Horizontal cavity, (befghijkl).
6) A hole, (eil).
7) Two vertical cavities lying on a common vertical line with the region between them consisting of points on the figure. For at least part of each cavity, no points on the figure are directly to the left of the cavity. (This latter requirement is a somewhat stricter version of "open to the left"), (e).
8) +45° concave, (defghijkl).
9) A region such that a vertical line segment can be drawn starting on the figure, passing down through a vertical cavity, passing through points on the figure again, then (still moving down) entering another vertical cavity, and finally terminating on the figure, (efghl).
10) Not used.
11) Same as 9), but with a horizontal instead of vertical orientation, (ijk).
12) Vertical cavity, (aefghikl).
13) −45° cavity, (cefghijkl).
14) −45° cavity open in a "left-bottomward" direction, (efghkl).
15) Horizontal cavity not part of a hole, (befghjk).
16) +45° cavity not part of a hole, (defghjkl).
17) Holes whose inverse (complement) is horizontally concave, (i).
18) −45 cavity not part of a hole, (cefghjkl).
19) A vertical left edge with right-angled corners above and below, (acdefjk).
20) Two holes, (i).
21) A horizontal top edge with inside corners on both ends, (ej).
22) Same as 7) except that the cavities are horizontal and they face upward, (j).
23) Same as 7) except that the cavities are horizontal and they face downward, (k).
24) A vertical cavity, the lower end of which is above a bottom edge connected to an upper-left inside corner, (the intersections of a bottom edge and a right edge), (ek).
25) A cavity which is both vertical and horizontal, (efghil).
26) Hole whose inverse is vertically concave, (e).
27) Same as 9) except that the lower vertical cavity is inside a hole, (el).
28) Leftmost point of a vertical cavity open to right higher than the rightmost point of a vertical cavity open to the left, (g).
29) Right vertical edge, (bcdefijk).
30) Not used.
31) Height of the left leg of a U-shaped figure less than half the height of the right leg. (Used only to distinguish a "J" from a "U".)
32) Vertical cavity open to the left. This differs from 3 in that it includes cases where the boundaries of the cavity have nearly vertical slopes. (A fuller explanation of this distinction will be presented in the text.)
33) A right vertical edge with no horizontal cavity on the same level with it. (A Y has this property—but not a V.)
34) Leftmost point of a vertical cavity open to the right lies in the upper two thirds of the figure.
35) Vertical cavity open to right. (See 32.)
36) Horizontal cavity above a vertical cavity separated by part of the figure (efh).

Some of the descriptions in the table are of a qualitative nature, since more detailed statements would be beyond the scope of this paper. Following the description of each feature in the table is a parenthetic note referring to just those parts of Fig. 18 which have that feature. It is hoped that these illustrations will serve to clarify some of the more complex descriptions.

Before discussing some of the interesting features of this problem and our solution let us see how the system would operate in a particular case. Suppose, for example, that the figure to be identified happens to be an

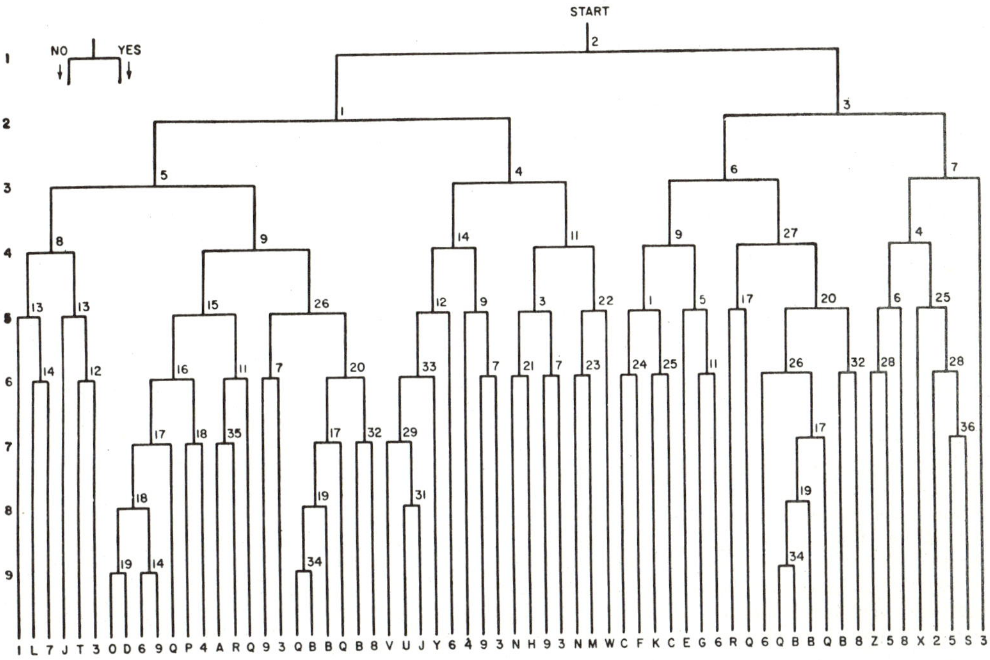

Fig. 17—Flow chart for recognition program.

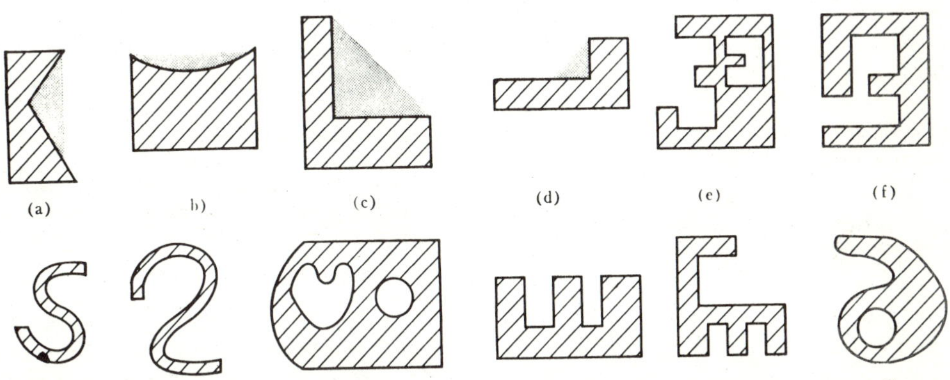

(a) (b) (c) (d) (e) (f)

(g) (h) (i) (j) (k) (l)

Fig. 18—Illustrations for recognition program features.

"E." Referring to Fig. 18 we see that the first question (2) tests whether there is a concavity open to the right. Since the answer is yes, the right branch is taken, and the next question is 3, "Is there a concavity open to the left?" The answer being no, the left branch is taken and the next question is 6. Questions 9 and 5 follow in succession and a negative answer to the latter leads to the conclusion that the input is an "E."

In order to allow for variations in the forms of certain characters, these characters (such as "3" and "Q") appear at several different terminal points of the flow chart. A "9" for instance may be successfully recognized as drawn in either (a) or (b) of Fig. 19. Thus there are 63 termination points for the 34 characters.

Tests for each characteristic listed in Table II can be carried out by means of subroutines for SPAC. An average of about forty-five orders are required for each test. Thus, roughly three to five hundred orders are re-

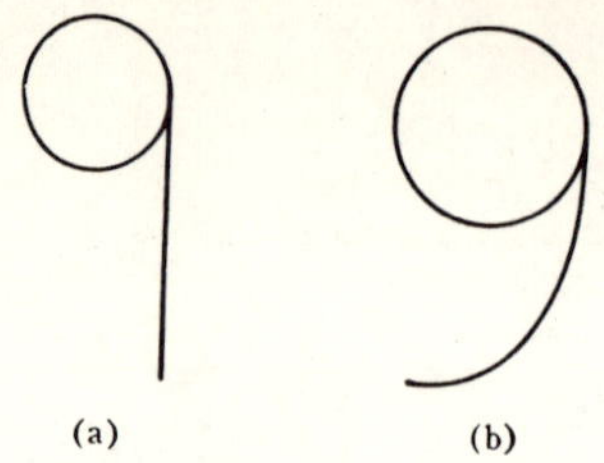

Fig. 19—Illustrating allowable style variations.

quired for each input figure (including one hundred orders to carry out the smoothing process described in Section III). There are about 1600 orders in the entire program, which has been successfully tested by means of the simulated SPAC. A lack of space precludes the presentation of the entire program in this paper, but a representative subroutine will be included.

The subroutine for each test consists of a series of operations carried out on the given figure so that at the end of the routine the field is cleared unless the figure has the property being tested for. Table III consists of a portion of a calling sequence that realizes the first few levels of the flow chart of Fig. 17. The order SBR XXX calls in the subroutine XXX. (For example, to test for property 2 we use the order SBR RO2.) After this subroutine has been executed the next order in the sequence is carried out. The order JMP PRY causes the computer to print a statment to the effect that the input character is a Y.

TABLE III

SBR RO2	TRZ 3
TRZ 1	JMP PR3
SBR RO3	TRA 60 (where a stop order is located)
TRZ 2	1 SBR RO1
SBR RO7	TRZ 4 etc.

An example of a SPAC program for carrying out a typical test is shown in Table IV.

TABLE IV

SPAC Subroutine for Test 9 (Table II)

WRT 1	MPY 9	ADD U
ADD L, R	EXP V (3)	STR 7
INV	ADD U	WRT 9
STR 9 (1)	SHF D	LNK
LNK	MPY 1 (4)	MPY 7
WRT 1	STR 7	EXP V
INV¯	WRT 1	ADD U
STR 8	LNK	SHF D
WRT 1	WRT 7	MPY 1 (6)
SHF D	EXP V	STP
MPY 8 (2)	SHF D	
ADD U	MPY 8 (5)	

The following explanatory notes refer to the numbered instructions in the program.

(1) Zeros, with zeros to the left and right of them.
(2) Points just below bottom edges.
(3) Zeros with upward projections touching ones.
(4) Zeros just below parts of the figure which are below vertical cavities.
(5) Zeros just below parts of the figure which are below vertical cavities.
(6) Ones below two vertical cavities, as required in Table II.

Note that the use of the points obtained in (1) as the possible vertical cavity points prevents a slightly crooked vertical line from being considered as vertically concave.

It will not be possible to discuss in detail all of the problems that lead to the use of the various tests employed in the system described here, but a few samples may serve to give the general flavor.

Consider first the test for a vertical cavity open to the right (test 2). A strict interpretation of this test would mean that a positive result would be obtained in cases typified by a "T" whose vertical member is slanted as shown in Fig. 20. In order to prevent this,

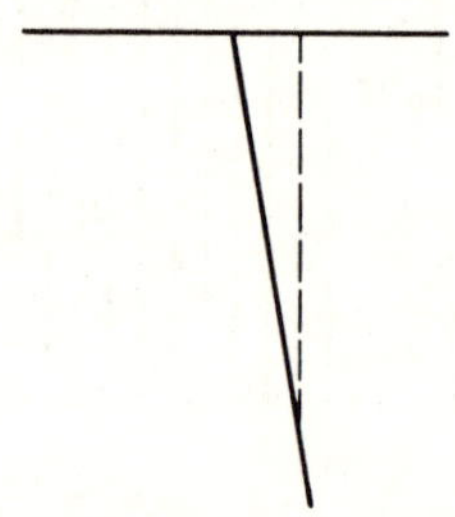

Fig. 20—Illustrating test 2.

the program for test 2 is written so that necessary conditions for a point to be considered as being in a vertical cavity are:

1) It must not be horizontally adjacent to a one-cell;
2) All zero-points in the cavity that are in the same column as the given point must meet condition 1, except possibly those at the top and bottom of the cavity.

These requirements insure that parts of the upper and lower borders of a vertical cavity must both be nearly horizontal. Hence Fig. 18(a) does *not* possess feature 2 as indicated in Table II. In certain cases it may be desirable to detect the presence of vertical cavities whose boundaries do not meet condition 2. Such a cavity is shown in Fig. 21. Test 35 accomplishes this function, in that it does not require the upper and lower cavity boundaries to be nearly horizontal. This characteristic is useful in distinguishing R's from A's.

In order to distinguish Y's from V's, it was found necessary to look for a right vertical edge below the V-shaped notch at the top of the figure. This is property 33 in Table II. A right vertical edge in this case is defined as an edge containing either one vertical strip of

Fig. 21—Illustrating need for test 35.

length at least equal to six or two vertical strips each of length at least equal to three.

The recognition program is preceded by the smoothing routine described earlier in this paper, which eliminates small irregularities. In addition, the various subroutines for detecting features are generally insensitive to fine details, so that the over-all system will operate fairly well in the presence of scattered noise. Fig. 22 is a photograph of a 704 print-out which consists of an input figure and the output statement produced by the recognition program. Such tests have been carried out on about 90 figures. The clumsiness of the procedure for generating input data has precluded more exhaustive experimentation, but the success of the program has been clearly established.

VII. Conclusion

Methods applicable to two classes of problems, pattern recognition and pattern detection, have been developed. Solutions to several specific problems in these areas have been described, namely the recognition of alphanumeric characters, and the detection of L-shaped patterns. The methods and solutions presented here have all been successfully tested by means of a 704 simulation program, and some of the results of these tests have been included.

The matrix size of 36×36 used in these experiments was chosen for its convenience in simulating on the 704, and because it is a reasonably satisfactory size for the complexity of the patterns used in the tests. For applications in which fine details of more complex figures must be studied, a larger matrix will be necessary. A smaller matrix might suffice for simpler applications, although for small matrices the permissible variation in the size of the input image is quite limited, and an important advantage of the techniques described here is lost. On the other hand, as was mentioned in Section II, a matrix that is not too fine will smooth out some of the random irregularities in the input. Of course the principal reason for limiting the matrix size is economic.

Since SPAC does not yet exist as hardware, it is not possible to give actual execution times for the programs included here. However, in view of the simplicity of the logic required for each SPAC order,[1] and the speed of components now in the development stage, it is not unreasonable to assume that, within five years, a speed of one microsecond per order will be attainable. Under this assumption, the character recognition program given here could operate at a rate of about 2500 characters per second (ignoring input time). The time required by the 704 simulation program to execute each SPAC order varies widely as a function of both the data and the instruction. A rough estimate of the time for a "typical" program is 10 msec per order.

In addition to being a fascinating field of study, automatic pattern processing has numerous conceivable applications. Primary interest today is in devices for character recognition, and it is easy to list applications such as transmitting hand written programs and input data to computers without the need for key punch operators, automatic sorting of mail, machine reading of telephone toll tickets written by operators, and machine reading of texts to be automatically translated into other languages.

Pattern detection methods might be useful in biological studies where searches must be made for particular cell structures, bacteria, or viruses among large numbers of microphotographs.[9] Organic chemistry is another field in which important data exist in pictorial form, namely molecular diagrams. Searches for particular kinds of molecular structures among large numbers of records (perhaps in a patent office) may well be facilitated by machines.[10] No doubt other applications will be found as the techniques improve.

VIII. Appendix

The Order Structure of the Spatial Computer (SPAC)

The order structure of SPAC is summarized in Table V, and a brief amplification of some of the descriptions follows. A more complete treatment will be found in a paper mentioned earlier.[1] (Note that some of the abbreviations in this paper will differ slightly from those used in the original description of SPAC.[1])

Suppose, for example, that the order ADD 1, 4 is given. Then, within every module, simultaneously, the contents of MR1 and MR4 will be added to the PR contents (Boolean additions). Note that each module operates on the data in its own memory cells, independently of what is going on in the other modules. The order ADD L, 2 results in the contents of the PR of each module being incremented (again Boolean addition) by the contents of MR2 and the *original* contents of the PR of the neighboring module to the left. Note that ADD L, 2 is not equivalent to ADD 2 followed by ADD L. Other references to neighboring modules used

[9] H. P. Mansberg, "Automatic particle and bacterial colony counter," *Science*, pp. 823–827; October 25, 1957.

[10] L. C. Ray, R. A. Kirsch, "Finding chemical records by digital computers," *Science*, pp. 814–819; October 25, 1957.

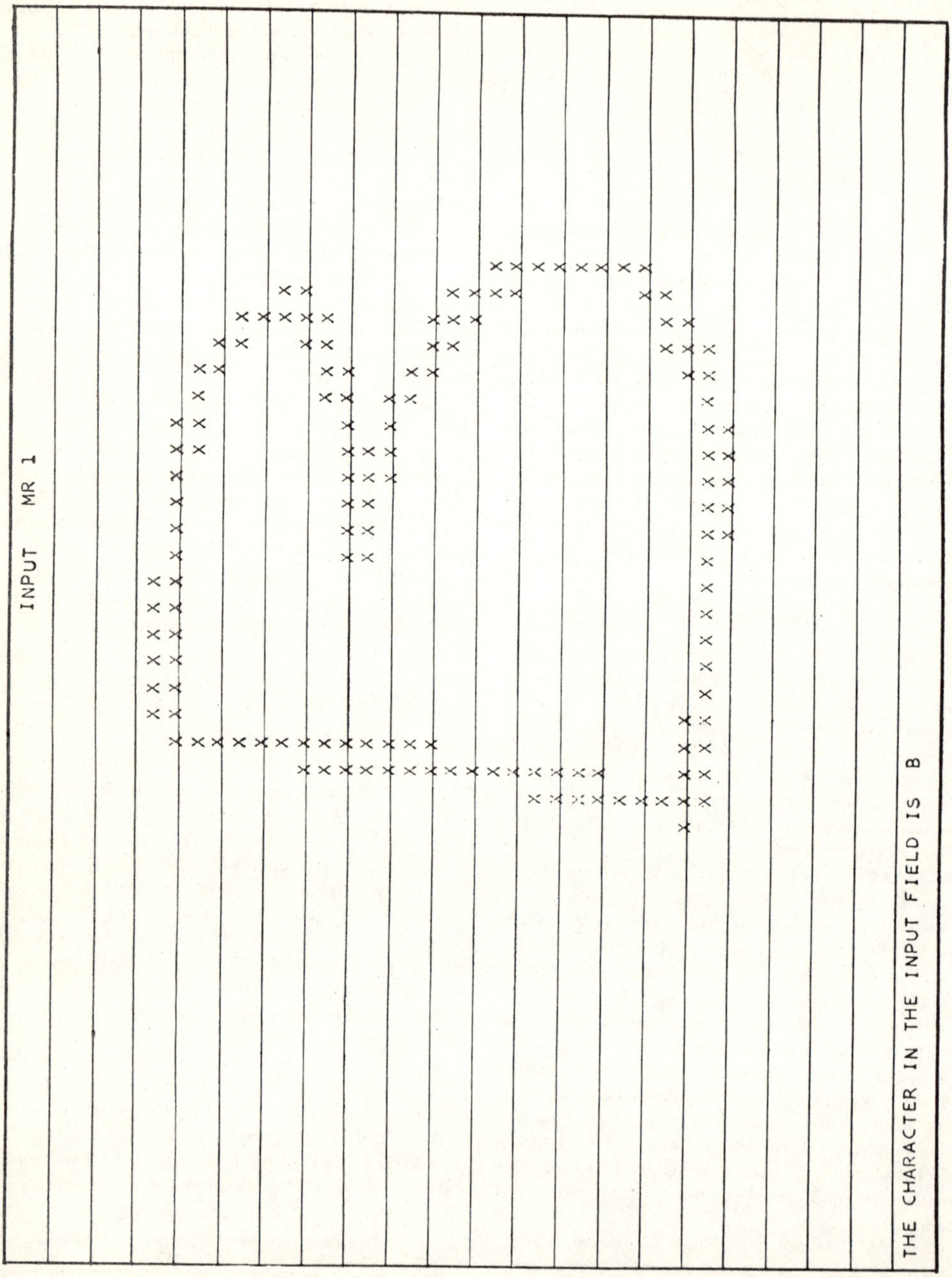

Fig. 22—Example of character recognition.

TABLE V
SPAC ORDER STRUCTURE

Order	Symbol	Interpretation
Write	WRT	Write the contents of the indicated MR into the PR without altering the MR contents.
Store	STR	Store the contents of the PR in each of the specified memory cells without altering the PR contents.
Invert	INV	Change the contents of every PR.
Add in memory	ADM	Add logically to the contents of each specified MR, the contents of the PR, without changing the latter.
Multiply in memory	MPM	Multiply logically the contents of each specified MR by the contents of the PR, leaving the PR contents undisturbed.
Add	ADD	Add logically to the contents of each PR, the contents of the specified MR's and neighboring PR's.
Multiply	MPY	Multiply logically the contents of the PR, the specified MR's and neighboring PR's, placing the result in the PR.
Add Reference	ADR	Add a one to the PR of the module in the lower left corner of the matrix.
Shift	SHF	Write the contents of each PR in the contents of the PR of the module in the specified direction (L, R, U, or D).
Transfer	TRA	Execute the instruction at the indicated address and then continue from there in sequence.
Transfer if zero	TRZ	If every PR contains a zero, then TRA to the indicated address. Otherwise continue with next order.
Link	LNK	Activate link elements between those adjacent pairs of modules in which both PR's contain ones. De-activate all other link elements.
Expand	EXP	Add ones to all PR's connected to PR's with ones through a chain of activated link elements of the orientation(s) specified in this order (H, V, P, N—or any combinations).
Stop	STP	End of program or subroutine.

with the ADD, MPY and SHF orders are R, U, and D referring to right, above (up) and below (down) respectively. Incidentally, it is assumed that a border of modules whose PR contents are permanently zero surrounds the entire matrix.

The link and expand orders require some further clarification. Although they are not shown in Fig. 1, there are one-bit memory elements between every adjacent pair of modules, including diagonal neighbors (so that each module shares eight such elements with its neighbors). These link cells become activated (or de-activated) only when a link order is given, in accordance with the description of that order in Table V. Note that there are four kinds of link cells, depending upon the orientation of the line connecting the two modules that they connect. These are horizontal (H), vertical (V), diagonal with positive slope (P), and diagonal with negative slope (N). An expand order can refer to any combination of these four orientations. When an expand order is given, the activated link cells of the specified orientation(s) establish two-way channels between the modules they connect. A propagation of ones takes place starting from those PR's which contained ones when the EXP order was given, and spreading to all other PR's connected to them via the network of channels.

Although not specifically discussed here, there are means for loading patterns into the module array prior to the executions of a program, and also means for unloading the output. There are also instructions making possible a printed output (required for the recognition program). At this time SPAC exists only in simulated form.

ACKNOWLEDGMENT

The author would like to thank Miss D. M. Habbart of the Bell Telephone Laboratories who wrote the SPAC simulation program which made possible the testing of the ideas described in this paper.

Reprinted from *IEEE Trans. Electron. Comput.*, **EC–12,** No. 5, 1963, pp. 791–813

The Illinois Pattern Recognition Computer—ILLIAC III*

25

BRUCE H. McCORMICK†

Summary—This report describes the system design of an all-digital computer for visual recognition. One processor, the Pattern Articulation Unit (PAU), has been singled out for detailed discussion. Other units, in particular the Arithmetic Unit and the Taxicrinic Unit, are treated in reports listed in the bibliography.

The PAU has been shown to be a processor of fundamentally new design—its logical organization has no analog in the central processing unit of existing computers. The PAU is the first modular parallel processor which because of its digital organization is capable of more reliable visual identification than part analog/part digital preprocessors of much less generality and potential virtuosity; is faster than any presently suggested alternative realizable today at comparable cost; and can serve as a prototype to a new generation of parallel computers that will capitalize upon thin film and integrated semiconductor circuitry of the immediate future.

Fig. 1—Main frame of the computer (as of June, 1963).

I. Introduction

THE ILLINOIS Pattern Recognition Computer (ILLIAC III), an all-digital processor for visual information, is under construction at the Digital Computer Laboratory, University of Illinois. This visual recognition digital computer (Fig. 1) is designed for automatic scanning and analysis of massive amounts of relatively homogeneous visual data. In particular, the design is an outgrowth of studies at this Laboratory of a computer system capable of scanning, measuring, and analyzing in excess of 10^7 bubble-chamber negatives[1] per year [8]–[13].

The computer, when complete, will comprise:

1) *High-speed oscilloscopic scanners* for the rapid ingestion into the visual recognition computer of photographic information digitized on a black-white raster. These devices also have a measuring mode capable of obtaining accurate coordinate digitization of points lying on tracks or other entities appearing in the picture.

2) *A Pattern Articulation Unit* (PAU), whose duty is to perform local preprocessing on the digitized raster, such as track thinning, gap filling, line element recognition, etc. The logical design of the all-digital processor has been optimized for the idealization of the input image to a line drawing. Nodes representing end points, bends, points of intersection are labeled in parallel by appropriate programming. The abstract graph describing the interconnection of labeled nodes is then extracted as a list structure, which comprises the normal output of the processing unit.

3) *A Taxicrinic Unit* (TU) [19], which assembles such graphs into coherent list structures subject to a manipulative grammar, and categorizes these graphs to complete the visual recognition function.

4) *An Arithmetic Unit* [20] for executing the mathematical analysis (stereoreconstruction, statistical summary, etc.) involved in processing photographic data.

5) *An Output Complex* consisting of printers, visual displays, etc., for presenting and storing the output of the system.

Every attention is being given to design and construct the system so that partial but increasing production capability is achieved at each earlier stage in the complete development, with simulation of uncompleted units provided by the attached ILLIAC II computer of the Digital Computer Laboratory.

Principally, this paper will discuss the use, design and fabrication of the PAU, since this processor of the computer is of fundamentally new design and therefore least familiar. The PAU employs a two-dimensional iterative array of 1024 (32×32) identical processing modules locally connected to execute Boolean functions, threshold logic and signal path building. It is augmented by an unconventional core memory, called a transfer memory, which, in conjunction with the iterative array, can operate as an associative memory.

* Received October 28, 1963. The work reported here was supported in part by the U. S. Atomic Energy Commission under Contract No. AT(11-1)-1018.

† Digital Computer Laboratory, University of Illinois, Urbana, Ill.

[1] Typically a stereoexposure of a bubble chamber comprises three negatives.

II. Mode of Visual Analysis

A. Scanning and Measuring

Visual material must be digitized before input to the pattern recognition computer proper. The input mechanism which performs this task will be referred to as the *scanning unit.* Input visual information is typically in *frames:* one frame per view of a bubble-chamber stereotriad, field-of-view of a neurohistological section, or microfilm frame of printed text (Fig. 2, page 794) [1].

All scanning units currently under construction at this Laboratory examine the film (or biological section, etc.) by a TV-like scan; that is, the input image has imposed upon it a two-dimensional rectangular (or rhombic) raster. Digital representation of the input material is normally one of two dominant forms: *bit,* or *coordinate.*

For example, one view of a bubble-chamber stereotriad can be digitally encoded *in bit form* by projecting a raster (1024×4096 cells) upon the frame. Each cell is examined to see if the negative locally is above some minimum opacity. If so, a "1" is recorded; alternatively, a "0" is recorded, indicating that the negative is locally transparent (*i.e.,* background only). Typically, for the bubble-chamber case, encoded tracks range from one to three cell lengths in width.

Alternatively the view can be digitally encoded *in coordinate form* by scanning the frame, again for the bubble-chamber case, with 4096 parallel sweeps (parallel to the X axis) and for each sweep recording the X coordinate for each leading (and trailing) edge of every black mass seen. In bubble-chamber case the total number of bits required is approximately equal for the two digital representations.

In the digitizing process it is convenient to distinguish between scanning and measuring. For some areas, *e.g.,* alphanumeric recognition, measuring normally plays no role. In general, measuring plays an ancillary role to scanning.

The first image filtering, or recognition processes, would appear nominally independent of mild image distortion. In fact a human scanner can find, without difficulty, events of interest in playback photographs of bit-encoded film even though the oscilloscopic scan/playback system has introduced distortions of 5 to 10 per cent (*cf.* Fig. 2).

In contrast, for measurement, resolution of one part in ten of a track width (4 μ on the film) is employed and comparable linearity held over the entire face of the film. This added coordinate resolution is typically required only for 10 per cent of the tracks in a frame. These slower-speed high-resolution procedures can be called into play where needed, without significant deterioration of the over-all processing rate. Accordingly, a traditional separation of visual data processing into a *scanning* and a precision *measuring* phase has grown up.

It is entirely consistent to use one instrument for both scan and measurement purposes. The second-generation oscilloscopic systems [14] under development at this Laboratory give promise of handling both functions: a very fast (open-loop) scanning mode applied universally; a slower (closed-loop, *i.e.,* spot referenced to an optical grating) measuring mode of those film areas singled out as a result of processed scan information.

Neither the scanning unit, nor the measuring unit, performs a pattern recognition function. Input bit patterns are arbitrary, as far as these units are concerned, and reflect the general purpose nature of the over-all recognition system. The interpretation of the input bit information (*i.e.,* visual recognition) is a function of the subsequent processor—the visual recognition computer proper.

B. Pattern Articulation

A scanning program set-up, for example, to process bubble-chamber negatives examines one view at a time [8]. Each negative is partitioned into a network of *windows,* a window representing a square raster of size 32×32 bits. For the particular case of exposures made of the 72-inch hydrogen bubble chamber made at 15:1 demagnification, it is our experience [9] that a partition of the picture into roughly 15 windows across and 60 windows in length provides marginally adequate resolution: approximations 10^3 windows per view. These windows are then processed sequentially, in a TV-like scan, starting with the bottom-left corner window and ending with the top-right window.

In this procedure all in-window processing is executed by the PAU; cross-window compilation of accumulated information, however, is delegated to the TU.

Within each window we require an iterative procedure to update any track segments previously named which enter the window, and to identify vertices and name new tracks which originate within that window. This boundary value information, and only this information, is then transmitted to the Taxicrinic Unit. Accordingly the input-output "black box" functional description of the PAU is specified by the input (a window) and this boundary value output (Fig. 3).

The image within each window must be idealized by edging, line thinning, gap filling and line smoothing algorithms. These transformations, dependent only upon local behavior of the image, can be performed in parallel on the image. When correctly selected, they idealize the original image to a line drawing (Fig. 4).

This line drawing can be converted to a linear graph by appropriate *labeling* (in parallel) of vertices, bends, crossovers, and terminals of the idealized image (Fig. 5). We have chosen to call the processor that performs these two functions (idealizing and labeling) the *Pattern Articulation Unit* (PAU), in line with the root meaning of the verb *articulate:* to utter distinctly, properly; to divide into joints. This labeled line drawing, or graph, is still embedded in the processing array, and procedures will now be introduced for its extraction and description.

A natural description of the graph is to list in turn

each edge, or branch. Each branch (connected line segment) is described by a pair of terminal points, or *nodes*, augmented on occasion by a tag: a few bits of qualitative information (crude orientation, thickness, etc.). Description of a line drawing by its labeled nodes implies a considerable data condensation. For example a 32×32 raster containing three nonintersecting tracks requires 1024 bits to describe as a retinal matrix, 60 bits to list as three branches (*i.e.*, pairs of 10-bit coordinates).

This loss of information, however, reflects in subsequent ambiguity about the curve spanning given end points. A straight-line segment between two nodes of the branch can be taken as a *model* of the actual arc, which can be considered in Fig. 6(a) and (b) to be in satisfactory agreement, but very inadequate in Fig. 6(c) and (d). In general, continuity established between two nodes is, of itself, insufficient information. It is for this reason that labeling procedures that mark nodes (in parallel in the PAU), not only at end points, but also at junction points and positions of high curvature, have been introduced. Introduction of open-circle nodes in Fig. 6(c) and (d) allow one again to fall back upon the linear graph approximation.

To mechanize a description procedure for these linear graphs it is necessary to provide a means to read out the coordinates (X, Y) of all nodes in the labeled image, and to give a pairing algorithm for listing together nodes sharing a common branch. Coordinate readout will be treated later, the pairing algorithm will be treated here.

A pairing algorithm reduces by definition to a *tracking procedure* to walk from one given node to one (or more) other terminal nodes linked to it by a continuous path of black points. This tracking procedure is inherently iterative and serial, and would appear ill-adapted to parallel processing. However, the following strategy is employed in the PAU: we build a *path* (in parallel) between terminal nodes. Each site position of the 1024-bit window raster is provided with a *selector switch*, preset in parallel by judicious programming, to link each cell to, for example, each black cell of its eight immediate neighbors. If now a logical "1" signal is impressed at one terminal, the entire path rapidly assumes this signal level (flash-through), thus identifying points common to this chain. In particular, all nodes connected to the initiating node are selected out. Tests of circuit design indicate that the delay per site of the propagated tracking signal can be held to approximately 60 nsec per site, or typical times to identify an associated node of approximately 2 μsec.

C. Bilateral List Processing

At the conclusion of the pattern articulation process the original image had been reduced, window by window, to an idealized line drawing. This line drawing, in turn, was labeled and further abstracted to a graph, *i.e.*, a set of nodes and branches (pairs of nodes sharing a simple line element). Nodal coordinates were then serially extracted, generating a list structure.

That portion of the list structure extracted from any one window, however, may reflect idiosyncracies of local order within that one segment of the total frame and only poorly reflect long-range (global) order of the picture. That is, the processor for pattern articulation can in no satisfactory way anticipate global order, and correctly so, for the data rate lies predominantly at the local recognition level. It is then necessary to take the elements found in successive windows and rearrange these sublists into descriptive categories of common speech: the tracks, electron spirals, etc., of bubble-chamber exposures or the alphanumeric characters of printed text.

In the Pattern Recognition Computer these tasks are delegated to a processor we shall refer to as the *Taxicrinic Unit* (TU)[2] to emphasize its principal activity: the manipulation, search, and systemization of abstract graphs (bilateral list structures). These processes can, of course, be carried on within a contemporary arithmetic computer, and programming techniques such as list processing have been introduced to expedite the writing of code here. It is increasingly recognized, however, that the contemporary arithmetic computer is poorly matched to analysis situations making virtually no use of arithmetic, in which the most commonly employed order is the transfer instruction. Processors specifically adapted to graph manipulation and interpretation can be expected within the next few years to take their place in importance and utility side by side with the arithmetic unit.

D. Syntactic Model of Visual Description

In summary a model, called the Syntactic Model, for the description of visual data has been implicitly proposed here [5]–[7]. In brief, this descriptive scheme is based upon assigning a hierarchical system of labels to the points which make up the picture. At each level the labeled outputs from lower levels serve as input to the current level of labeling. At the lowest level (executed by the scanning unit) each point is assigned one of the labels, black or white. In the next level (executed by the PAU) all, for example, black points are locally connected together in road-like elements and assigned an orientation: north-south, east-west, right-diagonal, left-diagonal.

Using the road segments so formed, higher order "phrases" are formed the sublists generated from each window. But at this level of synthesis it is increasingly obvious that the rules of grammar (syntax) for optimally joining elements together in the list structure are highly *class* dependent: the description of bubble-chamber negatives and the description of handwriting, though both composed of road-like elements, clearly part at this level if not earlier.

[2] From the Greek, ταξισ, rank, arrangement (originally, pattern) and κρινω, to judge.

It would not serve our purpose here to further elaborate the Syntactic Model of visual recognition. This model, however, was originally developed to answer a very specific problem: the identification of patterns that occur in bubble-chamber negatives. Toward this end a prototype high-resolution oscilloscopic scanner was constructed, and to firm the design, a simulator of the Pattern Articulation Unit for the IBM 7094 has been written and provided with a fairly complete set of programming macroinstructions [3], [4]. Using these tools a variety of specific labeling and list processing algorithms have been developed [8]–[13]. A comprehensive program for bubble-chamber automatic scanning is currently being written.

(a) (b) (c)

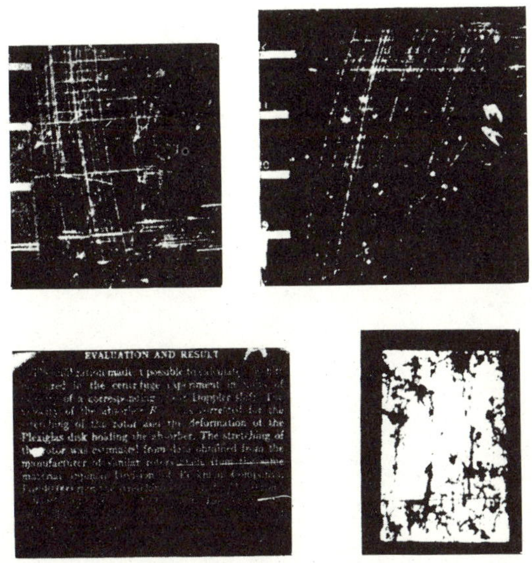

Fig. 2—Scope playback of flying spot scanned material (1024 line scan). (a) Bubble-chamber negatives. (b) Scientific text. (c) Stained rat-brain tissue.

(a) (b)

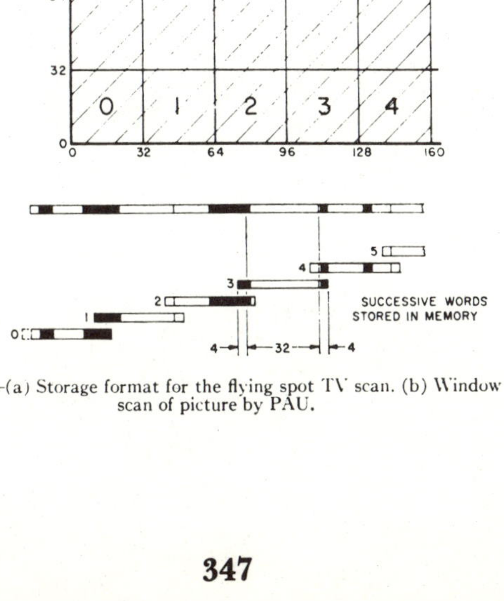

Fig. 3—(a) Storage format for the flying spot TV scan. (b) Window scan of picture by PAU.

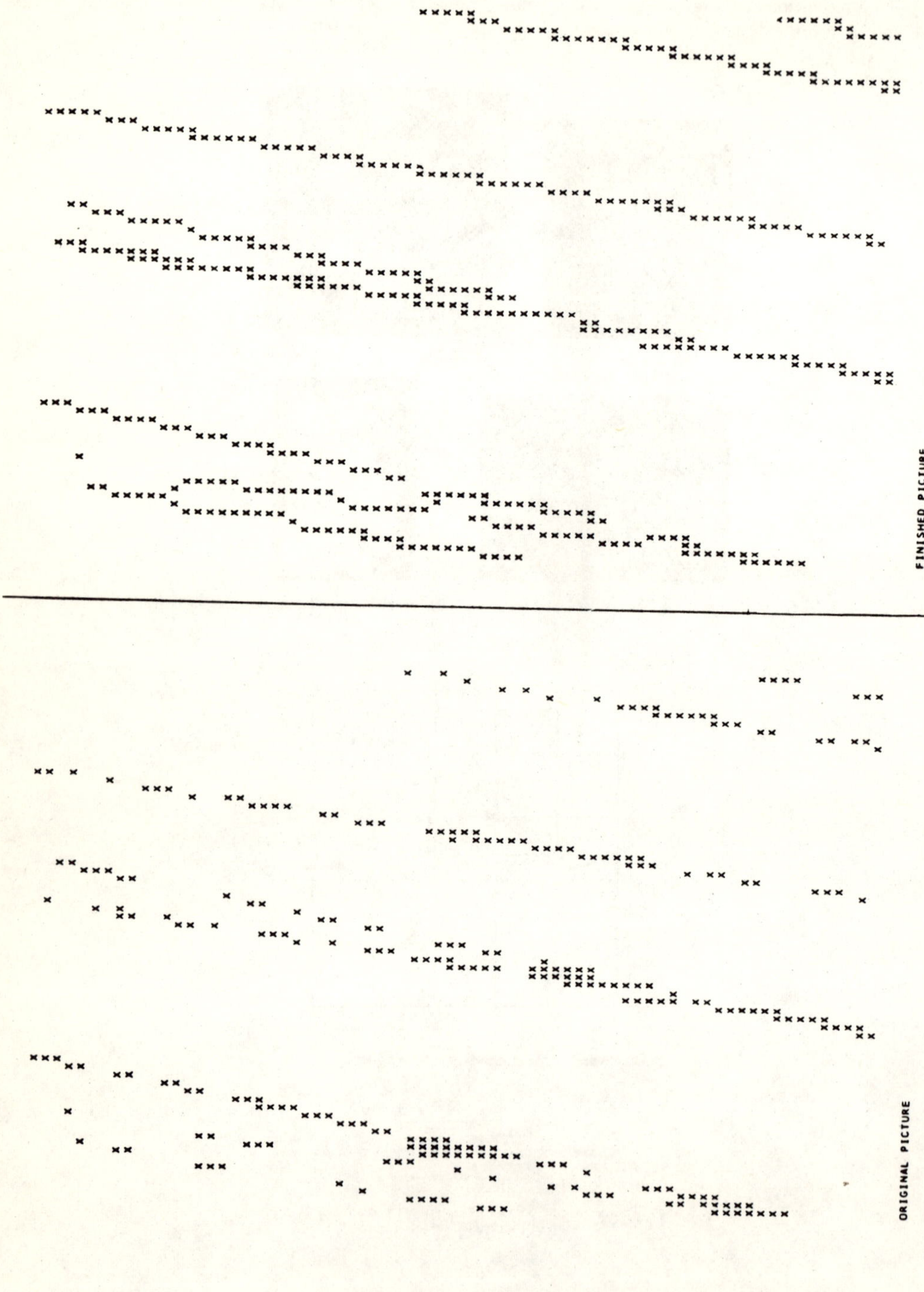

(a)

Fig. 4—Image idealized to a line drawing (*Cont'd*).

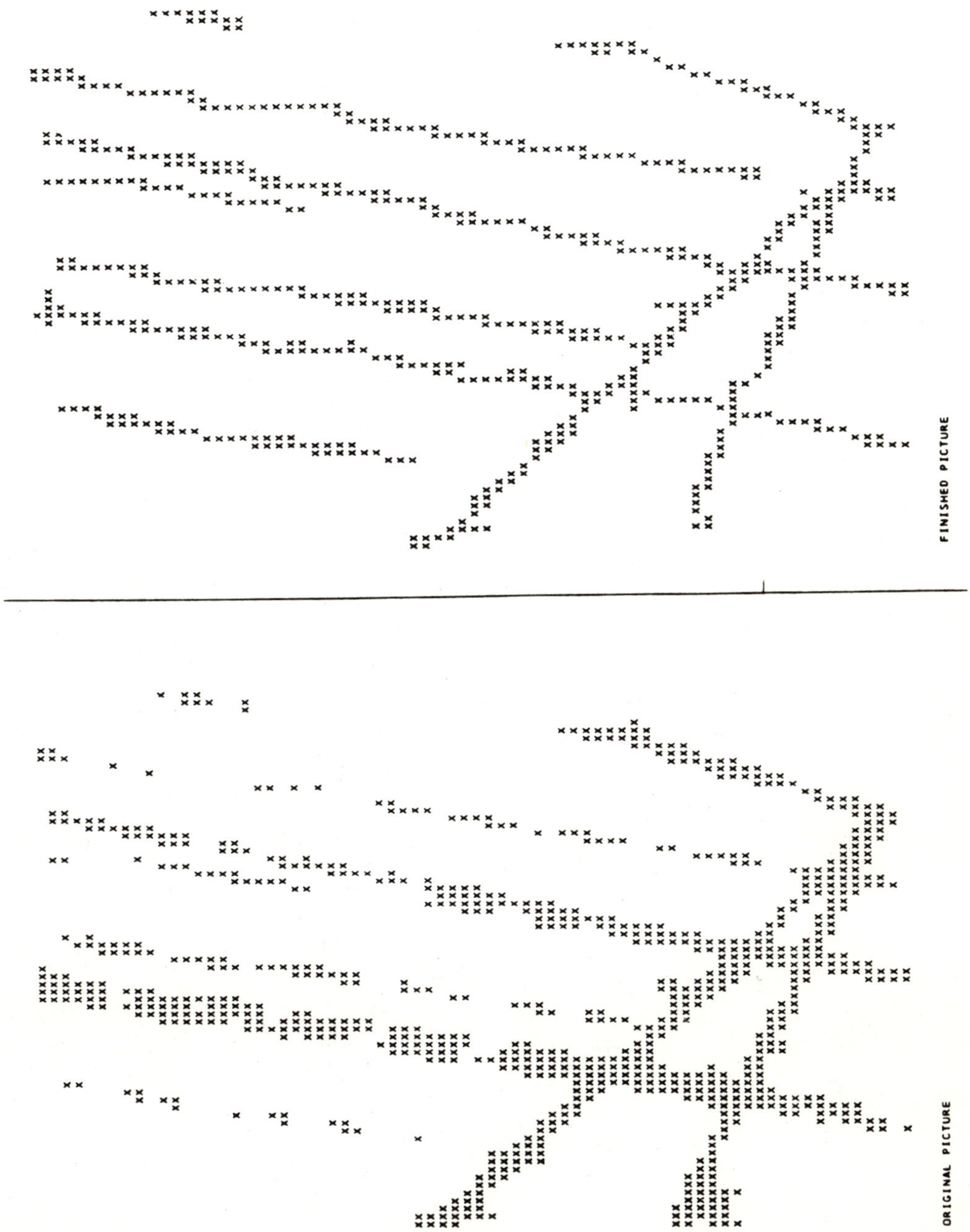

Fig. 4 (b)

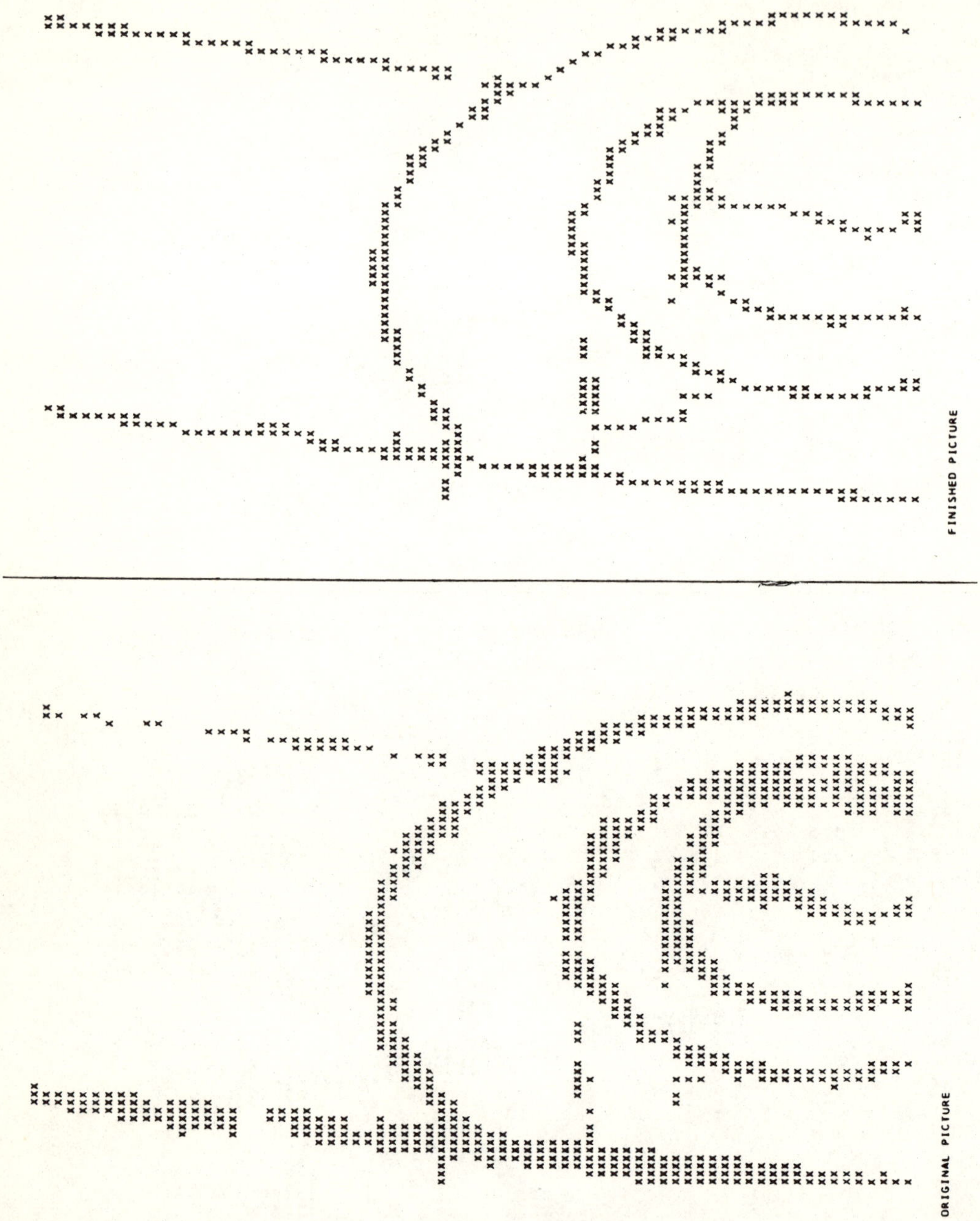

Fig. 4 (c)

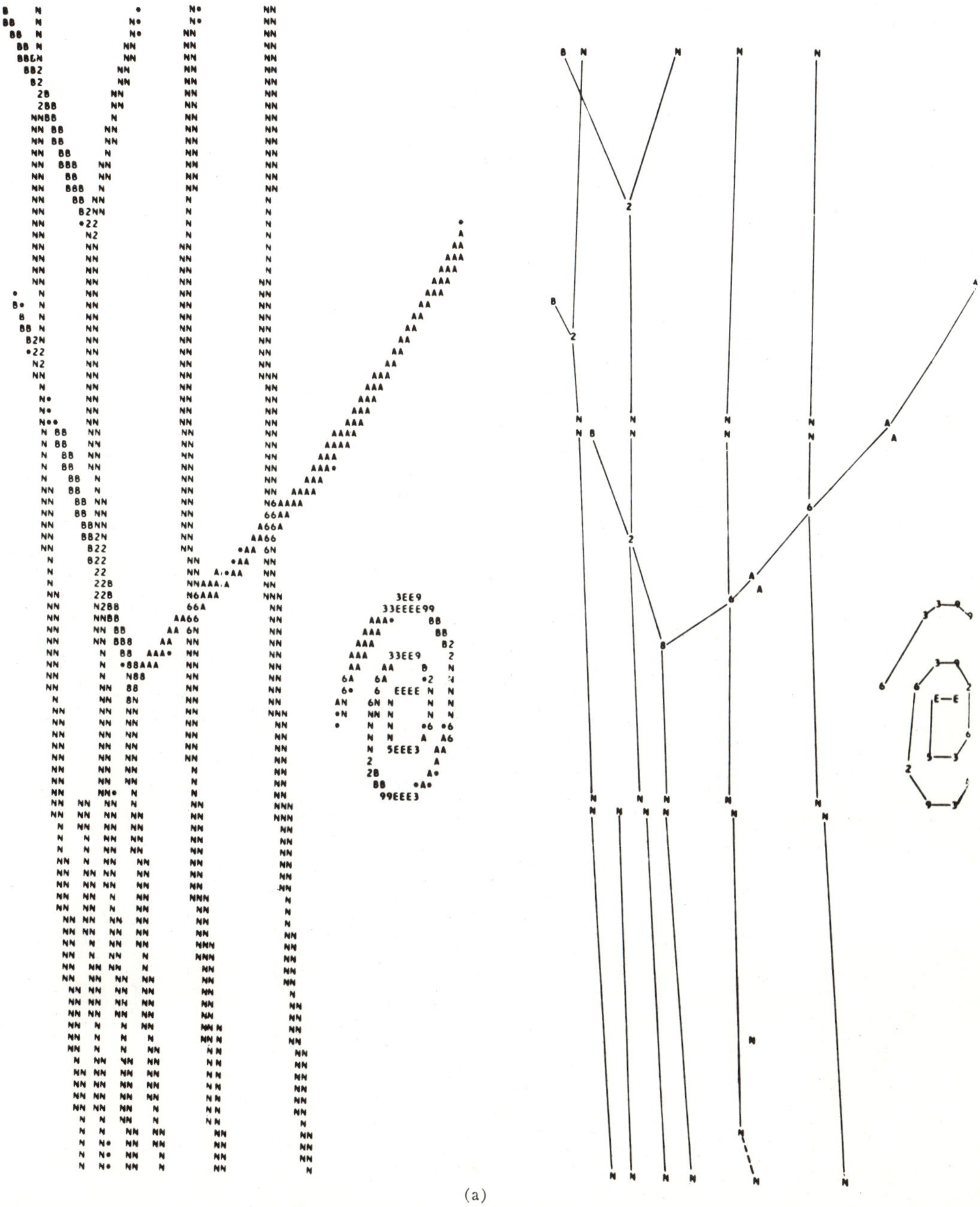

(a)

Fig. 5—Labeled bubble-chamber negatives (*Cont'd*).

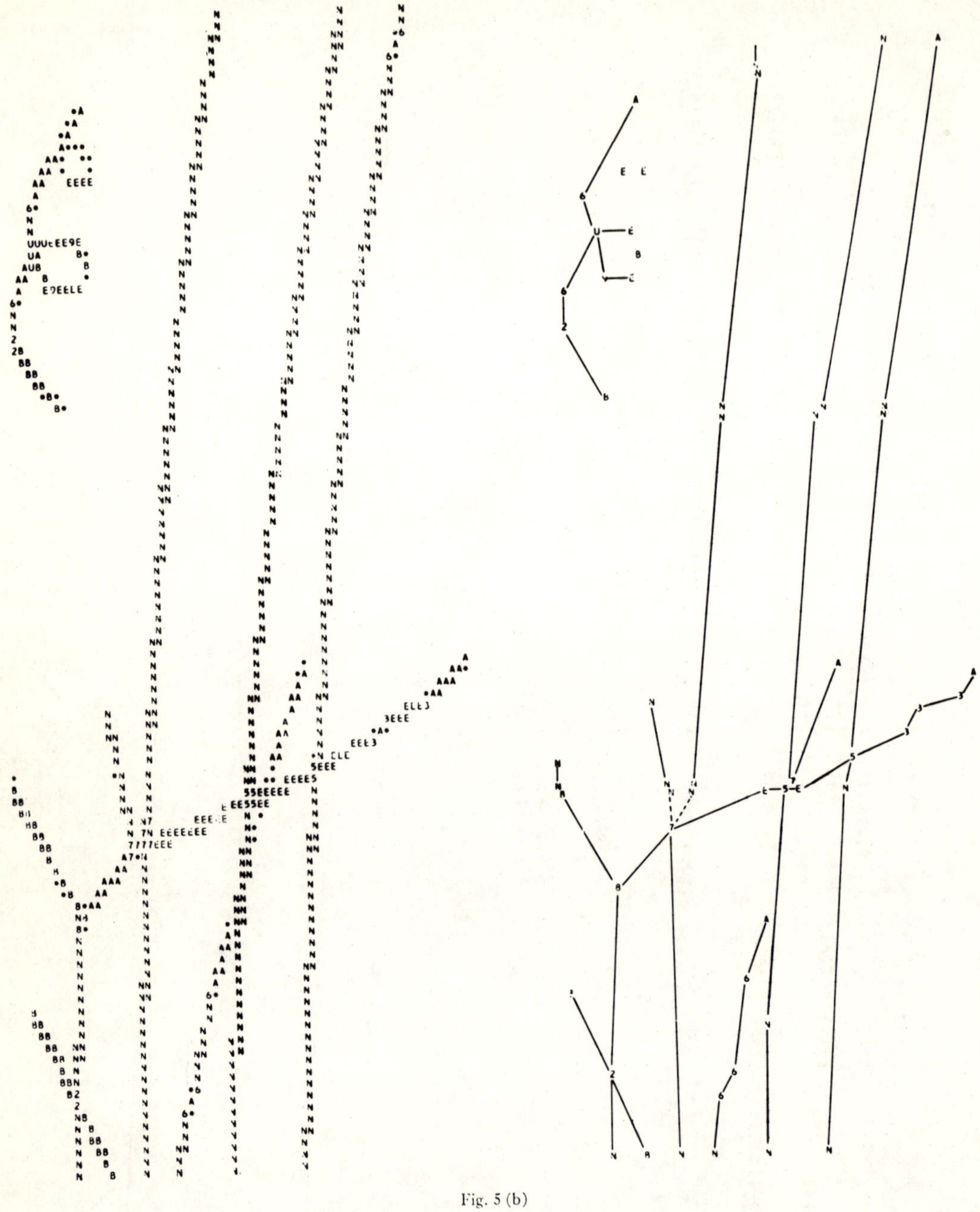

Fig. 5 (b)

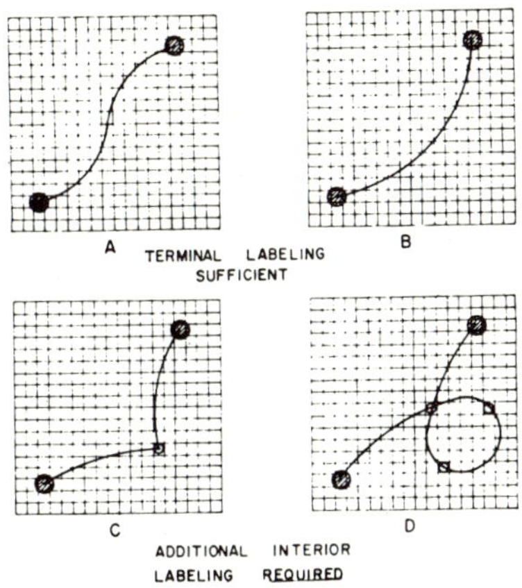

Fig. 6—Representation of curve by end points and additional labeling nodes.

III. Realization of the Pattern Articulation Unit

A. The Iterative Array

The PAU is a parallel processing unit for the automatic scanning of bit-encoded visual images. The iterative array of the PAU consists of 1024 identical processing modules (Fig. 7) called stalactites, placed at sites of a two-dimensional Bravias net (32×32). Accordingly the internal word size in this processor of the computer is 32×32=1024 bits. The logical design of the all-digital processor has been optimized for the idealization of the input image to a line drawing. Nodes representing end points, bends, points of intersection, etc., of this idealized line drawing are then labeled by appropriate programming. Finally, the abstract graph describing the interconnection of labeled nodes is extracted as a list structure, which comprises the normal output of a processing unit.

Initially the digitized input image is transferred line-by-line to the stalactite array. It is observed from empirical simulation studies that the input image (window) can be idealized to a line drawing by a sequence of simple Boolean functions of the output of nearest neighbors; *i.e.*, the new value ("0" or "1") assigned to a site is a specified Boolean function of the output of neighboring sites. In particular the array can function as a two-dimensional shift register. Neither the selection of relative neighbors involved nor the Boolean dependence is allowed to change site-to-site. Accordingly, common control signals are sent to all modules. The number of control lines is independent of the array size (*i.e.*, number of stalactites).

1) *Thinning:* Parallel preprocessing of the window image, the noise-cleaning operations mentioned above, can be largely accomplished by means of ***homogeneous logical transformations***, *i.e.*, by means of specific Boolean operations performed in parallel on the immediate neighbors of each digitized point of the picture.

Elementary homogeneous logical transformations can be subdivided into symmetric and asymmetric Boolean functions of the content of neighboring cells. Symmetric functions, including the large class of matching operations, implicitly reduce to a counting operation, and are treated in Section III-A, 2). Asymmetric Boolean functions occur more commonly in the context of thinning operations.

Intuitively the idea behind digital image thinning is to "shrink" an original digitized image to a line drawing, while preserving all connectivity of the original. The utility of the thinning process is readily apparent. Thinning projects to the *local* neighborhood of a point certain *global* aspects of the picture. For example, imagine a process by which all black track-like elements are thinned to "unit" thickness, massive black areas are reduced to mere peripheries, while intersection junctions of the original are preserved. For a rectangular (or rhombic) raster we can then classify all black cells of this "thinned" image into four categories, merely by counting the number of black points in the eight (six) cells immediately surrounding the cell in question:

Class of Point	Number of Black Points in Immediate Surround
Isolated point	0
End point	1
Interior point (of a line segment)	2
Junction point	3 or more

This mode of classification, applicable only for thinned images, is an immense simplification of the equivalent procedure for unthinned images. Positions noted by eye as end, interior, or junction point on the original (unthinned) digitized image are selected, in general, on the basis of elaborate decision criteria often involving a knowledge of neighboring points over an extensive area.

Simulation studies to date show that linewidth normalization (thinning) can be efficiently realized by simple AND, OR, NOT Boolean functions of the output of nearest-neighbor stalactites.

2) *Bubble Logic:* Certain noise-cleaning operations, in particular gap filling, implicitly involved an estimation of size a counting operation.

The neighboring bits in question are transferred to eight bits of the internal storage register of the stalactite. These cells of the stalactite are made "self-ordering"; a fixed number of identical operations will order the contents of the register so that all "0's" rise to the top, all "1's" precipitate to the bottom of the vertically aligned stalactite (Fig. 8). Once in this canonical form, threshold logic is achieved by sampling (in parallel) contents of all internal flip-flops of given depth.

For a physical description of the bubbling process consider a vertically oriented register containing mixed "1's" and "0's." Examine all adjacent pairs of digits and everywhere replace each $\binom{1}{0}$ pair by a $\binom{0}{1}$ pair. All

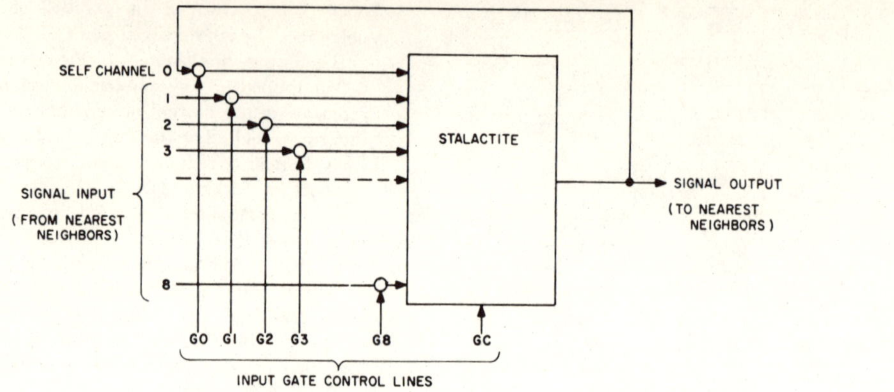

SIGNAL & INPUT GATE CONTROL LINES OF STALACTITE

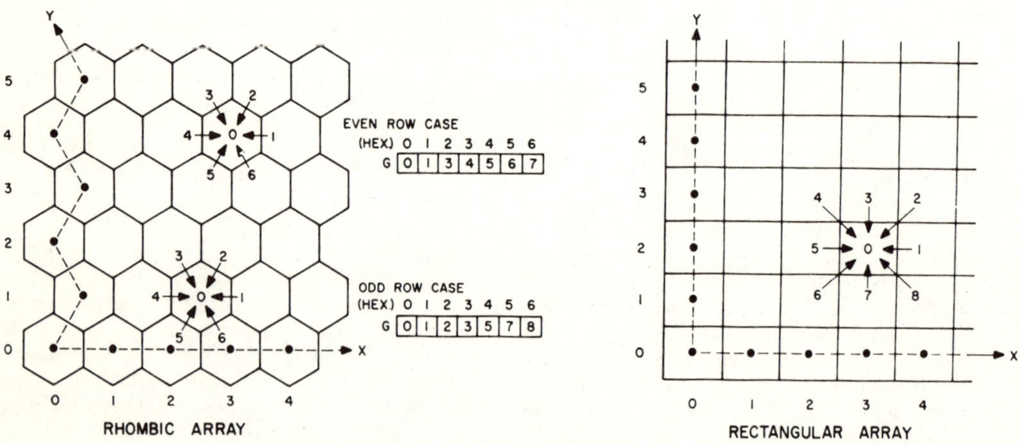

Fig. 7—Connectives of the iterative array.

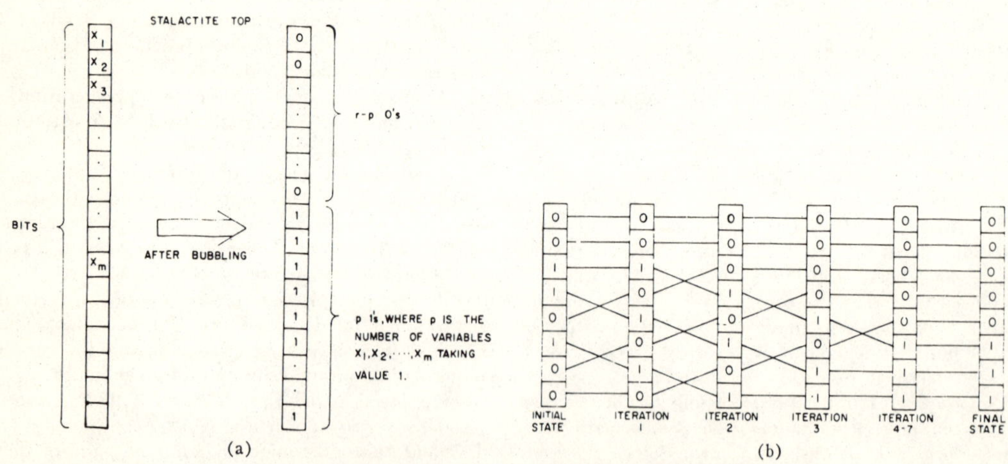

(a) (b)

Fig. 8—(a) Canonical form for symmetric Boolean functions of m variables ($m \leq r$). (b) Successive steps in the bubbling process.

other digits remain unchanged. Clearly this operation neither creates nor destroys "1's" but, if iterated, "1's" ultimately move to the bottom-most cells. For an r-bit register a maximum of $r-1$ iteratives of the bubble operation are required to order completely the contents of the register.

Fig. 8 shows an example of bubbling in which four operations completely order the register. Subsequent operations do not change the contents of the register so it is not necessary to sense the completion of ordering. The register is shown oriented vertically to strengthen the analogy that "0's" are bubbles moving to the top, hence the term "bubbling."

To describe the logical function involved let A, B, C be any three consecutive positions of the register (counting downward). The basic bubbling operation (B1D) is then given by

$$\text{Bubble "1's" Downward (B1D)}\begin{cases}\text{top} & B'=BC\\ \text{all interior} & B'=A\bar{B}\vee BC\\ \text{bottom} & B'=A\vee B\end{cases}$$

where B is any register position, A and C are adjacent positions (A above, C below) and B' is the new contents of the register B.

In addition bit stacking (and unstacking) facilities are built into the stalactite logic. These prove to be special cases of the bubble logic.

3) *Structure of the Stalactite:* The iterative array of stalactites can be connected in either rectangular or rhombic symmetry at programmer's option (Fig. 7). Each stalactite can be visualized as having a sole transmitting channel (the signal output line). In turn the stalactite can receive information from any (or all) of its immediate neighbors: eight for a rectangular array, six for a rhombic array (see Fig. 7). In addition the stalactite can sense its own output (input channel 0 in Fig. 7).

The internal symmetry of each stalactite module reflects all translational, rotational, and reflectional symmetries of an (infinite) planar array, and employs a minimum number of active elements consistent with efficient realization of processing macroinstructions.

The generic stalactite contains ten one-bit registers of internal storage (Fig. 9). These flip-flops, labeled M, $0, \cdots, 8$ serve as the buffer register of the transfer memory (M); an auxiliary nonbubbling register (0); and eight consecutive bubbling flip-flops $(1, 2, \cdots, 8)$.

If we ignore intrastalactite processing (bubbling, etc.), the simple structure of the stalactite for communicating with its neighbors can be understood from the following constraints:

1) The new value of every internal flip-flop is a function of only the normal nine inputs (eight neighbor, one self) and of control lines common to every stalactite of the array.
2) The new input signal is a function only of the present contents of the internal flip-flops and of control lines common to every stalactite of the array.

In addition to avoid race conditions, we will insist

3) In any one instruction an internal flip-flop is not both read from and written into. (Of course in any one instruction flip-flops may be inert and ignorable: neither read from nor written into.)

Construction of the above type can be called unconditional transfer orders—unconditional, because the execution of the instruction does not depend on the internal state of the stalactite.

Let us partition the generic stalactite into three blocks labeled TRANSMIT, RECEIVE and STORE as shown in Fig. 9. Blocks TRANSMIT and RECEIVE, as implied by the constraints 1) and 3), are pure combinatorial nets (*i.e.*, without internal storage).

A given internal flip-flop can in any one machine instruction be written into, or read from, but not both, *i.e.*, the RD control signals and the LD control signals must be *partitioned* into two disjoint sets. Alternatively one could partition the set of internal flip-flops, marking some for "intermediate storage" as in the traditional double-ranked shift register. We will find it faster (one machine cycle rather than two) to have the control assign (in common for the whole array) internal flip-flop numbers to intermediate results, and permute these assignments from one instruction to the next.

The ten registers of internal storage, the block STORE, are not differentiated, and therefore fed from a common bus. The TRANSMIT combinatorial net must be a symmetrical Boolean function of the output of the ten internal registers, if these are to be undifferentiated. The AND function of outgated flip-flops, with or without subsequent complementation, has been chosen for the TRANSMIT net.

That the net RECEIVE must be a symmetric net of its nine inputs is less obvious. We have proved a theorem that asserts "a generic stalactite, capable of being embedded in an (ideally infinite) array of either rectangular or (at programmer's option) rhombic array, and exhibiting all translational, rotational, and reflectional symmetries of the embedding space, must be a symmetric function of its eight input terminals (from nearest neighbors)." The 0 or self-input terminal is shown to be distinguished by this proof, and could be treated separately. Notice that inputs from diagonally connected neighbors are in no way distinguished, even though for the rectangular array alone there exists no rotation or reflection interchanging diagonal and horizontal/vertical axis inputs. This symmetry is in force only because the stalactite array can be viewed (at the option of the programmer) with *either* rectangular or hexagonal packing. The OR function of all ingated signal lines, with or without subsequent complementation, has been selected for the RECEIVE net.

B. The Transfer Memory [15]

The central core of the pattern articulation unit (PAU) has been introduced above as an iterative array of processin modules with word size 32×32. These

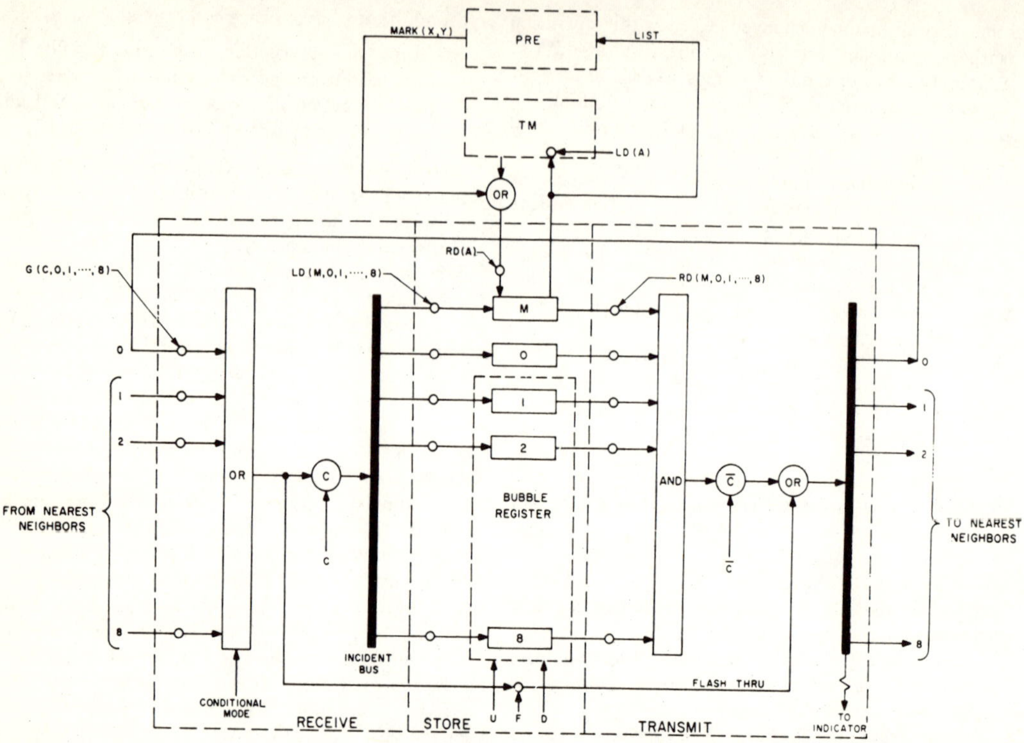

Fig. 9—Schematic of generic stalactite.

modules require individual access to memory. This memory can be partitioned into a part intrinsic to the stalactite, *i.e.*, those flip-flops implicit in the realization of threshold logic, etc., and into a remaining part extrinsic to the iterative array proper. Collectively this latter memory will be referred to as the transfer memory (TM) and is logically inert.

1) *Use of Auxiliary Memory:* Demands for intermediate storage are seen to arise naturally, either from the nature of the input visual image, or from the necessity to retain intermediate partial results. Examples of the former situation arise when successive input images are continuous in time sequence (neighboring motion picture frames, television scans, etc.), tone (successive slices of gray scale), or color (the digitization implicity in four-color printing). Here congruent storage is essential if the processing routine is to exploit similarities of image shape from frame to frame.

The necessity to store intermediate results of the iterative array stems directly from the means of executing homogeneous logical transformations in the processor. The complexity of the iterative array can obviously be greatly simplified if various digital filtering operations can be performed not in parallel, but serially, and intermediate results ($32 \times 32 = 1024$ bit words) stored. For example, local track segment orientation can be designated as being predominantly horizontal, vertical, left-diagonal or right-diagonal in four serial tests, whereas simultaneous identification requires approximately four times as much hardware.[3]

To this end the transfer memory supplies 54 planes of 1024 bits each of random access memory. In this mode of operation one bit from each of the 1024 processing modules (stalactites) is transmitted in parallel to (from) the TM in any one memory cycle.

2) *Extraction of Information at a Labeled Point:* Normally a processing routine can be cast into a form where relatively few stalactites are labeled, *i.e.*, singled out for detailed examination. All tracking operations culminate in this form—labeling of terminal nodes, points of intersection, etc. The essential point is that ancillary information (most naturally associated with each labeled node) can be extremely useful. For example, in bubble-chamber data processing, local orientation can help distinguish track segments of an electron spiral from segments of an intersecting beam track.

Such information, perhaps aimed at improved tracking by assisting selection of the next point of readout, is extracted from the transfer memory by a second

[3] The intrinsic speed advantage of contemporary digital circuitry over neutral response rates strongly suggests that a different schema (time-multiplexed use of one processing array with facilities (TM) for storage of intermediate results) be used in the man-made recognition machines, in contrast to the extreme filtering parallelism found, for example, in the frog's eye. See H. R. Maturana, J. Y. Lettvin, W. S. McCulloch, and W. H. Pitts, "Anatomy and Physiology of Vision in the Frog," *J. General Physiology*, vol. 43, pp. 129–175; July, 1960.

mode of reference. Rather than a global view of one bit from each of the 1024 stalactites, parallel output of the contents of *one* stalactite is sampled. In this latter node the transfer memory is viewed as a random access memory of 1024 words, one word (54 bits) associated with each cell of the processing array.

C. List Compilation

1) *List and Mark Instructions:* The problem of extracting an abstract graph description of a line drawing embedded in a plane of the stalactite array has been introduced in Section II-B. Once each node of the line drawing has been *labeled* in parallel by local Boolean processing, the list compilation facilities required to read out (and thus generate the abstract graph) can be reduced to two principal operations:

a) *List Instruction:* All points (*i.e.*, black cells of a sparsely populated plane) are sequentially identified by 10-bit coordinates $Z=(X, Y)$ with five bits X, five bits Y. Sequential readout implies a linear ordering of all 1024 cells of the array, and that an algorithm for finding the first black point is known.

b) *Mark Z Instructions:* A single cell specified by address Z is *marked* (*i.e.*, set = "1"). Marking, as will be shown below, can also be used for erasing points of the sparsely populated plane as found. Iteration of the search algorithm to find the "first" black point, alternated with subsequent erasure of each point as found, eventually lists all points of the plane.

2) *Use of the M Register:* From engineering considerations[4] it is convenient to specialize the mark and list instructions to the M plane of the stalactite array. The two coordinate instructions then take the form:

MARK (Z): sets to "1" the M flip-flop of the stalactite at coordinate $Z=(X, Y)$.

LIST: serially compiles a list of all coordinates Z of stalactites having "0" in the M flip-flop.[5] Coordinate Z of the next point found is transferred to the LIST register automatically upon storage of the previous contents of the register.

In use, a sparsely populated plane is complemented, loaded into the stalactite M register, and a first black point identified by the LIST instruction. Each coordinate of this list, once compiled, is used to MARK its associated M flip-flop (and thus erase the point). Black points connected to this point (found by flash-through) are in turn listed. This technique (for isolated track segments each LIST instruction brings down only one entry) builds a paired list of nodes, *i.e.*, the branches of the associated abstract graph (Fig. 10, page 806).

3) *Search Algorithm Ordering*: The list instruction as mentioned above implies a linear ordering of all 1024 cells of the two-dimensional array. A point in this array is specified by coordinate (X, Y) with five bits of X, five bits of Y. Rather than the customary integer representation it is convenient to visualize $(X+iY)$ as a point within the unit square: $0 \leq X < 1$, $0 \leq Y < 1$ with X, Y proper binary fractions. All "M" cells with an output signal "0" are lexicographical ordered first on Y, then X. The cell of lowest order is then LISTed first (Fig. 10).

4) *An Associate Memory:* Coordinate readout, in conjunction with the logical processing facilities of the stalactite array, combines to transform the transfer memory into a versatile *associative memory*. Consider the transfer memory initially filled with ≤ 1024 words, each of 54 bits. Let any specified subset of bit positions $(0, 1, \cdots, 53)$ be designated a *code field*. The associative property in simplest form asserts that the addresses of all words (if any) having as contents of their code field an (arbitrary) requested bit pattern are directly identified. In the PAU design parallel associative search is done by transferring the bit plane of the code field in turn to the stalactite array with appropriate complementation such that the ideal pattern, so manipulated, is identically zero. After stacking (or bubbling), the M bit of all blank stalactites is marked and the corresponding addresses compiled. The logical flexibility of the stalactite array permits obvious generalizations of this technique: in particular, the addresses of those words whose code field bits satisfy some simple Boolean function can be selected by appropriate intrastalactite programming.

D. PAU Order Code

For purposes of control the instruction set of the PAU can be partitioned into seven basic types of instructions:

1) Stalactite transfer orders (conditional/unconditional, with/without simultaneous border transfer);
2) Stalactite bubble orders;
3) Transfer memory orders;
4) Flash-through;
5) Pyramidal readout (*i.e.*, list, mark instructions);
6) Border input/output;
7) Special instructions.

In the interest of brevity we will treat in detail only the stalactite transfer and bubble orders. Instructions requiring communication between the stalactite array and the transfer memory will be momentarily ignored. We emphasize that the instructions described below are machine *micro*instructions. Programming *macro*instructions, on the other hand, are discussed in [3] and [6]. A sample code is illustrated in Fig. 11.

For pedagogical reasons it is convenient to introduce two redundant bits and subdivide the resulting 40-bit

[4] Coaxial cable connects the transfer memory (TM) and the M plane. It is convenient to make the MARK and LIST instructions adjuncts of the TM gating arrangement and to capitalize upon the close juxtaposition of M-plane signal lines at the TM.

[5] As we normally complement a plane before transferring it to the M register and initiating the LIST instruction, we will refer to a "0" in this M plane as a "black point."

stalactite μ instruction into four *control groups* of 10 bits each. The first of these is called the *flow control* as the first five bits of the group specify the information flow through the stalactite as a whole:

Flow group (first five bits):

←— 5 bits —→									
$\bar{C}$	G	C	F	B					
$\bar{C}$ out	Gates	C in	Flash-through	Bubble					

Here $\bar{C}$ and C specify whether the outgoing or incoming signal, respectively, or both, are to be complemented (see Fig. 9). Bit G, when "1" and only then, indicates that the gate input control group must be examined as at least one input gate is opened (gate control$\neq 0$). Bit F, when "1," indicates that the flash-through bypass is to be called into play.

The fifth, or B bit, when "1," evokes a bubble logical operation, the selection of which is given by the second five bits of the flow group:

Flow group (second five bits):

					←— 5 bits —→				
					U	D	N_2	N_2	N_0
					Up	Down	Number of Iterations		

Bits U and D (positions 6 and 7) define the type of bubble logic. Here the number of iterations to be applied (0, 1, 2, · · · , 7) is given by the binary number $N_2N_1N_0$. When $B=1$, the three bits of iteration number N are transferred to a control counter to control iterations of bubbling.

Having set up the flow, it is appropriate to interrogate which flip-flop outputs are to be sent as a confluence (AND/$\overline{\text{AND}}$) out over the output channel. The appropriate flip-flops are specified by the *FF Read Control group:*

FF Read Control group:

←—— 10 bits ——→									
M	0	1	2	3	4	5	6	7	8

Having thus established the output signal of every stalactite, we sum (OR) together the requisite input signals to the stalactite, as specified by the *Input Gate Control group:*

Input Gate Control group:

←—— 10 bits ——→									
C	0	1	2	3	4	5	6	7	8

Here the significance of the C bit needs re-emphasis. C (="1") signifies that conditional input gating is to be used, *i.e.*, each gate 0, 1, · · · , 8 marked with a "1" in the input gate control group is, in fact, open *only* if the correspondingly numbered stalactite flip-flop contains a "1" at the beginning of this instruction.

It will be remembered that the iterative array can operate in two connectivities: rectangular or rhombic. For the rectangular case all 10 bits of the input gate control group are used; for the rhombic array, the last two bits are ignored and the input gates, as associated internal flip-flops, renumbered to conform to the conventions.

Finally, the output signal of the input combinatorial net (called the *incident bit*) is, after possible complementation, ready to be stored, or interrogated as the conditional control bit for a bubble-logic operation (if specified by $B=$"1"). If the former situation obtains, then and only then, is the fourth and final control group examined—the *FF Load Control group:*

FF Load Control group:

←—— 10 bits ——→									
M	0	1	2	3	4	5	6	7	8

Here each of the 10 bits corresponds, respectively, with the 10 internal flip-flops of the generic stalactite.

In summary the intrastalactite microinstructions are specified by four control groups of 10 bits each, placed in the 40-bit stalactite instruction register (SIR):

Stalactite Instruction Register:

I	II	III	IV
10	20	30	40
Flow	FF Read	Input Gate	FF Load

The interpretation of the individual control groups has been described above.

E. Fabrication of the PAU

1) *Layout:* From a packaging point of view the PAU consists of six subdivisions, listed below:

Iterative array,
PAU control,
Transfer memory and pyramidal readout encoder,
SCR power supplies,
Final voltage regulators,
Air-conditioning unit.

All units are housed in the computer main frame with the exception of the SCR power supplies (basement), relay wall boxes (wall-mounted in computer room), and air-conditioning unit (roof-mounted directly above main frame). The distribution of the remaining units as housed in the main frame is shown in Fig. 12. Each of these units is discussed briefly below.

2) *The Iterative Array:* There are six basic circuit boards of the iterative array. Each circuit board is packaged on a 3.984 inches wide$\times$4.750 inches long photoceram board. A total of 1360 boards are required. Of these 1024 are used to house the stalactites of the iterative array, one per board.

The distribution of circuit boards of the iterative array as housed in the four front transistor bays of the computer main frame is shown in Fig. 13. Control drivers are placed largely in the middle of the transistor bays to keep wiring length to a minimum. Drivers to even and odd rows of the array are separated, consistent with the potentiality of using either rectangular or rhombic connectivity.

Every stalactite board has two coaxial connections (respectively, to/from the TM, and hence PRE). This integrates to a massive arterial network of miniature coaxial cable which is fanned into the TM (front central rack). Coaxial connections to (from) the border of the 40$\times$40 array, though extensive, are nominal in comparison.

3) *The Stalactite:* Because the stalactite plays a role of central importance in the array, its design configuration is shown in Fig. 14.[6]

Certain features of the design warrant emphasis. First it should be observed that virtually no decoding of control signals is done within the stalactite; that is, each control line is directly identified with a bit in the general microinstruction.

Secondly, almost half the circuitry of a module is expended on control, or routing of the signal, reflecting the wide range of admissible orders that a module can execute.

That portion of the stalactite of high symmetry, *i.e.*, the ten internal flip-flops with associated gates and bubble logic, are realized in ten thin-film microcircuits, each 0.42$\times$2 inches (Fig. 15).[7] Conventional silicon transistors and microdiodes are used. Parts of low symmetry, *i.e.*, the control portions of the stalactite, are packaged on printed-circuit chips using conventional discrete components.

[6] This circuit design of Prof. K. C. Smith will be reported separately in more detail by him at a later date [18].

[7] Dr. H. Bilger materially assisted in these layouts.

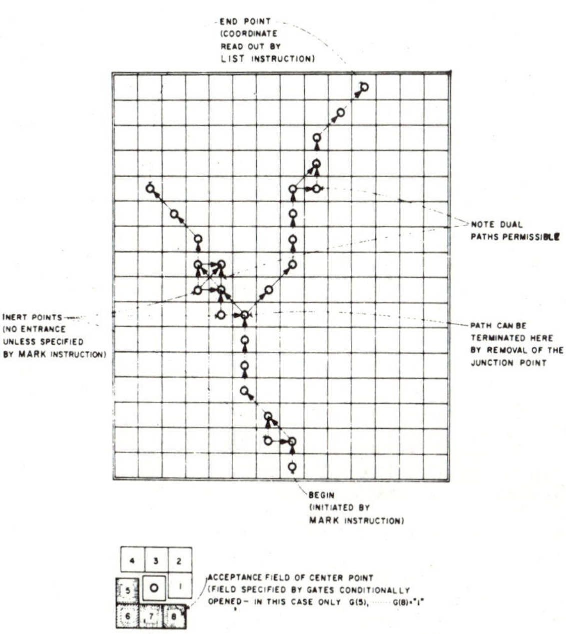

Fig. 10—Path building with multiselection switch arrangement.

```
              FORNANGO, J. P.                                                 31022

*
*  INITIAL PRE-PROCESSING ROUTINE FOR BUBBLE CHAMBER PICTURES
*
        SETMOD   72
        LETTER   ( X)
        BCOLOP   M0,,CLEAR,,,,,BAR          COMPLETELY FILLED CONTEXT PLANE
START   READ     M1
        PRINT    M1,,72,72
        CCCMMT   (-ORIGINAL PICTURE)

*******      FILLING ROUTINE      *******

        INDEX    SET,1,0
FILL    BCOFUN   M2,,M0,,M1,,(37$)          FILL SINGLE HOLES IN N. DIR.
        BCOLOP   M1,,OR,M1,,M2
        TMARK    DLSUR,,M2,,M0,,M1,,GE,7    FILL HOLES WITH 7 OR 8 NEIGHBORS
        BCOLOP   M1,,OR,M2,,M1
        BCOFUN   M2,,M1,,M1,,(2/5/6/7$)     CORNER FILL
        BCOFUN   M2,,M0,,M2,,(5+7$)
        BCOFUN   M3,,M1,,M1,,(4/7/8/1$)
        BCOFUN   M3,,M0,,M3,,(7+1$)
        BCOFUN   M4,,M1,,M1,,(6/1/2/3$)
        BCOFUN   M4,,M0,,M4,,(1+3$)
        BCOFUN   M5,,M1,,M1,,(8/3/4/5$)
        BCOFUN   M5,,M0,,M5,,(3+5$)
        BCOLOP   M1,,OR,M1,,M5
        BCOLOP   M1,,OR,M1,,M4
        BCOLOP   M1,,OR,M1,,M3
        BCOLOP   M1,,OR,M1,,M2
        INDEX    INCR,1,1
        JUMP     LESS,FILL,1,2
        BCOFUN   M2,,M1,,M1,,(5/1$)         EAST FILL
        BCOFUN   M3,,M1,,M1,,(1/5$)
        BCOLOP   M2,,OR,M2,,M3
        BCOFUN   M2,,M0,,M2,,(15$)
        BCOLOP   M1,,OR,M1,,M2
        INDEX    SET,1,0

*******      THINNING ROUTINE      *******

        BOOLOP   M7,,EQUAL,M1
THIN    TMARK    DLSUR,,M2,,M1,,M1,,LE,3    SAVE POINTS WITH 3 OR LESS NEIGH
        BCOFUN   M3,,M1,,M1,,(37$)
        BCOFUN   M4,,M1,,M1,,(15$)          REMOVE P IF IT IS A BOUNDARY PT
        BCOFUN   M5,,M1,,M1,,(3/7+7/3$)           NEXT TO 2 INTERNAL PTS.
        BCOFUN   M6,,M1,,M1,,(1/5+5/1$)
        BCOFUN   M3,,M3,,M3,,(1+5$)
        BCOFUN   M4,,M4,,M4,,(3+7$)
        BCOFUN   M5,,M5,,M3,,(3+7$)
        BCOFUN   M6,,M6,,M4,,(1+5$)
        BCOLOP   M3,,OR,M5,,M6
        BCOLOP   M4,,AND,M1,,M3,,BAR
        TMARK    DLSUR,,M5,,M2,,M3,,EQ,2    PUT BACK SAVED PTS WHICH DID NOT
        BCOLOP   M6,,AND,M2,,M5,,BAR              HAVE 2 NEIGHBORS REMOVED.
        BCOLOP   M2,,OR,M6,,M4
        BCOFUN   M1,,M7,,M2,,(26+48$)       PUT BACK REMOVED PTS WHICH WOULD
        BCOLOP   M1,,OR,M1,,M2                    BE DIAG. INTERNAL IF KEPT.
        INDEX    INCR,1,1
        JUMP     LESS,THIN,1,3
```

Fig. 11—Sample PAU simulator program [13] (using macroinstruction set).

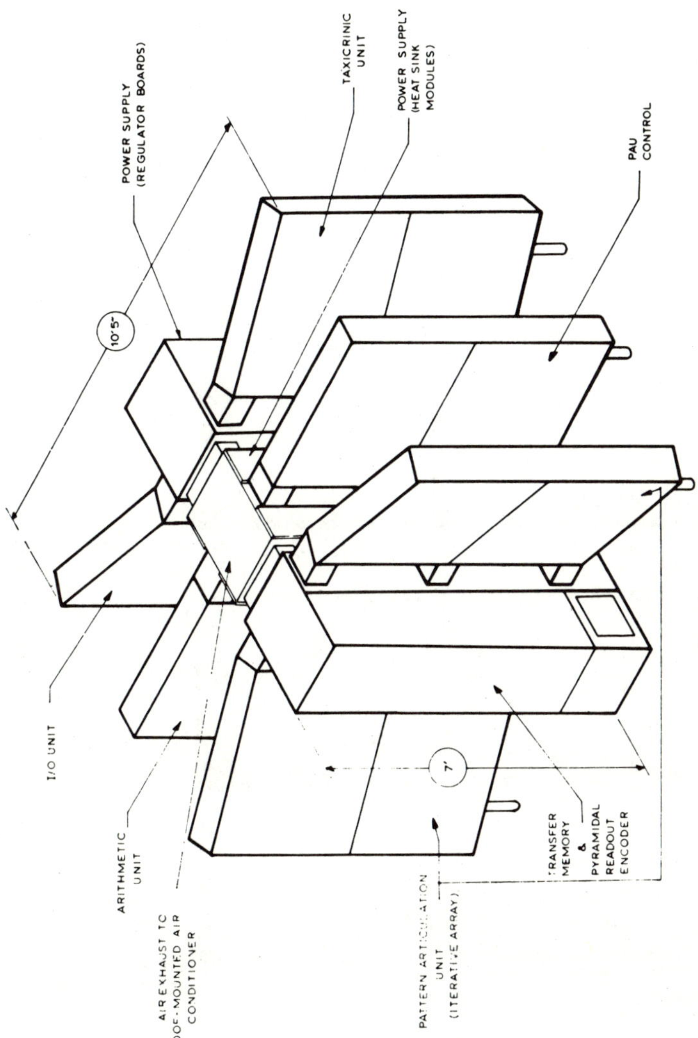

Fig. 12—Illinois pattern recognition computer (ILLIAC III).

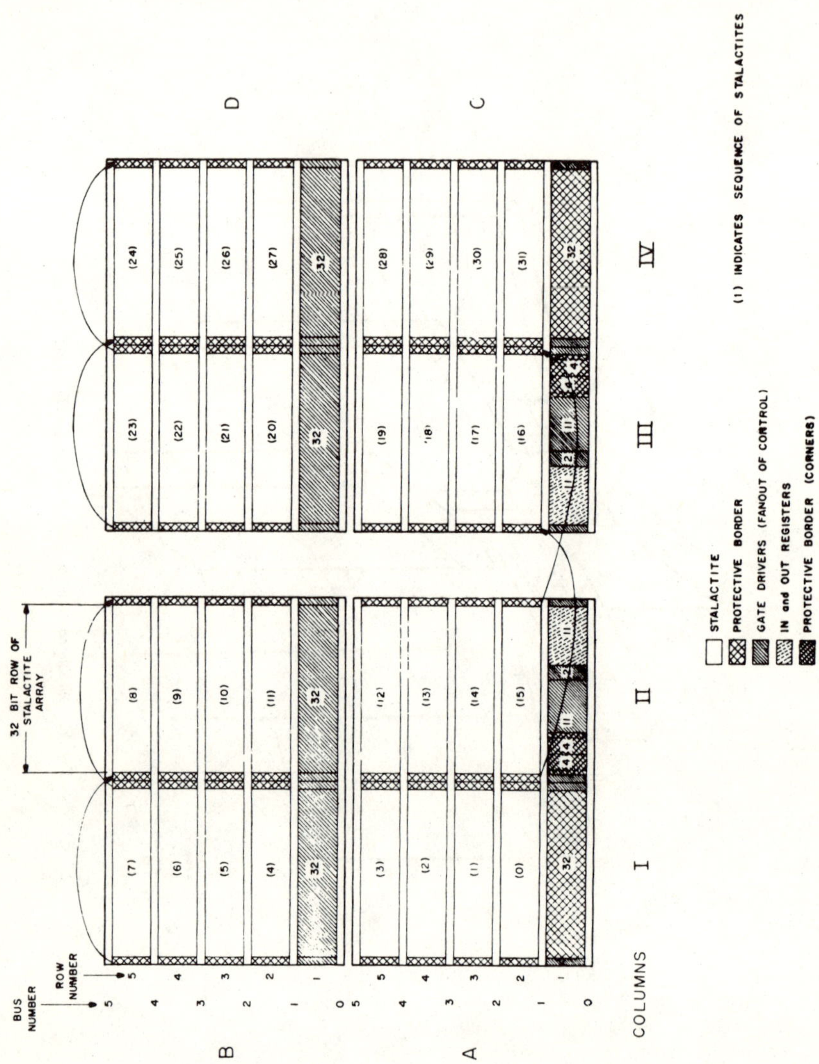

Fig. 13—Layout of PAU iterative array.

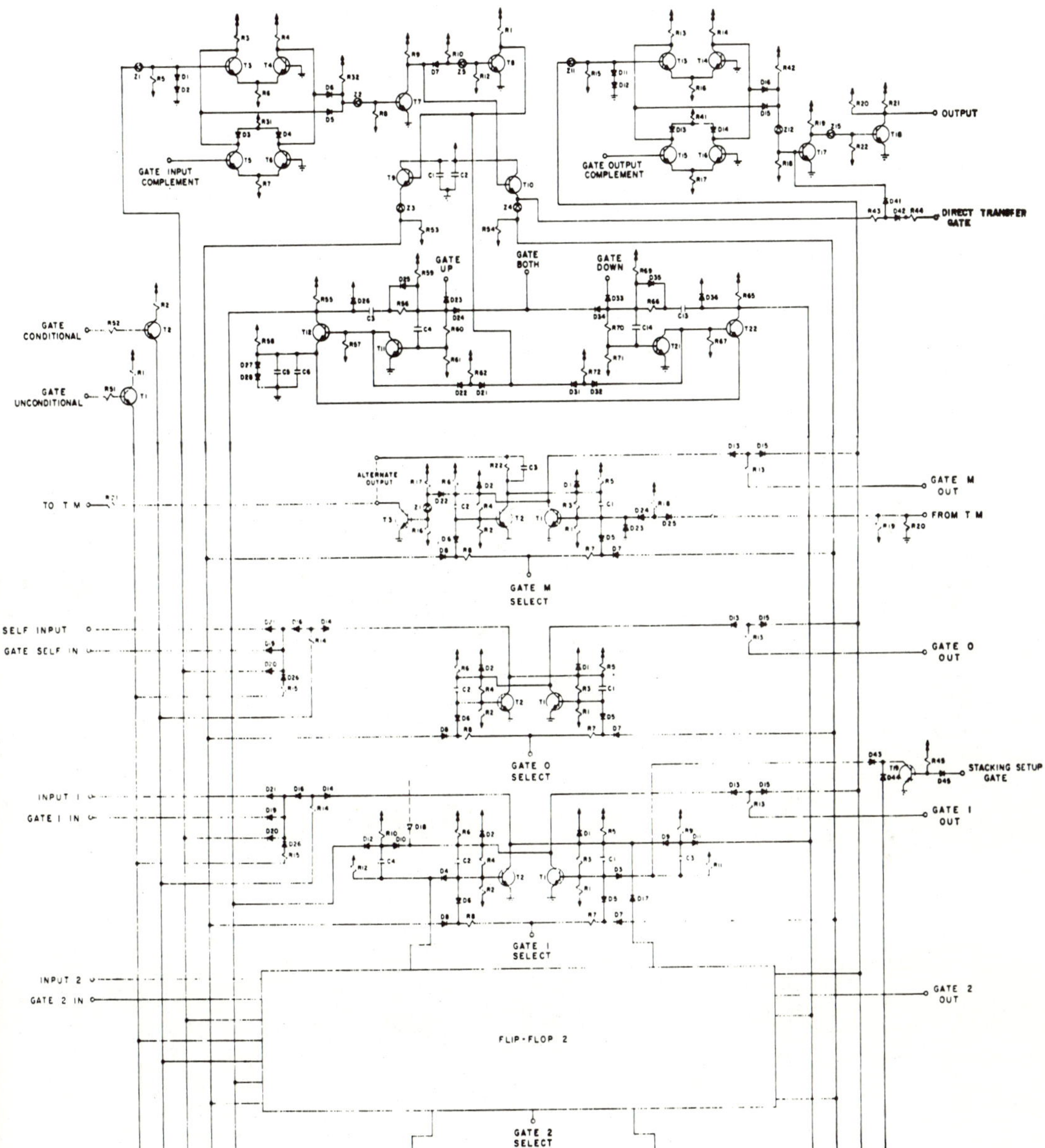

Fig. 14—PAU stalactite layout (*Cont'd*).

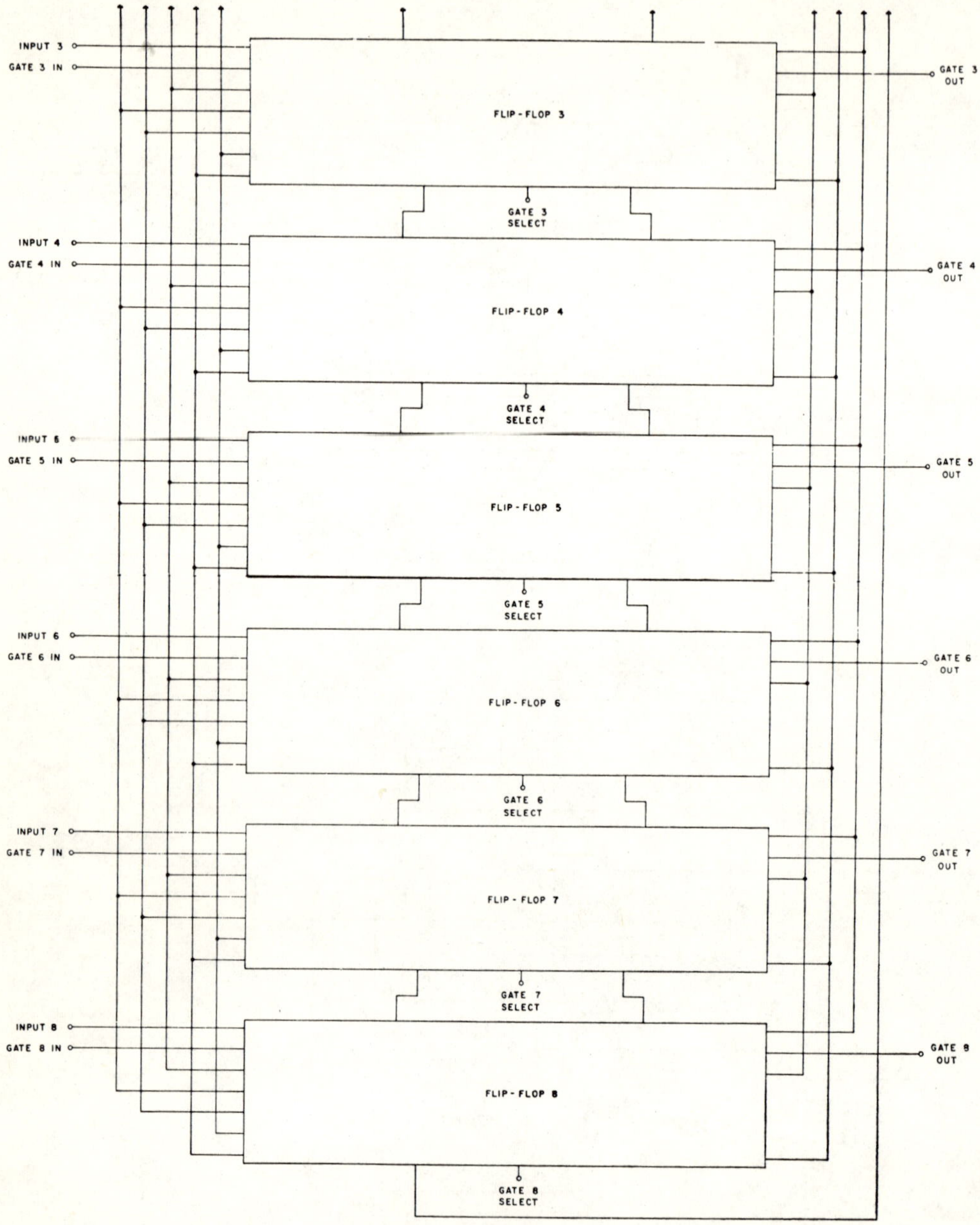
INPUT 3
GATE 3 IN
FLIP-FLOP 3
GATE 3 OUT
GATE 3 SELECT
INPUT 4
GATE 4 IN
FLIP-FLOP 4
GATE 4 OUT
GATE 4 SELECT
INPUT 5
GATE 5 IN
FLIP-FLOP 5
GATE 5 OUT
GATE 5 SELECT
INPUT 6
GATE 6 IN
FLIP-FLOP 6
GATE 6 OUT
GATE 6 SELECT
INPUT 7
GATE 7 IN
FLIP-FLOP 7
GATE 7 OUT
GATE 7 SELECT
INPUT 8
GATE 8 IN
FLIP-FLOP 8
GATE 8 OUT
GATE 8 SELECT

Fig. 14.

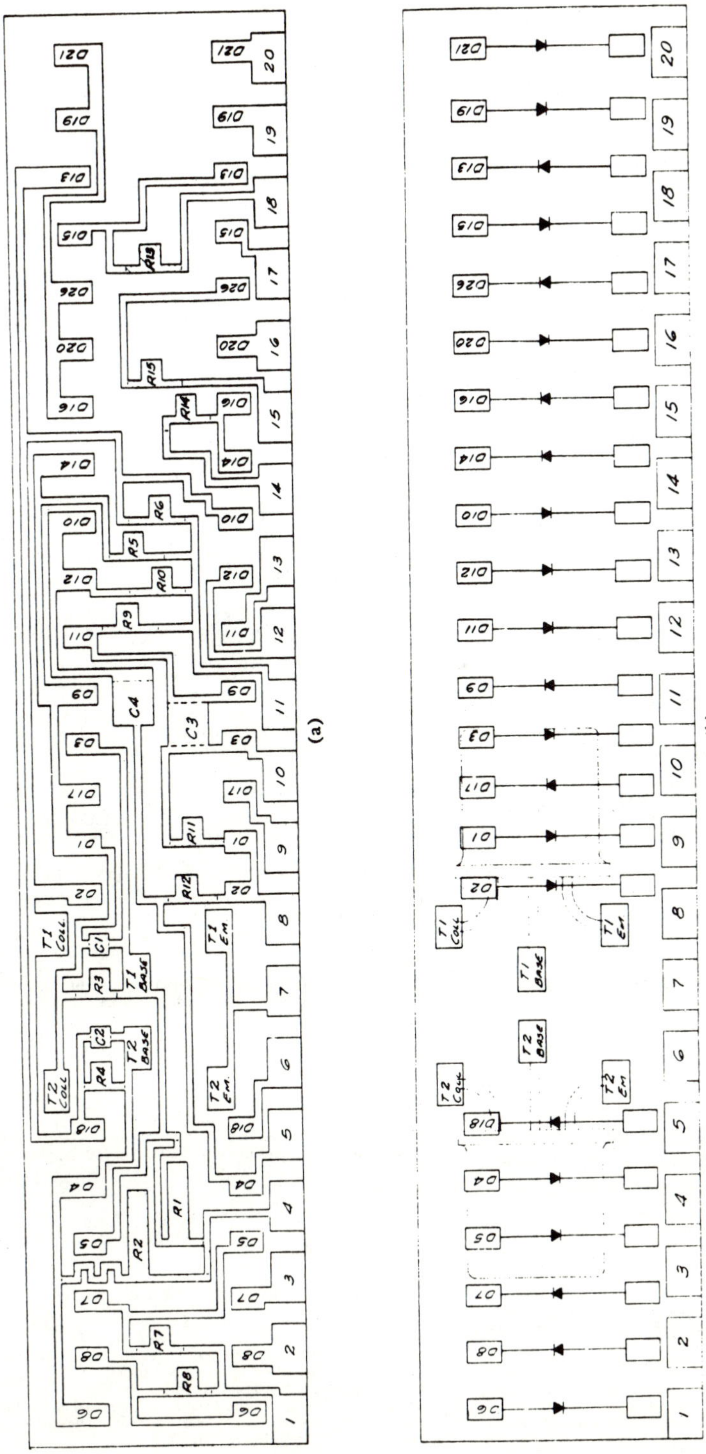

1 Gate select
2 Signal driver-left
3 Signal driver-right
4 −6 volts
5 Flip-flop below left
6 Flip-flop above left
7 Ground
8 +6 volts
9 Flip-flop below right
10 Flip-flop above right
11 +12 volts
12 Up and down driver left
13 Up and down driver right
14 Conditional driver right
15 Conditional driver left
16 To input OR and complement
17 To output AND and complement
18 Gate out
19 Gate in
20 Input

Fig. 15—(a) Conductor and passive component layout. (b) Location of diode and transistor attachment.

4) *Transfer Memory and Pyramidal Readout Encoder:* The transfer memory and the pyramidal readout encoder function together as an associative memory. For this reason they are packaged together in the entire front center rack and share the 1024 coaxial cables entering from and the 1024 coaxial cables exiting to the 1024-bit M register of the stalactite array.

Packaging the circuitry of the transfer memory in close superposition with the core matrix stack requires considerable ingenuity. A drawer arrangement holding the transfer memory circuitry, pyramidal readout encoder circuitry, the matrix stack, as well as the interconnecting coaxial cable, is planned.

Acknowledgment

Five of my colleagues on the faculty of the Digital Computer Laboratory have made major contributions to the design and fabrication of ILLIAC III: K. Ibuki (taxicrinic unit), Prof. R. Narasimhan (programming and the syntactic model), Prof. S. R. Ray (transfer memory), Prof. K. C. Smith (circuit design of the pattern articulation unit and computer power distribution), and Prof. S. Yamada (fast circuits and the automatic test console). A selected bibliography will be found appended to this paper, where the original reports of these associates are noted.

I would also like to acknowledge the contribution of former graduate students, particularly those who weathered the days when neither the structure nor the feasibility of the computer was very certain: J. L. Divilbiss (the bubble register), D. Hall (stalactite circuitry), J. H. Stein, B. Mayoh and R. K. Rice (simulation programming), C. P. Bates (scanner digital control), and S. Matsushita (arithmetic unit).

The structure of the Pattern Articulation Unit (PAU) is an outgrowth of the recent interest in cellular automata, in particular the work of S. H. Unger.[8] Prof. A. H. Amon was instrumental in the importance given to continuity in the machine which developed into the flash-through mechanism.

In addition, I would like to acknowledge the assistance of J. V. Wenta, who has been responsible for supervising the checkout, operation and maintenance of our prototype flying spot oscilloscopic system and the construction of the second generation device. F. P. Serio has ably supervised the fabrication of the main frame and power distribution system of the computer.

[8] S. H. Unger, "A computer oriented toward spatial problems," Proc. IRE, vol. 46, pp. 1744–1750, 1958, and "Pattern detection and recognition," Proc. IRE, vol. 47, pp. 1737–1752; 1959.

Bibliography

Summary Articles

[1] B. H. McCormick and R. Narasimhan, "Design of a pattern recognition digital computer with application to the automatic scanning of bubble-chamber negatives," *Nuclear Instruments and Methods*, vol. 20, pp. 401–406; January, 1963.

[2] B. H. McCormick, "The Illinois Pattern Recognition Computer (ILLIAC III)," Digital Computer Lab., University of Illinois, Urbana, Rept. No. 148; August 20, 1963.

Programming (PA U Simulator)

[3] J. H. Stein, "User's Manual for PAX, an IBM 7090 Program to Simulate the Pattern Articulation Unit of ILLIAC III," Digital Computer Lab., Rept. No. 147; July 29, 1963.

[4] J. H. Stein, "Program Description of PAX, an IBM 7090 Program to Simulate the Pattern Articulation Unit of ILLIAC III," Digital Computer Lab., File No. Rept. No. 151; September 16, 1963.

Programming (Syntactic Model)

[5] R. Narasimhan, "A Linguistic Approach to Pattern Recognition," Digital Computer Lab., Rept. No. 121; July 10, 1962.

[6] R. Narasimhan, "A Programming Language for the Parallel Processing of Pictures," Digital Computer Lab., Rept. No. 132; January 9, 1963.

[7] R. Narasimhan, "Syntactic Descriptions of Pictures and Gestalt Phenomena of Visual Perception," Digital Computer Lab., Rept. No. 142; July 25, 1963.

Programming (Bubble-Chamber Automatic Scanning)

[8] R. Narasimhan, "A Programming System for Scanning Digitized Bubble-Chamber Negatives," Digital Computer Lab., Rept. No. 139; June 24, 1963.

[9] R. K. Rice, "A Preliminary Study of PAU Microlists in Bubble-Chamber Photographs," Digital Computer Lab., File No. 506; February 1, 1963.

[10] R. Narasimhan and B. H. Mayoh, "The Structure of a Program for Scanning Bubble-Chamber Negatives," Digital Computer Lab., File No. 507; February 7, 1963.

[11] Brian H. Mayoh, "Bubble-Chamber Scanning Program: Syntax Table for the Compilation Phase of the Main Program," Digital Computer Lab., File No. 538; May 28, 1963.

[12] R. K. Rice and R. Narasimhan, "Bubble-Chamber Scanning Program: 1. LABEL, 2. SEARCH, Stage 1," Digital Computer Lab., File No. 542; June 10, 1963.

[13] R. Narasimhan and J. P. Fornango, "A Preprocessing Routine for Digitized Bubble-Chamber Pictures," Digital Computer Lab., File No. 558; July 22, 1963.

Oscilloscope Scanner Design

[14] C. P. Bates, K. Breeding and B. H. McCormick, "Scanner Digital Control," Digital Computer Lab. Rept. (in preparation).

Pattern Articulation Unit (PA U) Engineering

[15] S. R. Ray, "The Transfer Memory," Digital Computer Lab., Rept. No. 145; August 16, 1963.

[16] B. H. McCormick, "Specifications for Thin Film, Passive Element Microcircuit Modules," Digital Computer Lab., File No. 563; July 31, 1963.

[17] K. C. Smith and D. Hall, "Observations of the Operation of a 3-Bit Bubbling Register," Digital Computer Lab., File No. 482; August 31, 1962.

[18] K. C. Smith, "The Pattern Articulation Unit: Circuit Design of the Iterative Array," Digital Computer Lab. Rept. (in preparation).

Taxicrinic Unit (TU)

[19] K. Ibuki, "The Taxicrinic Unit of ILLIAC III: A Tentative Design," Digital Computer Lab. Rept. No. 150; August 16, 1963.

Arithmetic Unit (A U)

[20] S. Matsushita and B. H. McCormick, "Logical Design of the Main Arithmetic Unit of ILLIAC III," Digital Computer Lab. Rept. (in preparation).

Semiconductor Evaluation and Fast Circuit Design

[21] S. Yamada, "Cable Driver and Terminator Design," Digital Computer Lab., Rept. No. 146; August 21, 1963.

[22] S. Yamada, "Performance Characteristics of Fast Logic for ILLIAC III: Basic NAND and NOR Circuits," Digital Computer Lab., Rept. No. 152; September 18, 1963.

[23] S. Yamada, "Design of the Program-Controlled Semiconductor and Printed Circuit Board Test Console," Digital Computer Lab., Rept. No. 154; October 21, 1963.

Reprinted from *IEEE Trans. Electron. Comput.*, **EC–12,** No. 3, 1963, pp. 251–262

26

A Parallel Computer Organization and Mechanizations*

J. K. HAWKINS†, MEMBER, IEEE, AND C. J. MUNSEY†, MEMBER, IEEE

Summary—**This paper describes a type of parallel computer organization which can be regarded as lying at one extreme of a spectrum of possible degrees of parallelism. The organization is dominated by two characteristics, namely, one-bit storage per computational cell and single-level logic at each computational step. The organization is directed specifically toward spatial problems, but is demonstrated to be of a general-purpose nature. Mechanizations appropriate to this type of organization are described and some simple examples of spatial computing are presented.**

INTRODUCTION

THE LOGICAL properties, programming and potential applications of networks consisting of large parallel arrays of identical combinational and memory cells have received the attention of a number of investigators [1]–[9]. The motivation has been two-fold. First, a large need exists for systems which are capable of performing various types of image data processing. Since image data is naturally encountered in a parallel form and consists of large numbers of bits, it appears attractive intuitively to handle it subsequently in the same form by means of a parallel multiple-processor organization. Second, electronic microminiaturization work offers the promise of economical fabrication of planar arrays of useful circuits. Such fabrication is most economical when individual circuit units in the array are identical in internal structure and repeated in some uniform pattern.

A typical form of parallel computer organization is illustrated by the rectangular iterative array of Fig. 1. Computational cells are regarded as identical. Connections go to and come from all nearest neighbors. The internal logic and memory of each cell have been specified by various workers in a number of ways.

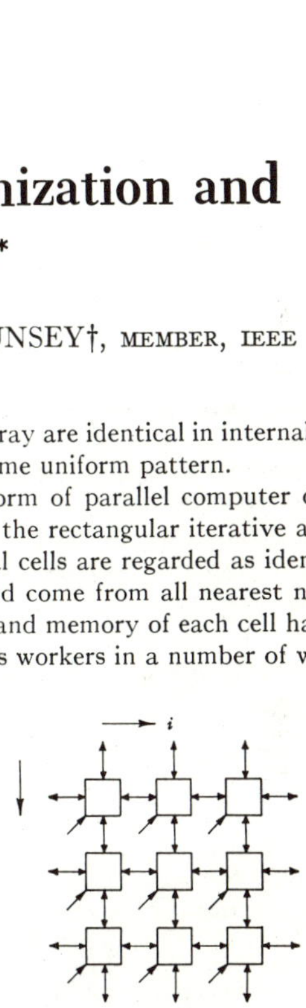

Fig. 1.

Previous investigators have almost universally assumed certain general properties for the cells making up the array. These properties include:

1) interconnections only with nearest neighbors
2) multistage combinational logic capabilities within each cell
3) more than one bit of storage.

* Received February 11, 1963.

† Aeronutronic Division, Ford Motor Company, Newport Beach, Calif.

The reasons for these assumptions are manifest. In terms of planar evaporated-circuit fabrication techniques, economy is served by restricting interconnections in such a way as to minimize crossovers. It also seems natural to build as much computational capacity into a cell as the fabrication technique will permit. Thus, incorporation of the logic corresponding to a full range of arithmetic commands appears as virtually the minimum acceptable level of computational capacity. In general, a number of memory bits in each cell ranging from a few to thousands has also been postulated. This seems in consonance with computational capacity.

It is the purpose of this paper to describe a somewhat different approach to the organization of parallel computers. While adhering to the general motivation behind such investigations, the authors considered three factors to be of such overriding importance as to warrant serious conceptual revisions. These factors are: 1) the number of bits per image which is practically useful to handle in many applications begins somewhere between 10^4 and 10^5 and rises rapidly to over 10^7, 2) the fabrication of an array of this number of individually complex active circuit units is still some years away and 3) some degradation of individual element performance can be readily tolerated in many image processing applications.

This paper therefore describes a parallel computer organization which, by deviating from usual concepts, opens up new approaches to hardware mechanizations. These have the general property of offering reasonable promise of achieving array sizes corresponding to image data in an economical manner. The organization makes this possible by sacrificing certain logical sophistication. A mechanization described below makes up for this drawback to some extent by increasing the flexibility of cell interconnections.

A Planar Computer Organization

Basic Specifications

Consider a computer organization in which the processing (arithmetic) section consists of two two-dimensional arrays, each of S binary cells, designated the input and output, respectively. Let the processor have the following properties (it will become apparent in the following section why this particular set of properties was chosen):

1) Interconnections occur only from input to output.
2) Each output cell receives inputs from N input cells with, in general, $N \ll S$, the number of cells in the array.
3) Each output cell has the same *pattern* of interconnections relative to its xy location in the array.
4) At each processing step, all output cells form the same combinational logic function with respect to their inputs.

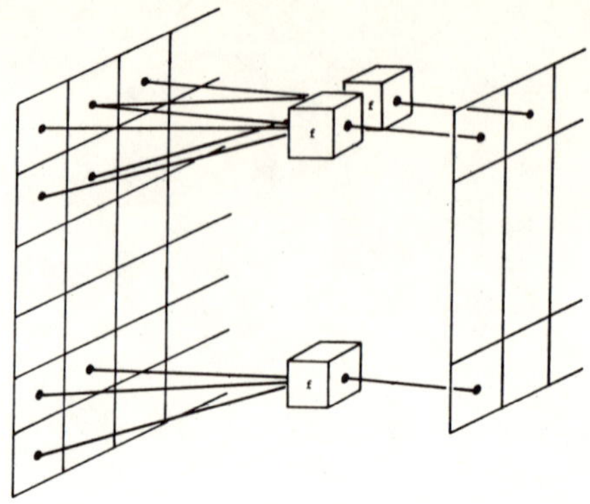

Fig. 2.

5) The logic functions which can be specified are limited, being the complements of linear input logic [10] functions.
6) The output can deliver its results to a memory and the input can receive arrays of bits from either the memory or an external input. The original two-dimensional ordering of bits within arrays is preserved throughout these transfers.

Some comments are in order on these specifications. The first four specifications can be represented as in Fig. 2, in which $N=3$ for simplicity. The label f is used to emphasize the fact that all cells perform the same logic function f at any given processing step. Not indicated in Fig. 2 is a constraint which has been implicitly lifted by the above specifications. Namely, no limit is imposed on N and, in particular, interconnections are not limited to near neighbors.

At each processing step, a *command* consists of two pieces of information (in addition to the address of the source of the input and the address at which the output is to be stored). These are: 1) the logic or truth table of the function f with respect to its input variables and 2) the *relative* locations of the input variables. An example is given in Fig. 3, in which f is the AND function $f=xyz$ for simplicity. In Fig. 3(b), the relative locations of x, y and z are given. An example of a single processing step is given in Fig. 4. When the function of Fig. 3 is applied to the input of Fig. 4(a),[1] the resulting output which is shown in Fig. 4(b) is given. It is left as an exercise for the reader to verify that the two locations containing 1's on the output are indeed the only ones at which the function f is satisfied.

[1] Edge effects enter to the extent that input variables may extend beyond the boundaries of S on the input field for those output bits located near the edge. In such cases the input is assumed to be identically 0 outside the region S.

x	y	z	f
0	0	0	0
0	0	1	0
0	1	0	0
0	1	1	0
1	0	0	0
1	0	1	0
1	1	0	0
1	1	1	1

or

$$f = AND(x, y, z) = x \cdot y \cdot z.$$

(a)

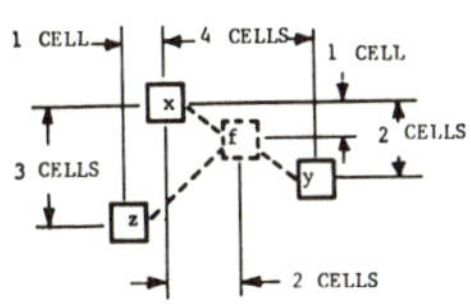

(b)

Fig. 3.

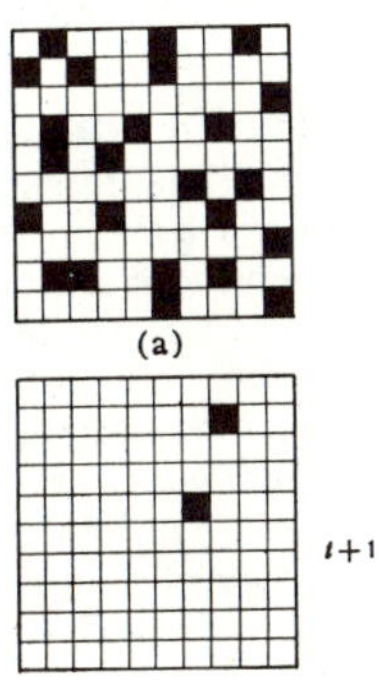

(b)

Fig. 4.

Linear Logic

The fifth specification can be stated in the following way:

$$f = -\operatorname{sgn}\left[\sum_{i=0}^{N} c_i x_i\right] \tag{1}$$

in which x_i are the input variables and c_i is any set of numbers. In (1), the values of the binary variables x_i and f are taken to be -1 and $+1$ rather than the usual 0 and 1. An identical expression for the latter case can be written in the form

$$f = \frac{1}{2}\left\{1 - \operatorname{sgn}\left[\sum_{i=0}^{N} c_i' x_i\right]\right\} \tag{2}$$

in which the values of the coefficients c_i and c_i' are related by a change of scale and translation.

Not all logic functions can be mechanized by a single function of the form of (1). Those functions which can be realized by (1) have been tabulated [11] for N up through six. However, any logic function whatever can be mechanized by an appropriate cascade of functions of the form of (1). This can readily be seen by noting, for example, that the NOR function is mechanized by letting $C_1 = C_2 = \cdots = C_N = +1$ and $C_0 = (N-1)$ for binary values -1 and $+1$ or $C_1 = C_2 = \cdots = C_N = +1$ and $C_0 = -\frac{1}{2}$ for binary values 0 and 1. In general, more sophisticated ways than simple NOR logic exist for mechanizing multilayer functions. A good example of such mechanizations for N up through four has been published [10].

Although the restriction of specifiable operations to linear input functions may appear serious, it compares favorably with single-level diode gate logic. For example, suppose input variables and their complements are available and either the function or its complement can be selected. The number of functions which can be mechanized in a single level of logic are given in Table I [11] for values of N, the number of input variables, through six.

Note that the formation of a multilevel logic function requires more than one program step. That is, the results of an operation appearing at the output and corresponding, for example, to the first logic level in a logic tree must be fed back (*e.g.*, via the memory) to the input in order that the second level can be formed and so on. While this implies that a programmer must pay attention to rather fine details of logic processing, it is felt that the processing power inherent in the large arrays which are made possible by this approach more than makes up for such an inconvenience. It is apparent that subroutines could be written for frequently used multilevel logic functions.

A difficulty arises when it is desired to mechanize a function in the form illustrated in Fig. 5. With the feed-through structure shown, it is necessary for the third array to receive inputs from both the first and second arrays simultaneously. A similar difficulty arises when it is desired to mechanize a structure without feed-through, but with more than one array serving as input to another, as in Fig. 6. This structure might correspond to a canonical NOR-NAND mechanization of a function in which each array in the second layer represents a NOR minterm.

These difficulties can be overcome in either of two ways. Since no restriction has been placed upon fan-in or near-neighbor connections, the input array of the basic processor can be made larger than the output array. If it is made three times as large, for example, then the three arrays 2, 3 and 4 of Fig. 6 can be accommodated simultaneously. With such an enlarged input array, if

TABLE I
NUMBER OF REALIZABLE FUNCTIONS

N	2^{2^N}	Linear Logic	AND or OR
2	16	14	14
3	256	104	48
4	65,536	1882	154
5	4,294,967,296	94,572	476
6	16×10^{18}	15,028,134	1446

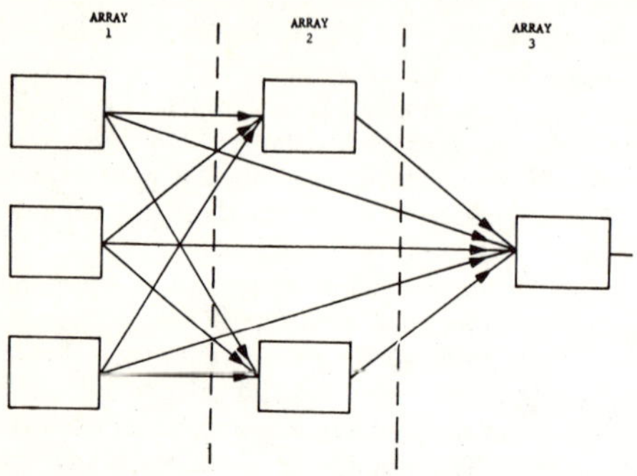

Fig. 5.

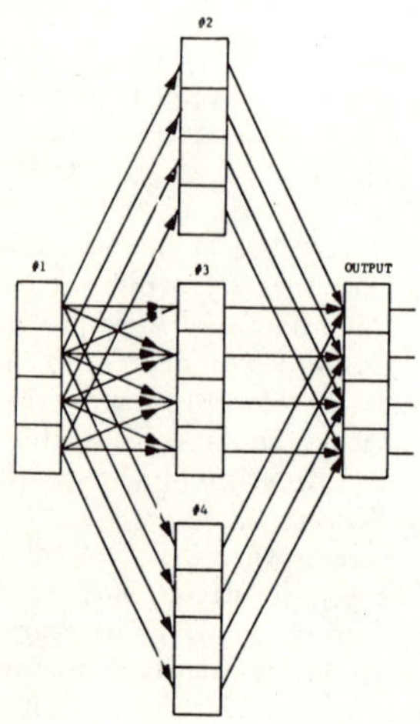

Fig. 6.

a simple 1:1 operation is desired (as illustrated in Fig. 2), then it is only necessary to avoid specifying function inputs from the unused portion of the input field. (It will be seen that this arrangement bears upon the problem of edge effects.)

There is another way out of the above difficulty, however, which is inherent in many mechanizations. As in most computing systems space can be traded for time, which is implied in the word "simultaneous" used above. Thus, many mechanizations inherently possess the property of storing the analog quantity $[\sum c_i x_i]$ in (1) before performing the decision operation corresponding to the "sgn" operator. If the storage time is long enough to accommodate several retrievals from memory, then multiple arrays can be presented at the input in sequence. At each presentation, only those c_i's corresponding to the particular array are nonzero. In this case (1) may be written

$$f = -\operatorname{sgn}\left[\sum_j \sum_i c_{ij} x_{ij}\right] \tag{3}$$

in which i refers, as before, to the variable and j to the time sequence of input arrays. For example, if the NOR of three variables is desired with x_1 on array 1, x_2 on array 2 and x_3 on array 3, the values of the c_{ij}'s may be tabulated as

$j(t)$ \ i	1	2	3
1	1	0	0
2	0	1	0
3	0	0	1

MECHANIZATIONS

Principles

The most salient feature of the computer organization postulated in the previous section is the huge number of interconnections which are involved in the processor. If S contains the number of bits compatible with high-resolution image data, even with N constrained to be the number of bits contained within relatively local regions (but more than nearest neighbors), the required number of interconnections can easily be on the order of 10^8 or 10^9. Making this number of connections is clearly impractical with conventional electronic techniques. This section describes one mechanization which accomplishes the required interconnection.

The high degree of parallelism and the repetitive nature of the logic suggests that some use may be made of optical techniques in mechanizing simple functions of the form of (1). Indeed, a simple optical system can be shown to produce a two-dimensional energy distribution which, at every xy coordinate, has a value corresponding to $[\sum c_i x_i]$ in (1).

A crude version of such an optical system is illustrated in Fig. 7. Let the input array represent binary values in the form of incoherent light intensity. Each distinguishable resolution element may therefore be regarded as one of the binary cells in the input array. Let a transparency, T, be placed between the input and output array. T is opaque everywhere except at certain locations corresponding to the *relative* locations of the input variables to the function being performed. Make the value of transmittance at these locations proportional to the coefficients c_i required to mechanize the function. Then, at every point on the output array, the light energy reaching that point is

$$\sum_{i=1}^{N} c_i x_i. \tag{4}$$

If the output field is also illuminated with a uniform energy proportional to c_0, then the index of summation in (4) can be taken from $i=0$ rather than $i=1$ and the quantity in brackets in (1) or (2) is thereby formed.

Note that the necessary sum for all elements in the array is formed simultaneously in parallel. No mechanical motion is involved other than placement of the transparency T.

The optical system of Fig. 7 can be looked at in a variety of ways. One is to regard it as a multiple pinhole camera, each transmittance region of T corresponding to a pinhole of selected aperture. The effect of the system is, therefore, simply to superimpose the input upon itself at a series of displaced locations determined by the geometry of the apertures in T.

The system may also be viewed from the fan-in, fan-out standpoint. For example, if the observer stands at P_1 on the output field, inputs (energy) are being received from all input elements within the dark-bordered region of the input. When standing at P_2, inputs are being received from the region surrounded by the dotted line. Because of the nature of light energy transmission, no interference between interconnections occurs at the transparency T and a large number of individual interconnections can thereby be made.

Finally, in order to complete the logic process specified by (1), the operation "$-$sgn" must be performed. This is, of course, the operation performed by transistors or other amplifying devices in conventional systems. By analogy, therefore, the output field must amplify the impinging light energy and must do so independently at each elemental area (or resolution element corresponding to a function value) on the field. For binary operation, the gain of the elemental amplifiers must be sufficient to cause the output to traverse the complete output range (from -1 to $+1$ or from 0 to 1) for the smallest change of input signal which can occur.

In general, the value of the smallest coefficient can be taken to be 1 and the input variable values as 0 and 1. The smallest input signal change is therefore 1. Generally, the maximum value of the input signal is limited in some way by the amplifying device. This maximum value is $\sum|c_i|$. Therefore, relative to the limit, the smallest input change is $1/\sum|c_i|$. The amplifier must make up for this effective attenuation and its minimum gain must therefore be $\sum|c_i|$. Table II lists the maximum value of this quantity as a function of the number of inputs, N, for linear input functions. There are, of course, many useful linear input functions which do not require this maximum sum of coefficients.

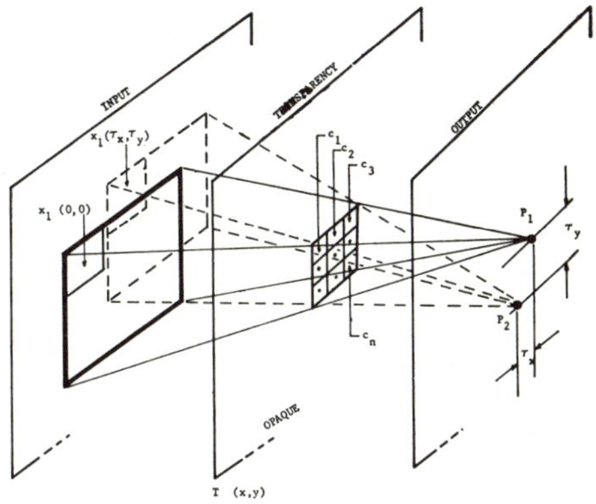

Fig. 7.

TABLE II
MAXIMUM COEFFICIENT SUMS

N	$\Sigma\|c_i\|$
2	3
3	5
4	9
5	17
6	35

Optical System Variants

It can be seen that the optical system described is identical in every respect to those employed in forming convolution integrals or in taking two-dimensional Fourier transforms [12], [13]. That is, optical systems have been shown to form an array of light intensities of the form

$$i(\alpha, \beta) = \int g(x, y)h(x + \alpha, y + \beta)dxdy. \tag{5}$$

For extracting spatial frequencies, g may be the input and h a two-dimensional transparency which varies, for example, as sine x (or sine r for radial frequencies). The technique described here simply treats (5) as a discrete rather than a continuous process.

It is worth noting that optical correlation has been widely used in studies of image processing applications. Generally, a nonlinear (binary) decision upon the output of the correlator is implicit in these approaches but not emphasized. Such a decision, of course, simply produces some linear input function of the input image. That is, we can always make the elemental area $dxdy$ in (5) as small as desired and regard the image value within this region as a binary variable. No loss in generality occurs since the values resulting from summation or integration processes can be made to approach one another as closely as desired by a sufficiently fine partitioning of the image.

A difficulty arises when some of the coefficients c_i

must be negative in order to mechanize the function. In fact, most of the functions of interest for image processing appear to be of this nature. The trouble results from the fact that, for incoherent optics, T cannot have negative transmittance values. It can, however, readily be overcome in a number of ways.

One technique is to employ coherent optics. By varying the thickness of T, the phase of light waves can be delayed or advanced relative to one another. If two signals of equal magnitude and opposite phase arrive at the output array, they cancel, producing the desired result. The effect is precisely that of inverting an electrical signal (*i.e.*, complementating a logical variable). The precision required in coherent optical systems and the difficulty of producing variable-thickness transparencies unfortunately make this solution unattractive.

The difficulty can also be overcome in incoherent optical systems by using both the input and its complement. This can be done either by doubling the size of the input array or by presenting first the input and then its complement in succession and taking advantage of some storage mechanism in the light-amplifying output array, as discussed in the previous section.

Since the values (light energies) of the input variables can only be positive, let

$$\begin{aligned} x_i^+ &= x_i \\ x_i^- &= 1 - x_i \\ c_i^+ &= c_i,\ c_i > 0;\ = 0,\ c_i \leq 0 \\ c_i^- &= -c_i,\ c_i < 0;\ = 0,\ c_i \geq 0. \end{aligned} \tag{6}$$

Then form

$$q = \sum_{i=1}^{N} c_i^+ x_i^+ + \sum_{i=1}^{N} c_i^- x_i^- \tag{7}$$

in which all quantities are positive. Substituting (6) in (7), the result is

$$q = \sum_{i=1}^{N} c_i x_i + \sum_{i=1}^{N} c_i^-. \tag{8}$$

The second term in (8) is positive. Therefore, let $c_0' = c_0 - \sum c_i^-$ and let $q' = q + c_0'$. Then

$$q' = \left[\sum_{i=0}^{N} c_i x_i \right],$$

as required by (1).

More sophisticated optical systems can be employed than the simple one illustrated in Fig. 7. In particular, greater resolution and less signal attenuation can be obtained with the simple-lens configuration illustrated in two dimensions in Fig. 8. The requirements of the system are, using geometric optics,

$$\frac{1}{d_2} + \frac{1}{d_1 + \Delta} = \frac{1}{f} \tag{9}$$

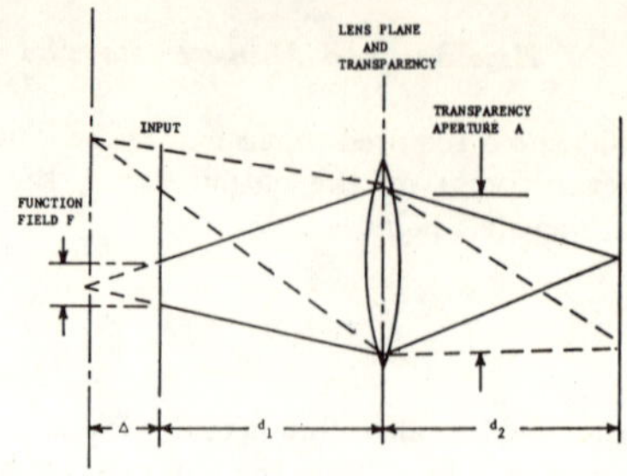

Fig. 8.

and, for 1:1 field sizes,

$$d_1 = d_2 = d. \tag{10}$$

The ratio of the size of the function field F on the input field to the size of the transparency aperture A is, therefore,

$$\frac{F}{A} = 2 - \frac{d}{f}. \tag{11}$$

The distance d can thus always be set to provide much greater light-gathering power by $A \gg F$.

Light Amplifiers

With $\sum c_i x_i$ formed everywhere on the output field, it remains to perform the operation "$-$ sgn" also everywhere on the output field in order to create the appropriate logical function f of (1) or (2) everywhere on the field. This calls for a high-gain decision amplifier having the following properties:

1) If $\sum c_i x_i$ is less than some value, the output should be 1.
2) If $\sum c_i x_i$ is greater than some higher value, the output should be 0 (or -1).
3) The output should be in the form of light energy in order to be useable as the input to a subsequent processing step.

The last requirement deserves some comment. Since memory storage intervenes between the output of one processing step and the input to a subsequent step, it is certainly possible to store results in non-optical form and convert them to optical form upon recall. In this case, however, the amplification burden is simply shifted from the processor itself to the complete output-memory-input loop. There is no loss in generality, therefore, if we ignore the particular form of memory storage and simply inquire into possible means for converting the field of $\sum c_i x_i$ (in light energy form) to a binary field of values, f, also in light energy form and suitable as an input field for a similar processor.

Amplifier properties (1), (2) and (3) above, therefore, simply specify a planar light-amplifying device. A number of potentially suitable devices exist. They include various types of image-intensifier tubes in which

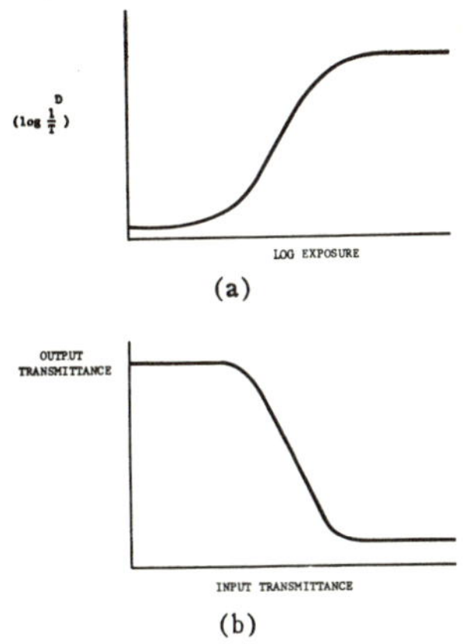

Fig. 9.

amplification is indeed achieved on a parallel basis. Television camera-display monitor combinations are also potential candidates. In this case, amplification is achieved electronically on a serial-scan basis, but the image spatial relationships are retained by appropriate scan synchronizing. An interesting and sometimes useful class of image amplifying devices is also represented by a variety of chemical or electrostatic reproduction processes. An example is ordinary high-contrast photographic film.

Photographic film has in fact been employed to simulate the computer system in some of the subsequent examples. It was selected because of its low cost and extremely high resolution compared to conventional electronics. Although impractical from a real-time standpoint, it provides a ready means of demonstrating the logical nature of this type of computer organization when applied to real image processing problems. Qualitatively, photographic film may be regarded as a light amplifier if the following sequence is considered: 1) expose film to input light L_1, 2) develop and 3) project a light source through the resulting transparency to produce light output L_o. As is well known, the ratio L_o/L_i can be extremely large and power amplification is therefore obtained. In effect, the "contrast" behavior of ordinary film is being employed to perform a decision operation. A typical exposure curve of film is plotted in Fig. 9(a) in the usual log-log manner. Exposure is given by

$$E = ItT \qquad (12)$$

with

I = intensity of source
t = time of exposure
T = transmittance of transparency through which I passes.

If we hold It constant and replot the exposure curve data on a linear scale (as the input-output characteristic of a transistor would be), the result is the transfer function of Fig. 9(b). Note that for a film sheet, therefore, each elemental region of the emulsion containing silver halide grains is acting as a small independent negative-gain light amplifier.

Examples of Image Computing

Parallel Addition

When one is devising a new form of computer organization, almost the first question propounded is how to carry out operations corresponding to basic arithmetic addition. It is seen that the system described should be universal in the sense that universal logical functions such as the NOR can be mechanized and memory in some form is present. Therefore, all arithmetic commands should be capable of being mechanized. To demonstrate this, a form of the add command is illustrated using basic NOR operators.

The logic for a binary sum of two numbers, A and B, is generally written in AND-OR form as

$$S_i = A_i\overline{B}_i\overline{C}_{i-1} + A_iB_i\overline{C}_{i-1} + A_i\overline{B}_iC_{i-1} + A_iB_iC_{i-1}$$

in which

S_i = ith bit of sum
A_i, B_i = ith bits of two numbers being added
C_{i-1} = carry from i-1 bit position.

The carry logic may be written as

$$C_i = A_iB_i + A_iC_{i-1} + B_iC_{i-1}.$$

Now write the above equations in terms of NOR logic. The carry bit will propagate (its correct value) with each successive logic operation. Therefore, putting all expressions in the NOR form $f = \overline{x+y}$, the following can be written:

$$C_1 = \overline{\overline{A}_1 + \overline{B}_1}$$

$$\overline{C}_2 = \overline{(\overline{\overline{A}_2 + \overline{B}_2}) + (\overline{\overline{A}_2 + \overline{C}_1}) + (\overline{\overline{B}_2 + \overline{C}_1})}$$

$$C_2 = (\overline{\overline{C}_2}), \text{ etc.} \qquad (13)$$

for $C_3 \cdots$. Clearly, these operations must be carried out successively since C_2 depends upon C_1, etc. The sum logic can be performed in parallel, however, when all carries have propagated:

$$\overline{S}_i = \overline{\overline{\overline{A}_i + B_i + C_i} + \overline{A_i + \overline{B}_i + C_i} + \overline{A_i + B_i + \overline{C}_i} + \overline{\overline{A}_i + \overline{B}_i + \overline{C}_i}}$$

$$S_i = (\overline{\overline{S}_i}).$$

To give a specific example, the *relative* locations must be identified on one or more two-dimensional fields of the variables A and B. The illustration chosen is a single field consisting of two columns of two-binary-bit numbers. The effective command (logic sequence) given is: *Add every number in the field to the number immediately above it.*

The binary number field is shown in Fig. 10(a). A blank is equivalent to a zero. Most of the field is zero

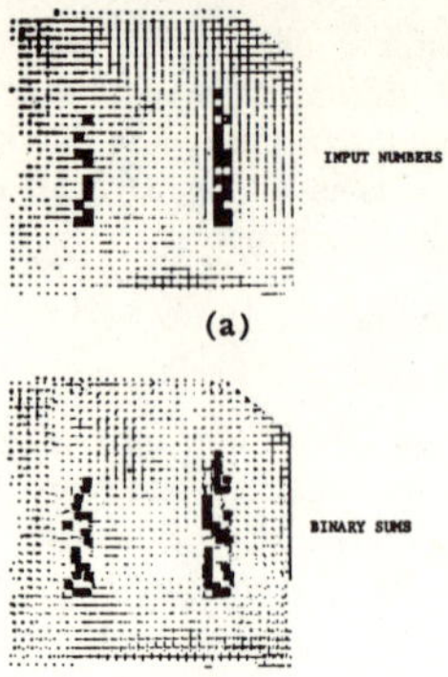

Fig. 10.

simply for ease of illustration. The numbers are two bits in length and the lower order bit is to the right.

We will not go through the tedium of reproducing all intervening steps, each corresponding to a particular logical term. It should be amply clear that by following the steps implied in (13) and (14) the over-all logical function corresponding to the sum can indeed be produced in this manner. The result is shown in Fig. 10(b).

Some consideration of the above example will convince the reader that this computer organization is not particularly appropriate for performing conventional arithmetic operations. That is, several field processing steps are required just to propagate carries one bit position (to the left in Fig. 10). Real-time feedback around the processing station (rather than via memory) would ameliorate this situation considerably since carries could then propagate at a rate limited only by the response time of the processor. Such a real-time feedback system has been tried using a television camera at the output field and a display monitor as part of the input field. In such a system, carries can indeed be made to propagate depending upon the values of other bits (input fields A and B) occupying other portions of the input field.

Angle Detection Logic

The real power of a highly parallel computer organization does not appear to lie in conventional numerical processing applications, however, but rather in image data processing. In the latter case, operations carried out within the system begin to merge into the analog area since discrete bit positions (and values) are not usually present in real image data. The possible configurations of input "bits" can, therefore, take on an almost continuous range of values of the quantity $\sum c_i x_i$ and the analog operation of (5) is perhaps a better representation of this portion of the system operation. The nonlinearity of the decision process is retained, however, so that the system takes on the nature of a complex linear-nonlinear filter network.

To illustrate this approach to image processing, a simple example of detecting acute angles in a field of geometrical shapes is presented. The input field is shown in Fig. 11. It is desired to provide a "yes" answer to all configurations containing an acute angle—black on white or white on black—and a "no" answer to all others. It would be expected, therefore, that a 1 (black dot) should appear at the locations of such acute angles in the field and a 0 (white) elsewhere. This is indeed the result of an appropriate process. However, as a visual aid, the black-dot "yes" outputs are converted into small circles as a final step in the process. The output of this step is shown in Fig. 12. When Fig. 12 and Fig. 11 are superimposed, the result is Fig. 13. Note that most acute angles are indeed correctly detected. There are some errors, notably of omission. Since the process was performed on photographic film under anything but optimum conditions, it is believed that these errors are due to dust, film and/or developing defects, fingerprints, etc. Another notable error occurs in the thin area connecting two otherwise separate triangles (center of each half-field of Fig. 13). This is due to the inability of the process to distinguish between thin lines and acute angles; a more sophisticated process would be required to make this distinction.

The processing steps in going from Fig. 11 to Fig. 12 can be described with reference to Fig. 14. Each box represents one step through the optical arithmetic processing station. Those labelled NOT are simple image polarity reversals. The NOR is a 1:1 (point-to-point) NOR operation on the two input fields. The circle generator converts a point input image to a small circle output image by means of a small donut-shaped transparency in the processing station. The functions f are specified by the transparency (pair) appearing in Fig. 15 and by the plot of Fig. 16. The transparency pair of Fig. 15(a) consists of a circular central area of positive transmittance and an annular area of negative transmittance (a separate transparency used with the negative of the input). Some consideration of this pair will convince the reader that the light-sum output vs the degree of an angle appearing across the transparency pair will vary roughly as the curve of Fig. 16 (θ defined by black). Two examples of acute angles (a black acute $<90°$ and black obtuse $>270°$) are illustrated in Fig. 15(b) and (c). If the decision amplifier threshold is set at the appropriate value (the exposure in the case of film), then only angles greater than a given angle will produce an output. The function f_1 is, therefore, repeated at two effective bias levels corresponding to $\theta_1(90°)$ and $\theta_2(270°)$, as indicated in Figs. 14 and 16. The transparency pair of Fig. 15 has long been known by photographers, incidentally, as the "unsharp mask technique" by means of which fine detail can be enhanced. It is also worth noting that the process is indeed quite angle sensitive since it succeeded in correctly rejecting a large number of 180° angles (straight edges) in the input field.

Fig. 11.

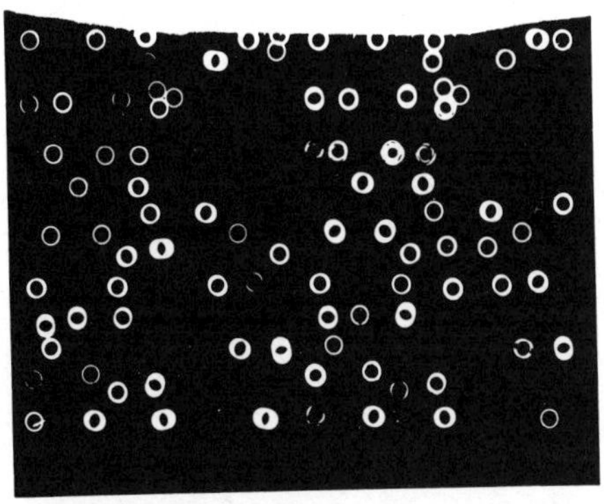

Fig. 12.

Fig. 13.

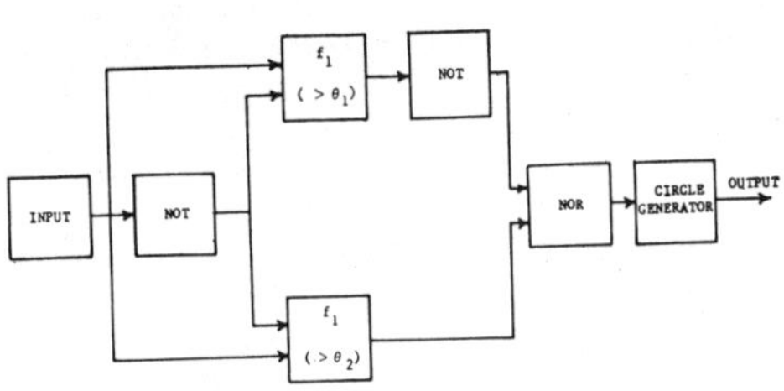

Fig. 14.

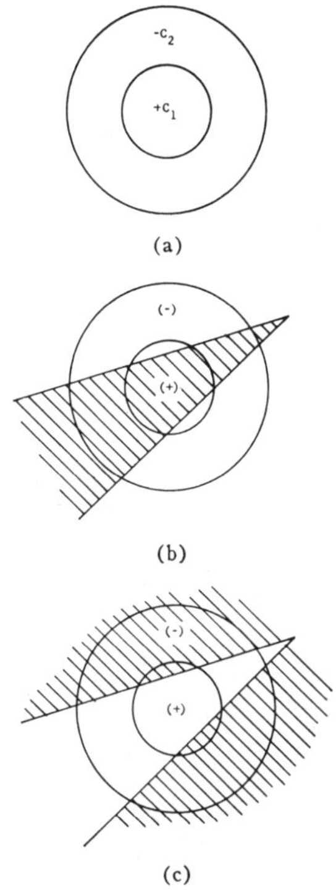

Fig. 15.

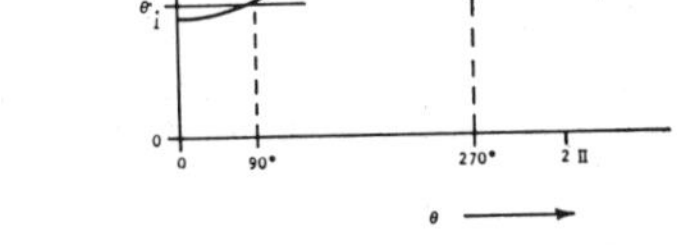

Fig. 16.

Object Detection in Real Images

In real image data, inputs seldom possess the ideal black-and-white binary values of Fig. 11 and the background is seldom so uncluttered. Therefore, experiments were conducted on a portion of a typical aerial photograph shown in Fig. 17. The object of the experiment was to find a processing sequence which would detect vehicles of standard passenger-car size. After some study of vehicle images and initial experimentation, it was concluded that a major fraction (more than 85 per cent) of the vehicles in this photograph could be detected by a straightforward process of testing (by a logical function) for appropriate line pairs of various polarities (black-white reversals) in about eight discrete ranges of angular direction. The complete process would, it is believed, have been able to take into account two-tone vehicles of both polarities as well as solid-color vehicles of both polarities. The complete process would, however, have been rather tedious to carry out without some automatic mechanization of the computer organization described in this paper. In order to test the approach, therefore, the logical sequence of the complete process was truncated and was then simulated by means of photographic film. This truncated version is described below.

Because of a certain overlap between functions performed at 90° relative rotation, the simplest possible process consisted of detecting vehicles aimed in orthogonal directions. Because of the predominance of roads, these directions were chosen in accordance with the arrows on Fig. 17. Attention was also restricted to dark vehicles. Processing may be listed in a verbal description as follows:

1) Long edges (corresponding to the length of vehicles) were detected by means of the transparency-pair function $f_1(\theta)$ of Fig. 18(a).

2) Pairs of 1) of the proper polarity for dark vehicles and separated by approximately the width of a vehicle were detected. This corresponds approximately to a spatially separated AND of $f_1(\theta)$ and $f_1(\theta+180°)$, according to the function pair of Fig. 18(b).

3) Short edges (corresponding to the width of vehicles) were detected by means of a transparency pair similar to f_1 but of different dimensions, as shown in Fig. 18(c). Call these $f_2(\theta)$.

4) Pairs of 3) of proper polarity and separated by approximately the length of a vehicle were detected. This corresponds approximately to a spatially separated AND of $f_2(\theta+90°)$ and $f_2(\theta+270°)$, according to the function pair of Fig. 18(d).

5) An AND of 2) and 4) was taken.

6) A circle generator was applied to 5).

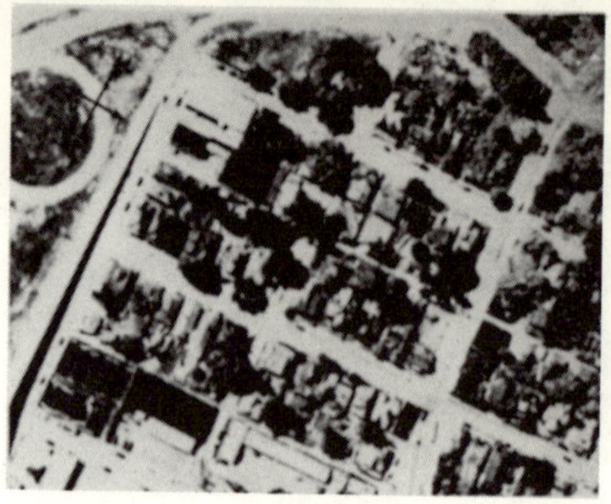

Fig. 17.

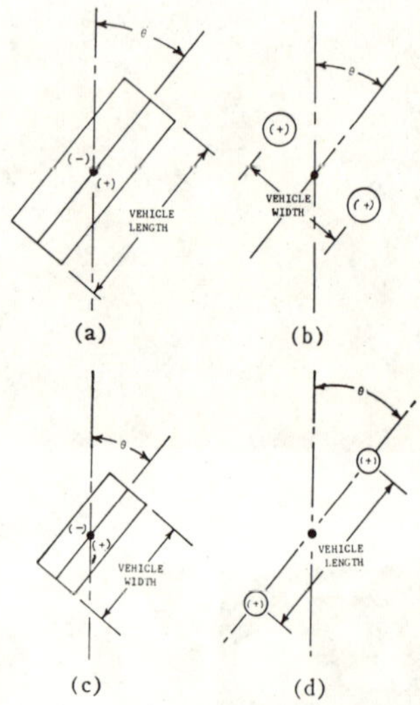

Fig. 18.

Some details of the processing inherent in amplifier reversals are left out of the above list for simplicity. The result of step 6) is shown in Fig. 19 and the superposition of Figs. 17 and 19 is given in Fig. 20. Some distortions due to the crude optical system employed have occurred at the lower left corner and caused the circle to miss the correctly detected vehicle in the lower right corner. Nevertheless, a significant proportion of the non-two-tone vehicles aimed in the two given directions have indeed been picked out by the process. In addition, a vast amount of background clutter corresponding to houses, trees, backyards, etc. has been correctly rejected.

It is worth noting that while the above does not represent the only possible solution to the stated problem, some simpler approaches have been tried and found to fail. For example, it appears that if vehicles are indeed small dark rectangular objects on a light field, then the

Fig. 19.

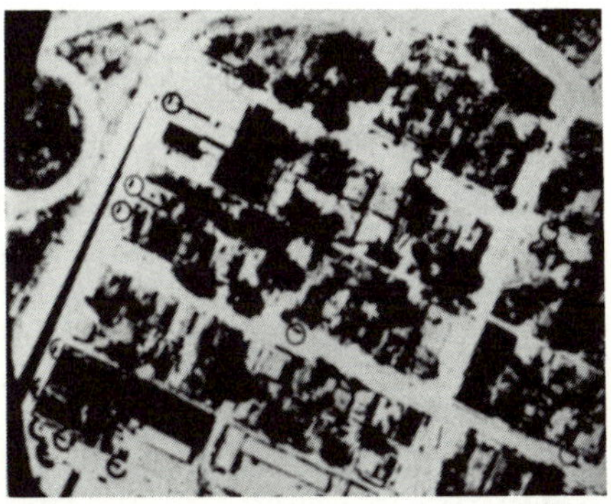

Fig. 20.

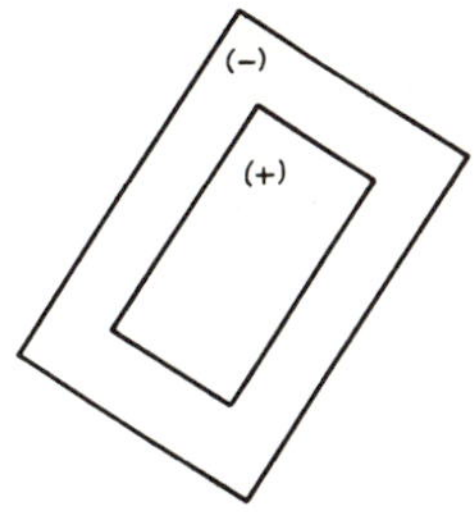

Fig. 21.

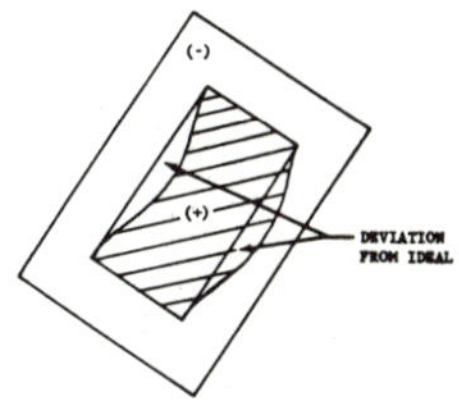

(a)

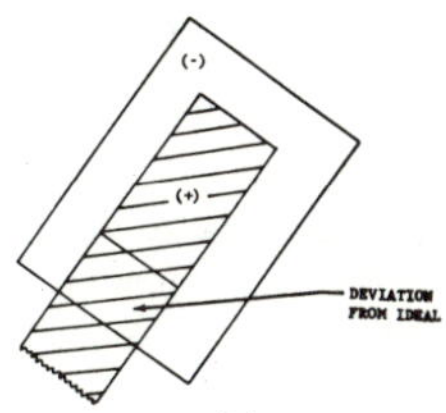

(b)

Fig. 22.

simple one-stage function pair of Fig. 21 should do a creditable job of detecting them. This is not the case, however, for the following reasons. The worst vehicle image fails to "match" the ideal of Fig. 21 by some percentage. Therefore, the decision level must be set somewhere below the total relative area of Fig. 21. Put another way, if elemental portions of the areas of Fig. 21 are regarded as individual bits, the appropriate logical function cannot be an AND but must be an m-out-of-N majority function with $m<N$ by some margin appropriate to the worst vehicle image. An example is given in Fig. 22(a). On the other hand, some non-vehicle objects in the photograph come close to matching the ideal rectangular image. Such an object is the dark shadow of approximately the width of a vehicle appearing about half way between dead center and the lower left corner of the picture. It possesses nearly square corners and deviates from a rectangular ideal only in that it extends too far, as shown in Fig. 22(b). If its deviation from the ideal is no greater than that of Fig. 22(a), the two cannot be distinguished in a single processing step. It appears that aspect-ratio discrimination, which comes so naturally to human beings, must be deliberately programmed into an image processing computer.

Comments and Conclusions

The organization of an extreme form of parallel computer has been described and its application to potentially practical image-processing tasks illustrated. Some mechanizations have been mentioned and two have been tested, but the possibilities are by no means exhausted. The reader will no doubt be able to generate several mechanizations of his own.

It may appear that the most difficult part of the mechanization is either the parallel light amplifier or the rather large image memory storage which may be required in practical processing applications. Some consideration of the available devices and media, however, lead the authors to believe that this is not so. Rather, attention is invited to the transparency which, in effect, specifies the logic function being performed at any instant of time.

Suppose that the computer consists of nothing but a single processing station and associated memory. The output field is given temporary storage properties so that forming a logic function of more than one field need not be a problem. At each processing step an image must be recalled from memory and presented at the input. The output must produce an amplified (binary) version of the resultant function field and deliver it to memory. These operations themselves are not trivial. However, between processing steps the transparency must be changed in readiness for the next operation. Since the transparency represents an image it should be handled in the manner of other images in the system. Thus, in memory there should be no distinction between images (data) and transparencies (commands). While it appears that components are readily available for performing high-speed memory and amplification operations on an image basis, the high-speed change of a transmissive image appears awkward at present.

The desirability of a stored-command (transmittance-image) system is, however, apparent from one final consideration. Command modification is an integral part of most modern computers. When changing a stored transmittance image is considered, it amounts to changing the coefficients c_i in a given linear input logic function from one value to another. But changing such coefficients is precisely the operation carried out in many simple learning-network processes and an algorithm (weight-change rule) exists for certain simple situations. Therefore, command modification in an image processing computer of the type described could be programmed to be equivalent to a learning process, carried out on a field of data in parallel—an occasionally powerful tool.

References

[1] S. H. Unger, "A computer oriented toward spatial problems," *Proc. Western Joint Computer Conf.*, May 6–8, 1958. pp. 234–239.

[2] E. J. McCluskey, Jr., "Iterative combinational switching networks—general design considerations," IRE Trans. on Electronic Computers, vol. EC-7, pp. 285–291; December, 1958.

[3] J. H. Holland, "Iterative circuit computers," *Proc. Western Joint Computer Conf.*, pp. 259–265; May 3–5, 1960. (This paper concerns iterative circuit computers constructed of microelectronic components and systems.)

[4] F. C. Hennie, "Iterative Arrays of Logical Circuits," John Wiley and Sons, Inc., New York, N. Y.; 1961.

[5] R. E. Griswold, "A Study of Iterative Switching Networks," Stanford Electronics Labs., Palo Alto, Calif., Tech. Rept. No. 098-2, ASTIA Doc. No. AD 274 349; January 15, 1962.

[6] W. Kilmer, "Iterative switching networks composed of combinational cells," IRE Trans. on Electronic Computers, vol. EC-11, pp. 123–131; April, 1962.

[7] B. H. McCormick and R. Narasimhan, "Design of a Pattern Recognition Computer with Application to the Automatic Scanning of Bubble Chamber Negatives," Digital Computer Lab., University of Illinois, Urbana, File No. 463; July, 1962.

[8] J. L. Divilbiss and B. H. McCormick, "Tentative Logical Realization of a Pattern Recognition Computer," Digital Computer Lab., University of Illinois, Urbana, File No. 403; 1961.

[9] D. L. Slotnick, W. C. Borck and R. C. McReynolds, "The Solomon computer," *Proc. Western Joint Computer Conf.*, pp. 87–107; 1962.

[10] R. C. Minnick, "Linear-input logic," IRE Trans. on Electronic Computers, vol. EC-10, pp. 6–16; March, 1961.

[11] R. A. Stafford, "A Magnetic Integrator for the Perceptron Program," Aeronutronic Div., Ford Motor Co., Newport Beach, Calif., ASTIA Doc. No. AD 264 227; September 29, 1961.

[12] H. C. Montgomery, "An optical harmonic analyzer," *Bell Sys. Tech. J.*, vol. 17, pp. 406–412; July, 1938.

[13] L. J. Cutrona, E. N. Leith, C. J. Palermo and L. J. Porcello, "Optical data processing and filtering systems," IRE Trans. on Information Theory, vol. IT-6, pp. 386–400; June, 1960.

Reprinted from IEEE TRANSACTIONS
ON *ELECTRONIC COMPUTERS*
Volume EC-12, Number 3, June, 1963

PRINTED IN THE U.S.A.

Appendix
Machine Intelligence

Editor's Comments on Paper 27

27 Turing: *Computing Machines and Machine Intelligence*

Because recognition machines can learn, can search and find objects, can describe these objects, and can summarize or compress information about these objects, recognition machines are often said to exhibit intelligence. It is therefore fitting to include in this volume the prophetic article by A. M. Turing, *Computing Machinery and Intelligence* [Tur].

In this article Turing constructs an eloquent rationale for the ultimate realization of thinking machines that compete effectively with human intelligence. This article also lays a foundation for philosophical discussions on the nature of thought and on the significance of machines in the evolution of cultures.

Reprinted from *The World of Mathematics,* Vol. 4, 1956, pp. 433–460

27

VOL. LIX. No. 236.] [October, 1950

MIND

A QUARTERLY REVIEW

OF

PSYCHOLOGY AND PHILOSOPHY

I.—COMPUTING MACHINERY AND INTELLIGENCE

BY A. M. TURING

1. *The Imitation Game.*

I PROPOSE to consider the question, 'Can machines think ?' This should begin with definitions of the meaning of the terms 'machine' and 'think'. The definitions might be framed so as to reflect so far as possible the normal use of the words, but this attitude is dangerous. If the meaning of the words 'machine' and 'think' are to be found by examining how they are commonly used it is difficult to escape the conclusion that the meaning and the answer to the question, 'Can machines think ?' is to be sought in a statistical survey such as a Gallup poll. But this is absurd. Instead of attempting such a definition I shall replace the question by another, which is closely related to it and is expressed in relatively unambiguous words.

The new form of the problem can be described in terms of a game which we call the 'imitation game'. It is played with three people, a man (A), a woman (B), and an interrogator (C) who may be of either sex. The interrogator stays in a room apart from the other two. The object of the game for the interrogator is to determine which of the other two is the man and which is the woman. He knows them by labels X and Y, and at the end of the game he says either 'X is A and Y is B' or 'X is B and Y is A'. The interrogator is allowed to put questions to A and B thus:

C: Will X please tell me the length of his or her hair ?

Now suppose X is actually A, then A must answer. It is A's

object in the game to try and cause C to make the wrong identification. His answer might therefore be

'My hair is shingled, and the longest strands are about nine inches long.'

In order that tones of voice may not help the interrogator the answers should be written, or better still, typewritten. The ideal arrangement is to have a teleprinter communicating between the two rooms. Alternatively the question and answers can be repeated by an intermediary. The object of the game for the third player (B) is to help the interrogator. The best strategy for her is probably to give truthful answers. She can add such things as 'I am the woman, don't listen to him!' to her answers, but it will avail nothing as the man can make similar remarks.

We now ask the question, 'What will happen when a machine takes the part of A in this game?' Will the interrogator decide wrongly as often when the game is played like this as he does when the game is played between a man and a woman? These questions replace our original, 'Can machines think?'

2. *Critique of the New Problem.*

As well as asking, 'What is the answer to this new form of the question', one may ask, 'Is this new question a worthy one to investigate?' This latter question we investigate without further ado, thereby cutting short an infinite regress.

The new problem has the advantage of drawing a fairly sharp line between the physical and the intellectual capacities of a man. No engineer or chemist claims to be able to produce a material which is indistinguishable from the human skin. It is possible that at some time this might be done, but even supposing this invention available we should feel there was little point in trying to make a 'thinking machine' more human by dressing it up in such artificial flesh. The form in which we have set the problem reflects this fact in the condition which prevents the interrogator from seeing or touching the other competitors, or hearing their voices. Some other advantages of the proposed criterion may be shown up by specimen questions and answers. Thus:

Q: Please write me a sonnet on the subject of the Forth Bridge.
A: Count me out on this one. I never could write poetry.
Q: Add 34957 to 70764
A: (Pause about 30 seconds and then give as answer) 105621.
Q: Do you play chess?
A: Yes.

Q : I have K at my K1, and no other pieces. You have only K at K6 and R at R1. It is your move. What do you play ?

A : (After a pause of 15 seconds) R-R8 mate.

The question and answer method seems to be suitable for introducing almost any one of the fields of human endeavour that we wish to include. We do not wish to penalise the machine for its inability to shine in beauty competitions, nor to penalise a man for losing in a race against an aeroplane. The conditions of our game make these disabilities irrelevant. The 'witnesses' can brag, if they consider it advisable, as much as they please about their charms, strength or heroism, but the interrogator cannot demand practical demonstrations.

The game may perhaps be criticised on the ground that the odds are weighted too heavily against the machine. If the man were to try and pretend to be the machine he would clearly make a very poor showing. He would be given away at once by slowness and inaccuracy in arithmetic. May not machines carry out something which ought to be described as thinking but which is very different from what a man does ? This objection is a very strong one, but at least we can say that if, nevertheless, a machine can be constructed to play the imitation game satisfactorily, we need not be troubled by this objection.

It might be urged that when playing the 'imitation game' the best strategy for the machine may possibly be something other than imitation of the behaviour of a man. This may be, but I think it is unlikely that there is any great effect of this kind. In any case there is no intention to investigate here the theory of the game, and it will be assumed that the best strategy is to try to provide answers that would naturally be given by a man.

3. *The Machines concerned in the Game.*

The question which we put in § 1 will not be quite definite until we have specified what we mean by the word 'machine'. It is natural that we should wish to permit every kind of engineering technique to be used in our machines. We also wish to allow the possibility than an engineer or team of engineers may construct a machine which works, but whose manner of operation cannot be satisfactorily described by its constructors because they have applied a method which is largely experimental. Finally, we wish to exclude from the machines men born in the usual manner. It is difficult to frame the definitions so as to satisfy these three conditions. One might for instance insist that the team of engineers should be all of one sex, but this would not really be satisfactory, for it is probably possible to rear a complete individual from a single cell of the skin (say) of a man. To do so would be a feat of biological technique deserving of the very highest praise, but we would not be inclined to regard it as a case of ' constructing a thinking machine '. This prompts us to abandon the requirement that every kind of technique should be permitted. We are the more ready to do so in view of the fact that the present interest in ' thinking machines ' has been aroused by a particular kind of machine, usually called an ' electronic computer ' or ' digital computer '. Following this suggestion we only permit digital computers to take part in our game.

This restriction appears at first sight to be a very drastic one. I shall attempt to show that it is not so in reality. To do this necessitates a short account of the nature and properties of these computers.

It may also be said that this identification of machines with digital computers, like our criterion for ' thinking ', will only be unsatisfactory if (contrary to my belief), it turns out that digital computers are unable to give a good showing in the game.

There are already a number of digital computers in working order, and it may be asked, ' Why not try the experiment straight away ? It would be easy to satisfy the conditions of the game. A number of interrogators could be used, and statistics compiled to show how often the right identification was given.' The short answer is that we are not asking whether all digital computers would do well in the game nor whether the computers at present available would do well, but whether there are imaginable computers which would do well. But this is only the short answer. We shall see this question in a different light later.

4. *Digital Computers.*

The idea behind digital computers may be explained by saying that these machines are intended to carry out any operations which could be done by a human computer. The human computer is supposed to be following fixed rules ; he has no authority to deviate from them in any detail. We may suppose that these rules are supplied in a book, which is altered whenever he is put on to a new job. He has also an unlimited supply of paper on which he does his calculations. He may also do his multiplications and additions on a ' desk machine ', but this is not important.

If we use the above explanation as a definition we shall be in danger of circularity of argument. We avoid this by giving an outline of the means by which the desired effect is achieved. A digital computer can usually be regarded as consisting of three parts :

(i) Store.
(ii) Executive unit.
(iii) Control.

The store is a store of information, and corresponds to the human computer's paper, whether this is the paper on which he does his calculations or that on which his book of rules is printed. In so far as the human computer does calculations in his head a part of the store will correspond to his memory.

The executive unit is the part which carries out the various individual operations involved in a calculation. What these individual operations are will vary from machine to machine. Usually fairly lengthy operations can be done such as ' Multiply 3540675445 by 7076345687 ' but in some machines only very simple ones such as ' Write down 0 ' are possible.

We have mentioned that the ' book of rules ' supplied to the computer is replaced in the machine by a part of the store. It is then called the ' table of instructions '. It is the duty of the control to see that these instructions are obeyed correctly and in the right order. The control is so constructed that this necessarily happens.

The information in the store is usually broken up into packets of moderately small size. In one machine, for instance, a packet might consist of ten decimal digits. Numbers are assigned to the parts of the store in which the various packets of information are stored, in some systematic manner. A typical instruction might say—

' Add the number stored in position 6809 to that in 4302 and put the result back into the latter storage position '.

Needless to say it would not occur in the machine expressed in English. It would more likely be coded in a form such as 6809430217. Here 17 says which of various possible operations is to be performed on the two numbers. In this case the operation is that described above, *viz.* ' Add the number. . . .' It will be noticed that the instruction takes up 10 digits and so forms one packet of information, very conveniently. The control will normally take the instructions to be obeyed in the order of the positions in which they are stored, but occasionally an instruction such as

'Now obey the instruction stored in position 5606, and continue from there'

may be encountered, or again

'If position 4505 contains 0 obey next the instruction stored in 6707, otherwise continue straight on.'

Instructions of these latter types are very important because they make it possible for a sequence of operations to be repeated over and over again until some condition is fulfilled, but in doing so to obey, not fresh instructions on each repetition, but the same ones over and over again. To take a domestic analogy. Suppose Mother wants Tommy to call at the cobbler's every morning on his way to school to see if her shoes are done, she can ask him afresh every morning. Alternatively she can stick up a notice once and for all in the hall which he will see when he leaves for school and which tells him to call for the shoes, and also to destroy the notice when he comes back if he has the shoes with him.

The reader must accept it as a fact that digital computers can be constructed, and indeed have been constructed, according to the principles we have described, and that they can in fact mimic the actions of a human computer very closely.

The book of rules which we have described our human computer as using is of course a convenient fiction. Actual human computers really remember what they have got to do. If one wants to make a machine mimic the behaviour of the human computer in some complex operation one has to ask him how it is done, and then translate the answer into the form of an instruction table. Constructing instruction tables is usually described as 'programming'. To 'programme a machine to carry out the operation A' means to put the appropriate instruction table into the machine so that it will do A.

An interesting variant on the idea of a digital computer is a 'digital computer with a random element'. These have instructions involving the throwing of a die or some equivalent electronic process; one such instruction might for instance be, 'Throw the die and put the resulting number into store 1000'. Sometimes such a machine is described as having free will (though I would not use this phrase myself). It is not normally possible to determine from observing a machine whether it has a random element, for a similar effect can be produced by such devices as making the choices depend on the digits of the decimal for π.

Most actual digital computers have only a finite store. There is no theoretical difficulty in the idea of a computer with an unlimited store. Of course only a finite part can have been used at any one time. Likewise only a finite amount can have been constructed, but we can imagine more and more being added as required. Such computers have special theoretical interest and will be called infinitive capacity computers.

The idea of a digital computer is an old one. Charles Babbage, Lucasian Professor of Mathematics at Cambridge from 1828 to 1839, planned such a machine, called the Analytical Engine, but it was never completed. Although Babbage had all the essential ideas, his machine was not at that time such a very attractive prospect. The speed which would have been available would be definitely faster than a human computer but something like 100 times slower than the Manchester machine, itself one of the slower of the modern machines. The storage was to be purely mechanical, using wheels and cards.

The fact that Babbage's Analytical Engine was to be entirely mechanical will help us to rid ourselves of a superstition. Importance is often attached to the fact that modern digital computers are electrical, and that the nervous system also is electrical. Since Babbage's machine was not electrical, and since all digital computers are in a sense equivalent, we see that this use of electricity cannot be of theoretical importance. Of course electricity usually comes in where fast signalling is concerned, so that it is not surprising that we find it in both these connections. In the nervous system chemical phenomena are at least as important as electrical. In certain computers the storage system is mainly acoustic. The feature of using electricity is thus seen to be only a very superficial similarity. If we wish to find such similarities we should look rather for mathematical analogies of function.

5. *Universality of Digital Computers.*

The digital computers considered in the last section may be classified amongst the 'discrete state machines'. These are the machines which move by sudden jumps or clicks from one quite definite state to another. These states are sufficiently different for the possibility of confusion between them to be ignored. Strictly speaking there are no such machines. Everything really moves continuously. But there are many kinds of machine which can profitably be *thought of* as being discrete state machines. For instance in considering the switches for a lighting system it is a convenient fiction that each switch must be definitely on or definitely off. There must be intermediate positions, but for most purposes we can forget about them. As an example of a discrete state machine we might consider a wheel which clicks round through 120° once a second, but may be stopped by a lever which can be operated from outside ; in addition a lamp is to light in one of the positions of the wheel. This machine could be described abstractly as follows. The internal state of the machine (which is described by the position of the wheel) may be q_1, q_2 or q_3. There is an input signal i_0 or i_1 (position of lever). The internal state at any moment is determined by the last state and input signal according to the table

		Last State		
		q_1	q_2	q_3
Input	i_0	q_2	q_3	q_1
	i_1	q_1	q_2	q_3

The output signals, the only externally visible indication of the internal state (the light) are described by the table

State	q_1	q_2	q_3
Output	o_0	o_0	o_1

This example is typical of discrete state machines. They can be described by such tables provided they have only a finite number of possible states.

It will seem that given the initial state of the machine and the input signals it is always possible to predict all future states. This is reminiscent of Laplace's view that from the complete state of the universe at one moment of time, as described by the positions and velocities of all particles, it should be possible to predict all future states. The prediction which we are considering is, however, rather nearer to practicability than that considered by Laplace. The system of the 'universe as a whole' is such that quite small errors in the initial conditions can have an overwhelming effect at a later time. The displacement of a single electron by a billionth of a centimetre at one moment might make the difference between a man being killed by an avalanche a year later, or escaping. It is an essential property of the mechanical systems which we have called 'discrete state machines' that this phenomenon does not occur. Even when we consider the actual physical machines instead of the idealised machines, reasonably accurate knowledge of the state at one moment yields reasonably accurate knowledge any number of steps later.

As we have mentioned, digital computers fall within the class of discrete state machines. But the number of states of which such a machine is capable is usually enormously large. For instance, the number for the machine now working at Manchester it about $2^{165,000}$, *i.e.* about $10^{50,000}$. Compare this with our example of the clicking wheel described above, which had three states. It is not difficult to see why the number of states should be so immense. The computer includes a store corresponding to the paper used by a human computer. It must be possible to write into the store any one of the combinations of symbols which might have been written on the paper. For simplicity suppose that only digits from 0 to 9 are used as symbols. Variations in handwriting are ignored. Suppose the computer is allowed 100 sheets of paper each containing 50 lines each with room for 30 digits. Then the number of states is $10^{100\times50\times30}$, *i.e.* $10^{150,000}$. This is about the number of states of three Manchester machines put together. The logarithm to the base two of the number of states is usually called the 'storage capacity' of the machine. Thus the Manchester machine has a storage capacity of about 165,000 and the wheel machine of our example about 1·6. If two machines are put together their capacities must be added to obtain the capacity of the resultant machine. This leads to the possibility of statements such as 'The Manchester machine contains 64 magnetic tracks each with a capacity of 2560, eight electronic tubes with a capacity of 1280. Miscellaneous storage amounts to about 300 making a total of 174,380.'

Given the table corresponding to a discrete state machine it is possible to predict what it will do. There is no reason why this calculation should not be carried out by means of a digital computer. Provided it could be carried out sufficiently quickly the digital computer could mimic the behaviour of any discrete state machine. The imitation game could then be played with the machine in question (as B) and the mimicking digital computer (as A) and the interrogator would be unable to distinguish them. Of course the digital computer must have an adequate storage capacity as well as working sufficiently fast. Moreover, it must be programmed afresh for each new machine which it is desired to mimic.

This special property of digital computers, that they can mimic any discrete state machine, is described by saying that they are *universal* machines. The existence of machines with this property has the important consequence that, considerations of speed apart, it is unnecessary to design various new machines to do various computing processes. They can all be done with one digital computer, suitably programmed for each case. It will be seen that as a consequence of this all digital computers are in a sense equivalent.

We may now consider again the point raised at the end of §3. It was suggested tentatively that the question, 'Can machines think ?' should be replaced by 'Are there imaginable digital computers which would do well in the imitation game ?' If we wish we can make this superficially more general and ask 'Are there discrete state machines which would do well ?' But in view of the universality property we see that either of these questions is equivalent to this, 'Let us fix our attention on one particular digital computer *C*. Is it true that by modifying this computer to have an adequate storage, suitably increasing its speed of action, and providing it with an appropriate programme, *C* can be made to play satisfactorily the part of A in the imitation game, the part of B being taken by a man ?'

6. *Contrary Views on the Main Question.*

We may now consider the ground to have been cleared and we are ready to proceed to the debate on our question, 'Can machines think ?' and the variant of it quoted at the end of the last section. We cannot altogether abandon the original form of the problem, for opinions will differ as to the appropriateness of the substitution and we must at least listen to what has to be said in this connexion.

It will simplify matters for the reader if I explain first my own beliefs in the matter. Consider first the more accurate form of the question. I believe that in about fifty years' time it will be possible to programme computers, with a storage capacity of about 10^9, to make them play the imitation game so well that an average interrogator will not have more than 70 per cent. chance of making the right identification after five minutes of questioning. The original question, 'Can machines think ?' I believe to be too meaningless to deserve discussion. Nevertheless I believe that at the end of the century the use of words and general educated opinion will have altered so much that one will be able to speak of machines thinking without expecting to be contradicted. I believe further that no useful purpose is served by concealing these beliefs. The popular view that scientists proceed inexorably from well-established fact to well-established fact, never being influenced by any unproved conjecture, is quite mistaken. Provided it is made clear which are proved facts and which are conjectures, no harm can result. Conjectures are of great importance since they suggest useful lines of research.

I now proceed to consider opinions opposed to my own.

(1) *The Theological Objection.* Thinking is a function of man's immortal soul. God has given an immortal soul to every man and woman, but not to any other animal or to machines. Hence no animal or machine can think.

I am unable to accept any part of this, but will attempt to reply in theological terms. I should find the argument more convincing if animals were classed with men, for there is a greater difference, to my mind, between the typical animate and the inanimate than there is between man and the other animals. The arbitrary character of the orthodox view becomes clearer if we consider how it might appear to a member of some other religious community. How do Christians regard the Moslem view that women have no souls? But let us leave this point aside and return to the main argument. It appears to me that the argument quoted above implies a serious restriction of the omnipotence of the Almighty. It is admitted that there are certain things that He cannot do such as making one equal to two, but should we not believe that He has freedom to confer a soul on an elephant if He sees fit? We might expect that He would only exercise this power in conjunction with a mutation which provided the elephant with an appropriately improved brain to minister to the needs of this soul. An argument of exactly similar form may be made for the case of machines. It may seem different because it is more difficult to "swallow". But this really only means that we think it would be less likely that He would consider the circumstances suitable for conferring a soul. The circumstances in question are discussed in the rest of this paper. In attempting to construct such machines we should not be irreverently usurping His power of creating souls, any more than we are in the procreation of children: rather we are, in either case, instruments of His will providing mansions for the souls that He creates.

However, this is mere speculation. I am not very impressed with theological arguments whatever they may be used to support. Such arguments have often been found unsatisfactory in the past. In the time of Galileo it was argued that the texts, "And the sun stood still . . . and hasted not to go down about a whole day" (Joshua x. 13) and "He laid the foundations of the earth,

[1] Possibly this view is heretical. St. Thomas Aquinas (*Summa Theologica*, quoted by Bertrand Russell, p. 480) states that God cannot make a man to have no soul. But this may not be a real restriction on His powers, but only a result of the fact that men's souls are immortal, and therefore indestructible.

that it should not move at any time " (Psalm cv. 5) were an adequate refutation of the Copernican theory. With our present knowledge such an argument appears futile. When that knowledge was not available it made a quite different impression.

(2) *The 'Heads in the Sand' Objection.* " The consequences of machines thinking would be too dreadful. Let us hope and believe that they cannot do so."

This argument is seldom expressed quite so openly as in the form above. But it affects most of us who think about it at all. We like to believe that Man is in some subtle way superior to the rest of creation. It is best if he can be shown to be *necessarily* superior, for then there is no danger of him losing his commanding position. The popularity of the theological argument is clearly connected with this feeling. It is likely to be quite strong in intellectual people, since they value the power of thinking more highly than others, and are more inclined to base their belief in the superiority of Man on this power.

I do not think that this argument is sufficiently substantial to require refutation. Consolation would be more appropriate : perhaps this should be sought in the transmigration of souls.

(3) *The Mathematical Objection.* There are a number of results of mathematical logic which can be used to show that there are limitations to the powers of discrete-state machines. The best known of these results is known as Gödel's theorem,[1] and shows that in any sufficiently powerful logical system statements can be formulated which can neither be proved nor disproved within the system, unless possibly the system itself is inconsistent. There are other, in some respects similar, results due to *Church, Kleene, Rosser,* and *Turing.* The latter result is the most convenient to consider, since it refers directly to machines, whereas the others can only be used in a comparatively indirect argument : for instance if Gödel's theorem is to be used we need in addition to have some means of describing logical systems in terms of machines, and machines in terms of logical systems. The result in question refers to a type of machine which is essentially a digital computer with an infinite capacity. It states that there are certain things that such a machine cannot do. If it is rigged up to give answers to questions as in the imitation game, there will be some questions to which it will either give a wrong answer, or fail to give an answer at all however much time is allowed for a reply. There may, of course, be many such questions, and questions which cannot be answered by one machine may be satisfactorily

[1] Author's names in italics refer to the Bibliography.

answered by another. We are of course supposing for the present that the questions are of the kind to which an answer ' Yes ' or ' No ' is appropriate, rather than questions such as ' What do you think of Picasso ? ' The questions that we know the machines must fail on are of this type, " Consider the machine specified as follows. . . . Will this machine ever answer ' Yes ' to any question ? " The dots are to be replaced by a description of some machine in a standard form, which could be something like that used in § 5. When the machine described bears a certain comparatively simple relation to the machine which is under interrogation, it can be shown that the answer is either wrong or not forthcoming. This is the mathematical result : it is argued that it proves a disability of machines to which the human intellect is not subject.

The short answer to this argument is that although it is established that there are limitations to the powers of any particular machine, it has only been stated, without any sort of proof, that no such limitations apply to the human intellect. But I do not think this view can be dismissed quite so lightly. Whenever one of these machines is asked the appropriate critical question, and gives a definite answer, we know that this answer must be wrong, and this gives us a certain feeling of superiority. Is this feeling illusory ? It is no doubt quite genuine, but I do not think too much importance should be attached to it. We too often give wrong answers to questions ourselves to be justified in being very pleased at such evidence of fallibility on the part of the machines. Further, our superiority can only be felt on such an occasion in relation to the one machine over which we have scored our petty triumph. There would be no question of triumphing simultaneously over *all* machines. In short, then, there might be men cleverer than any given machine, but then again there might be other machines cleverer again, and so on.

Those who hold to the mathematical argument would, I think, mostly be willing to accept the imitation game as a basis for discussion. Those who believe in the two previous objections would probably not be interested in any criteria.

(4) *The Argument from Consciousness.* This argument is very well expressed in *Professor Jefferson's* Lister Oration for 1949, from which I quote. " Not until a machine can write a sonnet or compose a concerto because of thoughts and emotions felt, and not by the chance fall of symbols, could we agree that machine equals brain—that is, not only write it but know that it had written it. No mechanism could feel (and not merely

artificially signal, an easy contrivance) pleasure at its successes, grief when its valves fuse, be warmed by flattery, be made miserable by its mistakes, be charmed by sex, be angry or depressed when it cannot get what it wants."

This argument appears to be a denial of the validity of our test. According to the most extreme form of this view the only way by which one could be sure that a machine thinks is to *be* the machine and to feel oneself thinking. One could then describe these feelings to the world, but of course no one would be justified in taking any notice. Likewise according to this view the only way to know that a *man* thinks is to be that particular man. It is in fact the solipsist point of view. It may be the most logical view to hold but it makes communication of ideas difficult. A is liable to believe 'A thinks but B does not' whilst B believes 'B thinks but A does not'. Instead of arguing continually over this point it is usual to have the polite convention that everyone thinks.

I am sure that Professor Jefferson does not wish to adopt the extreme and solipsist point of view. Probably he would be quite willing to accept the imitation game as a test. The game (with the player B omitted) is frequently used in practice under the name of *viva voce* to discover whether some one really understands something or has 'learnt it parrot fashion'. Let us listen in to a part of such a *viva voce*:

Interrogator: In the first line of your sonnet which reads 'Shall I compare thee to a summer's day', would not 'a spring day' do as well or better?

Witness: It wouldn't scan.

Interrogator: How about 'a winter's day' That would scan all right.

Witness: Yes, but nobody wants to be compared to a winter's day.

Interrogator: Would you say Mr. Pickwick reminded you of Christmas?

Witness: In a way.

Interrogator: Yet Christmas is a winter's day, and I do not think Mr. Pickwick would mind the comparison.

Witness: I don't think you're serious. By a winter's day one means a typical winter's day, rather than a special one like Christmas.

And so on. What would Professor Jefferson say if the sonnet-writing machine was able to answer like this in the *viva voce*? I do not know whether he would regard the machine as 'merely artificially signalling ' these answers, but if the answers were as satisfactory and sustained as in the above passage I do not think he would describe it as 'an easy contrivance '. This phrase is, I think, intended to cover such devices as the inclusion in the machine of a record of someone reading a sonnet, with appropriate switching to turn it on from time to time.

In short then, I think that most of those who support the argument from consciousness could be persuaded to abandon it rather than be forced into the solipsist position. They will then probably be willing to accept our test.

I do not wish to give the impression that I think there is no mystery about consciousness. There is, for instance, something of a paradox connected with any attempt to localise it. But I do not think these mysteries necessarily need to be solved before we can answer the question with which we are concerned in this paper.

(5) *Arguments from Various Disabilities.* These arguments take the form, " I grant you that you can make machines do all the things you have mentioned but you will never be able to make one to do X ". Numerous features X are suggested in this connexion. I offer a selection :

Be kind, resourceful, beautiful, friendly (p. 448), have initiative, have a sense of humour, tell right from wrong, make mistakes (p. 448), fall in love, enjoy strawberries and cream (p. 448), make some one fall in love with it, learn from experience (pp. 456 f.), use words properly, be the subject of its own thought (p. 449), have as much diversity of behaviour as a man, do something really new (p. 450). (Some of these disabilities are given special consideration as indicated by the page numbers.)

No support is usually offered for these statements. I believe they are mostly founded on the principle of scientific induction. A man has seen thousands of machines in his lifetime. From what he sees of them he draws a number of general conclusions. They are ugly, each is designed for a very limited purpose, when required for a minutely different purpose they are useless, the variety of behaviour of any one of them is very small, etc., etc. Naturally he concludes that these are necessary properties of machines in general. Many of these limitations are associated with the very small storage capacity of most machines. (I am assuming that the idea of storage capacity is extended in some way to cover machines other than discrete-state machines.

The exact definition does not matter as no mathematical accuracy is claimed in the present discussion.) A few years ago, when very little had been heard of digital computers, it was possible to elicit much incredulity concerning them, if one mentioned their properties without describing their construction. That was presumably due to a similar application of the principle of scientific induction. These applications of the principle are of course largely unconscious. When a burnt child fears the fire and shows that he fears it by avoiding it, I should say that he was applying scientific induction. (I could of course also describe his behaviour in many other ways.) The works and customs of mankind do not seem to be very suitable material to which to apply scientific induction. A very large part of space-time must be investigated, if reliable results are to be obtained. Otherwise we may (as most English children do) decide that everybody speaks English, and that it is silly to learn French.

There are, however, special remarks to be made about many of the disabilities that have been mentioned. The inability to enjoy strawberries and cream may have struck the reader as frivolous. Possibly a machine might be made to enjoy this delicious dish, but any attempt to make one do so would be idiotic. What is important about this disability is that it contributes to some of the other disabilities, *e.g.* to the difficulty of the same kind of friendliness occurring between man and machine as between white man and white man, or between black man and black man.

The claim that " machines cannot make mistakes " seems a curious one. One is tempted to retort, " Are they any the worse for that ? " But let us adopt a more sympathetic attitude, and try to see what is really meant. I think this criticism can be explained in terms of the imitation game. It is claimed that the interrogator could distinguish the machine from the man simply by setting them a number of problems in arithmetic. The machine would be unmasked because of its deadly accuracy. The reply to this is simple. The machine (programmed for playing the game) would not attempt to give the *right* answers to the arithmetic problems. It would deliberately introduce mistakes in a manner calculated to confuse the interrogator. A mechanical fault would probably show itself through an unsuitable decision as to what sort of a mistake to make in the arithmetic. Even this interpretation of the criticism is not sufficiently sympathetic. But we cannot afford the space to go into it much further. It seems to me that this criticism depends on a confusion between two kinds of mistake. We may call them 'errors of functioning' and 'errors of conclusion'. Errors of functioning are due to some mechanical or electrical fault which causes the machine to behave otherwise than it was designed to do. In philosophical discussions one likes to ignore the possibility of such errors; one is therefore discussing 'abstract machines'. These abstract machines are mathematical fictions rather than physical objects. By definition they are incapable of errors of functioning. In this sense we can truly say that 'machines can never make mistakes'. Errors of conclusion can only arise when some meaning is attached to the output signals from the machine. The machine might, for instance, type out mathematical equations, or sentences in English. When a false proposition is typed we say that the machine has committed an error of conclusion. There is clearly no reason at all for saying that a machine cannot make this kind of mistake. It might do nothing but type out repeatedly '$0 = 1$'. To take a less perverse example, it might have some method for drawing conclusions by scientific induction. We must expect such a method to lead occasionally to erroneous results.

The claim that a machine cannot be the subject of its own thought can of course only be answered if it can be shown that the machine has *some* thought with *some* subject matter. Nevertheless, 'the subject matter of a machine's operations' does seem to mean something, at least to the people who deal with it. If, for instance, the machine was trying to find a solution of the equation $x^2 - 40x - 11 = 0$ one would be tempted to describe this equation as part of the machine's subject matter at that moment. In this sort of sense a machine undoubtedly can be its own subject matter. It may be used to help in making up its own programmes, or to predict the effect of alterations in its own structure. By observing the results of its own behaviour it can modify its own programmes so as to achieve some purpose more effectively. These are possibilities of the near future, rather than Utopian dreams.

The criticism that a machine cannot have much diversity of behaviour is just a way of saying that it cannot have much storage capacity. Until fairly recently a storage capacity of even a thousand digits was very rare.

The criticisms that we are considering here are often disguised forms of the argument from consciousness. Usually if one maintains that a machine *can* do one of these things, and describes the kind of method that the machine could use, one will not make

29

much of an impression. It is thought that the method (whatever it may be, for it must be mechanical) is really rather base. Compare the parenthesis in Jefferson's statement quoted on p. 21.

(6) *Lady Lovelace's Objection.* Our most detailed information of Babbage's Analytical Engine comes from a memoir by *Lady Lovelace.* In it she states, "The Analytical Engine has no pretensions to *originate* anything. It can do *whatever we know how to order it* to perform" (her italics). This statement is quoted by *Hartree* (p. 70) who adds : "This does not imply that it may not be possible to construct electronic equipment which will 'think for itself', or in which, in biological terms, one could set up a conditioned reflex, which would serve as a basis for 'learning'. Whether this is possible in principle or not is a stimulating and exciting question, suggested by some of these recent developments. But it did not seem that the machines constructed or projected at the time had this property".

I am in thorough agreement with Hartree over this. It will be noticed that he does not assert that the machines in question had not got the property, but rather that the evidence available to Lady Lovelace did not encourage her to believe that they had it. It is quite possible that the machines in question had in a sense got this property. For suppose that some discrete-state machine has the property. The Analytical Engine was a universal digital computer, so that, if its storage capacity and speed were adequate, it could by suitable programming be made to mimic the machine in question. Probably this argument did not occur to the Countess or to Babbage. In any case there was no obligation on them to claim all that could be claimed.

This whole question will be considered again under the heading of learning machines.

A variant of Lady Lovelace's objection states that a machine can 'never do anything really new'. This may be parried for a moment with the saw, 'There is nothing new under the sun'. Who can be certain that 'original work' that he has done was not simply the growth of the seed planted in him by teaching, or the effect of following well-known general principles. A better variant of the objection says that a machine can never 'take us by surprise'. This statement is a more direct challenge and can be met directly. Machines take me by surprise with great frequency. This is largely because I do not do sufficient calculation to decide what to expect them to do, or rather because, although I do a calculation, I do it in a hurried, slipshod fashion, taking risks. Perhaps I say to myself, 'I suppose the voltage here ought to be the same as there : anyway let's assume it is'

Naturally I am often wrong, and the result is a surprise for me for by the time the experiment is done these assumptions have been forgotten. These admissions lay me open to lectures on the subject of my vicious ways, but do not throw any doubt on my credibility when I testify to the surprises I experience.

I do not expect this reply to silence my critic. He will probably say that such surprises are due to some creative mental act on my part, and reflect no credit on the machine. This leads us back to the argument from consciousness, and far from the idea of surprise. It is a line of argument we must consider closed, but it is perhaps worth remarking that the appreciation of something as surprising requires as much of a 'creative mental act' whether the surprising event originates from a man, a book, a machine or anything else.

The view that machines cannot give rise to surprises is due, I believe, to a fallacy to which philosophers and mathematicians are particularly subject. This is the assumption that as soon as a fact is presented to a mind all consequences of that fact spring into the mind simultaneously with it. It is a very useful assumption under many circumstances, but one too easily forgets that it is false. A natural consequence of doing so is that one then assumes that there is no virtue in the mere working out of consequences from data and general principles.

(7) *Argument from Continuity in the Nervous System.* The nervous system is certainly not a discrete-state machine. A small error in the information about the size of a nervous impulse impinging on a neuron, may make a large difference to the size of the outgoing impulse. It may be argued that, this being so, one cannot expect to be able to mimic the behaviour of the nervous system with a discrete-state system.

It is true that a discrete-state machine must be different from a continuous machine. But if we adhere to the conditions of the imitation game, the interrogator will not be able to take any advantage of this difference. The situation can be made clearer if we consider some other simpler continuous machine. A differential analyser will do very well. (A differential analyser is a certain kind of machine not of the discrete-state type used for some kinds of calculation.) Some of these provide their answers in a typed form, and so are suitable for taking part in the game. It would not be possible for a digital computer to predict exactly what answers the differential analyser would give to a problem, but it would be quite capable of giving the right sort of answer. For instance, if asked to give the value of π (actually about 3·1416) it would be reasonable to choose at random between the values 3·12, 3·13, 3·14, 3·15, 3·16 with the probabilities of 0·05, 0·15, 0·55, 0·19, 0·06 (say). Under these circumstances it would be very difficult for the interrogator to distinguish the differential analyser from the digital computer.

(8) *The Argument from Informality of Behaviour.* It is not possible to produce a set of rules purporting to describe what a man should do in every conceivable set of circumstances. One might for instance have a rule that one is to stop when one sees a red traffic light, and to go if one sees a green one, but what if by some fault both appear together ? One may perhaps decide that it is safest to stop. But some further difficulty may well arise from this decision later. To attempt to provide rules of conduct to cover every eventuality, even those arising from traffic lights, appears to be impossible. With all this I agree.

From this it is argued that we cannot be machines. I shall try to reproduce the argument, but I fear I shall hardly do it justice. It seems to run something like this. 'If each man had a definite set of rules of conduct by which he regulated his life he would be no better than a machine. But there are no such rules, so men cannot be machines.' The undistributed middle is glaring. I do not think the argument is ever put quite like this, but I believe this is the argument used nevertheless. There may however be a certain confusion between 'rules of conduct' and 'laws of behaviour' to cloud the issue. By 'rules of conduct' I mean precepts such as 'Stop if you see red lights', on which one can act, and of which one can be conscious. By 'laws of behaviour' I mean laws of nature as applied to a man's body such as 'if you pinch him he will squeak'. If we substitute 'laws of behaviour which regulate his life' for 'laws of conduct by which he regulates his life' in the argument quoted the undistributed middle is no longer insuperable. For we believe that it is not only true that being regulated by laws of behaviour implies being some sort of machine (though not necessarily a discrete-state machine), but that conversely being such a machine implies being regulated by such laws. However, we cannot so easily convince ourselves of the absence of complete laws of behaviour as of complete rules of conduct. The only way we know of for finding such laws is scientific observation, and we certainly know of no circumstances under which we could say, 'We have searched enough. There are no such laws.'

We can demonstrate more forcibly that any such statement would be unjustified. For suppose we could be sure of finding such laws if they existed. Then given a discrete-state machine it should certainly be possible to discover by observation sufficent about it to predict its future behaviour, and this within a reasonable time, say a thousand years. But this does not seem to be the case. I have set up on the Manchester computer a small programme using only 1000 units of storage, whereby the machine supplied with one sixteen figure number replies with another within two seconds. I would defy anyone to learn from these replies sufficient about the programme to be able to predict any replies to untried values.

(9) *The Argument from Extra-Sensory Perception.* I assume that the reader is familiar with the idea of extra-sensory perception, and the meaning of the four items of it, *viz.* telepathy, clairvoyance, precognition and psycho-kinesis. These disturbing phenomena seem to deny all our usual scientific ideas. How we should like to discredit them! Unfortunately the statistical evidence, at least for telepathy, is overwhelming. It is very difficult to rearrange one's ideas so as to fit these new facts in. Once one has accepted them it does not seem a very big step to believe in ghosts and bogies. The idea that our bodies move simply according to the known laws of physics, together with some others not yet discovered but somewhat similar, would be one of the first to go.

This argument is to my mind quite a strong one. One can say in reply that many scientific theories seem to remain workable in practice, in spite of clashing with E.S.P.; that in fact one can get along very nicely if one forgets about it. This is rather cold comfort, and one fears that thinking is just the kind of phenomenon where E.S.P. may be especially relevant.

A more specific argument based on E.S.P. might run as follows: "Let us play the imitation game, using as witnesses a man who is good as a telepathic receiver, and a digital computer. The interrogator can ask such questions as 'What suit does the card in my right hand belong to?' The man by telepathy or clairvoyance gives the right answer 130 times out of 400 cards. The machine can only guess at random, and perhaps gets 104 right, so the interrogator makes the right identification." There is an interesting possibility which opens here. Suppose the digital computer contains a random number generator. Then it will be natural to use this to decide what answer to give. But then the random number generator will be subject to the psycho-kinetic powers of the interrogator. Perhaps this psycho-kinesis might cause the machine to guess right more often than would be expected on a probability calculation, so that the interrogator might still be unable to make the right identification. On the other hand, he might be able to guess right without any questioning, by clairvoyance. With E.S.P. anything may happen.

If telepathy is admitted it will be necessary to tighten our test up. The situation could be regarded as analogous to that which would occur if the interrogator were talking to himself and one of the competitors was listening with his ear to the wall. To put the competitors into a 'telepathy-proof room' would satisfy all requirements.

7. *Learning Machines.*

The reader will have anticipated that I have no very convincing arguments of a positive nature to support my views. If I had I should not have taken such pains to point out the fallacies in contrary views. Such evidence as I have I shall now give.

Let us return for a moment to Lady Lovelace's objection, which stated that the machine can only do what we tell it to do. One could say that a man can 'inject' an idea into the machine, and that it will respond to a certain extent and then drop into quiescence, like a piano string struck by a hammer. Another simile would be an atomic pile of less than critical size: an injected idea is to correspond to a neutron entering the pile from without. Each such neutron will cause a certain disturbance which eventually dies away. If, however, the size of the pile is sufficiently increased, the disturbance caused by such an incoming neutron will very likely go on and on increasing until the whole pile is destroyed. Is there a corresponding phenomenon for minds, and is there one for machines? There does seem to be one for the human mind. The majority of them seem to be 'sub-critical', *i.e.* to correspond in this analogy to piles of subcritical size. An idea presented to such a mind will on average give rise to less than one idea in reply. A smallish proportion are super-critical. An idea presented to such a mind may give rise to a whole 'theory' consisting of secondary, tertiary and more remote ideas. Animals minds seem to be very definitely sub-critical. Adhering to this analogy we ask, 'Can a machine be made to be super-critical?'

The 'skin of an onion' analogy is also helpful. In considering the functions of the mind or the brain we find certain operations which we can explain in purely mechanical terms. This we say does not correspond to the real mind: it is a sort of skin which we must strip off if we are to find the real mind. But then in what remains we find a further skin to be stripped off, and so on.

Proceeding in this way do we ever come to the 'real' mind, or do we eventually come to the skin which has nothing in it? In the latter case the whole mind is mechanical. (It would not be a discrete-state machine however. We have discussed this.)

These last two paragraphs do not claim to be convincing arguments. They should rather be described as 'recitations tending to produce belief'.

The only really satisfactory support that can be given for the view expressed at the beginning of § 6, will be that provided by waiting for the end of the century and then doing the experiment described. But what can we say in the meantime? What steps should be taken now if the experiment is to be successful?

As I have explained, the problem is mainly one of programming. Advances in engineering will have to be made too, but it seems unlikely that these will not be adequate for the requirements. Estimates of the storage capacity of the brain vary from 10^{10} to 10^{15} binary digits. I incline to the lower values and believe that only a very small fraction is used for the higher types of thinking. Most of it is probably used for the retention of visual impressions. I should be surprised if more than 10^9 was required for satisfactory playing of the imitation game, at any rate against a blind man. (Note—The capacity of the *Encyclopaedia Britannica*, 11th edition, is 2×10^9.) A storage capacity of 10^7 would be a very practicable possibility even by present techniques. It is probably not necessary to increase the speed of operations of the machines at all. Parts of modern machines which can be regarded as analogues of nerve cells work about a thousand times faster than the latter. This should provide a 'margin of safety' which could cover losses of speed arising in many ways. Our problem then is to find out how to programme these machines to play the game. At my present rate of working I produce about a thousand digits of programme a day, so that about sixty workers, working steadily through the fifty years might accomplish the job, if nothing went into the waste-paper basket. Some more expeditious method seems desirable.

In the process of trying to imitate an adult human mind we are bound to think a good deal about the process which has brought it to the state that it is in. We may notice three components,

(*a*) The initial state of the mind, say at birth,

(*b*) The education to which it has been subjected,

(*c*) Other experience, not to be described as education, to which it has been subjected.

Instead of trying to produce a programme to simulate the adult mind, why not rather try to produce one which simulates the child's? If this were then subjected to an appropriate course of education one would obtain the adult brain. Presumably the child-brain is something like a note-book as one buys it from the stationers. Rather little mechanism, and lots of blank sheets. (Mechanism and writing are from our point of view almost synonymous.) Our hope is that there is so little mechanism in the child-brain that something like it can be easily programmed. The amount of work in the education we can assume, as a first approximation, to be much the same as for the human child.

We have thus divided our problem into two parts. The child-programme and the education process. These two remain very closely connected. We cannot expect to find a good child-machine at the first attempt. One must experiment with teaching one such machine and see how well it learns. One can then try another and see if it is better or worse. There is an obvious connection between this process and evolution, by the identifications

Structure of the child machine = Hereditary material
Changes ,, ,, = Mutations
Natural selection = Judgment of the experimenter

One may hope, however, that this process will be more expeditious than evolution. The survival of the fittest is a slow method for measuring advantages. The experimenter, by the exercise of intelligence, should be able to speed it up. Equally important is the fact that he is not restricted to random mutations. If he can trace a cause for some weakness he can probably think of the kind of mutation which will improve it.

It will not be possible to apply exactly the same teaching process to the machine as to a normal child. It will not, for instance, be provided with legs, so that it could not be asked to go out and fill the coal scuttle. Possibly it might not have eyes. But however well these deficiencies might be overcome by clever engineering, one could not send the creature to school without the other children making excessive fun of it. It must be given some tuition. We need not be too concerned about the legs, eyes, etc. The example of Miss *Helen Keller* shows that education can take place provided that communication in both directions between teacher and pupil can take place by some means or other.

We normally associate punishments and rewards with the teaching process. Some simple child-machines can be constructed or programmed on this sort of principle. The machine has to be so constructed that events which shortly preceded the occurrence of a punishment-signal are unlikely to be repeated, whereas a reward-signal increased the probability of repetition of the events which led up to it. These definitions do not presuppose any feelings on the part of the machine. I have done some experiments with one such child-machine, and succeeded in teaching it a few things, but the teaching method was too unorthodox for the experiment to be considered really successful.

The use of punishments and rewards can at best be a part of the teaching process. Roughly speaking, if the teacher has no other means of communicating to the pupil, the amount of information which can reach him does not exceed the total number of rewards and punishments applied. By the time a child has learnt to repeat ' Casabianca ' he would probably feel very sore indeed, if the text could only be discovered by a ' Twenty Questions ' technique, every ' NO ' taking the form of a blow. It is necessary therefore to have some other ' unemotional ' channels of communication. If these are available it is possible to teach a machine by punishments and rewards to obey orders given in some language, *e.g.* a symbolic language. These orders are to be transmitted through the ' unemotional ' channels. The use of this language will diminish greatly the number of punishments and rewards required.

Opinions may vary as to the complexity which is suitable in the child machine. One might try to make it as simple as possible consistently with the general principles. Alternatively one might have a complete system of logical inference ' built in '.[1] In the latter case the store would be largely occupied with definitions and propositions. The propositions would have various kinds of status, *e.g.* well-established facts, conjectures, mathematically proved theorems, statements given by an authority, expressions having the logical form of proposition but not belief-value. Certain propositions may be described as ' imperatives '. The machine should be so constructed that as soon as an imperative is classed as ' well-established ' the appropriate action automatically takes place. To illustrate this, suppose the teacher says to the machine, ' Do your homework now '. This may cause " Teacher says ' Do your homework now ' " to be included amongst the well-established facts. Another such fact might be,

[1] Or rather ' programmed in ' for our child-machine will be programmed in a digital computer. But the logical system will not have to be learnt.

" Everything that teacher says is true ". Combining these may eventually lead to the imperative, ' Do your homework now ', being included amongst the well-established facts, and this, by the construction of the machine, will mean that the homework actually gets started, but the effect is very satisfactory. The processes of inference used by the machine need not be such as would satisfy the most exacting logicians. There might for instance be no hierarchy of types. But this need not mean that type fallacies will occur, any more than we are bound to fall over unfenced cliffs. Suitable imperatives (expressed *within* the systems, not forming part of the rules *of* the system) such as ' Do not use a class unless it is a subclass of one which has been mentioned by teacher ' can have a similar effect to ' Do not go too near the edge '.

The imperatives that can be obeyed by a machine that has no limbs are bound to be of a rather intellectual character, as in the example (doing homework) given above. Important amongst such imperatives will be ones which regulate the order in which the rules of the logical system concerned are to be applied. For at each stage when one is using a logical system, there is a very large number of alternative steps, any of which one is permitted to apply, so far as obedience to the rules of the logical system is concerned. These choices make the difference between a brilliant and a footling reasoner, not the difference between a sound and a fallacious one. Propositions leading to imperatives of this kind might be " When Socrates is mentioned, use the syllogism in Barbara " or " If one method has been proved to be quicker than another, do not use the slower method ". Some of these may be ' given by authority ', but others may be produced by the machine itself, *e.g.* by scientific induction.

The idea of a learning machine may appear paradoxical to some readers. How can the rules of operation of the machine change ? They should describe completely how the machine will react whatever its history might be, whatever changes it might undergo. The rules are thus quite time-invariant. This is quite true. The explanation of the paradox is that the rules which get changed in the learning process are of a rather less pretentious kind, claiming only an ephemeral validity. The reader may draw a parallel with the Constitution of the United States.

An important feature of a learning machine is that its teacher will often be very largely ignorant of quite what is going on inside, although he may still be able to some extent to predict his pupil's behaviour. This should apply most strongly to the later education of a machine arising from a child-machine of well-tried design (or programme). This is in clear contrast with normal procedure when using a machine to do computations : one's object is then to have a clear mental picture of the state of the machine at each moment in the computation. This object can only be achieved with a struggle. The view that 'the machine can only do what we know how to order it to do ',[1] appears strange in face of this. Most of the programmes which we can put into the machine will result in its doing something that we cannot make sense of at all, or which we regard as completely random behaviour. Intelligent behaviour presumably consists in a departure from the completely disciplined behaviour involved in computation, but a rather slight one, which does not give rise to random behaviour, or to pointless repetitive loops. Another important result of preparing our machine for its part in the imitation game by a process of teaching and learning is that ' human fallibility ' is likely to be omitted in a rather natural way, *i.e.* without special 'coaching'. (The reader should reconcile this with the point of view on pp. 24, 25.) Processes that are learnt do not produce a hundred per cent. certainty of result : if they did they could not be unlearnt.

It is probably wise to include a random element in a learning machine (see p. 438). A random element is rather useful when we are searching for a solution of some problem. Suppose for instance we wanted to find a number between 50 and 200 which was equal to the square of the sum of its digits, we might start at 51 then try 52 and go on until we got a number that worked. Alternatively we might choose numbers at random until we got a a good one. This method has the advantage that it is unnecessary to keep track of the values that have been tried, but the disadvantage that one may try the same one twice, but this is not very important if there are several solutions. The systematic method has the disadvantage that there may be an enormous block without any solutions in the region which has to be investigated first. Now the learning process may be regarded as a search for a form of behaviour which will satisfy the teacher (or some other criterion). Since there is probably a very large number of satisfactory solutions the random method seems to be better than the systematic. It should be noticed that it is used in the analogous process of evolution. But there the systematic method is not possible. How could one keep track

[1] Compare Lady Lovelace's statement (p. 450), which does not contain the word ' only '.

of the different genetical combinations that had been tried, so as to avoid trying them again ?

We may hope that machines will eventually compete with men in all purely intellectual fields. But which are the best ones to start with ? Even this is a difficult decision. Many people think that a very abstract activity, like the playing of chess, would be best. It can also be maintained that it is best to provide the machine with the best sense organs that money can buy, and then teach it to understand and speak English. This process could follow the normal teaching of a child. Things would be pointed out and named, etc. Again I do not know what the right answer is, but I think both approaches should be tried.

We can only see a short distance ahead, but we can see plenty there that needs to be done.

BIBLIOGRAPHY

Samuel Butler, Erewhon, London, 1865. Chapters 23, 24, 25, *The Book of the Machines.*

Alonzo Church, " An Unsolvable Problem of Elementary Number Theory ", *American J. of Math.*, 58 (1936), 345-363.

K. Gödel, " Über formal unentscheidbare Sätze der Principia Mathematica und verwandter Systeme, I ", *Monatshefte für Math. und Phys.*, (1931), 173-189.

D. R. Hartree, *Calculating Instruments and Machines*, New York, 1949.

S. C. Kleene, " General Recursive Functions of Natural Numbers ", *American J. of Math.*, 57 (1935), 153-173 and 219-244.

G. Jefferson, " The Mind of Mechanical Man ". Lister Oration for 1949. *British Medical Journal*, vol. i (1949), 1105-1121.

Countess of Lovelace, ' Translator's notes to an article on Babbage's Analytical Engine ', *Scientific Memoirs* (ed. by R. Taylor), vol. 3 (1842), 691-731.

Bertrand Russell, *History of Western Philosophy*, London, 1940.

A. M. Turing, " On Computable Numbers, with an Application to the Entscheidungsproblem ", *Proc. London Math. Soc.* (2), 42 (1937), 230-265.

Victoria University of Manchester.

Additional References

[Abr]
N. Abramson and D. Braverman, Learning to Recognize Patterns in a Random Environment, *IRE Trans. Inform. Theory,* Vol. **IT-8,** Sept. 1962, pp. 58–63.

[Bus]
R. R. Bush and F. Mosteller, *Stochastic Models for Learning,* Wiley, New York, 1955.

[Chi]
Y. T. Chien and K. S. Fu, A Modified Sequential Recognition Machine Using Time-varying Stopping Boundaries, *IEEE Trans. Inform. Theory,* Vol. **12,** No. 2, 1966, pp. 206–214.

[Chom]
N. Chomsky, Three Models for the Description of Language, *IRE Trans. Inform. Theory,* Vol. **IT-2,** No. 3, Sept. 1956, pp. 113–124.

[Chow-1]
C. K. Chow, An Optimum Character Recognition System Using Decision Functions, *IRE Trans. Electron. Comput.,* Vol. **EC-6,** No. 4, Dec. 1957, pp. 247–254.

[Chow-2]
C. K. Chow, On the Characterization of Threshold Functions, *Switching Circuit Theory and Logical Design,* AIEE Spec. Publ. S-134, Sept. 1961, p. 34–38.

[Coh]
M. Cohn and R. Lindaman, Axiomatic Majority-Decision Logic, *IRE Trans. Electron. Comput.,* Vol. **EC-10,** No. 1, Mar. 1961, pp. 17–21; also *ibid.,* Sept. 1961, p. 530.

[Din]
G. P. Dinneen, Programming Pattern Recognition, *Proceedings of the Western Joint Computer Conference,* Los Angeles, Mar. 1955, pp. 94–110.

[Est]
W. K. Estes, A Random-Walk Model for Choice Behavor, *Mathematical Methods in the Social Sciences,* K. J. Arrow, S. Karlin, and P. Suppes (eds.), Stanford University Press, Stanford, Calif., 1960, Chap. 18.

[Fre]
H. Freeman, On the Encoding of Arbitrary Geometric Configuration, *IRE Trans. Electron. Comput.,* Vol. **EC-10,** No. 2, June 1961, pp. 260–268.

[Fu]
K. S. Fu, *Sequential Methods in Pattern Recognition and Machine Learning,* Academic Press, New York, 1968.

[Haw]
J. Hawkins and C. J. Munsey, A Parallel Computer Organization and Mechanizations, *IEEE Trans. Electron. Comput.,* Vol. **EC-12,** No. 3, June 1963, pp. 251–262.

[Hil]
C. J. Hilditch, Linear Skeletons from Square Cupboards, *Machine Intelligence IV,* B. Meltzer and D. Michie (eds.), American Elsevier, New York, 1969, pp. 403–420.

[Ho]
Y. C. Ho and R. L. Kashyap, An Algorithm for Linear Inequalities and Its Applications, *IEEE Trans. Electron. Comput.,* Vol. **EC-14,** No. 5, Oct. 1965, pp. 683–688.

[Kai]
T. Kailath, The Divergence and Bhattacharyya Distance Measures in Signal Selection, *IEEE Trans. Commun. Tech.,* Vol. **COM-15,** No. 1, Feb. 1967, pp. 52–60.

[Kem]
J. G. Kemeny and J. Laurie Snell, *Finite Markov Chains,* Van Nostrand, New York, 1960.

[Kir]
R. A. Kirsch, Computer Interpretation of English Text and Picture Patterns, *IEEE Trans. Electron. Comput.,* Vol. **EC-13,** No. 4, Aug. 1964, pp. 363–376.

[Kof]
K. Koffka, *Principles of Gestalt Psychology,* Harcourt Brace, New York, 1935.

[Mar]
T. Marill and D. M. Green, On the Effectiveness of Receptors in Recognition Systems, *IEEE Trans. Prof. Tech. Group Inform. Theory,* Vol. **IT-9,** No. 1, Jan. 1963, pp. 11–17.

[McCo]
B. H. McCormick, The Illinois Pattern Recognition Computer—ILLIAC III, *IEEE Trans. Electron. Comput.,* Vol. **EC-12,** No. 5, Dec. 1963, pp. 791–813.

[McCu]
W. S. McCulloch and W. Pitts, A Logical Calculus of the Ideas Immanent in Nervous Activity, *Bull. Math. Biophys.,* 1943, Vol. **5,** pp. 115–133.

[McK]
R. McKeon (ed.), *The Basic Works of Aristotle,* Random House, New York, 1941, pp. 700ff.

[McN]
R. McNaughton, Unate Truth Functions, *IRE Trans. Electron. Comput.,* Vol. **EC-10,** No. 1, Mar. 1961, pp. 1–6.

[Min]
R. C. Minnick, Linear Input Logic, *IRE Trans. Electron. Comput.,* Vol. **EC-10,** No. 1, Mar. 1961, pp. 6–16.

[Mur-1]
S. Muroga, I. Toda, and M. Kondo, Majority Decision Functions of Up to Six Variables, *J. Math. Comp.,* Oct. 1962; Also in Japanese in 1959 and 1960.

[Mur-2]
S. Muroga, I. Toda, and S. Takasu, Theory of Majority Decision Elements, *J. Franklin Institute,* Vol. **271,** May 1961, pp. 276–418.

[Nar-1]
R. Narasimhan, A Linguistic Approach to Pattern Recognition, *Digital Computer Laboratory, Rept. 121,* University of Illinois, Urbana, Ill., 1962.

[Nar-2]
R. Narasimhan, Syntax-Directed Interpretation of Classes of Pictures, *Commun. ACM,* Vol. **9,** No. 3, March 1966, pp. 166–173.

[New]
A. Newell and H. A. Simon, The Logic Theory Machine: A Complex Information Processing System, *IRE Trans. Inform. Theory,* Vol. **IT-2,** No. 3, Sept. 1956, pp. 61–79.

[Pal]
G. Palmieri and R. Sanna, Automatic Probabilistic Programmer/Analyzer for Pattern Recognition, *Estratto Rivista Methods,* Vol. **12,** No. 48, 1960.

[Nil]
N. J. Nilsson, *Learning Machines,* McGraw-Hill, New York, 1965.

[Pau]
N. C. Paull and E. J. McCluskey, Jr., Boolean Functions Realizable with Single Threshold Devices, *Proc. IRE,* Vol. **48,** July 1960, pp. 1335–1337.

[Paz]
A. Paz, *Introduction to Probabilistic Automata,* Academic Press, New York, 1971.

[Rab]
M. O. Rabin and D. Scott, Finite Automata and Their Decision Problems, *IBM J. of Res. Develop.,* Vol. **3,** No. 2, Apr. 1959, pp. 114–125.

[Ros-1]
F. Rosenblatt, The Perceptron: a Probabilistic Model for Information Storage and Organization in the Brain, *Psychological Rev.,* Vol. **65,** No. 6, 1958, pp. 386–408.

[Ros-2]
F. Rosenblatt, Two Theorems of Statistical Separability in the Perceptron, *Proceedings of a Symposium on the Mechanization of Thought Processes,* H. M. Stationary Office, London, 1959, pp. 421–456.

[Ros-3]
F. Rosenblatt, *Principles of Neurodynamics: Perceptrons and the Theory of Brain Mechanisms,* Spartan Books, Washington, D.C., 1962.

[Rose]
A. Rosenfeld and J. L. Pfaltz, Sequential Operations in Digital Picture Processing, *J. Ass. Comput. Machinery,* Vol. **13,** No. 4, Oct. 1966, pp. 471–494.

[Seb-1]
G. S. Sebestyen, Recognition of Membership in Classes, *IRE Trans. Inform. Theory,* Vol. **IT-7,** No. 1, Jan. 1961, pp. 44–50.

[Seb-2]
G. S. Sebestyen, Pattern Recognition by an Adaptive Process of Sample Set Construction, *IRE Trans. Inform. Theory,* Vol. **IT-8,** No. 5, Sept. 1962, pp. S82–S91.

[Sin]
R. C. Singleton, A Text for Linear Separability as Applied to Self-Organizing Machines, *Self Organizing Systems 1962,* M. C. Yovits et al. (ed.), Spartan Books, Washington, D.C., 1962, pp. 503–524.

[Skl-1]
J. Sklansky, R. L. Chazin, and B. J. Hansen, Minimum-Perimeter Polygons of Digitized Silhouettes, *IEEE Trans. Comput.,* Vol. **C-21,** No. 3, Mar. 1972, pp. 260–268.

[Skl-2]
J. Sklansky and P. Merryman, A Continuous Two-Dimensional Model of Threshold Learning. *IEEE Trans. Systems, Man, and Cybernetics,* Jan. 1973, pp. 51–61.

[Skl-3]
J. Sklansky, Threshold Learning of Two-Mode Signal Detection, *IEEE Trans. Inform. Theory,* Vol. **IT-11,** No. 3, July 1965, pp. 353–362.

[Skl-4]
J. Sklansky, Measuring Concavity on a Rectangular Mosaic, *IEEE Trans. Comput.,* Vol. **C-21,** No. 12, Dec. 1972, pp. 1355–1373.

[Ste]
K. Steinbuch and U. A. W. Piske, Learning Matrices and Their Applications, *IEEE Trans. Electron. Comput.*, Vol. **EC-12,** Dec. 1963, pp. 846–862.

[Tur]
A. M. Turing, Computing Machinery and Intelligence, *Mind,* Vol. **59,** pp. 433–460. Also *The World of Mathematics,* Vol. 4, Simon and Schuster, New York, 1956.

[Ung]
S. H. Unger, Pattern Detection and Recognition, *Proc. IRE,* Oct. 1959, pp. 1737–1752.

[Van]
A. Vander Lugt, Signal Detection by Complex Spatial Filtering, *IEEE Trans. Inform. Theory,* Vol. **IT-10,** No. 2, Apr. 1964, pp. 139–145.

[Von]
J. Von Neumann, Probabilistic Logics and the Synthesis of Reliable Organisms from Unreliable Components, *Automata Studies,* Princeton University Press, Princeton, N. J., 1956, pp. 43–97.

[Wat]
S. Watanabe, Karhunen–Loève Expansion and Factor Analysis—Theoretical Remarks and Application, *Transactions of the Fourth Prague Conference on Information Theory, Statistical Decision Functions and Random Processes,* Prague, Aug.–Sept. 1965, pp. 635–660.

[Wid]
B. Widrow, Pattern Recognition and Adaptive Control, *IEEE Trans. Appl. and Ind.,* Vol. **83,** No. 74, Sept. 1964, pp. 269–277.

[Wie]
N. Wiener, *Cybernetics,* Wiley, New York, 1948.

[Win-1]
R. O. Winder, Enumeration of Seven-Argument Threshold Functions, *IEEE Trans. Electron. Comput.,* Vol. **EC-14,** No. 3, July 1965, pp. 315–325.

[Win-2]
R. O. Winder, Threshold Logic in Artificial Intelligence, *Artificial Intelligence,* IEEE Publ. S-142, 1963, pp. 107–128.

Author Citation Index

Subject Index